CLASSICS IN PSYCHOLOGY

CLASSICS IN PSYCHOLOGY

A NOTE ABOUT THE AUTHOR

WILHELM THIERRY PREYER was born in Manchester, England, in 1841 but was educated in Germany. First an exploring scientist, who visited Iceland in 1860, Preyer then studied physiology at Bonn and worked in Paris with Claude Bernard. He became Dozent, and later Professor of Physiology at Jena. Though his work was chiefly in embryology, Preyer became increasingly interested in child psychology during the 1870s and, after carefully observing his son, published two of the first and most important works in the field in 1881. Indeed Preyer has been credited with being the scientist who launched the child study movement. After moving to Berlin in 1888, he became ill and died in 1897.

THE MIND OF THE CHILD

W[illiam] Preyer

Parts I and II

ARNO PRESS
A New York Times Company
New York ★ 1973

Reprint Edition 1973 by Arno Press Inc.

Reprinted from a copy in
The University of Illinois Library

Classics in Psychology
ISBN for complete set: 0-405-05130-1
See last pages of this volume for titles.

Manufactured in the United States of America

————◆————

Library of Congress Cataloging in Publication Data

Preyer, William, 1841-1897.
  The mind of the child.

  (Classics in psychology)
  Translation of Die Seele des Kindes.
  Reprint of parts 1 and 2 which were published
separately by D. Appleton, New York in 1890 and 1889,
respectively, and were issued in series: International
education series.
  CONTENTS: pt. 1. The senses and the will.—
pt. 2. The development of the intellect.
  1. Child study. I. Title. II. Series.
[DNLM: LB P944s]
BF431.P68413 1973   155.4'13   73-2985
ISBN 0-405-05156-5

INTERNATIONAL EDUCATION SERIES

THE MIND OF THE CHILD
PART I

THE SENSES AND
THE WILL

OBSERVATIONS CONCERNING
THE MENTAL DEVELOPMENT OF THE HUMAN BEING
IN THE FIRST YEARS OF LIFE

BY

W. PREYER

PROFESSOR OF PHYSIOLOGY IN JENA

TRANSLATED FROM THE ORIGINAL GERMAN

By H. W. BROWN
TEACHER IN THE STATE NORMAL SCHOOL AT WORCESTER, MASS.

NEW YORK
D. APPLETON AND COMPANY
1890

EDITOR'S PREFACE.

A CAREFUL study of this work will do much to put one in possession of the method of studying mental growth in children. Parents and teachers will find this method of observation invaluable, inasmuch as it will make experience constantly profitable.

Experience, it is true, marshals its train of facts before us in an endless succession every day of our lives. But, without scientific method, one fact does much to obliterate all others by its presence. Out of sight, they are out of mind. Method converts unprofitable experience, wherein nothing abides except vague and uncertain surmise, into science. In science the present fact is deprived of its ostentatious and all-absorbing interest, by the act of relating it to all other facts. We classify the particular with its fellow-particulars and it takes its due rank. Such classification, moreover, eliminates from it the unessential elements.

The method of science, as Herbart pointed out involves the ascertainment and fixing of quantitative relations. "Every theory," says he, "to admit of comparison with experience, must be developed until the same embodies the modifications of quantity found in that experience." *

---

* See "Journal of Speculative Philosophy," vol. xi, p. 251, J. F. Herbart on the application of mathematics to psychology.

The characteristics of accuracy and precision which make science exact are derived from quantity. Fix the order of succession, the date, the duration, the locality, the environment, the extent of the sphere of influence, the number of manifestations, and the number of cases of intermittence, and you have exact knowledge of a phenomenon. When stated in quantitative terms, your experience is useful to other observers. It is easy to verify it or to add an increment. By quantification, science grows and grows continually, without retrograde movements.

One does not forget, of course, that there is something besides the quantitative and altogether above the quantitative. The object itself is more important than its quantitative relations. The soul as a self-active essence is the object in psychology. Science determines the quantitative relations of its phenomenal manifestation. In other words, science determines exactly the time when, the place where, the duration and frequency, the extent and degree of the manifestation of this self-activity in the body and through the body.

The nature of feelings, volitions, and ideas in themselves, is the object of introspective psychology and metaphysics. But all will concede that parents and teachers are directly interested in the order of development of the soul from its lower functions into its higher ones, and are consequently concerned with these quantitative manifestations.

The author's comparisons between the steps of progress in the child and the same in other animals constitute one of the most valuable features in this book.

It is worth repeating that the supreme interest to us

in these observations is the development from lower degrees of intelligence to higher ones. The immense interval that separates plant life from animal life is almost paralleled by the interval between the animal and the human being. From mere nutrition to sensation is a great step; from mere sensation to the conscious employment of ethical ideas and the perception of logical necessity and universality, is an equal step. Yet it is to be assumed that the transitions exist in all degrees, and that the step from any degree to the next one is not difficult when the natural means is discovered. It is this means that comparative psychology is discovering.

The infant is contemplated in the process of gaining command over himself. His sense-organs gradually become available for perception; his muscles become controllable by his will. Each new acquisition becomes in turn an instrument of further progress.

Exact science determines when and where the animal phase leaves off and the purely human begins— where the organic phase ends and the individual begins. The discrimination of impulsive, reflexive, and instinctive movements, all of them organic, throws light on the genesis of mind out of its lower antecedent. Imitation is the first manifestation of the transition from the organic to the strictly spiritual.

In this connection it is, before all, an important question, What is the significance of the relapse into unconscious instinct through the formation of habit? We do an act by great special effort of the will and intellect; we repeat it until it is done with ease. It gradually lapses into unconscious use and wont, and has become instinctive and organic. We need not suggest the bear-

ing of this question on education, which deals so much
with the formation of habits, and yet seems to aim
always at bringing to consciousness in the pupil all of
his unconscious presuppositions. Education deals in
explanations. It exhumes for the individual his social
history, his cosmical evolution, and sets before him in a
systematic form the logical structure of his thinking, of
his language, of his ethical and æsthetical motives. It
turns his attention through mathematics upon the necessary forms which all phenomena assume. Everywhere
education proceeds from the particular being before the
senses to the general form of its existence, and drags
into consciousness what has been hitherto merely organic
—involved and implied but unperceived. Education,
in fact, lifts us to the contemplation of the universal
in each individual. Then by the aid of general ideas
we are able to recall the particular facts, or drop them
out of sight, at our pleasure. Learning by science
to comprehend principles—which may be defined as
energies moving according to their own laws—we become independent of memory to a great degree, and may
let the instances which formed our ladder of discovery
drop away. We thus arrive at what the School-men
called the angelic form of knowing.

The work of Professor Preyer before us contains
three parts, respectively devoted to (a) the development of the senses, (b) the will, and (c) the intellect.
Parts first and second are contained in this volume; and
part third, with three appendices, forms a second volume, to follow immediately.

WILLIAM T. HARRIS.

CONCORD, MASS., *February, 1888.*

AUTHOR'S PREFACE TO THE FIRST EDITION.

I PROPOSED to myself a number of years ago, the task of studying the child, both before birth and in the period immediately following, from the physiological point of view, with the object of arriving at an explanation of the origin of the separate vital processes. It was soon apparent to me that a division of the work would be advantageous to its prosecution. For life in the embryo is so essentially different a thing from life beyond it, that a separation must make it easier both for the investigator to do his work and for the reader to follow the exposition of its results. I have, therefore, discussed by itself, life before birth, the "Physiology of the Embryo." The vital phenomena of the human being in the earliest period of his independent existence in the world are, again, so complicated and so various in kind, that here too a division soon appeared expedient. I separated the physical development of the newly-born and the very young child from his mental development, and have endeavored to describe the latter in the present book; at least, I hope that, by means of personal observations carried on for several years, I have furnished facts that may serve as material for a future description.

A forerunner of the work is a lecture, "Psycho-genesis" (the Genesis of Mind), given before a scientific association at Berlin on the 3d of January, 1880, and soon after made public * in my book, "Naturwissen-schaftliche Thatsachen und Probleme" ("Facts and Problems of Natural Science") Berlin, 1880.

This sketch has given manifold incitement to fresh observations. But great as is the number of occasional observations in regard to many children, I do not thus far know of diaries regularly kept concerning the mental development of individual children. Now precisely this chronological investigation of mental progress in the first and second years of life presents great difficulties, because it requires the daily registering of experiences that can be had only in the nursery. I have, notwithstanding, kept a complete diary from the birth of my son to the end of his third year. Occupying myself with the child at least three times a day—at morning, noon, and evening—and almost every day, with two trifling interruptions, and guarding him, as far as possible, against such training as children usually receive, I found nearly every day some fact of mental genesis to record. The substance of that diary has passed into this book.

No doubt the development of one child is rapid and that of another is slow; very great individual differences appear in children of the same parents even, but the differences are much more of time and degree than of the order in which the steps are taken, and these

---

* See Jour. Spec. Philos. for April, 1881, for an English translation of this lecture of Professor Preyer.—ED.

steps are the same in all individuals; that is the important matter. Desirable as it is to collect statistics concerning the mental development of *many* infants— the activity of their senses, their movements, especially their acquirement of speech—yet the accurate, daily repeated observation of *one* child—a child sound in health, having no brothers or sisters, and whose development was neither remarkably rapid nor remarkably slow—seemed at least quite as much to be desired. I have, however, taken notice, as far as possible, of the experiences of others in regard to other normal children in the first years of life, and have even compared many of these where opportunity offered.

But a description of the gradual appearance of brain-activity in the child, along with the most careful observation of his mental ripening, would be only a beginning. The development of mind, like the development of body, must be regarded as dating back far beyond the origin of the individual being.

If the infant brings into the world a set of organs which begin to be active only after a long time, and are absolutely useless up to that time—as, e. g., the lungs were before birth—then the question, To what causes do such organs and functions owe their existence? can have but one answer—*heredity*.

This, to be sure, explains nothing; but dim as the notion is, much is gained toward our understanding of the matter, in the fact that some functions are inherited while others are not.

What is acquired by experience is only a part. The question whether a function of the brain, on which everything depends in the development of the child's mind, is inherited or acquired, must be answered in each individual case, if we would not go astray in the labyrinth of appearances and hypotheses.

Above all, we must be clear on this point, that the fundamental activities of mind, which are manifested only after birth, do not originate after birth.

If they had previously no existence at all, we could not discover whence they come or at what time. The substance of a hen's egg that has been fecundated, but is frozen as hard as a stone, certainly has no sensation; but after thawing and three weeks' warming, that same substance, changed into a living chicken, has sensation.

The capacity of feeling, in case of the fulfillment of certain outward conditions, if it be not a property of the egg, must have originated during incubation from matter incapable of sentiency; that is, the material atoms must not only have arranged themselves in a different order, receiving through their union and separation different chemical properties, as actually happens; must not only have changed their physical properties—e. g., elasticity, solidity, etc., which are partly dependent on the chemical, partly independent of them—as likewise happens; but these atoms must have gained entirely new properties which were neither chemically nor physically indicated beforehand, were not to be assumed or predicated. For neither chemistry nor physics can attribute to the substances that constitute the egg other than chemical and physical properties. But if the warming, ventilation, evaporation, and liberation of carbonic acid have had their normal course during incubation, then these new mental properties present themselves, and that without the possibility of their being gained by imitation in the incubator. And these properties are similar to those of the beings that produced the egg. Hence, it must be admitted that these beings have imparted to the egg matter which contained, in addition to the known or physically and chemically discoverable properties, latent properties not chemically and physically discoverable—psychical, therefore, physiological—these being potential, so that warming, airing, etc., are necessary to their development. The same conditions are required for the development of the tissues and organs of the embryo, which likewise were not contained in the albumen, sugar, and fat, in the water and the salts of the egg; neither do their properties belong to those with which chemistry and physics are concerned, but they are like those of the generators of the egg.

Some parts of the contents of the egg, then, possess potentially properties unquestionably mental—the capacity of sensation, at least. And these parts must, at the same time, be those from which originate the cotyledons (of plants), the foundation of the embryo. As is well known, they are cellular forms with the power of independent movement, to which can not be denied, any more than to the lowest zoöphytes, the capacity of discrimination. They grow and move by putting out and drawing in pseudopodia; * they undoubtedly appropriate nourishment, require oxygen, multiply by division, conduct themselves in general like *amœbœ*, or other simple living beings. The opinion that they possess a

---

* Filaments thrust out from any part of the body, serving as organs of locomotion.

certain crude psychical endowment, sensation of an obscure sort, can not be refuted.

Everything goes to show a continuity in the capacity of sensation. This capacity does not spring afresh each time in the human being out of material incapable of sensation, but, as a hereditary property of the parts of the egg, is differentiated in these, and by stimulus from without is brought into action—the process being hardly discernible in the embryo protected from this stimulus, but plainly visible in the new-born child.

The mind of the new-born child, then, does not resemble a *tabula rasa*, upon which the senses first write their impressions, so that out of these the sum-total of our mental life arises through manifold reciprocal action, but the tablet is already written upon before birth, with many illegible, nay, unrecognizable and invisible, marks, the traces of the imprint of countless sensuous impressions of long-gone generations. So blurred and indistinct are these remains, that we might, indeed, suppose the tablet to be blank, so long as we did not examine the changes it undergoes in earliest youth. But the more attentively the child is observed, the more easily legible becomes the writing, not at first to be understood, that he brings with him into the world. Then we perceive what a capital each individual has inherited from his ancestors—how much there is that is not produced by sense-impressions, and how false is the supposition that man learns to feel, to will, and to think, only through his senses. Heredity is just as important as individual activity in the genesis of mind. No man is in this matter a mere upstart, who is to achieve the development of his mind (Psyche) through his individual experience alone; rather must each one, by means of his experience, fill out and animate anew his inherited endowments, the remains of the experiences and activities of his ancestors.

It is hard to discern and to decipher the mysterious writing on the mind of the child. It is just that which constitutes a chief problem of this book.

PREYER.

JENA, *October* 6, 1881.

AUTHOR'S PREFACE TO THE SECOND EDITION.

THE first edition of this book appeared in October, 1881. Just two years afterward, a second became necessary. This differs from the former chiefly in abbreviation of the statements coming from other persons, and not indispensable; in improvements in form; in a more careful and exact formulation of general conclusions; and in a considerable enlargement of the material of facts in support of these conclusions. In respect to the last point, the communications that have come to me by letter, from the most various sources, have been of great value.

To all those who have gratified me by sending their observations concerning the mental development of the child during his earliest years, I here express my thanks for the interest they have taken in my presentation, and for the help they have afforded me in the laborious work.

The mental life of the human being is, in fact, so hard to investigate in its development, that very many persons must co-operate in the work; the individual can oversee but little of it. The evolution of the mind resembles a stream into which no one descends twice. Like that, it issues from obscure depths as a clear spring; the water trickles but scantily at first into the light of day, and gathers slowly and in stillness to a murmuring brook. Soon, however, its waves beat with increasing movement against the banks. The bottom is no longer clearly visible. Farther on, foaming gorges pour themselves into the still clear, but agitated waters, which only the solid rocks can restrain. In like manner self-will breaks against the resisting order of the world. When, at length, the torrent has victoriously opened its path in the mountains, and has adapted itself to its environment, then it hastens on, sometimes sparkling and smooth, sometimes roaring powerfully, as if, like the turbulent boy, it would reach distant goals, and yet would cling to the heart of the mother, to moderate the spring-tide of the gushing life.

At last, mirror-like in its calmness, powerfully dispensing blessings and diffusing life, it becomes master of itself, and loses itself in the ocean out of which it once arose.

Throughout the whole course, from the spring to the river's mouth, the spectator sees the flow, sees the before and the after; he knows, too, that it is the same elements that are hastening forward, though often united with new ones, and becoming changed; that many of these, indeed, pass off into vapor, but the river is ever the same. So is it also with the mind. From birth to death, the play of its waves does not cease; new impressions are mingled with old ones, many are forgotten and changed, yet the individuality remains to the last, and before the self (*Ich*) has come to the knowledge, whither the restless hastening forward is really leading, the hastening is at an end.

Thus, the highest questions of themselves press upon the observer of the child, upon the physiologist and the philosopher, the teacher and the educator, the physician and the psychologist, the philanthropist and the pastor, in the joyous form of the smiling, rosy face of the child, but at the same time these questions are as impenetrable as is in general the great mystery of becoming and of ceasing to be.

THE AUTHOR.

JENA, *April* 28, 1884.

CONTENTS.

INTRODUCTION TO THE AMERICAN EDITION.

IF one would train and break horses, however un-
manageable, like Willis J. Powel, who perhaps ex-
celled all others in this art before or since, he must, like
him, study long and patiently the nature of the horse.
If one would raise sheep with greatest success, he must,
like the English herdsman who said that he and his
family were Cotswold people and knew nothing whatever of Southdowns, serve a long apprenticeship in
learning the habits, instincts, and all the conditions that
affect sheep development favorably or unfavorably.
The principle has long been a commonplace with breed-
ers and trainers of domestic animals, although many
. naturalists now believe that for him who will long and
patiently study and think and feel his way down and
back into the soul of a particular animal, there are possibilities both of scientific discovery and of control and
modification of brute instinct undreamed of before.
The trained agent of charity organizations, who la-
bors among the poor, must prepare himself for efficiency by careful study of the way in which individual
poor people, and even beggars, think, feel, live, and act.
The modern prison-keeper studies criminals till he becomes an expert in the psychology of crime. The mis-

sionary first studies the existing beliefs and superstitions of the savage races among whom he is to labor, or, if not, his work is but little more effective than if he did not take the trouble to learn their language.

Teachers as a rule do not study the nature of the children they instruct in any such way, and that for the following reasons : First, their business, as too often viewed, is not to educate or unfold, a process to which all have a right, but to instruct, or infuse set courses and sums of information to which the nature of the child may or may not have a right. Secondly, many think they have all the knowledge of childhood they require, from memory of their own childish years. This is wrong. Mental and moral growth necessarily involves increasing oblivion of everything of childhood save mere incidents, and even these are, other things being equal, remembered inversely as the degree of development to fullness of maturity. What remains from this source often misleads and has no regulative value for the teacher. Thirdly, many think a course in a text-book in psychology supplies this need. This is probably the gravest mistake of all. All such books I know are far too abstract and schematic, too much devoted to definition or in some cases even controversy, too commonplace and traditional in their subject-matter, so as to be sometimes an impediment to the fine tact and instinct that, in minds of finest fiber, divine, perhaps half unconsciously, the needs and individual nature of children.

The living, playing, learning child, whose soul heredity has freighted so richly from a past we know not how remote, on whose right development all good

causes in the world depend, embodies a truly elementary psychology. All the fundamental activities are
found, and the play of each psychic process is so open,
simple, interesting, that it is strange that psychology
should be the last of the sciences to fall into line in the
great Baconian change of base to which we owe nearly
all the reforms, from Comenius down, which distinguish schools of to-day from those of the sixteenth
century. It is a striking fact that nearly every great
teacher in the history of education who has spoken
words that have been heeded has lived for years in the
closest personal relations to children and has had the
sympathy and tact that gropes out, if it can not see
clearly, the laws of juvenile development and the lines
of childish interests.

Among all the nearly fourscore studies of young
children printed by careful empirical and often thoroughly scientific observers, this work of Preyer is the fullest
and on the whole the best. It should be read by teachers and parents even of older children, as the best example of the inductive method applied to the study of
child-psychology. The development of each sense, and
the unfoldment of the power of voluntary motion, are
traced with great fullness; and still more attention is
devoted to the growth of the ability to speak, with a
suggestive co-ordination of the progressive stages of
decay of the linguistic centers in aphasia and allied
forms of disease.

A work on the whole so good awakens a desire for
still further advance along the same lines. Not only
does Preyer not continue his studies into school age,
but he has not attempted, like Perez, to trace the un-

foldment of sentiments and emotions, nor, like Herbart and Ziller, to tabulate the spontaneous interests of children. The most hopeful effort yet made in this direction was begun three years ago in the institution with which the translator of this work is connected, and may be described as follows, as characterized substantially in the words of the principal, E. H. Russell: Systematic observation of children is made a part of the regular work of this normal school, with a view of enlarging the scope of the ordinary study of psychology, to render it more objective and useful, to bring the prospective teachers into closer and better relations to children, and to gather a store of facts whereby in time to increase and rectify our present unsatisfactory knowledge of child-nature. The method is: First, to explain to the students, at the beginning of the second half-year in school, how to improve their opportunities on the street, at home, in families of friends, of noticing minutely the spontaneous, unconstrained activities, bodily and mental and physical, of children of all ages, at play, study, or work, etc. Then, at the earliest convenient moment, concise record is made on blanks with printed headings, and colored—e. g., white for personal observation, red for second-hand facts, etc. The records, now some five or six thousand in number, are classified, so far as can be, under memory, imagination, deceit, ignorance, mechanical construction, moral sense, etc., etc. Precisely what the value of this material will be it is now too soon to say, but as to its good effects on the powers of observation, tact, psychologic knowledge and interest of those who make them, there can be no question whatever. The students soon become more interested in children and their ways, and more skillful in dealing with them; and some acquire much ingenuity in following out the more complicated and obscure processes of child-life. They also acquire right habits of observation and investigation generally, learning in some degree the caution, discrimination, and veracity required in studying nature. It is so interesting that students must be rather restrained than impelled to the work; and graduates are believed to be distinctly guided toward best success and pleasure in their vocation by these studies, and display intelligence and sympathy in dealing with troublesome children. Many of the essays of the graduating class are based on this work.

While commending this book to American teachers generally, the writer desires to commend the Worcester method of psychogenetic study to the careful attention of principals of normal schools.

G. STANLEY HALL.

JOHNS HOPKINS UNIVERSITY, *January 7, 1888.*

EXPLANATION OF ABBREVIATED CITATIONS.

Kussmaul: "Untersuchungen über das Seelenleben des neugeborenen Menschen" ("Investigations concerning the Mental Life of the New-Born Human Being"), 1859 (38 pp.); and "Störungen der Sprache" ("Disturbances or Obstructions of Speech"), 1877.

Genzmer: "Untersuchungen über die Sinneswahrnehmungen des neugeborenen Menschen" ("Investigations concerning the Sense-Perceptions of the New-Born Human Being"), 1873 (reprinted 1882, 25 pp.).

Sigismund: "Kind und Welt" ("The Child and the World"), 1856.

Gustav Lindner: in Twelfth Annual Report of the "Lehrerseminars in Zschopau," 1882, and in the periodical "Kosmos," 1882.

Frau Dr. Friedemann; Frau Professor von Strümpell; and Herr Ed. Schulte—to these the author is under particular obligation for MSS.

All other references, sources of information, and names of authors are given without abbreviation.

THE MIND OF THE CHILD.

FIRST PART.

DEVELOPMENT OF THE SENSES.

THE foundation of all mental development is the activity of the senses. We can not conceive of anything of the nature of mental genesis as taking place without that activity.

Every sense-activity is fourfold in its character: First, there is an *excitement of the nerves;* then comes *sensation;* and not until the sensation has been localized in space and referred to some point in time, do we have a *perception.* When, further, the cause of this is apprehended, then the perception becomes an *idea.*

The adult human being is a person who is responsible, who acts according to his own pleasure, and is capable of independent thought. For our understanding of his psychical states and processes, it is of great importance to know what is the condition of things as to the above stages of sense-activity, in the newly-born, and in the infant, who is not responsible, who does not act according to his pleasure, and does not think at all.

I have therefore instituted many observations concerning the gradual perfecting of the senses at the beginning of life, and I commence with a description of them. In these observations I have had especially in mind the prominent part played in the mental development of the child, at the earliest period, by the sense of sight.

CHAPTER I.

SIGHT.

THE observations with regard to the development of the sense of sight during the first years relate to sensibility to light, discrimination of colors, movements of the eyelids, movements of the eyes, direction of the look, seeing of near and distant objects, and interpretation of what is seen. To these are attached some statements concerning sight in new-born animals.

1. Sensibility to Light.

My child's sensibility to light, when he was held toward the window in the dusk, five minutes after birth, did not seem unusually great. For he opened and shut his eyes, with alternate movement, so that the space between the lids was about five millimetres wide. Soon after, I saw in the twilight both eyes wide open. At the same time the forehead was wrinkled.

Long before the close of the first day, the child's expression, as he was held with his face toward the window, became suddenly different when I shaded his eyes with my hand. The dim light, therefore, undoubtedly made an impression, and, to judge from his physiognomy, an agreeable one; for the shaded face had a less contented look.

On the second day the eyes close quickly when a candle is brought near them; on the ninth, the head is also turned away vigorously from the flame, when the candle is brought near, immediately after the awaking of the child. The eyes are shut tight. But, on the following day, the child being in the bath, when a candle was held before him at a distance of one metre, the eyes remained wide open. The sensitiveness to light is, therefore, so much greater at the moment of waking than it is a short time afterward, that the same object causes at the one time great annoyance and at the other time pleasure.

Again, on the eleventh day, the child seemed to be much pleased by a candle burning before him at a distance of one half a metre, for he gazed at it steadily with wide-open eyes, as he did also, later, at a shining curtain-holder, when the bright object was brought into his line of vision, so that it was in the direction in which he seemed to be gazing. If I turned the child away, he became fretful and began to cry; if I turned him to the light again, then his countenance resumed the expression of satisfaction. To verify this, I held the child that same day at the same distance before a burning candle, once immediately after his waking, and again after he had been awake some time in the dark. In both cases he shut his eyes.

That he liked moderately bright daylight was apparent from the frequent turning of his head toward the window when I turned him away from it. This twisting of the head became the rule on the sixth day; on the seventh it was often repeated, and every time that the face was turned toward the window the expression of satisfaction was unmistakable.

I have repeatedly made the observation that, when the light falls upon the face of sleeping infants they suddenly close the eyes more tightly, without waking, and this from the tenth day on.

In the case of my child, I found the pupils in ordinary daylight for the most part more contracted than is the case in adults—certainly less than two millimetres in diameter; and the lessening of the space between the lids, at sight of a bright surface of snow or of a shining summer cloud, was likewise more frequent and more persistent than with adults, during the whole period of observation.

Brightly-shining objects, appearing in the field of vision, often produce, from the second month on, exclamations of delight. But other highly-colored objects also easily rouse the attention of the infant. In the tenth month he is pleased when the lamp is lighted in the evening; he laughs at the light, and reaches after the bright globe.

Of the observations of others concerning the sensibility of new-born human beings to light, the following are to be mentioned:

1. Fully-matured children just born shut the eyes quickly and convulsively when exposed to bright light. Individuals, also, among children born two months too soon, distinguish between light and darkness on the second day.

2. In the very first hours the pupil of the eye contracts in a bright light, and expands in light less bright.

3. If one eye of the new-born child is shut while the other is open, then the pupil of the latter expands.

4. Infants from two to four days old, sleeping in the dark, shut the lids tightly, and even awake with a start when the bright light of a candle comes very near their eyes.

To these statements of Prof. Kussmaul, the first of which, in particular, I can confirm, Dr. Genzmer adds that the eyes of the newly-born, when suddenly exposed to bright light, make a movement of convergence; and that sensitive infants are brought into a state of general discomfort and made to cry, by a sudden glare of light, or by a quickly-changing, dazzling light; this I can confirm. The alternate shutting and opening of the eyes, that is often to be seen in infants exposed to bright light, was seen by Genzmer even in a sleeping child two days old—a remarkable observation, which waits confirmation. On the other hand, I never saw a new-born child bear dazzlingly bright light quietly with open eyes. Assertions of an experience contrary to this may, perhaps, rest on the observation of children born blind.

From all the foregoing statements we conclude that, with fully-matured new-born human beings, sensibility to light is normally present either directly after birth, or a few minutes, or at most a few hours, after birth; that light and darkness are discriminated in sensation; further, that the reflex arc from the optic nerve to the *oculomotorius* already performs its function— especially is this true of the filaments that contract the pupils. Here, then, we have an inborn reflex, and that of a double sort, since both pupils contract when the light reaches one of them. Further, at the beginning,

3

sensibility to light on awaking, or after being awhile in the dark, amounts to an aversion to light; yet a dim light is already sought, and therefore is not unpleasant. Finally, we infer that after some days ordinary daylight, or a brilliant and brightly-shining object, excites cheerfulness, the aversion to light disappears, and the head is turned oftener to the window.

2. Discrimination of Colors.

At what age the child is capable of distinguishing colors, at least red, yellow, green, and blue, it is hard to determine. In the first days, it is certain that only the difference of light and dark is perceived, and this imperfectly; moreover (according to Flechsig), the *tractus opticus*, which in the matured child is still gray at first, does not get its nerve medulla, and with that its permanent coloring, till three or four days after birth. And even then the differentiation of simultaneous bright and dark impressions proceeds slowly.

The first object that made an impression on account of its color, upon my boy, was probably a rose-colored curtain which hung, brightly lighted by the sun but not dazzlingly bright, about a foot before the child's face. This was on the twenty-third day. The child laughed and uttered sounds of satisfaction.

As the smooth, motionless, bright-colored surface alone occupied the whole field of vision, it must have been on account either of its brightness or of its color that it was the source of pleasure. In the evening of the same day, the flame of the candle, at the distance of one metre, caused quite similar expressions of pleasure when it was placed before the eyes, which had been gazing into empty space; and so did, on the forty-second day, the sight of colored tassels in motion, but in this case the movement also was a source of pleasure.

In the eighty-fifth week, when I undertook the first systematic tests, with counters alike in form but unlike in color, no trace of discrimination in color was as yet to be discerned, although without doubt it already existed. Different as were the impressions of sound made by the words " red," " yellow," " green," " blue " (these were certainly distinguished from one another), and well as the child knew the meaning of " give," he was not able to give the counters of the right color, even when only " red " and " green " were called for. We are not to infer from this, however, an inability of the eye to distinguish one color from another, for here it is essential to consider the difficulty of associating the sound of the word " red " or " green " with the proper color-sensation, even when the sensation is present.

At this time, before the age of twenty-one months, there must have been recognition not only of the varying intensity of light (white, gray, black), but also of the quality of some colors, for the delight in striking colors was manifest. Yet in the case of little children, even after they have begun to speak, it can not be determined without searching tests what colors they distinguish and rightly name.

In order, then, to ascertain how the separate colors are related to one another in this respect, I have made several hundred color-tests with my child, beginning at the end of his second year. These I used to apply every day in the early morning, for a week; then, after an interval of a week, again almost every day, but in a different manner—as will be shown directly.

In all these tests I made use of the colored ovals which Dr. H. Magnus, of Breslau, gives in his "Tafel zur Erziehung des Farbensinnes" (1879), ("Chart for the Training of the Color-Sense").

After the names "red" and "green" had been repeatedly pronounced while the corresponding colors were presented, then these two colors were simply presented and the questions, "Where is red?" and "Where is green?" were put, always in alternation. The trials were absolutely without result in the eighty-sixth and eighty-seventh weeks. After an interval of twenty-two weeks, on the seven hundred fifty-eighth day, I received eleven times a right answer, six times a wrong answer. On the following day the answers were right seven times, wrong five times; on the day after that, nine times right, five times wrong. From this it seemed probable, already, that the two colors were distinguished, either on account of their quality or on account of their brightness, and that the right names were often associated with them. To my surprise, however, on the seven hundred sixty-third day the answers were right fifteen times and wrong only once, and on the following day ten times right and not once wrong. The child had therefore firmly grasped the connection of the sound-impressions "red" and "green" with two different light-impressions. For such proportions as those of the above numbers exclude the possibility of chance.

I carried the test further. To red and green I added yellow, and when the three colors were lying near one another, each one was rightly pointed out in answer to the question where it was. Then came a disinclination on the part of the child to continue, such as often makes color-tests impossible in children so young. When the trial was repeated, he was inattentive, and he confounded the three colors with one another. On the following day, the seven hundred sixty-fifth, green especially was confounded with yellow. The answers on five days of the one hundred tenth week were:

	Right.	Wrong.
Red..........................	26	10
Green........................	24	7
Yellow.......................	23	5
Total......................	73	22

Blue was now added as a fourth color. The answers in eight trials, during the time from the end of the one hundred tenth to the beginning of the one hundred twelfth week, were:

	Right.	Wrong.
Red..........................	32	14
Green........................	31	8
Yellow.......................	34	2
Blue.........................	27	12
Total......................	124	36

Often, especially on being asked "Where is blue?" the child would consider long, observe the four colors attentively before deciding, and then give me the color quickly. It appears evident that yellow is recognized more surely than are the other colors. Yellow seems to be the easiest to distinguish, and hence the easiest also to retain in memory. I made other tests of the same sort, which showed the superiority of yellow. Then violet was added as the fifth color, called "lila," as easier to speak, and a different way of conducting the experiment was adopted.

I laid each color separately before the child and asked, "What is that?" He answered, *rroot* [Eng. pronunciation *wrote*] (for *roth*, red), *delp*, *depp*, *gelp* (for *gelb*, yellow), *rihn*, *ihn* [Eng. pr. *reen*, *een*] (for *grün*, green), *balau* (for *blau*, blue), and *lilla* (for *lila*, violet).

In the one hundred twelfth week the answers in four trials were:

	Right.	Wrong.
Red...	10	2
Yellow..	9	0
Green...	9	1
Blue...	5	7
Violet...	11	1
Total.......................	44	11

Here, too, yellow is foremost; it was named correctly nine times, not once wrongly named. Blue comes last. It was confounded especially with green and violet. If the child's attention failed, I broke off.

Afterward the tests were continued in both ways combined; but these proved to be great consumers of time. It often happens that the child takes no interest in the colors. Sometimes, from roguishness, he *will* not name the color he knows, and will not point out or give me the one I ask for. At other times he himself brings the box that holds the color-ovals, and says *wawa* = "Farbe" (color), in expectation of a lesson. The trials in which the attention is undivided are, however, not numerous.

Gray is added. In the one hundred twelfth and one hundred thirteenth weeks five tests yielded the following answers:

	Right.	Wrong.
Red.................................	16	3
Yellow..............................	22	1
Green..............................	14	5
Blue...............................	10	15
Violet..............................	18	1
Gray...............................	10	2
Total....	90	27

Yellow maintains the first place, being rightly named in twenty-two instances, and wrongly only once. The judgment in regard to blue is the worst; fifteen wrong judgments to ten right ones. It is noteworthy that in this series, as in the preceding, violet is rightly named oftener than green.

I now bade the child, repeatedly, to place together the ovals of the same color. After much moving hither and thither, he succeeded with yellow, red, rose, green, and violet, but very incompletely. The expressions "light" and "dark," before the names of the colors, were beyond the child's understanding. So the saturated and the less saturated colors, the light and the dark, were, as before, indicated by the common name of the quality alone. Four trials with the colors mixed, during the time from the one hundred fourteenth to the one hundred sixteenth week, resulted as follows:

	Right.	Wrong.
Red......	15	1
Yellow..............................	13	0
Green.........................	4	7
Blue...............................	3	10
Violet..............................	11	2
Gray...............................	6	0
Brown........................	4	0
Rose...............................	1	2
Black..............................	2	0
Total........................	59	22

Blue was especially confounded with violet, also with green. All very pale colors were confounded with gray, all dark ones with black. The order in which the colors were recognized, i. e., rightly named, is now the following: Yellow best of all, then red, violet, green; and worst of all, blue.

On other days I laid before the child, as I had done previously, a single color, with the question, what it was, and marked the answer wrong if it were not given right immediately. The colors are now called by the child *rott, delp, drün, blau, lila, grau, swarz, rosa, braun.*

Four trials in the one hundred fourteenth and one hundred fifteenth weeks yielded the answers:

	Right.	Wrong.
Red..................................	13	0
Yellow...............................	11	0
Green................................	7	9
Blue.................................	5	13
Violet...............................	10	3
Gray.................................	1	3
Brown................................	4	1
Rose.................................	3	3
Black................................	4	0
Total.....................	58	32

For the first five colors this trial gives the same order of succession as above. Blue and green are very uncertain; blue is called *drün* (meant for grün) and *lila* (violet), green is called gray; and, oftener still, neither blue nor green is named at all; while yellow, and red, and black, are given correctly and quickly.

I now let the child take out of the box of colored ovals one after another of them, at pleasure, name it, and give it to me. At the first trial he seized at random ; at the second he sought his favorite color, yellow.

Two trials in the one hundred fifteenth week :

	Right.	Wrong.
Red..	6	0
Yellow.....................................	8	0
Green......................................	1	2
Blue.......................................	0	5
Violet.....................................	4	1
Gray.......................................	1	5
Brown.....................................	0	1
Rose.......................................	3	2
Black......................................	2	0
Total........................	25	16

The result is the same as above. Red, yellow, and black are the only colors that are surely recognized.

I now made no more trials for two months. The child spent the larger part of the day in the open air, with me, on a journey ; the greater part of the time was spent in the neighborhood of Lake Garda.

In the one hundred twenty-first week, an occasional examination showed a greater uncertainty than before. Blue was scarcely once named rightly, in spite of the most urgent cautions. When the trials were resumed, after our return, the result was bad. I took the colored counters in my hand and put questions. At the very first questioning, yellow was indeed named rightly three times, and not wrongly at all ; but red was twice wrongly and not once rightly named.

I got the following answers in the one hundred twenty-fourth week, in the first four trials with all the colors after the interval :

	Right.	Wrong.
Red......................................	17	0
Yellow....................................	22	0
Green.....................................	0	18
Blue......................................	0	13
Violet....................................	9	4
Gray.....................................	0	5
Brown....................................	4	3
Rose.....................................	3	4
Black....................................	3	0
Orange...................................	0	2
Total...........................	58	49

Here it is still more evident than before that red
and yellow are already more surely recognized and more
correctly named than green and blue. On the eight
hundred sixty-sixth day the child, without being constrained, took colors out of the box and gave them to me,
naming them as he did so. The colors that were mistaken
for one another were rose, gray, and pale green; brown
and gray; green and black; finally, blue and violet.

In the following experiments, also, the child every
time took the colors out of the box and gave them to
me, telling the names at the same time, without the least
direction. Five trials out of the one hundred twenty-
fourth and one hundred twenty-fifth weeks gave:

	Right.	Wrong.
Red......................................	29	1
Yellow....................................	16	0
Green.....................................	0	4
Blue......................................	0	6
Violet....................................	14	0
Gray.....................................	0	8
Rose.....................................	14	5
Brown....................................	7	2
Black....................................	0	2
Orange...................................	0	6
Total...........................	80	34

Red and yellow are eagerly sought and almost always rightly named; blue and green avoided and always named wrongly (e. g., as *lila, swarz*). I now removed all the red and yellow colors from the collection, and let the child give to me, and name as many of the remaining ones as he could on a stretch. Now that red and yellow are wanting, however, he shows from the first a less degree of interest, and in the case of green he says "Papa tell!" In all other cases he had a name for the color he took. If that was wrong, it was always corrected by me, often by the child himself; but it was always entered in the record as wrong, if the first answer was wrong. In the one hundred twenty-fifth and one hundred twenty-sixth weeks six trials were made in which this method was strictly observed and the following judgments were registered:

	Right.	Wrong.
Green	2	19
Blue	6	20
Violet	20	3
Gray	0	6
Rose	19	6
Brown	15	0
Black	7	2
Orange	11	7
Total	80	63

The brighter colors were at first selected. The child confuses orange (*oroos*, as he calls it) with yellow, blue with violet, green with gray, black with brown.

I tried repeatedly to induce the child to place together the colors that seemed to him alike, but it was a total failure. Then I asked for single colors by their names, but the results of this procedure were likewise

poor. (This on the eight hundred seventy-ninth day.)
Finally, I took a single color at a time and asked, " What
is that ? " In four trials in the one hundred twenty-
sixth, one hundred twenty-seventh, and one hundred
twenty-eighth weeks, the answers were :

	Right.	Wrong.
Red..	11	(1)
Yellow.....................................	11	0
Green......................................	1	14
Blue.......................................	1	11
Violet.....................................	12	1
Gray	6	1
Rose.......................................	11	2
Brown......................................	10	0
Black......................................	6	1
Orange.....................................	6	2 and (1)
Total..........................	75	34

For green and blue—which are confounded with
gray when they are light, and with black when they
are dark—there is probably a less degree of sensibility,
certainly a less interest. Blue is still called *lila*. Besides, it is very difficult to direct the attention persistently to the colors. The child, although tested only in
the early hours of morning, seeks now other means of
entertaining himself. Now and then he makes a mistake in speaking. (Errors of this kind are indicated by
parentheses). But on the eight hundred ninety-eighth
day every color was rightly named—green and blue, to
be sure, only after some guessing. In six trials in the
one hundred twenty-ninth, one hundred thirty-fifth, one
hundred thirty-sixth, one hundred thirty-seventh, and
one hundred thirty-eighth weeks the child took the colors
and gave them to me, naming them. The answers were :

	Right.	Wrong.
Red	27	1
Yellow	27	0
Green	2	14
Blue	2	13
Violet	15	2
Gray	5	1
Rose	10	3
Brown	14	0
Black	5	1
Orange	12	3
Total	119	38

There is confounding of colors as before. The only thing new is the designation *garnix* (for *gar nichts*, " nothing at all ") for green and blue. Unknown colors are now often named green—e. g., blue. In a bouquet of yellow roses these were designated as yellow, but the leaves were obstinately called *garnix*, and so likewise were very whitish colors, whose quality is, however, recognizable at once, in a moderate light, by adults acquainted with colors.

On the nine hundred thirty-fourth day there was this remarkable utterance when green and blue were placed before the child: *grin blau kann e nicht, grosse mann kann grin blau,* which meant (as appeared from similar utterances), " I can't give green and blue rightly; a grown person can." Green was mostly called gray; very rarely (inquiringly) it was called red; blue was named *lila*. In the one hundred thirty-first and one hundred thirty-fourth weeks I made three trials, asking for colors which I laid out; in the one hundred thirty-eighth and one hundred thirty-ninth weeks, in three trials, sometimes the child took the colors himself, sometimes I put them before him. The answers were:

	Right.	Wrong.
Red....................................	14	1
Yellow.................................	24	0
Green..................................	4	13
Blue...................................	0	15
Violet..................................	9	5
Gray...................................	5	0
Rose...................................	9	2
Brown..................................	11	1
Black..................................	7	1
Orange.................................	10	1
Total.........................	93	39

Here begins at last the right naming of green, while
blue is not yet so often correctly designated. The child
took the colors of his own accord and named them in
three trials, in the one hundred thirty-ninth, one hundred
forty-first, and one hundred forty-sixth weeks, as follows:

	Right.	Wrong.
Red....................................	19	2
Yellow.................................	12	0
Green..................................	2	2
Blue...................................	2	11
Violet..................................	6	1
Gray...................................	1	2
Rose...................................	3	0
Brown..................................	10	0
Black..................................	3	0
Orange	8	1
Total.........................	66	19

The red twice misnamed was dark. The word
"green" was now rightly applied continually to leaves
and to meadows, and, before the completion of the third
year, blue also was almost invariably designated correctly, if the attention was not diverted.

With regard to the order in which the colors were rightly named up to the thirty-fourth month, the total result is as follows:

	JUDGMENTS.		PER CENT.	
	Right.	Wrong.	Right.	Wrong.
I. Yellow...............	232	8	96·7	3·3
II. Brown...............	79	8	90·8	9·2
III. Red.................	235	36	86·7	13·3
IV. Violet...............	139	24	85·3	14·7
V. Black...............	39	7	84·8	15·2
VI. Rose...............	76	29	72·4	27·6
VII. Orange.............	47	23	67·1	32·9
VIII. Gray...............	35	33	51·5	48·5
IX. Green...............	101	123	45·0	55·0
X. Blue...............	61	151	28·8	71·2
Total..............	1,044	442	70·3	29·7

Thus, of the four principal colors, yellow and red are *named rightly much sooner* than are green and blue; and yellow first—brown is (dull) yellow—then red. That the color-sensations, green, blue, and violet, exist in very different proportions, is probably not a peculiarity of the individual. Violet, which was much oftener named rightly than were green and blue, contains the already well-known red, and may appear to the child as a dirty red, or as dark red. For it is in fact probable that blue and greenish-blue were perceived in the earliest period, not as blue and greenish-blue, but as gray and black. That green of every sort is not named rightly till very late, may be owing, in part, to a stronger absorption of light, by means of the blood of the vessels of the retina. Although the place of the clearest vision, in the back part of the eye, is free from blood-vessels, yet the other colors which, like yellow, orange, red, and brown, reach the retina undimmed, in great extension, have, on that account, an advantage over green and blue, which are most easily confounded with gray.

Even in the fourth year, blue was still often called gray in the dusk of morning, when it appeared to me distinctly blue. The child would wonder that his light-blue stockings had become gray in the night. This I observed on three days.

Gray is, without doubt, along with white and black, rightly known long before the first discrimination of colors, but is often wrongly named, for the reason that green and blue are probably perceived as gray. The right naming of it became the rule before the end of the third year, whereas yellow was rightly named, almost invariably, nearly a year earlier. To this color the pigment of the yellow spot is most helpful. Red may also have an advantage, in the fact that in bright daylight, when the eyes are shut, especially when snow is on the ground, that is the only color in the field of vision [i. e., the eyelids are translucent, and we perceive red]; as black is the only one before we fall asleep in the dark.

On the whole we must, accordingly, declare the child to be still somewhat lacking in sensibility to the cold colors in the second year and the first half of the third year; a conclusion with which occasional observations concerning other children harmonize. At any rate, by very many children, yellow is first rightly named and blue last. One boy began, before he had reached the age of four months, to prefer a brilliant red to other colors.* All children prefer, like him, at this

---

* According to Genzmer: "Untersuchungen über die Sinnes-wahrnehmungen des neugeborenen Menschen," 1859.

age and long after, the whitish colors, without regard to their quality.

The incapacity of the two-years-old child to name blue and green correctly can not be attributed solely to his possible inability to associate firmly the names "blue" and "green" (which he has heard and which he uses fluently) with his possibly distinct sensations; for "yellow" and "red" have already been used correctly many months before. If green and blue were as distinct as yellow and red in his sensation, then there would not be the least occasion for his giving them wrong names, and preferring red and yellow to them in all circumstances. The child does not yet *know* what green and blue signify, although he is already acquainted with yellow and red. Neither does he yet know what "green" means when, in the one hundred ninth and one hundred twelfth weeks of his life, he apparently distinguishes "red" and "green" correctly. Green is at this time, for him, merely something that is not red.

I have yet to mention that my child, at the beginning of his third year, moved and handled himself with surprising sureness and quickness in the semi-darkness of twilight; he thus discriminated well between light and dark. And at the beginning of his fourth year he named correctly all the colors except the very dark or the pale ones, particularly even the most varying shades of green and blue, to the astonishment of those who had been occasionally present at the color-lessons here described, and who had witnessed his numerous errors.

Other children, with sound eyes, are likewise perfectly sure in their naming of colors at the age of three

4

years, though very uncertain at the age of two years. A boy of two and two-thirds years was impressed by the colors in the following order:

1, dark violet; 2, yellow; 3, red; 4, blue; 5, green. Here the first named was singled out before the others on account of its being dark.*

A boy of four years, who had received no regular instruction in observing colors, was asked by his father what colors he saw in a brilliant rainbow that was just then defining itself sharply upon the gray sky. The child answered slowly, but with decision, "Red, yellow, green, blue"; and he afterward, as I am informed by his father, Prof. Bardeleben, of Jena, always picked out these principal colors easily among paints, whereas the naming of violet, reddish-yellow, and other mixed colors, was difficult for him.

3. Movements of the Eyelids.

The eyelids are not often kept apart long in the first days of life. Newly-born children, even when awake, keep their eyes shut far more than they keep them open. And, when the lids are raised, there appears for the most part a strange asymmetry. One eye remains open while the other is shut. Alternate shutting and opening were seen by me frequently from the first to the eleventh day; afterward more seldom. Yet my child, before the first twenty-four hours were passed, had both eyes wide open, once, at the same time, in the twilight. During the first month the rule was, that when both eyes were open at the same time, they were not open

---

* Frau Dr. Friedemann.

equally wide; this was still strikingly noticeable on the thirty-first day. At this time, too, the occasional keeping open of one eye only had not ceased. Further, even when both eyes were closed, the movements of the left and right upper lids were frequently not simultaneous.

Other remarkable irregular (atypische) movements of the lids were seen in connection with the raising and lowering of the look on one side and on both sides. Especially, in the fifth week, the lids were often raised while the look was directed downward, so that the white sclerotic was visible over the cornea; a movement that an adult imitates with difficulty, and that lends to the countenance an expression almost of a character to cause anxiety. But long before the third month the lid followed the pupil regularly when the look was downward. When, on the contrary, the child, as he lay on his back, directed his glance toward his forehead, which he did without wrinkling his forehead in the least, the lid was not always raised, but it often covered the iris close up to the pupil, sometimes even partially covering the latter; and this I saw repeatedly as late as the eighth week.

The "rolling of the eyes" by sick children, the pupils going upward and the upper eyelid downward, so that only the white sclerotic remains visible in the space between the lids, is an advanced stage of this physiological irregularity, which appears also in hysterical patients. Even toward the end of the third month I saw that when the child looked up (as he was carried on the arm in an upright position), e. g., to a lamp standing high, the eyelid was not completely raised, but here, too, the pupil was touched by the edge of the lid at a tangent. At this time the forehead, which, in the first days, appeared often in horizontal folds, as is the case with monkeys, was either not wrinkled at all or very little, and in exceptional cases, when the look was directed upward. Not till the ninety-eighth day was my boy's brow wrinkled when he looked upward, and then not to such a degree as that of an adult, and even in the eighth month the brow was not wrinkled invariably; but from the end of the ninth month it was regularly so. This co-ordinate movement is therefore acquired, probably because it enlarges the field of vision when one is looking upward, without making it necessary to bend back the head.

The raising of the lid along with the downward look was seen in the first days of infant life, up to the tenth day, by Raehlmann, and Witkowski also, and they rightly call attention to the fact that the relation of compulsory dependence between the raising of the lid and the elevation of the cornea does not yet exist at the beginning. The muscle that raises the lid can contract at the same time with the lower rectus muscle of the eye; the upper rectus muscle of the eye may contract without the one that lifts the lid: later, this can no longer be done. There must be, then, at the beginning, within the province of the oculómotorius, an independence of the separate branches, that is afterward lost. The co-excitement of the branch that goes to the elevator of the lid (levator palpebræ), on occasion of the excitement of the branch going to the elevator of the glance (rectus superior), in the upper division of the oculomotorius, is accordingly something acquired—is

learned afresh by each individual human being—on account of the help it gives in the act of seeing. Just so,
according to our observations, the perfectly useless excitement of the elevator-branch on occasion of the excitement of the branch that goes to the muscle that
depresses the glance (rectus inferior) in the lower division of the oculomotorius, though frequent at first, is
so persistently omitted farther on, that adults are hardly able to contract at the same time the lid-elevator and
the eye-depressor (rectus inferior), i. e., to direct the
look downward with the eye wide open. Consequently,
the movements under consideration—of the upper eyelid upward in looking up, and downward in looking
down—are not inborn in human beings.

On the other hand, the closing of the lid when it is
exposed to a strong light, as well as the contracting of
the pupil in light, is inborn. But the case here is one
of reflex action of the optic nerve: on the one hand,
upon the orbicularis branch of the facialis; on the
other hand, upon the *iris* branch of the oculomotorius,
not therefore a case of associated movements, but of
purely sensori-motor reflexes.

The quick shutting of the eye by a sudden movement of the lid, followed immediately by the opening
of it—what is called winking—does not appear, as is
well known, in new-born or in very young infants.
The fact is well established that they bear the sudden
approach of a hand to the eye without moving the lid;
whereas, later in life, every one in such circumstances
shuts the eye for an instant, or even starts back at the
first approach, just as after an actual touch—and this
even when there is a pane of glass before the face—un-

less special practice in the control of this reflex movement leads in manhood to the voluntary inhibition
of it.

I have determined the time in the case of my child
at which the first winking occurred as a sign of fright
at any sudden impression, and as an expression of surprise at a new impression made upon the sense of
sight. My experience is as follows:

I put my hand suddenly near the face of the child,
as he lay quiet with open eyes, without the least reaction
on his part, on the sixth, eighth, eleventh, twelfth,
twenty-second, twenty-fifth, fiftieth, and fifty-fifth days.
During this period the softest touch of the lashes, of
the edges of the lids, of the conjunctiva, or the cornea,
occasioned an immediate closing of the lid. The dropping of the lid up to the twelfth day was, however,
decidedly slower than it is in adults. On the fifty-
seventh and fifty-eighth days I noticed that winking
made its appearance for the first time, occurring when
I put my head quickly near the child's face; but, on
repeating the experiment several times, both eyes remained open. On the sixtieth day, the quick, simultaneous shutting and opening of both eyes in case of
fright at a quick approach to the face (just as in case of
a sudden loud sound), is already the rule. At such
times the child often throws up both arms quickly, alike
whether he is lying down or is held in the arms. This
is the case especially as late as the fourteenth week. At
this time, however, there was not observable any starting back with the head, or the upper part of the body,
at the rapid approach of my face to his; whereas the
winking now invariably appears promptly, even when

the approach is repeated several times in close succession. It was the same in the fifteenth and sixteenth weeks. Other children, however (according to Sigismund), do not yet close their eyes in the fourteenth and even the sixteenth week, when you thrust at them with the finger as if you meant to hit them. The difference is probably owing to the fact that the finger occupies too small an area in the field of vision compared with the palm of the hand and with the face. O. Soltmann found that the seventh and eighth weeks marked the first appearance of the lid movement in the experiment of the "attacking hand," and my observations accord with this.

Not till after the first three months did I observe that the eyes were closed when, in the bath, water touched the cornea or even the lashes; in the first days the wetting of the eyes, even when it was repeated, having occasioned no closing of the lid at all. Probably it is experiences of this kind—of disagreeable sensation when the exposed parts of the eye are touched—that caused in the ninth week, for the first time, the closing of the lid when a large object suddenly approached the eye without touching it; for the rapid approach is in itself not pleasing. For the rest, the winking on occasion of a strong, unexpected impression remained, after it had once appeared, as an acquired reflex movement, which returned on every provocation of that sort. Thus, it followed with uncommon quickness upon a puff of wind in the face (e. g., in the twenty-fifth week). The child stared with an inquiring gaze in the direction whence the current of air came, after he had responded to it with the eyelids.

It is not allowable to assume, in explanation of this reflex movement, that the idea of danger must first be formed in order to produce the closure of the eyes, as many suppose. In that case there would be no purely reflex action, but a habit. But the time is too short for the production of an idea along with the volitional impulse to lower the lid, and a child of nine weeks has not yet the idea of danger. He does not know that, with the sudden change in the distribution of light and shade in the field of vision, at the approach of the hand, there may be joined a danger to himself; and he winks just the same at a sudden noise, even on the twenty-fifth day of his life.

Had he the idea of danger, he would start back with the head or the upper part of his body at the quick approach of my hand or my head, as he does later. We should be forced to adopt the auxiliary hypothesis that an experience made by the child's ancestors in a more mature period of life led to a habit which then manifested itself in the descendants early in life as an hereditary habit. This Darwinian view is superfluous, because *the disagreeable feeling* that is connected with every unexpected, sudden, and strong sense-impression, is of itself sufficient to induce the closing of the lid. For so long as the child can not rightly separate his sense-impressions, especially those of sight, so long as he does not plainly discern the rapid changes in a moderately bright field of vision, he can not be disagreeably affected by these changes. But if he is sufficiently developed to observe sudden and important changes, then he will experience a disagreeable feeling, will be frightened, and the immediate consequence of this will be the warding off of that which offends him—he will shut the eyelids. Thus, the shutting of the eyes at the sudden impression of light is seen to be akin to the keeping of them tightly shut when exposed to bright light during the first days of life; and it remains only to explain the difference, that at the beginning the eye remains closed longer, for the newly-born do not wink. This difference, merely quantitative, is probably due to the less rapid propagation of the nerve-excitement, to the greater extent of time involved in the reflex, and especially to the greater intensity and duration of the stimulus. Dazzling light causes to adults likewise a more disagreeable feeling than does the rapid approach of a strange hand. Lightning produces a momentary closing of the lids; a surface of snow, brightly illuminated by the sun, occasions shutting of the eyes and blinking, and even the tight compression of the eyelids.

The lessening of the space between the lids, and the complete closing of the eyes, in shutting them tightly, is effected, upon the whole, by the contraction of the muscle that closes the eye (musculus orbicularis), whereas the dropping of the upper lid in winking is produced by the contraction of the lid-muscles (musculi palpebrales) alone; and blinking, proper, at the sight of a dazzlingly bright object, by the contraction of the external parts of the orbicular muscle (particularly the orbital and cheek muscle). All these orbicular filaments are supplied by the facial nerve (nervus facialis) as their only motor nerve. As the reflex from the optic nerve is perfect from the first day of existence, since bright light causes tight closing of the eyes, it follows that the reflex arc from the optic nerve to this branch of the

facialis, as well as that to the iris branch of the oculomotorius, must be inborn.

The quick shutting and opening of the eye in case
of surprise also becomes more intelligible if we dismiss
the hypothesis of the idea of danger—an idea that is as
yet foreign to the child—and consider rather that every
surprise, even a joyous one, is at the first instant akin to
fright, on account of the unexpectedness it brings with
it—the sudden impression on the senses.   Sudden danger is only a special case.   Even in adults an unexpected
loud sound occasions invariably the winking movement
of the lids.

On the twenty-fifth day my child fixed his eyes for
the first time upon the face of his nurse, then upon mine
and his mother's, and when I nodded he opened his eyes
wider, and shut and opened the lids several times.   The
same movements appeared when I for the first time
spoke to him in a deep voice, as I did on the day mentioned.   It was a reflex movement of surprise.

At the end of the seventh month, a green fan being
rapidly opened and clapped together at a distance of
half a metre from his face, my child shut and opened
his eyes quickly every time with an expression of the
greatest astonishment, until I had repeated the experiment a good many times in succession; and even then
there remained a boundless surprise at the disappearance
and reappearance of the large, round surface.   This was
discernible in his immovability, following upon previous
agitation, and in the intensity of his gaze.   The play
of the lid is also observed in case of other new movements, especially rhythmical ones, as in hearing new
noises; and then the mouth often remains open, and

the eyes are wide open, yet there is no lifting of the eyebrows (in the eighth month).

But not only surprise, strong desire is likewise associated with the keeping of the lids open to the maximum extent. When, in the thirty-fourth week, I took away from the babe his milk, he gazed at it rigidly, and opened his eyes wide, and they took on an expression of indescribable longing. Moreover, sounds of desire were often expressed imperfectly, with closed lips, and this continued as a habit with him in the second year. The eyes were, besides, noticeably more lustrous than usual, when the child was mastered by strong desire, surprise, or joy, which is to be explained as the consequence of an excitement of the secretory nerve of the lachrymal gland (ramus lacrymalis trigemini) accompanying the psychical excitement, rather than as the result of compression of the gland through increased supply of blood.

More important in regard to psychogenesis is the fact, established by me concerning all infants, that from birth they manifest a high degree of pleasurable feeling by wide-open eyes; unpleasant feeling by shutting the eyes and holding them firmly together. In reference to the first, it surprised me that when the child was placed at his mother's breast, and even just before being placed there, the eyes were regularly stretched open, and almost always remained wide open when he began to suck. This was observed in increasing measure on the third, sixteenth, and twenty-first days. But also, in a warm bath of 35° C., the eyes were wide open in the first three weeks, and, although the child did not laugh, his countenance took on a pleasant expression

from the widening of the opening between the lids.
Audible and visible laughing, which appeared first on
the twenty-third day, is simply an advanced stage of
this expression of pleasure, in which "the eyes laugh."
Certain mild impressions of light also produce a wide
opening of the eyes; this was often observed from the
first day on, as has been already stated. In the case of
another child, which cried out immediately after its
head emerged from the womb, I put my finger, three
minutes later, into the child's mouth and pressed on the
tongue. At once all crying ceased, a brisk sucking began, and the expression of the countenance, which had
been hitherto discontented, became suddenly altered.
The child, not yet fully born, seemed to experience
something agreeable, and therewith—during the sucking of the finger—the eyes were widely opened. All
these observations decidedly support the opinion that
pleasure is expressed by wide-open eyes, so far as these
will bear the light of day—in twilight and moderate
artificial light, even from the moment of birth. Equally certain is it that discomfort is manifested by shutting
the eyes.

The eyes are generally shut together at the first cry
of the child, and later the rule is that all outcry on account of painful or unpleasant feelings, e. g., hunger,
brings with it a gripping of the eyes together, or, at any
rate, a considerable lessening of the opening between
the lids. And the screwing up of the eyes without
crying and without any vocal utterance, but often with
turning away of the head—e. g., in the second half of the
first year, when the teeth are coming or when the gums
are examined—is an indubitable sign of discomfort.

Afterward follows the closing of the lids at all sudden strong sense-impressions, because these bring in their train unpleasant feelings; and with feelings of pleasure the eyes are opened. If that inborn expressive movement is frequently repeated, then it takes place with greater and greater rapidity, and becomes at last pure reflex movement, occurring at all sufficiently strong, new, sudden impressions, before feelings of pleasure or of discomfort can be developed.

The already mentioned hereditary reflex from the trigeminus to the orbicular branch of the facialis—the existence of which is manifested on the first day by the closing of the lid when the hairs of the eyelash are touched, or when the conjunctiva or the cornea is touched—this, too, might be, at first, a defense against the disagreeable, an expressive movement of displeasure; since every touch, even the lightest, of the exposed parts of the eye, so abundantly supplied with nerves, is unexpected and disagreeable. The corresponding reflex path is traveled with less swiftness at first, because at this time the feeling of displeasure probably inserts itself between the centripetal and the centrifugal processes—not to mention the less rapid propagation of the nerve-excitation. Later, the reflex closing of the lid will come mechanically, after contact, without previous feeling of discomfort, and even with the appearance of the most deliberate purpose of defense. It is as if one said, " I shut my eye because it might be hurt "—in reality, however, there is no deliberation.

The difference between this hereditary trigeminus-facialis - reflex and the hereditary opticus - iris - reflex shows plainly the difference between reflexes of ancient inheritance (palæophyletic) and reflexes inherited more recently (neophyletic). For the adaptation of the pupil to bright light, which appears at once and invariably in the newly-born, and in animals without eyelids, must have been inherited at an earlier epoch than was the closing of the lid upon the eye's being touched, because the latter does not occur so promptly in the newly-born. But the new-born holds the eyes shut when dazzlingly bright light is thrown upon them, and in general when it feels discomfort, as does the maltreated frog. Out of this act of holding the eyes tightly shut has probably been differentiated the sudden, brief closing of the lid (opticus-facialis-reflex) that follows all sudden sense-impressions, and that still in the present generation, as an acquired reflex, even one that may be inhibited by the will, stands in contrast with the two other hereditary reflexive movements of defense.

4. Movements of the Eyes.

The eye-movements of the newly-born and of infants are of great interest in their bearing upon the history of the origin of the perceptions of space. The contending parties, the Nativists and the Empiricists,* in support of their views, make their appeal expressly to the child that has had no experience. The Nativists maintain that a pre-established mechanism produces from the beginning co-ordinated, associated eye-movements in the newly-born. The Empiricists hold that this is not the case, but that the eye-movements of the newly-born are

---

* See "Elements of Physiological Psychology," by George T. Ladd (1887), for explanation of these terms.

asymmetric and non-coördinated; that the intentional use of the muscles of the eye is learned only through experience, and that binocular vision, such as adults have, becomes afterward possible through the association of the movements of both eyes in "fixating" an object.

My observations show that, with regard to the simple matter of fact, both parties are right. Some new-born children actually make associated, co-ordinated movements of the eyes several times on the first day; others do not. In some cases I saw both these facts in the same child, but I never found in any child co-ordinated movements exclusively.

I saw my child before the close of the first day of his life turn both eyes at the same time to the right, then to the left, frequently, hither and thither, his head being still; then, again, he would do it moving the head in accord. During the whole time his face was turned toward the window, in the twilight. Nay, only five minutes after his birth, when I held him in the dusk toward the window, an associated movement of the eyes took place. And when I began to observe new-born children, it happened that I saw a child thirty-five minutes after birth (January 4, 1869) move his eyes only as an adult is accustomed to do, in accord.

Donders and Hering, also, have perceived such movements of the eyes in the newly-born. The observation requires only patience, because the newly-born spend the first twenty-four hours mostly in sleep, and when awake they cry a good deal, and their eyes do not remain open.

If we were to rest satisfied with noticing such facts as these, we should come to quite erroneous results.

More accurate and often repeated observation of the eye-movements of the child, especially during the first six days, taught me that the simultaneous turning of both eyes to the right or to the left is not co-ordinated with complete symmetry, as it is in adults. In the cases of a child ten hours old, and of one of six days, their eyes being wide open, I saw eye-movements that were associated, and only such, but which showed themselves, on more accurate observation, to be not perfectly in accord. On the whole, I have found that, in the newly-born, one eye very often moves independently of the other, and the turnings of the head take place in a direction opposite to that in which the eyes move. The unintentional character of both movements is plainly recognizable, and the combination of the two is, at the beginning of life, accidental. The turning of both eyes to left and right, also, which is established on the first day, takes on the appearance of accident, coming in as one among all possible movements.

As the other muscles of the body and of the face are contracted, without intention, by the very young infant, so also are the muscles of the eye.

For this reason we may observe all sorts of non-coördinated movements of the eyes accompanying grimaces, wrinkling of the brows, and movements of the lips, in cases where there is no possibility of sight or of sensibility to light, the lids being closed—e. g., on the tenth day—while the child is not crying, but is lying still. Sometimes it falls asleep with eyes half open, as may be known by its regular breathing and by the repose of its limbs, and then also are seen various unintentional movements of the eyes. Among those which attract

notice when the child is awake are movements of decided convergence. The child looks like a squinting
child. But at the beginning of the third week of life
the maximum degree of convergence and the strabismus are by no means so frequent as in the first; the
irregularity of the movements of the eyes, which others
also have observed in many new-born children, is still
clearly pronounced. Schœler saw in the first days, until the fourth, only non-coördinated movements, and until the tenth day no perfectly correct fixation. Here
his observation ceased. On the thirty-first day, in my
child, strabismus was noticed as rare; on the forty-sixth,
as very rare; on the forty-eighth and fiftieth, the same;
and irregular movements in general, as very rare from
the fifty-fifth day on; but they did appear until the
tenth week, while the child was awake. During sleep,
however, he moved his eyes asymmetrically as late as
the sixtieth day in a lively manner, often the lids, too,
on both sides, the eyes being half open and his snoring
uninterrupted. When he had attained the age of three
months, non-coördinated movements of the eyes were no
more to be observed. After this I watched the sleeping child, however, only now and then, and in the ninth
month I noticed an occasional slight irregularity.

This consolidation of the mechanism of the muscles
of the eye does not, however, by any means involve the
cessation of useless co-ordinated movements of the eyes,
as is shown by several experiences. Thus, the gaze of
one child in the twenty-third week was almost regularly
directed toward his forehead. This child, troubled with
an itching eczema on the head, would, at that time, let
his head swing hither and thither when his hands were

5

held, in case anything whatever, were it only a pillow, touched his head.

The eyes of my child easily converged in the ninth month without any assignable cause, and upon objects held before his nose at a distance of one or two inches.

In the tenth month the convergence of the lines of vision seemed disturbed; a very insignificant squinting inward appeared, but this anomaly vanished completely a few weeks later, after I had directed that he should spend more time out-of-doors, in order to favor his seeing at a distance. From that time the movements of the eyes continued to be normal. The readiness with which convergence of the eyes, upon my finger, held at the end of my boy's nose, occurred (as late as the twentieth month), is remarkable, as well as the fact that at the beginning such high degrees of convergence occur along with pupils relatively very wide open, which is not the case with adults.

All these observations are absolutely favorable to the opinion that conscious vision has decisive influence upon the regulation of the eye-movements; that only after discrimination of the light-impressions by the optic nerve-center do harmonious centro-motor impulses proceed from the nerves of the muscles of the eye (the motor oculi, abducens, trochlearis of both eyes), and that at the beginning, before the faculty of sight manifests itself—i. e., so long as only the function of sensibility to light is active—the eye-movements are not associated and not co-ordinated. Even when they are found symmetrical we can not, in face of a majority or of a very great number of irregular eye-movements, infer a pre-established, complete nerve-mechanism, having bilateral symmetry and capable of functioning at birth, such as exists in the case of sucking. For, if man brought such a mechanism with him into the world (as the chicken and other animals do), how could he come to make so many irregular, purposeless movements of the eyes before making permanent use of this mechanism?

The general rule is, that out of concurring non-co-ordinated movements of the muscles there grow gradually co-ordinated ones; so, here, with the muscles of the eyes. And, after the co-ordinated movements have become confirmed in the act of sight, there takes place, little by little, an elimination of the superfluous ones, a preference of those that are useful for distinct vision with both eyes. Just so the unregulated movements of the legs at the time of learning to walk become more and more rare, and of the co-ordinated ones, the most useful alone are retained, those which do the most service with the least effort.

It is surprising that representatives of the nativistic theory should, notwithstanding, urge in their own support the results of the investigations in regard to the newly-born—e. g., Raehlman and Witkowski, as follows: " As for the character of the eye-movements in the newly-born, they are in some respects similar to those made in sleep, but in many respects not similar. They are so far similar that they are often entirely non-coördinated; sometimes, though more seldom, of one side only; not similar, in that they generally follow much more rapidly, and in a very great majority of cases appear to be of both sides and often co-ordinated. Even at the first spontaneous opening of the space between the lids, following directly upon birth, we saw apparently co-ordinated lateral movements, which, however, in extent and intensity, were of irregular character. The eyes moved for some minutes incessantly hither and thither with a vast range, such as they do not take later in the regulated act of vision. Among these we saw, to be sure, non-coördinated movements enter suddenly, movements in which the principle of association had absolutely no part."

With this my observations are in full accord. And what the observers report of the eye-movements of sleeping children (whose lids were lifted up without their waking) also agrees in many particulars therewith and with the statements of Schœler: "As to the form of such movements we find, first, lateral turnings that are associated—i. e., they take place bilaterally and with seeming co-ordination. These are rare in sleep, yet they seem to occur; at any rate, it may be said decidedly that non-coördinated movements of the eyes are the most frequent ones. We see, e. g., both eyes move slowly to the right; the apparently associated side-movement is, however, not equal on the two sides, but is of varying force, now in one eye now in the other, so that convergences and divergences are introduced alternately.

Moreover, there are frequently quite abnormal, diametrically opposed movements of the two eyes; one eye moves slowly to the right, the other to the left; or the right eye upward to the right, while the left moves upward to the left. Finally, there occur vertical variations of both eyes of such sort that, e. g., while the right eye turns to the left and somewhat downward, the left eye turns to the left and at the same time somewhat upward. The most remarkable observation, however, is that absolutely one-sided movements occur. While, e. g., the right eye seems to fix the observer, the left eye is seen to move sidewise."

Although all these observations relate to the eyes of children (and adults) in sleep, they are all, according to my experience, perfectly applicable to waking infants in their first days.

5. Direction of the Look.

The ability to "fixate" a bright object is utterly lacking in the new-born child, because he is not yet in condition to move the muscles of the eye at his pleasure, and every fixation is an act of will. On the other hand, the ability to turn the head toward a bright object so that this can produce an image on the retina is often present on the first day of life. And the gaze of a new-born child as he lies quiet, with open eyes, is seen directed to the candle that is held before him in passing. But, in fact, the very young babe *stares*, motionless, with a stupid expression of countenance, into empty space, and merely *seems* to "fixate" the object that is brought into his line of vision. For the staring with unchanged position of the eyes does not cease when the object is removed. The look does not yet follow the removed object, neither does the head. Yet the eyes move on the seventh day independently of the turnings of the head, and converge strongly.

It has indeed been observed by Kussmaul that individuals among children prematurely born (two months too soon) lying with head turned away from the window in the dusk of evening on the second day of life, repeatedly turned the head to the window and the light when a change was made in their position ; and I have observed the same thing in the fully-matured infant regularly on the sixth day ; but this is merely a case of desire in a primitive form, not a case of the gaze following an object. The object that is apparently sought is motionless, and is not a recognized cause of sensation. The nature of the experience is rather this : such and such a position of the body or of the head is associated with an agreeable sensation—in this instance an agreeable sensation of light—and is therefore preferred ; another position, a disagreeable one, in which the face is shaded, is avoided. Just so the head is turned to the warm, smooth breast of the mother, and the turning away from it is felt as disagreeable, even in the dark.

Accordingly, the turning of the head toward a motionless, moderately bright light, that has been noticed in some children even in the first days, can not be regarded as a voluntary direction of the gaze. At the beginning there is nothing but staring when the eyes are opened, and even on the ninth day the turning away from dazzling light is no sign of knowledge of direction.

Here again I agree entirely with Raehlman and Witkowski, when they report that they have never seen movements of real fixation up to the tenth day. "It may occasionally happen that upon a certain change of the position of the lighted candle, or through some movements of the child's eyes, the eye is accidentally put in position for the light ; i. e., an image arises on the yellow spot, but this apparently intentional relation of position between the eye and the object is a purely accidental one, and assuredly is not based upon a conscious fixation."

When Darwin says that on the ninth day the eyes were directed to the lighted candle, the meaning is simply that the flame was placed in the line of the fixed gaze ; but when he adds that up to the forty-fifth day nothing has seemed thus to fasten the eyes, it must be that the critical period of the beginning of fixation passed unnoticed.

The second stage is made known by the turning of the head from one motionless, extended, bright surface in the field of vision to another. On the eleventh day my child held his gaze from one to two minutes steadily upon my face, and turned his head toward the light, which appeared close by in the field of vision. In like manner behaved a female child, who on the fourteenth day directed her gaze, which had been fastened upon her father's face, to some one who came up, and at the sight of this person's head-covering the child's gaze became rooted as if with surprise.*

At this time and later it is noticed also that the infant gazes preferably upward toward the white ceiling of the room. But the upward look that grows out of this, through which the human infant is said to be essentially distinguished from the animal, depends without doubt upon his horizontal position in the arms of his mother or nurse. If the babe were never carried in this manner, it would hardly look upward often.

The *third* stage is attained with the following of a bright object in motion, and is characterized by the associated movement of the eyes while the head is motionless.

It was on the twenty-third day of his life that my

---

* Frau Prof. von Strümpell.

child, who was gazing at the candle burning steadily at the distance of one metre before him, turned both his eyes to the left when I moved the candle to the left, and to the right when the candle was moved to the right. As soon as I held the burning candle up, both his eyes were directed upward toward the light, without any movement of the head. At the same time his face suddenly assumed a surprisingly *intelligent* expression, not before observed. When the light was moved side-wise the head was moved, often; but generally the eyes alone moved. It would also happen that the movements of the eyes were accompanied by a slight sympathetic movement of the head. The motion of the candle had to be very slow always, otherwise it was not followed.

Twenty times that day, certainly, I repeated the experiment, the result of which greatly surprised me, as other children do not follow a moving light with their eyes till after many months. I had, to be sure, made the trial almost every day since the birth of my child, and thereby the mechanism of convergence may have got an earlier start.

Two days later, and seven days later, the same trial was made with the slowly-moved candle or with my hand only. Whenever the movement was slow enough, the child followed it with his look, moving sometimes the eyes only, sometimes head and eyes in accord. Every time that both eyes moved with the light, the countenance assumed again the contented, intelligent expression which it had never worn until the twenty-third day. With that day began also active looking (as distinguished from staring). The outstretched hand, the flame of the candle, faces when they came into the field of vision, were looked at, one can not yet say "fixated," because with this word is associated the notion of voluntary, distinct vision. But from this time forth the gaze of the child was actively directed, daily, without any contrived occasion, to bright surfaces in the field of vision such as have been mentioned.

It is to be noted that no part is played in this progress by the cerebral cortex. For Longet removed carefully the cerebral hemispheres of a pigeon, sparing the corpora quadrigemina and the rest of the brain, kept the bird alive for eighteen days, and saw that in the dark not only did the sudden approach of a light produce contraction of the iris and blinking, but also as soon as he moved the burning candle in a circle the creature made a corresponding movement of the head. To this act, then, the cerebrum is not indispensable. But after the destruction of the corpora quadrigemina the trial yields no results.

While by means of such observations the transition from staring to looking could be marked with tolerable accuracy, the passage from looking to observing and "fixating" objects was not so sharply defined. In the fifth week the Christmas-tree, with its many lights, was looked at with pleasure; in the seventh the child followed with both eyes a lamp carried by some one, a glittering gold chain, or the movements of his mother's head, much more quickly and exactly than before. When looking persistently at a face quite near, his mouth is pursed in a remarkable manner, as is often seen to be the case in adults when there is a great strain of the attention.

A week earlier even, on the thirty-ninth day, the

swinging movement of tassels close in front of the child's face would elicit a pleased expression and a cry of delight. It happened also that the child, when he had been moving actively in his bed, and so had unintentionally shaken it, suddenly became still, and laughed when the blue tassels over his face were set swinging in consequence of the shaking.

In the following weeks, gilded picture-frames, that shone brightly as they reflected the light of the lamp, were looked at for minutes at a time, and the gaze was lifted accordingly. Such strong impressions of light produced gayety, just as swinging objects did. On the sixty-second day, for example, the child looked for almost half an hour at a swinging lamp hanging from the ceiling, with continuous utterances of pleasure. The eyes did not, however, in this case, follow closely the separate oscillations. Both eyes, indeed, often moved simultaneously to the left or to the right, but not in time with the lamp. His pleasure manifested itself by movements of the arms, and by sounds such as are made by a child only when he is pleasurably excited; his interest was shown by an unwavering gaze.

The day before, the child had looked upon the friendly face of his mother for some minutes and then given a cry of joy. It was as if for the first time he had discovered his mother. The face of his father, too, which always exerted a quieting influence on the child when " worrying," became at this time—before the tenth week—an occasion of gayety. In the case of a little girl, the same thing took place in her sixth week.*

---

* Frau von Strümpell.

All these facts indicate that motionless images on the retina are distinguished from moving ones, although distinct sight is not yet attained; accommodation, indeed, is still wanting.

With this the fourth stage is reached, marked by the ability, which is retained from this time forth, to direct the eyes toward an object. Right and left, above and below, are distinguished, and very soon the most extended use is made of this ability. For now the child *seeks* with his eyes untiringly for new objects, when he is awake and well. This seeking, i. e., primarily the endeavor to give *a definite direction to the look* and to hold it there, dates back to the first three months. In the tenth week, a girl-child looked for the face of the person calling her, although it was with difficulty that she held her head erect. On the other hand, a boy of the same age,* who was lying on his back, could not follow with his eyes a cane that I moved hither and thither before him, but simply stared at it.

A third child began, after the end of the sixteenth week, to look at its hands, and in the twenty-third week carried to its mouth the finger of another person that had been put into its hand.†

When, on the eighty-first day, at a distance of about one metre from my child, I rubbed with my wet finger a tall drinking-glass, and produced high tones new to the infant, he immediately turned his head, but did not hit the direction with his gaze; sought for it, and, when it was found, held it fast. From this time forth he followed with a more animated look, much more accurate-

---

* Frau von Strümpell.　　　　† E. Schulte.

ly, even without movements of the head, an outstretched hand not in rapid motion. When the hand was moved very quickly, however, the eye did not follow at all (thirteenth week). What the child seemed to like best of all to follow with his eyes, was a person walking back and forth in the room; he would turn the head more than ninety degrees, and look attentively after the moving figure (fourteenth week).

On the one hundred first day a pendulum, which was making just forty complete oscillations to the minute, was for the first time followed surely and with machine-like regularity. This proves that less than three eighths of a second is needed for the lateral movement of the eye. But for the present such quick movements are not preferred. When, in the sixteenth week, the infant went with us on a journey by rail, he directed his gaze, not at the images that were swiftly passing by the windows, but persistently and attentively at the sides and ceiling of the carriage, and (after our arrival) at the new, motionless objects in the room into which he was brought. The persistent gazing at the ceiling with head leaning back, peculiar to many infants, was especially frequent at this time and in the nineteenth week (p. 43). Yet it is becoming easier for him all the time to follow objects moved quickly. When I have been occupied with the child, if I suddenly get up to leave the room, the child always turns his head round exactly toward me very quickly, and looks after me with great eyes, one might almost say with thoughtful, inquiring eyes (fifth month). But it was not till the twenty-ninth week that I saw the child look distinctly, beyond all doubt, after a sparrow flying by.

But a much longer time passed before objects thrown on the floor, playthings which had served to amuse for a time, were followed with the eyes. Inasmuch as the point concerned here is of a discovery made afresh by every individual human being, viz., that bodies are heavy, and fall if they are not supported, I directed my attention particularly to this, and I give here some observations concerning it in the case of my child :

30th week.—The child very often lets fall to the floor objects held a short time in the hand, but up to this time he has not once looked after them.

31st week.—If the child sees or hears anything fall, he sometimes turns his gaze in the direction where the fall took place.

33d week.—The falling and letting fall of an object make no impression, although objects moved slowly downward are followed with especially close gaze of both eyes.

34th week.—The child but rarely looks after an object that falls out of his hand.

36th week.—Objects thrown to the ground are not yet followed by the child regularly, or with any expression of attention, whereas he fixes his gaze with the greatest interest on any slowly-moving objects that he can hold in view, e. g., tobacco-smoke.

43d week.—The child looks after objects thrown on the floor, oftentimes as if in wonder.

47th week.—The child throws down objects of all sorts that are put into his hands, after busying himself with them some moments, and frequently looks after them. Once he threw a book on the floor eight times in succession, with eager attention, which was manifested by the protruding of the lips.

63d–65th weeks.—Very often the child throws down objects that displease him, or with which he has played awhile, and generally looks after them.

78th week.—The throwing away of playthings is rare (giving up of the habit).

124th week.—Throwing the ball, of all plays, yields by far the greatest pleasure, and the gaze follows the ball with special precision.

The knowledge that bodies are heavy would begin, according to this, in my child, with the forty-third week, when for the first time the fall of an object previously held in his own hand causes astonishment. It would be interesting to know how it is with other children in this respect. Darwin observed that a child, even in the eighth month, could not properly follow with his gaze an object swinging only moderately fast; on the other hand, at the age of thirty-two days, this child perceived his mother's breast three or four inches away; for without touching it he protruded his lips, and his eyes were "fixed" (cf. p. 32), just as happened on the forty-ninth day at sight of a brightly-colored tassel, which made him stop moving his arms when it appeared in the field of vision.

6. Seeing Near and Distant Objects.

The approach of the flame of a candle or of a shining metallic surface to the face of an infant that has not yet moved its eyes, produces, in the first two to six weeks, convergence of the lines of vision and strabismus. This convergence seems to be associated with a strain of the muscle of accommodation, as Genzmer ascertained by observation of the lens-images. He examined one eye while the other was alternately brightly lighted and shaded, and he concludes that a previously-formed connection exists between the position of convergence and the strain of accommodation. This conjecture is, in fact, very probable. For the ante-natal existence of the reflex arc from the optic nerve to the motor oculi is proved by the contraction of the pupil exposed to light immediately after birth. Now, the motor oculi, through the excitement of which the pupil is contracted, is also the nerve of accommodation, which strains the ciliary muscle when near objects are seen, and is at the same time the nerve which supplies the internal rectus muscle of the eye and so the muscle of convergence.

When a bright object approaches the eye, accordingly, through the mere excitement of the motor oculi from the retina outward, the whole machinery of adaptation, accommodation, and convergence is at once set in action. Contraction of the pupil, thickening of the lens, and looking inward, occur together when a light is brought near the child, without justifying the supposition of the least choice or intention in the case, solely through the reflex excitement of the motor oculi from the optic nerve outward. At any rate, vision is introduced through the concurrence of these three processes with the sensation of brightness. Indistinct as the muscular sensation of the ciliary and convergence muscle may be, it will associate itself with the sensation of light the more perceptibly the oftener a bright object approaches the eye. The contraction of the pupil, moreover, does not invariably take place along with convergence in the newly-born (p.38).

But thus far the conditions are not fulfilled for securing a sharply-defined image on the retina, nor if such an image were to arise could the object be distinctly seen as a bounded surface.

For, as to the first point, it is evident that only seldom does the flame of the candle (or any bright object whatever) come directly within the distance at which the child's eye sees plainly. The infant seems to recognize distinctly, earliest of all, the face of his mother or nurse, since this is light, pictures itself oftenest on his retina, and is at the same time so near that it comes most frequently within the range of distinct vision. In this way the difference between a faint retinal image (of objects distant or too near) and sharply-defined images is impressed upon the child. The diffusion circles must assert themselves less when the moderately bright object is at a certain small remove from the eye; at all other distances they make their appearance.

As to the second point, it is certain that in the first days or weeks, even if the diffusion images should be utterly wanting, still the form of the object can not be plainly seen; the only distinct sensation is that of brightness. All experiences with people born blind, but after some years operated on successfully, point in this direction. And although learning to see is with such persons a different thing from what it is with normal infants, because the long repose of the central organs of the sense of sight causes a partly quicker, partly slower, functional development of these, yet no radical essential difference between the two developments of the process of sight can be established if the operation is performed during childhood. Even the experiences of space gained through seizing and touching can not be directly made available at the first attempt at accommodation by one born blind and gaining sight late in life. By him, as by the infant, among the countless retinal images must be preferred above all others, those which are of moderate brightness and those in which the diffusion circles amount to a minimum. For very great brightness is disagreeable, like every over-strong nerve excitement, and the dark involves a weaker nerve excitement than the moderately bright, and thus seems less adapted to arouse the attention of the eye. Of the images of medium intensity of light, that which is sharply defined is observed before all others, for the reason that this one, apart from the pleasurable feeling it causes, is distinguished from all others—precisely through its sharp outlines—the relative position is better ascertained, and the object is more easily recognized when seen again. Thus when the retinal images all appear together the brighter and sharper ones are preferred; these impress themselves first and most enduringly upon children, the others being consequently neglected. In this way the function of accommodation is set in operation. Then the eye can fixate, one after another, objects that are at unequal distances from it.

Still the step, from the reflex accommodation at the approach of an object to the eye in repose to the voluntary accommodation at the sight of two unequally distant objects, remains obscure. Probably it is first taken upon the ground of a logical process, after the child has moved himself, or at least his head and his arms, toward the object. Then first will the knowledge dawn upon

6

him, " I do not need to be nearer the object in order to see it plainly."

This experience can not, however, be turned to account before the development of the power of choice. For " fixation " is the *voluntary* bringing of an illuminated point on the place of clearest vision, the yellow spot, to a distinct image. The child that for the first time gazes at the flame of the candle has no power of choice; for him, therefore, fixation is not possible. He simply stares spell-bound by the new sensation.

Binocular fixation must, however, be inexact long after the first voluntary act of accommodation, because irregular movements of the eyes are still frequent. Fixation, properly speaking, does not in any case take place before the day on which for the first time a moving object is voluntarily followed with the gaze—not before the close of the third month (according to my observations and those of Cuignet).

But for a long time after this critical point, the perception of objects unequally distant from the eye, as also the estimate of distances, remains imperfect. How slowly the third dimension of space gets established in perception, in spite of daily practice, appears from the following observations, separated by great intervals of time, made in regard to my boy, whose sight was afterward very keen.

In the ninth week the apparatus of accommodation was already in action. At least I inferred so, from the fact that, while head and eyes were motionless and the amount of light remained unvarying in good daylight, the pupils expanded and contracted alternately several times, although this was done also even when my face remained at the same distance from that of the child. He was evidently experimenting here, letting his eyes converge more and less strongly, allowing my face to become distinct and less distinct before them.

17th week.—Objects accidentally seized are moved toward the eyes. The child often grasps at objects which are twice the length of his arm away from him; indeed, at the same object several times in succession.

18th week.—Reaching too short for the distance is very frequent.

44th week.—New objects are no longer, as was the case earlier, carried to the eyes (and to the mouth), or, at any rate, only rarely; on the other hand, they are attentively regarded and felt with the hands, the mouth being pursed. When the child regards a stranger near him (in the seventh month) his countenance takes on an expression of the greatest astonishment, mouth and eyes being wide open, all the muscles becoming suddenly rigid in the exact position they were last in. The new retinal image must therefore be quite clear, to be so easily distinguished from other retinal images of human faces—i. e., the accommodation is perfect.

47th week.—Playing with a single hair (a woman's), on which the eyes were long fixed, proves the same thing.

51st week.—Some men sawing wood, at a distance of more than one hundred feet, attract the attention of the child and give him pleasure. His sight, therefore, is keen at a distance, as it is for near objects. But that things plainly seen are at unequal distances he has not yet comprehended; for, in the—

58th week.—The child grasped again and again, with

great perseverance, at a lamp in the ceiling of a railway-carriage in which he was passing some hours, and was unusually merry over it.

68th week.—He continues to come short, very often, in his attempts to seize objects; he also reaches too far to the left or to the right, and too high and too low.

96th week.—I stood at the window in the second story and threw a piece of paper to the child, who was in the garden below. He picked it up, looked at it, and held it toward me a long time, with uplifted arm, expressing his desire that I should take it—a convincing proof how little he appreciates distance.

108th week.—Looking at small photographic likenesses of persons known to him, the child at once knows whom they represent; he must, therefore, have good power of accommodation, since only in well-defined retinal images can be perceived the differences, often slight, by which human faces are recognized.

113th week.—Articles of household furniture known to the child are also recognized at once when represented in the picture-book, and at a distance of three inches, and of three feet.

It follows from these observations that the accommodation is perfect long before the perception of distance begins—i. e., the child is able to see plainly objects at very unequal distances from the eye without knowing how unlike their distance is, nay, even without any knowledge of their being at unequal distances. He becomes acquainted with distance only at a later period, probably through the movement of his body toward the object seen, and through the failure of his attempts to seize what lies at a distance.

Yet, for all children, probably the correct estimate of distance is first established by this very act of seizing, because in this there is abundant experience, the number of the attempts being great. On the contrary, by the act of offering things to others a correct estimate of distance is not formed till much later, because there is a lack of experience at the beginning. *Giving* makes its appearance much later than *taking*.

In any case the child is much longer in getting his bearings in space, even after he has the power of visual accommodation, than are many animals, e. g., the chicken, which, after a few hours, correctly perceives the distance of a grain of corn at which it pecks (p. 67). The human being must *infer*, by a roundabout way, from many individual experiences, the third dimension of space, whereas those animals inherit a nervous mechanism which makes this appear by no means a thing to be learned. In man, right and left, over and under, are given by means of the arms and legs, as these are separated from one another; but extent from before to behind is not thus given, because the child does not see or feel itself behind. For the knowledge of extent from front to rear, i. e., of the dimension of depth, there is need of movements, especially of seizing; hence, this is not acquired until later.

The old, much-mooted question, whether the child supposes the objects it first sees distinctly (but not yet as at unequal distances from the eye) to be *in* the eye or outside of it, is answered by John Stuart Mill (1859), according to the Berkeleyan theory of space-perception, for he says that a person born blind and suddenly enabled to see would at first have no conception of *in* or *out*, and would be conscious of colors only, not of objects. When, by his sense of touch, he became acquainted with objects, and had time to associate mentally the objects he touched with the colors he saw, then, and not till then, would he begin to see objects.

The correctness of this view is shown by all the earlier and later reports of oculists in regard to blind children who learn to see after being operated upon. The same thing is true of newly-born children that have their sight; for, whenever two impressions belonging to different departments of the senses occur together in our experience, then from the presence of the one we infer the other. The knowledge of *outness* is hence much earlier awakened and established than that of the unequal distances of objects from the eye. "At the age at which a child first learns that a diminution in brightness and in apparent magnitude implies increase of distance, the child's ideas of tangible extension and magnitude are not faint and faded, but fresh and vigorous." In the beginning, however, the perception of distance, as well as perception by touch, does not exist at all, and the former is still utterly lacking when the latter has reached a comparatively advanced stage. For the experiences with persons born blind that have afterward learned to see, show that some of these patients supposed the objects seen to be touching their eyes, as objects felt touch the skin. Here Stuart Mill is quite correct in saying, "That the objects *touched* their eyes was a mere supposition which the patients made, because it was with their eyes that they perceived them." From their experiences of touch, perception of an object and contact with it were indissolubly associated in their minds. The patient would certainly not say, however, that all objects seemed to touch his eyes, if some of them appeared farther off than others. Cases of this sort, therefore, fully prove that children are at first incapable of seeing things at unequal distances. But because the patients show great zeal in learning to judge of impressions of sight by means of the sense of touch, they must also learn to judge of distances.

One question more belongs here: Are newly-born children oftener myopic (near-sighted) or hypermetropic (far-sighted)?

We have the observations of Von Jäger (1861) and of Ely concerning the eyes of the newly-born and of infants, but these observations are in part contradictory. The first observer is of opinion that the configuration of the eye in the earliest days is myopic, there being an inborn prolongation of the axis of the eye, which lasts, however, but a few weeks. Evidence of this he found also in measurements made in post-mortem examinations. He maintains, on the evidence of his ophthalmoscopic and anatomical investigations, that at the beginning the adjustment for shorter distances prevails, but in the more matured child the adjustment for greater distances (in the early years). Ely, on the contrary, who (1880) tested newly-born children and infants of a few weeks (living children only) with the ophthalmoscope, making use of belladonna (whereby a higher per cent can be obtained for inborn hypermetropia, as he himself remarks), found that emmetropia, myopia, and hypermetropia are all innate, with a preponderance of the last condition. König-stein, who examined nearly three hundred children, states that the eye of the child is probably hypermetropic ex-

clusively (1881). Renewed observations, without the
use of belladonna, are desirable, though they are, of
course, attended with great difficulties.

I saw the eyes of my child, on the twelfth day of
his life, shine very brightly (both pupils dark-red) when
the flame of a candle was behind my head at one side.
This glow of the eye indicates hypermetropia at that
time. Later, this child's eyes became emmetropic.

It can not be without influence on the whole mental
development of the child whether he distinctly sees near
objects only, or distant ones also, in the first years of his
life, but there is as yet a lack of data for estimating this
influence.

One thing only I would lay down as settled, viz.,
that the protracted occupation of little children with
fine work, such as the pricking of paper, the placing and
drawing through of threads, etc.—notwithstanding the
fact that these exercises are warmly recommended in
the so-called Kindergartens of Germany, and are practiced daily for a long time—must be injurious to the
eyes. The prolonged strain of looking at near objects
is for children from three to six years old, even in the
best light, unqualifiedly harmful. All strain of attention to near objects in the evening, when lamp-light must
be used, should especially be forbidden, otherwise the
apparatus of accommodation will get a one-sided use too
early, and near-sightedness will be invited.

7. The Interpretation of what is Seen.

Many suppose that the infant, if he distinguishes
at all any individual visible thing, sees "all objects as
if painted upon a flat surface"—that he has as yet no

conception of anything external, existing outside of his
eye; at any rate, no suspicion that anything moves toward him; that his seeing seems to be at this time
merely a dim sense of light and of darkness; the finger
appears to him only as a dark patch in a bright field of
vision, and does not project in relief from the surface
of the picture.*

In opposition to this I must contend—while I agree
with the view in relation to the newly-born and the first
days of life—that in the second quarter of the first year,
when this is also said to hold good, there must be already something more than a mere "dim sense of light
and dark." For, in the first place, the convergence of
the lines of vision exists much earlier; so that the attention is directed to individual points in the field of
vision. Secondly, the glance of both eyes follows moving objects much earlier, though not voluntarily. Thirdly, it is early announced, by exclamations of pleasure
and displeasure over single objects held before the face,
that the discovery has been made of the demarcation in
space of the changing fields, colored, or dark and light,
in the visual plane.

Withal a considerable time elapses before the child
is capable of *interpreting* the colored, light and dark,
large and small, disappearing and reappearing mosaics
—before he can understand and appreciate, before he
ceases to wonder at transparency and luster, reflection
and shadow. In this the normal babe is inferior, in
learning to see, to the person born blind but gaining

---

* Sigismund's work on "The Child and the World" ("Kind und
Welt"), 1856.

sight through a surgical operation; the latter learns
much more rapidly to interpret the field of vision, by
reason of his more abundant experiences of touch.

Some of my observations concerning the interpretation of the more common retinal impressions of the
child, made at various times, may be brought together
here for illustration.

6th month.—When I nod with a pleasant look to
my child, he laughs with unmistakable signs of pleasure,
moving his arms up and down. (When strangers accost
him, however, he does not do this.) Once he observed
my image in the mirror, became very attentive, and
suddenly turned around toward me as if he were about
to compare the image in the glass with the original,
or wished to convince himself of the doubling of the
face.

7th month.—The infant stares at a strange face near
him fully a minute, and longer, with eyes fixed and
with an expression of the greatest astonishment: he
therefore interprets it at once as something strange.

8th month.—The greatest interest is aroused by bottles—nursing-bottles, wine-bottles, and bottles for water.
They are "fixated" with a protracted gaze; the child
wants them, and they are recognized even at a distance
of two or three metres. The interest is to be explained
by the circumstance that the child now gets his nourishment from the bottle, which he takes hold of several
times a day and sees near by. For this reason he recognizes objects like it in the field of vision more easily
than other objects (except human faces).

9th month.—Just as it is with bottles that resemble
nursing-bottles, so it is now with boxes that resemble an

infant's powder-box; these are gazed at fixedly, and are desired, with outstretched arms and wide-open eyes. More and more, however, the child shows his interest in other things and occurrences in his neighborhood; in particular, he turns his head quickly toward the door when it is opened or shut, and observes attentively new objects that he holds, or that are moving, for a longer time than formerly.

10th month.—Visual impressions that are connected with food are, however, most quickly and surely interpreted correctly. The child follows the preparation of his food with lips protruded and with wide-open, glistening, eager eyes.

11th month.—When the child is awake he hardly remains quiet a moment; is always moving the eyes hither and thither, and in like manner the head, while he tries to fixate with his gaze every one who comes in or goes by.

If these facts in regard to isolated sight-impressions show an early faculty of perception by the eye, since faces, bright and large moving objects, are soon distinguished from other parts of the field of vision and are easily recognized again, yet the following facts, although they come from a still later period, prove how far from correctly new impressions are interpreted.

15th month.—The child grasped repeatedly at the lighted candle, but not far enough to reach it, and when he was near enough put his hand into the flame; but never again afterward.

16th month.—In the bath the child grasps at the jets of water that flow from his head when the sponge is squeezed upon it, as if these were strings. He tries to catch them in his fingers in a pretty way, and seems surprised at his failure.

17th month.—The child grasped, at various times, generally with a laugh, at some tobacco-smoke a few feet away from him, bent his fingers and exerted himself to seize the smoke, which floated between him and a lamp. Only imperfect conceptions are formed, then, even yet, of the distance and the substantiality of objects.

18th month.—At the unexpected sight of a tall man dressed in black, the child becomes suddenly still, stares at the man about a minute, flees to his father and gazes, motionless, at the tall figure. Immediately after the man had withdrawn, the child said *atta*, and was unrestrainedly merry and loud as before.

Here an unexpected visual impression had evidently caused anxiety, without any assignable reason, for the man whose appearance the child did not know how to interpret was friendly toward him. It was not till the end of his second year that the child ceased to be so easily embarrassed by strangers in black dress.

22d month.—New impressions seem to enchain his attention in increased degree; the mysterious grows more and more attractive.

24th month.—The child observes very attentively animals that are moving, even the slowly-creeping snail and the beetle. These objects, easily followed with the eye, appear not to be at all understood, to judge from the inquiring expression of countenance. The child is surprisingly tender with them, almost timid.

At this period the understanding of actions, and of

the use of all sorts of utensils, is further developed than the ability to interpret representations of them, although an inexhaustible fancy in play has been manifested a long time already in various ways. Sigismund's child, at the end of the second year, understood a circle as representing a plate, a square as a *bonbon*, and had in his twenty-first month recognized the shadow of his father, of which he was at first afraid, as a picture, for he pointed at it joyously, crying "Papa!" Much later than this my boy called a square, *window ;* a triangle, *roof ;* a circle, *ring ;* four points, *little birds.*

Not till after the third year is the ability to represent known objects, even by lines on paper or by cutting out, manifested. Before this the child wants to " write," *raiwe* (schreiben), i. e., to draw; and thinks that by all sorts of marks he is representing a locomotive, a horse, a spoon, a plate, a bottle; but does not succeed without help. I have had information of one child only that, in its fourth year, without instruction, could cut animals out of paper with the scissors (giraffes, greyhounds, horses, lions, camels, fishes) in such a fashion, and draw them so on the slate with a pencil, that everybody knew at once what the lines inclosed (even in the case where he had sketched a man sitting). Such a talent is very rare, and indicates an inherited sense of form. An average child can not, before the end of the third year, draw an approximately circular line returning upon itself. This boy of three and a half years, however, bites animals out of bread, draws them with a stick in the sand, models them in clay, sees animal forms in the clouds, and devotes himself to his art with the greatest perseverance for months, without direction, without the least stimulus from parents or brothers and sisters.*

The surprisingly persistent desire of my boy (in his thirtieth month), repeated daily (often several times in the day), to " write" locomotives, *Locopotiwe raiben* (he meant " draw "), sprang from his seeing locomotives frequently. These objects interested him in a remarkable degree in his third and fourth years, evidently because greater changes in the field of vision excite the special attention of the infant very early, on account of the great number of optical nerve-fibers excited by the change of light and dark. In the country the locomotive is one of the largest moving objects. It also moves swifter than horses. That this, the largest moving mass perceived, became the most interesting of all, as was the case with the steamer on the sea, seems therefore natural.

As to the rest I have not been able to determine in what way little children represent to themselves such movements. Many regarded the locomotive as tired when it stood still, as thirsty when its tank was filling with water, as a stove when it was heated; or they were afraid of every steam-engine near them, so long as it was in operation.

8. Sight in Newly-born Animals.

The perfection of sight in quite young fowls, without experience, is astonishing as compared with the incomplete development of this sense in new-born human beings. Let their eyes be kept shut, without injuring

---

* Frau Dr. Friedemann.

them, from one to three days, and, in many cases, within two minutes after the removal of the bandage, they will follow the movements of creeping insects with all the accuracy of old fowls. Within from two to fifteen minutes they peck at any object, estimating the distance with almost infallible accuracy. If the object is out of reach, they will run to it and hit it every time, so to speak, for they never miss by more than a hair's breadth, even when the kernel of grain at which they pecked is no larger than the smallest dot of the letter *i; seizing* at the moment of pecking is a more difficult operation. Although an insect is sometimes caught with the bill and swallowed at the first attempt, they generally peck five or six times, and pick up crumbs once or twice, before they succeed in swallowing food for the first time. So Spàlding reports.

His statements hold good, also, according to my observations, for fowls one day old, not bandaged but kept in the dark one day; these, without mother or companions, at once find their way of themselves wherever they are, in the incubator or on the table in the laboratory. But I can not admit the supposed infallibility to within a hair's breadth. They miss in pecking by as much as two millimetres, though seldom. On the other hand, the attempts at swallowing frequently fail. Here it should be considered that even grown fowls are not sure in their pecking, seizing, or swallowing, as any one that observes closely may easily perceive. The accuracy is, however, marvelous at the very beginning. A duckling of a day old snapped at a fly that was just flying by, and caught it; a turkey of only a day and a half directed its bill, after the manner of the elders of its race, atten-

tively and deliberately, at flies and other small insects.
(Spalding.)

Many new-born mammals have likewise in the very
first hours of life the ability to move not only the head
but the whole body toward a visual impression—e. g.,
young pigs. Spalding bandaged the eyes of two pigs
just born. One of these was brought immediately to
the mother; it soon found the teats and began to suck.
Six hours afterward the other was placed at a short distance from the mother. It found her in half a minute,
after going about in a rather unsteady manner. After a
half-minute more it found the teats. In both cases smell
and taste must, therefore, have determined the direction of the movement; in the last case probably hearing
also. But it is not expressly stated whether the mother
made her voice heard. On the following day it appeared that the one of the young ones that had been
left with the mother no longer had on the bandage.
The other was wholly unable to see, but walked about,
bumping against things. In the afternoon the bandage
was taken off. Then the creature ran about as if it had
already been able to see before it was bandaged. Ten
minutes later it was hardly to be distinguished from
another young one that had enjoyed the use of its eyes
without interruption. "Placed on a chair, it saw that
the height required considering," knelt down and
jumped off. After ten minutes more this animal was
placed, together with another, twenty feet from the
sty. Both got to their mother in five minutes, at the
same instant.

If, in the last-mentioned experiment, smell and hearing not being excluded, imitation of the animal whose

sight has not been interrupted is possible to the one that has been for only twenty minutes able to see, yet the very remarkable fact of the jumping down from the chair after the previous kneeling must be based on an act of sight. The operation of estimating distance, however imperfect it be in the brain of an animal not yet two days old, and not able to see till within ten minutes before jumping down, proves that even thus early the third dimension of space comes to consciousness through the eye, as the result of retinal impressions, otherwise the animal would not have knelt before jumping. Now, since it had hitherto had no sight-perceptions, and in those ten minutes none that gave occasion for jumping, the association of retinal excitement, estimate of distance, muscular movement for kneeling and for the jumping that followed, must be inherited. For no one would attribute to a pig so young, blind ten minutes before, such a gift of invention, as to initiate, out of independent deliberation, a proceeding so rational and so well adapted to its purpose. The animal jumps because its ancestors have jumped countless times without waiting long or estimating carefully the distance. A human infant does not possess this association of retinal excitement and coordinated muscular movement. It moves without purpose and falls from the chair. The young Guinea-pig, on the other hand, does not jump and does not fall by accident, but lets itself drop, as I have often proved.

Kids kneel and see on the first day of life, without any example for imitation and without guidance, yet quickly and efficiently. I have seen them suck in this manner before they were twenty-two hours old. They

7

stride rather awkwardly up to the mother, snuff at her
teats, kneel down and suck, wagging their tails continually and pushing with their heads.

In the human being so many more associations of
sight with co-ordinated muscular movements are possible than in the brute at the moment of birth, that it
takes a longer growth after birth for these all to be developed.

Not before the sixth week, as O. Binswanger has discovered, are fully-formed ganglionic cells present in the
human cerebrum, and at the same period are first developed the cerebral convolutions, according to the investigations of Sernoff. Therefore, not only does the
human brain continue to grow after birth, but it differ-
entiates itself after birth, not before; since not until the
second month does it receive its characteristic morphological marks.

Such complicated mechanisms of associations as those
mentioned can not be developed before birth, because too
many other established inherited mechanisms go along
with them. They are all present potentially, but which
of them finally become most easily operative depends on
experience—i. e., on provocation from without, the more
or less often repeated treading of the separate paths of
association in the cerebro-spinal system. In other words,
the child learns much more than the animal.

The philosopher, Eduard von Hartmann, as early as
1872, used the following striking language with reference to this difference: "The human child seems to
bring nothing at all with him, but to learn everything;
in reality, however, he brings everything, or at any rate
far more than does the lower animal that creeps all com-

plete out of the egg; but he brings everything in an immature condition, because there is in him so much to be developed that in the nine months of embryonic life it can only be prefigured in the germ. So, then, in the progressive development of the infant brain the maturing of tendencies goes hand in hand with learning—i. e., with the modification of these tendencies by exercise; and the result is far richer and finer than can be attained in the brutes by mere inheritance."

The superiority of the animal, which utilizes at once its retinal excitations for its own advantage in jumping, is thus merely an apparent one, for it lacks the aptitude to learn other ways of utilizing experiences. This utilization may be conceived of as an inherited logical process—i. e., as *instinctive;* since the animal is born more mature than the human being, it is, unconsciously, earlier capable of performance such as the human being learns later through individual experience and accomplishes only with consciousness.

The same holds true of the association of seeing and touching, seeing and seizing, and other associations of which we have yet to speak.

Still, it is not to be denied that in man also the attainment of complicated combinations of this sort—of movements of the muscles of the eye and the arm upon receiving certain sense-impressions—is essentially assisted by inherited endowment. The muscular movements fall into the required groove without imitation the more quickly, in proportion as these have been the habitual combinations in the life of the race.

CHAPTER II.

HEARING.

THE observations concerning the gradual development of the faculty of hearing in early childhood relate
to the deafness of newly-born children—which is normally of only short duration—and to the babe's first
sensations and perceptions of sound. Then follow some
statements concerning the hearing of new-born animals.

1. The Deafness of the Newly-born.

All children immediately after birth are deaf. It
was formerly conjectured merely that the reason why
the new-born child can not hear is the filling of the
cavity of the tympanum with mucus, and that this
physiological deafness lasts until the cavity is emptied.
It is now settled that the temporary deafness is occasioned, also, and chiefly, by the lack of air in the cavity
before respiration.

Several investigators have found in the middle ear
of the fœtus a yellowish liquid, others a peculiar gelatinous substance. Gellé thinks that the latter comes
from a strong œdematous infiltration of the mucous
membrane of that part, and has its place supplied soon
after birth with air, by means of the respiratory movements, after it has become liquid—as he proved that it
does become, shortly before birth. He found in a cat,
half an hour after birth, both tympanic cavities filled
with air, and no remaining trace of the gelatinous magma.

The animal had cried out, and its lungs contained a good deal of air.

The question how far this gelatinous tissue, hyperæmia and swelling of the mucous membrane of the tympanic cavity, a sub-epithelial layer of the membrane, fill up the tympanic cavity before the first respiration, is not yet decisively answered. Neither has the point of time been ascertained, after how many respirations the Eustachian tube, in the human being, is permeable.

Probably the advent of respiration is not alone sufficient to accomplish the emptying of the tympanic cavities after birth and the filling of them with air; rather are repeated swallowing and breathing essential to it, and a few respirations are not sufficient, as Lesser proved, to replace with air the liquid contents of the tympanic cavity of the fœtus, or to change their character. Only after several hours' respiration can air be proved to exist in the middle ear along with the liquid; but Lesser found that the rapidity with which the liquid gave place to air did not sustain a constant relation to the duration of the extra-uterine existence. As Lesser examined forty-two new-born human beings, of whom thirteen were still-born, sixteen had lived a few minutes after birth, and thirteen had lived several hours or days, greater value is to be attributed to his results than to the isolated experiences of others. His results are of practical importance, and are especially remarkable in that they show that the fœtal condition of the middle ear in children prematurely born may persist more than twenty hours after birth. Such children, according to this, must be deaf somewhat longer than those born at the full time.

As to the rest, the old view of Scheel (1798), according to which the amniotic fluid comes directly into the
middle ear before birth through the Eustachian tube, as
the air does after birth, namely, through swallowing, is
not improbable. And we can not help agreeing with
him when he observes that because some of the amniotic
fluid remains in the tympanic cavity during the first
days after birth, a loud sound is less injurious to the
organ of hearing than if the cavity were at once filled
with air.   The collection of fluid in the middle ear
makes adults also hard of hearing. It was well said by
Herholdt (1797): "Experiments made on animals have
convinced me that in the fœtus the tympanic cavity is
completely filled with mucus and amniotic fluid, which
enters and is renewed through the Eustachian tube. So
the remainder of the amniotic fluid and that in the
tympanic cavity are in equilibrium and the tympanum
is pressed equally from all sides. By this the tympanic
cavity is relieved during the growth of the fœtus from
the obstacles that might stand in the way of its proper
development, and the tender tympanic membrane is protected from harm.   After birth the liquor flows out
slowly through the same channel, and the atmospheric
air takes its place.   Then first can the organs of hearing perform their functions, though not perfectly until
their development has become complete and the bones
of the head are firm and in reciprocal connection.   The
older physicians, who did not know this, dreamed of
an hereditary or inborn atmosphere."

In accord with this are the investigations of Moldenhauer and Von Tröltsch (1880).   The latter is of
opinion that the hyperplastic mucous membrane, which

in the fœtus almost fills up, like a cushion, the aperture of the tympanic cavity, often shrinks together before birth; the mucous cushion may even disappear within the uterus, in which case something else must occupy its place, and this can only be the amniotic fluid.

Besides the lack of air in the tympanic cavity, there is also to be taken into account, as a cause of the deafness of the human being at birth, the temporary closing of the external auditory canal, which is due, according to Urbantschitsch, not to epithelial agglutination, but to absolute contact of the coatings of the auditory canal. Many animals, also, but probably no birds, are for this reason deaf, or hard of hearing, directly after birth. So much the more surprising is the sensitiveness of others, e. g., of the Guinea-pig, of which something will be said by-and-by.

If the tympanic cavity in the new-born child is already filled with air, a deafness of half an hour, or of several hours, or even of several days, may be caused by the closing of the external auditory canal (the obstruction does not very quickly disappear), or by the narrowness of the canal. The difference in the results of observations according to which infants from one to three days sometimes react distinctly upon the stimulus of sound, sometimes ignore it completely, seems intelligible, however, if we only take into account the varying rapidity with which the Eustachian tube and the auditory canal are pervious to air, apart from all other obstacles, even possible cerebral ones. On the other hand, I must positively pronounce false the statements according to which children from three to four months old possess normally very slight capacity of hearing, and according to which it is hard to give a decided opinion as to whether such children hear at all or not. My observations upon many infants and my information from trustworthy mothers leave no doubt that, long before the third month, in the normal condition, the human voice is heard ; and in fact mature and sound children before the close of the first week of life react, in unmistakable fashion, upon the stimulus of loud sound, as Dr. Kroner, of Breslau, also found.

The longer continuance of difficulty of hearing is certainly of great advantage to the infant, as it stands in the way of the multiplication of reflex movements, and so of the tendency to convulsions.

But if children born at the right time make no movement in the fourth week when a loud sound is made behind them, then there is reason to suspect that such children will remain deaf and dumb.

2. The First Sensations and Perceptions of Sound.

How many hours, days, or weeks after birth the very earliest sensations of sound are experienced it is not easy to determine very accurately, for the reason that an unmistakable sign that a sensation of sound has been experienced is lacking. Movements of the eyelids, starting, throwing up the arms, and screaming, which appear in the child at the stimulus of sudden loud sound, appear readily at fright caused by any strong impression, while slight noises and soft tones remain unnoticed. The turning of the head toward the invisible source of sound does not take place till later.

Frequently-repeated attempts to test the ability of the newly-born to hear, leave no doubt that it is in-

creased by exercise, and that an occasional temporary
dullness occurs. But the experiments made thus far
are too scanty and uncertain.

Kussmaul could make the loudest discordant noises
near the ears of new-born children during the first days,
while they were awake, without any reaction on their
part. Numerous experiments made by him in this direction had only a negative result. But he adds that
another cautious observer, Feldbausch, has seen sleeping
children more than three days old start when he broke
the silence by clapping his hands hard. Champney's
child, on the contrary, did not react before the fourth
week upon any noise, however loud, not even clapping
of the hands, if there was no vibration of the room or
of the bed. If a door was slammed-to, the child started, just as it did directly after birth when the scales of
the balance in which it lay suddenly sprang up. When
fourteen days old, this child turned its eyes toward its
mother when she spoke to it, but as it did not at that
time stir at any noise, however loud, if there was no
shaking, this turning may be attributed to the feeling
of warmth at being breathed upon; for the movement
took place only when the mother's face was turned toward the babe, and it was presumably a movement of the
head rather than of the eyes.

Genzmer was the first to make experiments by
measuring. He ascertained the greatest distances at
which infants' eyelids quivered at the striking of a little
bell, which was done in just the same way always, with
a small iron rod. It appeared that almost all children
of one day, or certainly of two days, react upon impressions of sound, but their sense of hearing is, without

much reference to the degree of their maturity, at first unequal, and grows more acute within the first weeks. The average distance at which the striking of the bell was heard was found to be eight to ten inches, but the figures varied from one to twenty. In one case, that of a very active child, the distance on the first day was eight, on the sixth eighteen, on the twenty-fourth twenty-four inches; with a phlegmatic child, the auditory reflexes were on the first day irregular, on the eighth they occurred at five, on the twenty-fourth at eleven inches distance from the bell. It may be seen from these figures how unequal the progress is. But as the sound could hardly be of exactly the same force in all the experiments, and as the quivering of the eyelids is not caused by the stimulus of sound exclusively, and as not every sound-stimulus is responded to by a quiver of the eyelids, this whole series of experiments, limited to about thirty observations, on fifteen children, is uncertain.

The observations of Dr. Moldenhauer likewise leave much that is doubtful, although his mode of proceeding is better. He made use, as a test of the hearing, of the French toy, *cri-cri*, which gives a loud, brief, disagreeable sound, with discordant high overtones. This sound continues almost exactly identical after many experiments, and can be made quite close to the ear without involving other stimulus. The most important result of this experiment was that, with very few exceptions, children distinctly reacted at once upon the sound-stimulus at the first trial. Yet the degree of the reaction was extraordinarily unequal in different individuals, and in the same individuals on different days. Fifty children were tested. Of these only ten were less than twelve hours old (these all reacted), and only seven from twelve to twenty-four hours old, all the rest older. The least degree of reaction was indicated by a distinct quiver of the eyelids, even without interruption of sleep; a stronger degree by wrinkling of the forehead. Then came head-movements, mostly single short twistings of the head; finally, starting, accompanied by violent quivering of the head, the arms, and the upper part of the body; sleeping children awoke and screamed. The reflexes occurred more plainly and more quickly after the end of the second day than on the first two days. In experiments that followed one another in quick succession, there was very often manifested a dullness, going as far as entire absence of reaction.

Children sleeping soundly, and babes nursing, reacted less distinctly than those awake or half asleep.

Most children, then, even those born three or four weeks too early, respond in the first days to strong impressions of sound by reflex movements in the region of the facialis. The action of those just born, in the first five hours, was not investigated. The four youngest were six hours old, as the author tells me. Deafness was in some few cases (four out of fifty) well established, even after more than twenty-four hours; thus my observation that no reaction follows upon sound-impressions immediately after birth is not modified by this discovery. In fact, I saw a strong child, of ten hours, that did not react in the least upon the *cri-cri*, and I saw one of six days react very slightly.

Moldenhauer found further that, of four children who were tested for the first time after more than twenty-four hours and did not react, three did distinctly react in later repeated experiments in the same hour or on the following day. A child of three days did not react even at the second trial.

When the bell that has been mentioned was struck by Genzmer softly, very near the ear of children that heard well (probably more than two days old), they sometimes turned the head to that side; if occupied with nursing, they broke off from their occupation. Very violent striking of the bell made them restless. I have likewise observed that infants are greatly disturbed by strong sound-stimulus, just as new-born animals are; e. g., the shrill whistle of a locomotive near by easily produces persistent lively movements and violent screaming in a child previously perfectly quiet. Not every infant, indeed, shows so strong a reaction, nor does any in the first hour of life. But on the ninth day the turning of the head (in my judgment accidental) toward the source of sound was observed by Moldenhauer.

Too great a range is, however, commonly allowed for individual differences. When some children are reported as starting at loud sounds, even on the first day, others after three days, others again not till after eight weeks, there is reason to attribute the last statements to inaccurate observation, unless they apply only to those hard of hearing or prematurely born; or, unless too deep sounds and unsuitable noises were employed.

If a small tuning-fork, in vibration, warmed and carefully placed on the head, produces no other reaction than that produced by a fork not in vibration, similarly placed, we may infer that the inner ear has some share in the deafness of the newly-born. But such experiments must be made on many individuals. Moldenhauer got no definite result with tuning-forks on account of the sensitiveness of the skin of the head.

A very vigorous male child, born after his time, was seen by Dr. Deneke, in the lying-in asylum at Jena, six hours after birth, to close his eyes tighter every time the doctor struck two metallic covers together close to his ear. In this case, however, the reflex may have been started by the current of air arising from the sudden motion. A very strong new-born child, weighing nearly four and a quarter kilogrammes, did not react upon any noise, when I tested it half an hour after birth. That is the way all ordinary children behave just after birth. By ever so loud a noise, clapping of hands close to the ear, whistling, very loud screaming, they are not within the first half hour, according to my experiments, brought to screaming from a state of quiet, nor quieted if they are screaming. But they cry out if you blow on them, if you press softly on their temples, or strike them upon the thigh, after they have begun to breathe. Only there is a noticeably longer interval between the contact and the outcry than at a later period.

I saw my child, in the twenty-first hour of life, move both arms symmetrically, at a loud call, but this is perhaps to be attributed to being breathed on; for clapping of hands, whistling, speaking, produced no result, and on the second and third days no reaction upon sound-stimulus could be induced. It was not until the first half of the fourth day that I was convinced that my child was no longer deaf. For hand-clapping, or whistling, close to him then produced sudden opening of the half-shut eyes, as the child lay warm and satisfied with food, and to all appearance comfortable. As this result followed every time on repeated trials the fourth day, but not once on the third day, there can be no doubt that in this case the sound was heard by means of the tympanum on the fourth day, but not before. It also happened for the first time on the fourth day, and indeed several times, that the child when crying stopped as soon as I began to whistle close to him. This observation was made also upon babes of two and three days old. On the eleventh and twelfth days I noticed that my child became quiet always at the sound of my voice, which seemed also to call forth a sort of intense expression of countenance that, however, can not be described.

On the twenty-fifth day pulsation of the lids often followed when I spoke to the child in a low voice, standing before and near him. On the following day he started suddenly when a dish that he could not see was noisily covered near him. He is frightened, then, already, at unexpected loud sounds, as adults are. On the thirtieth day this fright was still more strongly manifested. I was standing before the child as he lay quiet, and being called, I said aloud, without changing my position, "Ja!" (yes). Directly the child threw both arms high up quickly, and made a convulsive start with the upper part of his body, while at the same time his expression, which had been one of contentment, became very serious. The same scene was enacted at another time on the slamming of a door.

In the fifth week the sensibility to sound has increased to such a degree that the child seldom sleeps in the daytime if any one walks about or speaks in the room; whereas, so late as the seventh day, a loud call did not wake the sleeping child. The increased sensibility is also proved by the quick turnings of the head when any one sits on the child's bed without being seen by him, and also by the starting at moderately loud noises.

In the sixth week I noticed this starting at quite insignificant noises, even when the child was asleep and did not wake. About this time he could already be quieted at once, when he was screaming, by his mother's singing. The first time this happened the child opened his eyes wide, evidently a symptom of astonishment at the new sensations of sound. On the following day, when his mother again quieted him by singing, he gazed at her with wide-open eyes (cf. p. 46), so that I already suspected he had associated the tones he heard with the oval of the face he saw, as is unquestionably the case with older children (e. g., of four months) when they laugh and utter joyous cries as soon as the mother sings anything to them.

In the seventh week the fright at a loud sound was still greater than before. Dishes fell to the floor several times while the child was asleep. Instantly both arms went up swiftly, and remained for more than *two minutes* upright in that strange position with fingers outstretched and parallel, without the child's waking. The attitude reminded one of the spreading of the wings of a frightened bird. There appears to be already a greater sensibility to tones, possibly to melodies, for an expression of the greatest satisfaction is perceived on the child's face when his mother hushes him with cradle-songs softly sung. It is worth noticing, also, that even when he is crying from hunger a low sing-song causes a pause in the crying and attracts attention. Speaking does not effect this invariably, by any means.

In the eighth week the infant heard, for the first time, the music of an instrument—the piano. He made known his satisfaction at the new sensation by an unusual straining of the eyes and by lively movements of arms and legs at every *forte*, as well as by smiles and laughter. The higher and softer tones made no such impression. This delight in music manifested itself in like manner in the following months, from which we may conclude that more than a year before the first imperfect attempt at speech there is discrimination between (musical) sounds and noises. The child of two or of three months often utters sounds of satisfaction when it hears music.

In the ninth week the sound of a repeating watch, which had earlier produced not the least impression on the child, now aroused his attention to the highest pitch. But his head was not turned with certainty toward the source of sound, whereas he would follow a moving hand accurately. At every sudden noise, scream, call, tones, clapping of hands, there is a quick shutting and opening of the eyes, and very often the arms are at the same time lifted quickly, no matter in what position the body is held. The same in the fourth month. In the seventh and eighth the closing of the lids predominates. The raising of the arms has already become rare.

In the eleventh week I noticed for the first time, what some others have not perceived before the second quarter of the year, though some have done so earlier, directly after the rise of a clear idea, is now repeated by the child accurately, or, in case it offers insurmountable difficulties of articulation for pronunciation, inaccurately. This fact of *sound-imitation* is fundamental. Beyond it we can not go. Especially must be noted here as essential that it appears to be an entirely indifferent matter what syllables and words are employed for the first designation of the child's ideas. Were one disposed to provide the child with false designations, he could easily do it. The child would still connect them logically. If taught further on that two times three are five, he would merely give the *name* five to what is six, and would soon adopt the usual form of expression. In making a beginning of the association of ideas with articulate syllables, such syllables are, as a rule, employed (probably in all languages) as have already been often uttered by the child spontaneously without meaning, because these offered no difficulties of articulation; but only the child's family put meaning into them. Such syllables are *pa*, *ma*, with their doubled form *papa*, *mama*, for "father" and "mother," in connection with which it is to be observed that the meaning of them is different in different languages and even in the dialects of a language. For *mamán*, *mamá*, *máma*, *mamme*, *mammeli*, *mömme*, *mam*, *mamma*, *mammeken*, *memme*, *memmeken*, *mammĕlĕ*, *mammi*, are at the same time child-words and designations for "mother" in various districts of Germany, whereas these and very similar expressions signify also the mother's breast, milk, pap, drink, nursing-bottle; nay, even in some languages the father is designated by *Ma*-sounds, the mother by *Ba*- and *Pa*-sounds.

9

invariably broke off from his occupation and turned about whenever a noise, not altogether too slight, was made near him.

After a half-year the babe often kept his gaze steadily directed for minutes at a time on my face, and with an expression of wonder, with eyes and mouth open, when I sang single notes to him. He utters a joyous cry at military music.

In the eighth month there is a quick closing of the lids, a single wink of the eyes for the most part, not only at every loud, sudden sound-impression, but even at every new one—e. g., when the voices of animals are imitated. This is no longer the expression of fright merely, but of astonishment also. In fright there has come, in place of the raising of the arms, a starting of the whole body and a convulsive movement of arms and legs together, which was also observed as early as the second month. The rapid shutting and opening of the eyes continued unchanged.

In the ninth month, when the child more than twelve times in succession shut down the cover of a large "caraffe," so that a loud slam was heard every time, this winking of the eyes and starting of the whole body took place every time, the countenance meanwhile expressing great attention. The reflex movements in this case were not, then, the expression of fright, for the child himself eagerly repeated the shutting down of the cover after I had raised it. The combined tactual and visual impression surpassed in interest the accompanying phenomenon of sound; the intensity of the latter, however, was so great as to involve the reflex movements. At this period I often saw, during the sleep of the child, lively movements of the hands after sound-impressions that did not waken the sleeper, the remains of an earlier reflex raising of the arm. Not only does the child turn his head round when he hears my voice without seeing me, but (as also in the tenth month) at every new loud noise—e. g., thunder. So, too, the turning of the head in the first and second weeks, when a loud sound is heard, is not a directing of the head toward the source of sound (p. 80); this does not take place till later (p. 85).

During teething, the sensibility to acoustic stimulus is, moreover, noticeably increased. A loud word then produces winking, fright, quicker breathing, screaming, and tears.

In the eleventh and twelfth months, the screaming child generally allows itself to be quieted in a few moments by a decided "Sh!" just as it did in the first month. No other spoken utterance has this effect, not even the sharp "ss" or "pst," but any singing, even false notes, will do it.

At this time—the three hundred nineteenth day—occurred a remarkable acoustic experience, which gives evidence of great intellectual advance. The child struck several times with a spoon upon a plate. It happened accidentally, while he was doing this, that he touched the plate with the hand that was free; the sound was dulled, and the child noticed the difference. He now took the spoon in the other hand, struck with it on the plate, dulled the sound again, and so on. In the evening this experiment was renewed, with a like result. Evidently the function of causality had emerged in some strength, for it prompted the experiment. The cause of the dulling of the sound by the hand—was it in the hand or in the plate? The other hand had the same dulling effect; so the cause was not lodged with the one hand. Pretty nearly in this fashion the child must have interpreted his sound-impression, and this at a time when he did not know a single word of his later language.

In the twelfth month the child was accustomed, almost every morning, to observe the noisy putting of coals into the stove, A. On the three hundred sixty-third day it took place in the next room, in the stove, B. The child at once looked in the direction of the sound, but as he discovered nothing he turned his head around nearly one hundred and eighty degrees, and regarded the stove, A, with an inquiring gaze: that stove had already been filled. This likewise shows logical activity applied to perceptions of sound, and this before the ability to speak.

Such experiments were from time to time carried on after this, entirely of the child's own accord; e. g., in the thirtieth month the child, while eating, held his hand by chance to his ear while a kettle of boiling water stood before him. At once he becomes attentive, notices the diminution in the force of the sound, takes his hand away, listens in silence, open-mouthed and with an expression of surprise, to the modification of the sound, holds his hand to his ear five or six times, and establishes the fact anew each time, like an experimenter, until the connection between the alteration in the sound and the movement of the hand no longer seems wonderful, because he has perceived it several times.

I note here that one of the earliest sound-perceptions in which causality operated without language, is the one mentioned (p. 87), occurring on the eighty-first day.

I have not been able, notwithstanding the greatest attention and very much outlay of time, to record any more observations of this sort concerning the activity of reasoning without speech, in the domain of sound.

After the end of the first year the child strikes with his hands on the keys of the piano, and looks around occasionally while doing it, as if to assure himself that somebody is listening to him. He takes pleasure in a canary-bird, laughing when it moves and listening in silence when it sings, and then laughing again. In general, laughing is frequent in the following months at new noises, like gurgling or clearing the throat (fifteenth month). Even thunder made the child laugh.

A favorite acoustic occupation consisted in holding a watch to his ear and listening to the ticking (sixteenth, seventeenth, and twenty-fourth months). But sometimes the watch was held behind the auricle and sometimes against his cheek. If I held it above, on his head, the ticking was heard (nineteenth month), as could be told by the look of attention. The conduction of sound by the bones must have been already established for some time past.

The pleasure in music, that showed itself even in the first three months, increased manifestly in the six following months. But it was nearly the end of the second year before the child, who was roused to the liveliest movements by hearing the most varied kinds of music, performed these movements in time. He did indeed dance, but in his own fashion, not rhythmically

(twenty-first month). Somewhat later, he would himself beat time with tolerable correctness with the arms,
or with one arm, trying meanwhile to sing over a song
that had been sung to him (twenty-fourth month), but
he did not succeed in this till later, and then imperfectly. Playing with fife and drum at that period gave
hardly more pleasure than striking some keys of the
piano, and that with both hands at once. But I must
add that it was absolutely impossible, notwithstanding
much pains, to teach the child to name rightly even the
three notes C D E (end of third year), though his
hearing for noises and vocal sounds was in general
acute.

Another child, on the contrary, a girl, could, in her
ninth month, sing correctly every note given her from
the piano, and seemed to find discords unpleasant; at
least she always wept bitterly at that age whenever any
one blew on a small tin trumpet. This child, and two
others of the same family, could sing before they could
talk, and sing correctly airs that had been sung to them.
Not only the *pitch*, but the stress and the shade of tone
are given by such musical children (in the eighth month),
who listen to all music with the greatest strain of attention. Such a child even sang itself to sleep (in the
eighth month), and later (in the nineteenth month), accompanied songs and pieces sung and played by others,
clapping its hands in correct time. (Frau Dr. Friedemann.)

Another little girl takes pleasure in hearing music
(in the eleventh month), likes to strike on the keys of
the piano, and when any one begins to sing airs that
have often been sung to her, she springs and accompa-

nies the singing with the movement of her body, and turns her hands this way and that. (Fr. v. Strümpell.)

Through the whole of the third year it was not easy to waken my child by sound-impressions alone. He often fell asleep even when there was a racket near him, and yet his hearing was acute enough when he was awake, as appears from the observations reported.

Even the knowledge of the direction of sound, though imperfect, still appeared earlier than in other cases. Darwin reports—e. g., that one of his acutely-hearing children, when more than seventeen weeks old, did not easily recognize the direction from which a sound came, so as to turn its gaze thither; with which should be compared the above statements (page 85); also that of Vierordt, that sometimes in the fourth month the child begins to turn his head in the direction of the sound; and that of R. Demme, who found that of about one hundred children only two, at the age of three and three and a half months, distinguished the voices of their parents from those of other persons calling to them; these children made animated movements and joyous utterances; all the other children were much later in making this distinction.

Individual differences, partly hereditary, partly acquired, are in this department very great.

3. The Hearing of New-born Animals.

Guinea-pigs not yet twelve hours old show unmistakably, by movements of the ears, as I found, that they hear all high tones of from one thousand to forty-one thousand double vibrations a second. For when, unseen by the animals, everything around being still,

I struck one of my forty small tuning-forks that ranged through that interval (from the C of the third octave to the E of the eighth) the ears of the animals were always immediately moved in time, either lowered or folded; and at loud tones the creatures invariably started. This reflex movement, nowhere mentioned hitherto, viz., the contraction of the auricles, took place with such machine-like regularity that I can compare no other movement with it in regard to precision, with the exception of the contraction of the pupil to light. In grown Guinea-pigs the auditory reflex for all these tones of the tuning-forks is likewise easy to prove; but it is sometimes very slight, especially after frequent repetition of the experiment. In the first half-hour after birth it is utterly wanting. New-born animals are accordingly deaf at the beginning.

On the other hand, it was at once demonstrable that all healthy Guinea-pigs an hour after birth, even those born some days before their time, respond to the most varied noises, both loud and soft—e. g., clapping of hands, by a quiver of the whole body; at first often by a spring and by movements that seem like attempts to flee. This behavior can have its origin only in heredity.

The reflex arc from the auditory nerve to the motor nerves has been so frequently used by their ancestors, when in moments of danger a noise made flight advisable, that the representatives of the present generation, without as yet any knowledge of danger, quiver at the first noise that comes. Even in the human babe of a few days old the starting at a sudden sound is a relic of this fright, and the same is true of adult human beings

and horses. The first movement of the eyelid upon
sudden noiseless sight-impressions is, on the contrary,
to be explained differently, as I showed above (page 28);
because the movements of flight, the starting and the
drawing back of the head, are wanting in the beginning.

New-born Guinea-pigs are especially sensitive to
sounds of slight intensity. They recognize their mother
by hearing on the first day of their life, even when she
grunts quite softly and interruptedly, whereas they do
not recognize her by sight after four or five days, as
I found (1878) by a series of laborious experiments.
As, moreover, the voice of the mother and that of the
other little ones of the same litter produces a direct
movement toward the source of the sound, when the
members of the family have been separated, the direction from which the sound comes must be perceived on
the first day.

The same is true of new-born swine. For Spalding
observed that, at the age of only a few minutes, if they
are removed several feet from their mother, they soon
find their way back to her, guided apparently by the
grunting she makes in answer to their squealing. The
mother, in one case that was observed, got up in less than
an hour and a half after giving birth to the young, and
went off to feed; the young ones went around and tried
in every way to get nourishment, followed the mother and
sucked while she ate standing. One of the young ones
was put in a bag the moment it was born and kept in
the dark till it was seven hours old. Then it was placed
outside the sty, a distance of ten feet from where the sow
lay concealed inside the house. The pig soon 'recog-

nized' the low grunting of its mother, went along outside the sty, struggling to get under or over the lower bar. At the end of five minutes it succeeded in forcing itself through under the bar, at one of the few places where that was possible. No sooner in than it went without a pause into the pig-house to its mother, and was at once like the others in its behavior. There can be no doubt that in this search the sensation of sound caused by the grunting was (for the creature that had not until five minutes before been exposed to the light) decisive of the direction to be pursued. Still, smell does not seem to have been excluded.

Among the animals that hear well at the very beginning must be counted the chicken just from the egg. For soon after leaving the shell, as soon as it can run, it follows the cluck of the hen; and even beforehand, in the egg after the shell has begun to burst, it responds by peeping to sounds of that kind. If it remains for a day or two in the dark after it has been hatched in the incubator, and is then exposed to the light at a distance of nine or ten feet from a box in which a brooding-hen is concealed, it will, after chirping one or two minutes, betake itself straight to the box, following the call of the hen, though it has never seen and never before heard her. This takes place, too, when it involves the overcoming of obstacles in the grass, the passage over uneven ground, when the little creatures are not in condition to stand on their feet. Even chickens deprived of sight from the first follow blindly the call of the clucking hen when they come within five or six feet of her. Mr. Spalding, who conducted both these experiments, also made chickens deaf before they left the shell by sealing their ears with several folds of gummed paper, uncovered their ears again after two or three days, set them free within call of the hen which was separated from them by a board, and then saw that, after turn. ing around a few times, they ran straight to the spot whence came the first sound they had ever heard. To them, therefore, the first sound-sensation could not be empty or meaningless. It became at once perception, and inherited memory asserted itself in a psycho-motor way. So thinks Spalding. But I have been able to prove in the case of thirty chickens hatched in an incubator, from one to three days out of the shell, that when food had been placed before them several times and a knocking upon wood made at the same time, they generally ran, every time I knocked in their neighborhood, to the spot whence the noise issued, although there was no food there. They had, therefore, recognized the direction of the sound already, and had learned something, or at least they had associated that special sound with the food. For they did not leave their place for other noises—e. g., whistling or the clucking of the hen, which they had never before heard; but they listened instantly to the clucking when I brought several clucking-hens successively into the neighborhood unseen by them, and they started at a loud report without moving from the spot. Besides, it is questionable whether the chickens with ears sealed were actually deaf, and whether they had not heard the voice of the hen before the stopping of the ears. The chick peeps before the shell has a crack in it, as I often perceived; has, therefore, heard its own voice, certainly, before emerging from the shell, and possibly the voices of others likewise.

At all events, the hearing of chickens just out of the shell, and of many new-born mammals, is vastly superior to that of the just-born human babe, both in regard to the discrimination of pitch and loudness of sound, and in respect to the perception of kinds of sound, the direction and perhaps the duration. It must be the case that the normal human being at birth hears nothing, then hears individual sounds indistinctly, then hears much indistinctly, and very gradually hears distinctly an individual sound out of the number of those indistinctly heard, finally hears much distinctly, and distinguishes strong, high tones earlier than deep ones. Every mother loses many thousands of words that she speaks, whispers, or sings to her child, without the child's hearing a single one of them, and she says many thousand words to him before he understands one. But if she did not do it, the child would learn to speak much later and with much more difficulty.

CHAPTER III.

FEELING.

THE observations concerning feeling in the newly-born and the infant relate chiefly to sensibility to contact, to the first perceptions of touch, and to sensibility to temperature.

1. Sensibility of the Newly-born to Contact.

The mature new-born child is known to be less sensitive to painful impressions than are adults. But it would be a mistake to infer from this a condition of anæsthesia or analgesia. For apart from anomalous cases, as of new-born children apparently dead, screaming and movements can be elicited from children and animals just born, when they are for the first time quiet and motionless, by pinching the skin; or, in the case of a child, by slapping the upper part of the thigh. I have convinced myself most fully of this in regard to children born at the right time, and prematurely born animals some minutes after birth, but at the same time I was convinced that the expressions of pain lack by a great deal the intensity and duration they have in older children. In this respect the newly-born resembles the fœtus, differing from it, however, to this extent, that immediately after pulmonic respiration begins, every sort of irritation of the skin produces stronger reflexes. Often the reflex mechanism starts into activity at once, the first time air is breathed. The clock was already wound up, as it were, but the pendulum gets its regular swing only through respiration. Before this it oscillated temporarily and with breaks, urged only by weak impulsions. By the act of birth the central nervous system is first literally awakened. And there is nothing against the assumption that the first contact, pressure in the act of birth, causes pain. I have twice heard a child scream whose head only was as yet born, and the expression of countenance in this half-born condition was one of extreme discomfort. The compression of the body, and the compression of the skull that had just preceded, probably awakened the child out of its intra-uterine sleep.

That rude contact in the act of birth may cause pain, in the strict sense of the word, to the mature fœtus, is probable, because the fœtus may in the same circumstances experience pleasure; for when I put into the mouth of the screaming child, whose head alone was as yet born, an ivory pencil or a finger, the child began to suck, opened its eyes, and seemed, to judge from its countenance, to be "most agreeably affected" (cf. p. 32).

Since in adults the sensibility of the skin and of the mucous membrane varies greatly according to the number of nerve-extremities of the part of the skin that is tested, we are especially interested to know whether such differences in sensibility to contact are already manifest in the newly-born. Kussmaul, whose experiments of the year 1859 were repeated and supplemented by Genzmer, 1873, was the first to investigate this question experimentally. He found several facts that indicate the hereditary character of certain differences. I will give the results of these observers on this point along with my own.

Tongue.—Tickling the tip of the tongue on the upper surface with a smooth glass rod occasions sucking movements; meantime the edges of the tongue curve upward on both sides of the rod and the lips protrude like a snout. At the same time appears the pantomime that indicates the sensation "sweet." When the middle of the tongue is touched on the upper surface, the eyes are shut tight, the nostrils and the corners of the mouth are raised; there is no sucking. Tickle the root of the tongue and of the palate, and the results are choking, opening the mouth wide, sticking out the tongue, lifting of the larynx, increased secretion of saliva, pantomime for "bitter" corresponding to the expression of nausea in adults.

These differences in the reflex movements and the sensations, according to the part of the tongue tickled by the rod, whether the tip of the tongue, the middle, or the root, may be regarded as established in general, but can not be proved in every individual case. Thus movements do not invariably follow the touching of the middle of the tongue. I have often been unable to elicit any movements at all from new-born children by using the glass rod. Yet in most cases children act exactly like just-born rabbits and Guinea-pigs in this respect, sucking at the rod when it presses in front, and pushing it out when it presses in the back part of the cavity of the mouth. When an infant has eaten enough, it does not suck at all, and when tired it sucks irregularly and feebly. But the results obtained in regard to new-born children whose stomachs are empty leave no doubt that even before birth the two paths from the sensory nerves of the tongue to the beginning of the motor nerves of the tongue, the nervus hypoglossus, and from there to its extremities in the tongue, are developed and passable, and that the sensibility of the upper surface of the tongue—from the tip to the root—to contact is, like that of the palate, inborn and already considerable, entirely apart from sensibility to taste. That along with the sucking at the rod there should be movements of swallowing is a further consequence of that practicability of the reflex path established before birth in the swallowing of the amniotic fluid. But none will assume the existence of the sensations "bitter" and "sweet" at the mere touching of the tongue, for they do not appear in such conditions even in adults. The mimetic movement for "sweet" is rather that of satisfaction associated with the agreeable feeling that comes with sucking, and the mimetic movement for " bitter " is that of discomfort associated with the disagreeable feeling manifested by choking.

Lips.—The sensibility of the lips to contact is great immediately after birth, for even very faint touches of them with a feather produce (on the sixth day) starting or movements of sucking, provided the newly-born are awake and hungry. Especially stroking of the lips with the finger easily produces sucking.

But I have not seen these sucking movements appear invariably in mature children just born or in animals. A machine-like certainty in their appearance is wanting, probably because those just born are not in every case hungry. The situation of the human fœtus makes it easy for the lips to be touched by the hands long before birth, and the swallowing of the amniotic fluid presupposes a streaming of it over the edges of the lips and so a frequent excitation of the nerve-extremities.

The reflex sensibility of the upper lip even outside the red border, which is surprising on the first day, I found also in the seventh week, when the touching of the lip produced an animated play of feature perceptibly greater than in adults.

Mucous Membrane of the Nose.—Irritation of the mucous membrane of the nose causes, in the mature newly-born, strong reflexes. The vapor of acetic acid and of ammonia occasions violent sneezing, or corrugation of the forehead, or at least blinking, sometimes rubbing of the face with the hands. Tickling the inner surface of the wing of the nose produces movements of the eyelids, stronger and appearing sooner on the side tickled than on the other. If the irritation is increased, the child moves its head and puts its hands toward its face. Sometimes, too, there is a secretion of tears, which is the more remarkable as children generally shed no tears in the first days of life.

The reflex excitement of the lachrymal nerves (ramus lacrymalis nervi trigemini) and the reflex secretion from the nerve-extremities in the mucous membrane of the nose outward, are accordingly possible at a surprisingly early period. Here we have, besides, a case of inborn reflex activity of a gland within the domain of one and the same nerve; for the centripetal and the centrifugal (secretory) fibers, which go to the tear-gland, belong to the fifth cranial nerve (trigeminus).

The great sensibility of the nasal mucous membrane to contact is, I must add, not present until the last weeks before birth, as children born at seven months make only doubtful responsive movements. Yet this sensibility has been found to be just as great in a child born at eight months as in those born at the right time. It is a purely hereditary peculiarity. Since there is hardly any occasion within the womb for an excitement of the inner surface of the nostril, this reflex arc from the nasal branches of the fifth cranial nerve to the face-nerve (facialis) must be a very firmly established one.

The same is true of the reflex paths that go from the extremities of the trigeminus in the nasal mucous membrane to the spinal motor nerves, inasmuch as a regular shaking has been observed by me to follow upon a gentle touch of the nasal mucous membrane. In the first three months of the second year, my

9

boy one day accidentally touched the septum of his nose with a raveled string. He at once made a wry face (excitement of the facialis), did not cry out, but shook, throwing his body violently this way and that, as if the certainly very disagreeable sensation of tickling in that spot were to be *shaken off*.

Conjunctiva and Cornea of the Eye and the Eye-lid.—If the conjunctiva, the edge of the cornea, or an eyelash be touched in the newly-born, a closure of the lid follows. Which of these parts are the most sensitive is matter of dispute. Kussmaul thinks the lashes, but Genzmer could touch these three or four times in some children without causing closing of the lid, whereas the closure never failed when the cornea was touched, and generally touching of the conjunctiva was followed by a bilateral closing of the lids. If we consider the fact that in adults the lashes can be touched without even an inclination to close the lid, but not so the conjunctiva or the edge of the cornea, we can not agree with Kussmaul in this case. I find also in new-born Guinea-pigs and in chickens just out of the shell the periphery of the cornea more sensitive to contact than the lashes or the lids and their edges. In all three cases, however, closing of the lid appears soon after birth, most quickly of all upon the touching of the cornea.

Blowing in the face of new-born children through a tube also causes closing of the lid, but only when the cornea or the conjunctiva or the lashes are reached by the air, and the eye of the side that is blown upon is shut tighter and more quickly than the other.

From my experiments upon new-born, normal chickens and Guinea-pigs, it appears that the closing of the lid does not follow quite so promptly immediately after birth as it does later. Still, the interval during which the inactivity of the reflex can be recognized, without arrangements for measuring the time, is very short, since with chickens, e. g., only a few hours after leaving the shell, the nictitating membrane is pushed forward when I touch the corner of the eye.

In a babe of eight days the eye shuts, when I touch the upper lid without touching the lashes; but in one of eleven days the closing of the lid upon the touching of the conjunctiva is considerably slower than in adults (p. 26).

On the fiftieth and fifty-fifth days the lightest touch of an eyelash produces an instant closing of the lid. In contrast with this sensitiveness stands the fact already mentioned (p. 27), that the child in the bath, during the first weeks of life, keeps its eyes open even when luke-warm water touches the cornea. In the seventeenth week the eyes were closed if even a drop of water touched the lashes. The persistent keeping of the eyes open in spite of wetting, at a considerably earlier period, which always surprised me afresh, considering the great sensitiveness of the cornea to the touch of the finger, suggests the surmise that even before birth the eyes have been accustomed to contact with liquid, through being sprinkled with the amniotic fluid, and so have sometimes been opened. The embryo chick occasionally opens its eyes many days before leaving the shell, as I perceived.

On the whole, it appears that this reflex arc from the trigeminus to the facialis is capable of performing its function before birth, inasmuch as the reflex closing of the eye upon being touched takes place immediately at birth even in animals born prematurely, and is thus an ancient inheritance; but sprinkling with water, as in the case of the adult, is not equal, as a reflex stimulus, to a dry touch; on the other hand, blowing induces a vigorous closing of the lid, and even sneezing, in the very young infant as well as in the one of six months.

Nose.—When the tip of the nose is touched, the new-born child shuts both eyes tight; if one wing of the nose is touched he closes, generally, only the eye on the side touched; at a stronger irritation both eyes are shut, the head being meanwhile somewhat drawn back: these being inborn reflexes of the nature of defense.

Palm of the Hand.—Put a finger into the hand of a new-born babe, and his hand closes around it. A fillip of the finger against the hand produces a withdrawal of the latter, and very likely a movement of the other arm. But I find the sensibility of the palm of the hand to be less than that of the skin of the face, for rude touches of the hand may often fail to call forth reflex movements.

Sole of the Foot.—Touching the sole of the foot of a new-born child causes spreading of the toes; slapping the sole causes a backward bending of the foot, a bending of the knee and of the hip joint. If the stimulus be greater, the same movements are generally made in addition, in the same order, with the other leg. The prick of a needle most easily causes, in the newly-born, reflex movements of pain, from the sole of the foot outward, viz., restlessness and screaming, but the time that elapses between the first touch and the beginning of the movement—the reflex period—is longer than in adults, and extends to two seconds.

The skin of the forearm and of the leg, in the newly-born, has an inferior sensibility to contact; that of the shoulders, the breast, the abdomen, the back, the upper part of the thigh, is less sensitive still. If the new-born child is not merely touched, but slapped with the hand, then general movements take place, often screaming and persistent restlessness, which indicate that the stronger sensation of touch has become painful. Yet, according to Genzmer, the prematurely born do not react at all upon moderate pricks of a needle, during the first days; the mature newly-born, immediately after birth, do so indeed only faintly or not at all, but after one or two days they do so plainly. This shows the dependence of the force of the stimulus upon the number of the nerve-extremities that are affected. The slap reaches many, the prick few extremities of the cutaneous nerves. But the sensibility to pricks of the needle, which is greater from the beginning in those born too late, increases noticeably during the first week.

I found in the case of my boy that the sensibility of the skin in different places was not so unequal in the first twenty-two hours as it was later, but it was surprisingly great; for the child reacted by movements upon the slightest touches of his face. On the second and third days, for instance, he started with a movement of the arms at gentle touches. On the seventh day the child is not waked by loud sound-stimulus, but is waked by a touch on the face. On the forty-first day, when the child had gone to sleep in my arms, I laid him on a sheet and then drew the sheet slowly away. At the first pull, both arms were moved quickly and simultaneously toward the head and back again, without the child's waking. Here we have not a localized touch, but a general slight agitation, calling forth the same reflex movement as a touch or a sound would do. In the fourteenth week, too, a sudden touch of the sleeping child occasioned a quick throwing up of both arms.

According to this, the reflex excitability for local tactile stimulus is undoubtedly greater in the first weeks than it is later. In the second year of life I found it a good deal dulled.

I may mention here also two remarkably sensitive regions in the skin of the infant. In the second quarter of the first year it appeared that the greatest disquiet, the loudest crying, the most distressed expression of countenance, as the child was turning and tossing hither and thither, at once vanished when a person put his little finger into the auditory canal. The child's eye assumed a peculiar expression of strained attention. If this sudden alteration had not invariably taken place even when the child was screaming, one might think rather of an acoustic than of a tactile excitation. Or, could the diminution of the loudness of his cries through the stopping of the ear attract his attention? In that case we can not understand why the child that is not crying but is quivering in the bath becomes quiet. For the rest, the experiment failed almost invariably after the end of the first six months; from that time on it always failed, and Kroner found that not all new-born children were quiet when the external auditory canal was tickled, but that some put their hands to the face and not to the ear.

How sensitive the dry skin of the forehead is to wet, is often shown by the reflex movements of babes at church-baptism. I once saw an infant of thirty-eight days, which remained tolerably quiet through the whole baptismal ceremony, make a sudden movement of both arms at once toward the head, without screaming, as soon as the lukewarm water trickled on its forehead. At the second wetting, directly afterward, there was a similar convulsive movement almost as of repulsion; and at the third, the child sneezed. According to this, the reflex excitability of the surface of the face in regard to wet is greater in the sixth week than it is in adult age. The adult can not be stirred to so vigorous reflex action by such a wetting as this of the christening with a few drops of water, although he may be by sprinkling.

Yet it seems difficult to determine the exact time when the great reflex excitability to contact manifested by the above facts, has so far subsided that a degree of excitability corresponding to the normal condition of adults is reached.

Apart from hereditary individual inequalities, and the frequent morbid development of the reflexes in early infancy into convulsions, the time when the reflexes begin to be inhibited is of the greatest account, no less than is the wearing out of the nerve-paths by frequent repetition of the excitements, in regard to the ultimate decline of the sensibility to touch. In the very earliest period, and before birth, the nerve-paths are not yet so easily passable as after repeated reflex excitation; hence the longer time occupied in the reflex. It appears from numerous experiments of mine upon unborn animals, and of Soltmann upon new-born and very young ones, that the sensibility of the nerves of the skin, estimated by the ease with which the reflexes take place upon slight stimulus, is continually on the increase, up to a certain point of time that may be designated as the beginning of inhibition of the reflex. But it is to be observed here that, while the central paths are traversed more and more easily through frequent use of them (and more rapidly, up to a certain limit), the peripheral extremities of the cutaneous nerves must be dulled through the inevitable stimulus of contact of wet and of cold, soon after the reflex activity has attained its maximum. For the permanent excitations of the skin of the infant must diminish the excitability of the nerves of the skin. What is gained, therefore, in central excitability (cranial and spinal activity and excitability) is lost in peripheral, and it is very probable that the reason of the slighter sensibility to pain in the newly-born is of a central character, because in the long repose before birth the extremities of the cutaneous nerves may have become very excitable while the brain was not yet active.

2. The First Perceptions of Touch.

From sensibility to contact it is a great step to the perception of touch. To the original consciousness belonging to sensation is added the experience of succession, and with that the consciousness of time; then the simultaneousness of the sensations of contact, and with this the consciousness of space; finally, the consciousness of the causal connection of two or more contacts that have come to consciousness in time and space, and with this the idea of the body touched.

If the new-born child is slapped, it has a sensation, for it cries out; but it knows nothing of the place where it is struck, and nothing of the cause of the blow. If it is struck again after an interval, then there is the possibility of a recollection, and so of a distinction of time. If the blow falls frequently upon different parts of the skin in like fashion, then distinctions of space will also come gradually into the child's consciousness besides the mere sensations of pain, since different extremities of the skin, different nerve-fibers, are each time excited by the blow. If the blow is renewed with intervals of freedom from pain, then the hand that strikes will gradually, only after considerable time, to be sure, be pushed away or avoided as the cause of the pain. If the sensation of contact is, on the contrary, pleasurable, then it will be desired. In both cases movements must be executed, and these lead again to new sensations of contact, which may be even more important in the genesis of mind.

Thus, the sensation of touch in the tips of the fingers, upon the first successful attempts at seizing, must assuredly be very interesting to the child, otherwise he would not, after grasping at and getting hold of an object, observe his own fingers persistently and attentively even when (in the twenty-third week) one hand accidentally gets hold of the other in moving the hands about. Here the discrimination between the mutual contact of two points of the skin of his own body and the contact of one point of the skin with a foreign object is undoubtedly a great step toward the cognition of the self (des Ich).

The earliest association, in time, of one sensation of

contact with another, is probably that which is given in the act of nursing. When the nipple comes between the lips, there follows upon this sensation of touch the sensation of wet (the milk) in the mouth (to which the new sensation of sweetness also joins itself). Herein is given the first perception of touch. The newly-born makes one of his first experiences, namely, this, that upon a certain contact of the lips follows a different, an agreeable sensation in the mouth. Hence the contact with the lips is desired. Every similar soft touch of the lips is therefore agreeable. But how far from being firm the association of the space-element with the time-element is, appears in this, that the newly-born sometimes, as I observed, after "trying" at the breast, take the skin of the breast near the nipple into the mouth and suck at it a long time. And how late in being established is the causal connection between the lip-contact with the nipple and the sensation of liquid sweetness in the mouth when nursing, is manifest from the fact that the infant keeps up for many months the habit of sucking his own fingers and foreign objects.

From this it appears, at the same time, how much more easily and more strongly the time-succession of two sensations impresses itself than does the connection in space or the causal connection. For the first act of sucking, after the first contact of the lips, brings countless other sucking movements in its train. Because it induced an agreeable sensation (of sweetness), it remains in the memory. The first causal connection of the lip-contact with the nipple, localized in space, with the sweet taste of milk, occurs not only later and so with more difficulty, but also is more easily forgotten. Else,

after seeing that the desired sensation of sweetness and
the flow of the milk occur only on sucking at the well-
distinguished breast or the nursing-bottle, the child
would not keep up so long the useless sucking at every
object, capable of being sucked, that is brought to the
mouth (even the fingers) when the feeling of hunger begins. However agreeable to the child the sucking at
the fingers may be, his hunger is not lessened by it, and
the sweet taste is not induced. Yet he sucks away obstinately, as if he thought the milk might be drawn from
the fingers too. The fact that the milk in the breast is
not visible may help to keep up the physiological error,
and it would be worth while to investigate whether infants that take milk exclusively from the breast of the
mother continue the useless sucking of all sorts of objects longer than do those who draw their milk exclusively from transparent bottles.

The habit of useless sucking seems the more strange,
as the infant shows very early a sort of activity of understanding in this field ; shows it by unambiguous
movements, viz., by opening wide the eyes at sight of
the mother's breast.

3. Sensibility to Temperature.

Concerning sensibility to differences of temperature
the observations are few.

Whether the sudden cooling of the child immediately
after birth, which may amount to several degrees, occasions a *sensation* of cold, is a question with regard to
mature newly-born children, as well as the prematurely
born, even in the cases where they shiver. For although
an unpleasant feeling is certainly associated with the with-

drawal of warmth, yet in this particular case the possibility is lacking of *comparing* temperatures. Within the womb the constant, unfelt temperature of the fœtus is somewhat higher than that of the mother. From the first instant of complete birth there begins a general and probably a pretty uniform cooling, because the air that surrounds the just-born child has only one temperature, and the child is wet all over the surface of its body, and so the evaporation must cool off the whole of the skin. Now, the great difference in the temperature of the skin, before and after birth, will be perceptible, in part indirectly, through contraction of the vessels, and in part directly, through peripheral excitation of the nerves, but at first only as an unpleasant feeling. As soon as the warm bath, into which the newly-born is usually dipped, brings back the skin nearly to the temperature that has been kept constant for months within the womb, the excitement (which had never before existed) of the nerves susceptible to temperature subsides, the contraction of the capillaries of the skin ceases, the feeling of discomfort passes away, and the first agreeable sensation of comfortable warmth is given; in general, the first agreeable sensation since birth, for most children. It is agreeable, through the contrast with the refrigeration, as the altered physiognomy of the newly-born in a bath of 36° C. shows, in comparison with that of the still wet, shivering, screaming, just-born babe, to whose head the vernix still adheres. Besides, I saw—at the second bath—that the dry fingers were spread out, a thing that could not be caused by the moisture. As early as the seventh day the expression of pleasure in the widely-opened eyes, immediately after the bath, was different. No sensuous impression of any kind is capable of calling forth such an expression of satisfaction, at this period, in the infants observed by me. Still, in addition to the sensation of warmth, there is the freedom from swaddling-clothes which are often associated with a disagreeable irritation of the skin.

In any case, the feeling of warmth and the feeling of cold are plainly manifest after the first bath, neither of these having been distinguished as such before birth, or probably directly after birth.

It is likely, also, that the powerful effect of a sudden general refrigeration upon the nerves of the skin, through the dipping of the just-born babe into ice-cold water, which has been made use of with the greatest success in restoring to life children apparently still-born, is attended with discomfort, even where the danger of strangling has been obviated. If the breathing has begun, this very strong stimulus produces a remarkable effect, the low whimpering being changed to a loud outcry. This cry is the same as that which follows upon a vigorous (painful) slap. From my experiences with newly-born animals, which cry out lustily on the application of electricity to the skin, and at other kinds of strong cutaneous stimulus, I can but regard this outcry as an utterance of pain; but it does not follow that the cooling of the child just born produces a sensation of cold. This can only come, as has been said, through contrast, where the possibility of comparison exists; therefore, after the first warm bath. The first cooling produces merely an unpleasant feeling.

We have but few experiences also with regard to *local warming* and *cooling*.

About twenty children were tested by Genzmer, who touched different parts of the surface of the skin with an ice-cold iron rod, and saw lively reflex movements invariably appear. But, as the stimulus of touch was not excluded in this case, his further experiments of wetting and then blowing on the skin in special places are of rather more account. This sort of stimulus, applied to the sole of the foot, produced withdrawal of the foot; applied to the hollow of the hand, it produced closing, then withdrawal of the hand. When the cheek was cooled the head was turned to one side. Unfortunately, nothing is said of the age of the children. In such cases the age should be reckoned by hours, and when new experiments are instituted, the blowing, which of itself acts as a reflex stimulus, is to be avoided; and, above all, the previous temperature of the skin ought to be determined. Little children very often have cold hands and feet without making any complaint. Possibly this in itself causes less reflex sensibility to the stimulus of cold and greater to the stimulus of warmth.

It is known that even quite young infants become restless and cry readily when they are wet anywhere with cold water. This dislike of the local withdrawal of warmth persists, during the first years of life, until at length the knowledge that a washing with cold water is refreshing overcomes the fear of cold (in the third year).

Moreover, how sensitive individual children are, in perfectly sound health, in regard to the discrimination of cold and warmth, was evident to me in the experiment of ordering the daily bath to be made colder gradually. The water could be cooled to $32\frac{1}{2}°$ C. without lessening the child's pleasure.. But every time the water was reduced to the neighborhood of 31¼° C. or less, the child screamed uninterruptedly until warmer water was added. The temperature of the skin, therefore, was presumably very near 32° C. But when the child was two and a half years old, he laughed and uttered joyous sounds in water of the temperature of the room—in a cold bath, therefore, such as formerly made him cry; and in his fourth year he objected to taking a warm bath 36° C. In the seventh month he became pale, always, at being put into water from 34° to 35° C., but regained his ordinary color within one or two minutes. The case here is not one of direct contraction of the capillaries of the skin through sudden withdrawal of warmth, but is a case of vaso-motor reflex action, because it was precisely the skin of the face, which was not dipped in the water, that became most pale, and this happened as late as the age of more than two years.

The sensibility of the mucous membrane of the mouth, of the tongue, of the lips, to cold and warmth is also surprisingly great in many infants during the first days. If the nursing-bottle is but a little more than blood-warm, it is refused, often with violent screaming; and if it is some degrees colder than the milk sucked from the breast of the mother, it is refused likewise. Therefore, in experiments designed to test the gustatory sensibility in new-born children, the liquids employed must have the exact temperature of 37° C. Yet infants learn easily to drink water and milk of the temperature of the room they live in, if their drink is given to them, when they are hungry, only at this temperature.

The sensibility of the lips to differences of temperature in liquids is in any case determined by the constant temperature of the amniotic fluid before birth,
and of the mother's milk after birth.

The difference in the neutral point of temperature
between the mucous membrane of the mouth (tongue),
and of the skin (e. g., the hand) which in the adult
amounts to 5° or 6° C. (whereas before birth it is zero),
can in general hardly establish itself in the first days of
life. The tongue and the mucous membrane of the
mouth maintain through life almost the same neutral
point they had before birth; whereas the external skin
only gradually gets its varying neutral points through
unequal refrigeration.

CHAPTER IV.

TASTE.

THE observations concerning the sense of taste relate chiefly to the question whether the newly-born
have a sensibility to taste such as makes possible at
once the distinction between different savors. Next
comes the comparison of gustatory impressions already
recognized as different. Then follow some statements
as to taste in newly-born animals.

1. Sensibility to Taste in the Newly-born.

We know, from mimetic reflex movements of the
same sort as those of adults, that the newly-born, and
even those born a month or two before their time, react
upon substances that have a taste, when these are intro-

duced into the mouth by means of a pencil. Kussmaul tested the sense of taste in this way in more than twenty newly-born children, making use of cane-sugar, quinine, common salt, and tartaric acid. Genzmer repeated these experiments with twenty-five children, most of whom he observed immediately after birth and from three to six days after, some up to the sixth week. Kussmaul found that the salt, the quinine, and the acid occasioned grimaces as an expression of dislike, but with much variation in the manifestation in individual cases. The sugar, on the other hand, produced movements of sucking. The liquids to be tested were all warmed, so that the reaction upon them can not be ascribed to a feeling of cold in the mouth.

As the acid, however, acted on the mucous membrane, it might cause pain in addition to the sour taste; yet the children did not cry out, and after the edges of the tongue were touched with a crystal of tartaric acid, the grimaces appeared instantaneously in two new-born children, while the crystal placed in the center of the upper surface of the tongue caused no change in the countenance for a considerable time, until the acid was sufficiently dissolved to reach the edges of the tongue that were sensitive to it. So that it is the sour taste, and not an incidental painful effect of the acid, that elicits the "sour" look. The suspicion that the latter is generated only by excitation of the nerves of taste through the acid, is not pertinent; accordingly, we have here a certain ability to distinguish sensations of taste, active directly after birth, before anything has been swallowed except the amniotic fluid swallowed before birth.

10

The psychogenetic importance of this fact demands a more detailed examination of the observations on which it rests.

Kussmaul found that the newly-born sometimes respond to the taste of sugar with the mimetic expression for bitter. It might thus be thought that the sensations were not distinguished, but were responded to irregularly, now with one, now with another, reflex movement. But the circumstances under which the reflex takes place are not irregular. " Some made a wry face at the first introduction of the solution of sugar, while they took in the rest of it with satisfaction. It was not the sensation of taste in itself apparently that was in fault, but another psychical experience, the surprise caused by the sudden effect on the sensitive nerves. One of the children even started directly with fright, when it came so suddenly to taste the unfamiliar liquid (which was warmed). Children that had reacted strongly upon quinine, commonly made a grimace again, or several times in succession, when a solution of sugar was introduced, but with decreasing animation, until finally a comfortable sucking and swallowing were substituted. This accords with the experiences that every adult has in his own case, viz., that a very bitter or nauseous taste does not allow itself to be at once supplanted by a sweet one, but at every fresh stimulus of the gustatory sense by substances of different savors, it recurs with decreasing force."

These deductions I must agree with, in every respect. I saw my child, the first day of his life, lick off the powdered cane-sugar that was put on the nipple, whereas he licked nothing else; so the sweet alone seemed desirable. On the second day, however, he licked at the mother's milk just as he had done at the sugar, with a calm, satisfied expression of countenance. When this child later received salted food and food of different kinds, the first thing that was remarkable at every new sensation of taste was the expression of surprise; and, as late as the second quarter of his second year (nay, occasionally in his fourth year), he would shudder, shut his eyes and distort his face in the strangest fashion, when he tasted a new food that was agreeable to him in spite of his grimaces; for he often wanted it directly afterward, and took it then soon with the expression of satisfaction. On the other hand, it was often easy to persuade the child, after he had learned to speak (as a hypnotized adult may be persuaded), that a sourish or generally unattractive food, which he at first refused, was very pleasant to the taste, so that he would then want more of it. It is necessary to distinguish sharply from the very first, on the one hand, the expression for the disagreeable manifested at the sudden new sensation, and the expression, not appearing till after this, of the agreeable that is excited by the pleasant taste; and on the other hand, the expression for the disagreeable at the bitter, the salt, or the sour taste, and that for the agreeable at the sweet taste.

It is certain, from all observations, that the newly-born distinguish the sensations of taste that are decidedly different from one another, the sweet, sour, and bitter.

But then Genzmer found in his experiments that individuals newly-born responded to an attenuated solution (one quarter to one per cent) of quinine, and one

of vinegar, by sucking movements, just as they did to
a solution of sugar.   In one case, indeed, a child on the
first day, as also in the sixth week, sucked at a five-per-
cent solution of quinine without any sign of dislike (Kussmaul's solution was of four per cent). If the solution was
more concentrated, the child made a wry face of complaint, as the others were wont to do at a weaker solution (beyond one degree), then began to cry, and made
it manifest that the disagreeable nature of the taste had
become perceptible to him.

Inasmuch as it has been established that there are
great individual differences among the newly-born in
their gustatory sensibility, and that, allowing for a considerable blunting of this through experimenting, there was
only in the case of individuals in the first week a refine-
ment of taste for differences in intensity, the hypothesis
is forced upon us that, in the case of the attenuated solutions the gustatory sensations of many children were too
weak to be found either agreeable or disagreeable ; that
new-born children especially are not yet in condition to
press the substance to be tasted against the hard palate
with the upper surface of the tongue, whereby the distribution to the end-organs of the nerves (these, moreover, being probably less numerous in the little tongue)
is favored and hastened.   In the case of these attenuated solutions there remains, then, only the effect upon
the sucking-mechanism, as in the case of touching the
tongue with the finger.   There is no need of the additional hypothesis that a weak bitter or sour taste is
agreeable to individuals among the newly-born, in order
to understand that the reaction upon a weak bitter or
sour is not accompanied with the same animated reflex

movements as a strong stimulus induces, but is accompanied with sucking. In general, the newly-born make a wry face after the introduction of a three to five per cent quinine solution; they shut the eyes tight, the throat is convulsively contracted, the mouth is opened wide, and the liquid is ejected along with the mucus of the mouth, which is generally secreted very scantily, but in this case abundantly. The "bitter" expression of countenance is thus quite a different one from the "sweet," even on the first day of life. But it is different also from the "sour," as in the case of adults, since in the movements of choking the corners of the mouth are drawn sharply up and sidewise; so they are, according to Genzmer, at the introduction of pretty strong acetic acid (which any way is unsuited to such experiments on account of its smell). The strongest solutions caused, besides, in his experiments, agitation and screaming for the most part; sugar, on the contrary, is tasted with satisfaction by all newly-born children, when it acts in sufficient quantity, after the first surprise is over. About this there is no doubt.

Since very sour and very bitter substances call forth in the newly-born different reflex movements under circumstances otherwise similar, and very sweet substances call forth quite different movements still, therefore these various gustatory qualities are distinguished.

The fact that weak solutions of bitter and of sour are by some taken in much the same way as weak solutions of sweet, with sucking movements, with no sign of discomfort, is explained by the slight sensibility of the tongue for degrees of intensity. The sensations of contact caused by the substances to be tasted, sensations which of themselves start sucking movements, over-power at that time the weak sensations of taste. But what to one child tastes strong, to another tastes weak. For many children one per cent of acetic acid was too sour, while they would suck away at a two-per-cent solution of quinine; with others it was the reverse. This fact, too, is in accord with the above statement.

The association of certain mimetic contractions of muscles with certain sensations of taste is a surprisingly strong one—it is inborn. Children born about two months or more too early are no less sensitive to the gustatory stimuli spoken of than are those born at the right time.

Accordingly, the opinion, often expressed, that the new-born infant possesses only a general sensation of taste, and that the qualitative differences of taste become perceptible to him only through his becoming accustomed to them—this opinion falls to the ground. Were it correct—did every moderate stimulus whatever of the nerves of taste cause sucking movements as a simple reflex, and did any strong stimulus whatever, on the other hand, cause choking, likewise as a simple reflex—then the most intensely sweet taste must be regarded as only a moderate stimulus, and the fact before recognized as established would be inexplicable, that under circumstances alike in other respects the mimetic expression for bitter is different from that for sweet and from that for sour, when the corresponding gustatory stimuli are strong enough.

Kussmaul's inference from his experiments is therefore correct, that the sense of taste in the newly-born is already capable of acting in its characteristic forms of

sensation; the sensation received by it is not one altogether undefined and vague.

2. Comparison of the Gustatory Impressions.

The sense of taste seems to be the first of all the
senses to yield clear perceptions, to which memory
directly attaches itself, as Sigismund rightly pointed
out. The gustatory impression of the milk to which the
child is accustomed abides, so that a comparison may
be made with strange milk. Of this ability to compare
the child soon makes use, for, during the whole nursing
period and even longer, the taste of sweet is preferred
by far to all other tastes, and these others are experienced with signs of disgust when they are strong, and
this from the first day on.

Burdach is wrong in affirming that not till the end
of the first month does the babe begin to object to
medicines, on the ground that then first is the child
disagreeably affected by astringent, bitter, salt, sour
tastes, whereas at the beginning he takes every liquid—
e. g., camomile-tea and tincture of rhubarb, just as willingly as milk, and does not yet manifest choice. If the
camomile-tea and the tincture of rhubarb are sweetened,
and are not cold or hot, he takes them; but liquids that
are not sweet, or that have a strong taste, or that are
cold or hot, he does not take so readily as he does
milk. The cavity of the mouth is, even for the newly-
born, something more than a mere "sucking-organ."
Although the food is not so mixed with saliva, by muscular movement, and so brought into contact with the
mucous membrane of the mouth as it is later, still it is
tasted and especially its temperature is noticed.

In fact, I have found the gustatory sensitiveness to-ward different degrees of intensity considerably in-creased very early. Thus, my child on the second day took, without hesitation, cow's milk diluted with water, which on the fourth day he stoutly refused. He must have compared the less degree of sweetness with that of his mother's milk. But an extremely small quantity of cane-sugar sufficed to make the bottle acceptable. It only needed a few grains applied to the mouth of the bottle.

Now, as bad-tasting medicines generally have some corrective, especially sugar, added to them, it is not sur-prising that infants often take them at once without discrimination. I have repeatedly convinced myself that this is the case, and at the same time that those medicines tasted sweet. If they are very sweet—e. g., one hundred parts sugar to one part calomel—they are taken willingly, even by the child of six months and more; the younger child does not need so great an ad-dition, precisely because it does not discriminate so nicely, but it rejects strong-tasting substances that are offered to it without any corrective.

Every new taste occasions in the babe of more than six months old a play of countenance which at first sug-gests surprise, then either a desire for more, or disgust. But very often the food that was at first desired is ejected after a second trial, with turning away of the head; and, as has been mentioned (p. 119), that which at first caused expressions of displeasure is directly aft-erward desired. Here are at least four different points to be noticed: 1, the stimulus of the new; 2, the sensa-tion of taste; 3, the sensation of touch and of temperature in the mouth; 4, the sense of smell. All four may act in harmony, but they may also counteract one another so that the child does not know whether the new thing tastes good to him or not, etc. Where the taste *alone* varies in two impressions of like sort, as with sweet and salt, the child of six months can discriminate accurately at once.

How far the comparison of the gustatory sensations discriminated may be carried after the weaning of a child has taken place, is shown, in the case of my child and some others, by the following observations:

From the one hundred fiftieth day on, the breast was to be given him only in the night. But after five nights the child refused to take the breast as hitherto, probably because in the days preceding so much cane-sugar had been added to the boiled and diluted cow's milk, that it tasted somewhat sweeter than milk from the breast.

At the end of the twenty-third week the child had a new nurse, whose milk it took eagerly. Then were taken, apparently with equal willingness, this milk and diluted, sweetened cow's milk, as well as meat-broth with yolk of egg, and yolk of egg beaten up in cow's milk.

From the one hundred and eighty-fifth day on, no more nurse's milk. Cow's milk boiled (one part water out of four parts), with a little egg, seems to relish. Water-gruel with yolk of egg was taken once, but not again; leguminous food of that sort is refused after a single trial.

From the eighth month on, the child was fed almost exclusively for months on Nestle's "prepared food" (Kindermehl), which was most agreeable to him. He utters a cry of joy, as if to make known his pleasure at the good taste, and this more loudly and persistently than over any food thus far tried. It would hardly be possible for an adult, owing to the sameness of the taste, to take for so long a time uninterruptedly, several times a day, nothing but this prepared food.

9th month.—With great surprise—at the new taste—the child took yolk of egg mixed with cane-sugar. He drinks water with liking, and sucks with pleasure at a piece of white bread. But in this the sucking doubtless yields more pleasure than the taste.

11th month.—The child takes, without pleasure, meat-broth with egg that has a slightly salt taste. He rejects obstinately scalded skimmed milk without sugar, but likes dry biscuit.

12th month.—The child is very fastidious (wählerisch) in regard to the taste of his food; refuses farinaceous food except "prepared food" and biscuit. Everything bitter was now, and for the two years following, detested, slightly salt food no longer so.

The idiosyncrasy of antipathy to many articles of food (even in the fourth and fifth years) went so far that even the sight of such food (e. g., peas) called forth lively demonstrations of disgust, even choking movements, a phenomenon exhibited by many children, and one that leads us to infer a largely developed capacity of discrimination in taste and smell.

As to the practical bearing of this, I hold, as a fixed rule—however much it may be at variance with the prejudices of a traditional method of training—that a young child should in no case be constrained to eat food that is distasteful to him. I can see no advantage whatever to the child from such severity, but it may very likely have an injurious effect upon the nutrition and the development of character, even if vomiting does not follow soon after the meal.

The refusal of the little child to eat certain kinds of food is by no means—as Heyfelder thinks it is—naughtiness. The babe is right in refusing to drink sour milk in the first place; and at the critical period of weaning it is not the child that deserves punishment when he rejects the salted food or food hard for him to digest, but the nurse that forces it on him who deserves it. Such constraint first develops often enough an antagonism to some dishes, and general willfulness. This is afterward vainly contended against as idiosyncrasy or naughtiness. But let the child's taste in the beginning have free course—guarding him always against excess—and he will of himself become accustomed to the food of the family. In this matter it should not escape notice that this last presupposes a certain blunting of smell as well as of taste, which the child gains only in the course of years.

3. Taste in Newly-born Animals.

In newly-born animals, also, whose sense of taste I tested, there is certainly a decided preference for substances of certain particular tastes, along with indifference to solutions that are qualitatively unlike and weak to the taste, and the memory of tastes is developed on the first day.

Experiments on little Guinea-pigs, only eight to sixteen hours old, and separated from the mother after two hours, proved to me absolutely that concentrated water-solutions of tartaric acid, soda, glycerine, introduced

into the mouth through glass tubes, are swallowed just
as greedily or eagerly as cow's milk and water, with
vigorous sucking. But then the empty tube, placed
with the end upon the tongue, occasioned just such
sucking. The experiments conducted in this manner
can not, therefore, yield much that can be depended
upon. Touch, as a reflex stimulus to sucking in hungry
new-born creatures, overpowers any taste-stimuli acting
at the same time. Newly-born animals that have eaten
enough do not, however, suck regularly in general.

For this reason another criterion, at least for the
recognition of an agreeable sensation of taste, is of especial value, viz., licking. This must be regarded as a
sure sign of enjoyment of the sweet in the case of new-
born human beings also—they lick persistently sugar,
but not crystals of tartaric acid, or the nipple-shell that
is not sugared.

A Guinea-pig, not yet seventeen hours old, was placed
by me in a glass box along with a bit of oil of thyme,
a bit of camphor, and a piece of sugar-candy. The
creature ran about, stayed longest by the sugar, gnawed
at a corner of that, and thereupon began to lick the
sugar very eagerly. One could see plainly how it
stretched forth the tongue and drew it along the smooth
surface of the crystal. After it had kept up this operation for some minutes, apparently with great satisfaction, I removed it, bandaged both its eyes, and repeated
the experiment after twenty-four hours. To my surprise the animal now again distinguished the sugar, although it had not touched the oil of thyme and the camphor, and although it could not see. This was probably
owing to the smell. The glass and the wood were not

licked, but the sugar was licked just as before, and just as it was after the animal was again allowed the use of its eyes. I have not seen other Guinea-pigs manifest on the first day such decision in taste. But the one instance proves that the sensation of sweet can be discriminated on the first day, can be desired and be found agreeable.

The chick just out of the shell also distinguishes different kinds of food by the taste. For when I placed before a chick boiled white-of-egg, boiled yolk, and millet, it pecked at all three, one after another, as it did at bits of egg-shell, grains of sand, spots and cracks in the wood floor; but only at the yolk-of-egg did it peck often and eagerly. When I took the last away, and then, an hour later than the first trial, placed it again before the chick, the creature ran directly to it and took some of it, whereas at the first trial it had tasted the white-of-egg only once, and had swallowed only one grain of millet, rejecting the rest obstinately afterward as before. This preference of the yolk-of-egg rests accordingly upon discrimination and taste-memory.

New-born animals, therefore, distinguish qualities of taste without having had any other gustatory impressions than those of the amniotic fluid swallowed in the egg.

This remarkable capacity can rest only on inherited recollection—on an *instinct* of taste.

Further experiments in this matter, especially upon newly-born human beings, are urgently to be desired, in order to ascertain in detail, better than hitherto, the gradual increase of sensibility according to the different degrees of concentration (in solution), and the characteristic reflexes for agreeable and disagreeable sensations of taste. Only chemically pure, odorless, strong-tasting substances should be used, in accurately graded quantities, for such experiments; preferably dissolved in luke-warm, distilled water; for sweet tastes, glycerine, cane-sugar, and sugar-of-milk; for bitter, sulphate of quinine; for salt, cooking-salt; for sour, tartaric acid and lactic acid ; for alkalines, soda.

CHAPTER V.

SMELL.

The observations concerning the faculty of smell relate first to the evidence of its existence in the new-born human being; next to the discrimination of impressions of smell on the part of the infant. These are followed by some statements concerning smell in new-born animals.

1. Faculty of Smell in the Newly-born.

The child can, even in its first days, be constrained, by strong-smelling substances, to mimetic movements. Kussmaul has ascertained that new-born children in sleep, when the odor of asafœtida or of the very bad-smelling Dippel's-oil enters their nostrils, frequently shut the eyelids tighter together, distort the face, become restless, move the head and the arms, awake ; and go to sleep again when the cause of the smell is removed. Genzmer observed that well-developed, lively children, are brought to screaming by strong impressions of smell. He made use of the ill-smelling aqua fœtida antihysterica, which was rubbed with a pencil upon the upper edge of the upper lip of sleeping and waking children. The infants made movements of sucking, when but little liquid was put on; of choking, when more was put on; the eyes, too, were screwed up and the countenance was distorted, as after strong gustatory impressions. How many hours old the children were, is not stated.

In these observations the sensation of wetness has been overlooked, and both investigators have failed to consider that in their experiments there was by no means an excitement of the nerves of smell exclusively. The failure of the first to obtain decisive results when he selected waking infants, and the circumstance that only strongly stimulating substances were found efficacious, as well as the appearance of strong reflex movements, points rather to an excitement of the sensitive nerve (the trigeminus) than of the nerve of smell (the olfactory). Still the tests with asafœtida are to be referred to the latter alone. Children born a month too soon likewise react on odorous substances in the above fashion (Kussmaul).

The proof of the existence of the faculty of smell in the newly-born child would be produced, if its mother or nurse would make up her mind to smear her breast with a strong-smelling substance that has no taste, or if some volatile stuff like petroleum, spirits of wine, cologne-water, asafœtida, in small quantity, were put upon a nursing-bottle or a nipple-shell. If the child then refuses to suck at the breast or the bottle that smells of the stuff, and does not refuse the source of milk that has been left in its natural state, then the

child can smell.   For in case of weak odors of this sort
it is not to be assumed that there will be perceptible
accompanying excitement of the nasal fibers of the trigeminus.   Such experiments are urgently to be wished.
A girl babe of eighteen hours obstinately refused the
breast upon the nipple of which a little petroleum, or
oil-of-amber, had been rubbed, but gladly took the other
breast.   This experiment of Kroner's alone corresponds
to my suggestion given above (made in 1878); only it
ought to be repeated with a number of very young
children.   For the observation that infants in the first
days reject the breast of the mother, when this has by
accident acquired a strange smell, was not instituted with
regard to infants just born.   And the fact that many
new-born children after having once tasted their mother's
milk, refuse for a long time, in spite of hunger and
thirst, to take any other food, is not convincing, for this
is not a case of sensations of smell exclusively, nor again
of children just born.

On the other hand, some of Kroner's observations
are decidedly in favor of the view that the normal child
can smell, a quarter of an hour after birth, and a few
hours or days after.   For it turns up its nose and makes
a wry face when Dippel's-oil or amber-oil is offered it,
and " children several hours old become generally restless, screw the eyelids tight together, open the mouth,
and thrust out the tongue."

In all experiments of this kind concerning the sense
of smell in the newly-born, care must also be taken that
the nostrils shall be perfectly open to the passage of the
air.   The child must breathe easily with his mouth shut.
The filling of the nostrils with amniotic fluid excludes

the possibility of a sensation of smell before birth. But directly after the beginning of respiration this liquid is displaced by air, and it is a question whether then the olfactory mucous membrane needs first a longer invigoration by the air before the olfactory cells can be the means of a sensation of smell, or whether a reaction follows immediately upon the inhalation of air that has an odor.

2. Discrimination of Impressions of Smell.

The sense of smell, when it has once been aroused to activity, continues to be of decisive importance to the infant in the choice of food, and this from the beginning. Sensations of smell are present, for the first time, not at the age of four weeks, or from the second month on, as many think, but even in the first days, and the pleasant and unpleasant feelings occasioned by them increase in intensity from day to day. Children of a few weeks sometimes do not take the breast of a nurse whose skin has a disagreeable smell, and they cry out as soon as the breast approaches them. There is no doubt that children born blind very early smell the spoon filled with milk or broth, and the disinclination of many infants, in the first week, to take cow's milk after they have had the breast, must be ascribed to the smell rather than to the taste, since they sometimes refuse the milk when it is brought near them without tasting it. In such a case the decisive experiment would be to hold the child's nose and bandage its eyes, to see whether it would not then take willingly the new food. At all events, the sense of smell in children born blind plays an essential part in the taking of food, and develops its own memory as early as does the sense of taste.

11

Whether the babe, however, knows its sleeping mother in the night by the smell, as animals undoubtedly do, must be left undecided. To me it is probable that the child does not recognize her when it does not see, hear, or feel her.

That the sense of smell is concerned in the seeking of the nipple, on the part of the babe that is merely laid by the nurse but not otherwise assisted (as is the case with animals), also seems to me improbable from my own observations in the lying-in hospital. For the children, indeed, push hither and thither (often with surprising quickness and violence), with the whole head against the breast (like young lambs, kids, calves, foals) with open mouth and intermittent movements of the lower jaw; but in my own child it was not till the eighth day of life that I saw this groping about; and whether the sense of smell co-operates in this is doubtful, for the child often sucked at the wrong place.

Later, long after weaning, the sense of smell is unquestionably the least turned to account for the knowledge of things. Impressions of smell are regularly confounded with impressions of taste. The following notes regarding the behavior of my child show how late in his case smell appeared distinctly:

In the fifteenth month, freshly-ground coffee and cologne-water, both of which he liked very much to smell in his third year, made no impression at all, or only a slight one. They were not desired, neither were any movements made to repel them if they were held under the nose of the child when his mouth was shut. At the end of this month, however, cologne-water held under his nose made the child laugh. He took pleasure in the odor as in any other new, agreeable sense-impression. In the sixteenth month he was affected in just the same way by the odor of oil-of-roses.

In the seventeenth month, however, the inability to separate smell and taste showed itself still in unmistakable fashion. For every time that I wanted to make the child smell something—for example, when I held a hyacinth or an essence to his nose—he would open his mouth, and in fact take the sweet-smelling flower into his mouth. He thought, therefore, that as he had hitherto had agreeable sensations of smell only in connection with taste (of milk), he must now, since he was smelling, also taste—a very interesting proof, in relation to the genesis of mind, that sensation is independent of the knowledge of the organ of sensation; and that the reasoning processes depend upon the preceding associations of sensation.

In the eighteenth month the child no longer carried regularly to his mouth the objects he was to smell or that he wanted to smell; he had therefore recognized the separation of smell from taste. If I gave him a rose, saying, "Smell of it!" ("Riech einmal!") he would put the flower to his nose, with his mouth shut, and inhale the aroma through the nose, though, to be sure, only after exhaling the breath many times against the flower. For a long time "smell" was understood to mean exhaling, probably because the nurse, in order to indicate smell, had always feigned a sneeze. Yet the opening of the mouth occasionally appeared later also, when the child was to smell anything. Genuine snuffing, taking in the air for the purpose of smelling, did not take place.

As no exercises in smelling are in general instituted for children, and as the infant almost always has a sourish smell of half-digested milk, and has little opportunity to smell anything except milk and his own perspiration and that of his nurse or mother, the late development of smell, as a conscious act, is not surprising. The importance of this function for testing the atmosphere and food, and for cleanliness, is unfortunately almost universally underestimated. We find, too, as is well known, in many, probably in most, adults, a great uncertainty as to whether they have a sensation of smell or a sensation of taste, or both. The civilized child ordinarily grows up without instruction in this respect, although it would be very useful to impress upon him early the various kinds of smell, in association with definite expressions for them, as is usually done with colors and tones.

3. Smell in New-born Animals.

Many mammals are capable of distinguishing different impressions of smell only a few hours after birth.

Especially in the case of new-born Guinea-pigs, no one of which was more than seventeen hours old, I was able easily to establish this fact. For when I put ill-smelling substances, like asafœtida, in not too small quantities, on the bottom of a wide-mouthed glass bottle, lying in a horizontal position, into which the animal under observation crept, the creature repeatedly wiped and rubbed its nose with the fore-feet. Further, the animals turned away, with a quick sidewise movement of the head, after concentrated propionic acid, or carbolic acid, or water-ammonia, had been held before them some seconds. Often they sneezed at the same time with a peculiar noise. The smell of camphor, on the other hand, seemed to be not disagreeable to young Guinea-pigs; for they stayed a long time in a glass half filled with pieces of camphor, when they might easily have left it, and they made none of those movements of repulsion. The same is the case with gum-benjamin. Here, to be sure, the rapid blunting of sensitiveness to odors should be taken into account.

I tested several more odorous substances in this way, especially oil-of-thyme, alcohol, ethylic ether, chloroform, prussic acid, and nicotine. Toward these last the Guinea-pigs did not act with so much decision on the first day as they did toward the first-mentioned, probably because the attenuation, in order to avoid its being poisonous, was too great. Thus much, however, is settled : new-born animals a few hours after birth discriminate between agreeable and disagreeable smells. The impressions must simply be strong enough. Any one who has seen how animals, when only half a day old, behave toward asafœtida and camphor, will not doubt that the former causes them discomfort, while the latter does not. Tobacco-smoke also is offensive to them, and when blown against the face causes, even before the close of the first day of life, shutting of the eyes and drawing back of the head—accordingly, purposive reflexes of defense.

We are not justified, indeed, in assuming that mammals just born perceive the odorous substances mentioned by means of their olfactory nerves only, for the sneezing, the rubbing of the nose with the fore-feet, the closing of the eyelids, the turning away and drawing back of the head from strong-smelling substances, the surprising indifference toward substances having a less intense but still a decided odor, indicate, in the experiments upon animals of one day old, an excitement of the nasal branch of the trigeminus. But it is demonstrated by other facts that mammals, dogs, rabbits, cats, can really smell directly after the first respirations.

Biffi bisected the olfactory lobes in very young puppies that had not yet their sight. They bore the operation well, and the mother's licking helped to heal the wound. Animals thus treated could no longer find the mother's teats, so long as they were blind. They crept about on her belly, trying to suck everywhere—*tentando quà e là col muso gli oggetti.* In most cases somebody had to open their mouths and put the teat in. On the contrary, blind puppies in the normal state find the teats at once, as if they saw them. Accordingly, it is not to be doubted that in trying to find the source of the milk, the young are guided by smell, for they could make use of touch (after being operated on) as they could before. We may conclude, then, that the olfactory nerve is excitable in other just-born mammals also, and that it was concerned in the above experiments.

This inference is confirmed by the experiments of Gudden, which show that in rabbits one or two days old, the closing of one nostril, or the removal of one hemisphere of the brain, hinders the development of the olfactory nerve, of the olfactory bulb, and of the tractus of that side. With the removal of one bulbus, the tractus almost entirely disappears. After the removal of both the olfactory bulbs, which makes a comparatively insignificant wound, the little creatures, entirely deprived of the sense of smell, soon perished

in consequence of deficient nourishment, since they no
longer found their way well to the old ones and their
teats, notwithstanding the assistance they got from the
nervi trigemini. It is then as it is in the case of simple bisection of both olfactory nerves. When, on the
other hand, the organs of smell were left unharmed, and
both eyes were taken from the newly-born, and both
ears stopped, then the sense of smell was developed in
a very high degree, the olfactory bulbs being demonstrably enlarged beyond the ordinary measure. In like
manner, the external ears of a rabbit, that had been deprived of both its eyes soon after birth, had a vigorous
development, and the hearing became acute beyond
what is normal.

From these experiments we infer both the dependence of the organic development upon stimulation from
without and the power of physiological concurrence,
but in particular we infer that rabbits very soon after
birth can smell and that they make abundant use of
this capacity in finding the teats. Otherwise it would
be incomprehensible that they can no longer find the
teats after the destruction of the olfactory nerves alone,
and that they perish of hunger.

Spalding has observed, further, that four kittens,
three days old, and still blind, when he put near them
his hand, which a dog had just licked, began to spit in
a way that was amusing. He infers from this that the
cat abhors her hereditary enemy even before she can see
him. Here the fact ought to be brought to notice that
on the third day the cat possesses a finely-developed
sense of smell.

At the same time, however, by this observation and

many others, especially that of the "pointing" and "setting" of young bird-dogs, the fact is proved that the memory of certain impressions of smell is inherited. In man such olfactory instincts probably no longer appear. With him the sense of smell plays in general a much less pronounced part in the genesis of mind than it does in the brutes, which are well known to surpass him greatly, at an early stage, in recognizing and discriminating odors, and which are occupied all their lives, much more than man is, with perceptions of smell.

CHAPTER VI.

THE EARLIEST ORGANIC SENSATIONS AND EMOTIONS.

WITH regard to the physiological conditions of the organic sensations and emotions of adult human beings, so little that is of general application is established, that an investigation of these in the child who can not yet speak seems premature. I have, therefore, directed my attention merely to a small number of sensations and emotions in the child. My observations are, unfortunately, as yet very fragmentary in this direction. But it is better to communicate them than to be silent about them, if only to show that here many new problems are, as it were, growing up out of the ground, close upon one another.

The whole behavior of the child is determined essentially by his feelings of pleasure and his feelings of discomfort. For this reason I shall speak first of these in general. Next appear in the life of the child, among the special feelings, the feeling of hunger, and the feeling of satiety, concerning which I append some observations. I have likewise considered the feeling of fatigue, which is much less marked in children.

Of emotions, fear and surprise are prominent in importance for the mental development of the very young child.

1. Feelings of Pleasure in General.

In the first three months the feelings of pleasure are not manifold. Besides the appeasing of hunger, with the enjoyment that ever recurs along with it, of sucking and of the sweet taste, there comes in the first month, and indeed from the first day on, a pleasurable feeling through the warm bath. The less intense but constant satisfaction in moderately bright impressions of light comes next, and, somewhat later, that in objects moved slowly before the eyes. The pleasure in both steadily grows, but is not so great as the pleasurable feeling in being undressed, which likewise makes its appearance in the first weeks. The release from clothing, etc., is followed regularly by lively movements, especially by alternate stretchings of the legs and visible comfort. Great satisfaction is also afforded the infant by the process of wiping it dry.

Acoustic impressions regularly produce pleasurable feelings in the second month. Singing, piano-playing, and all sorts of musical sounds, sometimes quiet the restless child, sometimes cause lively expressions of joy in the child, as he is lying comfortably or is held in the arms. So it is when he is spoken to by members of the family. The large, bright oval of the face, that moves close in front of the child's face, and speaks and sings and laughs, arouses attention and produces cheerfulness early through its peculiarity, being different from all other optical impressions, yet the human child hardly knows its mother before the third month.

In the fourth month, the pleasure of grasping at all possible objects comes gradually into view, becomes plain in the fifth, and continues to increase in the sixth. The delight of being taken out-of-doors at this period is probably occasioned more by the change, the greater brightness, and the fresher air, than by the sight of trees and houses. The child's own image in the mirror was in one case observed with unquestionable signs of pleasure in the seventh month; animals and watches do not generally excite the child's pleasurable interest till later.

A new sort of pleasurable feelings, in which an intellectual element already mingles, appears when the child begins himself to produce some change, especially of form, through his own activity, so that he gradually acquires the knowledge of his own power. Here belong not only the effects of the voice, especially of screaming and of the first sounds uttered by himself, but also the first plays. First of all, and that in the fifth month, in the case of my child, it was the act of crumpling a sheet of paper, that was taken up and repeated with evident gratification. Tearing newspapers to pieces and rolling them up into balls afforded him great pleasure from that time to his third year. A like enlivening effect was produced by the long-continued pulling of a glove this way and that (practiced from the fifth month to the fourth year, from time to time), also by pulling at the hair of one's beard (at the same period), then by the ringing of a little bell, continued an intolerably long time. Later it was the movements of his own body in locomotion (in marching), and purely intellectual pleasures that amused him: putting things in and out, cutting with scissors, turning the leaves of books, looking at pictures. Last came the inventive, embellishing and yet moderate imagination, that gives life to shapeless blocks of wood, transforms the leaves of trees into savory food, and so on.

On the whole, however, it is manifest in the case of all children in the first part of their life, that much more happiness comes through relief from disagreeable conditions than through the provision of positively agreeable conditions. Hunger, thirst, wet, cold, swaddling-clothes—the getting rid of these produces pleasurable feelings, which are in part stronger, in part not weaker, than those occasioned by mild light, moving tassels, lukewarm baths, song, and the friendliness of parents. It is not until the second three months that wholly new scenes of enjoyment are entered upon with the first successful attempts at grasping objects.

The first period of human life belongs to the least agreeable, inasmuch as not only the number of enjoyments is small, but the capacity for enjoyment is small likewise, and the unpleasant feelings predominate until sleep interrupts them.

The *expressions* of pleasurable feeling are at the beginning not very various; but from the first day signs of pleasure are open eyes, and soon after an animated gleam in them—a slight excitation of the secretory nerve of the lachrymal gland.

The voice is in the first days an altogether different one when pleasurable feelings are expressed from what it is when the child is hungry, and high, crowing tones, as a sure sign of joy, have in fact been observed by me in the fourth month. They were always employed with the same significance even in the fourth year. Toward the end of the first year there appeared in the case of my boy, as an acoustic expression of pleasure, a peculiar grunting, caused probably by oscillations of the uvula with the mouth shut. This made its appearance especially when the child had a joyous anticipation, was expecting something agreeable, and it used to be associated frequently with a movement of abdominal pressure. A genuine pressure or straining, accompanied by a strong expiration, or by that grunting with shut mouth, was for months an indubitable expression of pleasure. I have not succeeded in finding an explanation of this peculiarity.

More commonly, movements of the extremities are found in infants as signs of pleasurable feelings—stretchings and bendings, drawing up and throwing out the arms and legs (especially in the bath, and when the piano was played, were these clearly manifested, even in the second month); at a later period these are multiplied and are associated with very loud, joyous shouting, as early as the third quarter of the first year. What is called "Strampeln" (kicking), is also frequently observed after the clothes are taken off, when the infant has been fed and is comfortable in a warm, dry bed, in a moderate light, not excited by new impressions. I saw also, in the sixth month even, the quick, bilateral, symmetrical movement, up and down, of the arms (not of the legs), joined with laughing, as an expression of pleasure, when one simply nodded to the child in a friendly manner. The striking of the hands together and laughing for joy, perhaps at the lighting of a lamp, does not occur till later (ninth and tenth months). But loud laughing from this time on is not always an expression of joy; for, from the end of the first half-year, my child very often laughed when others laughed to him, and from the end of the first year almost invariably when any one laughed near him, merely in imitation, and quite mechanically, vacantly, without knowing why. If he crowed meantime, with vigorous employment of abdominal pressure, then, indeed, he had some special reason for joy. But when (in the second month) he laughs on being tickled upon the sole of the foot, the laughing is reflexive. Intentional laughing for pleasure—e. g., at the repetition of an agreeable play, or of a musical chord (in the first quarter of the second year)—is, even for the practiced ear, difficult to distinguish from reflexive laughing, but the countenance of the child, smiling as he regards the face of his mother, is easily distinguishable, even in the third month (by the direction of the look), from that of the child smiling vacantly, upon a full stomach. In both cases the smile is a sign of pleasure; but in the first case it is a sign of a special sensation—in the last, of nothing more than a general sensation.

With regard to the connection of all these muscular actions with the nervous processes underlying the joyous emotion, nothing is as yet known. Screaming from pain and laughing from pleasure are modified expirations, and not the least help is to be elicited from the relation of the respiratory apparatus to the sensorium for the explanation of these expressions of antagonistic emotions. The excessive inclination to movement as a symptom of joy, in little children and young animals, seems mysterious, and the hysterical leap from crying to laughing in a moment, in children three to four years old, which has nothing morbid in it, can not lessen the difficulty of the attempt at a physiological explanation. It is probably true of little children in general, that every strong feeling brings in its train a motor discharge. It is, in fact, very difficult, even for older children—nay, for many adults as well—not to betray great joy, just experienced, by some look, or by the brightness of the eyes, or an increased animation, and not to make some movement on hearing merry dance-music.

2. Unpleasant Feelings in General.

In the first half-year of life, unpleasant feelings are more frequent than afterward. Even with the most careful nursing, ventilation, regulation of the temperature of the air and of the bath, control of the milk of mother, nurse, or cow, or of the substitute for this, and with the most favorable surroundings, it is not often granted to a human child to continue in perfect health, without a day of suffering. Birth itself may be painful to the child, or may involve inevitable treatment of a painful character; and the number of children's diseases that are in part accompanied by severe pain is not small. In no period of life is the mortality anything like so great as in the first year. Through this tendency to illness, which is shown in the helpless, defenseless, inexperienced infant, many unpleasant feelings must arise, for only the healthy organism can experience unalloyed pleasure.

But I do not mean to speak here of the numerous unpleasant feelings caused by illness, and by attempts at cure, but only of such as even the perfectly healthy child can not be spared, not even under the most favorable circumstances. To these belong hunger and thirst, discomfort in consequence of inconvenient position in lying or in being held, or of cold, or wet, or ill-smelling air; then the discomfort arising from the tight swathing that unfortunately still prevails far too widely in Germany; the pain of teething, the disagreeable effects of driveling (" drooling," *Geifern*), and of sucking at objects not fit to be sucked; later, the pain of being denied things eagerly craved.

It is an error to maintain that the very young child is not yet capable of having the genuine feeling of pain or even a high degree of unpleasant feeling; for he who can enjoy must also be able to suffer, otherwise he could not enjoy. And that the new-born child experiences pleasure in sucking at a full, healthy breast, nobody doubts. The outward signs of unpleasant feeling in the infant are also unmistakable for every diligent observer.

Above all, crying is characteristic: it is piercing, and persistent in pain; a whimpering in an uncomfortable posture; uninterrupted and very loud in the cold bath; interrupted by frequent pauses in hunger; suddenly waxing to unexpected intensity, and again decreasing quickly, when something is desired and not obtained. Soon are added, as expressions of discomfort, inarticulate and articulate sounds. The infant can not yet moan and groan, he only utters cries, and in the first days does not feel pain at many kinds of treatment that would cause pain to older children—treatment confined to a small area of the skin; for example, pricks of a needle, cooling with ice, sewing up of wounds after operations (Genzmer)—for he often keeps perfectly quiet under such treatment, and even falls asleep. All new-born infants, besides, react much more slowly by crying, in response to the strongest impressions, than do older infants.

A second sign is the shutting of the eyes and holding them tightly closed, which often takes place in adults also in the same fashion. In the first year the child regularly closes his eyes when he manifests a strong feeling of discomfort by screaming. He often shuts the eyes (especially in the ninth month) without screaming, with corrugated brow, when he has to endure something disagreeable; e. g., when he is dressed, or when a finger is put in his mouth, at the period of teething, in order to feel the coming of a tooth.

A further symptom of discomfort is the turning away of the head, which I likewise perceived unaccompanied by crying, under the circumstances just mentioned (distinctly marked in the first as in the ninth month).

The most delicate index of the child's mood is, however, the form of the mouth, as even the least degree of unpleasant feeling is surely expressed at once by drawing down the angles of the mouth. But this alteration of the child's countenance, which appears more and more distinctly up to the fourth year in every single case, is not developed so early as the three previously mentioned expressions of discomfort. In my child, whom I observed carefully, this action of the muscle that depresses the angles of the mouth was not perceived at all before the eighteenth week. But during and before the twenty-third week, whenever the child was addressed in a harsh tone, the stern countenance of the speaker was stared at a moment, then both angles of the mouth were drawn down. Hereupon began for the first time the plaintive cry, accompanied by the appearance of the naso-labial corrugation; the cry, however, ceased as soon as the countenance that had been severe toward the child changed to friendliness. Very soon the previous cheerfulness returned. Darwin saw even earlier this form of the mouth, from about the sixth week to the second and third month.

Accordingly, the first appearance of this peculiar sign of discomfort is in some cases in the first three months; in others, in the first half of the second three months. From this time on, every vexation, but nothing else, is announced by this sign, which is especially pronounced from the sixth month on. Finally, from the eighth month to the end of the third year, appears also, together with violent screaming, another singular form of the mouth. The mouth becomes, viz., as I often observed, quadrangular, a parallelogram, sometimes almost a square—a form which presents itself at once (even with perfectly deaf children, to judge from the mere look) as a sure sign of the highest degree of discomfort, as Darwin rightly brings to notice.

In spite of all these signs of the existence of unpleasant feelings, it is often extraordinarily difficult,

12

especially in the first year, to find out what causes underlie them.

Why does the little girl (of four months) weep when her mother comes near her with a great hat on her head, whereas the child smiles at her when the mother appears without a hat or lays the hat aside? (Frau Dr. Friedemann). Probably fear mingles with the surprise at the strange, as is the case with brutes.

I once had a good horse, that knew me well, but was afraid and began to tremble somewhat when I dismounted and crouched down upon the ground (to get a shot at a bird without being seen). The beast was evidently afraid of the new phenomenon. His master in that hitherto unseen attitude had become to him a strange being. In like manner the very young child will often fail to understand an alteration in persons whose image is well impressed upon his mind, and will be afraid. Children may turn away with horror from hands they like to kiss, if these hands are covered with black gloves, and they may be brought to weeping just by the sight of a figure, well known to them, if it be clothed in black. It was not till the nineteenth month that my child ceased to be reserved toward strangers, and occasionally condescended to give his hand to them when asked, provided only they were not dressed entirely in black (cf. pp. 145–147).

In many children a high degree of uncomfortable feeling may exist, and in a fashion decidedly comical for adults, especially through pity. When figures of all sorts—e. g., human forms—were cut out of paper with scissors for the amusement of my child, he would often weep if a paper figure was in danger, through hasty cutting, of losing an arm or a foot (twenty-seventh month). A like account has been given me of a little girl.

When an infant, fed, warm, and dry, one that we are justified in declaring to be perfectly healthy, nevertheless screams, screws up his eyes, draws down the corners of his mouth, and does not suffer himself to be quieted—we can not easily assign an external cause of his discomfort. It must, therefore, be an internal, unknown cause. I once let my child, of three months, in such a situation, cry on. It was not quite twenty minutes before he fell asleep, and he awoke in good spirits after several hours. Often it is not mere ill-humor that expresses itself in such cases, but an unconquerable impulse to cry out, which can not be called morbid. In some children it is sleepiness, weariness, even after nursing, that manifests itself in crying, especially when anything hinders them from going to sleep. Screaming also is a substitute for the deficient movement of the limbs in the case of children in swaddling-clothes.

When no one of the symptoms mentioned of a strong feeling of discomfort is present, a state of discontent of a low grade may be announced by a lack of luster in the eyes, indolent movements, cessation of the play of countenance, or a somewhat paler complexion. But in this case the cause is usually some disturbance of the health, however slight, just as it is with orang-outangs and chimpanzees. In the babe, as in the weaned and even the older child—nay, even in adults that have not toned down the natural play of feature, or concealed it by self-control—even in this case I am compelled to designate the drawing down of the angles of the mouth as the most delicate form of reaction, one which does not fail even in sleep, since it continues after the falling asleep, in case of illness, and imparts to the countenance an extremely doleful, piteous expression. Whether a cheerful or a sad mood prevails, may be discerned, without seeing any other part of the face, from the appearance of the angle of the mouth alone.

3. The Feeling of Hunger.

Soon after birth hunger and thirst assert themselves. They are unmistakably recognizable in this, that, after objects capable of being sucked are put into the mouth, sucking movements appear, whereas the babe that has had enough does not suck, as I very often proved.

If the feeling of hunger and thirst continues, the child cries and becomes restless. But the restlessness always disappears temporarily during the first days of life when something to suck is put into the mouth, be it only the corner of a pillow or a finger, so that we are justified in assuming that the discomfort that is joined with hunger is displaced by the pleasure that belongs to sucking. Yet in many children, even a week after birth, the crying from hunger can not so surely be checked by letting the child suck at strange objects as it could earlier (Genzmer). So early as this, then, the child has had a useful experience. In the first days, almost every hungry child sucks at its own fingers. Then the crying begins again. This is from the beginning a different thing from the crying caused by pain, and is distinguished from it especially by the fact that it does not continue so long uninterrupted; on the contrary, I have always found—and I am confirmed in this by experienced nurses—that very small children, when hungry, cry with short and long intervals. The voice, too, has a different ring; the cry of pain is higher than that of hunger. The cry of hunger is, likewise, easily distinguished from the cry of satisfaction, even during the first days: for, when the child cries from hunger, the eyes are generally tightly closed; when it gives a cry of joy, they are open. Moreover, my child, when crying with hunger, used to draw back the tongue and spread it out; this does not take place in other kinds of crying. (In my boy this appeared plainly as late as the twenty-ninth week.)

The reflex excitability of the infant is, as others also have observed, increased during the condition of hunger, especially in regard to touches, most of all on the lips and cheeks.

A sure sign of hunger, or of the lively desire arising from it, is, further, the opening of the eyes widely on being brought near the breast, even before being placed at it, a thing which occurs regularly in the first weeks of life, but not before the very first experience of the breast. Experience, then, is necessary for this also.

I have not seen any other than the hungry child, directly before beginning to suck at the breast, make the peculiar shaking movements of the head, which take place in the same way when an artificial nipple is put to the lips of the babe (in the first and second months); these movements, however, become fainter and cease if the rubber is often removed from the mouth and again put in, as if the uselessness of those movements were perceived. Although these movements soon cease entirely, the animal eagerness for food manifestly increases in the first year. While draining the bottle the eyes are opened wide, and the gaze is never turned from the bottle (especially in the sixth and seventh months). If the child of six months is very hungry, he turns the head and the gaze vigorously and persistently toward the bottle, held before him at a small or a great distance, and at once cries violently if it be taken out of the room. On the other hand, he opens his mouth eagerly if the bottle be brought near him. This object, and in general everything connected with it, has in the third quarter of the first year by far the greatest interest for the infant, who stretches out his arms toward it with sparkling eyes if he has not had enough.

From the fifth month on, however, we succeeded in diverting his attention temporarily from the taking of food by means of new noises and movements (page 86); in the last three months of the first year his eating was not so hurried as before; hunger no longer prevailed so much over all other feelings. This progress, apart from the fact that under normal circumstances his hunger is always appeased without delay, is also due to the increase in the quantity of nourishment taken at a single meal. The smaller the stomach, the oftener it becomes empty. The more it can hold, the longer will hunger be postponed, there being no lack of nourishment. In healthy new-born infants the stomach holds (according to Beneke) only thirty-five to forty-three cubic centimetres; after two weeks, one hundred and fifty-three to one hundred and sixty; after two years, seven hundred and forty (leaving out great individual variations).

Thus the intervals between the meals become gradually longer, and the meals less frequent, and there remains in the intervals more time for the infant to turn its attention to other things than food, since the child, the older it grows, sleeps so much the less and consumes its food so much the less rapidly. In the tenth week, to be awake and hungry three times in a night (from eight to six o'clock) is little; in the fifteenth week, the intervals between meals are prolonged in the daytime to three or four hours, against two hours at the beginning of life; and in the eighteenth week—and perhaps earlier —there are nights of ten to eleven hours without the taking of any nourishment at all. Great differences exist, to be sure, among perfectly healthy infants in this respect. Still, it is true of all that they are hungry more frequently at the beginning of life than in the second, and certainly in the third, quarter of the first year. If one busies himself too much with the child, allows too many new sense impressions to act upon him, brings too much strain on his attention, then hunger arrives unseasonably, accompanied with crying, although during "play"—that is, in my case, during my observation of the child, and my experiments upon him—his cheerfulness may have been undisturbed. This sudden access of fretfulness and hunger I have often observed, and, indeed, even from the sixth week on. Later, however, viz., in the eighth and ninth months, the craving for food was less and less manifested by crying, and was often expressed by a peculiar cooing (*Girren*) with the mouth shut tight. This cooing, joined with movements of the larynx, always bore the character of desire, even for those who were not acquainted with its significance.

It does not seem to appear in many children. The origin of it is quite obscure. The child made the strange sound only when hungry, when he saw the food directly before him, which he could not at once take, because it was perhaps still too hot or not warm enough.

Notwithstanding the fact that the feeling of hunger is by far the strongest of all the feelings of the new-born and of the quite young infant, as appears from his whole behavior, yet it would be an error to suppose this feeling to be capable of producing a voluntary movement in the first weeks. I observed a child that, on the fourth and sixth days, obstinately refused, in spite of seven hours' abstinence from food, to take the left breast, whereas it took the right gladly every time, because the left was not so convenient for sucking, though it supplied milk enough. But even with the very convenient artificial nipple, this breast was often declined, and on the nineteenth day persistently, even after a fast of six to seven hours. On the other hand, the child sucked a long time at the skin near the nipple, then cried, and finally fell asleep, tired out with its vain effort. Manifestly in this by no means solitary instance the hunger is indeed great, but the knowledge that it might easily be appeased does not exist; and does not exist for this reason, because, at the first attempt to suck on the left side, the child's experience was that sucking was not so easy there as on the right. That this discrimination could be made so early as the fourth day of life is just as remarkable as the persistence with which it was held to by the infant, who regarded the difference as still existing in all following trials, even when the greatest convenience was attained.

4. The Feeling of Satiety.

Opposed in every respect to the expressions of the feeling of hunger and of thirst are the expressions of the feeling of satiety in the infant. The same food and source of food that were before desired with the greatest eagerness are now abhorred. When the child has sucked enough at the breast that yields milk in great abundance, so that his stomach is full, then he actually pushes the nipple away with his lips (third to fifth week). Just so, the child pushes out the mouth-piece of the nursing-bottle when he has sucked at it (fourth week). In the seventh month I plainly saw that the mouth-piece was vigorously thrust out with the tongue, almost with disgust. The head had already been turned away some time before, after the child had nursed abundantly. These movements are to be regarded as sure signs of the presence of the feeling of satiety. Other signs besides are early added to these.

As early as the tenth day, when the child had fallen asleep after eating his fill, I saw his mouth unmistakably take on the form of a smile, by which the expression of great satisfaction was imparted to the countenance. Later, this was frequently perceived. In the fourth week were added still other signs of the highest satisfaction, between the close of the child's feeding and the beginning of sleep: laughing, opening the eyes, then half-shutting them, inarticulate sounds, in which every person, even those who did not see the child, discerned satisfaction. In the first months, and even in the eighth, the expressions of pleasure and of discomfort are the most pronounced when the feeling of satiety has come or just before. The appeasing of hunger is the greatest pleasure; the increase of the feeling of hunger and of the feeling of thirst, which is not yet separated from that of hunger, is the greatest discomfort for the healthy infant.

Yet I have not been able in any case to attain the conviction that the infant is as yet capable, as Kuss-maul thinks, of feeling nausea. Neither overfullness nor vomiting, neither the greatest uncleanliness nor the most repulsive, foul smell, calls forth in the child in the earliest period the physiognomy associated with the feeling of nausea. The repugnance to bitter substances may, as Genzmer rightly observes, express itself even without that feeling, although the corresponding de-fensive reflexes in the adult are accustomed to be asso-ciated with that feeling.

5. The Feeling of Fatigue.

In spite of the lethargy of the newly-born or of the infant, it might seem doubtful whether he is easily fatigued, because he *apparently* makes but little effort, mental or physical. A closer consideration shows, how-ever, that several causes of fatigue must be operative directly after birth; that a feeling of weariness may come soon after that event; and that the physiological lethargy of the infant is connected with that feeling.

For the waking condition there is need of stimuli—i. e., excitations of the sensory nerves. Now, if these nerves are but little excitable, as is the case before birth, and if few stimuli are present, then the opposite of wak-ing—viz., sleep—will be persistent and sound. But when after birth the excitability of the nerves and the

number of the stimuli are increased, by the very opening of the eyes and ears and the activity of the nerves
of the skin, then sleep is interrupted. The longer this
interruption lasts, the greater must be the accumulation
of the products of the activity of the central and peripheral portions of the organs of sense, on the one hand,
and on the other hand of the muscles, which contract
more strongly and more frequently in the waking condition than in sleep. Now, these materials of fatigue,
as I have attempted to show in my treatise on the
causes of sleep ("Uber die Ursachen des Schlafes,"
Stuttgart, 1877), hinder prolonged waking, because they
withdraw from the blood the oxygen required for activity, in order to unite themselves with it, so that they
may be oxidized, and finally expelled. What are the
substances formed through the activity of the muscles
and the brain, and inducing the feeling of fatigue, we
have yet to ascertain.

In the new-born and the infant, whose muscles in
and of themselves are but little serviceable, and resemble the muscles of tired adults, as Soltmann proved by
comparative experiments upon animals, there are two
actions especially that require strong muscular effort—
viz., crying and sucking. The crying of the hungry
child is a sign of the waking condition that quickly
produces weariness. For, let the child have his cry out,
and he usually falls asleep soon, even without having
been fed. Sucking at a breast that contains little milk
is likewise tiresome; and I repeatedly within the first
three months saw sleep take possession of the child
while he was sucking thus at a scanty breast of the
nurse; and the sucking was frequently interrupted by

long intervals, even when the child must have been hungry.

Then there is the fatigue of the organs of sense. After the first two or three weeks are past, so that the attention can begin to be directed to something else than the milk, manifold changing impressions of light and sound, along with strong, cutaneous stimuli through touch and temperature from the beginning, act with rapidly fatiguing power upon the infant, especially when his relatives busy themselves too much with him. Thus, with my boy the hearing of piano-playing, in his eighth week, was followed by an unbroken sleep of six hours, whereas up to that time sleep had not once lasted so long.

But the weariness brought on by crying, sucking, manifold sense-impressions, is hardly sufficient to account for the brief duration of the waking periods in the first half-year, even if we make the largest allowance for the movements of the extremities, and add to that the labor performed by the respiratory muscles and by the heart. There must be still another cause that produces sleep, inasmuch as under normal conditions the greater part of the first two years of human life is actually spent in sleep. This other cause is, probably, the relatively smaller supply of oxygen (on account of the smaller quantity of blood and the less energy of the respiratory process) and the need of oxygen for growth; so that, on the one hand, less work is done and less warmth is produced; on the other hand, less oxygen can be spared for keeping up the change of matter in the ganglionic cells during the waking hours. We must also take into account the character of the food, which regularly consists uniformly of milk alone in the period of much sleep. Milk and whey in large quantities exert a somnific influence even upon adults. They contain sugar of milk, which, in the stomach produces lactic acid. This unites in the intestines with alkali, and thus after every meal larger quantities, relatively, of lactates must enter the blood in the infant than in the adult. These become oxidized, and thereby withdraw from the brain, according to the above-mentioned theory of sleep, in great measure the oxygen required for the waking condition, and for this reason, perhaps, the infant regularly falls asleep not long after each abundant supply of milk. The milk may also contain somnific materials from the blood of the mother. Finally, the almost uninterrupted act of digestion of the milk, scarcely ever discontinued more than two hours at a time, may, by collecting blood in the vessels of the digestive organs, withdraw from the brain temporarily, larger quantities of blood (which are necessary for the waking condition).

With these hypotheses accords the universal experience that in the first three months the duration of the period of sleep between two meals is much shorter than in the second three months, and that it continually increases. At first the period of digestion is shorter than it is afterward, on account of the smallness of the stomach. I found the sleep of the infant the sounder and more lasting, the more concentrated the milk was, other circumstances being the same. Mother's milk, abundant and good, produces a sounder and longer sleep than diluted milk of the cow, or scanty milk of the wet-nurse. But even if the mother's milk be given exclusively, the periods of sleep are shorter than in the first weeks, the waking more frequent than later; yet the whole time spent in sleep is longer. The frequent waking is doubtless favored by other causes than hunger, especially by the greater uncleanliness of the early period, and by wet—that is, by cutaneous irritation.

The notes I wrote down concerning the duration of sleep in the case of my boy show clearly the decrease of the duration of sleep as a whole, and the increase of duration of the single period of sleep, from the first day until the close of the third year. I extract the following particulars:

In the first month sleep lasted without interruption not often longer than two hours; but of the twenty-four hours, sixteen at least, and generally much more, were spent in sleep.

In the second month, a three-hours' sleep often appeared; now and then a sleep of five to six hours.

In the third month the child often sleeps four hours, frequently even five in succession, without waking.

In the fourth month, the sleep often lasts five to six hours; the intervals between the times of eating, three and four hours (against two hours at an earlier period). Once the sleep lasted nine hours.

In the sixth month, a sleep of six to eight hours is not infrequent.

In the eighth month, restless nights, on account of teething.

In the thirteenth month, as a rule, fourteen hours of sleep daily, in several separate periods.

In the seventeenth month, prolonged sleep began; ten hours, without interruption.

In the twentieth month, prolonged sleep became habitual, and sleep in the daytime was reduced to two hours.

From the thirty-seventh month on, the night's sleep lasted regularly eleven to twelve hours, and sleep in the daytime was no longer required.

Thus, from the fourth year, the waking period is longer than that of sleep, and sleepiness does not come on so quickly as before. The child, when walking, no longer says, "swer" ("schwer") for "müde" (tired), as he often did in the third year; and although the feeling of weariness sometimes asserts itself, yet drowsiness and sleep no longer follow directly upon it. The unwearied springing and running of older children is well known. The varied food taken at present, as contrasted with the milk-diet of an earlier period, unquestionably contributes to this, but chiefly the increased functional ability of the respiratory apparatus, of the blood, of the muscles, and ganglionic cells. The sleep itself is now in general more quiet, inasmuch as dreams, accompanied by movements and outcries, no longer occur so often.

I consider it as exceedingly important in the case of little children not to interrupt sleep artificially—to give them milk, it may be—and not to wake larger children either. By waking them a condition of real distress, accompanied with trembling and convulsions, is easily induced in perfectly healthy children, and a lasting depression of spirits generated. I know of no advantage to the child from being waked. It ought the more to be avoided, inasmuch as almost invariably a fright is given to the child, and all fright is absolutely harmful, whether caused by harsh address, or by threatening the child with the "black man," so called, or by catching the child, pouring water on him, and the like, in the way of fun. Older children like to show their superiority to younger ones by such misdeeds, and even ignorant nurses not seldom adopt such means. Thereby they arouse timidity, which may easily be increased by grewsome stories ("gräusige Geschichten") and foolish tales, and then it leads early to a morbid excitability.

6. Fear.

The time at which a child first betrays fear depends essentially upon his treatment, in so far as the avoidance of occasions of pain prolongs the period that is marked by unconsciousness of fear; whereas the multiplication of such occasions shortens the period.

There is, however, an hereditary timidity, which manifests itself as opportunity offers. How happens it that many children are afraid of dogs, pigs, and cats, before they know the dangerous qualities of these animals? A little girl was afraid of cats as early as the fourteenth week of life (Sigismund). Thunder makes many children cry—for what reason?

If there is in this case the co-operation of ideas, either clear or obscure, of danger, or of reminiscences of pain after a noisy fall, or of disagreeable sensations at loud rumbling and the like (I observed that my child in his second year cried with fear almost every time that heavy furniture was pushed about), yet in the expressions of fear on the part of inexperienced animals factors of this sort are excluded.

A hen with her first brood, about a week old, was

frightened by Douglas Spalding, who let fly a young hawk. "In the twinkling of an eye most of the chickens were hid among grass and bushes"; and when the bird of prey touched the ground, at a distance of twelve yards from the hen, the hen attacked it, and would undoubtedly have killed it. I have repeated this experiment. A young kestrel, very lively, as large as a domestic cock, was by me held by the wings and brought near to thirty-three chickens, three and a half weeks old, hatched in the incubator and raised in an inclosed space, without intercourse with other fowls. At first they did not appear to notice the bird. But as soon as they heard its voice, they all became still and attentive, and moved but little. Then I let the falcon loose : instantly the chickens scattered in all directions, and concealed themselves. How, except through inheritance, did the chicks arrive at the point of hiding themselves at seeing and hearing the falcon? They had never seen it or its like before, and a mother could not have described it to her offspring. But when, after a long interval, I let a pigeon, instead of a falcon, fly away over the thirty-three chickens, they were just as much frightened ; they scattered and hid themselves. On the other hand, they were not in the least frightened at their first sight of a hen which cackled loudly. The hereditary enemy must therefore be known through inborn memory. Yet I will not conceal that I do not regard the experiments, or this inference from them, as sufficiently conclusive (the check experiment with the pigeon prevents that), although no imitation by the chicks of the behavior of a hen was possible. When I put a kitten into a box in which there were eighteen

13

chickens not yet four hours old and two about twenty hours old, not one of the chicks made the least movement of flight. Even after the kitten had bitten a chicken, had been taken away, and afterward put into the box with the twenty chickens again, there was no stir at all among them; the one that had been bitten did not even turn away. The same thing took place on the third day. A turkey ten days old behaved as the chickens did in the above experiments. When he heard the voice of the hawk for the first time, and close to him, he "shot like an arrow to the other side of the. room, and stood there, motionless and dumb with fear," for ten minutes, as Spalding reports. Chickens show unmistakable signs of fear in regard to bees also as a general thing, according to him, although they have not been stung. They bring the timidity with them, then, from the egg, as an hereditary property. Yet against this inference it might be urged that every sudden, strong sense-impression elicits the same symptoms as do the impressions that excite fear. The behavior of the inexperienced chickens was the same at the sudden appearance of the dove as at the cry and the approach of the falcon. But when I let the latter loose among a great number of fowls that were busily pecking, the warning cry of the cock at once sounded; and when the falcon made toward a hen, they all flew off, except one that prepared to attack the bird of prey. A peahen did the same thing directly afterward. We see from this that fear and courage are very unequally distributed among creatures of the same kind. Timidity and bravery are accordingly to be admitted as hereditary qualities.

The case must be similar in the human child, who is afraid of all sorts of things not at all dangerous, as well as of things really dangerous, before he knows danger of himself, and before he can be infected by the timidity of mqther or nurse. It is altogether wrong to maintain that a child has no fear unless it has been taught him. The courage or the fear of the mother has indeed extraordinary influence upon the child, to the extent that courageous mothers certainly have courageous children, and timid mothers have timid children, through imitation ; but there are so many cases of timidity and of courage in the child, without any occasion of that sort, that we must take into account, as in the case of animals, an element lying further back, hereditary. Thus, Champneys observed (1881) that his boy, when about nine months old, showed signs of fear for the first time, becoming attentive to any unusual noise in a distant part of the room, opening his eyes very wide and beginning to cry. A month or so later this child had a toy given him, that squeaked when it was squeezed. The child at once screamed, and screamed afterward again and again, when it was offered to him. But after some time he became accustomed to the squeaking ; then he was pleased by it, and would himself make the toy squeak.

Among the observations that I made on my boy, a boy not particularly timid in his fourth year, but rather one who would defend himself against two or three older children together, are some that certainly are not to be referred to imitation, as the fear of machines and of small animals when near.

In the ninth month I observed him for the first

time crying, turning away, and drawing back from fear, when a small dog barked at the nurse, who was carrying my child on her arm. The same thing happened just a hundred days afterward, and again in the seventeenth month. In the second quarter of the third year the fear of all dogs is very conspicuous, although the child has never been bitten by such an animal, and, so far as can be determined, has never seen a dog bite a child. Even in the thirty-third month, his crying at the approach of even the smallest dog, of a few weeks old, is remarkable. Yet soon after this period the timidity was gradually overcome, and on one occasion the child, in my presence, actually took an apple out of the teeth of the dog, which had taken it away from him.

How little this fear of dogs, so late to be overcome, was a result of education, appears from the behavior of the child toward other small animals. To give pleasure to him, when he was two and a quarter years old, a number of very young pigs were shown to him. He at once became serious at the sight. But, when the queer creatures proceeded to suck at the teats of the mother that lay there perfectly quiet, then the child began to scream, to shed tears, to cling, and to turn away with fright. He thought, as it afterward appeared, that the sucking pigs were biting the mother. That he should himself be thrown into a state of genuine fear every time he was brought near them is the more strange, as they were all shut up in a pen with a high, strong fence about it. This fear became so great in the course of the fourth and fifth years in my child that he sometimes cried out in the night, and imagined that a pig was going to bite him. He seemed to see the animal as if it were actually there, and he could not be convinced that it was not there, even after his bed was brightly lighted up. The explanation offered by Heyfelder for similar cases may apply to some. He supposes that when children cry out in falling asleep, and believe themselves to be bitten by a dog, a sudden jerk of the leg or arm occasions a feeling out of which the imagination constructs the animal. But when a child that is sleeping in perfect quiet suddenly cries out, "Go away, pig!" and this without waking, we must assume that the dream-image appears without any external movement. A little girl was so afraid of doves in the seventeenth week and in the eleventh month that she could not make up her mind to stroke them; in the thirteenth month she ventured to stroke a dove, but immediately drew back her hand; in the fourteenth month her fear was overcome.

Just as remarkable as this fear of animals is the fear of falling at the first attempt to walk. Although the child never had fallen, so far as could be determined, he did not dare, in the fourteenth month, when he could not yet go alone, to take a step without support, and became fearful if he was not held. The child had before this bruised himself repeatedly, but in this case he cried from fear of falling, without having had the experience of being bumped in falling.

Two more examples: In the sixteenth month my child was afraid (to my surprise, for I thought to please him) when I drew tones of high pitch from a drinking-glass by rubbing with the finger, as I had done once at an earlier period (p. 47). His fear, which did not at that time—in the third month—appear, now increased to the point of shedding tears, whereas the ring of the glasses when struck was greeted with a cry of joy. Did the unusual tone in the sixteenth month seem uncanny on account of ignorance of the cause? Yet the same child laughed at the thunder and lightning (in the eighteenth and nineteenth months); another child even in the thirty-fifth month did the same, and imitated cleverly with the hand the zigzag movement of the lightning (Gustav Lindner).

In the twenty-first month my child showed every sign of fear when his nurse carried him on her arm close by the sea (in Scheveningen). He began to whimper, and I saw that he clung tighter with both hands, even during a calm and at ebb-tide when there was but a slight dashing of the waves. Whence the fear of the sea, which the child is not acquainted with? The water of the Eider Canal, of the Saale, of the Rhine, he was not in the least afraid of in the same year. The greatness of the sea could not of itself excite fear, for the symptoms of dread were shown only close by the water. Was it, then, the roaring heard in advance?

The fear of persons in black, too (seventeenth month), even when they are friendly, as well as the fear of a deep voice, of masked faces, of strange faces (Frau von Strümpell), (in the seventh month and in the twenty-fourth week), is not derived from education (Herr Ed. Schulte). It expresses itself in this way: The infant cries at the sight of strangers or at hearing strange voices, a thing he did not do in the first three months. On the other hand, the fear of punishment—a fear that has been bred in him—appearing in the second year, may easily be distinguished from natural dread. The child that for the first time disobeys a well-known prohibition does not cry, or tremble, or cling closer, or cower down, but he tries to get away. The fear of being chastised, however often it appears, through many successive generations, in the same form, at the same age, is always acquired anew. A proof of this I find, as do others, in the fact that my child is not in the least afraid in the dark, no doubt for the reason that he has never been punished by being shut up in a dark place.

How the special symptoms of fear, e. g., the characteristic trembling, are developed, is wholly unknown. It is asserted, in regard to little children, that they can not tremble (in fact, Darwin says this). But children just born, and those of four years, can tremble, as I have myself perceived. A perfectly healthy child, of good weight, not yet a quarter of an hour old, trembled almost incessantly, sometimes more, sometimes less, during my observation, although it was comfortably warm in the room (in the lying-in hospital). The child had already had a warm bath. Many just-born children, to be sure, do not tremble.

Many new-born animals—dogs, mice, rabbits, Guinea-pigs, and chickens, which I have often observed in regard to this point—tremble in a warm nest. But they have not at first the least fear at being laid hold of with the hand. The behavior of the chicken hatched in the incubator is very different in the first days of its life from what it is afterward; in the following days you have often the greatest difficulty in catching it. In the beginning it does not run away, though it knows how to run well enough; but later it runs away invariably.

Bird-dogs are likewise entirely without fear of man at the beginning of life, even after they can see. But, after they have once become acquainted with the whip, they manifest fear of man in the most marked manner— badger-dogs, in individual cases, in a striking degree, as Romanes reports, without their having ever been whipped, so far as appears. How inherited endowment is united here with individual experience we can not at present say, for lack of facts. But that fear of man is not originally present, but is introduced into many animals in common by inoculation through man's own agency, appears from the behavior of many animals, which in the wilderness unvisited by man are not in the least shy, whereas their fellows of the same species, where they are hunted, hide themselves with the greatest caution, or flee, even when they are not pursued, if they get scent of human beings. Of the graceful phalaropes, especially, I know this to be true, from personal observation. They have no fear at all of man in the uninhabited interior of Iceland, where I frequently observed them, whereas on the inhabited coast they are anything but tame.

So, with man also, it is, on the one hand, ignorance of danger, on the other hand, the becoming accustomed to it, that makes him fearless.

7. Astonishment.

It is exceedingly difficult to determine the moment when a human being is for the first time in his life astonished. *Surprise*, which manifests itself by a reflex movement of the arms, and that in the first week, after a sudden loud noise, is essentially different from *aston-*

ishment. And the great concentration of *attention* that the infant bestows on his own fingers, after he has begun his attempts at touching and seizing (in the fourth and fifth months), is different from the state of being overpowered by a high degree of astonishment at some new impression. But precisely at this period I could, not seldom, distinguish accurately the astonishment of the infant from that strain of attention—and this in the twenty-second week. When the child was in a railway-carriage, and I suddenly entered after a brief separation, so that at the same moment he saw my face and heard my voice, he fixed his gaze upon me for more than a minute, with *open mouth* (the lower jaw dropped), *with wide-open, motionless eyes*, and in other respects absolutely immovable, exhibiting the typical image of astonishment.

Just so he stared at a stranger (in the sixth and seventh months), who suddenly entered the room, for more than a minute, motionless, with open mouth and eyes. In the eighth and ninth months these symptoms seemed to be still more pronounced, and appeared not unfrequently at new impressions of sight and sound—not at new impressions of smell and taste—and in remarkable uniformity. E. g., the child was thus astonished in the thirty-first week at the clapping together of a fan; in the thirty-fourth, at an imitation of the voices of animals; in the forty-fourth, at a strange face near; in the fifty-second, at a new sound; in the fifty-eighth, at a lantern (after waking). I do not remember to have perceived along with this a raising of the eyebrows; but this may have been overlooked on account of its being slight at this early period. Often, when the

mouth was opened, an *ah* was heard. The attitude of
the astonished child was in every case that which he had
in the moment just before the new impression. This
attitude was retained, with eyes stretched wide apart
and with the mouth very widely open. But when a less
degree of astonishment than in the cases mentioned was
felt, then in every instance a pulsation of the eyelid or
a succession of such movements indicated wonder; the
eyes, indeed, were opened wide, but not the mouth.

Toward the end of the second year, the symptoms
of the highest degree of astonishment made their appearance, in general, more seldom than before, especially the dropping of the lower jaw. It took more,
therefore, at this time, to turn the entire attention to a
single impression of sight or hearing so powerfully that
the lower jaw could not be kept up. The child had
been astonished too often, and had become accustomed
to the once new impressions.

The whole behavior of the child when astonished is
completely original with him, not being in the least
acquired by imitation or through training, for it was in
the fifth month at latest that his astonishment was of
the sort described. His immobility is the consequence
of the sudden, powerful, new impression, and resembles
the cataplexy of animals, caused by the arrest of the
will through fright. For particulars, see my treatise on
"Cataplexy and Animal Hypnotism" ("Die Kataplexie
und der thierische Hypnotismus," Jena, 1878).

Individual animals, however, may be astonished at
new impressions without being so frightened as to lose
their will completely. I have repeatedly seen a bird-
dog stand motionless before the stove-door, in which

there was isinglass, after the fire had been kindled, staring at the flames and hearkening to the blowing noise and the crackling. The dog was astonished, as a child is at the fire in a stove, not yet knowing what it is. Astonishment is certainly not an emotion peculiar to mankind alone.

Animals experience also the mingling of fear and astonishment, just as children do, especially when some quite new and incomprehensible thing happens. Romanes gives us (1878) the following observations, made by himself, which he adduces as proofs that animals form concepts, but which I use as proofs that fear and astonishment are mingled when the understanding fails —i. e., when insight into the connection of new perceptions with old is lacking:

A dog was afraid of thunder, and became frightened when one day a noise like thunder was made in the house by pouring apples upon the floor of the garret. But when he was taken up there, and had seen what occasioned the uproar, he was again as lively as usual. Horses that are easily frightened behave in a similar manner, showing fear only so long as the cause of a noise remains unknown to them.

Another dog was in the habit of throwing dry bones about. Romanes one day fastened a long, fine thread to a bone, and while the dog was playing with the bone began to draw this away slowly, standing apart. The whole bearing of the dog changed; he started aside, and observed with terror how the bone seemed to move of itself. The same dog was frightened by soap-bubbles on the floor, but touched one of them with his paw, and when it vanished he ran away, manifestly horrified by the incomprehensible disappearance of the large ball.

In these cases, just as in the examples of the child above given (also p. 150), want of knowledge generates fear, but at the same time the novelty of the impressions generates astonishment. In the first case, fear came first and disappeared in astonishment at the recognized cause; in the second, both were present together; in the third, astonishment came first, then fear, on account of lack of comprehension.

If we were to try these three experiments with little children, we should certainly find many who would behave like the dogs—only it would not be easy to select those of the right age. There is no doubt that astonishment makes its appearance earlier than fear.

CHAPTER VII.

SUMMARY OF GENERAL RESULTS.

It is very difficult for the matured human being to place himself in thought in the condition of a child that has had as yet no experiences, or only vague ones; because every individual experience leaves in the brain, without doubt, after the first epochs of growth are successfully passed, an organic modification—as it were a scar—so that the previous condition of the sensorium in the newly-born, a condition as yet undisturbed by individual impressions—affected only by the traces of the experiences of past generations — can not be reconstructed without employing the help of imagination. For the mental state of each man is so much the product of his experiences, that he can not picture himself to himself at all as being without these experiences.

And yet I believe that, on the basis of the facts comprised in the previous chapters, something may be laid down as probable.

With regard to sense-activity in general, we may note, as in the highest degree probable, that before birth no sensation of light exists, no luminous image produced by pressure on the eye, or by pulling upon the optic nerve or the retina, and yet immediately after birth light and darkness are distinguished. It is certain that no sensation of smell is experienced before birth, and yet the newly-born react upon strong-smelling substances in the first hour of life. No human being, certainly, can hear before birth; but several hours (with animals half an hour) after birth reflex movements upon strong impressions of sound have been, in individual cases, regularly demonstrated by me. A sensation of taste, in the strict meaning of the word, can hardly be possessed by the child before birth, but directly after birth he behaves quite differently toward very bitter substances from what he does toward sweet. There remains, then, only the sense of touch, as a probably active one in the fœtal state. Yet the unborn human being, beyond a doubt, is not in condition to distinguish warmth from cold. Accordingly, unless general sensations may exist, it is only sensations of contact that the human being just born has experienced before he comes into the world.

In regard to the development of the separate senses, the following results are especially to be mentioned :

Seeing.—The human child can not see, in the proper meaning of the word, during the first weeks. At the beginning, the child merely distinguishes light from darkness, and discerns the change from one to the other only when a large part of the field of vision is illumined or shaded. But if the light object is much brighter than the surroundings, as the flame of a candle in a dark room, then it produces the sensation of light in the very first week, even if the object be small.

The discrimination of colors is in the first months exceedingly imperfect, and is, perhaps, restricted to the discerning of unequal degrees of light. The first colors to be rightly named are yellow and red, and the sensations of brightness, white, gray, and black; green and blue, on the contrary, are not correctly named till much later. Probably the child of one year continues to perceive green and blue almost as gray, at any rate as not so different from each other as at a later period. A child will hardly name correctly the four primitive colors mentioned before the end of the second year; while, on the other hand, every normal child will, in the fourth year, even without special training of the color-sense, recognize and name them better than the compound colors.

The winking of the eyelid on a sudden approach to the face is wanting in the first weeks, and is a reflex movement of the nature of defense, which originates only after a disagreeable feeling, in consequence of a sudden hitherto unobserved change in the field of vision, has been able to be developed. Accordingly, the rapid opening and shutting of the eyes is, from the second month on, a sign of perfected sight, especially a sign of the perception of rapid movements. Further, it is true in general, that the eyes are opened wider when impressions and conditions are agreeable than when disagreeable.

The eye-movements of new-born human beings are not co-ordinated, not associated as they are later in distinct vision, but are in the first days predominantly irregular; yet it often happens that, among the manifold unregulated movements of the eyes, there even appear turnings of both eyes at the same time to the left, or to the right, or upward, or downward. These originally rare and not quite symmetrical eye-movements, soon become more frequent and quite symmetrical, and gradually displace the irregular movements entirely, because they favor clearer vision.

The "fixation" and distinct seeing of an object are slowly developed. In the first stage the child stares into empty space. In the second, he turns the eye frequently from an object that is in the line of his gaze, e. g., a face, to a remarkably bright object that emerges near by, e. g., the flame of a candle, and then stares at this. In the third stage he follows a slowly-moving object with eye and head, or with the eyes only.

The transition from staring to looking is complete; that from looking to observing is attained in the fourth stage. Accommodation is now effected; objects unequally distant from the eye are distinctly seen in succession, whereas, at the beginning, all seemed to be blended in the same plane. The contraction of the pupil comes with convergence of the lines of vision in seeing near objects, whereas, at the beginning, the contraction of the pupil to light, even without near vision, and without convergence, is noticed, and dilated pupils are often present along with convergence. The expression, when there are convergence and binocular vision of a slowly-moving object, is always "intelligent."

The longest delay of all in the child is in the gradual development of the ability to interpret what is seen. Transparency, lustre, shadow, are for years incomprehensible, and lose the mystery that clings to them only through very frequently repeated perception.

The thickness of objects seen remains long unknown, and the third dimension of space becomes a constituent part of perceptions late and imperfectly, in comparison with the first two (the length and breadth). The failures of attempts at seizing objects show how imperfectly (even in the second and third years) the estimate of distance still is; the erroneous interpretations of ordinary sight-impressions, as of steam and flame, prove that the establishment of a relation between the impressions of touch and those of sight is effected but slowly in the first years; and that in particular the perception of the difference between a surface-extension and an extension in three dimensions begins late and is established slowly. Yet the ability to recognize pictures of known objects and persons as such, is developed early.

As to the theory of space-perception, the facts prove directly that there does not exist in the human being immediately after birth a ready-made, inborn mechanism to be set in regular activity by impressions of light; but that the impressions themselves really develop the inherited mechanism, which is but incomplete at birth. In this the empirical theory is correct. The foundations only are innate, not the entire apparatus. And yet this proposition can by no means be admitted to be exclusive, to be invariably true. It is true for mankind; but, on the other hand, many animals that see at birth—especially chickens and pigs, but many others, too—bring with them into the world a mechanism for space-perception that is completely capable of performing its function—that needs only some luminous impressions in order to operate at once nearly or quite as perfectly as in the adult animal. In this case, which supports the most extreme nativism (see p. 34), the possibility of any considerable perfecting of sight by practice on the part of individuals is, it would seem, excluded, to begin with; the chicken, which, when just hatched, pecks accurately at a grain of millet does not learn to see much better through frequent seeing. Man, on the contrary, learns, from the time of birth on, to see better day by day, and, even in later life, can, by much seeing, vastly improve his visional apparatus in more than one direction. The hereditary mechanism is, therefore, still plastic in him— still highly capable of differentiation—because not so far advanced and one-sidedly developed as in the fowl, which is sharp-sighted immediately after being hatched, having a visual organ that is complete, and no longer so plastic, and also relatively much larger.

HEARING.—The hearing of the new-born child is so imperfect that it must be called deaf. All mammals are also incapable of reacting upon impressions of sound immediately after birth. The cause of this peculiarity is partly peripheral. Previous to respiration, air is wanting in the middle ear, and the outer auditory

14

passage is not yet permeable, the tympanum being set too obliquely.

Even after the sound-conducting parts of the ear have become open, from a quarter of a day to several days after birth, there is no discrimination of sounds; but before the end of the first week we notice, in normal children, the characteristic winking of the eyelid after a sudden loud noise. The starting at powerful sound-impressions, which continues for several months, proves the growth of the faculty of hearing. Meanwhile, although particular kinds of sounds, not previously observed, are perceived as different even in the first months of life—e. g., deep voices and high voices, hissing sounds and *s*-sounds, singing and speaking—still, it is three quarters of a year, at least, before a child *knows* the notes of the piano, and it is questionable whether he can learn to name correctly *c, d, e, f, g, a, b* before the end of the second year. Many children, notwithstanding, learn to sing before they talk, and all distinguish the noises and tones of speech long before they can produce them themselves. At the same time the intensity of the sound-impression made, in the case of great differences, is recognized by the attentive observer, by the varying liveliness of the reflexes, even in sleep. The direction of the sound is perceived by the child as early as the second and the third month.

The great superiority of the ear to the eye, from the psychogenetic point of view, is but slightly prominent upon superficial observation of the child that does not yet speak; but we need only compare a child born blind with one born deaf, after both have enjoyed the most careful training and the best instruction, to be convinced that, after the first year, the excitements of the auditory nerve contribute far more to the psychical development than do those of the optic nerve.

Further, many mammals and fowls are provided, at their entrance into the world, with a more developed, much more correctly-working auditory apparatus than that of man, and are far superior in perception of pitch, intensity, and direction of sound, to the human child; but in no animal is the cerebral portion of the organ of hearing capable of so fine differentiation after birth, for none reacts with anything near the precision with which the child reacts upon the subtile variations of intensity and quality of the sounds of human speech.

SENSIBILITY TO CONTACT is, in the first hour of life, much inferior to what it is later; the sense of *temperature* does not yet exist. The latter probably leads, but not till after repeated alternations of warm baths and the cooling off of the whole surface of the skin and of particular places, to discrimination of the sensations "hot, warm, cool, cold," inasmuch as the neutral point of the temperature of the skin, always the same before birth, can not at once be established.

To painful assaults that reach only a few nerves of the skin, the newly-born show an inferior degree of sensibility; yet it can not be doubted that they are capable of highly unpleasant sensations after they have exhibited unambiguous signs of comfort (in nursing and in the warm bath).

The inferior degree of sensibility to contact, as well as to temperature and to pain, in the newly-born, are to be referred (as with the fœtus) to the as yet incomplete development of the brain, not of the skin. On the contrary, the nerves of the skin are very excitable, no doubt because they alone, of all the nerves of sense, are very frequently excited before birth, the movements of the child causing contact at many points of the skin.

TASTE.—Of all the organs of sense that of *taste* is best developed in the new-born child at birth. Sweet is at once distinguished from bitter, sour, or salt, and the sour gives a different sensation from the bitter. Here we have one of the cases, rare in mankind, of innate capacity to distinguish among qualities in the same department of sense. Many animals can likewise immediately after birth distinguish sweet from other tastes. On the other hand, the ability to distinguish unequal intensities of taste is very slightly developed in the child at the beginning of life.

SMELL.—Probably the newly-born can not smell anything immediately on its entrance into the world, because the cavity of the nose has been previously filled up with amniotic fluid; and in the adult, when the cavity has been filled with liquid, there is for some time inability to smell, or a dullness of the sense of smell. But, after some hours, and it may be even in the first hour after birth, normal children can distinguish between agreeable and disagreeable smells. Of many animals, it is known that they do not delay to make use of their sense of smell when the nasal cavity has once been filled with air by breathing. And the normal child, too, early distinguishes clearly different kinds of milk; accordingly, he very likely distinguishes some odors at the end of the first day of life.

FEELINGS.—As to the feelings of the child in the first period of life, it is certain that they are not manifold, indeed (because the activity of the senses is still incomplete), but they may be very intense. Every sensation, when it is compared with a different sensation, produces a feeling. All feelings are either agreeable or disagreeable. In the first case, they awaken in the child the desire for a repetition of the sensation concerned, since the very lack of the agreeable produces discomfort; in the second case, the desire for repetition is not stirred. It is, however, a peculiarity of all agreeable feelings that, after a certain duration, they are no longer agreeable, doubtless because they depend upon excitations of the ganglionic cells, and these cells are soon fatigued when they are intensely excited—i. e., when the feeling is very vivid. In little children this is shown by the rapid change in what they think desirable.

The feelings that are not agreeable are either disagreeable or indifferent. The former are wont to be expressed by vigorous, loud expirations of the breath, by cries, and, even at the earliest period, by an unmistakable play of the countenance, especially by the shape the mouth takes.

Little as is known thus far of the emotions and feelings of the young child, one thing may, however, be declared as certain—that these are the first of all psychical events to appear with definiteness, and that they determine the behavior of the child. Before a sure sign of will, of memory, judgment, inference, in the proper sense, is found, the feelings have expressed themselves in direct connection with the first excitations of the nerves of sense, and before the sensations belonging to the special departments of sense can be clearly distinguished as specifically different. But through repetition of feelings, opposed in character, are gradually unfolded memory, power of abstraction, judgment, and inference.

The most powerful agent in the development of the understanding at the beginning is astonishment, together with the fear that is akin to it.

Out of the desire of everything that has once occasioned pleasurable feelings is gradually developed the child's will.

SECOND PART.

ACTIVITY of will is possible only after perceptions have been had. What is desirable must necessarily have been set off from what is to be repelled, through repeated comparison of sensations, before willing can show itself. For whoever wills, knows what he wills and what he does not will; has previously ascertained what is to him desirable and what is repulsive. The new-born child knows nothing of this, and hence has as yet no will. He has not yet had any experiences in regard to his own states; has not compared any sensations; perceived anything of the external world; and so has obtained no knowledge of what will be to him agreeable or disagreeable. He who wills has gained this knowledge through his own experience, and regulates accordingly his behavior—i. e., his movements.

In order to follow the very slow transition, accomplished not by steps but in a continuous flow, from the one condition to the other, all movements made by the human being while he is still feeble must, as far as possible, be observed, with the question in view, how far they may be expressions of a will.

I therefore put together, in this second part, my ob-

servations touching the movements of the child, and
some conclusions that follow directly from them, bearing upon the formation of the will.

* * *

CHAPTER VIII.

THE MOVEMENTS OF THE CHILD AS EXPRESSIONS OF WILL.

It is only through movements that the will directly
expresses itself.   The possibility of recognizing the will
of the child in his movements must, therefore, be established, and the manifold character of the child's movements be set forth, before we consider the observations
upon the gradual development of will.

1. Recognition of the Child's Will.

Widely different as are the phenomena within the
domain of will, that owe their origin directly to it, every
expression of will is first recognized in movements, viz.,
words, acts, looks, gestures.   Not every spoken sound,
nor every act performed, nor every look or gesture, is
the expression of an act of will: for sleeping persons
can talk ; somnambulists do various things without willing, without knowing what they do; and expressions of
countenance may be produced artificially, by electrical
stimulus, in opposition to the influence of the will ; and
infants that have no will often make gestures, the significance of which as expressions of will (to adults) is
wholly unknown to them.   But, conversely, it is true
strictly and universally, that the will, in the ordinary
sense, during its development, announces itself only

through the language of words, acts, looks, and gestures.

After its first stages of development it can reveal
itself indirectly, also, by the opposite means, to wit,
by the suppression of these very movements. No one
doubts that a man is capable of expressing his will indirectly by silence and by inactivity, without altering
his countenance and without gestures, precisely by the
inhibition of movements. In this, however, we have to
do, not with a particular kind of willing which is to be
classed with those positive expressions of will that have
been spoken of, but we have to do with the exact opposite. It is clear that in all these cases in which the
will has been already much developed beforehand, the
person that inhibits the movement is in the state of non-
willing, noluntas, or nolentia, in contrast with voluntas.
To this state of being-unwilling belongs the voluntary
inhibition of a movement, this inhibition being nothing
else than the non-willing of the movement. Non-willing is not, however, characterized by the absence of
symptoms of willing, as the mere negation of that, but
is a peculiar condition of excitement in that it checks a
movement, or is intended to check one.

The will-apparatus, or the complex organism of centro-motor structures of the highest rank, which is to be
looked for in the cerebrum, must be so organized that,
when it is in activity, some muscular contraction results ;
when it is not active, either nothing happens, because
there are no ideas (without prejudice to the possibility
of immediate activity of will in case a motor idea presents itself), or nothing can happen, because the apparatus is brought to a standstill by other ideas. This

last is the state of inhibition, which, as so-called voluntary inhibition or nolition, also controls, from the brain outward, motor centers of lower rank (in part).

To the state of willing is opposed, in general, the state of not-willing; in particular, the state of inhibition of a movement. Not-willing is the excluding or contradictory opposite of willing; inhibition in the physiological sense, the contrary opposite of willing. An illustration will make this clear. Take a bar of soft iron and make it magnetic by means of an electric current that incloses it, and it attracts another piece of iron; but let a second electric current of the proper strength, in a second spiral wire, circulate around the bar in an opposite direction to the first, and the bar no longer attracts the iron. When this second inhibitory current is interrupted, then the attraction is present again. Here the attraction of the iron represents a muscular movement in the condition of willing; the non-attraction represents muscular rest in the condition of not-willing; while in general a bar of iron does not attract another, so, too, in a particular case, a bar of iron encircled by two properly-graded electric currents having opposite directions, likewise does not attract another, but regains its magnetism at once when the second current ceases. Thus, when a child expresses no will—i. e., makes no voluntary movement—two cases are to be distinguished from each other: either the child has as yet no will, or he checks his movements with a will already much developed: he wills, namely, that a movement shall not be made. As soon as the inhibition or nolition passes away, movement appears again, in case the antecedents of it in the brain have not in the mean

time vanished. For voluntary inhibition has influence
in general only on those muscles the nerves of which
are in organic connection with the cerebrum, the seat of
the will.

This distinction between willing and voluntary inhibition may seem an idle one, but it is necessary, because
it refutes the notion that one can will a non-activity.
One can merely will-not-to-be, inhibit, prevent activity;
for it lies in the nature of willing to be always positive.
It can, therefore, be recognized only by positive expressions; where these are wanting, we are authorized to
deny its actual presence, and we have then to investigate
not-willing (or willing not-to-be, or not-to-act).

Now, according to experience, the expressions of will
are four only—word, act, look, gesture. If, then, it is
to be ascertained whether a child is in the state of willing, at least one of the four forms of expression must
be proved by observation to be present. Failing in this,
we must conclude that, invariably, at the time of observation, the individual observed was demonstrably not
in the state of willing.

But, granting that we succeed, the inference as to
the presence of the will continues still to be uncertain,
inasmuch as in some circumstances the phenomena
mentioned appear without will. Hence, we need more
exact criteria.

In the first place, it is settled that all willing is recognized exclusively by movements of contractile parts
of the willing being—in man and the higher animals
by muscular contractions induced by excitement of
nerves. But there are various classes of nervo-muscular
movements, and in beings of low order without nerves

and muscles there are movements of contractile tissues to which choice can not in advance be denied. Finally, in all cases where a contractile tissue exists, direct stimulus of this is capable of producing contraction, which may take precisely the same course as if, instead of the artificial stimulus, the will itself had caused it.

In order to ascertain in the midst of these manifold movements of contractile structures those to which the predicate "willed" applies, we should be obliged to have an objective sign once for all present in those very movements, and wanting in all others. But such a criterion can not be given.

Only subjective means of distinguishing can be given, and the four following are, in my view, characteristic:

1. Every willed movement is preceded directly by ideas, one of which, finally, as cause of the movement, acquires motor force.

2. Every willed movement is previously known in general, or in its kind, to the one who executes it, and it has—

3. An aim, more or less clearly represented in his mind; finally, the movement may—

4. Even at the instant of the rise of the voluntary impulse, be inhibited by new ideas.

The three first-named signs accompany every willed movement; the last makes its appearance only after the will is completely formed, and stamps the willed movements as voluntary in the stricter sense.

Every movement to which these four characteristics do not apply is involuntary. Accordingly, all muscular movements of man may, in fact, be distinguished as

willed and not-willed, voluntary and involuntary. Many
willed movements are executed by adults involuntarily
also—e. g., talking in sleep; many involuntary movements voluntarily, especially by actors; but, for all that,
the essential difference of the two remains. For the impulse to an involuntary movement has something added
to it when it is changed into a voluntary; and the impulse to a voluntary movement has something subtracted
from it when it becomes involuntary. This something
is precisely the purely psychical element of the previous
motor idea, the knowledge of the movement and of its
aim, and the possibility of its being inhibited by new
ideas.

When do these attributes appear in the child?

The answer to this question, as I shall attempt to
give it, presupposes that shortly before birth, and in a
higher degree immediately after birth, the motor centers possess a variable excitability, of such a sort that
in certain conditions, especially the first agreeable ones,
they supply fewer motor impulses; in certain other conditions—the first disagreeable ones—they supply more
such impulses. By this the irregular, manifold, inborn
movements of the very young babe are influenced necessarily—e. g., they are increased in the condition of hunger; and this influence appears as the manifestation of
an innate faculty of desire, so called. The movements
continue until the increased excitability (e. g., that
caused by hunger) is lessened. Then the assumed desire
seems satisfied. With repeated variation in the central
excitability (due purely to organic causes—nutrition,
supply of oxygen, etc.), the feeling that now appears,
of satisfied or unsatisfied desire, will work upon the

motor central organs in opposite ways, and will impart to the innate movements the character of longing or of repulsion. But these movements can not be transformed into willed movements until ideas are formed.

Thus the will does not arise out of nothing, and does not pre-exist as such, but is developed out of that desire, which on its part is not a fundamental, simple function of the ganglionic cell, but the result of the variations in the excitability of that cell by means of feelings and then of ideas. The will, as such, is not inborn, but it is hereditary. The variable excitability of the motor central organs, and, associated with that, a succession of primitive (impulsive) movements, which adults designate as movements of "longing," and ascribe to a faculty of desire; this is inborn in every one as the first germ of willing. The question is, When does this germ manifest itself in such a way that no doubt can exist of the presence of will?

Evidently we must, in order to find the answer, test the normal infant, proceeding chronologically in our experiments, to ascertain whether a new movement, as, e. g., the first grasping at an object seen, is accidental or intentional; i. e., whether the grasping movement is known to the child that desires as well as grasps, and whether its aim actually hovers before him. But even then the movement is not yet necessarily voluntary. It is so, however, when it can be omitted; say, on account of the idea of disagreeable consequences.

Although the discovery of the appearance of such activity of will in the child has an element of uncertainty in it, because it comes at a time when verbal language is still wanting, yet the determination of the first

instance of excitement in non-willing is much more difficult. Here, however, the earliest independent inhibition of accustomed movements presents something for
us to lay hold of.

Both taken together—the development of will in
the actually-executed movements of the child, and the
development of non-willing in the inhibition of frequently - repeated movements—furnish the foundation
for the formation of character. Both demand for their
investigation, above all, a careful observation of the
movements of the child from the beginning of its life.
No one has up to the present time even attempted this.

2. Classification of the Child's Movements.

A principle of classification for the movements of
the human being, sufficient for all actual cases, has not
yet been found. I must, therefore, attempt a new one,
in order simply that the movements of the child that
appear in the first years of life may be brought into
groups for a synoptical presentation.

If in this scheme of classification we regard the process immediately preceding the movement as the exclusive criterion of distinction, then there will be four
different kinds of movements, according to the com-
plexity of this process, to be separated from one another
—movements of the first, second, third, and fourth rank
—further movements may be derived from these, as
will appear in what follows.

The accompanying diagram will serve for illustration. It lays claim only to a general significance—i. e.,
it is true anatomically only of the relation of each case
to the following case :

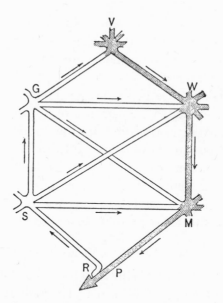

R represents the extremities of all the nerves of sense (in the eye, ear, mouth, nose, skin).

R S, the nerves of sense in their course (e. g., the paths of the optic nerve, auditory nerve, cutaneous nerves, in the upper portion of the peduncle of the cerebrum).

S, the lower sensory centers (e. g., optic thalami, corpora quadrigemina, corona radiata).

G, the higher sensory or emotional centers in the cerebral cortex (parietal region).

V, the ideational centers in the cerebral cortex.

W, the higher motor or volitional centers (centro-motor and inhibitory) in the cortex also.

M, the lower motor centers.

P, the extremities of the motor nerves (muscles).

I. *Impulsive Movements.*—These may be distinguished from all other movements by this, that they are caused without previous peripheral excitement, exclusively by the nutritive and other organic processes that go on in the motor centers of the lowest rank (M P). They are movements which the fœtus already executes, and earlier than any others, at a time when, as it can not possibly be incited to movement by peripheral stimulus, its centripetal paths are not yet practicable or not yet formed at all, and the ganglionic cells from which the excitations proceed are not yet developed. After birth such purely centro-motor impulses may continue long after complete development of the centers, especially in sleep. All these movements are unconscious.

II. *Reflex Movements.*—These require peripheral excitation—i. e., sense-impressions and centripetal, intercentral, and centrifugal paths (R S M P); they make their first appearance, therefore, in the embryo of the higher animals, after two sorts at least of centers of lower rank connected with each other are formed— sensory and motor. All reflex movements, in normal conditions, follow the sense - impression with great promptness and become conscious only after they have taken place.

III. *Instinctive Movements.* — These likewise require the presence of certain sense-impressions, and of at least three sorts of centers that have morphological connection with one another. Lower sensory, higher sensory, and lower motor centers must co-operate, in order that the simplest instinctive movement may take place (R S G M P). For these movements arise only after a sensation, and then an emotion, that supplied the motor impulse, have preceded. The instinctive movement must be preceded by a condition for which I find no more fitting designation than the word disposition (*Stimmung*). Yet the development of the ganglionic cells of the cerebral cortex is not required for all in-

15

stinctive movements—e. g., for sucking, which on that account comes near to the genuine reflexes. All instinctive movements have an aim, but are unconscious, as such, before and while they take place; and all are hereditary. Accordingly, when a human being or an animal executes a movement that was never executed by his ancestors, this movement can not be instinctive. This serves to distinguish instinctive from other movements, though it is to be borne in mind that many movements of the child may have been executed by his ancestors, which are not in the least instinctive. The ideo-motor movements of Carpenter are instinctive movements that lack the characteristic of heredity.

IV. *Ideational* (*Vorgestellte*) *Movements*. As the lowest form and the point of departure of this group, already characterized, are to be taken *imitative movements* or copies of others. These are necessarily dependent on sense-perceptions, and require at least four sorts of centers—lower and higher sensory, and lower and higher motor (R S G V W M P and V W M P; five, therefore, when G and V are separated). The centrifugal paths probably go, according to Meynert, all of them, from the cortex through the corpora striata and the lower portion of the peduncle of the cerebrum, but according to others directly also to the anterior columns of the spinal marrow. For the production of the most simple imitation, and so of the simplest ideational movement, the sense-impression must be previously elaborated as to time, space, and cause, i. e., wrought out to the formation of an idea, and this idea then works with motor force; it is determinative for the excitement of the motor centers and the muscles that reproduce the sense-impression. Imitations are, therefore, in the normal waking condition, always conscious; they can be unconscious only in various conditions of partial sleep. But in this case many conscious imitations have gone before. A participation on the part of the cerebral cortex is certain, whereas all movements of the first and second, and many of the third rank, take place without that.

From these four kinds of movement of the child may be derived all other centro-motor movements—passive and peripheral, caused by artificial stimulus of the motor nerves in their course are not considered—since we may suppose not only the expressive movements, but also the whole of the specifically voluntary, i. e., deliberate movements, to have arisen partly out of the frequent repetition, concurrence, and union of the four kinds named, partly from modifications of these according to the variation in the sense-impressions, feelings, and ideas. Physical causes only lie at the foundation of the first two kinds of movement; the last two have also psychical causes. Inhibitions of the discharges of motor impulses in the child whose will is completely developed, come to pass, as in the adult, in the following manner:

(1) R S M,   (2) R S W M,   (3) R S G M,
(4) R S G W M,   (5) R S G V W M,

and after very frequent repetition also without an immediately preceding excitement of the nerves of sense, R S, of which later.

No direct causes of the child's movements can be named beyond these four: (1), central, purely physical, stimuli; (2), peripheral, purely physical, stimuli; (3), feelings; (4), ideas. They correspond to the above groups. If, notwithstanding, the expressive, or expressional movements, and the deliberate movements, are hereafter treated by themselves, it is because of merely external reasons, in order not to complicate too much the presentation of the facts, a matter difficult at best. The intentional, voluntary, deliberate movements can not be separated physiologically from others, because no decisive objective criterion of distinction can be given; on the contrary, an involuntary movement becomes voluntary, simply by taking on something psychical, a particular activity of the central organs of the highest rank, which alters nothing in the movement itself (unless by incidentally delaying it somewhat and making it less harmonious). In truth, a physical difference no more exists between a voluntary and an artificial, electrical, nervo-muscular excitation than between the vibrations of the air from a vowel-sound sung and one artificially produced. The cock of the gun once set going, the shot follows invariably in the same fashion, no matter whether it was willed or not, whether it had an aim or not.

Only the muscular movements before birth, and in the earliest period after birth, take a somewhat different course from that of the later ones; for, according to Soltmann, the excitability of the motor nerves of the newly-born is inferior to that of adults, and does not surpass that in domestic mammalia until several weeks after birth. The muscles of the newly-born are like the wearied muscles of adults. With this is doubtless connected the peculiar sluggishness of the movements in the earliest period—a sluggishness that forms the greatest contrast to the vivacity of a later period, and that is interrupted in the transition period (as in the case of the marmot waking from his winter sleep) by surprising stretchings of the arms and legs, following one another almost in jerks.

CHAPTER IX.

IMPULSIVE MOVEMENTS.

ALTHOUGH the movements of the extremities in the unborn and the just-born child lack a characteristic mark by which these movements might at once be recognized as impulsive, they must, as must all later impulsive movements, be sharply distinguished from the reflex, the instinctive, the imitative, and other ideational movements, because they lack all the characteristic signs of the latter, as the following comparison will show:

The movements of the arms and legs of the fœtus and of the newly-born are of a *reflex* character, when a peripheral stimulus, be it only contact with the wall of the uterus, immediately precedes them. But how does the first movement of the embryo come to pass? That it can not be occasioned by passive contact has been proved to me by means of a close observation of the chick in the egg—the creature moves of itself, as I found, from the beginning of the fifth day. Here occur first only movements of the trunk, then also of the extremities and head—exactly as in the unharmed embryo of the trout, and like what occurs in the embryo of the frog in the egg—without the least change in the surroundings, and long before the reflex excitability is

present at all, the details of which are given in my book
on the "Physiology of the Embryo."

The cause of these remarkable primitive movements
of the trunk in unborn animals must exist in the animals
themselves, therefore, and can not be derived from a reaction of the superficial portions upon the central ones.
The same must be the case with the human embryo.

The impulsive movements are not *instinctive*, because they have no aim. They can not be designated
as directly useful or advantageous, appearing, as they do,
in an extremely irregular manner, nor can they, in general, be styled movements answering to a purpose. It
happens, in fact, that the very young child, by throwing
his arms and legs violently about, directly harms himself. In sleep he strikes his eye with his hand, rolls
himself aimlessly hither and thither when fast asleep,
so that he beats his head against the hard wood, and
wakes himself up, or cries out in a dream. Once I saw
my child (of sixteen months), when sound asleep, suddenly raise his left hand and put it against his left eye,
evidently by pure accident, so that the lid was raised.
The child slept on with one eye open—the pupil much
contracted—for a long time, and then removed his hand
without waking, just as accidentally, upon which the
lid dropped again. The eye did not move, notwithstanding the stimulus of the light. In this case the
convulsive raising of the arm first into the air and then
to the eye is to be called impulsive and almost dangerous, but not instinctive; besides, all purely instinctive
movements are co-ordinated, the impulsive movements
—the greater part of them—not co-ordinated.

The impulsive movements can not be *expressive*, for

the reason that, before birth, states of feeling which might be expressed by these are not to be assumed, and the presumable seat of such excitations in the brain—in fact, the whole brain—may be wanting without the appearance of the least change in the impulsive movements of the extremities, as I have proved in the case of the animal embryo, and as has been demonstrated by the movements of headless and brainless human abortions. Neither does the attribute *voluntary* apply to them, because no ideas, as yet, exist of their possible results; nor the term *imitative*, because a model is wanting. Moreover, Soltmann has proved, by many experiments, that in the new-born dog, after manifold stimulus of the cerebral cortex no movements at all of the muscles of the extremities—the face, neck, back, belly, or tail—are produced, but that, on the contrary, these appear only from the tenth day, after the animals have got their sight. Corresponding to this, the destruction of the parts answering to the motor departments of the cortex in older animals had also no effect in creatures from one to nine days old. No ataxy followed—no paralysis or disturbance of the muscular sense, or the like, even up to the time when the electric excitability of the brain existed. The muscular movements of new-born blind dogs are thus, for this very reason, quite independent of the gray cerebral cortex, as well as of peripheral stimulus—i. e., they are impulsive.

There is nothing left but to assume a cause of the impulsive movements that is internal, given in the organic constitution of the motor ganglionic cells of the spinal marrow, and connected, in the early embryonic stages, with the differentiation and the growth of those structures and of the muscular system. With the formation of the motor ganglionic cell in the spinal marrow and cervical marrow a certain quantity of potential energy must accumulate, which, by means of the flow of blood or of lymph, or possibly through the rapidly advancing formation of tissue, is, with remarkable ease, transformed into kinetic energy.

Difficult as it is to specify with certainty, in later life, movements of the human being that take place without peripheral excitement of any sort, direct or indirect, here we have them. And it is worthy of notice that impulsive movements, which outnumber others before birth and perpetually appear in all the newly-born, diminish even during the nursing period, and withdraw in proportion as the will develops, until finally, with ever-increasing voluntary inhibition of the original youthful impulse of movement, such muscular activity appears, in the adult, almost solely in dreamless sleep.

In the text-books hardly any notice is to be found of these peculiar centro-motor excitations, yet these are precisely of the very highest importance in the formation of the will. Alexander Bain alone has (1859) distinguished them definitely from other movements. He calls them automatic and spontaneous; but, as he reckons among these the movements that result from muscular sensations also, in young children and animals —movements which are to be referred to the condition of the muscles, and so to peripheral excitations—I can not entirely agree with him; for I give the name of "purely impulsive," and have given it (in my treatise "Psychogenesis," * 1880) exclusively to the muscular

---

* See "Jour. Spec. Phil.," April, 1881, for English translation.—ED.

contractions, proceeding from the fœtal constitution of the motor centers, that take place before centripetal stimuli operate, and so before muscular sensations can exist and assert themselves in stimulating movement.

The number of such movements is not great. Aside from those of the unborn, which are not to be taken into account here, the following may be specified : The out-stretching and bending of the arms and legs of the child just born, with movements sometimes quick, sometimes slow, generally non-coördinated, often co-ordinated, is nothing else than a continuation of the intra-uterine movements, and has, according to my observations, a striking resemblance to the extensions and flexions of the limbs of animals suddenly waking from their deep winter sleep. These, like sleeping children (and, indeed, in the first half of the second year it is still plainly marked), make genuine fœtal movements, which look as if they were directed against some invisible resistance. Convulsive motion is generally not so frequent in sleep as slow contractions, along with spreading and bending of the fingers, movements which likewise become more rare toward the end of the second year (probably with all sound children), and are from the beginning mostly asymmetrical.

The stretching of the limbs immediately after waking, which I have seen repeatedly in the second week, is often not distinguishable from these movements. It remains for years almost unchanged. In the twentieth month I saw it appear well marked, without being followed by waking.

The movements of the eyes before opening them at waking, especially the lateral turnings of the pupil, are impulsive. I have seen these movements, which can not be dependent on light, even in adults. The pupils moved rapidly under the lids this way and that, and indeed asymmetrically also. The lids, too, were meanwhile half opened, without any interruption of the snoring (in the second month).

The movements of the newly-born and of the infant in the bath, which has very nearly the same warmth as the amniotic fluid that perpetually surrounds the child before birth, can not be regarded as simply reflexive in character. We may, indeed, see in them already the beginning of expressive movements, especially expressions of pleasure, the more so since they are regularly accompanied by an extremely contented expression of countenance (protrusion of the lips also); but these movements in the bath are for a long time (so late as the fourth month)—-the greater part of them—just as purposeless, senseless, and asymmetric as on the first day. Sometimes the trunk also takes part in them, with half twistings and raisings, and this as early as the second month.

There is nothing expressive in this. The infant is accustomed, also, as late as in the period from the fourth to the sixth month, just as on the first day, when he is left to himself, in the warm bath and in falling asleep, to give to his arms and legs by preference the same position almost that they had before birth. The position of the legs continues to be that of the fœtus even much longer. The muscular contractions required for that are impulsive.

A further impulsive muscular activity is brought to our acquaintance by observation of the play of feature, still empty of meaning, in sleeping babes. They very often move the facial muscles without waking, especially the lips and eyelids, and, indeed, for the most part, with bilateral symmetry, although grotesquely, and this without any interruption of their snoring.

Babes that are awake also strike very vigorously about them with their arms (in the third quarter of the first year) quite aimlessly, while for the legs, as a rule, more frequently, in bed and bath especially, there is a pretty symmetrical alternation of stretching and bending.

Yet it must be noted that the bilaterally symmetrical movement of the facial muscles and of the arms in reflexes appears very much earlier and is more pronounced than that of the legs. And the abductions, adductions, supinations, and rotations of the arms unquestionably appear plainly at an earlier period than do those of the legs in manifold variety. In the case of a very vigorous child, I saw that even in the first half-hour of its life the lips were protruded, and the mouth opened and shut, with perfect co-ordinate symmetry. The corrugation of the forehead, and the screwing up of the eyes, in the first hour of life, however, is not always impulsive; the latter, especially, is often of a reflex character. Only the strange asymmetrical grimaces of new-born children when awake are probably purely impulsive. In connection with this, I have been surprised at the immobility of the nose, which I have not seen moved earlier than in the seventh month; of course, I except the very early dilating of the nostrils by means of the levator alæ nasi, as a reflex and an accompanying movement in snoring, sucking, and difficult breathing.

Crowing and other similar exercises of the voice are in the first year to be regarded in many cases as discharges of accumulated motor impulses, which, as well as the squeaking of new-born animals, and the peeping of the chick in the egg, can not have their origin merely in peripheral excitement. Precisely as the muscles of the arms and legs, of the face and of the eyes, so those of respiration, of the tongue, and of the larnyx are set in activity without purpose by a centro-motor impulse. In the first year the exercise of the muscles is with all healthy children the beneficial result of such animation, which, considered in itself, seems entirely purposeless. An adult lying on his back could not make these persistent movements, that are made by the seven-to-twelve months child, without a decided feeling of fatigue; and, when we consider that the child, in addition, turns his head attentively, and cries at every noise, at every change in his neighborhood, the total of the nervous excitements seems relatively much greater in the one-year-old child than in the adult, who makes fewer superfluous movements, and has become dull to ordinary sense-impressions.

Here belong, further, " accompanying "-movements made by little children.

In individual cases it can hardly be determined whether movements wholly useless (like those described on pages 23 and 24), especially of the facial muscles, are merely impulsive, or are the remains of an extinct instinct, or are accompanying-movements. We have an example in the holding out of the little finger apart from the others at the first attempts of the child to carry the soup-spoon to the mouth without help. In the eighteenth month this graceful movement was executed by my boy without the least incitement, and without any one's having made the movement before in his neighborhood, absolutely "of himself." Surprising as it seemed at the beginning—it occurred often from that time on—I can not admit that an imitation of unknown examples is at the bottom of this, because the child did not give the least attention to his finger, but, on the contrary, was wholly absorbed in carrying the contents of the spoon to his mouth. The extending of the little finger straight into the air probably came in as an accompanying-movement, but not in accord with the movement of the other fingers, without the cognizance of the child. In the third year it was only very rarely to be seen, and then also it was manifestly unconscious.

Another still more surprising movement, wholly purposeless, and withal quite bilaterally symmetrical, was observed by me frequently in the first year, and even in the last month of it. When my child, namely, lying on his back on a soft couch, received the nursing-bottle which the nurse tilted for him holding it in her hand, he used almost invariably to stretch out his closed hands upward, with the lower arm bent at right angles to the upper arm, which rested on the cushion or the coverlet. And in this strange attitude the child remained until he had drained the bottle. If he was obliged (toward the end of the first year) to use one hand for giving the bottle a different direction or for holding it, then the arm that did not take part in this remained in its peculiar position. This has no resemblance at all to the position of seizing; seems rather to be an accompanying-movement going along with extreme strain of the attention. When the child was allowed to drink out of a glass (in the sixteenth month) that was held to his mouth, he would then stretch out his hands and spread all the fingers, and while drinking would not cease from the muscular contractions necessary to those movements; this had a very peculiar look, and was more suggestive of grasping.

Further, all little children make unsteady accompanying-movements of various sorts, especially when they hear new sounds—music, singing. They like to move the arms up and down at such times. In play, too, when the cover of a pitcher is put on and off before their eyes, there is often a corresponding movement with the hand, executed while the cover is clapped to and subsequently (eighth and ninth months), after the first observations have once been made by the children. Here we have to do not with attempts at imitation, but with pure accompanying-movements. The child sees and hears or tastes something new, strains his attention, and has a feeling (an agreeable one) of gratified curiosity. This feeling leads to the motor discharge. Such a movement showed itself in my boy frequently in the fourth year, especially with new impressions of taste. His right forearm would go sidewise hither and thither from two to four times in a second, while he was tasting a new kind of food that he desired.

All accompanying-movements of this kind, which approximate to the reflexes, are no more purely impulsive, because they require a peripheral excitement, and because feelings co-operate in them. On the other hand, the movements of the head and legs in new-born puppies, and of most new-born mammals in general (movements called droll and comical on account of their striking awkwardness), are probably purely impulsive. And the trembling of these creatures in a warm bed belongs here also (p. 171).

CHAPTER X.

REFLEX MOVEMENTS.

The fact firmly established by me in the case of numerous animal embryos, that no reflex movements can be elicited in early stages of development by however strong and varied stimulus, whereas movements, especially bendings and stretchings of the trunk, regularly take place from internal causes, proves the untenableness of a wide-spread view, according to which all movements of the newly-born are of a reflex character. The human being just born has, in fact, in many respects, a less reflex excitability than the infant manifests later, and yet he moves in a lively manner.

Notwithstanding this, many reflex movements of the newly-born are already strongly marked, answering to the reflex excitability that increases rapidly before birth in the last stage of the fœtal development; and they have a very great psychogenetic significance, because through their frequent repetition the harmonious co-working of many muscles as means of warding off what might injure or be unpleasant is soon perfected, and the development of the will is made possible through these co-ordinations. Then, later, is manifested, in unmistakable fashion, the power of the growing cerebral will-mechanism in the inhibition of reflexes. These must, for this reason, have occurred previously in great numbers, so that again and again harmful results have arisen, and the experience, e. g., has been made, "Crying does no good, crying brings harm; better, then, keep down the violent, loud expiration." Through logical operations of this sort—long before gaining the power of speech—the foundation is laid for self-control, which rests essentially upon the inhibition of reflex movements.

The beginning of reflex muscular contractions comes in the period before birth. For it is possible through outward impressions, even by means of continued gentle stroking (*Palpiren*), to produce and to augment movements of the fœtus in the more advanced fœtal period. From my observations, I regard it as certain, also, that rough handling during the birth, especially where the amniotic fluid is scanty, may produce premature respiratory movements in the child, and thereby endanger its life—a thing for midwives and physicians to heed. The embryo begins early to swallow. The chick in the egg makes movements of swallowing on the eleventh day; and before anything of the creature is visible—on the twenty-first day of the brooding, according to my observations—can be brought, by means of a prick of a needle, by cooling, and other harsh treatment, to loud peeping; the prematurely-born rabbit may be made to squeak by electric stimulation, provided only respiration has begun. I have even seen the embryo of the Guinea-pig in an unbroken ovary (in a warm, very much diluted solution of common salt) before a breath had been drawn—the placental circulation being maintained—not only make bilaterally symmetrical reflexes with the extremities on being lightly touched, but I have repeatedly proved, also, that in this case the touching of the lips, especially of the whiskers (*Spürhaare*), produces an extremely well-adapted movement of rubbing with the fore-paw of the same side—in the amniotic fluid—a movement, accordingly, which is, later, very frequent with the Guinea-pig, and which is proved by this observation to be absolutely hereditary. But if the touching of the lip or any portion of the skin is carried so far as to become pricking or pressure, then an inhalation takes place, and with that the reflex activity is modified.

A series of new reflexes begins also with the birth of the human being, through breathing.

The first cry of the new-born child was, indeed, formerly regarded as anything but reflex, yet it is in the highest degree probable that this first loud expiration is a pure reflex effect. Kant wrote (certainly without having himself observed children and animals just born): " The outcry that is heard from a child scarcely born has not the tone of lamentation, but of indignation and of aroused wrath ; not because anything gives him pain, but because something frets him ; presumably because he wants to move, and feels his inability to do it as a fetter that deprives him of his freedom. What can be the intent of Nature in causing the child to come with loud outcry into the world, when both for child and mother in a savage condition of nature, this is attended with the utmost danger? No animal, however, except man (as he now is), makes loud announcement of his existence at the time of his birth."

This remarkable view has been commented on in

16

various ways, and even at the present time many persons think that the whimpering and crying of the child just born have a higher psychical significance. All interpretations of this sort go to wreck upon the repeatedly established fact that new-born children without any brain at all cry out, and many healthy new-born children at their coming into the world, as Darwin reports, do not cry, but sneeze. In both cases the expirational reflex must be occasioned by a strong peripheral excitement— e. g., the sudden cooling off of the skin, and the rubbing of the back. For I have observed in the case of many new-born animals, especially Guinea-pigs, that they make their voice heard, with the same machine-like regularity as does the frog deprived of brain, if you simply stroke their backs. It is known, too, that many animals cry out during birth, and immediately thereafter. Calves especially bleat normally, not only directly after they have left the bodies of the mothers, but, as experienced farmers assure me, often even during birth. Goats often cry out directly after birth.

The purely reflexive movement of sneezing is frequent with the newly-born and with infants. It demonstrates the existence of a very firm connection, long hereditary, of the nasal branches of the trigeminus with the motor expiratory nerves, and is remarkable, as sobbing is, for the reason that it requires an inborn complex co-ordination of many muscles. In observations concerning reflex excitability, the sneezing of infants is a much better sign of the effect of stimulus than are other movements. On the thirty-eighth day I saw sneezing produced by some drops of lukewarm water that trickled over the forehead ; on the forty third day I saw that particles of witch-meal caused sneezing; on the hundred and seventieth mere blowing on the child had the same effect. Adults do not readily show such sensibility. In sneezing, the eyes even of little children are invariably closed (just so it is with apes, according to Darwin); why, is not satisfactorily explained. Donders found that the contents of the blood-vessels of the eye are lessened by the closing of the lid. The shutting of the eyes in violent expiration of breath seems from this to have a purpose. But it is purely reflex in character. F. H. Champneys, who observed his son throughout the first nine months, found that sneezing was always accompanied by violent movements of all the limbs, the legs being drawn up, and the forearms bent with the elbows pushed forward; noteworthy symmetrical accompanying-movements, which, however, do not appear in all infants.

Other innate forms of loud expiration of breath are common with very small children, as is well known, but are likewise of very little or no psychogenetic significance; thus, wheezing or snuffling, a phenomenon accompanying sucking; snoring (first observed by me on the twenty-fourth day), yawning with wide-stretched mouth, a striking habit in all infants in the early period, and which, merely as an augmented and intensified manner of drawing in the breath, helps to bring the respiratory apparatus, little by little, into regular activity, inasmuch as it probably comes on invariably after a succession of scanty inhalations, by way of compensation, after a stronger respiratory stimulus, or because the excitability of the respirational center has in the mean time increased. I once saw a child yawn on the seventh day of its life, stretching its mouth very wide, and at the same time screwing the eyelids together; and it kept this attitude for some seconds. This child generally distorted its face in a remarkable manner when it had been disturbed in going to sleep. But a direct physiological connection of yawning with the dropping of the lids and with sleepiness is not demonstrated, unless we count as such the increased demand for oxygen, caused by the fatigue of the respiratory muscles also, which may produce a deeper inspiration. Here, too, belongs the coughing that I, in one case, heard with perfect distinctness, in the first hour of life. Clearing the throat is, on the contrary, acquired, as Darwin rightly observes. Still, in very young babes, who cough somewhere about the fourth day, involuntary coughing has, as a matter of fact, the same effect as voluntary clearing the throat has later. The early involuntary pushing out of the nipple by means of the tongue, after nursing, is, in fact, much more adroit than the later voluntary spitting out of the skin of a grape or gooseberry that has been crushed and sucked out in the mouth. Yet the latter complicated movement was executed quite skillfully in the nineteenth month (Sigismund).

Sobbing and sighing, two psychically characteristic forms of expiration in later life, have in the infant not the least expressional significance. Both make their appearance late, under normal conditions. I observed sighing in the seventh month, and that repeatedly after the child had been brought from the recumbent to the upright, half-sitting position. Sighing often appeared in my child—even in the second year—when he was in a contented mood, and this without its being an imitation.

The respiratory movements go on at the beginning of life, in general, without any relation whatever to the emotions. The heaving of the bosom in mental agitation, the holding of the breath under the strain of attention—these things do not take place in the very earliest youth. The respiration of the infant is, however, very irregular in the first weeks, so that there is an illusory appearance of such phenomena. In the newly-born, the breathing, now violent, now again quite weak, interrupted by intervals in which the breathing ceases, then rhythmical, then soon after alternately deep and light, approaches but slowly the later type.

At the close of the seventh week the number of respirations made by my boy in sleep was twenty-eight to the minute; in the thirteenth week twenty-seven. But for months yet the breathing was irregular. After four or five quick inspirations, would often follow a cessation interrupted by separate, deep breathings. The older the child, so much the more regular the movements of breathing and the less their frequency. During the teething-fever the number went up (in the ninth month) temporarily to forty and forty-two in a minute, and in the sixteenth and seventeenth months, during sleep, amounted to twenty-two and twenty-five a minute. From this period on, the character of it was predominantly regular: in the twentieth month it was twenty-two and twenty-three. But whenever there is a noise made that is not quite loud enough to wake the quietly-sleeping infant, then the frequency of the breaths immediately increases to twenty-five and twenty-six, to fall again soon to twenty-two and twenty-three. This extraordinary reflex sensibility of the respiratory apparatus I have often observed (p. 83). It is noteworthy because it proves the existence of a reflex arc from the auditory nerve to the inspiratory nerves (of the intercostal muscles and the diaphram).

The very slow consolidation of the entire respiratory mechanism in all infants is certainly connected with this great reflex excitability. In later life stronger and more numerous stimuli may operate without the least change in the respiration. Moreover, since breathing, like the activity of the heart, gradually settles into a regular rate without the participation of the will, it affords an excellent example of the development of a very complicated, co-ordinated, involuntary muscular activity of which no trace exists, under normal conditions, before birth. This co-ordination, however, as it begins directly after birth, in consequence of sufficiently strong excitement of the cutaneous nerves, as an imperfect periodical reflex, is not only hereditary but inborn, yet not so perfect as after it has been longer manifested.

Of reflexes not periodical those especially frequent in other departments are, in infants, vomiting, choking, and hiccough—all three inborn movements, which are performed at once in the same manner as they are later.

In choking, children of one to five days old stretch forth the tongue, with a reflexive elevation of the larynx, and make grimaces, as adults do when they wish by a choking movement to throw out a foreign substance from the œsophagus. The usual occasion of choking in infants seems to be accumulation of mucus, but it may also be produced by tickling the palate and the roots of the tongue, or by moistening them with sort, as these observations have made clear, through the *becoming accustomed to the parts of one's own body.* These, which at first are foreign objects, affect the child's organs of sense always in the same manner, and thereby become uninteresting after they have lost the charm of novelty. Now, his own body is that to which the attractive objective impressions (i. e., the world) are referred, and with the production by him of new impressions, with the changes wrought by him (in the experimenting which is called "playing"), with the experience of being-a-cause, is developed more and more in the child the feeling of self. With this he raises himself higher and higher above the dependent condition of the animal, so that at last the difference, not recognizable at all before birth and hardly recognizable at the beginning after birth, between animal and human being attains a magnitude dangerous for the latter, attains it, above all, by means of language.

But if it is necessary for the child to appropriate to himself as completely as possible this highest privilege of the human race and through this to overcome the animal nature of his first period ; if his development requires the stripping off of the remains of the animal and the unfolding of the responsible " I "—then it will conduce to the highest satisfaction of the thinking man, at the summit of his experience of life, to go back in thought to his earliest childhood, for that period teaches him plainly that he himself has his origin in nature, is intimately related to all other living creatures. However far he gets in his development, he is ever groping vainly in the dark for a door into another world ; but the very fact of his reflecting upon the possibility of such a has been made in the first part of this book; in regard to the last I was in hopes of finding, by frequent observation of sleeping children, confirmation of the conformity to law that Pflüger discovered, such as exists in animals deprived of their brain. I was strengthened in my view after the first experiment (on the fourteenth day of my child's life), for, upon touching the *left* temple of the sleeping child, he started, and directed the *left* hand toward the place that was touched (law of the conduction on the same side for unilateral reflexes). This experiment, repeated at intervals, yielded the same result three times. In the same way, in the fourteenth week, when I touched the right eye on the inner corner with the finger-nail, the right hand of the child went directly to that spot and rubbed the eye; but, when I made the touch on the left, the left hand remained quiet. It is any way an accident that the little hand found exactly the right place, for in other cases it went by. When the child was awake, no convulsive, no reflex movement took place upon the same sort of contact, and the repetition of the touching of the sleeping child on other days had likewise often this negative result, or else irregular movements of rubbing as a consequence (p. 101). When in the seventh week I touched the *left* temple of the child as he lay quiet, his *left* arm remained motionless, but the *right* arm made an energetic movement forward, upward, and to the left, although the left arm lay perfectly free. Whence this contra-lateral response? Perhaps the sensorium was active and did not yet localize accurately, or the reflex path of the same side was less easily passable. Such unexpected responsive movements I have often perceived in the first two years, and that as late as the thirty-fifth month in a sleeping child, even when the tickling was on the left, the *right* arm lying under the body of the sleeping child and the left arm being free.

This observation is thus exactly opposed to that of Pflüger (1853), who tickled a sleeping boy of three years, on the right nostril, and saw that he raised the right hand in defense, and rubbed the right nostril. When tickled on the left, the child took the left hand. Then Pflüger laid both arms of the boy, who lay on his back asleep, gently near the body, held the left arm firmly with a light pressure, on a pillow placed upon it, and holding a feather in his free hand, tickled the left nostril of the little fellow. Immediately the left arm was moved, but could not be brought to the face. The child then made a grimace, and tried, after repeated tickling on the left, to press the left nostril with the right hand, "whereas he had at other times always chosen the hand of the same side, however much and however long he was tickled, until he awoke." The "always" can not hold good universally.

But I often saw the reflex of the same side in the second year also. Thus, in the seventeenth month, I touched the right nostril on the inside, while the child was asleep; at once the right hand went to it and rubbed, and, when I had touched the left nostril, that was immediately rubbed with the left hand. Then, on the repetition of the experiment, there was no longer any responsive movement of the sleeping child.

O. Rosenbach also has observed the action of reflexes in sleeping children, and has ascertained especially that some of them are lacking during sound sleep (those of the abdomen, the cremaster, and patella), but he does not give the age of the children.

At any rate, the experiments that I instituted suffice to show that, without detriment to the general validity of Pflüger's laws of reflexes, circuitous reflex routes must often be tried by little children, many experiences must first be had before those laws are manifested in their purity. Many times, to be sure, the experiments upon children sleeping soundly surprised me at once by their conformity to law. Yet simple experiments of that sort that I repeated upon several children, and the observation of the independent movements of arms and hands in the newly-born, have given me but few evidences of the existence of perfectly-developed inborn reflexes of the corresponding side after stimulus on one side. The trigeminus facialis reflex is such a case, since upon the touching of one eye, in the first hour of life, very often this one only is shut; another case is the spreading of the toes when the sole of the foot is touched (pp. 104, 225). The law of symmetry of the reflexes is recognized as valid for the just-born, in the dilatation of both pupils, when only one eye is shaded; in the closing of both eyes at the rude touch of one eye or one nostril; in movements of both feet when the sole of one foot is touched (p. 104); so likewise the appearance of the reflex in unequal degrees of intensity on both sides in bilateral reflexes following stimulus of one side is confirmed by the stronger movements of the eyelid (after the tickling of one nostril) as well as of the leg upon the irritated side (p. 104). But the law of inter-sensitive motor movement still needs proof; for, according to it, no reflex from the trigeminus to the

motor oculi ought to occur. But if a child be waked
by a touch of the eyelid, the raising of the lid seems
to occur through reflexive action. The question comes
up whether movements do not always take place before
the opening of the eyes. I have not liked to experiment in regard to this, as I do not wake children without urgent reasons.

Further, in the case of two children, who in the
first half-year suffered from local itching eruptions of
the skin (milk-crust), the reflexive movements of the
limbs were quite irregular and at the beginning absolutely unsuited, afterward not in all cases suited, to re-
lieve the pain or the feeling of tickling; at all events,
apart from the turnings of the head, which was the
most tormented, and which was moved hither and
thither like a pendulum when the arms were confined
(fourth month). Many times when the arms had escaped from the tethers in the night, the face was
scratched to bleeding in several places that were evidently not troublesome (fourth to sixth month). At
every unguarded moment the hands went to the head;
and the skin, even the sound part of it, was rubbed and
scratched. These scratching movements can not be inborn, they must be acquired. The result of an accidental contact of the head and hand appearing in the
diminution of the tickling sensation must have induced
a preference of the movement of the hand to the head
among all sorts of movements; for in the concurrence of
all muscular movements those are preferred—i. e., most
frequently repeated—which bring with them feelings of
pleasure, and which remove whatever excites unpleasant
feeling, while the movements that prevent feelings of

pleasure and those that cause unpleasant feeling become more and more rare.

The mentioned reflexive reaching toward the head had now, in one of the two cases before us, a peculiar association as its further consequence (in regard to the other case there is lack of observation). When, namely, the eczema became less and at last had entirely disappeared, the lifting of the arms along with the carrying of the hands to the head still continued, showing itself every time that anything disagreeable occurred to the child, or when he refused to do anything—e. g., when he did not want to play any more or to play at all. Manifestly we have to do here with a primitive process of induction or generalization. Formerly that movement was regularly executed in connection with the disagreeable cutaneous sensation on the head (up to the sixth month); now that sensation, indeed, is wanting, but the movement is so firmly associated with the quality "disagreeable" of that feeling, that it is executed even when something else appears with the same quality (ninth month). Thus individual expressional movements arise from acquired reflexes, which disappear again later because they remain individual.

In direct contrast to the acquired reflex movements, stands the inborn spreading of the toes that follows the touching (tickling, stroking) of the soles of the feet, which I saw just as plainly marked in new-born children five minutes after birth, and in the first days, as in the fourth week. Darwin mentions that, after the touching of the sole with a bit of paper on the seventh day, the foot was suddenly jerked away, and the toes curled up. I have not been able to find out under what circumstances this reflex or the spreading of the toes at the touch of the sole of the foot occurs (cf. p. 104), but I observed that as early as the eighth week, tickling of the sole was followed by laughing. This so-called reflexive (*"reflectorische"*) laughing (p. 145) is not a regular, absolutely pure reflex act, because it is dependent upon the previously existing mood.

The reflexive starting, quivering, and stretching out of the arms at a sudden, unexpected, strong impression, especially a sound-impression, the starting back with the head and the upper part of the body at a sudden approach—fright, in fact—is wholly lacking in the first hours of life. The human child just born can not, properly speaking, experience fright any more than can animals just born, although many sensations, such as that of a dazzlingly bright light, are surprising and disagreeable to him. But this stage of inferior sensibility scarcely outlasts the first days in vigorous children; in some (born after their time) it may in the case of sudden impressions (p. 80), have given place, even before the second day, to the susceptibility to fright that is more or less characteristic of the infant.

This has already been spoken of repeatedly, so far as the bilaterally symmetrical reflexes, occasioned by all sorts of acoustic, optical, tactile impressions (e. g., by taking hold of the child, or blowing upon him), especially the extending and raising of the arms, the starting and the quick pulsation of the eyelid, are symptoms of being frightened (p. 82). Apart from the starting, which is not always regular, these reflexes are distinguished above others by their perfect symmetry. *Both* arms are raised exactly simultaneously, *both* eyes close for a moment after a sudden impression, even when this is made only on one side (as in pulling at the blanket on which the child is lying). This reflex mechanism, that unites the motors of the extremities with the organs of sense, must have an easy action from the beginning, although no direct advantage from it to the child can be affirmed.

Another constant symptom of fright in children is their silence. For example, when a child has had a fall, screaming does not begin till after an interval It is probable that this condition of not being able to scream, like that of apthongia or reflex aphasia, rests upon tetanic excitement of the motor nerves, especially of the nerves of the tongue, in consequence of which every attempt to form a sound may result in spasm of the tongue. In children this occurrence is by no means so rare as in adults. Children, both before and after they have begun to learn to speak, do not begin to scream until some time after the effect of the sudden impression; for this reason, probably, because by that impression the will is completely paralyzed, so that at first they do not even get so far as to the attempt to form a sound. All the muscles that at other times are voluntarily movable are no longer moved becauses the impulses of will are wanting; so it is also with the tongue and the muscles of the larynx. Even the reflex excitability is diminished. Hence, probably, the silence of those frightened in the first moment. The very strong excitement of particular centers brings with it an arrest of the other central functions. Finally, the motor impulse becomes operative, but produces that spasm of the tongue, and not till after that passes, screaming.

It takes a long series of experiences, which each individual must go through for himself anew, before such fright-reflexes and infringements upon the activity of the will can be controlled, and many persons never learn to control them. Still, it is of the greatest importance for the cultivation of the child's will to exercise children as early as possible in the conscious inhibition of reflex movements.

At the beginning, probably, no reflex is inhibited, but there exists a peculiarity discovered by Soltmann, which counteracts the disadvantages arising from this defect. The excitability of the nerve-muscle, namely, in cats, dogs, rabbits, gradually increases from birth on (in man probably until toward the sixth week of life, as it then about equals that of adults, or somewhat surpasses it). The inferior excitability of the motor nerves in the earliest period exerts a beneficial counter-influence to the tendency to convulsions after physiological stimulation. Here I must agree with Soltmann, and attribute to this factor, as he does, great importance, especially on account of the absence of will and of the inhibition of reflexes; but my experiments and observations upon new-born Guinea-pigs, and on those born prematurely, leave not the least doubt that in these animals inhibitions of reflexes take place through strong peripheral stimuli even before birth, or with the first drawing of breath. For when, in such a fœtus or new-born creature, I pinch sharply with the forceps any spot whatever on the skin after breathing has begun, the auricle does not react in the least, or reacts only very feebly upon the strongest impressions of sound; but if the peripheral stimulus ceases, then both auricles plainly move at once upon the same acoustic stimulus. Here exists, then, soon after the beginning of respiration (in the prematurely and the normally born) an inhibition of a reflex through strong localized cutaneous stimuli. A paralysis of the reflex, or paraplegia, after contusion— e. g., of a kidney—it has not been possible, thus far, to produce in new-born creatures (dogs and rabbits). The inhibitory effect of the excitement of the vagus upon the activity of the heart is, on the other hand, present in the new-born mammal.

It is highly desirable now to fix, by observation and simple experiments, the date of beginning of inhibitions of reflexes in the human being. I saw a sixteen-days-old child, that was screaming violently, become quiet in an instant when it was laid face downward on a pillow; and I have observed, even in very young babes, the quieting effect of singing, making a hushing sound, and playing on the piano. But in these cases we have not to do with inhibitions of reflexes in the strict sense of the term, but with the supplanting of a feeling of discomfort, along with its motor consequences, or a reflex activity, by means of a new impression. A brainless new-born child, even, that was screaming violently, could be easily quieted, as Pflüger relates, by letting him suck the finger. The cerebral activity of the newly-born can not yet influence the reflexive and impulsive activity of the spinal cord, because the brain is not yet sufficiently developed. Soltmann has proved, by experiments on new-born dogs, that at the beginning of life no excitements pass from the brain to the spinal cord, which would be capable of arresting the reflex operations effected by the cord. And I have no doubt that the very same thing is true of many other new-born animals. But it is not true of all, and whether it is precisely in the human being that immediately after birth no trace of the inhibition of reflexes exists, is doubtful. The Guinea-pig, which is much more mature at birth, comes into the world, according to the previously-mentioned observations, with a complete apparatus for inhibition of reflexes.

Genuine inhibitions of reflexes may first be observed with certainty in little children at the time when they no longer (as they do in the first six to nine months), without the least sign of self-control, excrete at once the products of nutrition when the accumulation of these stimulates them reflexively to do so. In all healthy infants this reflex excitability is great. But I lack observations as to when for the first time the reflex stimulus, that shows itself normally on the first day of life, is overcome, or the immediate response to it is at least delayed. At the beginning of the first year children are accustomed to scream after the evacuation; later, to scream before it, formally announcing it. In the latter case they have had the experience that the threats, the chastisements, and the natural disagreeable consequences of the immediate reflex activity cause more discomfort than waiting does. We have here one of the strongest effects of early training, as is proved by the behavior of animals and many insane persons.

The point of time at which control of the *sphincter vesicæ* begins, allowed itself in one case to be approximately determined. From the beginning of the tenth month, viz., the desire to evacuate the bowels was, in the daytime, in a healthful and waking condition, almost

17

invariably announced by great restlessness. If the
child was then attended to, the evacuation took place
invariably not till *several seconds* after giving him the
proper position. The child needed so much time,
therefore, in order to annul the inhibition by means of
his now unquestionably authenticated will.

Here we have two proofs of the existence of choice:
first, the inhibition of a reflex never inhibited in the
first half-year, the non-willing of it; second, the removal of the inhibition, the willing of the reflex. The
first inhibitory act, which, for that matter, does not
last long when it is not regarded, seems to occur seldom before the last three months of the first year
(sometimes much later). It is lacking, as a rule, when
the child does not enjoy undisturbed health, when his
attention is strongly claimed, and when he is tired.
The overcoming of the reflex stimulus in sleep, which
takes place independently of will by means of habit,
requires for that very reason a much longer period of
time. It is to be borne in mind, however, in this case,
that a pretty strong pressure, like other peripheral
stimuli, first interrupts the sleep, and thereby makes
room for the influence of the will.

Those reflexes which during the whole of life are
not inhibited by the will, appear, notwithstanding, to
be in part more distinct in the new-born and the infant
than in the following years of life. At least Eulenburg
found (1878) in two hundred and forty-one children
under twelve months the reflex of the tendon of the
patella at the beginning not quite so frequent, indeed,
as in adults; where it did appear, however, it was
more distinct than it was later, especially in forty-one

children examined in the first month, and in sixteen (out of seventeen) one day old. Later observations of the same investigator and his assistant Dr. Haase (1882) confirmed the relatively more frequent absence of the knee-phenomenon in one hundred and sixteen children from one to twenty-four months old. In seven cases it was wanting on both sides, in three cases on one side. The foot - phenomenon was wanting, in fact, in the great majority of the cases. It was distinctly seen only in twenty-two out of the one hundred and sixteen children. The osseous reflexes were still more rare (tibia reflex observed in fifteen, radius reflex in fourteen of the one hundred and sixteen). On the other hand the reflex of the abdomen, of the nose, of the cornea, and of the pupil were not missing in a single case. The ear-reflex was only in five cases indistinct. (In seventy-eight boys, from one to sixty months old the cremaster reflex was lacking in twenty cases.) It appears from this that the tendon-reflexes are not so easily inherited as those of the skin and mucous membrane. The latter are more useful to the organism.

The decrease of the general reflex tendency ("*Reflexdisposition*") in the earliest years is identical in ultimate effect with the increase of an inhibition of reflexes. To be sure, the individual efficient factors in both cases can not yet be isolated. The tendency to spasms that has its origin partly in the lack of all reflex inhibition in the earliest period, and the heightened reflex sensibility easily to be established physiologically in every teething child, which gives occasion for the strangest grimaces, find their counterpoise only after the development of the will—i. e., after far advanced development of the gray substance of the cerebrum, upon the removal of which there appear in animals reflex phenomena similar to those in new-born and quite young individuals. But in older children, too (in the fourth year) many reflexes are found, especially the mimetic and the defensive (such as that mentioned, p. 101—"shuddering"), more strongly expressed than after their training has been carried further.

The pain-reflexes that are most strongly manifested in later life are, according to the experiments of Genzmer, already in part mentioned, least developed precisely in the earliest period. Through observation of some sixty new-born children, it was established by him that they are, on the first day, almost insensible to the prick of a needle, and in the first week they still have an inferior degree of sensibility. Prematurely-born infants were in the course of the first days so sharply pricked with fine needles in the nose, upper lip, and hand, that a little drop of blood flowed from the puncture, and yet they gave no sign of discomfort; indeed, often not even a slight quivering could be noticed. To pricks that are acute for the adult, normal children responded after one to two days, seldom earlier, merely with reflex movements as upon being touched. "The pain-reflexes differ from those reflexes of touch in this, that the movement is wont to follow the stimulus only after a longer pause (up to two seconds), while in the touch-reflexes the physiological period is considerably shorter." The sensibility to needle-pricks was found to be somewhat greater in children born after their time, and it increases generally in the first weeks. It is of great interest, in connection with this, that in children of some weeks there followed occasionally upon a prick in the sole of the foot a distortion of the countenance without local reflexes. "They seemed to become conscious of the feeling of pain. In the first week this was never the case." A reflexive lachrymal secretion could not be produced at that period by any prick, but only by irritation of the mucous membrane of the nose; "at pricks on the skin of the face, the moisture of the eyes did seem, but only at times, to increase."

Now from all these facts it does not follow that the newly-born are sensible of no pain at all, but it follows that the pain-reflexes are still wanting when the painful impression is circumscribed—reaches but few nerves—as in the prick of a fine needle. Fifty simultaneous needle-pricks would doubtless bring pain-reflexes in their train immediately after birth. So much is made certain by my experiments on prematurely-born rabbits and Guinea-pigs, which responded, with unmistakable pain-reflexes, only to very strong local, and to weaker extended, painful assaults—to electric, thermal, mechanical, chemical cutaneous stimuli. Distortion of the face and loud screaming appear also in mature or nearly mature new-born human beings upon strong electrical stimulation of the skin, as Kroner found (1882).

It would be of great interest to draw up a list, as complete as possible, of the reflex movements of the newly-born, the infant, and the child not yet able to speak; to separate the inborn movements from the acquired, those capable of being inhibited from the purely physical reflexes and the pain-reflexes; and to test whether there is a single reflex that belongs to the human child alone. A thorough-going comparison of new-born chimpanzees and orangs with new-born negro children in regard to the reflexes would perhaps disclose no differences.

In the human infant there have been proved—to adduce only one sensory and one motor nerve as example —six different regular reflex movements from the optic nerve to the motor oculi alone, which appear in case of light-impressions, viz. :

1. Contraction of the superior rectus muscle of the eye in raising the glance, when bright light appears above; in the fourth week or earlier (p. 44).

2. Contraction of the elevator of the lid in moderate light; immediately after birth (p. 4).

3. Contraction of the internal rectus muscle of the eye (movement of convergence) at a moderately bright impression of light just before the tip of the nose; in the second week (p. 50).

4. Contraction of the inferior rectus muscle of the eye in lowering the gaze when bright light appears below; in the fourth week (p. 44).

5. Contraction of the muscle of accommodation at the approach of bright light to the eye; after the third week (p. 51).

6. Contraction of the sphincter of the iris under the influence of bright light; immediately after birth (pp. 4 and 51).

Anatomy has not yet discovered the paths of connection for any one of these six reflexes from the retina to the muscles of the orbit that are supplied by the motor oculi. And the same thing is true also of the mimetic reflex movements of the infant from the nerve of hearing, smell, and taste to the facial nerve, and from the sensitive nerve of the face to the facial nerve. Microscopic investigation has, in fact, thus far been unable to demonstrate in a single embryonic reflex the two centers—the sensory and motor ganglionic cells— in full development. Complete ganglionic cells have not been seen in the brain till after birth (p. 70). Probably the paths of the embryonic reflexes are still, in general, imperfectly isolated.

CHAPTER XI.

INSTINCTIVE MOVEMENTS.

The instinctive movements of human beings are not numerous, and are difficult to recognize (with the ex- ception of the sexual ones) when once the earliest youth is past. So much the more attentively must the in- stinctive movements of the newly-born and of the infant and of the little child be observed. In order to under- stand them, accurate observation of the instinctive movements of new-born animals is necessary. I will first group and present some statements upon that point.

1. Instinctive Movements of New-born Animals.

Movements unquestionably instinctive are manifested by chickens in the very first hours after leaving the egg —in fact, even while they are still engaged in breaking the shell. For what else was it but such a movement when a chick that had worn an opaque hood from the moment of breaking the shell until the lapse of some days, moved its head, six minutes after it was unhooded, in the right way to follow with its gaze a fly twelve inches distant? After ten minutes the insect came within reaching distance of the neck, and was seized and swallowed at the first effort. At the end of twenty minutes this chick was placed, on uneven ground, at some distance from a hen with which was a chick of the same age as the one under observation, in such a way that it could see and hear the hen. After chirping for about a minute, it ran straight to the hen (Spalding). The very young chick does not invariably succeed in seizing the insect or the kernel, at which it pecks, between its upper and its under mandibles, in such a way that the object can be swallowed, but almost all peck at it. Chickens one day old, and those of several days, according to my observations, often peck six, even nine and ten, times inaccurately, and very often toil in vain, with all sorts of movements of the head (p. 67), even after a successful seizure of the kernel, to swallow it.

Here, then, are in complete development—1. Head-movements at the sight of objects in motion. 2. Pecking, when these objects are capable of being reached. 3. Running or scudding (*Rutschen*), when the cluck of the hen is heard for the first time or she is for the first time seen. 4. Bill- and head-movements, when a small object is got ready for swallowing. All these movements may, indeed, fail to be made, even when the external conditions of their appearance are completely fulfilled, as I have several times seen in chicks from one to three days old hatched in the incubator; but they are not to be looked upon as acquired or voluntary, for they are still new to the chick itself, and are executed without a previous idea of the result. Otherwise, the little creatures would not, as I have seen them do, peck at their own nails. The very young chick, which has never yet seen the movements mentioned, can have no self-acquired idea of them beforehand, because no experience preceded them; but its ancestors had the idea, and the chick itself inherited, without knowing it, a memory-image (Erinnerungsbild) of that. The chick thus acts skillfully, and with seeming intelligence, not out of its own deliberation, but through the inherited association of the sensuous recollection with the motor recollection, not through the idea of the movement itself executed by the creature, this movement being rather involuntary. If the movement be omitted—under external conditions otherwise similar—then, in the concurrence of the inherited sensory-motor associations with one another and with the new connections of sensation and movement arising from individual sense-impressions, another association has appeared in greater force than those spoken of, or a new *feeling* prevails. Likewise the diligent pluming of the down with the bill by the chicken not yet one day old, and the scraping of the head with the foot, that I saw on the third day (the creature never having seen the thing done), and the scratching, appearing on the second day (without a model for imitation), can be nothing else than hereditary, instinctive movements. Spalding says forcibly: " The instinct of present generations is the product of accumulated experiences of past generations. The permanence of such associations in the individual life depends upon the corresponding impression on the nervous system. We can not, strictly speaking, experience any individual fact of consciousness twice; but, as by pulling at the

bell we can produce the same ring that we heard yesterday, so we are capable, as far as the established connection of nerves and nerve-centers holds, of living over
again our experiences. Why should not these modifications of the substance of the brain (which, persisting
from hour to hour, from day to day, make permanent
acquirement possible) pass on from parents to their offspring just like any other physical peculiarity? Instinct
is inherited memory."

It is no objection to this conception of instinct as an
hereditary association that not all the sensory-motor connections of the parents pass over to their posterity. For
very many of them are not firm enough The firmest
in the chicken are the movements of pecking, swallowing, peeping, running, scratching, and scraping, and the
beating with the future wings in scudding forward,
which last I saw very lively in the fourth hour, without
possibility of its being an imitation. Yet some of these
movements, long hereditary, may also vanish, or at least
may not appear, if the external occasions are wanting.
Chickens that were hatched by Allen Thomson upon a
carpet, and were kept on it for some days, showed no
inclination to scratch, because the stimulus that was exercised upon the soles of their feet by the carpet was
new, and was not adapted to set in activity their inherited mechanism for scratching. As soon, however, as
a little gravel was spread upon the carpet, the scraping
began at once (as Romanes reports). We see clearly
from this that chickens do not from the beginning of
their life scratch with the purpose of seeking grains of
seed. For the quite thinly spread gravel could not
furnish the prospect of finding such in the carpet. I

have even seen chickens that were hatched in the incubator, and then brought up in an inclosed space by themselves away from all other fowls, make vigorous scratching movements on smooth white paper without spots, especially in the fourth week of life, as if the brightness of the great surface might be scraped away. The scratching of fowls thus takes place without deliberation, after certain visual and tactile impressions, as a purely instinctive movement, like peeping, pecking, running, and flying.

Swallows do not *learn* to fly; they receive no instruction as to how they have to contract their muscles in order to speed through the air for the first time from the maternal nest, but they fly of themselves. The young redstarts, also, which I have observed daily before they were fledged, receive no directions for flying. But they exercise their wings in the nest before their first attempt at flight, often spreading them and making them whir. The first excursion is slower than the flight of the parents; the young creature flies downward, but it never hits against anything, and after a few days the certainty of its flight is worthy of admiration. Confidence grows with practice.

These flight-movements of quite young birds can not be voluntary movements; they are instinctive, precisely as is the pecking of the chicken that has been hatched a few hours, which, having come into the world alone in the incubator, without mother or companions, in the utmost quiet (without guiding noises), pecks at every single visible object capable of being pecked at, or at a spot or hole in the wooden floor on which the creature stands, as well as at its own nails, with astonishing address. Pecking is not, therefore, according to these observations of mine, set agoing by hearing, as has been suspected, when the noise made by the pecking of the mother was imitated with the finger-nail (Darwin). I have, in fact, observed that chickens between three and twenty hours old, hatched in the incubator, almost all of which had pecked at the yolk and white of egg put before them cut into small bits (after being hard boiled), and were now pausing—I have noticed that, when I let two large fowls close by them pick up the same food upon hard wood, noisily and persistently, the young ones were not in the least affected by the hammering of the bills, although they had hearing, for they started, at sudden loud noises, all simultaneously, like one fowl—a strange sight.

If a drop of water be put on the eye of a chicken on the twenty-first day, before the creature has left the shell, it shakes off the drop briskly, like a hen; put the drop on the tip of the bill, and the chick makes many movements of swallowing, as I often observed.

All these movements are, like pecking, inherited. They appear, in fact, not exceptionally, but very frequently, when nearly the same conditions, internal and external, are fulfilled that were fulfilled when their ancestors executed them—executed them times innumerable. How easily in this case instinctive activity takes on the stamp of great individual intelligence is shown especially in the following observation made by A. Agassiz (1876): Very young hermit-crabs, not long after leaving the egg, rush with extraordinary animation for suitable shells that are given to them in the water. They examine the opening at the mouth, and

take up their quarters inside with remarkable alacrity.
But, if it chances that the shells are still occupied by
mollusks, then they stay close by the opening, and wait
till the snail dies, which generally occurs soon after the
beginning of the imprisonment and the strict watch.
Upon this the small crab pulls out the carcass, devours
it, and moves into the lodging himself. What fore-
sight! On account of the preference of the empty
shells, the whole proceeding can not be hereditary. But
the young animals are not instructed. They were from
the beginning separated from their parents, and had no
time or opportunity for experiences of their own. They
must, therefore, have inherited their practice of waiting
from their ancestors, as a rule of conduct for the case
where a shell is occupied, and they can at once distinguish such a one from an empty one.

Now, precisely as it is true of these animals that are
sagacious in one direction, and of the chicken, and, in
general, of all animals, that they come into the world
with a good share of inherited memory for movements
(p. 71)—i. e., with instinctive motility (Motilität)—so it
will be true of the human child. Which of its movements are instinctive? First, seizing.

2. Development of Seizing.

Of all movements of the infant in the first half-year,
no one is of greater significance for its mental development than are the seizing movements. I have on this
account observed these with special attention.

It is supposed by many that the moving of the
hands hither and thither in the first days of life is a
kind of seizing, since the fingers are carried not only

to the face, but also to the mouth. Such a view is irreconcilable with the ordinary meaning of the word *seize* and with the facts. For seizing presupposes the perception of an object desired, and, in addition, a control of the muscles, both of which are wanting in the first days.

The first putting of the hand into the mouth has nothing in common with the later seizing, except that it requires a movement of the arm. The hand is not even *carried* to the face, but, in its random movements about, it gets to and into the mouth, as well as elsewhere, which, on account of the position of the arms in the fœtus long before birth, seems perfectly natural. Newborn children, left to themselves, keep this attitude, and move their hands to the face and to the lips, as they must have done already before birth. If the lips are touched, then sucking movements readily appear in the hungry infant; therefore nothing of purpose can be found in the early sucking of the child at its own fingers (observed by Kussmaul on the first, by me on the fifth, day), which is followed later by the biting of the fingers. The position of the arms and hands in the uterus is conditioned by the restricted space. Every other position would involve an enlargement of the superficies of the fœtus.

It appears, therefore, that we are not justified in seeing in the first approximation of the hand to the mouth, the beginning of seizing-movements. In the first days of his life the infant moves his hands about his face and into his eyes, in a very different way from that of seizing, which comes later as a gesture expressing a desire. Young infants, whose fingers have accident-

ally, in the random movements of the arms, come to
the mouth, are not able, if anybody takes the fingers
away, to put them to the mouth again. Nay, even if
some one carries their fingers to their lips for them, the
infants can not hold their own fingers there, in case
gravity makes the arm drop (Genzmer). Later, however,
babes are often seen to suck at their own fingers in sleep.

Neither does the fact that the infant, as I noted on
the ninth day, when he is sleeping, does not, as he does
when awake, clasp my fingers placed in his hand—
neither does this fact indicate a seizing as a purposive
movement; but the clasping is to be regarded as a reflex, just like the spreading of the toes when the sole of
the foot is touched (pp. 104, 224). The proof of this I
see herein, that the older child—e. g., of seventeen
months—when I put my finger in the hollow of his
hand during his sleep, does not clasp it either, but when
I move my finger with a gentle rubbing movement
back and forth upon the flat of his hand, he often
clasps it quickly, almost convulsively, with his fingers,
without waking. The foot behaves like the hand in
this respect, in the earliest period, as it responds less
readily in sleep. The absence of the clasping in sleep
is thus to be ascribed simply to the insufficient excitement of the nerves of the skin, and the diminution of
the reflex excitability in sleep; in no case is the clasping of the finger, by a child that is awake, intentional
within the first two weeks.

The first grasping at objects, with manifest desire to
have them, was seen by Sigismund in a boy nineteen
weeks old; by me, in a girl in her eighteenth week,
and in my boy in his seventeenth week.

The contraposition of the thumb, an indispensable condition to the completion of the act of seizing—which is said to be an easy matter for young monkeys, even within the first week of life—is very slowly learned by the human child, as I noticed; he does not learn at all to place the great-toe opposite the other toes. It is a question, indeed, whether human beings born without arms, can learn to use the great-toe as a thumb, as the quadrumana do. I once saw a young man without arms make a drawing with his foot. But in doing it the pencil was held between the great-toe and the second, without contraposition, as one would hold it between the forefinger and the middle finger, in case one wanted to draw or write without the help of the thumb. Adults succeed easily in doing the latter, even without practice.

Having the opinion that possibly at the beginning of life seizing might be done with the great-toe as with the thumb, I tested hands and feet in the case of my boy in the earliest period, and I present here my observations concerning the development of seizing, in chronological order:

First to third day: movements with the hands to the face predominate.

On the fourth day, a pencil was decidedly not held firmly by the foot.

On the fifth day his fingers clasp my finger very firmly; his toes do not. For the rest, his hands often move to the face, at random, without getting hold of it.

On the sixth day, the same. The hands even go into the eye.

On the seventh day, it appears that a thin pencil is

held with the great-toe and the other toes exactly as with the thumb and fingers. But in this there is no seizing; of a contraposition of the thumb there is just as little to be observed as of the great-toe, but in case of convenient position of the pencil between thumb and forefinger, and between the great-toe and its neighbor, fingers as well as toes are vigorously bent and the object is held.

On the ninth day the finger is not clasped by the sleeping child.

In the third to seventh weeks, the child has not yet clasped my finger with his thumb, but only with his fingers.

In the eighth week I am convinced that the thumb is still put around the pencil, as the fingers are, but it may more easily than before be bent passively for seizing, so that my finger is held firmly. The four fingers of the child's hand, directly without co-operation of the thumb, embrace my finger when I put it in the hollow of the hand of the child.

Up to the eleventh week no noticeable advance. If I put a pencil into the child's hand, he holds it firmly, indeed, but without heeding it (without knowing it, one would say of an adult, i. e., mechanically, as in absen' of mind), and can not perfectly use the thumb clasping. Another child, of exactly the same age, could not even clasp and hold the stick that was put into his hand.

End of the twelfth week: when the child was moving his hands about in the air, it often happened that my finger, held near, came into one of the little hands. On the eighty-fourth day I saw, in connection with this,

18

for the first time, a placing of the thumb opposite, so that it looked just as if the child had purposely seized the finger, which was not presented to him, but merely held motionless within reach, and allowed to follow passively the movements of the child's arm hither and thither. This experiment was repeated several times on the same day, with like result. Then first I gained the firm conviction that the contraposition of the thumb and the seizing of the finger, followed reflexively, without intention, as a consequence of the cutaneous stimulus occasioned by the contact.

In the thirteenth week, the thumb already follows more readily the bending fingers, when a pencil is put into the child's hand.

In the fourteenth week, seizing that is undoubtedly intentional is not yet present, but the little hand holds objects that come accidentally into it, or that are put into it, longer and more firmly than at an earlier period, and with a decided contraposition of the thumb, by which many have doubtless been misled to suppose that "proper grasping at objects" begins in this week—a thing which certainly is not universally true. I, at least, detected no trace of intentional seizing after objects seen, in the fifteenth and sixteenth weeks, and on the one hundred and fourteenth day. While the babe is nursing, however, a finger is reflexively clasped by thumb and fingers more often than formerly. Others, also, whose attention I directed to this point, confirm my opinion that in the third month seizing is merely apparent. It does not begin, as Vierordt also found, before the fourth month.

In the seventeenth week (one hundred and seventeenth day) I saw for the first time earnest efforts to take hold of an object with the hand.   It was a small rubber ball that was within seizing distance, but the child missed it.   When now it was put into his hand he held it for a long time very firmly and moved it to his mouth and *to his eyes*, and that with a peculiar, new, more intelligent expression of countenance.   On the following day, the awkward but energetic attempts to seize upon all sorts of objects held before the child were more frequent.   He fixated the object—e. g., my fin-ger—and grasped three times in succession at an object distant twice his arm's length from him, (p. 55)—and also fixated his own hand (cf. p. 109), especially when this had once successfully seized.   His expression of countenance meantime indicated great attention. Again, after a day, the repeated grasping at every-thing that comes within reach of the arms seems to give the child pleasure.   But wonder is mingled with it, for—

In the eighteenth week, in the attempts to seize, when they fail, his own fingers are attentively regard-ed.   Probably the child has expected the sensation of contact, or if it occurred has wondered at the nov-elty of the sensation of touch.   He continues to hold firmly, regard, and carry to the mouth objects once seized.   But at this time the outstretching of the arms, as if to seize, becomes also the expression of the strongest desire.   On the one hundred and twenty-first day the child, for the first time, stretched out both arms toward me at the morning greeting, and that with an indescribable expression of longing.   On the day before, nothing of this sort was yet to be perceived.   The progress from grasping at inanimate things to grasping at members of the family came suddenly.

In the nineteenth week the child took a bit of meat that was offered to him on the point of a fork and carried it with his hand to his mouth.

In the thirty-second week seizing with both hands, at the same time directing the line of vision to the object, was more sure and more frequent than before, the attention at the same time being more active. The child lying on his back, raises himself without help to a sitting posture and bends over forward, reaching out with both hands to lay hold of anything that is before him. The straining of the attention expresses itself especially by the protruding of the lips, which I saw besides on the one hundred and twenty-third day for the first time, in connection with the act of seizing.

During all this time the seizing is still imperfect, as the four fingers do not all work in harmony with the thumb. When the child sees an object that he wants, he generally spreads out all the fingers of both hands while stretching out the arms. But when he has clasped the pencil or my finger, it often happens that in doing so the thumb and one finger only are employed; frequently the thumb with two fingers or with three or with all. Very often, too, the co-operation of the thumb is entirely wanting. But the ability to seize accurately with thumb and fingers is so far developed that nothing more is wanting but the co-ordinating will to do it in every suitable case. Thus far it depends much more on the situation and form of the object and on the accident of the position of the hand, than it does on the purpose, how many and what fingers, as they bend in the act of seizing, actually take part in this act.

In the thirtieth week the seizing was noticeably quicker and more perfect, but the lack of certainty in getting hold of objects seized was still great. The hands still often pass by the object gazed at, with fingers spread. Grasping at objects at the distance of a metre becomes more frequent. Very often, probably always, whenever form, color, or luster has excited the child's gratification, the thing seized is at once carried to the mouth, the tongue is put far out, and the object licked. Probably we have here a case of primitive logical inference; up to this time sucking and tasting were the most important strong, agreeable, sensations the young being has known; when, therefore, he has a new agreeable sensation (e. g., of a bright color, a round, smooth body, a soft surface), it is brought into association with the lips and tongue, through which the pleasurable feeling at taking in the sweet milk was received.

The quick moving of the hands to a new object presented for the first time—e. g., a brush—must unquestionably be interpreted as a sign of desire. The parts of his own body, moreover, appear to the child as foreign objects. For in the thirty-second week, as he lies on his back, he likes to stretch his legs up vertically, and observes the feet attentively as he does other objects held before him. Then he grasps with the hands at his own feet, and often *carries his toes to his mouth with his hand.*

The child also expresses interest, by protruding the lips, his gaze being firmly directed to the object seized, presumably in the now discovered fact that the thing be-

fore seen and desired is at the same time the thing which
is touched, and which yields new sensations. The bright,
colored, long, short, appears now to him as also smooth,
rough, warm, cold, hard, soft, heavy, light, wet, dry,
sticky, slippery. The combination of two departments
of sense in one object gratifies. Such an object is likewise his own foot seen and touched. In case the object
seen and touched stands immovably firm, and so can not,
like the ball and the toes, be brought to the mouth, the
child tries, notwithstanding, in unmistakable fashion, to
get hold of it, to pull it to him, and to bring it to his
mouth, the source of his greatest feeling of pleasure, no
matter whether it is large or small. At the same time
it often happens, as I perceived to my astonishment on
the occasion of his taking hold of a firmly-standing carved
post, that the child (borne upon the arm) draws himself
with the arms to the desired object and puts his mouth
close up to it. The pleasure obtained in this way, also,
through the touching of the object seen, which is the occasion of renewed seizing movements, is probably likewise
the occasion of the desire to taste it. For now, after
the nursing-bottle is presented to the child, he grasps
at it with his hand; whereas he used to suck at it with
arms inactive, he now tries to hold it fast, sometimes
with the expression of eagerness. In this case the remembrance of the taste, or what in this regard amounts
to the same thing, the gratification in the appeasing of
hunger, stimulates the seizing movement. The order
of succession originally is: tasting, then tasting and
seeing, then seeing and desiring, tasting and desiring
more, thereupon seeing, seizing, tasting. Through
repetition of these associations, probably, the remem-

brance of the taste has, as it were, become amalgamated with seeing and seizing in general, until experience has taught that the things touched and seized have no taste or have a bad taste.

It is worthy of notice in this connection, that precisely during the first attempts at seizing, the greatest strain of attention, along with protrusion of the lips was observed, and later—in the thirty-fourth week, when the seizing was done more quickly—the mouth was opened before or directly after the seizing and then the object was put into it. At the first attempts the putting into the mouth followed without being intended beforehand, but now the hand is stretched out with the purpose of bringing the thing seen to the mouth, and the mouth is open ; here it is to be borne in mind that the very thing that excites pleasure, the nursing-bottle, was especially often carried to the mouth. If the child at this period and afterward was allowed to carry a crust of bread to the mouth without assistance, it was often seen that in spite of accuracy in laying hold of the crust, it was carried not into the already-opened mouth, but against the cheek, chin, or nose—an uncertainty of touch that appeared still in the first attempts to eat with a small spoon, in the seventeenth month.

Failure to grasp, grasping too short, and grasping at objects very far off, disappear so gradually that I can not assign a definite period of disappearance.

Neither could it be ascertained at what time the putting of the fingers into the mouth and the grasping at the face without getting hold of any part of it ceased. Invariably, shortly before and after a tooth comes through, the child moves his fingers about in the mouth a good deal, keeping three or four fingers in the mouth. When alleviation had been experienced several times through chewing of the fingers, these no longer went accidentally—after moving about the hands in the air at random—but went regularly during teething into the mouth; and it must come, finally, through frequent repetition of the movement, to a reflex process, as the hand is brought near to every approachable place that feels pain. The first experience that biting the fingers, even before the teeth are there, moderates the pain or the tickling, appears as a consequence of the putting of the hand into the mouth; other painful impressions likewise become, therefore, later, the occasion of movements of the hand which may simulate seizing-movements.

In the forty-third week the child without help not only grasps properly with both hands at a nursing-bottle, but carries it correctly to the mouth; the same with a biscuit lying before him. He pulls strongly at the beard of a face that he can reach.

On the other hand, he grasped at the flame of the lamp in the forty-fifth week; in the forty-seventh, and later, at objects separated from him by a pane of glass, as if they were attainable, and that persistently, with attention and eagerness, as if the pane were not there. The discovery of the transparency of glass, which assuredly appears wonderful to every child, requires many such fruitless attempts at seizing.

The greatest progress in the movement of the muscles of the arm manifested itself at just this time, in the fact that often very small shreds of paper on the floor were grasped at and deftly laid hold of by thumb and forefinger. But precisely this frequent play with the bits of paper afforded occasion to observe the above-mentioned uncertainty of the sense of touch when unsupported by sight. For whereas before this, when the child used to take pleasure in biting pieces out of a newspaper, these had to be taken out of his mouth by some one, in the fourteenth month he could be allowed to bite the paper to pieces undisturbed, because he now of himself took out of his mouth with his right hand every piece he had bitten off, and handed it to me. In connection with this, I made the observation that the shred of paper in the mouth on or near the lips was not always found by the child when he touched with the tips of his fingers. Without the guidance of the sense of sight, therefore, touch was still quite imperfect. Both senses united, on the other hand, did astonishing things even much earlier than this, in spite of the failure to grasp, especially the failure to grasp far enough, as late as the second year (p. 55), and the numerous attempts to get hold of what could not be laid hold of (p. 63). Thus I saw the child, at the age of ten months, amuse himself, entirely of his own accord, by taking deliberately from one hand into the other a long hair that he had found on the carpet, and by gazing at it.

Of the many thousand nerve-fibers and muscle-fibers that must come into harmonious activity in order that such a movement may take place, the child knows nothing, but he directs already the whole nervo-muscular mechanism with his will, which was generated by desire. Before he is capable of this, the sensuous stimulus that starts the seizing-movements must have been repeated many hundreds of times, so that one and the same sensation often returned, an agreeable feeling arose, a perception at first indistinct, then gradually more and more distinct, and finally an idea of the objectivity of the thing seizable could be formed. Secondly, the movement of the arm, also, which, before as well as after birth, is directed to the mouth or the face, must have been very often repeated before it came to consciousness—i. e., before an idea of it could be formed, because in the beginning it was not perceived at all by the child. When, however, the desired object is represented in idea, and the movement of the arm is represented, the rapid succession of both representations favors their union, which calls into life the will. In fact, the distinct representation of the movement is not required any more at a later period, provided only that the aim is clearly recognized. Too much importance has often been attributed to the representation of the movement, the representation not being necessary beforehand except for a new purposive movement; this mistake has been made by W. Gude and Lotze; the representation of the aim remains the principal thing. For many voluntary movements—e. g., those of the eyes—are generally not clearly represented beforehand, at any period, while the end and aim of them fill the consciousness. At that time the kind of movement necessary to the attainment of the aim is known only in a general way.

But, in order to be able to execute a simple voluntary movement, such as reaching after objects, similar movements must previously have been often executed involuntarily, because only through these can muscular sensations or sensations of innervation be developed.

These are, however, necessary pioneers for the voluntary motor impulses, and they play an important part in other movements also besides the voluntary ones of the child and of the adult, viz., the instinctive ones. For the memory-images of the innervation-sensations, or muscular sensations, which the contraction of the muscle in contrast with its repose brings with it, determine which muscles are to be contracted, and how strongly each is to be contracted, after the kind of movement to be executed is settled upon.

Now, if the repetition of a voluntary movement—e. g., a seizing movement—occurs very often, then the turning to account of those memory-images is hastened and simplified to such a degree that, without the co-operation of the brain-sensorium, the brain-motorium alone sets the muscles in activity after a sensory impression has acted upon it. Herein consists the chief characteristic of the cerebro-motor acquired reflexes; to these belongs also the grasping at a hat caught by a gust of wind, at a later period of life.

But, on the other hand, in dreams—e. g., with the child (and with the hypnotic subject) after exclusion of the will—the sensory impression may affect only the brain-sensorium in such a way that complex movements go on just as if they were voluntary. Such movements Carpenter has called ideo-motor movements. The cerebral-motor impulses are accordingly not purely reflexive, as are those of the spinal reflexes, for in the latter no center of higher rank, no brain-sensorium, no brain-motorium, is originally concerned.

Moreover, for both these last there comes into consideration a cerebral inhibitory apparatus, which, wanting to the infant, arrests more and more easily, with his increasing development, the voluntary, or ideo-motor or purely reflexive (spinal-motor) movement that follows the sensory impression, and becomes manifest at the period when self-control begins.

That movement of the quite young child, which from the beginning is commonly called " seizing," originates, accordingly, in the following manner:

The moving of the hands hither and thither, especially to the face, is inborn, impulsive, determined by the position of the child within the womb.

The clasping of the finger laid in the hand in the first days is purely reflexive.

Then follows the "absent-minded " (in the adult) or "mechanical" holding fast of objects put into the hand as an unconscious, instinctive movement (in the adult, a movement that has become unconscious or no longer conscious; in the child, a movement not yet conscious).

Next is observed the holding fast of the object with contraposition of the thumb, when the object is so situated that the hand, moving hither and thither, accidentally grasps it. As the thumb now co-operates, the pure reflex has become complicated, and the central separation of the previously united impulses has been attained. As the holding-fast lasts much longer than in case of the reflex, and the attention, although only very imperfectly and transiently, is directed to the new experience of holding fast, the movement has now no longer taken place without the consciousness of the cerebral sensorium, but it is not yet voluntary; this kind of primitive holding-fast (not seizing) still approximates to the instinctive (ideo-motor) movements.

In the seventeenth to the nineteenth weeks the participation of the will of the brain-motorium in this act begins to attain its full force; the child does not yet stretch out its arm, but wills to hold fast the object that has accidentally come into his hand. He looks at it and forms an idea of it. From this fixation of the held object to the seizing of the object fixated is only a step. With that, willed-seizing is present, since the path of connection is at last passable from the brain-sensorium to the brain-motorium.

Years now pass before this seizing, which is indispensable for the development of the understanding (i. e., for having experiences) is perfected, and the voluntary inhibition of it by new, chiefly inculcated ideas, becomes possible.

Most of the voluntary inhibitions, the first acts of self-control, come into existence at a period that lies outside of the scheme of this exposition.

3. Sucking, Biting, Chewing, Teeth-Grinding, Licking.

Sucking belongs to the earliest co-ordinated movements of man; it is associated directly with swallowing, and has been repeatedly perceived even before the child was fully born, in case an object that could be sucked got into the mouth, and upon the upper surface of the tongue, at the same time touching the lips. When (December, 1870) I touched with my finger the tongue of a child, born at the right time, and moved my finger to and fro, or turned it on the upper surface of the tongue, three minutes after the head had emerged —the child was already crying feebly as soon as the mouth was free—the babe immediately stopped crying and sucked briskly, but not when I merely touched the lips or put the finger between them. Without doubt, every normal child has become acquainted with the swallowing of the amniotic fluid before birth, but has hardly sucked as yet at his own fingers. Still, it is a matter of absolute indifference, for the performance of the act of sucking, whether liquid comes into the cavity of the mouth or not, and the sucking for hours at empty rubber-bottles—a vicious, highly reprehensible practice —encouraged in Thuringia for the purpose of keeping infants quiet, shows, just as the sucking at cloths and at the fingers a few minutes after birth (according to Champneys) shows, that swallowing is not required for prolonged sucking. Yet under normal conditions, swallowing is the muscular action that attaches itself directly to sucking.

Of what kind is this movement, which is to so high a degree indicative of adaptation to an end? As human abortions without brain, and puppies without a cerebrum, can suck, the participation of the intellect, any choice or purpose, is excluded in advance. But since in the normal condition only the hungry, or, at least, only the not completely satisfied infant, sucks (the one that is full rejecting the nipple forcibly), we have here something other than a purely reflex movement. For the absence of the sucking movement can not be ascribed in the satisfied child to fatigue caused by previous sucking, because frequently the act is not renewed for a long time after the previous sucking has been finished. No more is it an impulsive movement, since it appears, in the waking condition at the beginning, only after lips, or tongue, or palate are touched by

an object capable of being sucked. The sucking movements of sleeping (dreaming) infants with empty, untouched mouth, however, show that the act may arise
from purely central causes, after it has once been ini-
tiated through peripheral stimuli.

Accordingly, sucking must be classed among the instinctive movements. A scruple concerning this may
easily be removed.

It has been maintained that young animals easily
forget how to suck, if they omit sucking for some days.
Such an assertion, however, relates either to such animals (like Guinea-pigs) as at the very beginning of life
bite and chew, digest other food than milk, and soon
have no more need to suck; or to the unlearning of
sucking at the breast, which is somewhat less easily accomplished than is sucking from the bottle. In both
cases, therefore, the question is not of a forgetting of
the act of sucking—an act which yields great pleasure
to older children also, as is well known, and even to
adults (in smoking).

Of all the movements of the " suckling," hardly any
is so perfect from the beginning as that which gave
him this name. It is not so productive on the first
day, indeed, as on the second; in fact, I found the
efforts at sucking in the first hour of life, with healthy,
new-born children, often quite devoid of effect (1869);
when an ivory pencil was put into the mouth, they
were found also non-coördinated; but again they may be
quite regular, and, as has been mentioned, effectual, at
the very moment of birth; they are based, therefore,
on hereditary movements, which take place after two
weeks with machine-like regularity, without imitation

or training, and without other movements, except swallowing. The intermissions in sucking that occur with shorter intervals in the first days of life than at a later period, depend in part upon fatigue, in part upon the quicker filling of the little stomach, where the milk itself is not of unsuitable quality. On the other hand, I once saw a babe of seven days (not fully satisfied, no doubt) after ceasing to suck, keep up the movements of the mouth as in sucking.

It has long been known that children do not at once find the nipple without help, when they are placed at the breast, but only after several days (in one case not till the eighth day), thus later than is the case with animals. Like the latter, the very young child, before the nipple is put into the mouth, makes lateral movements of the head, which sometimes look like a groping about; the opening wide of the eyes before being placed at the breast and the keeping of them open during the nursing (very surprising in the first week, in a light not glaring) has, however, no connection with the finding of the nipple, since even those born blind, it appears, are no later in finding it. The action of the eyes is rather, in the first week, simply the expression of pleasurable feeling (pp. 32 and 143).

It often happens that, when the child is placed at the breast, the nipple does not get into the mouth; but the child sucks hard at the skin near it as late as the third week—a proof of the lack of discernment at this period. Yet the connection of the breast, as a whole, with nursing is known, for as early as the twenty-second day I saw the babe open wide its mouth at a distance of an inch and a half from the nipple. That the sense of smell is less decisive in the matter than the sense of sight is proved beyond question by observations upon infants whose eyes are bandaged, and upon those born blind. In animals born blind (dogs), the sense of smell is, on the contrary, recognized as an indispensable guide. The stretching out of the arms and the straining open of the eyes by the older infant, at sight of the breast at a distance, is against the participation of the smell. In the first period, the nipple is probably found by means of the sense of touch in the lips.

Besides, the sense of touch plays an important part in even the act of nursing, from the beginning. For it is not any object whatever put into the mouth that is sucked, but only certain objects, not too large, not too rough, not too hot or too cold, and not of a strongly bitter, or sour, or salt taste. In general, hungry children suck at their own fingers from the first days; if they are not hungry, they like to hold the fingers in the mouth, especially when teething, without sucking at them, and in the bath they suck at a sponge (in the eighth month), which they hold to the lips like a piece of bread.

Biting is not less instinctive than sucking. In the tenth month my child no longer sucked at the finger put into his mouth, but bit it almost invariably. Yet I can not give the exact date at which biting begins and sucking at the finger first ceases. In the seventeenth week the finger was already plainly bitten—i. e., compressed firmly between the toothless jaws; in the eleventh and twelfth months the child seized my hand, carried it to his mouth, and bit the skin till it hurt, as he did in general with the fingers of others which he

19

himself put into his mouth. Just so he tried at this period to bite to pieces a cube of solid glass. In the tenth month he had learned without instruction to crunch, with his four teeth, bread, which he then swallowed. After his teeth came, almost everything desirable was brought into contact with them as far as this was possible, and was then bitten, and he liked to smack his lips (eleventh month).

Before the infant gets his first tooth, he already makes frequent movements of chewing, which are especially multiplied after a hard bread-crust has been put into the mouth. The flow of blood that is increased before the teeth come through is, toward the end of the first three months, when driveling has begun, doubtless associated with disagreeable sensations, which are referred to the gum. But the fact that the toothless babe makes perfect chewing-movements—he who has never had in his mouth an object capable of being chewed, except his own fingers, that have often got in there—goes to prove that the function of chewing comes into activity, without practice, as soon as the requisite nerves and muscles and the center are developed. Chewing is a purely hereditary function; it is instinctive.

Another movement, absolutely original, and probably practiced for a while by all teething babes, is grinding the teeth. In the ninth month it affords the child great satisfaction to rub an upper and a lower incisor together, so as to be heard at the distance of a metre. The infant seems to be interested in the sudden appearance of his teeth in quick succession. For he makes comical movements of the mouth—e. g., protrudes both lips far out, makes perfect chewing-movements, and performs gymnastics with the tongue without the utterance of sound. But the grinding is practiced chiefly with four teeth.

Another movement that belongs here is absolutely original — licking. If this were not innate, how could the new-born human child within the first twenty-four hours of its life lick sugar? I have myself observed it, and have also seen licking for milk on the second and third days, and that hardly less adroit than in the seventh month. At this period not only are desired objects, whether stationary or seized, stroked with the tongue, but the lips of the mother in kissing; and, *vice versa*, the tongue is stroked with the objects.

All the movements of the infant here enumerated — sucking, biting, smacking, chewing, tooth-grinding, licking — must be designated as typical instinctive movements, like the pecking of the chicken. All are useful to him, for even the grinding with the first teeth is of use in making the child familiar with them. All are hereditary and involuntary.

4. Holding the Head.

All new-born children, and chickens just hatched, probably all new-born mammals, and all birds just hatched, are unable to hold the head up and to keep it balanced. It falls forward, to the left or the right, even backward, when it is held up straight by some one else. In this respect the helplessness of the human child is not greater than that of the chick hardly clear of the shell; but the latter learns in a few hours to control better the muscles required for holding the head than the child does in many weeks.

This muscular activity is especially adapted to help us in following the growth of the child's will. For weakness of the muscles can not be the cause of the inability to balance the head, because other movements of the head are quickly executed. At the end of the first and at the beginning of the second week I saw the babe, on being placed at the breast, continually make vigorous lateral movements of the head, which are made in like fashion by very young Guinea-pigs, calves, foals, and other animals in sucking. But during the first ten weeks no trace could be discovered, in the case of my boy, of an attempt to hold the head in equilibrium. In the eleventh week the head no longer bobs about, absolutely unsteady, when the child is made to sit up straight, but rather is balanced occasionally, although very imperfectly as yet. In the twelfth week the head often falls forward, also backward and sidewise, and is only for moments in equilibrium; yet a gain may be perceived from day to day in this respect, as the short duration of the holding erect becomes daily somewhat longer on the average. In the thirteenth week the head falls but seldom to one side, even when it is entirely free; rather is it for the most part tolerably well balanced. In the fourteenth week (in the case of another child not till the twenty-first) it falls forward also, but seldom (when the child is held up straight), and in the sixteenth week the bobbing of the head has altogether ceased; the holding up of the head is now settled for life.

In this important step is expressed an unquestionable, vigorous act of will. For the contractions of the muscles that balance the head are at first not willed; they are not reflexive, not imitative, but impulsive, and then, as the purpose of them soon becomes discernible, they are instinctive. The benefit of these contractions is not recognized by the infant, but the muscular feelings that go with them are distinguished from other muscular feelings by their agreeable consequences; since, for example, the child can see better when the head is erect, and food can be taken more conveniently; therefore, these muscular contractions are preferred. Among all possible positions of the head, then, that of equilibrium gradually appears oftenest in the upright position of children, because it is the most advantageous, and when children establish it we say they possess *will.* Adults let the head fall when they go to sleep sitting, just as infants do when awake. Their will is extinguished when they cease to be awake. There is thus, during the waking period, a certain outlay of will permanently necessary for balancing the head, and the new-born and the very young child, though awake, do not yet possess this small quantum of will. We may, therefore, without hesitation, refer the period of the first distinct manifestation of activity of will in the infant in this field to that week in which the head, while he is awake, no longer bobs hither and thither—i. e., the sixteenth week in the case of my child, the only one accurately observed as yet; in general, the fourth to the fifth month. R. Demme observed—not so accurately, to be sure—one hundred and fifty children in reference to this, and found that " very powerfully-developed infants carry the head properly balanced as early as toward the end of the third or within the first half of the fourth month of life; children moderately strong do this for the first time in the course of the second half of the fourth

month ; and more delicate individuals that fall somewhat below the normal standard in their nutrition do
not attain to this before the fifth or the beginning of
the sixth month of life." The statement of Heyfelder,
that even after six or eight weeks attempts were made
to hold the head erect, I can not confirm.

Observations are lacking, also, concerning the first
attempts of the infant, who at the beginning lies
straight or keeps the position it had before birth, to
lie on the side. One child did not accomplish it until
the fourth month, and only by great effort. When I
laid my boy, in the ninth and tenth months, on a pillow
face downward, the unusual position seemed to be extremely uncomfortable to him. He behaved in a very
awkward fashion, but turned over without any help, so
that after a minute or so he lay on his back again, or
supported himself on his hands. Something similar to
this happened, however, even in the sixth week of life.
The infant, when laid upon a pillow face downward,
propped himself even at that time on his forearms,
turning his head meantime to one side, without crying, thus exchanging the uncomfortable attitude for
one less uncomfortable. But in this there is as yet no
choice.

In the first three months no voluntary movement
appears. New-born children can not so much as free
the face by turning the head when any one covers
the face with his hand or lays them on a pillow with
the face downward. They cry and move the extremities
aimlessly, so that it can not be told with certainty
whether the new position is agreeable to them or not.
Some of them, indeed, retain for some time, without

moving, every position that is given to them—a thing which I have observed also in new-born animals.

5. Learning to Sit.

The first successful efforts to sit alone are referred (by Ploss) to the fourth month, or (by Sigismund) to the period from the seventeenth to the twenty-sixth week. Heyfelder also states that vigorous children of five to six months sit with the whole of the upper part of the body erect. R. Demme found, on the other hand, that very powerfully developed children, " without specially remarkable strain of their muscular powers, could sit all alone toward the end of the seventh or at the beginning of the eighth month for several minutes." Those of moderate strength did not achieve the same thing till the ninth and tenth months; weakly ones in the eleventh and twelfth months.

With my child, who was vigorous, we succeeded with surprising ease in the first attempt to have him take a sitting posture contrived for him so that his back would be well supported. This was in the fourteenth week. In the twenty-second week the child actually raised himself to a sitting posture when he wanted to grasp at my face; but it was not till the thirty-ninth week that he could sit alone for any length of time; then he liked sitting, but not without a support. Even in his baby-carriage he needed that (in the fortieth and forty-first week still) in order to keep sitting. But although he could sit only for moments, at most, without any support, yet he always kept trying, manifestly to his own gratification, to maintain his equilibrium.

Finally, in the forty-second week the child sits up,

naked in the bath, without support, holding his back straight; so likewise in the carriage, where the clothes, coverings, and pillows essentially facilitate the balancing. The more difficult sitting upright in the bath, with its smooth sides, demands in the following period his entire attention. So long as his attention is not claimed by fresh impressions, the child does not fall to one side. He gains day by day in certainty in maintaining his equilibrium, so that after some days he sits for a full minute undressed in the bath, or in the carriage, without any support. From the eleventh month on, sitting becomes a habit for life.

In the beginning there appears along with this a peculiarity that is also found in monkeys, as was brought into notice by Lauder Brunton (1881). When, viz., little children are allowed to sit alone on the floor, they turn the soles of the feet toward each other, a habit that perhaps comes from the position of the legs before birth; for every child, when it is left to itself, undressed and unswathed, in a warm bed, takes for a long time after birth an attitude resembling the intra-uterine attitude—legs drawn up and arms bent and drawn in.

The sitting apparatus used by different nations in earlier times and at present—children's chairs with and without provision for locomotion—have been described by H. Ploss in his book "The Little Child from the Cushion to the First Step" ("Das Kleine Kind vom Tragbett bis zum ersten Schritt," 1881), and illustrated with cuts. These contrivances all serve rather the convenience of those who have the care of the child than that of the child itself. In fact, they are injurious when used too early. It is an important rule in orthopedy and in pedagogy that no child be habituated to a sitting posture before he has of himself raised himself with the upper part of the body from the recumbent position, in attempts to seize objects, *without aid*—in other words, before he *wills* to sit.

That the time at which this is done is, as appears from the above statements of different observers, very different with different children—the earliest time being generally in the fourth and the latest in the twelfth month—is explained in part by the premature attempts of the relatives to bring on the sitting by artificial means; in part by imitation, where brothers and sisters are growing up together—the latter, however, applies only to the later stages; in part, finally, through muscular weakness also, unequal nourishment, lack of care, or neglect. But, apart from all these influences, variation in the statements about the first sitting is caused also by different conceptions on the part of the observers. The attempt to sit is still very far removed from actual sitting; and this difference has been often overlooked.

6. Learning to Stand.

The first successful attempts to stand, in which my child stood on his feet without support, but only for a moment, were made in the thirty-ninth week. In the following weeks he needed only slight aid, and he seemed to prefer to occupy himself with learning to stand rather than with learning to sit, although it must have been more of a strain upon him.

In the eleventh month he can stand without any support, and even stamps with his foot, but for all that he is not at all sure on his feet. Only when chairs that

offer support, or watchful arms are close by, is the upright posture maintained longer than a moment. In fact,
until some time after the first year of life has been
completed, the child does not stand for a longer time
than that, except when he leans back in a corner. I
have not ascertained that in the numerous attempts, repeated daily, to have him stand, he actually fell down a
single time in the first year; and yet he gave us exactly
the impression of being afraid of falling, as soon as he
was to stand without leaning or being held. Finally,
however, at the beginning of the second year, the child
could stand for some moments without a hand to hold
him. Then he gained gradually more confidence in
himself through his efforts to walk, which were undertaken at the same time.

A little girl, who in the nineteenth week had raised
herself for the first time alone to a sitting posture,
could from the eleventh month on hold herself upright
for some moments without any help, and could get up
alone; her sister could do it from the tenth month (Frau
von Strümpell).

R. Demme found that only very vigorous children
were able, at about the thirty-fifth to the thirty-eighth
weeks of life, with slight support (given by taking hold
of their hands or arms) to stand for some minutes; and
not before the fortieth to the forty-second week could
they stand entirely unsupported for two or three minutes.
Children of moderate strength arrived at this only about
the forty-fifth to the forty-eighth week; those more
feeble not till the twelfth month or later. These observations relate to one hundred and fifty Swiss children.

Sigismund puts the date of the first attempts to stand

at the eighteenth to the twenty-sixth week. "At that time children like much to stand, if they are grasped under the arms." But standing without support does not begin before the seventh month, and generally begins after the eighth.

Imitation co-operates in this, for in families in which several children grow up together the younger ones usually learn to stand somewhat earlier than the first-born does.

7. Learning to Walk.

Learning to walk is mysterious in its beginnings, because the reason for the alternate bending and stretching of the legs at the first placing of the infant upright is not apparent to him. But the possibility of learning to walk rests solely on the invariably repeated lifting and putting down of the feet by the child when standing or held erect. The flexions and extensions occur, to be sure, when the child is lying down, in bed or in the bath; but the regular bending and stretching which appear even months before the first successful attempt to walk, when the child, held upright on the floor, is pushed forward, is a different thing—it is instinctive. If infants could sustain life without coming in contact with human beings, they would of themselves doubtless adopt, but considerably later, the upright walk, because it is advantageous for command of the surrounding region through eye and ear. In the nursery, walking is almost always induced, and with unspeakable pains, earlier than can be good for children with regard to the growth of the bones. Children's go-carts (Kinderlaufstühle) and walking-frames (Gehkörbe) that favor such premature exercises are objectionable contrivances, because they help to make children bow-legged. Creeping, the natural preparatory school for walking, is but too often not permitted to the child, although it contributes vastly to his mental development. For liberty to get to a desired object, to look at it and to feel of it, is much earlier gained by the creeping child than by one who must always have help in order to change his location. Mother and nurses, in many families, prevent children from creeping before they can stand, through mere prejudice and even superstition, even when it is not the convenience of the elders, their disinclination to be observing watchfully the freely-moving child, that determines the unjustifiable prohibition. It can not be a matter of indifference for the normal mental development of the child not yet a year old, whether it is packed in a basket for hours, is swathed in swaddling-clothes, is tied to a chair, or is allowed to creep about in perfect freedom upon a large spread, out-of-doors in summer, and in a room moderately heated in winter.

When it is that a child tries to creep for the first time can not be accurately stated, just because he is generally hindered in such attempts. The date is besides very different for children of the same family, according to the nutrition and the firmness of the bones, the muscular power, and the desire of movement, which depend upon the nutrition. Some infants do not creep at all. Moreover, the manner of creeping is by no means the same in all children, nor do even European children all drag on both knees. My child dragged as a rule on one knee only, and used the other for an advance movement, putting forward the proper foot, as Livingstone reports of the Manyuema children in Africa. But like all children he learned to kneel down only a long time after he could walk, whereas animals a day old kneel of themselves (p. 68). So, too, it was long after he could walk, that he learned to move forward on hands and knees.

The date of the first successful attempts to walk also varies much, even with children of the same family, with approximately the same nourishment. One weakly child (according to Sigismund) could run alone cleverly when it was eight months old, another at sixteen months; many do not learn till after they are a year and a half or even two years old. Much depends on the surroundings. If a child grows up among other little children, some of whom are walking, some learning to walk, then he will, as a rule, be able to stand erect and to run, without any support from the mother, earlier than if he grows up alone. But in this case the frequent repetition of the instruction in walking may shorten considerably the natural period. Thus Demme saw (1882) out of fifty children two at the end of the ninth month of life walk alone for some minutes—unsteadily, to be sure; on the other hand, seven not till between the eighteenth and twenty-fourth month; the remaining forty-one in the third half-year. A vigorous female child with whom no experiments in standing and walking were undertaken, began to creep with the fifth month. " Up to the end of the tenth month she moved forward very briskly on all-fours, like a monkey, and up to this time, according to the express statement of the trustworthy parents, she had made no attempt to raise the body upright. With the fourteenth month she began first to raise herself up by firm objects, and from the sixteenth to the eighteenth learned to walk properly without any assistance, keeping up meantime the frequent practice of going on all-fours. The girl was intelligent, and her development in other respects was regular."

In general, the first attempt of the child that can hold himself erect by means of firm objects, to stand free of support, to trot, to walk, comes into the time including the last quarter of the first year and the first three quarters of the second year, although proper walking-movements of an infant supported from above appear even in the second quarter of the first year. Champney's child was held upright for the first time at the close of the nineteenth week, so that the feet just touched the ground, and was moved forward. The legs moved themselves fitly all the time, in alternation. Every step was taken perfectly, and that without delay or irregularity, even when the feet were held too high; only, that when the boy was held too high, the alternating movement was interrupted, as the foot remaining in the air made a new step. The touching of the ground on the part of one foot seemed to furnish the stimulus for the movement of the other. These perfectly correct observations—out of the nineteenth week—support absolutely my view of the act of walking as an instinctive movement.

It was after the close of the first quarter of the second year that my child, standing unsupported on his feet, suddenly trotted for the first time around the table, swaying, to be sure, or staggering like a drunken man that wants to run, but without falling. And from that day forth he could walk upright, at first only rapidly, hardly except on a trot, as if the only thought were to prevent the falling forward, and with arms extended in front — then slower and more securely. Within the next ten weeks, however, the child went over a threshold hardly an inch high, between two rooms, only by holding on, and was often seen at this period to fling with a jerk the foot that was put down in advance, like a tabetic patient, or to lift it too high and set it down too hard. The muscular sense was not yet developed.

In order to give a clear idea of the gradually progressing development, I place together here a few more observations which I made upon my child concerning the first sitting, creeping, standing, walking, and running:

22d and 23d weeks.—Lying on his back the infant often lifts himself up to a *sitting* posture, and is pleased when he is *placed upright* on the knees of his nurse.

28th week.—The child of his own accord *places himself upright*, but only on the lap of his mother, holding on to her.

35th week.—The child, while being carried, places himself on the arm and the hand of the nurse, and looks over her shoulder.

41st week.—First attempts at walking. The child was held under the arms so that his feet touched the floor. Then he lifted his legs alternately and stretched them imperfectly, in alternation. What induced these movements in him is beyond finding out. Sitting and standing without support are impossible.

42d week.—Whence it comes that the child, held

under the arms, his feet touching the floor, sets these to moving *forward*, and in the beginning *sidewise* also, now more regularly, is the harder to comprehend, for the reason that there is no pushing from behind, and usually nothing is before the child that he would desire. The inclination to walk is very great. From this time on the child *sits* without support.

43d week.—Whereas the child at the beginning put his feet irregularly over, by, and before each other, he now *lifts* the foot high up and generally puts it down firmly on the floor without crossing the legs. These remarkable movements occasion him the greatest pleasure. If he is very restless, he is speedily quieted if he is placed with his feet on the floor and held so. He begins then at once, without the least urging, *to move himself forward.*

45th to 47th weeks.—The exercises in walking, practiced almost daily, were at this period entirely omitted, in order to ascertain whether that which had been hitherto attained would be forgotten.

At the end of the forty-seventh week, however, the child when held up places his feet remarkably correctly, and seldom over each other; but the needed estimate of the amount of muscular force to be employed is still lacking, for he often lifts the foot too high, and puts it down too hard.

48th week.—The child often stands now a moment without support and stamps with his foot. He takes hold of a chair and *pushes* it forward somewhat, with only the slightest support.

49th week.—If the child is left to himself on a soft blanket, surrounded with pillows, he can not raise himself without help, and he can not stand more than an instant without help.

50th week.—The child can not yet of himself place himself upon his feet, when he is sitting or lying, nor can he walk without help.

53d week.—The child can *creep*, or rather drag himself along somewhat, but can not walk alone.

54th week.—He can *walk* when held by *one* hand. When creeping on the carpet, he moves but little and slowly from his place, and this with *asymmetrical* movements and stretchings of arms and legs.

57th week.—He hitches along hither and thither quite nimbly on hands and knees, but walking without being led (by one hand) is quite impossible.

60th week.—The child can raise himself alone from the floor by a chair, first to his knees and then to his feet. But he can stand all alone only a few moments; always clings tightly when he is put down.

62d week.—The child is still unable to stand longer than a moment without being supported, or at least touched. This inability depends no longer on the difficulty of maintaining the equilibrium, but on the lack of confidence in himself, for the only time when he is still unable to stand is when he knows he is not held. But when, without his knowledge, I have withdrawn from his back the support of my hand, having gradually reduced the pressure, then he *stands* for several seconds upright, and *without support*. Just so in the—

63d week.—The child still walks only when he can hold on with both hands (on the sides, fifty-five centimetres high, of a rectangular wooden structure of one

20

and a quarter metres length on the side, made by me on purpose for my child in 1878, and cushioned).

64th week.—When the child is led by one of his arms, so loosely that the arm is as if put through a loose ring, he walks properly and steadily; he can therefore walk without being held; but if he is left entirely free from one's touch, then he does not walk, but falls or stumbles into the arms of the person sitting or standing before him. Co-ordinating ability is not lacking, therefore, but self-confidence; whereas the inability to speak depends on lack of co-ordinating power. By altogether too frequent support, by too much telling how and showing how, by training, independent development is hindered and self-confidence is smothered in its origin.

65th week.—The child can not yet walk alone, indeed; but when he clasps only one guiding finger with his thumb and finger, he strides swiftly and securely forward. He raises himself, if he is laid down, first to the knees, and while he holds fast to something he *stands up*, but can not stand up without holding on.

66th week.—Suddenly—on the four hundred and fifty-seventh day of his life—the child can run alone. The day before, he was entirely unable to take three steps alone—he had to be led if only by means of a stick, perhaps a lead-pencil. Now, he ran alone around a large table, unsteadily indeed, and staggering and not holding his head in a stable position, but without falling. On the following day the little traveler is manifestly pleased at his new accomplishment, runs staggering, at random, with arms now hanging down, now lifted as if he wanted to hold on, now mute, again crying out,

"Hey! hey-ey!" (this he continued to do for months), and laughing. He likes to hold on by the furniture. On the day following, the child frequently stops during his hasty walking, and stamps, changing position from one foot to the other without any help. On the four hundred and sixty-first day he can walk *backward* also if he is led, and without leading can *turn round* quickly and cleverly. In walking he strikes about him at random with his arms. At the end of this week he can, *during his walking*, already direct his attention to other things, move his hands hither and thither for pleasure, hold objects and look at them during the *slow* walking, which has just been learned.

67th week.—Although a fall appears inevitable frequently in his walking alone, yet it rarely occurs—in the first five days of walking scarcely more than three times. In falling forward, both arms are now stretched straight out, which must be instinctive, as a falling person has not yet been seen by the child. In falling backward there is no protective movement. Whether the arms were extended at the *first* fall I have not been able to settle.

68th week.—The act of walking no longer requires so great attention as at the beginning. During his advance his look is already turned sidewise; and he even chews, swallows, laughs, and calls out. Walking is already becoming mechanical.

70th week.—The child raises himself from the floor alone—i. e., he stands up himself.

71st week.—Now first can a threshold—only an inch high, at the door between two rooms—be stepped over without help (not yet invariably, in the seventieth week, the child holding by the wall and the door-post). If he is sitting, he can now stand up without help.

77th week.—One day the child ran, without inter-vals of more than five seconds, nineteen times around a large table, calling out meantime, " Mamma! " and " Bwa, bwa, bwa! " Great liking for running.

78th week.—If he is holding something in his hands, then he walks over the threshold an inch high without holding on by anything.

85th week.—The thresholds are stepped over quick-ly without hesitation. In *running* he inclines forward, as if, at every step, falling were consciously prevented by carrying forward the center of gravity.

89th week.—Running is still somewhat awkward—with asymmetrical movements of the arms—so that it looks as if the child must fall. But a fall is very rare.

In the twenty-fourth month the child turns of him-self, *dancing* in time to music; also beats the time with tolerable correctness, when he hears a hand-organ or a bag-pipe.

In the twenty-eighth month he first learned to " go on all-fours "—that is, on hands and feet (playing " bear "). Before this he had (in creeping) dragged himself along on hands and knees, never on hands and feet. In this period came the first exercises in *jumping*, which were continued to the point of ex-haustion. In this month, too, and in the previous one, begins pleasure in climbing (on tables, chairs, benches).

In the thirtieth month, *mounting a staircase* of twenty-five steps without help—the right hand, on the balustrade, rather directing than holding. After ten days the same, with both hands free in the air.

In the thirty-fourth month, the first gymnastic exercises, which, like climbing and jumping, afford extraordinary pleasure. Also the throwing of any kind of objects (out of a window); the hurling of stones into the air or into a pond; the moving or setting in motion of objects within reach (on the table) are absolutely original, and must consequently be traced back to hereditary tendencies to produce changes in movable objects.

On the whole, it appears from the observations concerning sitting, standing, creeping, running, walking, jumping, climbing, throwing, which are rapidly but unequally developed in all children in like fashion, that these movements are predominantly or exclusively instinctive. They are not imparted by education. If any one insists on saying that they are learned, he must admit that they are only in the smallest degree learned by imitation; for a child that sees no one drag himself along, jump, climb, or throw, will without fail perform these movements, even when he is not trained. The progenitors of man must have found these especially useful, so that they grew to be fixed habits and became hereditary. At the same time, as it appears, those harmonious movements remained oftenest in use which, like those of the muscles of the eye that are used in seeing (p. 35), are of most service with the least strain.

CHAPTER XII.

IMITATIVE MOVEMENTS.

To determine as exactly as possible the date of the first imitative acts is of especial interest in regard to the genesis of mind, because even the most insignificant imitative movement furnishes a sure proof of activity of the cerebrum. For, in order to imitate, one must first perceive through the senses; secondly, have an idea of what has been perceived; thirdly, execute a movement corresponding to this idea. Now, this threefold central process can not exist without a cerebrum, or without certain parts of the cerebrum, probably the cortical substance. Without the cerebral cortex, certain perceptions are possible, to be sure; many movements are possible, but not the generation of the latter out of the former. However often imitation has the appearance of an involuntary movement, yet when it was executed the first time, it must have been executed with intention —i. e., voluntarily. When a child imitates, it has already a will. But the oftener a voluntary movement is repeated, always in the same way, so much the more it approximates reflex movement. Hence many imitative acts, even in the child, occur involuntarily quite early. But the first ones are willed. When do they make their appearance?

If we make, for the infant to see, a movement that he has often practiced of his own accord, he can make a successful imitation much earlier than is commonly supposed. Such a movement, which I employed as suitable for early imitation, is the *pursing of the mouth*, the protruding of the closed lips, which often occurs, (even in adults) along with a great strain of the attention.

This protruding of the lips occurred with my child on the tenth day of life (in the bath, when a burning candle was held before him at the distance of a metre); in the seventh week it was decidedly marked at sight of a new face quite near him; in the tenth week, at the bending and stretching of his legs in the bath. It was as if the letter *u* were to be pronounced—and yet the child was wholly unable to imitate this movement so easily made by him (as late as the fourteenth week) when I made it for him under the most favorable circumstances. At the end of the fifteenth week appeared for the first time the beginnings of an imitation, the infant making attempts to purse the lips when I did it close in front of him. That this was a case of imitative movement is shown by the imperfect character of it in comparison with the perfect pursing of the lips when he makes the movement of his own accord in some other strain of the attention. Strangely enough, the imitation was attempted on the one hundred and fifth day, but not in the following days.

Further attempts at imitation occurred so seldom and were so imperfect, notwithstanding much pains on my part to induce them, in the following weeks, that I was in doubt whether they might not be the result of accidental coincidences. Not till the seventh month were the attempts to imitate movements of the head, and the pursing of the lips already spoken of, so striking that I could no longer refer them to accidental coincidence. In particular the child often laughed when one laughed to him (p. 145). The attention is now more and more plainly strained when new movements are made for the infant to see—he follows these with evident interest, but without coming to the point of an attempt at imitation in a single instance. This indolence was the more surprising, as even in the seventeenth week the protruding of the tip of the tongue between the lips (customary with many adults at their work) was perfectly imitated once, when done by me before the child's face, and the child in fact smiled directly at this strange movement which seemed to please him. Imitative movements thus appear in the fourth month, which in the seventh, and even the ninth, do not succeed or are quite imperfectly achieved. Yet in the tenth month correct imitations of all sorts of movements were frequent, and it is certain that these were executed with distinct consciousness; for, when he is imitating movements of hand and arm frequently repeated before him—e. g., *beckoning* [in the general sense of making a sign] and saying—" Tatta "—the child looks fixedly at the person concerned, and then often suddenly makes the movement quite correctly.

Beckoning (*Winken*) is in general one of the movements of the infant acquired early by imitation. In my child it appeared for the first time at the beginning of the tenth month. When he was going to be taken out, his mother used to make a sign to him, and now he likewise made a sign, almost invariably, in the doorway, with one arm, frequently with both arms, yet with an expression of face that indicated that he moved the arms or arm without understanding, upon the opening of the

door. The proof of this lies in the fact, that when I
enter the room, the child, so long as the door is in
motion, makes that movement which he at first only
imitated, and does it regularly—no hint of leave-taking
in it therefore. The beckoning movement is made also
at other times—e. g., on the opening and shutting of a
large cupboard; it has, therefore, completely lost its
purely imitative character. The movement consists essentially of a rapid raising and dropping of the extended arm; it is not, therefore, genuine beckoning.
Not till after some weeks were motions of the hand
added, and this more skillful imitation made it seem as
if the machine-like movements that were made at the
opening of the door were less and less involuntary,
were more and more intentionally performed as genuine
signs of leave-taking. But at this period (tenth month)
such an action is not yet admissible; for when I make
the same beckoning movement for the child without
opening the door, he repeats it often in a purely imitative fashion without deliberation, though, to be sure,
the eye has an expression of great strain of attention,
on account of the difficulty of comprehending so quick
a movement.

Not every imitative movement can be so clearly
perceived to be willed as can this one. When one
enters a room in which there are a good many infants,
all quiet, one can easily observe the contagious influence
of crying. For, if only one child begins to cry, then
very soon several are crying, then many, often all of
them. So, too, when one single infant (in the ninth
month) hears other children cry, he likewise, in very
many cases, begins to cry. The older the child becomes,

the more seldom appears this kind of undesirable imitation; but even in children four years old, quite aimless imitative movements may often be perceived (as in mesmeric patients) if the children are observed without their knowledge. For example, they suddenly hold the arms crossed, as a stranger present is doing, and bow as he does at leaving.

A little girl in the last quarter of her first year imitated, in the drollest fashion, what she herself experienced in her treatment by the nurse, giving her doll a bath, punishing it, kissing it, singing it to sleep; and before the end of the first year she imitated the barking of the dog and the bleating of the sheep (Frau Dr. Friedemann).

Another female child imitated the following movements in a recognizable manner: in the eleventh month she threatened with the forefinger if any one did so to her, used a brush after she had seen brushes and combs, used a spoon properly, and drank from a cup, and made a kind of cradling movement with her doll, singing, "Eia—eia." In the thirteenth month the child made the motion of sewing, of writing (moistening the point of the pencil in her mouth) and of folding the arms. In the fifteenth month she fed the doll as she was fed herself, imitated shaving, on her own chin, and reading aloud, moving her finger along the lines and modulating her voice. In the eighteenth month she imitated singing, and made the motion of turning a crank like a hurdy-gurdy player when she heard music; in the nineteenth she went on hands and feet, crying "Au, au!" (ow, ow), in imitation of a dog; in the twentieth she imitated smoking, holding a cane firmly with her fingers exactly as is done in smoking a pipe. Her younger sister, in her fifteenth month, first imitated the movement of sewing and of writing; while the elder, in the nineteenth month, after repeated attempts at imitation, sewed together two pieces of cloth, without instruction, drawing the needle through correctly (Frau von Strümpell).

Toward the end of the first year of life the voluntary imitative movements, more numerous than before, are executed much more skillfully and more quickly. But when they require complex co-ordination they easily fail. When (at the beginning of the twelfth month) any one struck several times with a salt-spoon on a tumbler so that it resounded, my child took the spoon, looked at it steadily, and then likewise tried to strike on the glass with it, but he could not make it ring. In such imitations, which are entirely new, and on that account make a deeper impression, as in the case of puffing (*Pusten*) it would happen that they were repeated by the child in his dreams, without interruption of his sleep (twelfth month), a proof that the experiences of the day, however unimportant they appear to the adult, have stamped themselves firmly upon the impressionable brain of the child. But it takes always some seconds before a new or partly new movement, however simple, is imitated, when it is made for the child to imitate—e. g., it was a habit of my child (in the fourteenth month) to move both arms symmetrically hither and thither, saying, " ay—ĕ, ay— ĕ " (altogether differently, much more persistently and rapidly, than when beckoning). If some one made this very swinging of the arms for the child to observe, with the same sound, there was always an interval of several seconds before the child could execute the movement in like fashion. The simplest mental processes of all, therefore, need much more time than they do later. But imitations of this kind are almost always performed more quickly when they are not sought, when the child-brain is not obliged first to get its bearings, but acts spontaneously. If I clear my throat, or cough purposely, without looking at the child, he often gives a little cough likewise in a comical manner. If I ask, "Did the child cough?" or if I ask him, "Can you cough?" he coughs, but generally copying less accurately (in the fourteenth and fifteenth months). The bow too tightly strained shoots beyond the mark.

Here, besides pure imitation, there is already understanding of the name of the imitated movement with the peculiar noise.

This important step in knowledge once taken, the movements imitated become more and more complicated, and are more and more connected with objects of daily experience. In the fifteenth month the child learns to blow out a candle. He puffs from six to ten times in vain, and grasps at the flame meantime, laughs when it is extinguished, and exerts himself, after it has been lighted, in blowing or breathing, with cheeks puffed out and lips protruded to an unnecessary degree, because he does not imitate *accurately*. For it can hardly be that a child that has never seen how a candle can be blown out would hit upon the notion of blowing it out. Understanding and experience are not yet sufficient to make this discovery.

I find, in general, that the movements made for imitation are the more easily imitated correctly the less complicated they are. When I opened and shut my hand alternately, merely for the purpose of amusing the child, he suddenly began to open and shut his right hand likewise in quite similar fashion. The resemblance of his movement to mine was extremely surprising in comparison with the awkward blowing out of the candle in the previous instance. It is occasioned by the greater simplicity. Yet, simple as the bending of the finger seems, it requires, nevertheless, so many harmonious impulses, nerve-excitements, and contractions of muscular fibers, that the imitation of simple movements even can hardly be understood without taking into account the element of heredity, since unusual movements, never performed, it may be, by ancestors— say, standing on the head—are never, under any circumstances, imitated correctly at the first attempt. The opening and shutting of the hand is just one of the movements by no means unusual, but often performed by ancestors. Still, it is to be noticed that at the beginning the imitation proceeded very slowly, although correctly. On the very next day it was much more rapid on the repetition of the attempt, and the child, surprised by the novelty of the experience, now observed attentively first my hand and then his own (fifteenth month).

Of the numerous more complicated movements of the succeeding period, the following, also, may be mentioned, in order to show the rapid progress in utilizing a new retinal image for the execution of an act corresponding to it: A large ring, which I slowly put on my head and took away again, was seized by the child, and put by him in the same way on his own head without fumbling (sixteenth month). But, when it is a case of combination of a definite action of the muscles of the mouth with expiration of the breath, innumerable fruit-less efforts at imitation are made before one of them succeeds, because, in this case, a part only of the working of the complicated muscular action can be perceived, while the rest must be found out by trial. Thus, the child could not, in spite of many attempts, get any tone out of a small hunting-horn. He put it to his mouth, and tried to imitate the tone with his own voice. Sud-denly the right manner of blowing was hit upon acci-dentally, and from that time was never forgotten (eight-eenth month).

After the child had seen how his mother combed her long dark hair before a glass, he took a hand-mirror and a comb and moved the comb around on his head, combing where there was no hair. So, too, he would now and then seize a brush and try to brush his head and his dress, but took special pleasure in brushing also all kinds of furniture. More than once he actually took a shawl, held it by a corner to his shoulder, and drew it behind him like a train, frequently turning around while doing this. He also put a collar round his neck; he tried to dry himself with a towel, but without success; whereas the washing of the hands with soap, without direction, was imitated, though not with much skill, yet tolerably well; none but very complicated imitative actions these, and all of them, in the case of my boy, belong to the third quarter of the second year—an ex-ceptionally important period in mental genesis—the same is true of seizing, holding things before him, and (what was observed by Lindner in the sixth month) the imitation of reading aloud from a newspaper or pamphlet, the feeding of deer—holding out a single spear of grass to them—scraping the feet upon entering the house (as if the shoes were to be cleaned).

But how little real imitation and understanding of the act itself there was, even in this period of perfect external imitations, appears from the circumstance that a map is held, as a newspaper, " to be read aloud," before the face, and upside down. Now, too, the child likes to take a pencil, puts the point in his mouth, and then makes all sorts of marks on a sheet of paper, as if he could draw.

Just as remarkable is the lively interest in everything that goes on in the neighborhood of the child. In packing and unpacking, setting the table, lighting the fire, lifting and moving furniture, he tries to help. His imitative impulse seems here almost like ambition (twenty-third month).

Toward the end of the second year various ceremonious movements, especially those of salutation, are also imitated. The child sees how an older boy takes off his hat in salutation; immediately he takes off his own head-covering and puts it on again, like the other boy.

All these movements last enumerated are distinguished from the earlier ones by this, that they were executed or attempted by the boy unsolicited, without the least inducement or urging, entirely of his own motion.

They show, on the one hand, how powerful the imitative impulse has become (in the second year); on the other hand, how important this impulse must be for the further mental development. For, if the child at this age passes the greater part of his time in company inattentive to manners, or unrefined, then he will imitate all sorts of things injurious to him, and will easily acquire habits that hinder his further development. It is, therefore, of the greatest importance, even at this early period, to prevent the intercourse of children with strangers, and to avoid everything that might open wrong paths to the imitative impulse.

The imitative movements of the muscles of speech, the child's imitations of sounds, syllables, and words are treated of in detail in the third part of this work. The first answer of the infant to the language addressed to him by his relatives, which is said to be made, in individual cases, as early as the eighth and ninth weeks (according to Sully, 1882), is no attempt at imitation, but a directly reflexive movement, like screaming after a blow, etc. Singing has already been mentioned as one of the earliest imitated performances. It is true of these, as of all later imitations, that the first imitation of every new movement is voluntary on the part of the child, and, in case an involuntary imitation seems to occur, then either this has already been often repeated as such, or it is a movement often practiced without imitation. The accuracy of the imitation depends little, however, upon the co-operation of a deliberative cerebral activity. On the contrary, children of inferior mental endowment among those born deaf sometimes possess (according to Gude) a purer and more distinct enunciation than those more gifted.

CHAPTER XIII.

EXPRESSIVE MOVEMENTS.

EXPRESSIONS of countenance and gestures arise chiefly, as is well known, from imitation. Not only persons born blind, but also those who become blind at an advanced age, are distinguished from those who have sight by their lack of the play of feature. Their expression of countenance shows only slight changes; their physiognomy appears fixed, uniform; the muscles of the face move but little when they are not eating or speaking. Little children also lack a characteristic play of feature, hence the difficulty of making portraits of them, or even of describing them. Different as is the contented face from the discontented, even on the first day, different as is the intelligent face from the stupid, the attentive from the inattentive, the difference can not be completely described. In the second half of the first year children act after the example of the members of the family. Speak gravely to a gay child of a year old, and it becomes grave; if it is sober, and you show a friendly face, the child in many cases brightens up in an instant. Yet it would be premature to conclude from this that all the means of expression by the countenance are acquired solely through imitation. Some mimetic movements, of which we have already spoken, are of reflex origin. The same is true of gestures. Others may be instinctive.

As every gesture is wont to appear in association with the expression of countenance appropriate to it, when it has a language value, it seems advisable to treat

21

together expressions and gestures which together form pantomime, and to separate the purely expressive muscular movements of the infant from its other movements, in our attempt to trace their origin.

So long as the child can not yet speak words and sentences, it effects an understanding with other children and with adults by the same means that are employed by the higher animals for mutual understanding, by demonstrative movements and attitudes, by sounds expressive of emotion or feeling, of complaining, exultation, alluring, repelling, or desiring, and by dumb looks. These very means of expression are employed by the child when it entertains itself in play with inanimate objects.

Of the expressive movements of the child I have especially considered, as to their origin, smiling and laughing, pouting and kissing, crying and wrinkling of the forehead, shaking the head and nodding, shrugging the shoulders, and begging with the hands, as well as pointing.

1. The First Smiling and Laughing.

The first smiling is the movement most often misunderstood. Every opening of the mouth whatever, capable of being interpreted as a smile, is wont to be gladly called a smile even in the youngest child. But it is no more the case with the child than with the adult that a mere contortion of the mouth fulfills the idea of a smile. There is required for this either a feeling of satisfaction or an idea of an agreeable sort. Both must be strong enough to occasion an excitement of the facial nerves. A smile can not be produced by a mere sensation, but only by the state of feeling that springs from it, or by the agreeable idea developed from it, however vague it may yet be.

Now, as has been shown already, the number of sensations associated with a pleasurable feeling in the first days of life is very small, and an idea, in the proper sense of the word, the new-born child unquestionably can not have as yet, because he does not yet perceive. The child that is satisfied with nursing at its mother's breast, or with the warmth of the bath, does not smile in the first days of life, but only shows an expression of satisfaction, because for the moment all unpleasant feelings are absent. But how easily such a condition of comfort manifests itself by a very slight lifting of the corner of the mouth, is well known. If we choose to call this a smile, then even sleeping babes smile very early. On the tenth day of his life I saw my child, while he was asleep, after having just nursed his fill, put his mouth exactly into the form of smiling. The dimples in the cheeks became distinct, and the expression of countenance was, in spite of the closed eyes, strikingly lovely. The phenomenon occurred several times. On the twelfth day appeared, along with the animated movements of the facial muscles, a play of features in the waking condition, also, that one might take for a smile. But this play of the muscles of the mouth lacked the consciousness that is required to complete the smile, as does the smile of the sleeping child. On the twenty-sixth day, first, when the child could better discriminate between his sensations and the feelings generated by them, did the smile become a mimetic expression. The babe had taken his milk in abundant quantity, and was lying with his eyes now open and now half-closed, and with an indescribable expression of contentment on his countenance. Then he smiled, opening his eyes, and directed his look to the friendly face of his mother, and made some sounds not before heard, which were appropriate to his happy mood. But the idea had not yet arisen of the connection of the mother's face with the mother's breast, the source of enjoyment (p. 46). Nor can we at this period assume an imitation, by the child, of the smile of the mother, because at first inanimate objects (tassels) are smiled at, and before the fourth month no imitative movements at all were attempted.

Not only the first-mentioned very early movements of smiling, but also this perfect smile is connected with a condition of contentment, and there is no reason to regard it as less hereditary in character than is screaming with pain, which no one would refer to imitation.

Later the child smiles when he is smiled at, but not always by any means. Strangers may smile at him in ever so friendly a manner, yet the wondering little face, usually merry, now sober, remains immobile. The first imitations of the smile in children are not so free from deliberation as the smiles of many adults, which through training and the conventional forms of greeting have degenerated into mere formality.

The original smile of satisfaction at new, agreeable feelings, a smile which may continue even in sleep, and which appears only in a cheerful frame of mind, remains in force still later. By an unusual expression of intensity in the more brightly gleaming eye, as well as by lively movements of the arms and legs, most plainly by laughing and smiling, the infant manifests his satisfaction—e. g., in music (in the eighth week)—without any one's giving him in any other way the least occasion for it.

The date of the first smile varies very much, therefore, according as we take for a smile a spontaneous expression of pleasure, or the communication of an agreeable condition, or the satisfaction at a pleasing idea; here belongs the first imitated smile, and the statements that the first smile appears in well-developed children about the fourth week, as the expression of pleasure (Heyfelder), in the sixth to the eighth week (Champneys), in the seventh and ninth week (Darwin), or that in the seventh to the tenth week (Sigismund) the babe smiles for the first time, are as indefinite as the statement that, at the end of the second week, his mouth takes on a lovely expression like a smile. It depends essentially on the nature of the occasion of the smile at what date the first smile shall be fixed.

One child first smiles at its image in the glass in the twenty-seventh week; another, in the tenth (see below); the one observed by myself, in regard to this point, in the seventeenth week, and not at all till that time. It was rather a laugh than a smile that surprised me on the one hundred and sixteenth day, whereas even on the one hundred and thirteenth the image in the mirror was regarded with a fixed and attentive look, to be sure, but without any sign of satisfaction. In these cases it is simply the joy at the distinct, new perception—an idea, therefore, that occasions the smile; in other cases it is pleasure in impressions of agreeable tastes, of softness or warmth, or joy in pleasing sound, or simply the feeling of satiety (fourteenth week), and then it is usually accompanied by a peculiar sound, which is always much softer in the first months than the expressions of displeasure. But, when the quite young child does not feel well, or is hungry, it can not smile any more. The surest sign of convalescence is the reappearance of this significant movement of the mouth.

From the smile to the laugh is but a step, and the laugh is often only a strengthened and audible smile. The first laugh upon a joyous sense-impression is, however, essentially different from that which springs from the heightened self-consciousness at the perception of the ludicrous; and the limit of time given for that, of six to seventeen weeks, is surprisingly late. Pliny thinks no child laughs before the fortieth day. I observed an audible and visible laugh, accompanied by a brighter gleam of the eye, in my child, for the first time, on the twenty-third day (p. 32). He was pleased with a bright, rose-colored curtain that was hanging above him, and he made peculiar sounds of satisfaction, so that I was first led by these to pay attention to him. The corners of his mouth were drawn somewhat upward. At this period no laugh yet appeared when the child was in the bath, but there also the expression of the little face with the widely-opened eyes was that of great satisfaction. Laughing appears at first simply as an augmentation of this expression of pleasure. It is often repeated in the same way in the fifth and sixth weeks—in the eighth especially—at the sight of slowly-swinging, well-lighted, colored objects, and on hearing the piano.

The child's laugh appeared for the first time, in the period from the sixth to the ninth week, as a sign of joy at a familiar, pleasing impression, his eyes being fixed on his mother's face.. But the laugh at the friendly nodding to him (p. 62), and singing (p. 84), of the members of the family, was then already much more marked, and was later accompanied by rapid raisings and droppings of the arms as sign of the utmost pleasure (sixth month). This last childish movement continued for years as an accompanying phenomenon of laughing for joy. But it is to be noticed that this laugh first began to be persistently loud in the eighth month (in play with the mother); every one could then at once recognize it as a laugh without looking in that direction. In this the child made a peculiar impression of gayety upon every one who saw him.

Loud laughing at new objects that please, and are long looked at, is still frequent in the ninth month; so also at new sounds in the fifteenth month (p. 89); then follows laughing at the efforts to stand with support. In the last three months of the first year, however, the character of the laugh appears to become different, as it becomes more conscious. The child laughs with more understanding than before. But he with a laugh grasps at his own image in the glass, and makes a loud jubilant noise, in the eleventh month, when he is allowed to walk, although he must be held firmly when doing so. At the end of the first year, to these independent utterances of pleasure had been added the purely imitative laughing when others laughed. Yet self-consciousness manifested itself also in this, through vigorous crowing with employment of abdominal pressure. Roguish laughing I first noticed toward the end of the second year. Scornful laughing and lachrymal secretion during

continuous laughter I have never observed in children
under four years of age.

From the sum total of my observations in regard to
the smiling and laughing of infants, it results unquestionably that both are original expressive movements,
which may be distinctly perceived in the first month,
which by no means take place the first time through imitation, and which, without exception, from the beginning
express feelings of pleasure; in fact, my child laughed
in his sleep at the end of his first year of life, probably
having a pleasant dream, and did not wake on account
of it.

The reasons are not yet known why feelings of pleasure are expressed just in this manner—i. e., by uncovering the teeth, and even before the teeth are present, by
lengthening the opening of the mouth, along with lifting the corners of the mouth, by peculiar sounds and a
brighter gleam of the eye (secretion of lachrymal fluid,
without its going so far as the formation of tears), and
lively accompanying movements of the arms (p. 145).
The causes must be hereditary. But Darwin rightly
urges that they do not operate so early as the causes of
crying and weeping, because crying is more useful to
the child than laughing. And if he saw two children
distinctly smile for the first time in the seventh week,
we ought to infer from that not so much a failure to
notice earlier attempts as the existence of individual differences. That he perceived the first decided laugh in
the seventeenth week shows how unlike individual infants are in this respect. Probably much depends on the
surroundings and on the behavior of the family. But
in all children the expression of pleasure begins with a

scarcely perceptible smile, which passes very gradually, in the course of the first three months, into conscious laughing, after the cerebral cortex has so far developed that ideas more distinct can arise. In the second month is perceived also the reflex laughing that follows tickling (p. 145) which I could besides (in the third year) distinguish almost invariably from expressive laughing by the sound alone, without knowing what was going on, although I was in a neighboring room when I heard it. This " thoughtless " laugh sounds, on the contrary, exactly like the child's laugh often heard continuously at this time, which occurred when he heard and saw adults laugh at jests unintelligible to him, and which was long continued without any meaning in it. Laughing incites still more to imitation and is more contagious than crying. The laughter of man seems even to have an enlivening effect on intelligent animals (dogs), which draw the corners of the mouth far back, and spring, with an animated gleam of the eye, into the air. I had a large Siberian dog that laughed in this manner. It is known that monkeys also laugh. These facts favor the hereditary character of the movement of laughing— all the more as tickling of the skin of the arm-pit excites laughing in children and monkeys in the same way, when they are gay, as Darwin informs us. But if a crying child is tickled in the same manner, it does not laugh.

2. Pouting of the Lips.

A peculiar expression of children and of many adults is the protruding of the lips when the attention is strained. I have seen old men, in playing on the piano, and in writing, protrude the lips in a still more striking manner—even putting out the tongue—than infants that are beginning to seize, and children that are examining a new toy. The external occasions of this remarkable alteration of the shape of the mouth may vary to whatever extent, yet they all agree in this, that after the first week they introduce a vigorous strain of attention. Yet the protruding of the lips appears long before the development of the ability to examine objects. I once saw a new-born child in its first hour of life protrude its lips which were as yet untouched (p. 207); but this protrusion was without the movement of sucking; it appeared along with many other movements of the facial muscles, and I should be inclined to explain it as purely impulsive. My child showed it on the tenth day of his life, distinctly, in the bath, when there was a lighted candle before him; and from that time on with extraordinary frequency until his fourth year. His lips were protruded almost like a snout, as in sucking (p. 98), then drawn back and again protruded (sixteenth month). The movements of the tongue exhibited by many children in learning to write, were not observed by me till much later than the protrusion of the lips; they appeared along with attempts to do with effort some new thing. Here it is worthy of notice that even in merely looking at an object without taking hold of it himself, the lips are pursed (fifth week, p. 50, and seventh week p. 45, also the tenth month, p. 63); later more protruded, when a testing (forty-fourth week, p. 55) or inquiring observation (forty-seventh week, p. 50) is combined with touching, in which the aim is to follow a moved object in various directions, or to put an object in motion or turn it around, to empty a box and fill it, or to open and shut it, or to put a number of small objects of the same kind, e. g., buttons, into rows and rolls or into envelopes (first half of second year).

In this the protrusion of the lips is quite different from the pouting of sullenness. The protruded lips of the cross child, resembling those, still further protruded, of the cross chimpanzee, which I observed in the zoological garden at Hamburg, as Darwin describes it and gives a picture of it, appear much later than this narrowing of the opening of the mouth that is combined with prolonged fixing of the gaze, and that lasts (with children not yet two years old) several minutes. It looks as if the vowel *u* were to be pronounced, whereas the children, whose hands are busy, are absolutely silent. Whence this expression? I will try to give an explanation of it. That this excitement of the facialis is hereditary is a fixed fact; for in the case, very carefully observed by me—a strongly marked case too—it can not have been acquired by imitation. My child neither associated intimately enough with other children nor saw pursing of the lips in the adults about him, and could not imitate it before the fifteenth week (see p. 283). But if it is hereditary, then it must be referred to the progenitors of man. All animals direct their attention first to food. Their first test is applied to things that may be reached with lips, feelers, snout, tongue. All testing of food is attended with a predominant activity of the mouth and its adjuncts. Especially in *sucking*, which first awakens the attention of the newly-born, is the mouth protruded. Later, when new objects, that excite the attention, come within reach, they are carried to the mouth, because the thing that was alone interesting previously, food, came to the mouth. The inference, that what is interesting belongs to the mouth, is first shaken by the experience that many beautiful and interesting objects do not go into the mouth or are disagreeable within it. But the association of the first movement of the mouth arising from sucking, the protruding of the lips, with strain of the attention, is confirmed by too frequent repetition of the taking of food, the most interesting occurrence to the infant, to be lost as quickly as is the carrying of new toys to the mouth. It is therefore not only transmitted to the child, but often remains for years, even into old age, and manifests itself in an extremely striking fashion when the attention is on the strain, at anything unusually interesting; particularly in case some personal activity, such as writing or drawing, causes the strain.

A particular kind of protrusion of the lips, different from the foregoing, takes place in—

3. Kissing.

This belongs to the very late acquired expressive movements, which, in general, do not seem to be inherited. As it is unknown to many nations, it is to be called conventional.

How little the child understands the significance of the kiss, although it is kissed by its mother probably more than a thousand times in its first year, is plainly apparent from many observations.

A little girl in the fourteenth month kissed "quite audibly the cheek or hand (stroking it at the same time) often from a pure fit of tenderness," but many times in order to obtain something or to pacify some one. In the fifteenth month this child kissed her mother one day twelve times in succession, entirely of her own accord; her sister kissed her mother's hand at the beginning of the fifteenth month without solicitation some eight times in succession; her brothers and sisters used to kiss one another, at the age of three and a half and one and a quarter years, for amusement (Frau von Strümpell). Another female child returned a kiss from the tenth month on, without any movement of warding off (Lindner); all this was learned.

I put together here, in brief form, some notes concerning my child:

11th day.—When the babe was kissed by his mother on the mouth, he fairly seized one of her lips with his, and *sucked* at it as if he had got the breast, putting out his tongue.

32d week.—The child no longer sucks at the lips when he is kissed, but *licks* them as he licks objects in general that please him.

33d week.—When he is kissed, the child no longer licks the lips, but allows himself to be kissed on the mouth without response or opposition. In the following months, also, there is no trace of an attempt to return the kiss, although signs of affection are not wanting. For in the fifty-first week the child hands to his mother the biscuit he is himself about to eat.

12th month.—The opening of the closed mouth that takes place in kissing is tolerably well imitated.

13th month.—The child has absolutely no idea of what a kiss signifies. Kisses are not agreeable to him, for he always turns away his head when he is kissed, no matter by whom.

15th month.—The words, " Give a kiss! " produce a drawing near of the head, and often a protruding of the lips. This proves an understanding of the words only, not of the thing.

19th month.—When strangers want to be kissed by the child, he holds off; accordingly, he is fastidious in his choice in regard to approach.

20th month.—The child shows by touching the face, especially the cheek, with his face, that proximity has come to appear to him as essential in kissing. Herein lies already an imperfect return of the kiss. The child also bends his head when some one says, " Kiss," toward the face of the speaker, without opening the mouth as hitherto, but does not always put out his lips.

23d month.—The child now knows the significance of the kiss as a mark of favor, and is fastidious in his choice in giving a kiss as he is in giving his hand. In kissing, his lips are put forward closed, and then the mouth is somewhat too widely opened after the contact.

34th month.—The feeling of thankfulness is awakened. When one has done something to please the child, he sometimes kisses, and has a gracious, thankful air, but says nothing.

At first, then, the lips of the mother, when she kisses her child, are treated like the finger held to the mouth, or like the breast, as objects to be sucked; then they are licked, as by a puppy; next, the kiss is endured; further on it is refused; soon afterward it is awkwardly, and only on request, returned; and, finally, it is spontaneously given as a sign of thanks and of affection— and this by a boy who is not in the least tender and is not trained. Assuredly this tedious schooling in learning to kiss furnishes the best evidence how little justified we should be in designating the kiss as an hereditary privilege of humanity.

4. Crying, Weeping, and Wrinkling the Forehead.

It is a fact long since familiar that newly-born and quite young babes do not weep—i. e., there is no external secretion of tears, however vigorously they cry. Later, children cry and weep at the same time, and can cry without weeping (e. g., in jest), but not till much later are they able to weep without crying out.

The date of the first external lachrymal secretion varies surprisingly in different children. Darwin puts together some observations on this point, from which it appears that in two cases the eyes were wet with tears for the first time at the end of the third and the ninth week; in another case tears flowed down the cheeks at the end of the sixth week. In two other children this was not the case as late as the twelfth and the sixteenth week; in a third child, however, it happened in the fifteenth week. One of his own children shed tears in crying in the twentieth week, but not yet in the eighteenth, and in the tenth the eyes were moist in violent crying. At the end of the eleventh week with this same child an accidental, rude touch of the eye with a rough cloth produced a flow of tears in this eye, but not in the other, which was merely moist. Champney's child shed tears for the first time in the fourteenth week.

I have seen tears flow from the eyes as early as the twenty-third day, in my boy, while he was screaming lustily.   Soon afterward, crying with shedding of tears, and whimpering, formed the most important sign of psychical events of different sorts.

What Darwin reports, that usually babes do not shed tears before they are two or four months old, is not true of German children in general.   Not weeping, but sobbing, comes so late, and even later, for the first time; and some causes of weeping, as willfulness, grief, anger, can not operate at first, because in general they are still wanting; whereas pain is expressed by tears from the first, when once the secretion of tears has begun.   Yet it is easy to prove that little children in the second and third years weep much more easily and shed more tears at impressions that cause displeasure than do children of six months or a year.   I suspect that in this matter more depends on the excitation of the lachrymal nerves through emotional cerebral processes than upon compression of the gland in screaming, as Darwin thinks.   For in the first place there sometimes appears, as Genzmer observed, in children just born, upon touching the mucous membrane of the nose, "an increased lachrymal secretion," which proves that through excitement of the nerves, especially reflexive excitation (and that without compression), lachrymal secretion may occur before weeping; secondly, tears may trickle over the cheeks in great drops without any compression of the lachrymal gland, without screaming; and in the second year also appears crying without weeping—that is, compression of the lachrymal gland without lachrymal secretion.   My child cried in his sleep, evidently dreaming, without shedding tears, and without waking, as early as the tenth month; another child (Lindner) in the eighteenth week.

Of crying—with tears (*Schreiweinen*)—in little children, on the other hand, two alterations of countenance are extremely characteristic, the observation and explanation of which offer many difficulties—viz., the drawing down of the corners of the mouth, and the wrinkling of the forehead.

The peculiar form of the mouth, arising from contraction of the depressors of the corners of the mouth, directly before and after a fit of crying, has already been spoken of in the description of childish expressions of discomfort (p. 149).

The wrinkling of the forehead is, indeed, likewise observed without exception in crying with the eyes held tightly together, but is in the beginning an impulsive movement frequently occurring without a fretful mood. I saw it on the first, second, sixth, seventh, tenth days (cf. pp. 2, 23, 36), exactly as in many monkeys, frequently appear without any assignable outward occasion. On the contrary, in young infants, the corrugation of the forehead is lacking just when we should expect to perceive it—judging from adults—e. g. (p. 24), at raising the glance (in the eighth and twelfth weeks). It is surprising, too, that in the first two weeks the horizontal corrugation of the brow appears much oftener than afterward. In the fourth month I saw for the first time in my child slight horizontal furrows in the brow when he was looking upward, but in the third quarter of the first year not invariably as yet; in the last three months invariably. Distinct vertical furrows, which lend a somber expression to the childish physiognomy, are always present in crying with tears, as has been mentioned, but often occur without that (plainly

22

in a boy of nine weeks; in my boy, in the seventh month).

A girl, one of twins, only six days and some hours old, was seen by me to wrinkle the brow twice very decidedly—once with, once without a simultaneous movement of the skin of the head. The mother said, "The child has serious thoughts." And, in fact, it looked peculiarly precocious, to see the skin of the forehead both times laid in deep, parallel folds, which extended over the whole breadth of the forehead, and the face take on a very serious expression. In this case, as in all similar cases, it does not, however, appear safe to attribute to the wrinkling of the brow the significance of an expressive movement, because the psychical states are as yet wanting that are expressed by horizontal folds of the brow.

The distinct wrinkling of the skin of the forehead in astonishment I have seen for the first time in the twentieth month. I have often seen, also, when new tricks were done before the child (in the fifteenth month), the characteristic transverse folds as an accompanying movement of laborious attempts at imitation. Yet we look in vain for physiological explanations of these facts. Darwin, who saw his children wrinkle the forehead, from the first week on, as an invariable antecedent to tearful crying, has expressed the conjecture that this expressive movement, inherited from of old (contraction of the corrugators), originally serving to protect the eyes when impressions were to be warded off, was finally associated with unpleasant feelings in general. The vertical folds that accompany effort would harmonize with this, but the transverse folds that accompany astonishment are connected with the wider opening of the eyelids.

That a purely reflexive corrugation of the brow— the vertical folds—occurs together with that early expressive movement in the first days, is certain. In the fourth year I saw, moreover, an actual contraction of the corrugators of a child fast asleep take place, sometimes without the least movement of the eyelid, when I let bright lamp-light fall upon the closed eyes, in a place otherwise dark. The sleep was not interrupted by it, nor even the snoring. This reflex may, like the screwing up of the eyes in the same circumstances, be inborn, like the corrugation of the brow after sound-impressions and contact in the first week.

5. Shaking the Head and Nodding.

Shaking the head as a sign of denial or refusal is in like manner practiced by many children early, without instruction and without opportunity for imitation. A forerunner of this expressive movement, which signifies dislike, disgust, much earlier than it does denial, is, as Darwin also declares, the sidewise movement of the head, the turning away when food is refused, whether the breast or the bottle.

Much in the same way, the head is turned to the window (p. 3) even in the first days (pp. 41, 42), and then toward objects moved (pp. 48, 49), but with a contented expression; later, in the direction of a new sound (pp. 84, 85, 88). In general I found, from the first day on, sidewise movements of the head without any reflex excitement (p. 260) frequently in my child (Von Ammon is wrong in the opinion that the infant does not move the head at all in the first days). The head-movements are, in fact, quite lively when the babe is placed at the breast, or is in the bath, or is lying down. They are sidewise movements, not nodding, absolutely irregular and "natural." At the beginning, however, the turnings of the head are, strangely enough, not always in harmony with the movements of the eyes (p. 36), which makes them seem "unnatural."

Further, I saw in the first week in my child regularly, when it was placed at the breast, a vigorous turning sidewise in both directions, almost a shaking of the head (cf. pp. 153, 260). On the eighth day of his life, when he for the first time took the breast without any help whatever, these lateral movements of the head made it seem just as if the child were trying to find something. On the twenty-seventh day, however, they took place just the same, when the bottle was put directly to his mouth; a strange association, caused possibly by this, that in the very first days the head is somewhat directed by helping hands, so that the nipple comes into the mouth. Later the head-movement, that has been always followed by the stream of milk, becomes for the infant a necessary preliminary condition of the taking of food, and is retained by him, although in connection with the bottle it is useless. Accordingly we have here not a case of an acquired movement of the head, one that has been learned, but an instinct that occasions the head-movements in sucking at the finger as well as in nursing at the breast.

It has been already mentioned that many mammals likewise move the head vigorously hither and thither when they begin to suck, so that we may assume an hereditary factor in mankind; the more so, as the turnings of the head were to be observed, very vigorous even in the eighth week, and invariably when the babe was placed at the breast, several times a day, before the nipple was firmly grasped. In spite of the great haste and greediness in sucking, these unnecessary previous movements were never forgotten. They are, as to their causes, different from the reflexive turning of the head.

When any one seats himself at the bedside of the child, the child's head is regularly turned toward him (fifth week). This is followed by the reflexive turning around at new sound-impressions (eleventh week), and when any one leaves the room noisily (twenty-second week).

All these lateral head-movements are not in the least forerunners of the denying or refusing shake of the head—are not in any way related to it; although they very frequently agree with it perfectly in appearance, if all the external circumstances and the physiognomy are left out of the account. The manifold variety of the lateral turnings of the head in the infant, from the first day, is astonishing. And yet the peculiar turning away of the head comes in as a well-marked expressive movement as early as the fourth day. My child refused to nurse at the left breast, which was somewhat more inconvenient for him than the right. He refused, turning his head away decidedly from it, and on the sixth day he screamed besides. On the seventh we first succeeded in overcoming his opposition. Yet a single averting of the head remained as a sign of refusal. It appeared almost invariably after the infant had nursed his fill and had thrust the nipple out of his mouth—a thing hardly to be accomplished by a reflex mechanism (very plainly done in the first as in the seventh month). The child was so dominated by the feeling of satiety that food was repulsive to him.

This single averting of the head to the left or to the right, according to the position, manifestly means "No more!" is, therefore, of the nature of refusal. But after the child had learned to balance his head there came, for the first time, numerous and very rapid turnings of it, exactly like the shaking of the head in denial by adults (in the sixteenth week). Then appeared also a nodding, but more seldom. It no more signified affirmation than the lateral turnings in that early period signified denial. This is rather an instance of exercise of the muscles simply. The turning away of the head in refusal, when the child had drunk enough, persisted. In the sixth month arm-movements were added, which seemed like movements of warding off, without my being convinced, however, that they were so. Rather was it many months before the appearance of unquestionable arm-movements of warding off, such as take place in the case of adults when something is held before the face too long. The child that does not want the offered object raises his arm sidewise from one to three times in refusal, and turns his head away toward the opposite side. This deprecating arm-movement (distinctly marked in the fifteenth month) may well be an acquired one, that is, imitated, as we may attribute to the child at this period a capacity of observation that would suffice for this. At any rate the raising of the bended arm is not in the beginning associated with the turning away of the head, and the nurse may in like manner have protected herself frequently when the child has put his hands into her face. To be sure, the execution of a defensive movement is quite early associated with an idea of defense. When the boy (in the eighteenth month) tries in anger to hit with his foot some one who has refused him a key that he wanted, we can not find for such a re-enforcement of the refusing head-movement any model that he has imitated; still less can we find one for his striking about him with arms and legs, throwing himself at the same time on the floor and screaming with rage (just like what I saw in the case of a chimpanzee from whom an apple that he wanted was withheld). There occur in children as early as the tenth month similar fits of rage (p. 323), in which the face becomes red in case their desire is not complied with (Frau von Strümpell).

Neither is the half-closing of the eyelid, when the head is turned away in refusal, to be traced to imitation. It did not occur invariably. I saw it in the eighth month distinctly in my boy when disinclination was expressed. Especially was antipathy (not fear) expressed by such turning away of the head at the approach of women dressed in black, no matter how friendly they were, up to the third quarter of the second year, and even the second quarter of the third year.

Long before this period, however, a repeated turning of the head, or a shaking of the head in denial, had arisen out of the simple averting of the head; this came through training. It appeared mostly in the thirteenth month when any one said, " No, no!" but there was no nodding at the " Yes, yes!" and there was no success in imitating nodding in the fourteenth month, in spite of much pains. Afterward the imitation often succeeded (in the sixty-fourth week), but the nodding of the head along with "No, no!" was also sometimes observed, and the shaking of the head with the "Yes, yes!" the meaning thus being confounded (a paramimy). In fact, it was months before the meaning of the affirmative inclination of the head was firmly impressed, after the negative one had been long practiced. When, on the four hundred and forty-fifth day of his life, the first movement had been correctly imitated for the second time—on the day before for the first time—the child made a peculiar movement of the hand in time with nodding of the head, a genuine supination, looking, the while, very attentively indeed at the head of the person before him—an unconscious accompanying movement, therefore. That the inclination of the head, learned with effort, meant "Yes" was wholly unknown to him; and yet, in the sixteenth month, the negative head-shaking meant for the child not only "No," but also "I do not know," and, in the seventeenth month, "I do not wish." This gesture continued now, while the nodding of the head in affirmation seldom occurred, unless it was specially asked for. It was not till the fourth year that an affirmative nod of the head meant "Thank you!" The difference is the more surprising as both movements have been frequently regarded as original. But children use the voice for denying and affirming much earlier than they do the inclination and turning of the head, and this whole exposition shows that these movements have not from the beginning an antagonistic relation to each other, but the sidewise turning away of the head, at first in refusal, later in denying, is in-

born, reflexive-instinctive, while the inclining and nodding of the head in affirmation or assent, or in the
expression of thanks, which appears much later, must
be called an acquired gesture of unknown origin.

6. Shrugging the Shoulders.

Little children show, at a very late period, a quick
raising of the shoulders, corresponding to the shrugging of the shoulders in the adult. In the fifteenth
month I saw my child, without any assignable cause,
shrug his shoulders for the first time, just as adults do,
only, perhaps, somewhat more quickly, and he did this
in similar fashion on several days. For a moment it
seemed as if the child's clothing were causing a disagreeable irritation of the skin; but the knowing expression of countenance did not at all harmonize with
this. And the shrugging of the shoulders also occurred
when I stood before the child and said, " Yes, yes! "
As I had nodded then affirmatively, the child nodded
also (four hundred and fifty-ninth day).

This led me to the conjecture that the shrugging of
the shoulders might already express inability, and I was
soon confirmed in this, for, on the following day even,
this gesture was the answer to my question, " Where is
your ear? " in reply to which the child, after some
hesitation, touched his eye. In the sixteenth month
this signification was beyond question; for if I ask,
"Where is your eye, ear, nose, forehead, chin?" and the
child does not know some one of these, then, to my surprise, he shrugs his shoulders. At the same date there
often follows upon this expressional movement another,
of waiting. When waiting—e. g., for a biscuit dipped

in hot water to become cool—the child plants both arms at the same time symmetrically against his sides, in such a way that his hands come against his hips with fingers bent, the back of the hand touching the hips. The whole attitude is that of waiting—not in the least of demanding—and is probably imitated, which can not be said of shrugging the shoulders. This became, moreover, in the second quarter of the second year, decidedly a sign, in the same sense as a shaking of the head in denial, of refusing, and of not knowing and of not being able. It must be counted among the as yet inexplicable hereditary expressive movements. Darwin also declares himself in favor of the hereditary character of the movement, but he did not see it in any very young English child, and reports it only in the case of two sisters (grandchildren of a Frenchman) who shrugged their shoulders between the sixteenth and eighteenth months.

7. Begging with the Hands and Pointing.

Putting the hands together in the attitude of begging belongs to the earliest gestures of German children that are acquired by training. This movement is, at the same time, one of the first of which the child understands the significance as language, and of which he makes use. He soon finds that the begging position of the hands brings him the desired food quicker than crying, and for this reason he makes the gesture of himself always when he wants anything, whether it be a biscuit, a toy, or a change of place. If continued crying, for a longer or shorter time, has proved wholly useless, then it is suddenly discontinued, and the child hastily puts his hands together in a begging attitude (fifteenth month), in case this childish trick happens to have been previously taught him. He also begs in this fashion without crying, and by making sounds of longing, with outstretched arms—e. g., when he desires the repetition of some new sort of fun. When some one had poised a spoon on the end of his nose, the (fourteen and a half months old) child laughed, seized the spoon, observed it carefully, put it from one hand into the other, and then handed it to the person with an indescribably beseeching tone of voice. Upon the repetition of the experiment he was again delighted.

Long even after learning the significance of the spoken "*Bitte*" ("I beg," or "Please"), which my boy pronounced "*bibi*" up to the twenty-second month, the accompanying raising and holding together of the hands did not cease; 'and what was especially surprising, when the child wished the continuance of a sight that pleased him, or of piano-playing, or when the railway train in which the child was traveling stopped, then he would strike his hands together repeatedly (twenty-third month), so that in a literal sense he manifested his applause and his desire for repetition or continuance by clapping the hands, just like a gratified public at the theatre. Nay, even in the tenth, as also in the seventeenth, month, this movement took place in sleep, no doubt, during dreaming.

It seems natural to assume that adults utter their applause by hand-clapping for the reason that the noise is greater; but the putting of the hands together in prayer in Christian churches, as well as the lifting of the arms in prayer by Mohammedans, agrees with the begging gestures of children. These express only indi-

rectly, by hand-clapping and also by noiseless putting
together of the hands, their satisfaction so far as they
thereby beg for repetition.

How it comes about that very small children are
artificially taught, along with the "giving of the hand"
(even in the twentieth to the twenty-fourth week sometimes [Lindner]), to raise and put together the hands
(not the feet), when they are to beg for anything, is not
hard to understand. This gesture is indeed acquired
by each individual through imitation and training, but
probably has its foundation in this, that in the act of
seizing, the arms are extended, and the hands, when
the desired object is grasped, place themselves about it.
Begging is also ultimately a desiring. And if we follow
the history of the development of the seizing movements from the beginning (p. 241), we are easily convinced that the arms, which must be extended for seizing, are, when this has been many times successful, extended in case of every strong desire (with and without
sounds expressive of desire), because the thing desired
is regarded as capable of being seized. What I have
stated as to the interpretation of the retinal images
(p. 62) confirms this view.

At first the child expresses his desire only by crying; after he has begun to seize, also by stretching out
the arms (in the case of my child for the first time on
the one hundred and twenty-first day); then, by extending the arms and putting the hands together. These
hereditary expressional movements, originating in the
practice of seizing, are made use of by educators, in order to teach the praying, begging attitudes, with folding
of the hands, which in the beginning are not in the least

understood by the child; he simply finds by experience that the joining of the hands along with the raising of the arms is sooner followed by the fulfillment of a wish than crying is, and for this reason he adopts the gesture. When, now, with the development of the faculty of sight, new objects that can not be seized are better distinguished from their surroundings, then the child manifests his lively interest in them—especially in moved and moving objects, e. g., horses—by this very gesture; he opens his mouth, breathes loudly by starts, fixates the object, and stretches out his hands (eighth month). Often at this period one can hardly tell whether the child means to *seize* or to *point*. When, before he can speak, at the question, "Where is the light?" he turns his head to the light, he thereby shows his understanding of the question as to the direction (ninth month); but when (in the fourteenth month) he lifts the right arm besides and points to the light with outspread fingers, then he has executed the gesture of *pointing*, absolutely distinct from desiring.

For the understanding of mental development it is an important fact that this pointing is already employed with perfect correctness before the first attempts at expression in words. A little girl of eleven months, who could not yet speak at all, answered the questions, "Where is papa?" "Where is Nannie?" etc., correctly, without a single mistake, by movements of the eyes and by indicating direction with the finger (Frau von Strümpell).

Later, this pointing is used as the expression of a wish, as it is by the deaf and dumb—e. g., my boy in the ninetieth week, at sight of the milk-pitcher, pointed at it with his hand, and directly after at the milk-bottle with the same hand—in fact, to my surprise, with the forefinger, the child unmistakably having the purpose of getting the milk poured out. Whence comes all at once the use of the forefinger in place of the spreading of all the fingers for pointing? Imitation alone hardly offers sufficient occasion for it; still less does the experimental touching. Rather, the whole complicated combination of " fixating," opening the mouth, raising the eyelids, lifting the arm, extending the fingers, must rest upon hereditary co-ordination, which, in case of hunger, has showed itself useful in obtaining food; so that *pointing* is thus to be traced back to *wishing to seize*. As is regularly the case in the tenth month, so in the second year, often the desired object that is pointed at is carried to the mouth, and as much as possible chewed up, after it is obtained.

From the success of the arm-movements expressing desire in case of hunger, soon arises the notion that these movements will also gratify other kinds of desire. Thus the child (in the twelfth month) sitting on a chair, when he desires to change his position, stretches out both arms longingly (cries if no attention is paid to him), and rejoices when taken up, as he does on getting an apple or a biscuit. In such cases, not unfrequently —e. g., in the fourteenth month—a " paramimy " is observed, since, instead of the begging position of the hands, one of the other little performances acquired by training and not yet understood by him, is executed— e. g., the hand is moved toward the head as an answer that has been learned to the question, " Where is the little rogue?" (*Trotzköpfchen*, "headstrong"). Here, with

the experience of success upon stretching out the hands
blends the experience of the agreeable (of friendliness,
it may be—of granting his requests) upon the right performance of those little tricks. The likeness of the results leads to confounding of the means.

But the more the voice is differentiated, so much the
more surely is a sound united with the gesture in the
first three months of the second year. Thus, with the
extending of the hands the begging sound "*hay-ŭh*"
(in the case of my child) was joined, this being associated
with the look and the forward inclination of the body,
as the expression of the strongest desire. But it passes
away and is lost, since with the growth of the understanding the gestures become more firmly established,
and are no longer confused with one another. Later
still, the speaking of the words learned takes the place
of the gestures, which they make less and less necessary.
In the fifteenth month, by striking with a ring I made
three glasses sound, the tones of which formed a chord.
The child was pleased, laughed, and when I paused,
he took the ring, handed it to me again, and directing
toward the glasses his arms, eyes, and head, announced
with his own peculiar *hay-ŭh*, his wish for a repetition.
Here, as yet, no *word-language existed, but the language
of gesture could not be misunderstood.*

When no response is made to a persistently-expressed
desire, then there may easily happen in lively children
a regular fit of rage; they throw themselves on the
floor, strike out when taken hold of, and scream furi-
ously and most angrily (observed by me for the first
time in the seventeenth month). But it may also happen if, e. g., the child pulls some one by the hand and

wants to be accompanied, that, on being denied the request, the child sheds tears of sorrow in place of being angry (twenty-third month). The spirit of invention may also be aroused, as in the following case: The child (of twenty-two months) wishes to sit at the table. No one listens to his entreaty or takes notice of his imploring gesticulations. Thereupon, he goes into the corner of the room, tries, with a great effort, to get a heavy chair, does not rest till it has been placed at the table, strikes with the flat of his hand on the seat of the chair, thus expressing plainly, without words, what he wants, and exults when he has been put up on the chair.

Besides the expressive movements discussed in this chapter, there are, in early childhood, several more that deserve a thorough investigation. They are generally hard to describe, however, although they are often easily understood, even when the child does not, as yet, speak a word. For the child's attitude, the direction of his look, the movements of his fingers, in varying combinations, make already a finely-developed *mute language.* Some examples may illustrate this.

In the fourteenth month affection is expressed by a gentle laying of the hand upon the face and shoulders [of others]—this movement is presumably acquired by imitation; anger and disobedience (willfulness) by very obstinate straightening of the body; this, in fact, in the tenth month even, when the child is laid down; shame —when he has soiled himself—by peculiar crying, with tears; pride (in a new baby-carriage in the nineteenth month). by a ridiculous bearing. The variety in the expression of countenance, when in the second and third years the separate passions gradually awake, is, however, indescribable, and, on account of the transitoriness of the phenomena, is hardly to be reproduced pictorially. Jealousy, pride, pugnacity, covetousness, lend to the childish countenance a no less characteristic look than do generosity, obedience, ambition. These states could not be recognized by the expression of countenance unless each of them had its own expressional movement, and, in fact, these movements appear in greater purity in the child, who does not dissemble, than they do in later life.

It is beyond the limits of this work to trace the connection of these mental states with the play of feature and with the growth of the will. Very many more observations must be instituted in regard to children before the influence of imitation and of inheritance upon the voluntary inhibition of emotional outbreaks, and upon the voluntary inducing of a state of mind at once self-contented and not disturbing to others can be understood.

CHAPTER XIV.

DELIBERATE (ÜBERLEGTE) MOVEMENTS.

THAT it is a very long time before we can perceive in the child a movement that is independent, proceeding from his own deliberation, follows from the foregoing chapters. Before *motives*, i. e., *reasons*, for movement can be added to the purely physical centro-motor impulses, to the peripheral reflex stimuli, to the inclination to imitate, to instinct, to the feelings as causes of muscular movements, not only must the motor experiences mentioned have been had countless times, but the

23

senses and the understanding must be a good deal developed. For he who moves no longer merely in *direct* dependence on his temporary feelings, moods, and mental and physical states in general—he who *represents to himself before the movement how the movement will be; in a word, he who acts must already have perceived very many movements of others and have felt very many movements of his own, in order to be able to originate in his mind a correct image of the purely voluntary, deliberate, or intentional movement that is to be executed.*

I should not be able to name any movement of the first three months to which this necessary condition applies well enough to exclude every doubt as to whether the movement might not be instinctive (and therefore inherited), or reflexive, or impulsive.

The *tactile* movements with the hands—not the feet—that occur in the first months, and have the appearance of *seeking*, are just as little voluntary as are the later *pulling* and *scratching* at the skin of a face touched; they are, as belonging to seizing, instinctive. Even *stamping* with the foot (in the eleventh month), pushing along a chair, at the same period, stretching the body out straight and stiff, as means of preventing being laid down by force (in the tenth month), as well as the much later movements of throwing, can not be styled intentional muscular movements, founded on independent deliberation. Rather do some plays, which are not to be referred either to imitation or instinct, either to reflex stimuli or emotions, point to the germination of choice and deliberation after the awakening of the function of causality. Thus my child, in the eleventh month, used frequently to strike a spoon against a newspaper or against another object held in his hand, and to exchange both objects suddenly, moving the spoon with the other hand, which gave exactly the impression of testing whether the noise proceeded from the one arm only, or would arise likewise in case this arm were motionless (p. 87). The restless *experimenting* of little children, especially in the first attempts at accommodation (p. 54) [of the eye]—even quite insignificant practices (like the crumpling of paper from the third to the sixth month), are not only useful but indispensable for the intellectual development. Moreover, it is essential to consider, in regard to the cultivation of the will, because thereby the understanding is gradually awakened, how inefficient most of the early, unrepresented, non-coördinated movements were, and how useful, on the contrary, are the co-ordinated movements with definite aims. Only when both occur together, the representation of the movement and the expectation of its result, is deliberate movement possible, which, unfortunately, is too often prevented through training from showing itself early. Often even in the second year we can tell only with difficulty, or can not tell at all, whether the child acts independently or not—e. g., when (in the sixteenth month) he opens and shuts cupboards, picks up from the floor and brings objects that he threw down. When, on the contrary, at this period, he holds, entirely of his own motion, an ear-ring that had been taken off, to the ear from which it was taken, I am inclined to see in that already a sign of deliberation—understanding and choice—whereas in the mere making of noise—it may be by opening and slamming-to the cover of a box, or by the eager tearing of newspapers—there is rather the co-operation of pleasure in noise and movement with gratification in the putting forth of power, than of deliberation and choice. Yet it seemed to me worthy of note that my child one day (in the fourteenth month) took off and put on the cover of a can not less than seventy-nine times, without stopping a moment. His attention, meantime, strained to the utmost, indicated that the intellect was taking part. "How does this noise happen?" the child would surely have thought, if he had been able to speak; for he often enough asked later, "What makes that?" when he heard a strange noise. But even the child not yet acquainted with speech might think thus, like an intelligent brute animal, only the latter would not lift the cover so often of his own accord.

It can not be doubted that the child wills and thinks long before the acquirement of speech; but independent activity joins itself to the unintentional, involuntary muscular movements quite imperceptibly, after long, incomplete manifestation of the power of co-ordination. The feelings that are determinative for all mental development, feelings of pleasure and displeasure, the attempts to seize that which excites desire—food, above all—and to keep off that which causes discomfort, must be looked upon as starting-points of the continuously-advancing development.

In this respect the history of the development of seizing, which has been portrayed, is a contribution at the same time to the knowledge of the development of volition. Especially the independent taking of food, that begins after the first attempts at seizing, offers interesting transitions from the imperfectly co-ordinated to the perfectly harmonious movement of the muscular apparatus of arm, mouth, tongue, and œsophagus. I group some observations concerning this point, made upon my own child, which show that the will is present before the co-ordination is complete.

5th month.—Meat offered with a fork is seized with the hand and carried slowly to the mouth; many times incorrectly, but once properly.

9th month.—Whatever can be brought to the mouth is put upon the tongue with astonishing celerity. In this operation fewer errors were made than before.

11th month.—The child, every day, of his own accord, takes a biscuit from the table with the hand, carries it correctly to his mouth—previously he often put it to his cheek or chin—bites off a bit, chews it fine, and swallows it; but he can not yet drink from a glass.

12th month.—Very seldom is there a failure to hit the mouth at the first trial with the biscuit. At the beginning of this month, too, the child can drink from a glass, only he still breathes into the water while drinking.

18th month.—The full spoon is carried to the mouth with tolerable skill.

19th month.—If the spoon is laid on the left side of the plate, then, after a little consideration, he takes it with his left hand, and no difference is noticeable between his use of the left and the right hand in eating.

20th month.—The child carries the spoon with food in it to the mouth more and more cleverly, quickly, and surely. For all that, he can not yet, without help or guidance, alone take food with the spoon—can not get it into the spoon. He does not always bestow attention enough on it; often pauses and grasps at shining objects of all sorts, when the things about him are such as he is not accustomed to.

In the months following, the child, being purposely remanded to his own resources, perfects himself in this line of action. What has been reported is, however, enough to show that intention is present long before co-ordination is perfected. Will, knowledge of consequences, representation of the whole movement—these are clear before the movement can be correctly executed. The reverse is the case with the characteristic pleasure taken by all boys in throwing; they hurl all sorts of things out of the window without a thought of the consequences.

This difference, often overlooked, between *willed* and instinctive movements of children, may be demonstrated in many other forms of movement, especially if the manner of playing, or the occupation from day to day, from week to week, is watched. But I have already presented so many particular instances, and the observations are so easy to make, if only time enough is given, and if several normal children are compared, that it seems unnecessary here to multiply examples. Only the movements of the tongue, which are the most important sign of the developed will, will be more fully treated as the foundation of learning to speak, in the description of that process (in the Third Part).

It suffices here, in order to ascertain approximately the date of the beginning of the manifestation of will, and of deliberation, in one child at least, to put together some of the movements treated in the previous chapters with reference to the questions: when the inborn movements are no longer purely impulsive; no longer purely mechanically reflexive; no longer purely instinctive; and when movements undoubtedly willed appear without the admixture of the others.

It holds good universally, that *willing can not take place until after the forming of ideas.* Up to that period the child is will-less, like an animal without a brain. After the beginning of the ideational or representative activity of the brain, a period is still necessary for the association of the idea or representation of a movement and the idea of an object (desired) as the aim of the movement. In this period of transition—from the incipient causative activity which changes the perceptions arising from sensuous impressions into ideas, to the combination of two ideas—a sensory and a motor— fall the movements of the infant that are the hardest to understand, those that have still a mixed character.

The following provisional synopsis is intended to help in determining the limits of this period in both directions:

MOVEMENT.	No trace existing.	First attempts.	With deliberation and effect.	Remarks.
Head-shaking....	....	4th day.	16th week.	In refusal.
Holding the head.	10th week.	11th week.	16th "	
Seizing...........	114th day.	117th day.	17th "	
Raising the upper part of body.	12th week.	16th(?) week.	22d "	Lying on back without help.
Pointing..........	4th month.	8th month.	9th month.	
Sitting...........	13th week.	14th week.	42d week.	Without being held or supported.
Standing.........	21st "	23d "	48th "	Wholly without support.
Walking..........	40th "	41st "	66th "	Alone, freely.
Raising one's self.	13th "	28th "	70th "	Without being held or helped.
Stepping over a threshold.	65th "	68th "	70th "	Without support.
Kissing...........	11th month.	12th month.	23d month.	
Climbing..........	24th(?) "	26th "	27th "	Without being held or helped.
Jumping	24th(?) "	27th "	28th "	

After this, will-power begins to show itself in co-ordinated movements of the larger muscular groups in the sixteenth and seventeenth weeks; so, too, the first imitations (p. 283) were successful, and, for the first time, his own image in the mirror was regarded with attention (twentieth chapter); willed contractions of the muscles of the eye, however, take place somewhat earlier (p. 46). Unquestionably deliberate, voluntary turning of the gaze to new objects I did not see, indeed, until the sixteenth week.

Thus, in the case of my child, the only one as yet regularly observed in the first months with reference to his movements, we shall have to postpone the beginning of the active manifestation of the will—i. e., of the activity of the cerebral cortex in the co-ordination of the muscles chiefly used later—to the fourth month. But, according to many experiments on other children, this very date probably holds good pretty generally, whereas later, in sitting, standing, walking, climbing, jumping, talking, the greatest variations as to time appear.

The first deliberate movements take place only after the close of the first three months.

Were there still need of proof that infants can not earlier execute voluntarily any movement whatever, on account of the as yet insufficient development of the cerebrum, it would be furnished by such facts as have been observed in microcephalous human beings. For in them the cerebrum remains deficient, and the will is not developed.

But that deliberate movements are made at the beginning of the second half-year, is proved by an instructive experiment that G. Lindner made upon his little daughter of twenty-six weeks. While the child at this age was taking milk as she lay in the cradle, the bottle took such a slant that she could not get anything to suck. She now tried to direct the bottle with her feet, and finally raised it by means of them so dexterously that she could drink conveniently. " This action was manifestly no imitation; it can not have depended upon a mere accident; for, when, at the next feeding, the bottle is purposely so placed that the child can not get anything without the help of hands or feet, the same performance takes place as before. Then, on the following day, when the child drinks in the same way, I prevent her from doing so by removing her feet from the bottle; but she at once makes use of them again as regulators for the flow of the milk, as dexterously and surely as if the feet were made on purpose for such use. If it follows from this that the child acts with deliberation long before it uses language in the proper sense, it also appears how imperfect and crude the child's deliberation is; for my child drank her milk in this awkward fashion for three whole months, until she at last made the discovery one day that, after all, the hands are much better adapted to service of this sort. I had given strict orders to those about her to let her make this advance of herself."

Other examples of deliberate movements made before the ability to speak exists are given later, in the Third Part. To this category belong also the attempts at imitation, rare, indeed, but well marked, that are observed in the fifth month; likewise, the first imitations of sounds and the attempts to repeat the speech of others, of which something will be said farther on.

CHAPTER XV.

SUMMARY OF GENERAL RESULTS.

In order to explain the formation and growth of the child's will, there is needed, above all, a careful observation of the muscular movements of the newly-born and of the infant. The inborn movements of every human being are of various kinds, but are of the same nature a short time after birth as they are a short time before birth—only freer than in the embryo, on account of greater room for motion, and modified by respiration.

These inborn, absolutely will-less movements are *impulsive*, when they are conditioned, as in the embryo, exclusively upon the organic processes going on in the central organs of the nervous system, especially in the spinal cord, and take place without any peripheral excitement of any of the sensory nerves. To these belong the remarkable, aimless, ill-adapted movements of the arms and legs of children just born, and their grimaces. All the motor nerves of the whole organism seem to take part in these impulsive muscular contractions. The opening of the eyes and the lateral movements of them, the rolling of the eyeball, the closing of the lid, and many contractions of the facial muscles immediately after birth, prove the excitement of the oculo-motorius, of the trochlearis, of the motor-trigeminus branches, of the abducens, of the facialis; the movements of the tongue show excitement of the hypo-glossus; the arm-and-leg-movements show excitement of the spinal motors without any assignable or admissible peripheral stimuli.

The inborn movements are, on the contrary, reflexive when they occur only upon peripheral impressions, such as light, sound, contact. In these, also, most of the motor nerves seem to be concerned, and, indeed, in general, in the manner that the laws of reflexes which have been found in brainless animals would lead us to expect. The reflexes of the newly-born are, however, slower in their operation at the beginning than after frequent repetition, and in individual cases show deviations from the condition found in full-grown men and animals. These deviations are probably to be referred partly to this, that the reflex-paths are developed to an unequal extent, so that a roundabout way sometimes offers less resistance to the reflex excitement than does the direct way. Hence, perhaps, the contra-lateral reflexes. From all the organs of sense, in the first days, reflexes go forth—viz., from the optic nerve, auditory nerve, olfactory, gustatory, the sensory branches of the trigeminus, and the cutaneous nerves, upon the whole surface of the body. But the stimuli must, in general, be stronger than at a later period, or (at least, in the skin and retina) must affect a greater number of extremities of nerve-fibers simultaneously, in case distinct reflexes are to take place. The reflex excitability of the skin of the face is relatively greater from birth on, than that of other parts.

A third kind of inborn movements is the *instinctive*, which, indeed, likewise occur only after certain sensory peripheral excitations, but neither with the mechanical uniformity of the reflexes, nor with the constancy of

those, even when reflex excitability is present.   Rather
is there need of a special psychical condition, which may
best be styled "disposition" (or "tone").   At any rate
there is required an activity of those central organs of
the nervous system, through which feelings have their
existence.   If the disposition, or the feeling is wanting,
then the instinctive movement is not made, even under
the strongest or most appropriate stimulus—as in the
case of laughter, when the sole of the foot of a child in
a sorrowful frame of mind is tickled by a stranger.   A
good example of the typical, instinctive, inborn movements of mankind is presented in sucking.   With this
is allied licking.   In new-born animals, especially chickens just hatched, many more complicated instinctive
movements appear, however, since perceptions producing directly a motor effect are followed by highly expedient co-ordinated movements; especially perceptions
of sight.   The eye of the bird, during the whole embryonic period, is much larger in proportion to the brain
than that of man, and can furnish accurately localized
impressions immediately after the bird is hatched.
These impressions are, by means of an hereditary mech
anism, at once (in pecking) turned to account, and thereby deliberate movements are simulated.   In fact, however, no movement of a new-born animal or child is deliberate; none voluntary.

   Willed movements can not take place until the development of the senses is sufficiently advanced, not only
to distinguish clearly the qualities belonging to the separate departments of sense, not only to feel every impression, to localize the sensation, and to compare it with
other sensations, to note its antecedents and consequents

—in a word, to perceive, but sufficiently advanced also to recognize the cause of the perception, whereby the perception becomes a representation, a mental picture or idea. Without the power of representation there is no will; without the activity of the senses there is no representation; thus the will is actually, inseparably bound up with the senses. It disappears when they are extinguished; it is wanting to the person who is fast asleep.

From this dependence of all will upon the senses, it by no means follows that a developed activity of the senses invariably brings with it the development of the will; on the contrary, something else is required for that. The representations, or ideas, formed in the first months of human life, by means of innumerable perceptions, must, in order to have a motor effect in general, find on hand a large number of movements, upon which they now operate with determinative force. It is only upon the central sources of the motor nerves, which have for a long time and often been excited, impulsively and reflexively or instinctively, that an idea can operate to co-ordinate or to modify. And this motor influence of ideas is greatest when the idea itself is that of a movement, particularly that of a movement leading to a desired object or a goal striven for. Only after the lapse of the first three months do such willed movements take place; but not in such a way as if a wholly new psychical agency suddenly appeared in the child as by inspiration; rather does the development of the will go on very gradually. Only to the spectator the transition seems sudden, from the will-less child to the child that wills, if he observes seldom. The first successful combination of a motor idea with the idea of an object or an aim, as in the case of the first successful attempt to seize—that is what seems sudden. But what is surprising here is the *result*, because that was wanting before in the numerous similar attempts. In fact, both the movements that are now willed, and the perceptions that also become willed later, were long ago and often made; at first without being willed, as a result of the heightened excitability of the central organs of the nervous system, and of the increasing paths of association; then each one for itself, which gave rise to ideas; and finally both together. The movement itself runs the same course in both cases. The willing of the movement is merely the willing of one of the impulses, as W. Gude well observes; one of the impulses that the child has already often allowed to operate in himself or that he had to let operate. But all this is true only of the first act of willing.

After the child, in the second three months, has begun to execute willed movements in greater number, he soon finds that the earlier combinations of muscular contractions no longer suffice for his desires, which have, in the mean time, become exceedingly manifold. Hence becomes necessary, on the one hand, a *separation* of nervo-muscular excitations hitherto combined; on the other hand, an *association* of those hitherto separated. In this, for the first time, is manifested the direct participation of the intellect in the occurrence of voluntary movements. The ordinary childish performances, the first attempts at imitation in the fourth month, and the greater independence in the taking of food (e. g., taking hold of the bottle) are proofs of this; but the essen-

tial character of the will is not to be found either in
separation alone, i. e., in the effort to make muscles contract separately that have hitherto always contracted together, or in association alone, i. e., in the effort to make
muscles contract together that have hitherto always contracted singly. The will is neither co-ordinating only
nor isolating only, but both ; and, what is most frequently overlooked, in both departments it performs
nothing absolutely new. As Gude has shown, it can
not "call forth primary movements." It finds completely co-ordinated movements—inborn ones, in fact—
like sucking, swallowing, already on hand, as well as
typically isolated movements—e. g., the lifting of the
eyelid with the look downward—which later it in part
can not call forth at all, in part can call forth only after
an enormous amount of practice.

In this important fact, that the will, as a reciprocal
action of motor ideas, can alter, isolate, combine, repeat,
strengthen and weaken, hasten and delay existing movements, lies, at the same time, the key to the understanding of the difficulty of *learning.*

On the one hand, the abundant material of inborn
impulsive, reflexive, and instinctive movements, which
are mingled together in the first three months and are
influenced by the increasing activity of the senses,
favors the development of will, since it alone supplies
the requisite representations of movement ; on the
other hand, however, this very material renders more
difficult the manifestation of the directing power of the
will. For the more that certain nerve-paths have been
made easily passable by frequent repetition of movements, the greater will be the resistance to the combina-

tions of these with others, and to the employment of isolated tracts; the best proof of this is furnished in the accuracy, never afterward reappearing, of children's imitations (in the fourth year) of the accent, pronunciation, intonation of words given to them from foreign languages and from various dialects of their mother-tongue. The first imitations are the first distinct, represented, and willed movements.

In order to give accuracy to the proposed outline of the development of will in the child, we have yet to set forth briefly its bearing with regard to four problems. To every perfect activity of will are indispensable desire, muscular sensations, voluntary inhibition, and attention.

Desire, in the ordinary meaning of the word, presupposes ideas. Therefore, when it is said of the newly-born that it desires something (or even that it is searching for and wishes something), this form of expression is false. The child's relatives merely infer from its movements, attitude, position, situation, a condition of discomfort, displeasure, or discontent (in case of hunger, thirst, wet), and out of their own subjective state reason to the existence of a similar objective state in the child. In fact, however, the behavior of the newly-born, like that of the unborn, is intelligible without the assumption of any mental process whatever when we consider that, with the greater excitability of the central nervous organs in the spinal cord and the medulla oblongata, not only do reflexes—after refrigeration, wet, and the like —occur more easily and more frequently, but instinctive movements also, like sucking, and especially impulsive movements, are multiplied, e. g., crying; but now, in the case of hunger and other disagreeable states, that excitability is, in fact, increased. After the removal of the causes of the discomfort it is diminished, and then the mobility is likewise diminished. Thus the child behaves as if it desired, although it does not desire. But the repetition of the alternation of great mobility along with discomfort—less mobility along with comfort —during the first days, leaves behind in the central organs traces that make possible, or favor, the association of the remembrance of movement with the sensuous impression (milk, warm bath, etc.) that relieved the discomfort. Then the thing that relieves the discomfort is perceived and represented, and now, for the first time, a movement of "desire" is made.

The *muscular sensations* probably begin to be developed before birth, with the movements of the child. They must be present in all later muscular actions, even the purely impulsive, and they exert their influence in the performance of all those which take place only when a psychical factor co-operates—hence in all instinctive movements and all represented movements, consequently in voluntary ones also; for if it were not so, then it would remain incomprehensible how, in the successful, often extremely complicated, harmonious contractions of the most different muscles, just the required degree of contraction, and no more than this, is attained. But from this it does not in the least follow that they determine the will itself, especially as they do not regularly enter into the consciousness. They belong rather to the machinery of nervo-muscular excitement, and to the impulse to it, upon which alone the will can operate. They remain below the threshold of the will when they do not generate ideas.

24

The *voluntary inhibition* of a movement pre-supposes willed movements; it therefore appears in the child only after well-advanced development of the representational or ideational stage. It is based on an excitement in the state of non-willing, and is produced in the child through ideas as to the result of a movement. When the child's will is completely at rest, the rise of no movement is arrested by it; a muscular contraction may occur at any moment. But when, in this state of rest, ideas are formed which prevent the motor ideas awakened by sense-impressions or memory-images from operating on the motor centers of highest rank, then this state is called *voluntary inhibition*. It does not come to a manifestation of will—i. e., in this case; the child does not will, because in him an inhibitory process takes place that neutralizes the motor ideas. When he is asleep he does not will, because there are no motor ideas and no inhibitory ones. I understand by ideas here, as always, psychical facts that are bound up with organic processes in the ganglionic cells of the cerebrum, and are, in part, causes of movements, in so far as the nerve excitations, by means of connecting fibers and intermediate ganglionic cells, reach the motor centers of lower rank. Through this, the voluntary inhibition of many reflexes also is then made possible. The simplest represented movement, viz., the first imitation, requires this co-operation of the cerebrum no less than it requires attention.

The *attention* of the child and of the adult is either compulsory—aroused by strong sense-impressions—or voluntary. In the first case—which happens in human beings only during the first three weeks—by means of

a reflex movement after an unexpected stimulus of
sound, of light, or other sensuous stimulus, a feeling is
generated that is immediately, or after several repetitions, distinguished as a feeling of pleasure or of discomfort. The strong feeling leaves behind it a remembrance, and leads, after the perfection of the perceptive
and then of the representative activity, to ideas (A) of
the object of that movement—i. e., of the reflex stimulus. If, meanwhile, the co-ordination and separation of
the muscular movements is sufficiently developed so that
movements can also be brought to pass through motor
ideas (B), then the latter (B) combine with the former
(A) upon the object in question, and the attention is
voluntarily directed to it. But we must not infer from
the early, isolated symptoms of the later voluntary attention—like pouting of the lips, directing the gaze,
cessation of crying or of uneasiness—an already existing
concentration of attention ; since this may be a case of
the supplanting of one movement by another without
will. The following of a moved light with the eye in
the fourth week is possible, too, without the co-operation of the cerebrum (p. 45), whereas, later, it is precisely the fixation, for the purpose of seeing distinctly, that
is voluntary. Not till the seventh week (pp. 54, 142)
and the ninth week (pp. 55, 84) did I become convinced
that my child was actually attentive—since his eye frequently showed a peculiar intensity of expression in
hearing and seeing—after the operation of strong stimuli ; but that he, of his own motion, turned to an object
and lingered on it attentively, I observed first in the
sixteenth and seventeenth weeks, when, of his own accord, he gazed at his own image in the glass. At this

time, and much later still, an uninterrupted strain of
his attention was impossible to the child. His attention lasted only for moments.

Every act of will requires attention, and every concentration of attention is an act of will. Hence an act
of attention without an accompanying muscular contraction is unrecognizable. But those muscular movements that take place without any co-operation whatever
of voluntary attention, are void of attention, either for
the reason that will is still wanting—in the first weeks
—or for the reason that will is no longer required to
keep in operation the oft-repeated, voluntary movement
—or, finally, because the will is inactive, as, e. g., in
sleep.

In conclusion, in regard to education, which always
has to control the motor ideas of the child, and, in case
these are improper ones, to substitute better, we have
especially to consider the *weakness of the will* even in
the complete waking condition. The surprising credu-
lity, docility, obedience, tractableness, the slight degree
of independence of will in young children, that attests
itself besides in many little traits of character, reminds
one of the similar behavior of adults in the mesmeric
sleep. For example, if I say to my two-and-a-half-year-
old child, after he has already eaten something, but is just
on the point of biting off a fresh piece from his biscuit—
if I say categorically, without giving any reason at all,
with a positiveness that will tolerate no contradiction,
very loud, yet without frightening him, " The child
has had enough now!" then it comes to pass that he at
once puts away from his mouth the biscuit, without fin-
ishing his bite, and ends his meal altogether. It is easy

to bring children even three or four years old to the opinion that a feeling of pain (after a hit) is gone, or that they are not tired or thirsty, provided only that our demands are not extravagant, and are not pressed too often, and that our assertion is a very decided one.

In this weakness of the child's will lies also the reason that little children can not be mesmerized. Their will-power does not suffice to keep their attention concentrated persistently in one direction, which is a necessary condition of hypnotism.

The weariness connected with the strain of attention makes intelligible also the rapid alternation of the plays of the child. Through too frequent yielding in this respect, which appears unobjectionable only in the first period of play, the later development of voluntary inhibitions, upon which most depends in the formation of character, is rendered essentially more difficult, and caprice is fostered. Exercises in being obedient can not begin too early, and I have, during an almost daily observation of six years, discovered no harm from an early, consistent guiding of the germinating will, provided only this guiding be done with the greatest mildness and justice, as if the infant had already an insight into the benefits of obedience. By assuming insight in the child, insight will be earlier awakened than by training; and by giving a true and reasonable ground for every command, as soon as the understanding begins, and by avoiding all groundless *prohibitions*, obedience is made decidedly more easy.

Thus, through cultivation of ideas of a higher order, the will may be directed even in the second year, and thereby the character be formed; but only through inexorable consistency, which allows no exception to a prohibition, is it possible to maintain the form once impressed upon the character.

[The third part of this work, treating of the Development of the Intellect, together with supplementary matter, is reserved for another volume of this series.— EDITOR.]

END OF VOL I.

INTERNATIONAL EDUCATION SERIES

THE MIND OF THE CHILD
PART II

THE DEVELOPMENT
OF THE INTELLECT

*OBSERVATIONS CONCERNING
THE MENTAL DEVELOPMENT OF THE HUMAN BEING
IN THE FIRST YEARS OF LIFE*

BY

W. PREYER
PROFESSOR OF PHYSIOLOGY IN JENA

TRANSLATED FROM THE ORIGINAL GERMAN
By H. W. BROWN
TEACHER IN THE STATE NORMAL SCHOOL AT WORCESTER, MASS.

NEW YORK
D. APPLETON AND COMPANY
1889

EDITOR'S PREFACE.

THIS second volume contains the further investigations of Professor Preyer on the mind of the child. The former volume contained the first and second portions, devoted respectively to the development of the senses and of the will. The present volume contains the third part, treating of the development of the intellect; and three appendixes are added containing supplementary matter.

Professor Preyer considers that the development of the power of using language is the most prominent index to the unfolding of the intellect. He differs with Professor Max Müller, however, on the question whether the operation of thinking can be carried on without the use of words (see the recent elaborate work of the latter on "The Science of Thought").

At my suggestion, the painstaking translator of this book has prepared a full conspectus, showing the results of Professor Preyer's careful observations in a chronological order, arranged by months. This considerable labor will render the book more practical, inasmuch as it will enable each reader to see at a glance the items of development of the child in the

several departments brought together in epochs. This
makes it possible to institute comparative observations
under the guidance of Professor Preyer's method. I
think that I do not exaggerate the value of this conspectus when I say that it doubles the value of the
work to the reader.

WILLIAM T. HARRIS.

CONCORD, MASS., *November, 1888.*

CONTENTS.

APPENDIXES.

A CONSPECTUS OF
THE OBSERVATIONS OF PROFESSOR PREYER ON THE MIND OF THE CHILD.

ARRANGED CHRONOLOGICALLY BY MONTHS, FOR THE CONVENIENCE OF
THOSE WHO WISH TO VERIFY THESE OBSERVATIONS, OR TO
USE THEM AS A GUIDE IN THEIR OWN INVESTIGATIONS.

By H. W. BROWN.

FIRST MONTH.

SENSES.*

SIGHT.—*Light.*—Five minutes after birth, slight sensibility to light (2). Second day, sensitiveness to light of candle (3). Sixth and seventh days, pleasure in moderately bright daylight (3, 4). Ninth and tenth days, sensitiveness greater at waking than soon afterward (3). Sleeping babes close the eyes more tightly when light falls on the eyes (4). Eleventh day, pleasure in light of candle and in bright object (3).

Discrimination of Colors.—Twenty-third day, pleasure in sight of rose-colored curtain (6).

Movements of Eyelids.—First to eleventh day, shutting and opening of eyes (22). Irregular movements (23). Lid closed at touch of lashes from sixth day on (26). Twenty-fifth day, eyes opened and shut when child is spoken to or nodded to (30).

Pleasure shown by opening eyes wide, displeasure by shutting them tightly; third, sixteenth, and twenty-first days (31).

Movements of Eyes.—First day, to right and left (35). Tenth

---

* Under "Senses" and "Will" the numbers in parentheses indicate pages in Vol. I.

lips: mouth-piece of bottle ditto. Tenth day, smile after eating. Fourth week, signs of satisfaction; laughing, opening and half shutting eyes; inarticulate sounds (157).

Fatigue.—From crying and nursing (159). Second and third weeks, from use of senses (160). First month, sleep lasts two hours; sixteen of the twenty-four hours spent in sleep (162).

WILL.

Impulsive Movements.—Outstretching and bending of arms and legs just after birth; contractions, spreading and bending of fingers (205). Grimaces (207). Wrinkling of forehead (309). First day, arms and legs take same position as before birth (206). Second week, stretching of limbs after waking (205).

Reflex Movements.—In case of light-impressions (34–42). First cry (213). Sneezing of newly-born (214). Coughing, ditto. (216). Seventh day, yawning (215). First day, spreading of toes when sole of foot is touched (224). First day, hiccough (219). First five days, choking (218). Wheezing, yawning (215). Seventh day, respiration irregular (217). Ninth day, clasping (243). Tenth day, lips protruded (283). Fourteenth day, movement of left hand toward left temple (220). Twenty-fourth day, snoring (215).

Instinctive Movements.—First to third day, hands to face. Fifth day, fingers clasp firmly; toes do not. Sixth day, hands go into eye (244). Seventh day, pencil held with toes, but no seizing. Ninth day, no clasping by sleeping child (245). Sucking (257–261). At end of first week, lateral movements of head (264). Third week, clasping with fingers, not with thumb (245).

Expressive Movements.—Twenty-sixth day, smile of contentment (296). Twenty-third day, tears flow (307). Crying, with tears, and whimpering, become signs of mental states (308).

INTELLECT.*

Memory first active in the departments of taste and of smell; then in touch, sight, hearing (5). Comparison of tastes (I, 123). Vowel-sounds in first month (67). Sounds in first six months (74). Sounds made in crying and screaming, *u-ä* (101). Twenty-second day, association of the breast with nursing (I, 260).

---

* Under "Intellect" the numbers in parentheses indicate pages from Vol. II, unless otherwise stated.

SECOND MONTH.

SENSES.

SIGHT.—*Light.*—Bright or highly-colored objects give pleasure (4).

Discrimination of Colors.—Forty-second day, pleasure in sight of colored tassels (7).

Movements of Eyelids.—Fifth week, irregular movements of lids. Eighth week, lid covering iris (23). Twenty-fifth day, opening and shutting eyes in surprise (30). Fifty-seventh and fifty-eighth days, winking. Sixtieth day, quick opening and shutting in fright (26).

Movements of Eyes.—Thirty-first day, strabismus rare. Forty-sixth to fiftieth day, very rare. Fifty-fifth day, irregular movements rare, but appearing in sleep till the sixtieth day (37).

Direction of Look.—Fifth week, toward the Christmas-tree (45). Thirty-ninth day, toward tassels swinging (46). Seventh week, moving lamp or bright object followed (45).

HEARING.—Fifth week, child does not sleep if persons walk or speak. Starting at noises. Sixth week, starting at slight noises even in sleep; quieted by mother's singing. Seventh week, fright at noise is greater (83). Sensibility to musical tones, ditto. Eighth week, tones of piano give pleasure (84).

TOUCH.—Thirty-eighth day, movements caused by touch of water (107). Forty-first day, reflex movement of arms caused by a general slight agitation (105, 106). Fiftieth and fifty-fifth days, closing of eyelid at touch of eyelash (103). Seventh week, upper lip sensitive (100).

ORGANIC SENSATIONS AND EMOTIONS.—Pleasure in musical sounds (141); in sight of human face (142). Reflexive laughing (145). Sixth week, fretfulness and hunger (155). Eighth week, fatigue after hearing piano-playing (160). Sleep of three, sometimes five or six hours (162).

WILL.

Impulsive Movements.—Of eyes before waking, also twistings and raisings of trunk (206). Seventh week, number of respirations twenty-eight to the minute (217).

Reflex Movements.—Of right arm at touch of left temple (220). Forty-third day, sneezing caused by witch-meal (215). Fifth week, vomiting (219). Eighth week, laughing caused by tickling (225).

Instinctive Movements.—Seventh week, clasping not yet with thumb. Eighth week, the four fingers of the child embrace the father's finger (245).

INTELLECT.

Speech.—Forty-third day, first consonant; child says *am-ma ;* also vowel-sound *ao.* Forty-fourth day, syllables *ta-hu ;* forty-sixth day, *gö, örö ;* fifty-first day, *ara ;* eighth and ninth weeks, *örrö, arra,* frequent (102).

THIRD MONTH.

SENSES.

SIGHT.—*Movements of the Eyelids.* — Eyelid not completely raised when child looked up (23). Irregular movements of eyes appear (though rare) up to tenth week; at three months are no more observed (37).

Direction of Look.—Sixty-first day, child looked at his mother and gave a cry of joy; the father's face made the child gay. Sixty-second day, look directed at a swinging lamp (46).

Seeing Near and Distant Objects.—Ninth week, accommodation apparent (54).

HEARING.—Ninth week, sound of watch arouses attention; other noises (84). Eleventh week, head moved in direction of sound (85). Eighty-first day ditto. (47). Twelfth week, sudden turning of head toward sounding body (85).

ORGANIC SENSATIONS AND EMOTIONS.—*Pleasure.*—Smile at sight of the mother's face (145).

Unpleasant Feeling.—From some internal cause (151).

Fatigue.—Sucking tiresome (159). Sleep of four or five hours without waking (162).

Hunger.—Tenth week, child hungry three times or more in a night (155).

WILL.

Reflex Movements.—Respirations, thirteenth week, twenty-seven to the minute (217). Hiccough frequent; stopped by use of sweetened water (219).

Instinctive Movements.—Eleventh week, pencil held, but mechanically; thumb not used in clasping (245). Twelfth week, eighty-fourth day, contra-position of thumb reflexive (245, 246). Thirteenth week, thumb follows fingers more readily (246). Eleventh week, head balanced occasionally. Twelfth week, some gain in holding head. Thirteenth week, head tolerably well balanced (264). Seizing merely apparent (246). No voluntary movement (266).

weeks, no intentional seizing. One hundred and fourteenth day, ditto (246). Seventeenth week, efforts to take hold of ball; ball moved to mouth and eyes. One hundred and eighteenth day, frequent attempts at seizing; following day, grasping gives pleasure (247). Fourteenth week, head seldom falls forward. Sixteenth week, head held up permanently (264), this the first distinct manifestation of will (265). Fourteenth week, child sits, his back supported (267). Seventeenth week, biting (261).

Imitative Movements.—Fifteenth week, beginnings of imitation; trying to purse the lips (283). Seventeenth week, protruding tip of tongue (284).

Expressive Movements.—Sixteenth week, turnings of head and nodding, not significant; head turned away in refusal (314).

Deliberate Movements.—Fourteenth week, attentive looking at person moving; one hundred and first day, at pendulum swinging (48). Fifteenth week, imitation, pursing lips (283). Sixteenth and seventeenth weeks, voluntary gazing at image in mirror (343).

INTELLECT.

Intellect participates in voluntary movements (I, 338).

Speech.—Fourteenth week, *ntö, ha, lö, na.* Fifteenth week, *nan-nana, nā-nā, nanna,* in refusal (103). Sixteenth week, in screaming, *ă-ŭ ă-ŭ ă, ā-ŭ ā-ŭ, ŭ-ā ŭ-ā, ū-ū-ā-ö, amme-a;* in discomfort, *ūă-ūă-ūă-ūă* (104).

Feeling of Self.—Seventeenth week, child gazes at his own hand (193). One hundred and thirteenth day, for the first time regards his image with attention (197). One hundred and sixteenth day, laughs at his image (198).

FIFTH MONTH.

SENSES.

SIGHT.—*Direction of Look.*—Looking inquiringly (48).

Seeing Near and Distant Objects.—Reaching too short (55).

HEARING.—Nineteenth week, pleasure in sound of crumpling of paper by himself. Twenty-first week, beating of gong enchains attention (85). Disturbed by noise (86).

TOUCH.—Auditory canal sensitive (106).

ORGANIC SENSATIONS AND EMOTIONS.—Pleasure in crumpling paper, tearing newspapers and rolling them into balls, pulling at glove or hair, ringing of a bell (142, 143). Eighteenth week, dis-

2

comfort shown by depressing angles of mouth (149). Eighteenth week, nights of ten to eleven hours without taking food (155). Eighteenth week, desire shown by stretching out arms (247).

WILL.

Instinctive Movements.—Eighteenth week, objects seized are held firmly and carried to the mouth (247). Nineteenth week, child takes bit of meat and carries to mouth. One hundred and twenty-third day, lips protruded in connection with seizing (248).

INTELLECT.

Speech.—Consonant *k*, *gö*, *kö*, *ăggĕggĕkö*. First five months, screaming sounds *u*, *ä*, *ö*, *a*, with *ü* and *o*; *m* almost the only consonant (104).

Feeling of Self.—Discovery by child that he can cause sensations of sound (192). Looking at his own fingers very attentively (194).

SIXTH MONTH.

SENSES.

SIGHT.—*Movements of Eyelids.*—Twenty-fifth week, winking caused by puff of wind in face (27).

Interpretation of what is seen.—Child laughs when nodded to by father; observes father's image in mirror, etc. (62).

TASTE.—Medicine taken if sweetened (124). One hundred and fifty-sixth day, child refuses breast, having had sweeter milk. End of twenty-third week, milk of new nurse taken, also cow's milk, meat-broth (125).

ORGANIC SENSATIONS AND EMOTIONS.—Pleasure in grasping increases (142). Arms moved up and down when child is nodded to (144). Twenty-third week, depression of angles of mouth and cry of distress caused by harsh address (149). Hunger apparent in persistent gaze at bottle, crying, and opening of mouth (154). Sleep of six to eight hours (162). Astonishment at seeing father after separation, and at sight of stranger (173).

WILL.

Reflex Movements.—Sneezing caused, on one hundred and seventieth day, by blowing on the child (215).

Instinctive Movements.—Twenty-second week, child raised himself to sitting posture (267). Twenty-third week, ditto: pleased at being placed upright (275).

Expressive Movements.—Laugh accompanied by raisings and droppings of arms when pleasure is great (299). Arm-movements that seemed like defensive movements (314). "Crowing" a sign of pleasure (II, 104).

INTELLECT.

Use of means to cause flow of milk (12).

Speech.—Twenty-second week, ögö, ma-ö-ĕ, hă, ā, ho-ich. "Crowing" and aspirate ha, and brrr-há, signs of pleasure (104). So aja, örrgö, ā-ā-i-ö-ā, eu and oeu (French) and ä and ö (German), also ijä; i and u rare (105).

Feeling of Self.—Twenty-third week, discrimination between touch of self and of foreign object (194; I, 109). Twenty-fourth week, child gazes at glove and at his fingers alternately (194). Twenty fourth week, sees father's image in mirror and turns to look at father. Twenty-fifth week, stretches hand toward his own image. Twenty-sixth week, sees image of father and compares it with original (198).

SEVENTH MONTH.

SENSES.

SIGHT.—*Movements of Eyelids.*—End of seventh month, opening and shutting of fan causes opening and shutting of eyes (30).

Direction of Look.—Twenty-ninth week, looking at flying sparrow (48). Thirtieth week, child does not look after objects let fall (49).

Seeing Near and Distant Objects.—Accommodation is perfect (55).

Interpretation of what is seen.—Staring at strange face (62).

HEARING.—Gaze at person singing; joy in military music (86).

FEELING.—Child became pale in bath (115).

TASTE.—New tastes cause play of countenance (124). One hundred and eighty-fifth day, cow's milk boiled, with egg, is liked; leguminous food not (125).

ORGANIC SENSATIONS AND EMOTIONS.—Pleasure in his image in mirror (142). Child laughs when others laugh to him (145). Twenty-ninth week, crying with hunger; spreading out tongue (153). Satiety shown by thrusting mouth-piece out (157).

WILL.

Impulsive Movements. — Nose becomes mobile.   Babes strike
about them vigorously (207).

Reflex Movements.—Sighing appears (216).

Instinctive Movements.—Thirtieth week, seizing more perfect
(249). Child places himself upright on lap, twenty-eighth week (275).

Imitative Movements.—Imitation of movements of head; of pursing lips (283).

Expressive Movements.—Averting head as sign of refusal; thrusting nipple out of mouth (313, 314).   Astonishment shown by open
mouth and eyes (55).

INTELLECT.

Child did not recognize nurse after absence of four weeks (7);
but children distinguish faces before thirtieth week (6).

Speech.—When hungry, child screams *mă, ă, ŭă, ŭăĕ;* when
contented, says *ŏrrŏ; lă, ŭ-ā-ŭ-i-i ; t* seldom, *k* only in yawning, *p*
very rarely (106).

EIGHTH MONTH.

SENSES.

Sight.—*Movements of Eyelids.*—Brow not wrinkled invariably
in looking upward (24).   Play of lid on hearing new noises; no lifting of eyebrows (30, 31).   Thirty-fourth week, eyes opened wide
with longing (31).

Direction of Look.—Thirty-first week, gaze turned in direction
of falling object.   Thirty-third week, objects moved slowly downward are followed with close gaze.   Thirty-fourth week, objects let
fall by him are seldom looked after (49).

Interpretation of what is seen.—Interest in bottles (62).

Hearing.—Quick closing of lids at new impressions of sound
(86).

Taste.—Pleasure in the " prepared food " (125).

Organic Sensations and Emotions.—Discomfort accompanied
by square form of the mouth (149).   Craving for food shown by
cooing sound (155).   Strongest feeling connected with appeasing of
hunger (157).   Restless nights (162).   Astonishment at new sounds
and sights; with fright (86).   Thirty-first week, at clapping of fan.
Thirty-fourth week, at imitation of voices of animals (173).

WILL.

Impulsive Movements.—Accompanying movement of hand (210). Thirty-fourth week, stretchings of arms and legs accompanying utterance (II, 108).

Instinctive Movements.—Thirty-second week, seizing with both hands more perfect; attention more active (248). In same week, legs stretched up vertically, feet observed attentively, toes carried to mouth with the hands (249). Pulling objects to him; grasping at bottle (250). Thirty-fourth week, carrying things to mouth (251).

Expressive Movements.—Laugh begins to be persistently loud (299). Thirty-second week, child no longer sucks at lips when he is kissed, but licks them (305). Eyelid half closed in disinclination (315). Interest in objects shown by stretching out hands (321).

INTELLECT.

Speech.—Variety of sounds made in the first eight months at random (76). Concept of bottle before language (79). Sounds in screaming different (106). Once the sound *hā-upp;* frequently *a-eî, a-aû, ă-hău-ă, hörrö.* Also *ntĕ-ö, mi-ja mija;* once *oŭăĕi* (107).

FEELING OF SELF.—Thirty-second week, child looks at his legs and feet as if they were foreign to him (194).

NINTH MONTH.

SENSES.

SIGHT.—*Movements of Eyes.*—Eyes converged easily (38).

Direction of Look.—Thirty-sixth week, objects that fall are not regularly looked after, but slowly moving objects, e. g., tobacco-smoke, are followed (49).

Interpretation of what is seen.—Boxes are gazed at (62). More interest shown in things in general (63).

HEARING.—Winking and starting at slamming noise (86).

TASTE.—Yolk of egg with cane-sugar taken with expression of surprise. Water and bread liked (126).

ORGANIC SENSATIONS AND EMOTIONS.—Striking hands together and laughing for joy (145). Eyes shut when something disagreeable is to be endured; head turned away also (148). Cooing, as in eighth month (155). Fear of dog (167, 168).

WILL.

Reflex Movements.—Number of respirations (in fever) forty and forty-two in a minute (217).

Instinctive Movements.—Teeth-grinding (262). Turning over when laid face downward (266). Thirty-fifth week, child places himself on arm and hand of nurse, and looks over her shoulder (275). Thirty-ninth week, likes to sit with support (267). Thirty-ninth week, stands on feet a moment without support (269).

Expressive Movements.—Loud laughing at new, pleasing objects (299). Turns head to light when asked where it is (321).

Deliberate Movements.—Things brought to mouth are put quickly on tongue (329).

INTELLECT.

Question understood before child can speak (I, 321).

Speech.—Voice more modulated : screaming varies with different causes (107). Delight shown by crowing sounds : *mä-mä, ämmä, mä*, are expressions of pleasure ; *ā-au-ā-ā, ā-ŏ, a-u-au, na-na ; apa, ga-au-ă, acha* (108).

FEELING OF SELF.—Feet are felt of, and toes are carried to mouth (190). Thirty-fifth week, foot grasped and carried to mouth. Thirty-sixth week, other objects preferred to hands and feet. Thirty-ninth week, in the bath his own skin is looked at and felt of, also his legs (194). Thirty-fifth week, his image in mirror is grasped at gayly (198).

TENTH MONTH.

SENSES.

SIGHT.—*Movements of Eyelids.*—Brow invariably wrinkled at looking upward (24).

Movements of Eyes.—Convergence of lines of vision disturbed (38).

Direction of Look.—Forty-third week, objects thrown down are looked at (49).

Interpretation of what is seen.—Visual impressions connected with food best interpreted (63).

HEARING.—Head turned at noise (87).

ORGANIC SENSATIONS AND EMOTIONS.—Joy at lighting of lamp (145).

WILL.

Reflex Movements.—Inhibition of reflex (229).

Instinctive Movements.—Forty-third week, carrying objects to mouth (252). Taking a hair from one hand into the other (253). Finger bitten (261). Bread crunched and swallowed (262). Turning over when laid on face (266). Fortieth and forty-first weeks, trying to sit without support (267). Forty-second week, sitting up without support in bath and carriage (267, 268). Forty-first week, first attempts at walking (275). Forty-second week, moving feet forward and sidewise; inclination to walk. Forty-third week, foot lifted high; moving forward (276).

Imitative Movements.—Beckoning imitated (285).

Expressive Movements.—Laughing becomes more conscious and intelligent (299). Crying in sleep (308). Striking hands together in sleep (319). Object pointed at is carried to mouth and chewed (322). Body straightened in anger (324). This not intentional (326).

INTELLECT.

Forty-third week, knowledge of weight of bodies (I, 50). A child missed his parents when they were absent, also a single nine-pin of a set (7, 8).

Speech.—Child can not repeat a syllable heard (77). In monologue, syllables are more distinct, loud, and varied when child is left to himself than when other persons entertain him: *ndăĕ, băĕ-băĕ, ba ell, arrŏ.* Frequent are *mă, pappa, tatta, appapa, babba, tătă, pa, rrrr, rrra.* Hints at imitation (108).

Feeling of Self.—Forty-first week, striking his own body and foreign objects (191). Forty-first to forty-fourth week, image in mirror laughed at and grasped at (198).

ELEVENTH MONTH.

SENSES.

SIGHT.—*Direction of Look.*—Forty-seventh week, child throws down objects and looks after them (49).

Seeing Near and Distant Objects.—Forty-fourth week, new objects no longer carried to eyes, but gazed at and felt. Forty-seventh week, accommodation perfect (55).

Interpretation of what is seen.—Trying to fixate objects (63).

HEARING.—Screaming is quieted by a "Sh!" or by singing.

Three hundred and nineteenth day, difference in sound of spoon on plate when plate was touched by hand (87).

TASTE.—Meat-broth with egg taken; scalded skimmed milk rejected; dry biscuit liked (126).

ORGANIC SENSATIONS AND EMOTIONS.—Forty-fourth week, astonishment at strange face (173).

WILL.

Instinctive Movements.—Forty-fifth week, grasping at flame of lamp; forty-seventh, at objects behind a pane of glass; gain in moving muscles of arm; shreds of paper handled (252). Biting father's hand (261). Smacking lips (262). Sitting becomes habit for life (268). Standing without support; stamping; but standing only for a moment (269). End of forty-seventh week, feet well placed, but lifted too high and put down too hard (276).

Expressive Movements.—Grasping at his image with laugh; jubilant noise at being allowed to walk (299).

Deliberate Movements.—Striking spoon against object and exchanging objects (326, 327). Child takes biscuit, carries it to mouth, bites off a bit, chews and swallows it; but can not drink from glass (329).

INTELLECT.

Syllables correctly repeated; intentional sound-imitation on the three hundred and twenty-ninth day. Forty-fifth week, response made for diversion: whispering begins (109). Three kinds of *r*-sounds: new syllables, *ta-heē, dann-tee, āa-neē, ngä, tai, bä, dall, at-tall, kamm, akkee, praï-jer, tra, ā-heē.* Some earlier sounds frequent; consonants *b, p, t, d, m, n, r; l, g, k:* vowel *a* most used, *u* and *o* rare, *i* very rare (110). Accentuation not frequent (111). Association of idea with utterance in one case (111, 122). Forty-fifth week, to word " papa," response *rrra* (113).

Feeling of Self.—Forty-fifth to fifty-fifth week, discovery of his power to cause changes (192).

TWELFTH MONTH.

SENSES.

SIGHT.—*Seeing Near and Distant Objects.* — Fifty-first week, pleasure in seeing men sawing wood at distance of more than one hundred feet (55).

HEARING.—Screaming quieted by " Sh!" (87). Three hundred

and sixty-third day, hears noise in next room and looks in direction of sound (88).

TASTE.—Fastidious about food (126).

ORGANIC SENSATIONS AND EMOTIONS.—Grunting as indication of pleasure (144). Fifty-second week, astonishment at new sound (173).

WILL.

Impulsive Movements.—Accompanying movement of hand in drinking (209).

Instinctive Movements.—Child seized father's hand, carried it to mouth and bit it (261). Forty-eighth week, standing without support a moment; stamping; pushing a chair (276). Forty-ninth week, child can not raise himself without help or stand more than an instant. Fiftieth week, can not place himself on his feet, or walk without help (277).

Imitative Movements.—Trying to strike with spoon on tumbler; puffing repeated in sleep (287).

Expressive Movements.—End of year, imitative laughing; crowing (299). Laughing in sleep (300). Opening of mouth in kissing (305). Arms stretched out in desire (322).

Deliberate Movements.—Biscuit put into mouth with few failures; drinking from glass, breathing into the water (329).

INTELLECT.

Ideas gained before language (78). Logical activity applied to perceptions of sound (I, 88). Abstraction, whiteness of milk (18).

Speech. — Imitation more successful, but seldom correct. Articulate sounds made spontaneously: *haja, jajajajaja, aja, njaja, naïn-hopp, ha-a, pa-a, dēwär, han-na, mömma, allda, alldaï, apa-u-a, gägä, ka, ladn; atta* is varied, no more *dada; w* for the first time. Ability to discriminate between words (112). Fifty-second week, child of himself obeys command, " Give the hand ! " Quieting effect of sounds " sh, ss, st, pst " (113).

Feeling of Self.—Striking hard substances against teeth ; gnashing teeth (189). Tearing of paper continued (192).

THIRTEENTH MONTH.
SENSES.

HEARING.—Child strikes on keys of piano ; pleased with singing of canary-bird (89).

ORGANIC SENSATIONS AND EMOTIONS.—Laughing almost invariably follows the laugh of others (145). Sleep, fourteen hours daily (162).

WILL.

Instinctive Movements.—Standing some moments without support (270). Fifty-third week, creeping. Fifty-fourth week, walking, with support; movements in creeping asymmetrical (277).

Expressive Movements.—No idea of kissing (305). Shaking head in denial (315). Begging sound along with extending of hands in desire (323).

INTELLECT.

Trying door after shutting it (15, 16). Hears the vowel-sounds in word (68).

Speech.—Desire expressed by *ă-na, ă-nananana* (112). Awkwardness continues; attention more lively. Tries to repeat words said for him. Three hundred and sixty-ninth day, *papa* repeated correctly (113, 114). Syllables most frequent, *nja, njan, dada, attu, mama, papaĭ, attaĭ, na-na-na, hatta, meenĕ-meenĕ-meenĕ, mŏmm, mŏmma, ao-u: na-na* denotes desire, *mama*, mother. Fifty-fourth week, joy expressed by crowing, some very high tones; first distinct *s*, three hundred and sixty-eighth day (114). Understanding of words spoken (115). Confusion of associations; first conscious act of obedience (116).

Feeling of Self.—Rapping head with hand (191). Finding himself a cause; shaking keys, etc. (192). Fifty-fifth week, strikes himself and observes his hands; compares fingers of others with his own (195).

FOURTEENTH MONTH.

SENSES.

SIGHT.—*Seeing Near and Distant Objects.*—Fifty-eighth week, grasping at lamp above him (55).

ORGANIC SENSATIONS AND EMOTIONS.—Fear of falling (169). Fifty eighth week, astonishment at lantern (173).

WILL.

Instinctive Movements.—Child could be allowed to bite paper to pieces; he took the pieces out of his mouth (253). Fifty-seventh week, he hitches along on hands and knees; can not walk without support. Sixtieth week, raises himself by chair (277).

Imitative Movements.—For imitating swinging of arms an interval of time was required (287). Coughing imitated (288). Nodding not imitated (315).

Expressive Movements.—Confounding of movements (322). Affection shown by laying hand on face and shoulders of others (324).

Deliberate Movements.—Child takes off and puts on the cover of a can seventy-nine times (328).

INTELLECT.

Wrong understanding of what is heard (89).

Speech.—No doubt that *atta* means " going "; *brrr*, practiced and perfected ; *dakkn, daggn, taggn, attagn, attatn ;* no special success in repeating vowels and syllables (117). Child tries and laughs at his failures, if others laugh ; parrot-like repetition of some syllables (118). Gain in understanding of words heard ; association of definite object with name (119). More movements executed on hearing words (120). Confounding of movements occurs, but grows rare ; begging attitude seen to be useful (121).

Feeling of Self.—Four hundred and ninth day, child bit himself on the arm (189). Pulling out and pushing in a drawer, turning leaves of book, etc. (192). Fifty-seventh week, child looks at his image in hand-mirror, puts hand behind glass, etc. (198). Fifty-eighth week, his photograph treated in like manner ; he turns away from his image in mirror ; sixtieth week, recognizes his mother's image in mirror as image (199).

FIFTEENTH MONTH.

SENSES.

SIGHT.—*Direction of Look.*—Sixty-third to sixty-fifth week, objects thrown down and looked after (50).

Interpretation of what is seen.—Grasps at candle, puts hand into flame, but once only (63).

HEARING.—Laughing at new noises, as gurgling or thunder (89).

SMELL.—Coffee and cologne make no impression till end of month (134).

WILL.

Instinctive Movements.—Sixty-second week, child stands a few seconds when support is withdrawn. Sixty-third week, walks, hold-

ing on to a support (277). Sixty-fourth week, can walk without
support, if he thinks he is supported; sixty-fifth week, walks holding by one finger of another's hand; raises himself to knees, stands
up if he can hold to something (278).

Imitative Movements.—Coughing. Learns to blow out candle
(288). Opening and shutting of hand (289).

Expressive Movements.—Laughing at new sounds (299). The
words "Give a kiss" produce a drawing near of head and protruding
of lips (306). Wrinkling of brow in attempts at imitation (310).
Deprecating movement of arm (314). Sixty-fourth week, nodding
sometimes accompanies the word "no"; four hundred and forty-fifth
day, an accompanying movement (316). First shrugging of shoulders (317). Begging gesture made by child when he wants something (318). Same made in asking for amusement (319). Wish expressed by handing a ring, looking at glasses to be struck, and saying *hay-üh* (323).

INTELLECT.

Hunting for scraps of paper, etc. (17). After burning his finger
in flame of candle, the child never put it near the flame again, but
would, in fun, put it in the direction of the candle. He allowed
mouth and chin to be wiped without crying (20).

Speech.—New sound *wa;* astonishment expressed by *hä-ä-ĕä-ĕ*,
joy by crowing in high and prolonged tones, strong desire by *häŏ*,
hä-ĕ, pain, impatience, by screaming in vowels passing over into one
another (121). The *atta* still used when a light is dimmed (122).
Advance in repeating syllables. Child is vexed when he can not repeat a word. One new word, *heiss* (hot) (123). The *s* is distinct;
th (Eng.) appears; *w;* smacking in sixty-fifth week; tongue the
favorite plaything (124). Understands words "moon," "clock,"
"eye," "nose," "cough," "blow," "kick," "light"; affirmative nod
at "ja" in sixty-fourth week; negative shaking at "no"; holding
out hand at words "Give the hand" or "hand"; more time required when child is not well (125).

Feeling of Self.—Child bit his finger so that he cried out with
pain (191). Sixty-second week, playing with his fingers as foreign
objects; pressing one hand down with the other (195). Sixty-first
week, trying to feel of his own image in the mirror (199).

SIXTEENTH MONTH.

SENSES.

SIGHT.—*Seeing Near and Distant Objects.*—Sixty-eighth week, reaching too short, too far to left or right, too high or too low (56), *Interpretation of what is seen.*—Grasping a⁺ jets of water (63).

HEARING.—Child holds watch to his ear and listens to the ticking (89).

SMELL.—Smell and taste not separated; a flower is taken into mouth (135).

ORGANIC SENSATIONS AND EMOTIONS.—Fear of high tones (169).

WILL.

Impulsive Movements.—Sleeping child raised hand to eye (202). Accompanying movement of fingers in drinking (210).

Reflex Movements.—Respirations, in sleep, twenty-two to twenty-five a minute (217).

Instinctive Movements.—Sixty-sixth week, four hundred and fifty-seventh day, child runs alone (278). Next day, stops and stamps. Four hundred and sixty-first day, can walk backward, if led, and can turn round alone. At the end of the week can look at objects while walking. Sixty-seventh week, a fall occurs rarely. Sixty-eighth week, walking becoming mechanical (279).

Imitative Movements.—A ring put on his head in imitation (289). Waiting attitude (318).

Expressive Movements.—Lips protruded almost like a snout (302). Shaking head meant "No" and "I do not know" (316). Child shrugs shoulders when unable to answer (317). Waiting attitude becomes a sign (318).

Deliberate Movements.—Opening and shutting cupboards, bringing objects, etc. Holding ear-ring to ear (327).

INTELLECT.

Child holds an ear-ring to his ear with understanding (I, 327). A begging movement at seeing box from which cake had come (11). Small understanding shown in grasping at ring (13).

Speech.—Progress in repeating words spoken for him and in understanding words heard. Desire expressed by *hä! hä-ö! hä-ĕ! hĕ-ĕ!* More seldom *hi, gö-gö, gö, f-pa, au;* more frequently, *ta, dokkn, tá-ha, a-bwa-bwa, bŭā-bŭā;* once *dagon.* Child "reads" the newspaper (126). Pain expressed by screaming; joy by crowing with vowel *i ;* *a* repeated on command ; *mŏ* and *ma ;* imitation tried (127). Touches eye, ear, etc., when these are named—not with certainty (128). Understands " bring," " give," etc. (129).

Feeling of Self.—Putting thumbs against the head and pushing, experimenting (191). Sixty-sixth week, child strikes at his image in mirror. Sixty-seventh week, makes grimaces before mirror ; turns round to see his father, whose image appeared in mirror (199). Sixty-ninth week, signs of vanity (200).

SEVENTEENTH MONTH.

SENSES.

SIGHT.—*Interpretation of what is seen.*—Child grasps at tobacco-smoke (64).

HEARING.—Holding watch to ear (89).

TASTE.—Surprise at new tastes (119).

SMELL.—Inability to separate smell and taste (135).

ORGANIC SENSATIONS AND EMOTIONS.—Prolonged sleep ; ten hours at a time (162).

WILL.

Reflex Movements.—Right hand moved when right nostril is touched (221).

Instinctive Movements.—Clasping of finger in sleep (243). Seventieth week, child raises himself from floor alone ; seventy-first week, steps over threshold (279).

Expressive Movements.—Shaking head means " I do not wish " (316). Throwing himself on floor and screaming with rage (323).

INTELLECT.

Child brings traveling-bag to stand upon in order to reach (12). Play of " hide and seek " (17).

Speech.—Screaming, whimpering, etc. (101). Increase of discrimination : *bibi, nă-nă-nă, t-tó, hŏt-tó ;* voluntary imitation (129). Associations of words heard with objects and movements (130).

Feeling of Self.—Making grimaces before mirror (200).

EIGHTEENTH MONTH.

SENSES.

SIGHT.—*Direction of Look.*—Seventy-eighth week, throwing away of playthings is rare (50).

Interpretation of what is seen.—Anxiety on seeing man dressed in black (64).

SMELL.—Objects no longer carried to mouth (135).

ORGANIC SENSATIONS AND EMOTIONS.—Laughing at thunder (170).

WILL.

Impulsive Movements.—Holding little finger apart from others (209).

Instinctive Movements.—Walks over threshold by holding on (275). Seventy-seventh week, runs around table; seventy-eighth, walks over threshold without holding on (280).

Imitative Movements.—Blowing horn (290).

Expressive Movements.—Trying to hit with foot, striking, etc. (315). Waiting attitude (318).

Deliberate Movements.—Full spoon carried to mouth with skill (329).

INTELLECT.

Memory of towel (8). Watering flowers with empty pot (16). Plays (17). Giving leaves to stag, etc. (18). Stick of wood put in stove (20).

Speech.—Understanding of words increases (130). Repeating of syllables is rare; *atta* becomes *tto, t-tu, ftu;* feeling recognized by tone of voice (131).

Feeling of Self.—Recognition of himself as cause of changes (192).

NINETEENTH MONTH.

SENSES.

HEARING.—Hearing watch on his head (89).

Organic Sensations and Emotions.—Fear of strangers ceases (´50). Laugh at thunder and lightning (170).

WILL.

Imitative Movements. — Combing and brushing hair, washing hands, etc. (290).

Expressive Movements.—Fastidious about kissing (306). Pride in baby-carriage (324).

Deliberative Movements.—Spoon taken in left hand (329).

repeat three syllables; laughs when others laugh (136). Single words more promptly understood (137). One new concept, expressed by *dā* and *ndā*, or *tā* and *ntā*. Eighty-seventh week, *attah* said on railway-train; *papa* and *bät* or *bit* (for " bitte ") rightly used; much outcry (138). Crowing tones not so high; loud readings continued (139).

TWENTY-FIRST MONTH.

SENSES.

HEARING.—Dancing not rhythmical (89, 90).
ORGANIC SENSATIONS AND EMOTIONS.—Fear of the sea (170).

WILL.

Instinctive Movements. — Eighty-ninth week, running is awkward, but falling rare (280).
Imitative Movements.—Imitation without understanding (290, 291).
Expressive Movements.—Ninetieth week, pointing as expression of wish (321).

INTELLECT.

Recognition of father (8). Association of biscuit with coat and wardrobe (11).
Speech.—Imitations more frequent. Eighty-ninth week, babbling different, more *consonants; ptö-ptö, pt-pt*, and *verlapp*, also *dla-dla;* willfulness shown in articulate sounds and shaking head (139). Unlike syllables not repeated, *dang-gee* and *dank-kee;* tendency to doubling syllables, *tete, bibi;* babbling yields great pleasure; *bibi* for " bitte " rightly used. New word *mimi*, when hungry or thirsty (140). Understands use and signification of sound, *neinein;* and answers of his own accord *jaja* to question in ninety-first week. Strength of memory for sounds; points correctly to nose, mouth, etc. (141). Astonishing progress in understanding what is said. Few expressions of his own with recognizable meaning, *jäĕ* excepted. *Att, att, att*, unintelligible. Tried to imitate sound of steam of locomotive (142).
Feeling of Self.—Placing shells and buttons in rows (193). Puts lace about him; vanity; laughs and points at his own image in mirror (200). The same on six hundred and twentieth day (201).

3

TWENTY-SECOND MONTH.

SENSES.

SIGHT.—New impressions enchain attention; the mysterious more attractive (64).

INTELLECT.

Speech. Progress in understanding; orders executed with surprising accuracy (142). Strength of word-memory; facility of articulation; spontaneous utterance of *pss, ps, ptsch, pth; pa-ptl-däpt;* greeting with *hāā-ö, ada* and *ana.* Singing, *rollo, mama, māmä,* etc. More certainty in reproducing sounds: "pst, anna, otto, lina," etc. Three-syllabled words correctly repeated, *a-ma-ma, a-pa-pa* (143). Words too hard are given back with *tapĕta, pĕta, pta, ptö-ptö* or *rateratetat. Ja ja* and *nein nein,* with *da* and *bibi* and *mimi,* used properly in request. Cry of pain a strong contrast with the crowing for joy (144).

TWENTY-THIRD MONTH.

SENSES.

SIGHT.—*Seeing Near and Distant Objects.*—Ninety-sixth week, does not appreciate distance (56).

WILL.

Imitative Movements.—Imitative impulse seems like ambition; ceremonious movements imitated (291).

Expressive Movements.—Kiss given as a mark of favor (306). Striking hands together in applause and desire for repetition (319). Tears of sorrow instead of anger; tries to move chair to table, etc. (324).

INTELLECT.

Joy at seeing playthings after absence of eleven and a half weeks (8). Concept of "cup" not sharply defined (16). Use of adjective for the first spoken judgment (96).

Speech.—*Heiss* (hot) means "The drink is too hot," and "the stove is hot" (144). *Watja* and *mimi; mimmi, mömö, māmä,* mean food; *atta,* disappearance; spontaneous articulation, *oĩ, eũ, ana, ida, didl, dadl, dldo-dlda;* in singing-tone, *opojö, apojopojum aui, heissa;* calls grandparents *e-papa* and *e-mama;* knows who is meant when these are spoken of. Understands words more easily, as "drink, eat, shut, open" (145). Word-memory becoming firm; imagination.

Great progress in reproducing syllables and words (146). Child's name, "Axel," is called *Aje, Eja.* "Bett, Karre, Kuk," repeated correctly. Echolalia reappears (147). Words are best pronounced by child when he is not called upon to do it (148).

Feeling of Self.—Child holds biscuit to his toes (190).

TWENTY-FOURTH MONTH.

SENSES.

SIGHT.—*Interpretation of what is seen.*—Moving animals closely observed (64).

HEARING.—Trying to sing, and beating time (90).

ORGANIC SENSATIONS AND EMOTIONS.—Astonishment more seldom apparent (174).

WILL.

Instinctive Movements.—Child turns, of himself, dancing in time to music; beats time (280).

Imitative Movements.—Ceremonious movements imitated, salutation, uncovering head (291).

Expressive Movements.—Roguish laughing first observed (299).

INTELLECT.

Understanding of actions and of use of utensils more developed than ability to interpret representations of them (I, 64, 65).

Speech.—Voluntary sound-imitations gain in frequency and accuracy; genuine echolalia (148). Imperfect imitations (149). Multiplicity of meanings in the same utterance (150). Distinguishing men from women. Combination of two words into a sentence, seven hundred and seventh day; words confounded; also gestures and movements; but not in the expression of joy and grief (151, 152).

TWENTY-FIFTH MONTH.

SENSES.

SIGHT.—*Discrimination of Colors.*—Color-tests, red and green; seven hundred and fifty-eighth day, eleven times right, six wrong; seven hundred and fifty-ninth, seven right, five wrong; seven hundred and sixtieth, nine right, five wrong (8). Does not yet *know* what blue and green signify. Moves and handles himself well in twilight (21).

Seeing Near and Distant Objects.—One hundred and eighth week, power of accommodation good; small photographic likenesses recognized (56).

INTELLECT.

Speech.—Progress is extraordinary. Does not pronounce a perfect "u." All sound-imitations more manifold, etc.; begins saying "*so*" when any object is brought to appointed place (152). Has become more teachable, repeats three words imperfectly. Evidence of progress of memory, understanding and articulation in answers given. No word invented by himself; calls his nurse *wolá*, probably from the often-heard "ja wohl." Correct use of single words picked up increases surprisingly (153). Misunderstandings rational; words better understood; reasoning developed (154). Inductive reasoning. Progress in forming sentences. Sentence of five words. Pronouns signify objects or qualities (155, 156).

TWENTY-SIXTH MONTH.

SENSES.

SIGHT.—*Discrimination of Colors.*—Seven hundred and sixty-third day, 15 right, 1 wrong. Three colors pointed out; disinclination to continue (8). Seven hundred and sixty-fifth day, green confounded with yellow. One hundred and tenth week, right 73, wrong 22. Blue added. End of one hundred and tenth week to one hundred and twelfth week, right 124, wrong 36. Yellow more surely recognized than other colors. Violet added (9). Colors taken separately. One hundred and twelfth week, right 44, wrong 11. Tests in both ways; attention not continuous. Gray is added. One hundred and twelfth and one hundred and thirteenth weeks, right 90, wrong 27 (10, 11). Child does not know what "green" means in one hundred and twelfth week (21).

Seeing Near and Distant Objects.—One hundred and thirteenth week, articles of furniture recognized in pictures at distance of three inches or three feet (56).

WILL.

Instinctive Movements.—First attempts at climbing (331).

INTELLECT.

Child points out objects in pictures, and repeats names given to them; list of results (156). Points out of his own accord, with certainty, in the picture-book. Appropriates many words not taught him, *tola* for "Kohlen," *dals* for "Salz." Others correctly said and used (157). Some of his mutilated words not recognizable; "sch" sometimes left out, sometimes given as *z* or *ss*. Independent thoughts expressed by words more frequently; "Good-night" said to the Christmas-tree (158). Verb used (in the infinitive) showing growth of intellect; learning of tricks decreases (159). No notion of number; does not understand "Thank you," but thanks himself. More names of animals, learned from adults; no onomatopœia (160).

TWENTY-SEVENTH MONTH.

SENSES.

SIGHT.—*Discrimination of Colors.*—Color-tests, from one hundred and fourteenth to one hundred and sixteenth week, four trials, colors mixed; result, 59 right, 22 wrong (11). Blue especially confounded with violet, also with green. Four trials in one hundred and fourteenth and one hundred and fifteenth weeks; result, 58 right, 32 wrong (12). Two trials in one hundred and fifteenth week; result, 25 right, 16 wrong (13).

ORGANIC SENSATIONS AND EMOTIONS.—Uncomfortable feeling through pity; child weeps if human forms cut out of paper are in danger of mutilation (150, 151).

WILL.

Instinctive Movements.—Pleasure in climbing begins (280).

INTELLECT.

Speech.—Activity of thought. Observation and comparison. Gratitude does not appear (161). Wishes expressed by verbs in the infinitive or by substantives. Adverbs; indefinite pronouns. Seven hundred and ninety-sixth day, makes the word *Messen* (162). *Wolà* and *atta* have almost disappeared. Independent applications of words (163). Monologues less frequent. Begs apple to give to a puppet. Echolalia prominent. Tones and noises imitated (164). Laughing when others laugh; fragments of a dialogue repeated. Feeble memory for answers and numbers. Eight hundred and tenth day, gave his own name for first time in answer to a question (165). No question yet asked by the child. The article is not used. Pronunciation slowly becoming correct (166).

TWENTY-EIGHTH MONTH.

SENSES.

SIGHT.—*Discrimination of Colors.*—One hundred and twenty-first week, greater uncertainty (13).

ORGANIC SENSATIONS AND EMOTIONS.—Fear of pigs (163).

WILL.

Instinctive Movements.—Going on all-fours; jumping, climbing gives pleasure (280).

INTELLECT.

Speech.—Rapid increase of activity in forming ideas, and greater certainty in use of words. Ambition; observation and combination; beginning of self-control; use of his own name and of names of parents; independent thinking (167). Increase in number of words correctly pronounced; attempt to use prepositions; first intelligent use of the article (168). Questioning active; first spontaneous question on eight hundred and forty-fifth day. "Where?" is his only interrogative word. Reproduction of foreign expressions (169). Imagination lively; paper cups used like real ones. Articulation better, but still deficient. Many parts of the body named correctly (170). Child makes remarks for a quarter of an hour at a time concerning objects about him, sings, screams in sleep (171).

TWENTY-NINTH MONTH.

SENSES.

SIGHT.—*Discrimination of Colors.*—One hundred and twenty-fourth week, right, 58; wrong, 49. Eight hundred and sixty-eighth day, child takes colors of his own accord and names them; confounding rose, gray, and pale-green, brown and gray, blue and violet. One hundred and twenty-fourth and one hundred and twenty-fifth weeks, right, 80; wrong, 34 (14). Red and yellow generally named rightly; blue and green not. Red and yellow are removed; child is less interested. One hundred and twenty-fifth and one hundred and twenty-sixth weeks, right, 80; wrong, 63. Orange confounded with yellow, blue with violet, green with gray, black with brown. Failure of attempt to induce child to put like colors together, or to select colors by their names (15).

Direction of Look.—One hundred and twenty-fourth week, gaze follows ball thrown (50).

ORGANIC SENSATIONS AND EMOTIONS.—Fear of dogs (168).

INTELLECT.

Personal pronoun used in place of his own name. Inflection of verbs appears, but the infinitive is generally used for imperative; regular and irregular verbs begin to be distinguished (171). Desire expressed by infinitive. Numbering active; numerals confounded. Eight hundred and seventy-eighth day, nine-pins counted "one, one, one," etc. (172). Questioning increases; "too much" is confounded with "too little." Yet memory gains (173). Sounds of animals well remembered. Slow progress in articulation (174).

Feeling of Self.—Personal pronoun in place of his own name; "me" but not yet "I" (202).

THIRTIETH MONTH.

SENSES.

SIGHT.—*Discrimination of Colors.*—One hundred and twenty-sixth, one hundred and twenty-seventh, and one hundred and twenty-eighth weeks, four trials with single color at a time; 75 right, 34 wrong. Eight hundred and ninety-eighth day, every color rightly named; some guessing on blue and green (16).

Interpretation of what is seen. — Persistent desire daily to "write" locomotives (66).

HEARING.—While eating, by chance puts hand to ear while kettle of boiling water stood before him; notices diminution in force of sound (88).

WILL.

Instinctive Movements.—Mounting a staircase without help; ten days later with hands free (280, 281).

INTELLECT.

Speech.—Independent activity of thought. When language fails, he considers well (174). Deliberation without words; concepts formed. Intellectual advance shown in first intentional use of language (175). Only interrogative word is still "Where?" "I" does not appear, but "me" is used. Sentences independently applied

(176). More frequent use of the plural in nouns; of the article; of the strong inflection; auxiliaries omitted or misemployed. Twofold way of learning correct pronunciation (177). Memory for words denoting objects good; right and left confounded (178).

THIRTY–FIRST MONTH.

SENSES.

Sight.—*Discrimination of Colors.*—Nine hundred and thirty-fourth day, child says he can not tell green and blue. Green mostly called gray; blue, violet (17).

Feeling.—*Sensibility to Temperature.*—Child laughs joyously in cold bath (115).

WILL.

Weakness of will shown by ceasing to eat when told that he has had enough (344).

INTELLECT.

Speech.—Onomatopœia; imitation of locomotive-whistle (91). Two new questions. Indefinite article more frequent. Individual formations of words, as comparative of "high"; "key-watch." Confounding of "to-day" and "yesterday" (178). Forming of sentences imperfect. Reporting of faults. Calls things "stupid" when he is vexed by them. Changes occupation frequently. Imitation less frequent. Singing in sleep. "Sch" not yet pronounced (179).

Feeling of Self.—Causing change in objects, pouring water into and out of vessels (193). Laughing at image of self in mirror (201).

THIRTY–SECOND MONTH.

SENSES.

Sight.—*Discrimination of Colors.*—One hundred and thirty-eighth and a few previous weeks, six trials, child taking colors and naming them; right 119, wrong, 38 (16, 17). Green and blue called "nothing at all." Unknown colors named green; leaves of roses called "nothing," as are whitish colors. One hundred and thirty-eighth and one hundred and thirty-ninth weeks, three trials; right, 93, wrong, 39 (17, 18). Green begins to be rightly named, blue less often (18).

INTELLECT.

Speech.—" I " begins to displace the name of child. Sentence correctly applied. Clauses formed. Particle separated in compound verbs. Longer names and sentences distinctly spoken, but the influence of dialect appears (180). Memory improved, but fastidious; good for what is interesting and intelligible to child (181).

Feeling of Self.—Fourfold designation of self (202).

THIRTY-THIRD MONTH.

SENSES.

SIGHT.—*Discrimination of Colors.*—One hundred and thirty-ninth, one hundred and forty-first, and one hundred and forty-sixth weeks, took colors of his own accord and named them; result of three trials, 66 right, 19 wrong (18).

ORGANIC SENSATIONS AND EMOTIONS.—Fear of even smallest dog (168).

INTELLECT.

Understanding that violations of well-known precepts have unpleasant consequences (21).

Speech.—Strength of memory shown in characteristic remarks Narrative of feeding fowls (181). Interest in animals and other moving objects; lack of clearness in concepts of animal and machine; meaning of word " father " includes also " uncle "; selfhood more sharply manifested. Confounds " too much " with " too little," etc. (182).

Feeling of Self.—" I " especially used in " I want that," etc. (202).

THIRTY-FOURTH MONTH.

SENSES.

SIGHT.—*Discrimination of Colors.*—" Green " rightly applied to leaves and grass (18). Order in which colors are rightly named up to this time; right, one thousand and forty-four; wrong, four hundred and forty-two: right, 70·3 per cent; wrong, 29·7. Yellow and red much sooner named rightly than green and blue (19).

WILL.

Instinctive Movements.—First gymnastic exercises (281).

Expressive Movements.—Kissing an expression of thankfulness (306).

INTELLECT.

Speech.—Repeating, for fun, expressions heard. Calls, without occasion, the name of the nurse; calls others by her name, sometimes correcting himself. Seldom speaks of himself in third person; gradually uses "Du" in address; uses "What?" in a new way. One thousand and twenty-eighth day, "Why?" first used; instinct of causality expressed in language (183). Questioning repeated to weariness. Articulation perfected, with some exceptions (184).

Feeling of Self.—Repeats the "I" heard, meaning by it "you" (202).

THIRTY-FIFTH MONTH.

WILL.

Reflex Movements.—Responsive movement in sleeping child (221).

INTELLECT.

Speech.—Fondness for singing increases; pleasure in compass and power of his voice (185).

THIRTY-SIXTH MONTH.

SENSES.

HEARING.—Musical notes C, D, E, could not be rightly named by child, in spite of teaching (90).

INTELLECT.

"When?" not used until close of the third year (184). Great pleasure in singing, but imitation here not very successful, though surprisingly so in regard to speech. Grammatical errors more rare. Long sentences correctly but slowly formed. Ambition manifested in doing things without help (185).

Invention in language rare. Participles well used (186).

THIRTY-SEVENTH MONTH.

SENSES.

SIGHT.—*Discrimination of Colors.*—Colors named correctly except very dark or pale ones (21).

ORGANIC SENSATIONS AND EMOTIONS.—Night's sleep from eleven to twelve hours; day-naps no longer required (163). Fear (in sleep) of pigs (168).

INTELLECT.

Speech. — Child's manner of speaking approximates more and more rapidly to that of the family (186).

FORTIETH MONTH.

INTELLECT.

Feeling of Self.—Fortieth month, pleased with his shadow (201).

THE MIND OF THE CHILD.

THIRD PART.

DEVELOPMENT OF THE INTELLECT.

THE development of the intellect depends in so great measure upon the modification of innate endowments through natural environment and education, even before systematic instruction begins, and the methods of education are so manifold, that it is at present impossible to make a complete exposition of a normal intellectual development. Such an exposition would necessarily comprise in the main two stages:

1. The *combination* of sensuous *impressions* into *perceptions* (Wahrnehmungen); which consists essentially in this—that the sensation, impressing itself directly upon our experience, is by the intellect, now beginning to act, co-ordinate in space and time.

2. The *combination* of *perceptions* into *ideas ;* in particular into *sense-intuitions* and *concepts.* A sense-intuition (Anschauung) is a perception together with its cause, the object of the sensation ; a concept (Begriff) results from the union of the previously separated perceptions, which are then called separate marks or qualities.

The investigation of each of these stages in the child

is in itself a great labor, which an individual may indeed begin upon, but can not easily carry through uniformly in all directions.

I have indeed tried to collect recorded facts, but have found only very little trustworthy material, and accordingly I confine myself essentially to my own observations on my child. These are not merely perfectly trustworthy, even to the minutest details (I have left out everything of a doubtful character), but they are the most circumstantial ever published in regard to the intellectual development of a child. But I have been acquainted with a sufficient number of other children to be certain that the child observed by me did not *essentially* differ from other healthy and intelligent boys in regard to the principal points, although the time at which development takes place, and the rapidity of it, differ a good deal in different individuals. Girls often appear to learn to speak earlier than boys; but further on they seem to possess a somewhat inferior capacity of development of the logical functions, or to accomplish with less ease abstractions of a higher order; whereas in boys the emotional functions, however lasting their reactions, are not so delicately graduated as in girls.

Without regard to such differences, of which I am fully aware, the following chapters treat exclusively of the development of purely intellectual cerebral activity in both sexes during the first years. I acknowledge, however, that I have found the investigation of the influence of the affectional movements, or emotions, upon the development of the intellect in the child during the first years so difficult, that I do not for the present enter into details concerning it.

The observations relate, first, to the non-dependence of the child's intellect upon language ; next, to the acquirement of speech ; lastly, to the development of the feeling of self, the "I"-feeling.

CHAPTER XVI.

DEVELOPMENT OF THE CHILD'S INTELLECT INDEPENDENTLY OF LANGUAGE.

A WIDE-SPREAD prejudice declares, "Without language, no understanding"! Subtile distinctions between understanding and reason have limited the statement to the latter term. But even in the restricted form, "Without verbal language, no reason," it is at least unproved.

Is there any thinking without words? The question takes this shape.

Now, for the thinker, who has long since forgotten the time when he himself learned to speak, it is difficult, or even impossible, to give a decided answer. For the thinking person can not admit that he has been thinking without words ; not even when he has caught himself arriving at a logical result without a continuity in his unexpressed thought. A break occurred in the train. There was, however, a train of thought. Breaks alone yield no thought ; they arise only after words have been associated with thoughts, and so they can by no means serve as evidence of a thinking without words, although the ecstasy of the artist, the profundity of the metaphysician, may attain the last degree of unconsciousness, and a dash may interrupt the thought-text.

But the child not yet acquainted with verbal language, who has not been prematurely artificialized by training and by suppression of his own attempts to express his states of mind, who learns *of himself* to *think*, just as he learns of himself to see and hear—such a child shows plainly to the attentive observer that long before knowledge of the word as a means of understanding among men, and long before the first successful attempt to express himself in articulate words—nay, long before learning the pronunciation of even a single word, he combines ideas in a logical manner—i. e., he *thinks*. Thinking is, it is true, "internal speech," but there is a speech without words.

Facts in proof of this have already been given in connection with other points (Vol. I, pp. 88, 327, 328); others are given further on.

It will not be superfluous, however, to put together several observations relating to the development of the childish intellect without regard to the acquirement of speech; and to present them separately, as a sort of introduction to the investigation of the process of learning to speak.

Memory; a causative combination of the earliest recollections, or memory-images; purposive, deliberate movements for the lessening of individual strain—all these come to the child in greater or less measure independently of verbal language. The, as it were, embryonic logic of the child does not need words. A brief explanation of the operation of these three factors will show this. Memory takes the first place in point of time.

Without memory no intellect is possible. The only

material at the disposal of the intellect is received from the senses. It has been provided solely out of sensations. Now a sensation in itself alone, as a simple fundamental experience affecting primarily the one who has the sensation, can not be the object of any intellectual operation whatever. In order to make such activity possible there must be several sensations : two of different kinds, of unequal strength ; or two of different kinds, of the same strength ; or two of the same kind unequally strong ; in any case, two unlike sensations (cf. my treatise " Elemente der reinen Empfindungslehre," Jena, 1876), if the lowest activity of the intellect, *comparison*, is to operate. But because the sensations that are to be compared can not all exist together, recollection of the earlier ones is necessary (for the comparison) ; that is, individual or personal memory.

This name I give to the memory formed by means of individual impressions (occurrences, experiences) in contrast with the *phyletic* memory, or instinct, the memory of the race, which results from the inheritance of the traces of individual experiences of ancestors ; of this I do not here speak.

All sensations leave traces behind in the brain ; weak ones leave such as are easy to be obliterated by others ; strong ones, traces more enduring.

At the beginning of life it seems to be the department of taste (sweet) and of smell (smell of milk) in which memory is first operative (Vol. I, p. 124). Then comes the sense of touch (in nursing). Next in order the sense of sight chiefly asserts itself as an early promoter of memory. Hearing does not come till later.

4

If the infant, in the period from three to six months of age, is brought into a room he has not before seen, his expression changes ; he is astonished. The new sensations of light, the different apportionment of light and dark, arouse his attention ; and when he comes back to his former surroundings he is not astonished. These have lost the *stimulus of novelty*—i. e., a certain *reminiscence* of them has remained with the child, they have *impressed* themselves upon him.

Long before the thirtieth week, healthy children distinguish human faces definitely from one another; first, the faces of the mother and the nurse, then the face of the father, seen less often ; and all three of these from every strange face. Probably faces are the first thing frequently perceived clearly by the eye. It has been found surprising that infants so much earlier recognize human faces and forms, and follow them with the gaze, than they do other objects. But human forms and faces, being large, moving objects, awaken interest more than other objects do ; and on account of the manner of their movements, and because they are the source from which the voice issues, are essentially different from other objects in the field of vision. "In these movements they are also characterized as a coherent whole, and the face, as a whitish-reddish patch with the two sparkling eyes, is always a part of this image that will be easy to recognize, even for one who has seen it but a few times" (Helmholtz).

Hence the memory for faces is established earlier than that for other visual impressions, and with this the ability to recognize members of the family. A little girl, who does not speak at all, looks at pictures with considerable interest in the seventh month, "and points meantime with her little forefinger to the heads of the human figures" (Frau von Strümpell).

My child in the second month could already localize the face and voice of his mother, but the so-called knowing ("Erkennen") is a recognition (Wiedererkennen) which presupposes a very firm *association of the memory-images*. This fundamental function attached to the memory can have but a slow development, because it demands an accumulation of memory-images and precision in them.

In the second three months it is so far developed, at least, that strange faces are at once known as strange, and are distinguished from those of parents and nurse; for they excite astonishment or fear (crying) while the faces of the latter do not. But the latter, if absent, are not yet, at this period, missed by most children. Hence it is worthy of note that a girl in her twelfth month recognized her nurse after six days' absence, immediately, "with sobs of joy," as the mother reports (Frau von Strümpell) ; another recognized her father, after a separation of four days, even in the tenth month (Lindner).

In the seventh month my child did *not* recognize his nurse, to whom he had for months been accustomed, after an absence of four weeks. Another child, however, at four months noticed at evening the absence of his nurse, who had been gone only a day, and cried lustily upon the discovery, looking all about the room, and crying again every time after searching in vain (Wyma, 1881). At ten months the same child used to be troubled by the absence of his parents, though he bore himself with indifference toward them when he saw them again. At this period a single nine-pin out of the whole set could not be taken away without his noticing it, and at the age of a year and a half this child knew at once whether one of his ten animals was missing or not. In the nineteenth and twenty-first months my boy recognized his father immediately from a distance, after a separation of several days, and once after two weeks' absence ; and in his twenty-third month his joy at seeing again his playthings after an absence of eleven and a half weeks (with his parents) was very lively, great as was the child's forgetfulness in other respects at this period. A favorite toy could often be taken from him without its being noticed or once asked for. But when the child—in his eighteenth month—after having been accustomed to bring to his mother two towels which he would afterward carry back to their place, on one occasion had only one towel given back to him, he came with inquiring look and tone to get the second.

This observation, which is confirmed by some similar ones, proves that at a year and a half the memory for visual and motor ideas that belong together was already well developed without the knowledge of the corresponding words. But artificial associations of this sort need continual renewing, otherwise they are soon forgotten ; the remembrance of them is speedily lost even in the years of childhood.

It is noteworthy, in connection with this, that what has been lately acquired, e. g., verses learned by heart, can be recited more fluently during sleep than in the waking condition. At the age of three years and five months a girl recited a stanza of five lines on the occasion of a birthday festival, not without some stumbling, but one night soon after the birthday she repeated the whole of the rhymes aloud in her sleep without stumbling at all (Frau von Strümpell).

It is customary, generally, to assume that the memory of adults does not extend further back than to the fourth year of life. Satisfactory observations on this point are not known to exist. But it is certainly of the first consequence, in regard to the development of the faculty of memory, whether the later experiences of the child have any characteristic in common with the earlier experiences. For many of these experiences no such agreement exists; nothing later on reminds us of the once existing inability to balance the head, or of the former inability to turn around, to sit, to stand, to walk, of the inborn difficulty of hearing, inability to accommodate the eye, and to distinguish our own body from foreign objects; hence, no man, and no child, remembers these states. But this is not true of what is acquired later. My child when less than three years old remembered very well—and would almost make merry over himself at it—the time when he could not yet talk, but articulated incorrectly and went imperfectly through the first, often-repeated performances taught by his nurse, "How tall is the child?" and "Where is the rogue?" If I asked him, after he had said "Frühstücken" correctly, how he used to say it, he would consider, and would require merely a suggestion of accessory circumstances, in order to give the correct answer *Fritick,* and so with many words difficult to pronounce. The child of three and even of four years can remember separate experiences of his second year, and a person that will take the pains to remind him frequently of them will be able easily to carry the recollections of the second and third years far on into the more advanced years of childhood. It is merely because no one makes such a useless experiment that older children lose the memory-images of their second year. These fade out because they are not combined with new ones.

At what time, however, the first natural association of a particular idea with a new one that appears weeks or months later, takes place without being called up by something in the mean time, is very hard to determine. On this point we must first gather good observations out of the second and third half-years, like the following:

"In the presence of a boy a year and a half old it was related that another boy whom he knew, and who was then in the country far away, had fallen and hurt his knee. No one noticed the child, who was playing as the story was told. After some weeks the one who had fallen came into the room, and the little one in a lively manner ran up to the new-comer and cried, 'Fall, hurt leg!'" (Stiebel, 1865).

Another example is given by G. Lindner (1882): "The mother of a two-year-old child had made for it out of a postal-card a sled (Schlitten), which was destroyed after a few hours, and found its way into the waste-basket. Just four weeks later another postal-card comes, and it is taken from the carrier by the child and handed to the mother with the words, '*Mamma, Litten!*' This was in summer, when there was nothing to remind the child of the sled. Soon after the same wish was expressed on the receipt of a letter also."

I have known like cases of attention, of recollection, and of intelligence in the third year where they were not suspected. The child, unnoticed, hears all sorts of things said, seizes on this or that expression, and weeks after brings into connection, fitly or unfitly, the memory-images, drawing immediately from an insufficient number of particular cases a would-be general conclusion.

Equally certain with this fact is the other, less known or less noticed, that, *even before the first attempts at speaking, such a generalizing and therefore concept-forming combination of memory-images regularly takes place.*

All children in common have inborn in them the ability to combine all sorts of sense-impressions connected with food, when these appear again individually, with one another, or with memory-images of such impressions, so that adaptive movements suited to the obtaining of fresh food arise as the result of this association. In the earlier months these are simple and easier to be seen, and I have given several examples (Vol. I, pp. 250, 260, 329, 333). Later such movements, through the perfecting of the language of gesture and the growth of this very power of association, become more and more complicated: e. g., in his sixteenth month my boy saw a closed box, out of which he had the day before received a cake; he at once made with his hands a begging movement, yet he could not speak a word. In the twenty-first month I took out of the pocket of a coat which was hanging with many others in the wardrobe a biscuit and gave it to the child. When he had eaten it, he went directly to the wardrobe and looked in the right coat for a second biscuit. At this period also the child can not have been thinking in the unspoken words, "Get biscuit—wardrobe, coat, pocket, look," for he did not yet know the words.

Even in the sixth month an act of remarkable *adaptiveness* was once observed, which can not be called either accidental or entirely voluntary, and if it was fully purposed it would indicate a well-advanced development of understanding in regard to food without knowledge of words. When the child, viz., after considerable experience in nursing at the breast, discovered that the flow of milk was less abundant, he used to place his hand hard on the breast as if he wanted to force out the milk by pressure. Of course there was here no insight into the causal connection, but it is a question whether the firm laying on of the little hand was not repeated for the reason that the experience had been once made accidentally, that after doing this the nursing was less difficult.

On the other hand, an unequivocal complicated act of deliberation occurred in the seventeenth month. The child could not reach his playthings in the cupboard, because it was too high for him ; he ran about, brought a traveling-bag, got upon it, and took what he wanted. In this case he could not possibly think in words, since he did not yet know words.

My child tries further (in the nineteenth and twentieth months) in a twofold fashion to make known his eager wish to leave the room, not being as yet able to speak. He takes any cloth he fancies and brings it to me. I put it about him, he wraps himself in it, and, climbing beseechingly on my knee, makes longing, pitiful sounds, which do not cease until after I have opened a door through which he goes into another room. Then he immediately throws away the cloth and runs about exulting.

The other performance is this : When the child feels the need of relieving his bowels, he is accustomed to make peculiar grunting sounds, by means of a strain of the abdomen, shutting the mouth and breathing loud, by jerks, through the nose. He is then taken away. Now, if he is not suited with the place where he happens to be, at any time, he begins to make just such sounds. If he is taken away, no such need appears at all, but he is in high glee. Here is the expectation, "I shall be taken away if I make that sound."

Whether we are to admit, in addition, an intentional *deception* in this case, or whether only a logical process takes place, I can not decide. In the whole earlier and later behavior of the child there is no ground for the first assumption, and the fact that he employs this artifice while in his carriage, immediately after he has been waited on, is directly against it.

To how small an extent, some time previous to this, perceptions were made use of *to simplify his own exertions*, i. e., were combined and had motor effect, appears from an observation in the sixteenth month. Earlier than this, when I used to say, " Give the ring," I always laid an ivory ring, that was tied to a thread, before the child, on the table. I now said the same thing—after an interval of a week—while the same ring was hanging near the chair by a red thread a foot long, so that the child, as he sat on the chair, could just reach it, but only with much pains. He made a grasp now, upon getting the sound-impression "ring," not at the thread, which would have made the seizure of the ring, hanging freely, very easy for him, but directly at the ring hanging far below him, and gave it to me. And when the command was repeated, it did not occur to him to touch the thread.

It is likewise a sign of small understanding that the mouth is always opened in smelling of a fragrant flower or perfume (Vol. I, p. 135). Deficiencies of this kind are, indeed, quite logical from the standpoint of childish experience. Because, at an earlier period the pleasant smell (of milk) always came in connection with the pleasant taste, therefore, thinks the child, in every case where there is a pleasant smell there will also be something that tastes good. The common or collective concept *taste-smell* had not yet (in the seventeenth month) been differentiated into the concepts taste and smell.

In the department of the sense of hearing the differentiation generally makes its appearance earlier ; memory, as a rule, later. Yet children whose talent for music is developed early, retain *melodies* even in their first year of life. A girl to whom some of the Froebel songs were sung, and who was taught appropriate movements of the hands and feet, always performed the proper movement when one of the melodies was merely hummed, or a verse was said (in the thirteenth month), without confounding them at all. This early and firm association of sound-images with motor-images is possible only when interest is attached to it—i. e., when the attention has been directed often, persistently, and with concentration, upon the things to be combined. Thus, this very child (in the nineteenth month), when her favorite song, " Who will go for a Soldier ? " ("Wer will

unter die Soldaten?") was sung to her, could not only
join in the rhyme at the end of the verse, but, no matter where a stop was made, she would go on, in a manner imperfect, indeed, but easily intelligible (Frau Dr.
Friedemann).

Here, however, in addition to memory and attention, heredity is to be considered ; since such a talent is
wholly lacking in certain families, but in others exists
in all the brothers and sisters.

In performances of this kind, a superior understanding is not by any means exhibited, but a stronger memory and faculty of association. These associations are
not, however, of a logical sort, but are habits acquired
through training, and they may even retard the development of the intellect if they become numerous. For
they may obstruct the formation, at an early period, of
independent ideas, merely on account of the time they
claim. Often, too, these artificial associations are almost
useless for the development of the intellect. They are
too special. On this ground I am compelled to cen-
sure the extravagancies, that are wide-spread especially in
Germany, of the Froebel methods of occupying young
children.

The *logic of the child* naturally operates at the beginning with much more extensive, and therefore less
intensive, notions than those of adults, with notions
which the adult no longer forms. But the child does
not, on that account, proceed illogically, although he
does proceed awkwardly. Some further examples may
illustrate.

The adult does not ordinarily try whether a door
that he has just bolted is fast ; but the one-year-old

child tests carefully the edge of the door he has shut, to see whether it is really closed, because he does not understand the effect of lock and bolt. For even in the eighteenth month he goes back and forth with a key, to the writing-desk, with the evident purpose of opening it. But at twelve months, when he tries whether it is fast, he does not think of the key at all, and does not yet possess a single word.

An adult, before watering flowers with a watering-pot, will look to see whether there is water in it. The child of a year and a half, who has seen how watering is done, finds special pleasure in going from flower to flower, even with an empty watering-pot, and making the motions of pouring upon each one separately, as if water would really come out. For him the notion "watering-pot" is identical with the notion "filled watering-pot," because at first he was acquainted with the latter only.

Much of what is attributed to imagination in very young children rests essentially on the formation of such vague concepts, on the inability to combine constant qualities into sharply defined concepts. When, in the twenty-third month, the child holds an empty cup to his mouth and sips and swallows, and does it repeatedly, and with a serene, happy expression, this "play" is founded chiefly on the imperfect notion "filled cup." The child has so often perceived something to drink, drinking-vessel, and the act of drinking, in combination with one another, that the one peremptorily demands the other when either appears singly; hence the pleasure in pouring out from empty pitchers into empty cups, and in drinking out of empty cups (in second to fifth years). When adults do the same in the play of the theatre, this action always has a value as language, it signifies something for other persons; but with the child, who plays in this fashion entirely alone, the pleasure consists in the production of familiar ideas together with agreeable feelings, which are, as it were, crystallized with comparative clearness out of the dull mass of undefined perceptions. These memory-images become real existences, like the hallucinations of the insane, because the sensuous impressions probably impress themselves directly — without reflection — upon the growing brain, and hence the memory-images of them, on account of their vividness, can not always be surely distinguished from the perceptions themselves. Most of the plays that children invent of themselves may be referred to this fact; on the other hand, the play of hide-and-seek (especially in the seventeenth and eighteenth months), and, nearly allied to this, the hunting after scraps of paper, bits of biscuit, buttons, and other favorite objects (in the fifteenth month), constitute an intellectual advance.

By practice in this kind of seeking for well-known, purposely concealed objects, the intelligence of little children can easily be increased to an astonishing degree, so that toward the end of the second year they already understand some simple tricks of the juggler; for example, making a card disappear. But after I had discontinued such exercises for months, the ordinary capacity for being duped was again present.

This ease with which children can be deceived is to be attributed to lack of experience far more than to lack of intelligence. When the child of a year and a half offers leaves to a sheep or a stag, observes the strange animal with somewhat timid astonishment, and a few days after holds out some hastily plucked grass-blades to a chaffinch he sees hopping across the road, supposing that the bird will likewise take them from his hand and eat them—an observation that I made on my child exactly as Sigismund did on his—it is not right to call such an act "stupid"; the act shows igno-rance—i. e., inexperience—but it is not illogical. The child would be properly called stupid only in case he did not *learn* the difference between the animals fed. When, on the other hand, the child of two and a half years, entirely of his own accord, holds a watch first to his left ear, then to his right, listens both times, and then says, "The watch goes, goes too!" then, pointing with his finger to a clock, cries with delight, "The clock goes too," we rightly find in such independent induction a proof of intellect. For the swinging of the pendulum and the ticking had indeed often been perceived, but to connect the notion of a "going clock" with the visi-ble but noiseless swinging, just as with the audible but invisible ticking of the watch, requires a pretty well advanced power of abstraction.

That the ability to *abstract* may show itself, though imperfectly, even in the first year, is, according to my observations, certain. Infants are struck by a quality of an object—e. g., the white appearance of milk. The "taking away" or "abstracting" then consists in the iso-lating of this quality out of innumerable other sight-im-pressions and the blending of the impressions into a concept. The *naming* of this, which begins months later, by a rudimental word, like *mum*, is an outward sign of this abstraction, which did not at all lead to the formation of the concept, but followed it, as will be shown in detail further on (in the two following chapters).

It would be interesting to collect observations concerning this reasoning power in the very earliest period, because at that time language does not interfere to help or to hinder. But it is just such observations that we especially lack. When a child in the twelfth month, on hearing a watch for the first time, cries out, "Tick-tick," looking meantime at the clock on the wall, he has not, in doing this, "formed," as G. Lindner supposes, "his first concept, although a vague and empty one as yet," but he had the concept before, and has now merely given a name to it for the first time.

The first observation made in regard to his child by Darwin, which seemed to him to prove "a sort of practical reflection," occurred on the one hundred and forty-fourth day. The child grasped his father's finger and drew it to his mouth, but his own hand prevented him from sucking the finger. The child then, strangely enough, instead of entirely withdrawing his hand, slipped it along the finger so that he could get the end of the finger into his mouth. This proceeding was several times repeated, and was evidently not accidental but intentional. At the age of five months, associations of ideas arose independently of all instruction. Thus, e. g., the child, being dressed in hat and cloak, was very angry if he was not at once taken out of doors.

How strong the *reasoning power without* words may be at a later period, the following additional observations show :

From the time when my child, like Sigismund's (both in the fifteenth month), had burned his finger in the flame of the candle, he could not be induced to put his finger near the flame again, but he would sometimes put it in fun toward the flame without touching it, and he even (eighteen months old) carried a stick of wood of his own accord to the stove-door and pushed it in through the open slide, with a proud look at his parents. There is surely something more than an imitation here.

Further, my child at first never used to let his mouth and chin be wiped without crying; from the fifteenth month on he kept perfectly quiet during the disagreeable operation. He must have noticed that this was finished sooner when he was quiet.

The same thing can be observed in every little child, provided he is not too much talked to, punished, yielded to, or spoiled. In the nineteenth month it happened with my child that he resisted the command to lie down in the evening. I let him cry, and raise himself on his bed, but did not take him up, did not speak to him, did not use any force, but remained motionless and watchful near by. At last he became tired, lay down, and fell asleep directly. Here he acquired an understanding of the uselessness of crying in order to avoid obedience to commands.

The *knowledge* of right (what is allowed and commanded) and of wrong (what is forbidden) had been long since acquired. In the seventeenth month, e. g., a sense of cleanliness was strongly developed, and later (in the thirty-third month) the child could not, without lively protest, behold his nurse acting contrary to the directions that had been given to himself—e. g., putting the knife into her mouth or dipping bread into the milk. Emotions of this kind are less a proof of the existence of a sense of duty than of the *understanding* that violations of well-known precepts have unpleasant consequences —i. e., that certain actions bring in their train pleasant feelings, while other acts bring unpleasant feelings. How long before the knowledge of words these emotions began to exist I have, unfortunately, not succeeded in determining.

But in many of the above cases—and they might without difficulty be multiplied by diligent observation —there is not the least indication of any influence of spoken words. Whether no attempt at speaking has preceded, or whether a small collection of words may have been made, the cases of child-intelligence adduced in this chapter, observed by myself, prove that without knowledge of verbal language, and independently of it, the logical activity of the child attains a high degree of development, and no reason exists for explaining the intelligent actions of children who do not yet speak at all—i. e., do not yet clothe their ideas in words, but do already combine them with one another—as being different specifically from the intelligent (not instinctive) actions of sagacious orangs and chimpanzees. The difference consists far more in this, that the latter can not form so many, so clear, and so abstract conceptions, or so many and complicated combinations of ideas, as can the gifted human child in the society of human beings—*even before he has learned to speak*. When he has learned to speak, then the gap widens to such an extent that what before was in some respects almost the equal of humanity seems now a repulsive caricature of it.

In order, then, to understand the real difference between brute and man, it is necessary to ascertain how a child and a brute animal may have ideas without words, and may combine them for an end : whether it is done, e. g., with memory-images, as in dreaming. And it is necessary also to investigate the *essential character of the process of learning to speak.*

Concerning the first problem, which is of uncommon psychogenetic interest and practical importance, a solution seems to be promised in the investigation of the formation of concepts in the case of those born deaf, the so-called deaf and dumb children. On this point I offer first the words of a man of practical experience.

The excellent superintendent of the Educational Institute for the Deaf and Dumb in Weimar, C. Oehlwein (1867), well says :

"The deaf-mute in his first years of life looks at, turns over, feels of objects that attract him, on all sides, and approaches those that are at a distance. By this he receives, like the young child who has all his senses, sensations and sensuous ideas ; * and from the objects themselves he apprehends a number of qualities, which he compares with one another or with the qualities of other objects, but always refers to the object which at the time attracts him. Herein he has a more correct or less correct sense-intuition of this object, according as he has observed, compared, and comprehended more or less attentively. As this object has affected him through

---

* Empfindungsvorstellungen.

sight and feeling, so he represents it to other persons also by characteristic signs for sight and indirectly for feeling also. He shapes or draws a copy of the object seen and felt with life and movement. For this he avails himself of the means that Nature has placed directly within human power—the control over the movement of the facial muscles, over the use of the hands, and, if necessary, of the feet also. These signs, *not obtained from any one's suggestion*, self-formed, which the deaf-mute employs directly in his representation, are, as it were, the given outline of the image which he has found, and they stand therefore in the closest relation to the inner constitution of the individual that makes the representation.

" But we find not only that the individual senses of the deaf-mute, his own observation and apprehension, are formative factors in the occurrences of sensation and perception, as is of course the case, but that the qualities of the objects observed by him, and associated, according to his individual tendencies, are also raised by him, through comparison, separation, grouping—through his own act, therefore—to general ideas, concepts, although as yet imperfect ones, and they are named and recognized again by peculiar signs intelligible to himself.

" But in this very raising of an idea to a general idea, to a concept—a process connected with the forming of a sign—is manifested the influence of the lack of hearing and of speech upon the psychical development of the deaf-mute. It appears at first to be an advantage that the sign by which the deaf-mute represents an idea is derived from the impression, the image, the idea, which the user of the sign himself has or has had ; he expresses by the sign nothing foreign to him, but only what has become his own. But this advantage disappears when compared with the hindrance caused by this very circumstance in the raising of the individual idea to a general idea, for the fact that the latter is designated by the image, or the elements of the image in which the former consists, is no small obstacle to it in attaining complete generality. The same bond that unites the concept with the conceiver binds it likewise to one of the individual ideas conceived—e. g., when, by pointing to his own flesh, his own skin, he designates the concept flesh, skin (in general also the flesh or the skin of animals) ; whereas, by means of the word, which the child who has all his senses is obliged to learn, a constraint is indeed exercised as something foreign, but a constraint that simply enforces upon his idea the claim of generality.

"One example more. The deaf-mute designates the concept, or general idea, 'red' by lightly touching his lips. With this sign he indicates the red of the sky, of paintings, of dress-stuffs, of flowers, etc. Thus, in however manifold connection with other concepts his concept 'red' may be repeated, it is to him as a concept always *one* and the same only. It is *common* to *all* the connections in which it repeatedly occurs."

But before the thinking deaf-mute arrived at the concept " red," he formed for himself the ideas " lip, dress, sky, flower," etc.

For a knowledge of intellectual development in the child possessed of all the senses, and of the great extent to which he is independent of verbal language in the formation of concepts, it is indispensable to make a collection of such concepts as uneducated deaf-mutes not acquainted either with the finger-alphabet or with articulation express by means of their own gestures in a manner intelligible to others. Their language, however, comprises " not only the various expressive changes of countenance (play of feature), but also the varied movements of the hands (gesticulations), the positions, attitudes, bearing, and movements of the other parts of the entire body, through which the deaf-mute naturally, i. e., *untouched by educational influences*, expresses his ideas and conceptions." But I refrain from making such a catalogue here, as we are concerned with the fact that *many concepts are, without any learning of words whatever, plainly expressed and logically combined with one another*, and their correctness is proved by the conduct of any and every untaught child born deaf. Besides, such a catalogue, in order to possess the psychogenetic value desired by me, needs a critical examination extremely difficult to carry through as to whether the " educational influences" supposed to be excluded are actually wholly excluded in all cases as they really are in some cases, e. g., in regard to food.

Degerando (1827) has enumerated a long list of concepts, which deaf-mutes before they are instructed represent by pantomimic gesture. Many of these forms of expression in French deaf-mutes are identical with those of German. It is most earnestly to be wished that this international language of feature and gesture used by children entirely uninstructed, born deaf, may be made accessible to psycho-physiological and linguistic study by means of pictorial representations—photographic best of all. This should be founded on the experiences of German, French, English, Russian, Italian, and other teachers of deaf-mutes.

For there is hardly a better proof that thinking is not dependent on the language of words than the conduct of deaf-mutes, who express, indeed, many more concepts of unlike content in the same manner than any verbal language does—just as children with all their senses do before they possess a satisfactory stock of words—but who, by gesticulation and pantomime before receiving any instruction, demonstrate that concepts are formed without words.

With reference to the manner in which uneducated deaf-mutes speak, the following examples are characteristic performances in gesture-language:

One deaf-mute asks another, "Stay, go you?" (look of inquiry). Answer: "Go, I" (i. e., "Do you stay or go?" "I go"). "Hunter hare shoots."

"Arm, man, be strong," means, "The man's arm is strong."

"N., spectacles, see," means, "N. sees with the spectacles."

"Run I finished, go to sleep," means, "When I had finished running, I went to sleep." "Money, you?" means, "Have you money?"

One of the most interesting sights I know of, in a psychological and physiological point of view, is a conversation in gesture and pantomime between two or three children born totally deaf, who do not know that they are observed. I am indebted to Director Oehlwein, of Weimar, for the opportunity of such observations, as also for the above questions and answers. Especially those children (of about seven years) not yet instructed in articulation employ an astonishing number of looks and gestures, following one upon another with great rapidity, in order to effect an understanding with one another. They understand one another very easily, but, because their gestures, and particularly their excessively subtilized play of feature, do not appear in ordinary life, these children are just as hard to understand for the uninitiated as are men who speak a wholly foreign language without any gestures. Even the eye of the deaf-mute has a different expression from that of the person who talks. The look seems more " interested," and manifestly far fewer unnecessary movements of the eyes and contractions of the facial muscles are made by the deaf-mute than by the child of the same age who has his hearing.

Further, deaf-mutes, even those of small ability, imitate all sorts of movements that are plainly visible much better, in general, than do persons with all their senses. I made, in presence of the children, several not very easy crossings of the fingers, put my hands in different positions, and the like—movements that they could not ever have seen—and I was surprised that some of the children at once made them deftly, whereas ordinary children first consider a long time, and then imitate clumsily. It is doubtless this exaltation of the imitative functions in deaf-mute children which makes it appear as if they themselves invented their gestures (see above, p. 23). Certainly they do not get their first signs through " any one's suggestion." they form them for themselves, but, so far as I see, only through imitation and the hereditary expressive movements. The signs are in great part themselves unabridged imitations. The agreement,

or "convention," which many teachers of deaf-mutes
assume, and which would introduce an entirely cause-
less, not to say mysterious, principle, consists in this,
that all deaf-mutes in the beginning imitate the same
thing in the same way. Thus, through this perfectly
natural accord of all, it comes to pass that they understand one another. When they have gained ideas, then
they combine the separate signs in manifold ways, as
one who speaks combines words, in order to express new
ideas; they become thereby more and more difficult to
be understood, and often are only with difficulty understood even among themselves; and they are able only in
very limited degree to form concepts of a higher order.
"Nothing, being dead, space"—these are concepts of a
very high order for them.

For this reason it is easy to comprehend that a deaf-
mute child, although he has learned but few words
through instruction in articulation, weaves these continually into his pantomimic conversation in place of
his former elaborate gestures. I observed that individual children, born totally deaf, preferred, even in conversation with one another, and when ignorant of the
fact that I was observing them, the articulate words just
learned, although these were scarcely intelligible, to their
own signs.

Thus mighty is the charm of the spoken word, even
when the child does not himself hear it, but merely feels
it with his tongue.

But the schooling the deaf-mute must go through in
order to become acquainted with the sensations of sight,
touch, and movement that go with the sound, is un-
speakably toilsome.

W. Gude says in his treatise, remarkable alike for acuteness and clearness, "Principles and Outlines of the Exposition of a Scheme of Instruction for an Institution for Deaf-Mutes " (" Grundsätze und Grundzüge zur Aufstellung eines Lehrplans für eine Taubstummen-Anstalt," 1881) : " The utterances of tones and of articulate sounds called forth by involuntary stimulus during the first years, in deaf-mutes, are such unimportant motor phenomena that they are not immediately followed by a motor sensation. But when the deaf-mute child is more awake mentally, he perceives that his relatives make movements of the mouth in their intercourse, and repeated attempts of those about him to make themselves intelligible by pronouncing certain words to him are not entirely without effect upon the deaf-mute that is intellectually active. When such deaf-mutes now direct their attention to the matter, they succeed in regard to only a part of the sounds—those that are conspicuous to the eye in their utterance—in getting a tolerable imitation. Individual deaf-mutes go so far, in fact, as to understand various words correctly without repeating them ; others succeed gradually in repeating such words as ' papa, mamma,' so that one can understand what is meant. Those who are deaf-mutes from birth do not, however, of themselves, succeed in imitating accurately other vocal sounds in general."

A deaf-mute, who had not been instructed, explained to Romanes, at a later period when he had learned the sign-language, that he had before thought in " images," which means nothing else than that he, in place of the words heard (in our case) and the digital signs seen (in his case), had made use of memory-images gained from visual impressions, for distinguishing his concepts. Laura Bridgman, too, a person in general the subject of very incorrect inferences, who was not blind and deaf from birth, could form a small number of concepts that were above the lowest grade. These originated from the materials furnished by the sense of touch, the muscular sense and general sensibility, before she had learned a sort of finger-language. But she had learned to speak somewhat before she became dumb and blind. Children with sight, born deaf, seem not to be able to perform the simplest arithmetical operations, e. g., 214 — 96 and 908 × 70 (according to Asch, 1865), until after several years of continuous instruction in articulate speaking. They do succeed, however, and that without sound-images of words, and perhaps, too, without sight-images of words; in mental arithmetic without knowledge of written figures, by help of the touch-images of words which the tongue furnishes.

In any case uneducated persons born deaf can count by means of the fingers without the knowledge of figures; and, when they go beyond 10, the notched stick comes to their aid (Sicard and Degerando).

The language of gesture and feature in very young children, born dumb and not treated differently from other children, shows also, in most abundant measure, that concepts are formed without words. The child born deaf uses the primitive language of gesture to the same extent as does the child that has his hearing; the former makes himself intelligible by actions and sounds as the latter does, so that his deficiency is not suspected. This natural language is also *understood* by the child born deaf, so far as it is recognizable by his eye. In the look and the features of his mother he reads her mood. But he very early becomes quiet and develops for himself, " out of unconscious gesticulation, the gesture language, which at first is not conventional, nay, is not in the strict sense quite a sign-language, but a mimetic-plastic representation of the influences experienced from the external world," since the deaf-mute imitates movements perceived, and the attitude of persons and the position of objects. Upon this pantomime alone rests the possibility of coming to an understanding, within a certain range, with deaf-mutes that have had no instruction at all. It can not, therefore, in its elementary form be conventional, as Hill, to whom I owe these data, rightly maintains. He writes concerning the child born deaf : " His voice seems just like that of other children. He screams, weeps, according as he feels uncomfortable; he starts when frightened by any noise. Even friendly address, toying, fun, serious threats, are understood by him as early as by any child." But he does not hear his own voice ; it is not sound that frightens him, but the concussion ; it is not the pleasant word that delights him, but the pleasant countenance of his mother. " It even happens, not seldom, that through encouragement to use the voice, these children acquire a series of articulate sounds, and a number of combinations of sounds, which they employ as the expression of their wishes." They not only *point out* the object desired, not only *imitate* movements that are to procure what they want, but they also outline the forms of objects wished for. They are able to conduct themselves so intelligently in this, that the deaf-mute condition is not discovered till the second year, or even later, and then chiefly by their use of the eye, because in case of distant objects only those seen excite their attention.

From this behavior of infants born deaf it manifestly follows that even without the possibility of natural imitation of sounds, and without the knowledge of a single word, qualities may be blended with qualities into concepts. Thus, *primitive thinking is not bound up with verbal language*. It demands, however, a certain development of the cerebrum, probably a certain very considerable number of ganglionic cells in the cerebral cortex, that stand in firm organic connection with one another. The difference between an uninstructed young deaf-mute and a cretin is immense. The former can learn a great deal through instruction in speaking, the latter can not. This very ability to learn, in the child born deaf, is greater than in the normal child, in respect to pantomime and gesture. If a child with his hearing had to grow up among deaf-mutes, he would undoubtedly learn their language, and would in addition enjoy his own voice without being able to make use of it; but he would probably be discovered, further on, without testing his hearing, by the fact that he was not quite so complete a master of this gesture-language as the deaf-mutes, on account of the diversion of his attention by sound.

The total result of the foregoing observations concerning the capacity of accomplishment on the part of uneducated deaf-mutes in regard to the natural language of gesture and feature, demonstrates more plainly than any other fact whatever that, without words and without signs for words, thought-activity exists—that thinking takes place when both words and signs for words

are wanting. Wherefore, then, should the logical combination of ideas in the human being born perfect begin
only with the speaking of words or the learning to
speak? Because the adult supposes that he no longer
thinks without words, he easily draws the erroneous
conclusion that no one, that not even he himself, could
think before the knowledge of verbal language. In
truth, however, it was *not language that generated the
intellect; it is the intellect that formerly invented language: and even now the new-born human being brings
with him into the world far more intellect than talent
for language.*

CHAPTER XVII.

LEARNING TO SPEAK.

No human being remembers how he learned his
mother-tongue in early youth, and the whole human
race has forgotten the origin of its articulate speech as
well as of its gestures; but every individual passes perceptibly through the stage of learning to speak, so that
a patient observer recognizes much as conformable to
law.

The acquisition of speech belongs to those physiological problems which can not be solved by the most
important means possessed by physiology, vivisection.
And the speechless condition in which every human
being is born can not be regarded as a disease that may
be healed by instruction, as is the case with certain
forms of acquired aphasia. A set of other accomplishments, such as swimming, riding, fencing, piano-play-

ing, the acquirement of which is physiological, are learned like articulate speech, and nobody calls the person that can not swim an anomaly on that account. The *inability to appropriate* to one's self these and other co-ordinated muscular movements, this alone is abnormal. But we can not tell in advance in the case of any new-born child whether he will learn to speak or not, just as in the case of one who has suffered an obstruction of speech or has entirely lost speech, it is not certain whether he will ever recover it.

In this the normal child that does *not yet* speak perfectly, resembles the diseased adult who, for any cause, *no longer* has command of language. And to compare these two with each other is the more important, as at present no other empirical way is open to us for investigating the nature of the process of learning to speak; but this way conducts us, fortunately, through pathology, to solid, important physiological conclusions.

1. Disturbances of Speech in Adults.

The command of language comprises, on the one hand, the understanding of what is spoken; on the other hand, the utterance of what is thought. It is at the height of its performance in free, intelligible, connected speech. Everything that disturbs the *understanding of words heard* must be designated disturbance of speech equally with everything that disturbs the *production of words* and sentences.

By means of excellent investigations made by many persons, especially by Broca, Wernicke, Kussmaul, it has become possible to make a topical division of most of the observed disturbances of speech of both kinds.

In the first class, which comprises the *impressive* processes, we have to consider every functional disturbance of the peripheral ear, of the auditory nerve and of the central ends of the auditory nerve; in the second class, viz., the *expressive* processes, we consider every functional disturbance of the apparatus required for articulation, including the nerves belonging to this in their whole extent, in particular the hypoglossus, as motor nerve of the tongue, and certain parts of the cerebral hemispheres from which the nerves of speech are excited and to which the sense-impressions from without are so conducted by connecting fibers that they themselves or their memory-images can call forth expressive, i. e., motor processes. The diagram, Fig. 1, illustrates the matter.

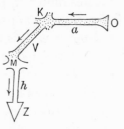

FIG. 1.

The peripheral ear *o*, with the terminations of the auditory nerve, is by means of sensory fibers *a*, that are connected with the auditory nerve, in connection with the storehouse of sound-impressions, K. This is connected by means of the intercentral paths *v* with the motor speech-center M. From it go out special fibers of communication, *h*, to the motor nerves of speech which terminate in the external instruments of articulation, *z*.

The impressive nerve-path, *o a* K, is centripetal; the expressive, M *h z*, centrifugal; *v*, intercentral.

When the normal child learns to speak, *o* receives the sound-impressions; by *a* the acoustic-nerve excitations are passed along to K, and are here stored up, every distinctly heard sound (a tone, a syllable, a word) leaving an impression behind in K. It is very remarkable here that, among the many sounds and noises that impress themselves upon the portions of the brain directly connected with the auditory nerve, a selection is made in the sound-field of speech, K, since all those impressions that can be reproduced, among them all the acoustic images necessary for speech, are preserved, but many others are not, e. g., thunder, crackling. Memory is indistinct with regard to these. From K, when the sound-images or sound-impressions have become sufficiently strong and numerous, the nerve-excitement goes farther through the connecting paths *v* to M, where it liberates motor impulses, and through *h* sets in activity the peripheral apparatus of speech, *z*.

Now, speech is disturbed when at any point the path *o z* is interrupted, or the excitation conducted along the nerve-fibers and ganglionic cells upon the hearing of something spoken or upon the speaking of something represented in idea (heard inwardly) is arrested, a thing which may be effected without a total interruption of the conduction, e. g., by means of poison and through anatomical lesions.

On the basis of these physiological relations, about which there is no doubt, I divide, then, all pure disturbances of speech, or *lalopathies*, into three classes:

(1) Periphero-Impressive or Perceptive Disturbances.

The organ of hearing is injured *at its peripheral extremity*, or else the acusticus in its course; then occurs *difficulty of hearing* or *deafness*. What is spoken is not correctly heard or not heard at all: the utterance is correct only in case the lesion happened late. If it is inborn, then this lack of speech, alalia, is called *deaf-mutism*, although the so-called deaf and dumb are not in reality dumb, but only deaf. If words spoken are incorrectly heard on account of acquired defects of the peripheral ear, the patient mis-hears, and the abnormal condition is called paracusis.

(2) Central Disturbances.

a. The higher impressive central paths are disturbed: *centro-sensory dysphasia and aphasia,* or *word-deafness.* Words are heard but not understood. The hearing is acute. " Patients may have perfectly correct ideas, but they lack the correct expression for them; not the thoughts but the words are confused. They would understand the ideas of others also if they only understood the words. They are in the position of persons suddenly transported into the midst of a people using the same sounds but different words, which strike upon their ear like an unintelligible noise." (Kussmaul.) Their articulation is without defect, but what they say is unintelligible because the words are mutilated and used wrongly. C. Wernicke discovered this form, and has separated it sharply from other disturbances of speech. He designated it sensory aphasia. Kussmaul later named this abnormal condition word-deafness (surditas verbalis).

b. The connections between the impressive sound-centers and the motor speech-center are injured. Then we have intercentral conductive dysphasia and aphasia. What is spoken is heard and understood correctly even when *v* is completely interrupted. The articulation is not disturbed, and yet the patient utters no word of

6

himself. He can, however, read aloud what is written. (Kussmaul.) The word that has just been read aloud by the patient can not be repeated by him, neither can the word that has been pronounced to him ; and, notwithstanding this, he reads aloud with perfect correctness. In this case, then, it is impossible for the patient of his own motion, even if the memory of the words heard were not lost, to set in activity the expressive mechanism of speech, although it might remain uninjured.

c. The motor speech-center is injured. Then we have centro-motor dysphasia and aphasia. If the center is completely and exclusively disturbed, then it is a case of pure ataxic aphasia. Spontaneous speaking, saying over of words said by another, and reading aloud of writing, are impossible. (Kussmaul.) On the other hand, words heard are understood, although the concepts belonging with them can not be expressed aloud. The verbal memory remains ; and the patient can still express his thoughts in writing and can copy in writing what he reads or what is dictated to him.

(3) Periphero-Expressive or Articulatory Disturbances.

The centrifugal paths from the motor speech-center to the motor nerves of speech and to their extremities, or else these nerves themselves, are injured. Then occurs *dysarthria*, and, if the path is totally impassable at any place, *anarthria*. The hearing and understanding of words are not hindered, but speaking, repeating the words of others, and reading aloud are, as in the last case (2, *c*), impossible. In general this form can not be distinguished from the foregoing when both are developed in an extreme degree, except in cases of peripheral dysarthria, i. e., dyslalia, since, as may be easily understood, it makes no difference in the resulting phenomena whether the motor center itself is extirpated or its connections with the motor outlet are absolutely cut off just where the latter begins; but if this latter is injured nearer to the periphery, e. g., if the hypoglossus is paralyzed, then the phenomena are different (paralalia, mogilalia). Here belongs all so-called mechanical dyslalia, caused by defects of the peripheral speech-apparatus.

Of these five forms each occurs generally only in connection with another; for this reason the topical diagnosis also is often extraordinarily difficult. But enough cases have been accurately observed and collected to put it almost beyond a doubt that each form may also appear for a short time purely by itself. To be sure, the anatomical localization of the impressive and expressive paths is not yet ascertained, so that for the present the centripetal roads from the acusticus to the motor speech-center, and the intercentral fibers that run to the higher centers, are as much unknown as the centrifugal paths leading from them to the nuclei of the hypoglossus; but that the speech-center discovered by Broca is situated in the posterior portion of the third frontal convolution (in right-handed men on the left, in left-handed on the right) is universally acknowledged.

Further, it results from the abundance of clinical material, that the acoustic-center K must be divided into a sound-center L, a syllable-center S, a word-center W, each of which may be in itself defective, for cases have been observed in which sounds were still recognized and reproduced, but not syllables and words, also cases in which sounds and syllables could be dealt with but no words; and, finally, cases in which all these were wanting. The original diagram is thereby considerably complicated, as the simple path of connection between K and M has added to it the arcs L S M and L S W M (Fig. 2).

The surest test of the perfect condition of all the segments is afforded by the repetition of sounds, syllables, and words pronounced by others.

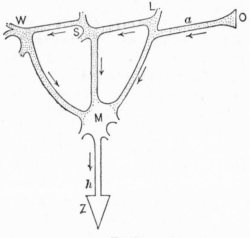

FIG. 2.

Syllables and sounds, but no words, can be pro- nounced if W is missing or the path S W or W M is interrupted; no syllables if S is missing or L S or S M is interrupted. If L is missing, then nothing can be re- peated from hearing. If L M is interrupted, then sylla- bles and words are more easily repeated than simple sounds, so far as the latter are not syllables. If L S is interrupted, then simple sounds only can be repeated. All these abnormal states have been actually observed. The proofs are to be found in Kussmaul's classic work on the disturbances of speech (1877). Even the strange case appears in which, L M being impracticable, syllables are more easily repeated than simple sounds.

If a is interrupted before the acquirement of speech, and thus chronic deafness is present in very early childhood, articulation may still be learned through visual and tactile impressions; but in this case the sound-center L is not developed. Another, a sound-touch-center, comes in its place in deaf-mutes when they are instructed, chiefly through the tactile sensations of the tongue; and, when they are instructed in reading (and writing), a sound-sight- (or letter) center. This last is, on the contrary, wanting to those born blind; and both are wanting to those born blind and deaf. Instead is formed in them through careful instruction, by means of the tactile sensations of the finger-tips, a center for signs of sound that are known by touch (as with the printed text for the blind).

Accordingly, the eye and ear are not absolutely indispensable to the acquirement of a verbal language; but for the thorough learning of the verbal language in its entire significance both are by all means indispensable. For, the person born blind does not get the significance of words pertaining to light and color. For him, therefore, a large class of conceptions, an extensive portion of the vocabulary of his language, remains empty sound. To the one born deaf there is likewise an extensive district of conceptions closed, inasmuch as all words pertaining to tone and noise remain unintelligible to him.

Moreover, those born blind and deaf, or those born blind and becoming deaf very early, or those born deaf and becoming blind very early, though they may possess ever so good intelligence, and perhaps even learn to write letters, as did the famous Laura Bridgman, will invariably understand only a small part of the vocabulary of their language, and will not articulate correctly.

Those born deaf are precisely the ones that show plainly how necessary hearing is for the acquirement of perfectly articulate speech. One who is deaf from birth does not even learn to speak half a dozen sounds correctly without assistance, and the loss of speech that regularly follows deafness coming on in children who have already learned to speak, shows how inseparably the learning and the development of perfect articulation are bound up with the hearing. Even the deafness that comes on in maturer years injures essentially the agreeable tone, often also the intelligibility, of the utterance.

2. The Organic Conditions of Learning to Speak.

How is it, now, with the normal child, who is learning to speak? How is it as to the existence and practicability of the nervous conduction, and the genesis of the centers?

In order to decide these questions, a further extension of the diagram is necessary (Fig. 3).

For the last diagram deals only with the hearing and pronouncing of sounds, syllables, and single words, not with the grammatical formation and syntactical grouping of these; there must further be a center of higher rank, the *dictorium*, or center of diction (Kuss-maul), brought into connection with the centers L S and W. And, on the one hand, the word-image acquired

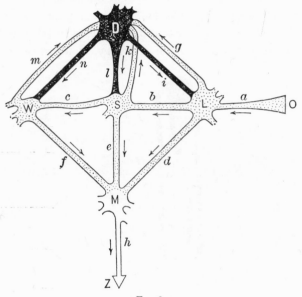

FIG. 3.

(by hearing) must be at the disposition of the diction-center, an excitation, therefore, passing from W to D (through *m*); on the other hand, an impulse must go out from the diction-center to pronounce the word that is formed and placed so as to correspond to the sense (through *n*). The same is true for syllables and sounds, whose paths to and from are indicated by *k* and *l*, as well as by *g* and *i*. These paths of connection must be of twofold sort. The excitement can not pass off to the diction-center D on the same anatomical path as the return impulse from D, because not a single case is known of a nerve-fiber that in natural relations conducts both centrifugally *and* centripetally, although this possibility of double conduction does occur under artificial circumstances. Apart, then, from pathological experience, which seems to be in favor of it, the separation of the two directions of the excitement seems to be justified anatomically also. On the contrary, it is questionable

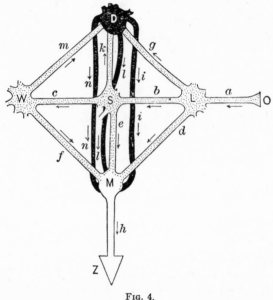

Fig. 4.

whether the impulse proceeding from D does not arrive directly at the motor speech-center, instead of passing through W, S, or L. The diagram then represents it as follows (Fig. 4). Here the paths of direct connection *i*, *l*, and *n* from D to M represent that which was just now represented by i L d and l S e and n W f, respectively; in Fig. 4, i conducts only sound-excitations coming from L, l only excitations coming from S, and n only those coming from W, as impulses for M. For the present, I see no way of deciding between the two possibilities. They may even exist both together. All the following statements concerning the localization of the disturbances of speech and the parallel imperfections of child-speech apply indifferently to either figure; it should be borne in mind that the nerve-excitement always goes *only* in the direction of the arrows, never in the opposite direction, through the nervous path corresponding to them. Such a parallel is not only presented, as I have found, and as I will show in what follows, by the most superficial exhibition of the manifold deviations of child-speech from the later perfect speech, but is, above all, necessary for the answering of the question : what is the condition of things in learning to speak ?

3. Parallel between the Disturbances of Speech in Adults and the Imperfections of Speech in the Child.

In undertaking to draw such a parallel, I must first of all state that in regard to the pathology of the subject, I have not much experience of my own, and therefore I rely here upon Kussmaul's comprehensive work on speech-disturbances, from which are taken most of the data that serve to characterize the individual deviations from the rule. In that work also may be found the explanations, or precise definitions, of almost all the names —with the exception of the following, added here for the sake of brevity—skoliophasia, skoliophrasia, and palimphrasia. On the other hand, the statements concerning the speech of the child rest on my own observations of children—especially of my own son—and readers who give their attention to little children may verify them all; most of them, indeed, with ease. Only the examples added for explaining mogilalia and paralalia are taken in part from Sigismund, a few others from Vierordt. They show more plainly (at least concerning rhotacism) than my own notes, some imperfections of articulation of the child in the second year, which occur, however, only in single individuals. In general the defects of child-speech are found to be very unequally distributed among different ages and individuals, so that we can hardly expect to find all the speech-disturbances of adults manifested in typical fashion in one and the same child. But with very careful observation it may be done, notwithstanding; and when several children are compared with one another in this respect, the analogies fairly force themselves upon the observer, and there is no break anywhere.

The whole group into which I have tried to bring in organic connection all the kinds of disturbances and defects of speech in systematic form falls into three divisions :

1. Imperfections not occasioned by disturbance of the intelligence — pure speech-disturbances or *lalopathies.*

2. Imperfections occasioned solely by disturbances of the intelligence—disturbances of continuous speech or discourse (Rede)—*dysphrasies.*

3. Imperfections of the language of gesture and feature—*dysmimies.*

I. LALOPATHY.

A. THE IMPRESSIVE PERIPHERAL PROCESSES DISTURBED.

Deafness.—Persons able to speak but who have become deaf do not understand what is spoken simply because they can *no longer* hear. The newly born do not
understand what is spoken because they can *not yet*
hear. The paths *o* and *a* are not yet practicable. All
those just born are deaf and dumb.

Difficulty of Hearing.—Persons who have become
hard of hearing do not understand what is spoken, or
they misunderstand, because they *no longer* hear distinctly. Such individuals easily hear wrong (paracusis).

Very young infants do not understand what is
spoken, for the reason that they do *not yet* hear distinctly; *o* and *a* are still difficult for the acoustic nerve-excitement to traverse. Little children very easily hear
wrong on this account.

B. THE CENTRAL PROCESSES DISTURBED.

Dysphasia.—In the child that can use only a small
number of words, the cerebral and psychical act through
which he connects these with his ideas and gives them
grammatical form and syntactical construction in order
to express the movement of his thought is *not yet* complete.

(1) The Sensory Processes centrally disturbed.

Sensory Aphasia (Wernicke), *Word Deafness*
(Kussmaul).—The child, in spite of good hearing and
sufficiently developed intelligence, can *not yet* understand spoken words because the path *m* is not yet

formed and the storehouse of word-images W is still empty or is just in the stage of origination.

Amnesia, Amnesic Dysphasia and Aphasia, Partial and Total Word-Amnesia, Memory-Aphasia.— The child has as yet no word-memory, or only a weak one, utters meaningless sounds and sound-combinations. He can *not yet* use words because he does not yet have them at his disposal as acoustic sound-combinations. In this stage, however, much that is said to him can be repeated correctly in case W is passable, though empty or imperfectly developed.

(2) The Sensori-motor Processes of Diction disturbed.

Acataphasia (Steinthal).—The child that has already a considerable number of words at his disposal is *not yet* in condition to arrange them in a sentence syntactically. He can *not yet* frame correct sentences to express the movement of his thought, because his diction-center D is still imperfectly developed. He expresses a whole sentence by a word ; e. g., *hot!* means as much as "The milk is too hot for me to drink," and then again it may mean "The stove is too hot!" *Man!* means "A strange man has come! "

Dysgrammatism (Kussmaul) *and Agrammatism* (Steinthal).—Children can *not yet* put words into correct grammatical form, decline, or conjugate. They like to use the indefinite noun-substantive and the infinitive, likewise to some extent the past participle. They prefer the weak inflection, ignore and confound the articles, conjunctions, auxiliaries, prepositions,.and pronouns. In place of "I" they say their own names, also *tint* (for "Kind" —child or "baby"). Instead of " Du, er, Sie " (thou, he, you), they use proper names, or man, papa, mamma. Sometimes, too, the adjectives are placed after the nouns, and the meaning of words is indicated by their position with reference to others, by the intonation, by looks and gestures. Agrammatism in child-language always appears in company with acataphasia, often also in insane persons. When the imbecile Tony says, "Tony flowers taken, attendant come, Tony whipped" (Tony Blumen genommen, Wärterin gekommen, Tony gehaut), she speaks exactly like a child (Kussmaul), without articles, pronouns, or auxiliary verbs, and, like the child, uses the weak inflection. The connection m of the word-image-center W with the diction-center D, i. e., of the word-memory with grammar, and the centers themselves, are as yet very imperfectly developed, unused.

Bradyphasia.—Children that can already frame sentences take a surprising amount of time in speaking on account of the slowness of their diction. In D and W m in the cerebral cortex the hindrances are still great because of too slight practice.

(3) The Motor Processes centrally disturbed.

a. Centro-motor Dysphasia and Aphasia, Aphemia, Asymbolia, Asemia. — Children have not yet learned, or have hardly learned, the use of language, although their intelligence is already sufficient. There is no longer any deficiency in the development of the external organs of speech, no muscular weakness, no imperfection of the nervous structures that effect the articulation of the separate sounds, for intelligence shows itself in the child's actions; he. forms the separate sounds correctly, unintentionally; his hearing is good and the sensory word-memory is present, since the child already obeys. His *not yet* speaking at this period (commonly as late as the second year) must accordingly be essentially of centro-motor character.

In the various forms of this condition there is injury or lack of sufficient relative development either in the centro-motorium M or in the paths that lead into it, *d*, *e*, *f*, as well as *i*, *l*, *n*.

a. Central Dysarthria and Anarthria.—In the child at the stage of development just indicated articulation is *not yet* perfect, inasmuch as while he often unintentionally pronounces correctly sounds, syllables, and single words, yet he can not form these intentionally, although he hears and understands them aright. He makes use of gestures.

Ataxic Aphasia (Verbal Anarthria).—The child that already understands several words as sound-combinations and retains them (since he obeys), can not yet use these in speech because he has not yet the requisite centro-motor impulses. He forms correctly the few syllables he has already learned of his future language, i. e., those he has at the time in memory as sound-combinations (sensory), but can *not yet* group them into new words ; e. g., he says *bi* and *te* correctly, learns also to say "*bitte*," but not yet at this period "tibe," "tebi." He lacks still the motor co-ordination of words.

At this period the gesture-language and modulation of voice of the child are generally easy to understand, as in case of pure ataxic aphasia (the verbal asemia or asymbolia of Finkelnburg) are the looks and gestures of aphasic adults. Chiefly n, f, and M are as yet imperfectly developed.

Central Stammering and Lisping (Literal Dysarthria).—Children just beginning to form sentences stammer, not uttering the sounds correctly. They also, as a rule, lisp for a considerable time, so that the words spoken by them are still indistinct and are intelligible only to the persons most intimately associated with them.

The paths d and i, and consequently the centro-motorium M, come chiefly into consideration here; but L also is concerned, so far as from it comes the motor impulse to make a sound audible through M.

The babbling of the infant is not to be confounded with this. That imports merely the unintentional production of single disconnected articulate sounds with non-coördinated movements of the tongue on account of uncontrolled excitement of the nerves of the tongue.

Stuttering (Syllabic Dysarthria).—Stutterers articulate each separate sound correctly, but connect the consonants, especially the explosive sounds, with the succeeding vowels badly, with effort as if an obstacle were to be overcome. The paths i and l are affected, and hence M is not properly excited. S, too, comes under consideration in the case of stuttering, so far as impulses go out from it for the pronunciation of the syllables.

Children who can not yet speak of themselves but can repeat what is said for them, exert themselves unnecessarily, making a strong expiratory effort (with the help of abdominal pressure) to repeat a syllable still unfamiliar, and they pause between the doubled or tripled consonant and vowel. This peculiarity, which soon passes away and is to be traced often to the lack of practice and to embarrassment (in case of threats), and which may be observed *occasionally* in every child, is stuttering proper, although it appears more seldom than in stutterers. Example : The child of two years is to say "Tischdecke," and he begins with an unnecessary expiratory effort, *T-t-itt-t*, and does not finish.

Stuttering is by no means a physiological transition-stage through which every child learning to speak must necessarily pass. But it is easily acquired, in learning to speak, by imitation of stutterers, in frequent intercourse with them. Hence, stutterers have sometimes stuttering children.

β. *Stumbling at Syllables.*—Children that already articulate correctly separate sounds, and do so intentionally, very often put together syllables out of the sounds incorrectly, and frame words incorrectly from the syllables, where we can not assume deficient development of the external organs of speech ; this is solely because the co-ordination is still imperfect. The child accordingly says *beti* before he can say *bitte ;* so too *grefessen* instead of *gefressen*.

The tracts *l* and *n* are still incompletely developed; also S and W, so far as impulses come thence to utter syllables by means of M.

b. Paraphasia.—Children have learned some expressions in their future language, and use them independently but wrongly ; they put in the place of the appropriate word an incorrect one, confounding words because they can *not yet* correctly combine their ideas with the word-images. They say, e. g., *Kind* instead of " Kinn," and *Sand* instead of " Salz " ; also *Netz* for

"Nest" and *Billard* for "Billet," *Matrone* for "Patrone."

The connection of D with M through *n* is still imperfect, and perhaps also M is not sufficiently developed.

Making Mistakes in Speaking (Skoliophasia).—In this kind of paraphasia in adults the cause is a lack of attention; therefore purely central concentration is wanting, or one fails to "collect himself"; there is distraction, hence the unintentional, frequently unconscious, confounding of words similar in sound or connected merely by remote, often dim, reminiscences. This kind of mis-speaking through carelessness is distinguished from skoliophrasia (see below) by the fact that there is no disturbance of the intelligence, and the correction easily follows.

Skoliophasia occurs regularly with children in the second and third years (and later). The child in general has not yet the ability to concentrate his attention upon that which is to be spoken. He *wills* to do it but *can* not yet. Hence, even in spite of the greatest effort, occur often erroneous repetitions of words pronounced for him (aside from difficulties of articulation, and also when these are wanting); hence confounding (of words), wrong forms of address, e. g., *Mama* or *Helene* instead of "Papa," and *Papa* instead of "Marie."

c. Taciturnity (Dumbness).—Individual human beings of sound physical condition who can speak very well are dumb, or speak only two or three words in all for several years, because they no longer *will* to speak (e. g., in the belief that silence prevents them from doing wrong).

This taciturnity is not to be confounded with the

7

paranoic aphrasia in certain insane persons—e. g., in catatonia, where the will is paralyzed.

It also occurs—seldom, however—that children who have already learned to speak pretty well are dumb, or speak only a few words—among these the word *no*— during several months, or speak only with certain persons, because they *will not* speak (out of obstinacy, or embarrassment). Here an organic obstacle in the motor speech-center is probable. For voluntary dumbness requires great strength of will, which is hardly to be attributed to the child. The unwillingness to speak that is prompted by *fun* never lasts long.

C. The Expressive Peripheral Processes disturbed.

(1) Dyslalia and Alalia (Peripheral Dysarthria and Anarthria).

The infant can *not yet* articulate correctly, or at all, on account of the still deficient development, and afterward the lack of control, of the nerves of speech and the external organs of speech. The complete inability to articulate is called alalia. The newly born is alalic. Dyslalia continues with many children a long time even after the learning of the mother-tongue. This is always a case simply of imperfections in *h* and *z*.

a. *Bulbo-nuclear Stammering (Literal Bulbo-nuclear Dysarthria and Anarthria).*—Patients who have lost control over the muscles of speech through bulbo-nuclear paralysis, stammer before they become speechless, and along with paralysis and atrophy of the tongue occur regularly fibrillar contractions of the muscles of the tongue. The tongue is *no longer* regulated by the will.

The child that has not yet gained control over his vocal muscles stammers before he can speak correctly, and, according to my observations, regularly shows fibrillar contractions of the muscles of the tongue along with an extraordinary mobility of the tongue. The tongue is *not yet* regulated by the will. Its movements are aimless.

b. Mogilalia.—Children, on account of the as yet deficient control of the external organs of speech, especially of the tongue, can *not yet* form some sounds, and therefore omit them. They say, e. g., *in* for "hin," *ätz* for "Herz," *eitun* for "Zeitung," *ere* for "Schere."

Gammacism.—Children find difficulties in the voluntary utterance of K and Ks (*x*), and indeed of G, and therefore often omit these sounds without substituting others; they say, e. g., *atsen* for "Klatschen," *atten* for "Garten," *asse* for "Gasse," *all* for "Karl," *ete* for "Grete" (in the second year), *wesen* for "gewesen," *opf* for "Kopf."

Sigmatism.—All children are late in learning to pronounce correctly S, and generally still later with Sch, and therefore omit both, or in a lisping fashion put S in place of Sch; more rarely Sch in place of S. They say, e. g., *saf* in place of "Schaf," *int* for "singt," *anz* for "Salz," *lafen* and *slafen* for "schlafen," *iss* for "Hirsch," *pitte* for "Splitter," *tul* for "Stuhl," *wein* for "Schwein," *Tuttav* for "Gustav," *torch* for "Storch" (second year), *emele* for "Schemel," *webenau* for "Fledermaus," but also *Kusch* for "Kuss." But in no case have I myself heard a child regularly put "sch" in place of *s*, as *Joschef* for "Josef." This form, perhaps, occurs in Jewish families; but I have no further observations concerning it as yet.

Rhotacism.—Many children do not form R at all for a long time and put nothing in place of it. They say *duch* for "durch," *bot* for "Brot," *unte* for "herunter," *tautech* for "traurig," *ule* for "Ruhe," *tänen* for "Thränen," *ukka* for "Zucker." On the contrary, some form early the R lingual, guttural, and labial, but all confound now and then the first two with each other.

Lambdacism.—Many children are late in learning to utter L, and often omit it. They say, e. g., *icht* for "Licht," *voge* for "Vogel," *atenne* for "Laterne," *batn* for "Blatt," *mante* for "Mantel."

(2) Literal Pararthria or Paralalia.

Children who are beginning to repeat intentionally what is said, often put another sound in place of the well-known correct (no doubt intended) one; this on account of deficient control of the tongue or other peripheral organs of speech. E. g., they say *t* in place of *p*, or *b* for *w* (*basse* for "Wasser" and for "Flasche"), *e* for *i* and *o* for *u*, as in *bete* for "bitte," and *Ohr* for "Uhr."

Paragammacism.—Children supply the place of the insuperably difficult sounds G, K, X by others, especially D and T, also N, saying, e. g., *itte* for "Rike," *finne* for "Finger," *tein* for "Klein," *toss* for "gross," *atitte* for "Karnickel," *otute* for "Kuk," *attall* for "Axel," *wodal* for "Vogel," *tut* for "gut," *tatze* for "Katze."

Parasigmatism.—Children are late in learning to

utter S and Sch correctly. They often supply the place of them, before acquiring them, by other sounds, saying, e. g., *tule* for "Schule," *ade* for "Hase," *webbe* for "Wasser," *beb* for "bös," *bebe* for "Besen," *gigod* for "Schildkröte," *baubee* for "Schwalbe."

Pararhotacism.—Most children, if not all, even when they have very early formed R correctly (involuntarily), introduce other sounds in place of it in speaking—e. g., they say *moigjen* for "morgen," *matta* for "Martha," *annold* for "Arnold," *jeiben* for "reiben," *amum* for "warum," *welfen* for "werfen."

Paralambdacism.—Many children who do not learn until late to utter L put in its place other sounds; saying, e. g., *bind* for "Bild," *bampe* for "Lampe," *tinne* for "stille," *degen* for "legen," *wewe* for "Löwe," *ewebau* for "Elephant."

(3) Bradylalia or Bradyarthria.

Children reciting for the first time something learned by heart speak not always indistinctly, but, on account of the incomplete practicability of the motor-paths, slowly, monotonously, without modulation. Sounds and syllables do *not yet* follow one another quickly, although they are already formed correctly. The syllables belonging to a word are often separated by pauses like the words themselves—a sort of dysphasia-of-conduction on account of the more difficult and prolonged conduction of the motor-impulse. I knew a boy (feeble-minded, to be sure) who took from three to eight seconds for answering even the simplest question; then came a regular explosion of utterance. Yet he did not stutter or stammer. When he had only *yes* or *no* to answer, the interval between question and answer was shorter.

Here belong in part also the imperfections of speech that are occasioned by too large a tongue (macroglossia). When a child is born with too large a tongue, he may remain long alalic, without the loss of intellectual development, as was observed to be the case by Paster and O. von Heusinger (1882).

II. DYSPHRASIA (DYSLOGICAL DISTURBANCES OF SPEECH).

The child that can already speak pretty correctly deforms his speech after the manner of insane persons, being moved by strange caprices, because his understanding is not yet sufficiently developed.

Logorrhœa (*Loquaciousness*).—It is a regular occurrence with children that their pleasure in articulation and in vocal sound often induces them to hold long monologues, sometimes in articulate sounds and syllables, sometimes not. This chattering is kept up till the grown people present are weary, and that by children who can not yet talk ; and their screaming is often interrupted only by hoarseness, just as in the case of the polyphrasia of the insane.

Dysphrasia of the Melancholy.—Children exert themselves perceptibly in their first attempts to speak, answer indolently or not at all, or frequently with embarrassment, always slowly, often with drawl and monotone, very frequently coming to a stop. They also sometimes begin to speak, and then lose at once the inclination to go on.

Dysphrasia of the Delirious (*Wahnsinnigen*).—

Children that have begun to speak often make new words for themselves. They have already invented signs before this; they are also unintelligible oftentimes because they use the words they have learned in a different sense.

Dysphrasia of the Insane (*Verrückten*).—The child is not yet prepared to speak. He possesses only non-co-ordinated sounds and isolated rudiments of words, primitive syllables, roots, as the primitive raw material of the future speech.

In many insane persons only the disconnected remains or ruins of their stock of words are left, so that their speech resembles that of the child at a certain stage.

Dysphrasia of the Feeble-minded.—The child at first reacts only upon strong impressions, and that often indolently and clumsily and with outcry; later, upon impressions of ordinary strength, without understanding—laughing, crowing, uttering disconnected syllables.

So the patient reacts either upon strong impressions only, and that indolently, bluntly, with gestures that express little and with rude words, or he still reacts upon impressions of ordinary strength, but in flat, silly, disconnected utterances.

Dysphrasia of Idiots.—Children have command at the beginning of no articulate sounds; then they learn these and syllables; after this also words of one syllable; then they speak short words of more than one syllable and sentences, but frequently babble forth words they have heard without understanding their meaning, like parrots.

Imbeciles also frequently command only short words and sentences or monosyllabic words and sounds, or, final-

ly, they lack all articulate sound. Many microcephalous
idiots babble words without understanding their meaning, like little children.

Echo-speech or Echolalia (Imitative Reflex Speech).
—Children not yet able to frame a sentence correctly
like to repeat the last word of a sentence they have
heard ; and this, according to my observations and researches, is so general that I am forced to call this echolalia a physiological transition stage. Of long words
said to them, the children usually repeat only the last
two syllables or the last syllable only. The feeble-
minded also repeat monotonously the words and sentences said by a person in their neighborhood without
showing an awakened attention, and in general without
connecting any idea with what they say. (Romberg.)

Interjectional Speech.—Children sometimes have a
fancy for speaking in interjections. They express vague
ideas by single vowels (like *ä*), syllables (e. g., *na, da*),
and combinations of syllables, and frequently call out
aloud through the house meaningless sounds and syllables. D and W are as yet undeveloped.

Often, too, children imitate the interjections used by
members of the family—*hop ! patsch, bauz !* an interjectional echolalia. Many deranged persons express
their feelings in like manner, in sounds, especially
vowels, syllables, or sound-combinations resembling
words, which are void of meaning or are associated
merely with obscure ideas (Martini). Then D is connected with M only through L and S, and so through *i*
and *e*.

Embolophrasia.—Many children, long after they
have overcome acataphasia and agrammatism, delight

in inserting between words sounds, syllables, and words
that do not belong there; e. g., they double the last
syllable of every word and put an *eff* to it: *ich-ich-eff*,
bin-in-eff, etc., or they make a kind of bleat between
the words (Kussmaul); and, in telling a story, put extra
syllables into their utterance while they are thinking.

Many adults likewise have the disagreeable habit of
introducing certain words or meaningless syllables into
their speech, where these do not at all belong; or they
tack on diminutive endings to their words. The syllables
are often mere sounds, like *eh*, *uh*; in many cases they
sound like *eng*, *ang* (angophrasia—Kussmaul).

Palimphrasia.—Insane persons often repeat single
sounds, syllables, or sentences, over and over without
meaning; e. g., " I am-am-am-am."

" The phenomenon in many cases reminds us of
children, who say or sing some word or phrase, a rhyme
or little verse, so long continuously, like automata, that
the by-standers can endure it no longer. It is often the
ring of the words, often the sense, often both, by which
the children are impressed. The child repeats them
because they seem to him strange or very sonorous."
(Kussmaul.)

Bradyphrasia.—The speech of people that are sad
or sleepy, and of others whose mental processes are indolent, often drags along with tedious slowness; is also
liable to be broken off abruptly. The speaker comes to
a standstill. This is not to be confounded with bradyphasia or with bradyarthria or bradylalia (see above).

In children likewise the forming of the sentence
takes a long time on account of the as yet slow rise and
combination of ideas, and a simple narrative is only

slowly completed or not finished at all, because the intellectual processes in the brain are too fatiguing.

Paraphrasia.—Under the same circumstances as in the case of bradyphrasia the (slow) speech may be marred and may become unintelligible because the train of thought is confused—e. g., in persons " drunk " with sleep—so that words are uttered that do not correspond to the original ideas.

In the case of children who want to tell something, and who begin right, the story may be interrupted easily by a recollection, a fresh train of thought, and still they go on ; e. g., they mix up two fairy tales, attaching to the beginning of one the end of another.

Skoliophrasia.—Distracted and timid feeble-minded persons easily make mistakes in speaking, because they can not direct their attention to what they are saying and to the way in which they are saying it, but they wander, allowing themselves to be turned aside from the thing to be said by all sorts of ideas and external impressions ; and, moreover, they do not notice afterward that they have been making mistakes (cf. p. 53).

Children frequently put a wrong word in place of a right one well known to them, without noticing it. They allow themselves to be turned aside very easily from the main point by external impressions and all sorts of fancies, and often, in fact, say the opposite of what they mean without noticing it.

III. DYSMIMIA.

Disturbances of Gesture-Language (Pantomime).

Perceptive Asemia.—Patients have lost the ability to *understand* looks and gestures (Steinthal).

Children can not yet understand the looks and gestures of persons about them.

Amnesic Amimia.—Aphasic persons can sometimes imitate gestures, but can not execute them when bid, but only when the gestures are made for them to imitate. Children that do not yet speak can imitate gestures if these are made for them to see, but it is often a long time before they can make them at the word of command.

Ataxic Dysmimia and Amimia (Mimetic Asemia).—Patients can *no longer* execute significative looks and gestures, on account of defective co-ordination.

Children can not express their states of desire, etc., because they do *not yet* control the requisite co-ordination for the corresponding looks and gestures.

Paramimia (Paramimetic Asemia).—Many patients can make use of looks and gestures, but confound them.

Children have not yet firmly impressed upon them the significance of looks and gestures; this is shown in their interchanging of these ; e. g., the head is shaken in the way of denial when they are affirming something.

Emotive Language (Affectsprache) in Aphrasia.— In Aphrasia it happens that smiling, laughing, and weeping are *no longer* controlled, and that they break out on the least occasion with the greatest violence, like the spinal reflexes in decapitated animals. (Hughlings-Jackson.)

Emotive language may continue when the language of ideas (Begriffssprache) is completely extinguished, and idiotic children without speech can even sing.

In children, far slighter occasions suffice normally

to call forth smiles, laughter, and tears, than in adults. These emotional utterances are *not yet* often voluntarily inhibited by the child that can not yet speak; on the contrary, they are unnecessarily repeated.

Apraxia.—Many patients are *no longer* in condition, on account of disturbed intellect, to make right use of ordinary objects, the use of which they knew well formerly; e. g., they can no longer find the way to the mouth; or they bite into the soap.

Children are *not yet* in condition, on account of deficient practice, to use the common utensils rightly; e. g., they will eat soup with a fork, and will put the fork against the cheek instead of into the mouth.

4. Development of Speech in the Child.

We may now take up the main question as to the condition of the child that is learning to speak, in regard to the development and practicability of the nerve-paths and of the centers required for speech. For the comparison of the disturbances of speech in adults with the deficiencies of speech in the child, on the one hand, and the chronological observation of the child, on the other hand, disclose to us what parts of the apparatus of speech come by degrees into operation. First to be considered are the *impressive* and *expressive* paths in general.

All new-born human beings are deaf or hard of hearing, as has already been demonstrated. Since the hearing but slowly grows more acute during the first days, no utterances of sound at this period can be regarded as responses to any sound-impressions whatever. The first cry is purely reflexive, like the croaking of the decapitated frog when the skin of his back is stroked (Vol. I, p. 214). The cry is not heard by the newly-born himself and has not the least value as language. It is on a par with the squeaking of the pig just born, the bleating of the new-born lamb, and the peeping of the chick that is breaking its shell.

Upon this first, short season of physiological deaf-mutism follows the period during which crying ex-presses bodily conditions, feelings such as pain, hunger, cold. Here, again, there exists as yet no connection of the expressive phenomena with acoustic impressions, but there is already the employment of the voice with stronger expiration in case of strong and disagreeable excitations of other sensory nerves than those of general sensation and of the skin. For the child now cries at a dazzling light also, and at a bitter taste, as if the un-pleasant feeling were diminished by the strong motor discharge. In any case the child cries because this loud, augmented expiration lessens for him the previously ex-isting unpleasant feelings, without exactly inducing thereby a comfortable condition.

Not until later does a sudden sound-impression, which at first called forth only a start and then a quiv-ering of the eyelids, cause also crying. But this loud sign of fright may be purely reflexive, just like the silent starting and throwing up of the arms at a sudden noise, and has at most the significance of an expression of discomfort, like screaming at a painful blow.

It is otherwise with the first loud response to an acoustic impression *recognized* as new. The indefinable sounds of satisfaction made by the child that hears mu-sic for the first time are no longer reflexive, and are not symptoms of displeasure. I see in this reaction, which may be compared with the howling of the dog that for the first time in his life hears music—I see in this reaction of the apparatus of voice and of future speech, *the first sign of the connection now just established between impressive* (acoustic) and *expressive* (having the character of emotive language) *paths.* The impressive, separately, were long since open, as the children under observation after the first week allowed themselves to be quieted by the singing of cradle-songs, and the expressive, separately, must likewise have been open, since various conditions were announced by various sorts of crying.

Everything now depends on a well-established *inter-central communication* between the two. This is next to be discussed.

The primitive connection is already an advance upon that of a reflex arc. The sound-excitations arriving from the ear at the central endings of the auditory nerve are not directly transformed into motor excitations for the laryngeal nerves, so that the glottis contracts to utter vocal sound. When the child (as early as the sixth to the eighth week) takes pleasure in music and laughs aloud, his voice can not in this case (as at birth) have been educed by reflex action, for without a cerebrum he would not laugh or utter joyous sounds, whereas even without that he cries.

From this, however, by no means follows the existence of a speech-center in the infant. The fact that he produces sounds easily articulated, although without choice, like *tahu* and *amma*, proves merely the functional capacity of the peripheral apparatus of articulation (in the seventh week) at a period long before it is inten-

tionally used for articulation. The unintentionally uttered syllables that make their appearance are, to be
sure, simple, at least in the first half-year. It is vowels
almost exclusively that appear in the first month, and
these predominate for a long time yet. Of the consonants in the third month *m* alone is generally to be
noted as frequent. This letter comes at a later period
also, from the raising and dropping of the lower jaw in
expiration, an operation that is besides soon easy for the
infant with less outlay of will than the letter *b*, which
necessitates a firmer closing of the lips.

But in spite of the simplicity of all the vocal utterances and of the defectiveness of the articulatory apparatus, the child is able (often long before the seventh
month) to respond to address, questions, chiding, either
with inarticulato sounds or with vowels or by means of
simple syllables, like *pa, ta, ma, na, da, mä, mö, gö,
rö* [*a* as in *father;* ä as in *fate;* ö like *i* in *bird.*]
Since these responses are entirely, or almost entirely,
lacking in microcephali and in children born deaf, they
are not purely reflexive, like sneezing, e. g.; therefore
there must be in the case of these a cerebral operation
also, simple indeed, but indubitably intellectual, in-
terposed between sound-perception and vocal utterance, especially as the infant behaves differently according to what he hears, and he discriminates very well
the stern command from the caress, forbidding from
allowing, in the voice of the person speaking to him.
Yet it is much more the *timbre*, the accent, the pitch,
the intensity of the voice and the sounds, the variation
of which excites attention, than it is the spoken word.
In the first half-year the child hears the vowels much

better than he does the consonants, and will imperfectly understand or divine the sense of a few sounds only— e. g., when his name is uttered in a threatening tone he will hear merely the accented vowel, for at the first performance taught him, purposely postponed to a very late period (in his thirteenth month), it made no difference to my child whether we asked without changing a feature, "Wie gross?" (how tall?) or "ooss?" or "oo?" In all three cases he answered with the same movement of the hand.

Now, although all infants in normal condition, before they can repeat anything after others or can understand any word whatever, *express* their feelings by various sounds, even by syllables, and *distinguish* vowels and many consonants in the words spoken to them, yet this does not raise them above the intelligent animal. The response to friendly address and loud chiding by appropriate sounds is scarcely to be distinguished as to its psychical value from the joyous barking and whining of the poodle.

The pointer-dog's understanding of the few spoken utterances that are impressed upon him in his training is also quite as certain at least as the babe's understanding of the jargon of the nurse. The correctly executed movements or arrests of movement following the sound-impressions "Setz dich! Pfui! Zurück! Vorwärts! Allez! Fass! Apporte! Such! Verloren! Pst! Lass! Hierher! Brav! Leid's nicht! Ruhig! Wahr Dich! Hab Acht! Was ist das! Pfui Vogel! Pfui Hase! Halt!" prove that the bird-dog understands the meaning of the sounds and syllables and words heard as far as he needs to understand them. The training in the

English language accomplishes the same result with "Down! Down charge! Steady! Toho! Fetch! Hold up!" as the training in the French language, with yet other words—so that we can by no means assume any hereditary connection whatever between the quality of the sound heard and the movement or arrest of movement to be executed, such as may perhaps exist in the case of the chick just hatched which follows the clucking of the hen. Rather does the dog learn afresh in every case the meaning of the words required for hunting, just as the speechless child comprehends the meaning of the first words of its future language without being able to repeat them himself—e. g., "Give! Come! Hand! Sh! Quiet!" Long before the child's mechanism of articulation is so far developed that these expressions can be produced by him, the child manifests his understanding of them unequivocally by corresponding movements, by gestures and looks, by obedience.

No doubt this behavior varies in individual cases, inasmuch as in some few the imitative articulation may be to some extent earlier developed than the understanding. There are many children who even in their first year have a monkey-like knack at imitation and repeat all sorts of things like parrots without guessing the sense of them. Here, however, it is to be borne in mind that such an echo-speech appears only after the *first* understanding of some spoken word can be demonstrated; in no case before the fourth month. Lindner relates that when he one day observed that his child of eighteen weeks was gazing at the swinging pendulum of the house-clock, he went with him to it, saying, "Tick-tack," in time with the pendulum; and when he

8

afterward called out to the child, who was no longer looking at the clock, "Tick-tack!" this call was answered, at first with delay, a little later immediately, by a turning of the look toward the clock. This proved that there was understanding long before the first imitation of words. Progress now became pretty rapid, so that at the end of the seventh month the questions, "Where is your eye? ear? head? mouth? nose? the table? chair? sofa?" were answered correctly by movements of hand and eyes. In the tenth month this child for the first time himself used a word as a means of effecting an understanding, viz., *mama* (soon afterward, indeed, he called both parents *papa*). The child's inability to repeat distinctly syllables spoken for him is not to be attributed, shortly before the time at which he succeeds in doing it, to a purely psychical adynamy (impotence), not, as many suppose, to "being. stupid," or to a weakness of will without organic imperfections determined by the cerebral development, for the efforts, the attention, and the ability to repeat incorrectly, show that the will is not wanting. Since also the peripheral impressive acoustic and expressive phonetic paths are intact and developed, as is proved by the acuteness of the hearing and the spontaneous formation of the very syllables desired, the cause of the inability to repeat correctly must be solely organic-centro-motor. The connecting paths between the sound-center and the syllable-center, and of both these with the speech motorium, are not yet or not easily passable; but the imitation of a single sound, be it only *a*, can not take place without the mediation of the cerebral cortex. Thus in the very first attempt to repeat something heard there exists an unquestionable advance in brain development; and the first successful attempt of this kind proves not merely the augmented functional ability of the articulatory apparatus and of the sound-center, and the practicability of the impressive paths that lead from the ear to the sound-center—it proves, above all, the establishment of intercentral routes that lead from the sound-center and the syllable-center to the motorium.

In fact, the correct *repeating* of a sound heard, of a syllable, and, finally, of a word pronounced by another person, is the surest proof of the establishment and practicability of the entire impressive, central, and expressive path. It, however, proves nothing as to the *understanding* of the sound or word heard and faultlessly repeated.

As the term "understanding" or "understand" is ambiguous, in so far as it may relate to the ideal content (the meaning), and at the same time to the mere perception of the word spoken (or written or touched)— e. g., when any one speaks indistinctly so that we do not "understand" him—it is advisable to restrict the use of this expression. *Understand* shall in future apply only to the *meaning* of the word; *hear*—since it is simply the perceiving of a word through the hearing that we have in view—will relate to the sensuous impression. It is clear, then, that all children who can hear but can not yet speak, repeat many words without understanding them, and understand many words without being able to repeat them, as Kussmaul has already observed. But I must add that the repeating of what is not understood begins only after some word (even one that can not be repeated) has been understood.

Now it is certain that the majority, if not all, of

the children that have good hearing develop the understanding more at first, since the impressive side is practiced more and sooner than the expressive-articulatory.
Probably those that imitate early and skillfully are the
children that can speak earliest, and whose cerebrum
grows fastest but also soonest ceases to grow; whereas
those that imitate later and more sparingly, generally
learn to speak later, and will generally be the more intelligent. For with the higher sort of activity goes the
greater growth of brain. While the other children culti-
vate more the centro-motor portion, the sensory, the intellectual, is neglected. In animals, likewise, a brief,
rapid development of the brain is wont to go along
with inferior intelligence. The intelligence gets a better development when the child, instead of repeating
all sorts of things without any meaning, tries to guess
the meaning of what he hears. Precisely the epoch at
which this takes place belongs to the most interesting
in intellectual development. Like a pantomimist, the
child, by means of his looks and gestures, and further
by cries and by movements of all sorts, gives abundant
evidence of his understanding and his desires, without
himself speaking a single word. As the adult, after
having half learned a foreign language from books, can
not speak (imitate) it, and can not easily understand it
when he hears it spoken fluently by one that is a perfect
master of it, but yet makes out *single* expressions and
understands them, and divines the meaning of the whole,
so the child at this stage can distinctly hear single words,
can grasp the purport of them, and divine correctly a
whole sentence from the looks and gestures of the speaker, although the child himself makes audible no articulate

utterance except his own, for the most part meaningless, variable babble of sounds and syllables and outcries.

The causes of the slowness of the progress in expressing in articulate words what is understood and desired, on the part of normal children, is not, however, to be attributed, as it has often been, to a slower development of the expressive motor mechanism, but must be looked for in the difficulty of establishing the connection of the various central storehouses of sense-impressions with the intercentral path of connection between the acoustic speech-centers and the speech-motorium. For the purely peripheral articulatory acts are long since perfect, although as yet a simple " *a* " or " *pa* " can not be repeated after another person ; for these and other sounds and syllables are already uttered correctly by the child himself.

The order of succession in which these separate sounds appear, without instruction, is very different in individual cases. With my boy, who learned to speak rather late, and was not occupied with learning by heart, the following was the order of the perfectly pure sounds heard by me :

On the left are the sounds or syllables indicated by one letter ; on the right, the same indicated by more than one letter ; and it is to be borne in mind that the child needs to pronounce only fourteen of the nineteen so-called consonants of the German alphabet in order to master the remaining five also ; for

$$c = \text{ts and k}$$
$$v = \text{f and w}$$
$$x = \text{ks and gs}$$
$$q = \text{ku and kw}$$
$$z = \text{ts and ds}$$

and of the fourteen four require no new articulation,
because

p is a toneless b
t is a toneless d
f is a toneless w
k is a toneless g

Of the ten positions of the mouth required for all
the consonants of the alphabet, nine are taken by the
child within the first six months : *

Months.
1. Indefinite
 vowels ; ä u, uä.
2. a, ö, o ; m,
 g, r, t ; h, am, ma, ta, hu, ör, rö, ar, ra, gö.
3. i ; b, l, n, ua, oa, ao, ai, c͡i, oä, äo, äa, äö ; öm, in, ab, om ; la, ho,
 mö, nä, na, ha, bu ; ng, mb, gr.
4. e, ä͡u, a-u, aö, ea ; an ; na, tö, la, me ; nt.
5. ü (y) ; k, ag, eg, ek, ge, kö.
6. j ; the lin- oi (eu, ä͡u), io, öe, eu (French) ; ij, aj, ög, ich ; ja, jä ;
 gual - labial rg, br, ch.
 sound,
7. d, p, äe, ui ; mä.
8. eö, aë, ou, a͡u ; up ; hö, mi, te.
9. ap, ach, äm ; pa, ga, cha.
10. el, ab, at, ät ; dä, ba, ta, tä ; nd.
11. ad, al, ak, er, ej, öd ; da, gä, bä, ka, ke, je, he, ne ;
 pr, tr.
12. w, än, op, ew, ür ; de, wä ; nj, ld.
13. s (ss), en ; hi ; dn.
14. mu ; kn, gn, kt.
15. z, oö, öa, is, iss, es, ass, th (English), ith (Engl.), it ; hä,
 di, wa, sse.
16. f (v), ok, on ; do, go ; bw, fp.
17. ib, öt, än ; bi.
18. äi, iä ; äp, im ; tu, pä ; ft.
19. ön, et, es ; sa, be ; st, tth (Engl.), s–ch, sj.

---

* Pronounce the letters in the tabular view as in German.

Months.

20.	ub, ot, id, od, oj, uf, ät; bo, ro, jo; dj, dth (Engl.).
21.	öp; fe; rl, dl, nk, pt.
22.	ol; lo; ps, pt, tl, sch, tsch, pth (Engl.).
23. q,	uo; id, op, um, em, us, un, ow, ed, uk, ig, il; jö, ju, po, mo, wo, fa, fo, fi, we, ku (qu), li, ti; tn, pf, gch, gj, tj, schg.
24.	ut, esch; pu, wi, schi, pi.
25.	oë, ul, il, och, iw, ip, ur; lt, rb, rt.
26.	nl, ds, mp, rm, fl, kl, nch, ml, dr.
27. x,	kch, cht, lch, ls, sw, sl.

Every such chronological view of the sequence of sounds is uncertain, because we can not observe the child uninterruptedly, and hence the first appearance of a new sound easily escapes notice. The above synopsis has a chronological value only so far as this, that it announces, concerning every single sound, that such sound was heard in its purity by me at least as early as the given month. The sound may, however, have been uttered considerably earlier without my hearing it. I know from personal experience that in other children many sounds appear much earlier; in my child, e. g., *ngä* was observed too late, and I have no doubt that the first utterance of *f* and *w* was unobserved, although I was on the lookout for them. When it is maintained, on the contrary, that *m* is not heard from a normal child until the tenth month, then the *am* and *mö* which appear universally in the first half-year have escaped notice. Earlier tabular views of this sort, which have even served as a foundation for instruction of deaf-mutes in speaking, do not rest exclusively on observation. Besides, in this matter, even two children hardly agree. According to my observations, I am compelled in spite of this disagreement to lay down the proposition as valid for all healthy children, that the greatly *preponderating majority of the sounds the child makes use of after learning verbal language, and many other sounds besides these, are correctly formed by him within the first eight months*, not intentionally, but just as much at random as any other utterance of sound not to be used later in speech, not appearing in any civilized language. I will only mention as an example the labio-lingual explosive sound, in which the tip of the tongue comes between the lips and, with an expiration, bursting from its confinement is drawn back swiftly (with or without tone). All children seem to like to form this sound, a sound between *p*, *b*, and *t*, *d ;* but it exists in few languages.

Among the innumerable superfluous, unintentional, random, muscular movements of the infant, the movements of the muscles of the larynx, mouth, and tongue take a conspicuous place, because they ally themselves readily with acoustic effects and the child takes delight in them. It is not surprising, therefore, that precisely those vibrations of the vocal cords, precisely those shapings of the cavity of the mouth, and those positions of the lips, often occur which we observe in the utterance of our vowels, and that among the child-noises produced unconsciously and in play are found almost all our consonants and, besides, many that are used in foreign languages. The plasticity of the apparatus of speech in youth permits the production of a greater abundance of sounds and sound-combinations than is employed later, and not a single child has been observed who has, in accordance with the principle of the least effort (*principe du moindre effort*) applied by French authors to this province, advanced in regular sequence from the

sounds articulated easily—i. e., with less activity of will
—to the physiologically difficult ; rather does it hold
good for all the children I have observed, and probably
for all children that learn to speak, that many of the
sounds uttered by them at the beginning, in the speechless season of infancy, without effort and then forgotten,
have to be learned afresh at a later period, have to be
painstakingly acquired by means of imitation.

Mobility and perfection in the *technique* of sound-
formation are not speech. They come into consideration
in the process of learning to speak as facilitating the
process, because the muscles are perfected by previous
practice ; but the very first attempts to imitate voluntarily a sound heard show how slight this advantage is.
Even those primitive syllables which the child of himself often pronounces to weariness, like *da*, he can not
at the beginning (in the tenth month in my case) as yet
say after any one, although he makes manifest by his effort—a regular strain—by his attention, and his unsuccessful attempts, that he would like to say them, as I
have already mentioned. The reason is to be looked
for in the still incomplete development of the sensori-
motor central paths. In place of *tatta* is sounded *tä* or
ata ; in place of *papa* even *taï*, and this not once only,
but after a great many trials repeated again and again
with the utmost patience. That the sound-image has
been correctly apprehended is evident from the certainty
with which the child responds correctly in various cases
by gestures to words of similar sound unpronounceable
by him. Thus, he points by mistake once only to the
mouth (Mund) instead of the moon (Mond), and points
correctly to the ear (Ohr) and the clock (Uhr) when

asked where these objects are. The acuteness of hearing indispensable for repeating the sounds is therefore present before the ability to repeat.

On the whole, the infant or the young child already weaned must be placed higher at this stage of his mental development than a very intelligent animal, but not on account of his knowledge of language, for the dog also understands very well single words in the speech of his master, in addition to hunting-terms. He divines, from the master's looks and gestures, the meaning of whole sentences, and, although he has not been brought to the point of producing articulate sounds, yet much superior in this respect is the performance of the cockatoo, which learns all articulate sounds. A child who shows by looks and gestures and actions that he understands single words, and who already pronounces correctly many words by imitation without understanding them, does not on this account stand higher intellectually than a sagaciously calculating yet speechless elephant or an Arabian horse, but because he already forms many more and far more complex concepts.

The animal phase of intellect lasts, in the sound, vigorous, and not neglected child, to the end of the first year of life at the farthest; and long before the close of this he has, by means of the *feelings* of pleasure and of discomfort, very definitely distinguishable by him even in the first days of life, but for which he does not get the verbal expressions till the second and third year, formed for himself at least in one province, viz., that of food, *ideas* more or less well defined. Romanes also rightly remarks that the *concept* of food arises in us through the feeling of hunger quite independently of language. Probably this concept is the very first that is formed by the quite young infant, only he would not name it "food," if indeed he named it at all, but would understand by it everything that puts an end to the feeling of hunger. It is of great importance to hold firmly to this fact of the origination of ideas, and that not of sensuous percepts only but of concepts, without language, because it runs contrary to prevailing assumptions.

He who has conscientiously observed the mental development of infants must come to the conclusion that *the formation of ideas is not bound up with the learning of words, but is a necessary prerequisite for the understanding of the words to be learned first, and therefore for learning to speak.* Long before the child understands even a single word, before he uses a single syllable consistently with a definite meaning, he already has a number of ideas which are expressed by looks and gestures and cries. To these belong especially ideas gained through touch and sight. Associations of objects touched and seen with impressions of taste are probably the first generators of concepts. The child, still speechless and toothless, takes a lively interest in bottles; sees, e. g., a bottle that is filled with a white opaque liquid (Goulard water), and he stretches out his arms with desire toward it, screaming a long time, in the belief that it is a milk-bottle (observed by me in the case of my child in the thirty-first week). The bottle when empty or when filled with water is not so long attractive to him, so that the idea of food (or of something to drink, something to suck, something sweet) must arise from the sight of a bottle with certain contents without the understanding or even utterance of any words. The formation of concepts without words is actually demonstrated by this; for the speechless child not only perceived the points of identity of the various bottles of wine, water, oil, the nursing-bottle and others, the sight of which excited him, but he united in one notion the contents of the different sorts of bottles when what was in them was white—i. e., he had separated the concept of food from that of the bottle. Ideas are thus independent of words.

Certain as this proposition is, it is not, however, supported by the reasons given for it by Kussmaul, viz., that one and the same object is variously expressed in various languages, and that a new animal or a new machine is known before it is named; for no one desires to maintain that certain ideas are *necessarily* connected with certain words, without the knowledge of which they could not arise—it is maintained only that ideas do not exist without words. Now, any object has some appellation in each language, were it only the appellation " object," and a new animal, a new machine, is already called " animal," " machine," before it receives its special name. Hence from this quarter the proof can not be derived. On the other hand, the speechless infant certainly furnishes the proof, which is confirmed by some observations on microcephalous persons several years old or of adult age. The lack of the power of abstraction apparent in these persons and in idiots is not so great that they have not developed the notion " food " or " taking of food."

Indeed, it is not impossible that the formation of ideas may continue after the total loss of word-memory, as in the remarkable and much-talked-of case of Lordat. Yet this case does not by any means prove that the formation of concepts of the *higher* order is possible without previous mastery of verbal language; rather is it certain that concepts rising above the lowest abstractions can be formed only by him who has thoroughly learned to speak: for intelligent children without speech are acquainted, indeed, with more numerous and more complex ideas than are very sagacious animals, but not with many more abstractions of a higher sort, and where the vocabulary is small the power of abstraction is wont to be as weak in adults as in children. The latter, to be sure, acquire the words for the abstract with more difficulty and later than those for the concrete, but have them stamped more firmly on the mind (for, when the word-memory fails, proper names and nouns denoting concrete objects are, as a rule, first forgotten). But it would not be admissible, as I showed above, to conclude from this that no abstraction at all takes place without words. To me, indeed, it is probable that in the most intense thought the most abstract conceptions are effected most rapidly without the disturbing images of the sounds of words, and are only supplementarily clothed in words. In any case the intelligent child forms many concepts of a lower sort without any knowledge of words at all, and he therefore performs abstraction without words.

When Sigismund showed to his son, not yet a year old and not able to speak a word, a stuffed woodcock, and, pointing to it, said, " Bird," the child directly afterward looked toward another side of the room where there stood upon the stove a stuffed white owl, repre-

sented as in flight, which he must certainly have observed before.   Here, then, the concept had already
arisen ; but how little specialized are the first concepts
connected with words that do not relate to food is
shown by the fact that in the case of Lindner's child
(in the tenth month) *up* signified also *down, warm* signified also *cold.* Just so my child used *too much* also
for *too little ;* another child used *no* also for *yes ;* a
third used *I* for *you.* If these by no means isolated
phenomena rest upon a lack of differentiation of the
concepts, "then the child already has a presentiment
that opposites are merely the extreme terms of the same
series of conceptions " (Lindner), and this before he can
command more than a few words.

But to return to the condition of the normal child,
as yet entirely speechless. It is clear that, being filled
with desire to give expression in every way to his feelings, especially to his needs, he will use his voice, too,
for this purpose. The adult likewise cries out with
pain, although the "Oh!" has no direct connection
with the pain, and there is no intention of making, by
means of the outcry, communication to others. Now,
before the newly-born is in condition to seek that which
excites pleasure, to avoid what excites displeasure, he
cries out in like fashion, partly without moving the
tongue, partly with the sound *ä* dominant, repeated over
and over monotonously till some change of external
conditions takes place. After this the manner of crying begins to vary according to the condition of the infant ; then come sounds clearly distinguishable as indi-
cations of pleasure or displeasure ; then syllables, at first
to some extent spontaneously articulated without mean-

ing, afterward such as express desire, pleasure, etc.; not until much later imitated sounds, and often the imperfect imitation of the voices of animals, of inorganic noises, and of spoken words. The mutilation of his words makes it seem as if the child were already inventing new designations which are soon forgotten; and as the child, like the lunatic, uses familiar words in a new sense after he has begun to learn to talk, his style of expression gets an original character, that of " baby-talk." Here it is characteristic that the feelings and ideas do not now first *arise*, though they are now first articulately expressed; but they were in part present long since and did not become articulate, but were expressed by means of looks and gestures. In the adult ideas generate new words, and the formation of new words does not cease so long as thinking continues; but in the child without speech new feelings and new ideas generate at first only new cries and movements of the muscles of the face and limbs, and, the further we look back into child-development proper, the greater do we find the number of the conditions expressed by one and the same cry. The organism as yet has too few means at its disposal. In many cases of aphasia every mental state is expressed by one and the same word (often a word without meaning). Upon closer examination it is found, however, that for the orator also, who is complete master of speech, all the resources of language are insufficient. No one, e. g., can name all the colors that may be perceived, or describe pain, or describe even a cloud, so that several hearers gain the same idea of its form that the speaker has. The words come short, but the idea is clear. If words sufficed to express clearly

clear conceptions, then the greater part of our philosophical and theological literature would not exist. This
literature has its basis essentially in the inevitable fact
that different persons do not associate the same concept
with the same word, and so one word is used to indicate different concepts (as is the case with the child). If
a concept is exceptionally difficult—i. e., exceptionally
hard to express clearly in words—then it is wont to receive many names, e. g., " die," and the confusion and
strife are increased ; but words alone render it possible
to form and to make clear concepts of a higher sort.
They favor the formation of new ideas, and without
them the intellect in man remains in a lower stage of
development just because they are the most trustworthy
and the most delicate means of expression for ideas.   If
ideas are not expressed at all, or not intelligibly, their
possessor can not use them, can not correct or make
them effective.   Those ideas only are of value, as a general thing, which continue to exist after being communicated to others.   Communication takes place with
accuracy (among human beings) only by means of
words.   It is therefore important to know how the
child learns to speak words, and then to use them.

I have above designated, as the chief difficulty for
the child in the formation of words, the establishment
of a connection between the central storehouse for sense-
impressions—i. e., the sensory centers of higher rank—
with the intercentral path of connection between the
center-for-sounds and the speech-motorium.   After the
establishment of these connections, and long after ideas
have been formed, the sound-image of the word spoken
by the mother, when it emerges in the center-for-sounds

that the child, beyond doubt, moved his head in the direction of the sound heard. I knocked on a mirror, being behind him. Immediately he turned his head round toward the source of the sound. At this period it is in general surprising with what ease single tones, scales, and chords attract the attention of the babe, to such a degree that the greatest restlessness subsides at once when these are sounded, and he hearkens with an intense gaze.

In the twelfth week the turning of the head toward the sounding body was sudden, even when the look did not take at once the right direction. When the direction was found, the child would hearken evidently with close attention (cf. p. 87.)

In the sixteenth week the turning round of the head toward a sound takes place with the certainty of a reflex movement. Before this time no notice at all was taken of more distant sound-stimulus—a hand-organ below in the garden, the voice of a person speaking aloud at the other end of the room; now both these sounds cause lively motions of the head, and an altered, not dissatisfied, expression of countenance.

The first noise artificially produced by the child himself, one that gave him apparent pleasure and was accordingly frequently repeated, was the crumpling of paper (especially in the nineteenth week). In the twenty-first week, at the beating of a gong, sounded for the purpose of taking his photograph, he became motionless—his attention was so enchained by the new noise—and stared with fixed gaze at the metallic plate. In general, his hearing became so much more acute in the fifth month that, when taking his milk, he almost

8

It is very much the same with other primitive syllables of the babe's utterance, e. g., *atta*. Where this does not denote the parents or grandparents it is frequently used (*táta, tatta, tatá*, also in England and Germany) in the sense of "gone" ("fort") and "good-by."

These primitive syllables, *pa-pa, ma-ma, tata* and *apa, ama, ata*, originate of themselves when in the expiration of breath the passage is stopped either by the lips (*p, m*) or by the tongue (*d, t*); but after they have been already uttered many times with ease, without meaning, at random, the mothers of all nations make use of them to designate previously existing ideas of the child, and designate by them what is most familiar. Hence occurs the apparent confounding of "milk" and "breast" and "mother" and "(wet-) nurse" or "nurse" and "bottle," all of which the child learns to call *mam, amma*, etc.

But just at this period appears a genuine echolalia, the child, unobserved, repeating correctly and like a machine, often in a whisper, all sorts of syllables, when he hears them at the end of a sentence. The normal child, before he can speak, repeats sounds, syllables, words, if they are short, "mechanically," without understanding, as he imitates movements of the hands and the head that are made in his sight. Speaking is a movement-making that invites imitation the more because it can be strictly regulated by means of the ear. Anything more than regulation is not at first given by the sense of hearing, for those born deaf also learn to speak. They can even, like normal children, speak quite early in dreams (according to Gerard van Asch).

Those born deaf, as well as normal children, when one turns quietly toward them, often observe attentively the lips (and also touch them sometimes) and the tongue of the person speaking; and this visual image, even without an auditory image, provokes imitation, which is made perfect by the combination of the two. This combination is lacking in the child born blind, pure echolalia prevailing in this case; in the one born deaf, the combination is likewise wanting, the reading-off of the syllables from the mouth coming in as a substitute. With the deaf infant the study of the mouth-movements is, as is well known, the only means of understanding words spoken aloud, and it is sight that serves almost exclusively for this, very rarely touch; and the child born deaf often repeats the visible movements of lips and tongue better than the hearing child that can not yet talk. It is to be observed, in general, that the hearing child makes less use, on the whole, of the means of reading-off from the mouth than we assume, but depends chiefly on the ear. I have always found, too, that the child has the greatest difficulty in imitating a position of the mouth, in case the sound belonging to it is not made, whereas he easily achieves the same position of the mouth when the acoustic effect goes along with it.

Accordingly, the connection between the ear and the speech-center must be shorter or more practicable in advance (hereditarily) than that between the eye and the speech-center. With regard to both associations, however, the gradually progressive shortening or consolidating is to be distinguished in space and time. With the child that does not yet speak, but is beginning to repeat syllables correctly and to associate them with primitive ideas, the act of imitation takes longer than with the normal adult, but the paths in the brain that he makes use of are shorter, absolutely and relatively— absolutely, because the whole brain is smaller ; relatively, because the higher centers, which at a later period perform their functions with consciousness and accessory ideas, are still lacking. Notwithstanding this, the time is longer than at a later period—often amounting to several seconds—because the working up of what has been heard, and even the arrangement of it in the center for sound-images, and of what has been seen in the center for sight-images, takes more time apart from a somewhat less swift propagation of the nerve-excitement in the peripheral paths. The child's imitation can not be called fully conscious or deliberate. It resembles the half-conscious or unconscious imitation attained by the adult through frequent repetition—i. e., through manifold practice—and which, as a sort of reminiscence of conscious or an abbreviation of deliberate imitation, results from frequent continuous use of the same paths. Only, the child's imitations last longer, and especially the reading-off from the mouth. The child can not distinguish the positions of the mouth that belong to a syllable, but can produce them himself very correctly. He is like the patients that Kussmaul calls " word-blind," who can not, in spite of good sight, read the written words they see, but can express them in speech and writing. For the same word, e. g., *atta*, which the child does not read off from the mouth and does not repeat, he uses himself when he wants to be taken out; thus the inability is not expressive-motor, but central or intercentral. For the child can already see very well the movement of mouth and tongue ; the impressive sight-path has been long established.

Herein this sort of word-blindness agrees fully with the physiological word-deafness of the normal child without speech, whose hearing is good. For he understands wrongly what he hears, when, e. g., in response to the order, " No ! no ! " he makes the affirmative movement of the head, although he can make the right movement very well. Here too, then, it is not centrifugal and centripetal peripheral lines, but intercentral paths or centers, that are not yet sufficiently developed—in the case of my child, in the fourteenth month. The path leading from the word-center to the dictorium, and the word-center itself, must have been as yet too little used.

From all this it results, in relation to the question, how the child comes to learn and to use words, that in the first place he. has ideas; secondly, he imitates sounds, syllables, and words spoken for him ; and, thirdly, he associates the ideas with these. E. g., the idea " white + wet + sweet + warm " having arisen out of frequent seeing, feeling, and tasting of milk, it depends upon what primitive syllable is selected for questioning the hungry infant, for talking to him, or quieting him, whether he expresses his desire for food by *möm, mimi, nana, ning,* or *maman,* or *mäm,* or *mem,* or *mima,* or yet other syllables. The oftener he has the idea of food (i. e., something that banishes hunger or the unpleasant feeling of it), and at the same time the sound-impression " milk," so much the more will the latter be associated with the former, and in

consideration of the great advantages it offers, in being
understood by all, will finally be adopted. Thus the
child learns his first words. But in each individual
case the first words acquired in this manner have a
wider range of meaning than the later ones.

By means of pure echolalia, without associating ideas
with the word babbled in imitation, the child learns, to
be sure, to articulate words likewise; but he does not
learn to understand them or to use them properly unless
coincidences, intentional or accidental, show him this
or that result when this or that word is uttered by him.
If the child, e. g., hearing the new word "Schnee,"
says, as an echo, *nee*, and then some one shows him
actual snow, the meaningless *nee* becomes associated
with a sense-intuition; and later, also, nothing can take
the place of the intuition—i. e., the direct, sensuous
perception—as a means of instruction. This way of
learning the use of words is exactly the opposite of that
just discussed, and is less common because more laborious. For, in the first case, the idea is first present, and
only needs to be expressed (through hearing the appropriate word). In the second case, the word comes first,
and the idea has to be brought in artificially. Later,
the word, not understood, awakens curiosity, and thereby generates ideas. But this requires greater maturity.

The third way in which the first words are learned
is this: The idea and the word appear almost simultaneously, as in onomatopoetic designations and interjections.
Absolutely original onomatopoetic words are very rare
with children, and have not been observed by me except after the children already knew some words. The
names of animals, *bow-wow*, *moo-moo*, *peep-peep* (bird),

hotto (horse, from the expression of the carter, "hott-
ho (*tt,*" instead of *Haut* (the skin), i. e., "left," in
contrast with "aarr"—*Haar, Mähne* (the mane)—i. e.,
"right"), are spoken for the child by the members
of his family. Some names of animals, like *kukuk*
(cuckoo), also *kikeriki* (cock) and *kuak* (duck, frog),
are probably formed often without having been heard
from others, only more indistinctly, by German, English
(American), and French children. *Ticktack* (*tick-tick*)
has also been repeated by a boy of two years for a watch.
On the other hand, *weo-weo-weo* (German, *ŭio*) for the
noise of winding a watch (observed by Holden in a boy
of two years) is original. *Hüt,* as an unsuccessful imitation of the locomotive-whistle by my boy of two and
a half years, seems also noteworthy as an onomatope
independently invented, because it was used daily for
months in the same way merely to designate the whistle.
The voice of the hen, of the redstart, the creaking of
a wheel, were imitated by my child of his own accord
long before he could speak a word. But this did not
go so far as the framing of syllables. It is not easy in
this to trace so clearly the framing of a concept as attaching itself directly to onomatopoetic forms as it is
in a case communicated by Romanes. A child that was
beginning to talk, saw and heard a duck on the water,
and said *quack.* Thereafter the child called, on the
one hand, all birds and insects, on the other hand, all
liquids, *quack.* Finally, it called all coins also *quack,*
after having seen an eagle on a French sou. Thus the
child came, by gradual generalization, to the point of
designating a fly, wine, and a piece of money by the
same onomatopoetic word, although only the first per-

ception contained the characteristic that gave the name.

Another case is reported by Eduard Schulte: A boy of a year and three quarters applied the joyous outcry *ei* (which may be an imitated interjection), modifying it first into *eiz*, into *aze*, and then into *ass*, to his wooden goat on wheels, and covered with rough hide; *eiz*, then, became exclusively a cry of joy; *ass*, the name for everything that moved along—e. g., for animals and his own sister and the wagon; also for everything that moved at all; finally, for everything that had a rough surface. Now, as this child already called all coverings of the head and covers of cans *huta*, when he saw, for the first time, a fur cap, he at once christened it *ass-huta*. Here took place a decided subordination of one concept to another, and therewith a new formation of a word. How broad the comprehensiveness of the concept designated *huta* was, is perceived especially in this, that it was used to express the wish to have objects at which the child pointed. He liked to put all sorts of things that pleased him upon his head, calling them *huta*. Out of the *huta*, for "I should like to have that as a hat," grew, then, after frequent repetition, "I should like that." There was in this case an extension of the narrower concept, after it had itself experienced previously a differentiation, and so a limitation, by means of the suffix *ass*. These examples show how independent of words the formation of concepts is. With the smallest stock of words the concepts are yet manifold, and are designated by the same word when there is a lack of words for the composition of new words, and so for fresh word-formation.

The formation of words out of interjections without imitation has not been observed. Here belongs the *rollu, rollolo,* uttered by my boy, of his own accord, on seeing rolling balls or wheels; and (in the twentieth month) *rodi, otto, rojo,* where the rotation perceived by the child occasions at once the one or the other exclamation containing *l* or *r.* In the case of Steinthal, it was *lu-lulu;* in the case of a boy a year and a half old, observed by Kussmaul, it was *golloh.* In these cases the first interjection is always occasioned by a *noise,* not simply by the sight of things rolling without noise. The interjection must accordingly be styled imitative. A combination of the original—i. e., inborn—interjectional sounds into syllables and groups of syllables, without the assistance of members of the family, and without imitation, for the purpose of communicating an idea, is not proved to exist.

On the whole, the way in which the child learns to speak not merely resembles the way in which he learns at a later period to write, but is essentially completely in accord with it. Here, too, he makes no new inventions. First are drawn strokes and blurs without meaning; then certain strokes are imitated; then signs of sounds. These can not be at once combined into syllables, and even after the combination has been achieved and the written word can be made from the syllables it is not yet understood. Yet the child could see, even before the first instruction in writing or the first attempt at scribbling, every individual letter in the dimensions in which he writes it later. So, too, the speechless child hears every sound before he understands syllables and words, and he understands them before he can speak them. The child commonly learns reading before writing, and so understands the sign he is to write before he can write it. Yet the sign written by himself is often just as unintelligible to him as the word he himself speaks. The analogy is perfect.

If the first germs of words, after ideas have begun to become clear by means of keener perception, are once formed, then the child fashions them of his own effort, and this often with surprising distinctness; but in the majority of cases the words are mutilated. In the first category belongs the comparative *hocher* for *höher* in the sentence *hocher bauen* (build higher)! (in the third year uttered as a request when playing with building-stones). The understanding of the comparative is plainly manifest in this. When, therefore, the same child in his fifth year, to the improper question, " Whom do you like better, papa or mamma ? " answers, " Papa and mamma," we should not infer a lack of that understanding, as many do (e. g., Heyfelder); but the decision is impossible to the child. Just so in the case of the question, " Would you rather have the apple or the pear ? "

Other inventions of my child were the verb *messen* for " mit dem Messer schneiden " (to cut with the knife); *schiffern*, i. e., " das Schiff bewegen " (move the ship), for " rudern," (row). And the preference of the weak inflection on the part of all children is a proof that *after* the appropriation of a small number of words through imitation, independent—always logical— changes of formation are undertaken. *Gegebt, gegeht, getrinkt* (gived, goed, drinked), have never been heard by the child; but " gewebt, geweht, gewinkt " (as in English, waved, wafted, beckoned), have been known to him as models (or other formations corresponding to these). Yet this is by no means to say that every mutilation or transformation the child proposes is a copy after an erroneously selected model ; rather the child's imagination has a wide field here and acts in manifold fashion, especially by combinations. " My teeth-roof pains me," said a boy who did not yet know the word " palate." Another in his fourth year called the road (Weg) the "go" (Gehe). A child of three years used the expression, "Just grow me" (*wachs mich einmal*) for "Just see how I have grown" (Sieh einmal wie ich gewachsen bin) (Lindner). Such creations of the childish faculty of combination, arising partly through blending, partly through transference, are collected in a neat pamphlet, " Zur Philosophie der Kindersprache," by Agathon Keber, 1868. The most of them, however, are from a later time of life than that here treated of. So it is with the two "heretical" utterances communicated by Rösch. A child said *unterblatte* (under-leaf) for " Oblate," because he saw the wafer (Oblate) slipped under the leaf of paper (Blatt) ; and he called the " American chair," " Herr - Decaner - chair," because somebody who was called " Herr Decan" used to sit in it. Here may be seen the endeavor to put into the acoustic impression not understood a meaning. These expressions are not inventions, but they are evidence of intellect. They can not, of course, appear in younger children without knowledge of words, because they are transformations of words.

On the other hand it is of the greatest importance for the understanding of the first stage of the use of

words in their real significance, after the acquirement
of them has once begun, to observe how many different
ideas the child announces by one and the same verbal
expression. Here are some examples: *Tuhl* (for Stuhl,
chair) signifies—1. " My chair is gone "; 2. " The chair
is broken "; 3. " I want to be lifted into the chair";
4. " Here is a chair." The child (Steinthal's) says (in
the twenty-second month), when he sees or hears a barking dog, *bellt* (barks), and thinks he has by that word
designated the whole complex phenomenon, the sight-
perception of the dog and of a particular dog, and the
sound-perception ; but he says *bellt* also when he merely
hears the dog. No doubt the memory-image of the
dog he has seen is then revived for him.

Through this manifold significance of a word, which
is a substitute for a whole sentence, is exhibited a much
higher activity of the intellect than appears in the mutilation and new formation of words having but one
meaning to designate a sense-impression, for, although
in the latter is manifested the union of impressions into
perceptions and also of qualities into concepts, wherein
an unconscious judgment is involved, yet a *clear* judgment is not necessarily connected with them. The
union of concepts into conscious clear judgments is recognized rather in the formation of a sentence, no matter
whether this is expressed by one word or by several words.

In connection with this an error must be corrected
that is wide-spread. It consists in the assumption that
all children begin to speak with nouns, and that these
are followed by verbs. This is by no means the case.
The child daily observed by me used an adjective for
the first time in the twenty-third month in order to ex-

press a judgment, the first one expressed in the language of those about him. He said "hot" for "The milk is too hot." In general, the appropriation and employment of words for the first formation of sentences depends, in the first instance, upon the action of the adults in the company of the child. A good example of this is furnished by an observation of Lindner, whose daughter in her fourteenth month first begged with her hands for a piece of apple, upon which the word "apple" was distinctly pronounced to her. After she had eaten the apple she repeated the request, re-enforcing her gesture this time by the imitated sound *appn*, and her request was again granted. Evidently encouraged by her success, the child from that time on used *appn* for "eat, I want to eat," as a sign of her desire to eat in general, because those about her "accepted this signification and took the word stamped by her upon this concept for current coin, else it would very likely have been lost." This also confirms my statement (p. 85) that a child easily learns to speak with logical correctness with wrong words. He also speaks like the deaf-mute with logical correctness with quite a different arrangement of words from that of his speech of a later period. Thus the child just mentioned, in whom "the inclination to form sentences was manifest from the twenty-second month," said, "hat die Olga getrinkt," when she had drunk!

But every child learns at first not only the language of those in whose immediate daily companionship he grows up, but also at first the peculiarities of these persons. He imitates the accent, intonation, dialect, as well as the word, so that a Thuringian child may be surely distinguished from a Mecklenburg child even in the second and third year, and, at the same time, we may recognize the peculiarities of the speech of its mother or nurse, with whom it has most intercourse. This phenomenon, the persistence of dialects and of peculiarities of speech in single families, gives the impression, on a superficial observation, of being something inherited; whereas, in fact, nothing is inherited beyond the voice through inheritance of the organic peculiarities of the mechanism of phonation. For everything else completely disappears when a child learns to speak from his birth in a foreign community.

Hereditary we may, indeed, call the characteristic of humanity, speech; hereditary, also, is articulation in man, and the faculty of acquiring any articulate language is innate. But beyond this the tribal influence does not reach. If the possibility of learning to speak words phonetically is wanting because ear or tongue refuses, then another language comes in as a substitute —that of looks, gestures, writing, tactile images—then not Broca's center, but another one is generated. So that the question whether a speech-center already exists in the alalic child must be answered in the negative; the center is formed only when the child hears speech, and, if he does not hear speech, no center is developed. In this case the ganglionic cells of the posterior third of the third frontal convolution are otherwise employed, or they suffer atrophy. In learning to speak, on the contrary, there is a continuous development, first of the sound-center, then of the syllable-center, then of the word-center and the dictorium. The brain grows through its own activity.

CHAPTER XVIII.

FIRST SOUNDS AND BEGINNINGS OF SPEECH IN THE CASE
OF A CHILD OBSERVED DAILY DURING HIS FIRST
THREE YEARS.

THE observations bearing upon the acquirement of speech recorded by me in the case of my boy from the day of his birth, the 23d of November, 1877, are here presented, so far as they appear worthy of being communicated, in chronological order. They are intended to serve as authenticated documents.

The points to which the attention is to be directed in these observations are determined by the organic conditions of the acquirement of speech, which have been treated previously. First, the expressive processes, next the impressive, last the central processes, claim the attention. (1) To the *expressive* beginnings of speech belongs the sum total of the inarticulate sounds—crying, whimpering, grunting, cooing, squealing, crowing, laughing, shouting (for joy), modulation of the voice, smacking, and many others, but also the silent movement of the tongue; further, articulation, especially before imitation begins; the formation of sound, and so the gradual perfecting of the vowels, aspirates, and consonants; at the same time the forming of syllables. The last is especially easy to follow in the babbling monologues of the infant, which are often very long. The reduplication of syllables, accentuation, and inflection, whispering, singing, etc., belong likewise here. (2) The *impressive* processes are discerned in the looks and gestures of the child as yet speechless; later, the ability to discriminate in regard to words and noises, and the connection of the ear with the speech-center, are discerned in the first imitations of sounds and in the repeating after others— i. e., in word-imitation. Here belong also the onomatopoetic attempts of children, which are simply a sort of imitation. Later, are added to these the answers to simple spoken questions, these answers being partly interjectional, partly articulate, joined into syllables, words, and then sentences. The understanding of words heard is announced especially by the first listening, by the association of certain movements with certain sound-impressions, and of motionless objects with other sound-impressions, before speaking begins. Hereby (3) the *central* processes are already shown to be in existence. The childish logic, especially induction from too few particulars, the mutilation of words reproduced, the wrong applications of expressions correctly repeated, the confounding of opposites in the verbal designation of concepts of the child's own formation, offer an abundance of noteworthy facts for the genesis of mind. Moreover, the memory for sounds and words, the imagination, especially in filling out, as well as the first acts of judging, the forming of propositions, questioning— all these are to be considered. As for the order in which the separate classes of words appear, the training in learning-by-heart, speculations as to which spoken word is first perfectly understood, to these matters I have paid less attention, for the reason that here the differences in the child's surroundings exert the greatest influence. My report must, in any event, as a rough draft of the history of the development of language in the child, be very imperfect. It, however, contains nothing but perfectly trustworthy matter of my own observation.

During the first weeks the child often cried long and vigorously from discomfort. If one were to try to represent by written vowels the screaming sounds, these would most nearly resemble, in the majority of cases, a short *u* (oo in book), with a very quickly following prolonged *ä* (*ai* in fair); thus, *uä, uä, uä, uä,* were the first sounds that may be approximately expressed. They were uttered after the lapse of five months exactly as at the beginning, only more vigorously. All the other vowel-sounds were at first undefined.

Notwithstanding this uniformity in the vowel-sounds, the sounds of the voice are so varied, even within the first five weeks, that it may be told with certainty from these alone whether the child feels hunger or pain or pleasure. Screaming with the eyes firmly closed in hunger, whimpering in slight indisposition, laughing at bright objects in motion, the peculiar grunting sounds which at a later period are joined with abdominal pressure and with lively arm-movements, as the announcement of completed digestion and of wetness (retained for the first of these states even into the seventeenth month), are manifold acoustic expressions of vitality, and are to be looked upon as the first forerunners of future oral communication, in contrast with the loud-sounding reflex movements of sneezing and of hiccough, and with the infrequent snoring, snuffling (in sucking), and other loud expirations observed in the first days, which have just as little linguistic value as have coughing and the later clearing of the throat.

10

The voice is very powerful as early as the sixth day, especially when it announces feelings of discomfort. Screaming is much more frequent, persistent, and vigorous also when diluted cow's milk is given instead of that from the breast. If one occupies himself longer than usual with the infant (in the first two months), the child is afterward more inclined to cry, and cries then (as in the case of hunger) quite differently from what he does when giving notice of something unpleasant— e. g., wetness. Directly upon his being made dry, the crying ceases, as now a certain contentment is attained. On the other hand, the inclination to cry serves very early (certainly from the tenth week on) as a sign of well-being (or increase in the growth of the muscles). At least a prolonged silence at this season is wont to be connected with slight ailment. But it is to be remarked that during the whole period no serious illness, lasting more than one day, occurred.

On the forty-third day I heard the *first consonant.* The child, in a most comfortable posture, uttering all sorts of obscure sounds, said once distinctly *am-ma.* Of vowels, *ao* was likewise heard on that day. But, on the following day, the child surprised me and others by the syllables, spoken with perfect distinctness, *ta-hu.*

On the forty-sixth day, in the otherwise unintelligible babble of the infant, I heard, once each, *gö* (*ö* nearly like *i* in bird), *örö*, and, five days later, *ara.*

In the eighth and ninth *weeks*, the two utterances, *örrö, arra*, became frequent, the *ö* and *a* being pure and the *r* uvular.

The syllable *ma* I heard by itself (it was during his crying) for the first time on the sixty-fourth day. But on the following day was sounded, during persistent, loud crying, often and distinctly (it returned in like manner months after), *nei, nei, nei,* and once, during his babbling, *a-omb.*

On the day after, distinctly, once each, *la, grei, aho,* and, besides, *ma* again.

On the sixty-ninth day, the child, when hungry, uttered repeatedly and very distinctly, *mömm* and *ngö.*

Of the syllables earlier spoken, only *örrö* is distinctly repeated in the tenth week. On the seventy-first day, the child being in the most comfortable condition, there comes the new combination, *ra-a-ao,* and, five days later, in a hungry and uncomfortable mood, *nä,* and then *näi-n.*

The manifest sign of contentment was very distinct (on the seventy-eighth day): *habu,* and likewise in the twelfth week *a-i* and *uāo,* as well as *ä-o-a,* alternating with *ä-a-a,* and *o-ä-ö.*

It now became more and more difficult to represent by letters the sounds, already more varied, and even to distinguish the vowels and repeat them accurately. The child cries a good deal, as if to exercise his respiratory muscles. To the sounds uttered while the child is lying comfortably are added in the fourteenth week *ntö, ha.* The last-was given with an unusually loud cry, with distinct aspiration of the *h,* though with no indication that the child felt any particular pleasure. At this period I heard besides repeatedly *lö, na,* the latter along with screaming at disagreeable impressions more and more frequently and distinctly; in the fifteenth week, *nannana, nä-nä, nanna,* in refusal. On the other hand, the earlier favorite *örrö* has not been heard at all for some weeks.

Screaming while waiting for his food to be prepared (milk and water) or for the nurse, who had not sufficient nourishment for the child, is marked, in the sixteenth week—as is also screaming on account of unpleasant feelings—in general by predominance of the vowels, *ä-ŭ, ä-ŭ ä, ā-ŭ, ā-ŭ, ŭ-ä, ŭ-ä, ū-ū-ā-ö*, but meantime is heard *amme-a*, and as a sign of special discomfort the persistent ill-sounding *ūǎ-ūǎ-ūǎ-ūǎ* (*ū*=Eng. $\overline{oo}$).

Screaming in the first five months expresses itself in the main by the vowels *u, ä, ö, a*, with *ü* and *o* occurring more seldom, and without other consonants, for the most part, than *m*.

In the fifth month no new consonants were developed except *k;* but a merely passive *gö, kö, aggeggĕkö*, the last more rarely than the first, was heard with perfect distinctness during the child's yawning.

While in this case the *g*-sound originates passively, it was produced, in connection with *ö*, evidently by the position of the tongue, when the child was in a contented frame, as happens in nursing; *ögö* was heard in the twenty-second week, as well as *ma-ö-ĕ, hǎ, ā, ho-ich*. The *i* here appeared more distinct than in the third month. The soft *ch*, which sounded like the *g* in " Honig," was likewise quite distinct.

About this time began the amusing loud " crowing " of the child, an unmistakable expression of pleasure. The strong aspirate sound *ha*, and this sound united with the labial *r* in *brrr-há*, corresponding in force to the voice, which had become exceptionally powerful, must likewise be regarded as expressions of pleasure.

So with the sounds *aja*, *örrgö*, *ā-ā-i-ŏ-ā*, which the child toward the end of the first half-year utters as if for his own gratification as he lies in comfort. With these belongs also the frequently repeated " eu " of the French " heure," and the " œu " of the French " cœur," which is not found in the German language, also the primitive sounds *ä* and *ö* (German). The lips contract very regularly, and are protruded equally in the transition from *ä* to *ö*. I heard also *ijä* cried out by the child in very gay mood. In the babbling and crowing continued often for a long time without interruption, consonants are seldom uttered, pure vowels, with the exception of *a*, less often than *ä* and *ö*; *i* and *u* are especially rare.

When the child lies on his back, he moves his arms and legs in a lively manner even without any external provocation. He contracts and expands all the muscles he can command, among these especially the muscles of the larynx, of the tongue, and of the aperture of the mouth. In the various movements of the tongue made at random it often happens that the mouth is partly or entirely closed. Then the current of air that issues forth in breathing bursts the barrier and thus arise many sounds, among them some that do not exist in the German language, e. g., frequently and distinctly, by means of labio-lingual stoppage, a consonant-sound between *p* and *t* or between *b* and *d*, in the production of which the child takes pleasure, as he does also in the labial *brr* and *m*. By far the greater part of the consonant-sounds produced by the exercises of the tongue and lips can not be represented in print; just as the more prolonged and more manifold movements of

the extremities, movements made by the child when he
has eaten his fill, and is not sleepy and is left to himself, can not be drawn or described. It is noteworthy
that all the utterances of sound are expiratory. I
have not once observed an attempt to form sounds while
drawing in the breath.

In the seventh month the child at one time screamed
piercingly, in very high tones, from pain. When hungry and desiring milk, he said with perfect distinctness,
mä, ä, ŭä, ŭäĕ ; when contented he would say *örrö* too,
as at an earlier period. The screaming was sometimes
kept up with great vigor until the child began to be
hoarse, in case his desire, e. g., to leave his bed, was not
granted. When the child screams with hunger, he
draws the tongue back, shortens it and thereby broadens
it, making loud expirations with longer or shorter intervals. In pain, on the other hand, the screaming is
uninterrupted and the tones are higher than in any
other screaming. During the screaming I heard the
rare *l* distinctly in the syllable *lä.* The vowels *ŭ-ā-ŭ-i-i*
also appeared distinctly, all as if coming by accident,
and not often pure. The *t* also was seldom heard ; *f, s,
sch, st, sp, sm, ts, ks, w,* not once yet; on the other
hand, *b, d, m, n, r,* often ; *g, h,* more seldom ; *k,* only in
yawning ; *p,* but very rarely, both in screaming and in
the child's babble to himself or in response to friendly
address.

In the eighth month the screaming sounds were for
the most part different from what they had been ; the disagreeable screaming no longer so intense and prolonged,
from the time that the food of the child consisted exclusively of pap (Kindermehl) and water. Single vowels,

like *u* and *ä*, are very often not to be heard pure. Often the child does not move the lips at all when with mouth shut he lifts and drops the larynx, and with eager desire for the pap howls, or coos like a dove, or grunts. The prattling monologues become longer when the child is alone, lying comfortably in bed. But definite consonants can only with difficulty be distinguished in them, with the exception of *r* in the *örrö*, which still continues to be uttered, though rarely and unintentionally. Once the child, while in the bath, cried out as if yawning, *hā-upp*, and frequently, when merry, *a-ei͡*, *a-au͡*, *ă-hau͡-ă*, *hörrö*. When he babbles contentedly in this manner, he moves the tongue quickly, both symmetrically, e. g., raising the edges equally, and asymmetrically, thrusting it forward to right or left. He often also puts out the tongue between the lips and draws it back during expiration, producing thereby the before-mentioned labio-lin·gual explosive sounds. I also heard *ntĕ-ö*, *mi-ja*, *mija* (*j* like Eng. *y*), and once distinctly *ouäĕi*.

In the ninth month it is still difficult to recognize definite syllables among the more varied utterances of sound. But the voice, often indeed very loud and inarticulate, is already more surely modulated as the expression of psychical states. When the child, e. g., desires a new, especially a bright object, he not only stretches both arms in the direction of it, indicating the direction by his gaze, but also makes known, by the same sound he makes before taking his food, that he wants it. This complex combination of movements of eye, larynx, tongue, lips, and arm-muscles appears now more and more; and we can recognize in his screaming the desire for a change of position, discomfort (arising from wet, heat, cold), anger, and pain. The last is announced by screaming with the mouth in the form of a square and by higher pitch. But delight at a friendly expression of face also expresses itself by high crowing sounds, only these are not so high and are not continued long. Violent stretchings of arms and legs accompany (in the thirty-fourth week first) the joyous utterance. Coughing, almost a clearing of the throat, is very rare. Articulate utterances of pleasure, e. g., at music, are *mä-mä, äm-mä, mä*.

Meantime the lip-movements of the *m* were made without the utterance of sound, as if the child had perceived the difference. Other expressions of sound without assignable cause are *ā-au-ā-ā, ā-ŏ, a-u-au, na-na*, the latter not with the tone of denial as formerly, and often repeated rapidly in succession. As separate utterances in comfortable mood, besides *örrö* came *apa, ga au-ă, acha*.

The tenth month is marked by the increasing distinctness of the syllables in the monologues, which are more varied, louder, and more prolonged when the child is left to himself than when any one tries to entertain him. Of new syllables are to be noted *ndäě, bāë-bāë, ba ell, arrö*.

From the forty-second week on, especially the syllables *mä* and *pappa, tatta, appapa, babba, tätä, pa*, are frequently uttered, and the uvular *rrrr, rrra*, are repeated unweariedly. The attempts to make the child repeat syllables pronounced to him, even such syllables as he has before spoken of his own accord, all fail. In place of *tatta* he says, in the most favorable instance, *tä* or *ata ;* but even here there is progress, for in the previous month even these hints at *imitating* or even responding to sound were almost entirely lacking.

In the eleventh month some syllables emphatically pronounced to the child were for the first time correctly repeated. I said "ada" several times, and the attentive child, after some ineffectual movements of the lips, repeated correctly *ada*, which he had for that matter often said of his own accord long before. But this single repetition was so decided that I was convinced that the *sound-imitation* was intentional. It was the first *unquestionable* sound-imitation. It took place on the three hundred and twenty-ninth day. The same day when I said "mamma," the response was *nanna*. In general, it often happens, when something is said for imitation, and the child observes attentively my lips, that evident attempts are made at imitation; but for the most part something different makes its appearance, or else a silent movement of the lips.

In the forty-fifth week everything said to the child, in case it received his attention, was responded to with movements of lips and tongue, which gave the impression of being made at random and of serving rather for diversion.

Further, at this period the child begins during his long monologues to *whisper*. He produces sounds in abundance, varying in force, pitch, and *timbre*, as if he were speaking an unknown tongue; and some single syllables may gradually be more easily distinguished, although the corresponding positions of the mouth pass into one another, sometimes quite gradually, sometimes rapidly. The following special cases I was able to establish by means of numerous observations:

In crying *rrra*, there is a vibration on both sides of the edges of the tongue, which is bent to a half-cylinder with the ridge upward. In this way the child produces three kinds of *r*-sounds—the labial, the uvular, and this bilateral-lingual.

New syllables of this period are *ta-hee*, *dann-tee*, *aa-nee*, *ngä*, *tai*, *bä*, *dall*, *at-tall*, *kamm*, *akkee*, *praï-jer*, *tra*, *ā-hee*. Among them *tra* and *pra* are noteworthy as the first combination of *t* and *p* with *r*. The surprising combinations *attall* and *akkee* and *praijer*, which made their appearance singly without any occasion that could be noticed, like others, are probably the first attempts to reproduce the child's own name (Axel Preyer) from memory. Of earlier sounds, syllables, and combinations of these, the following are especially frequent: *Mammam*, *apapa*, *örrö*, *papa*, *tata*, *tatta*, *naa*, *rrrc*, *pata*, *mmm*, *nă*, *ā*, *ä*, *au*, *anna*, *attapa*, *dadada*, *ja*, *ja-ja*, *eja*, *jaë*. The last syllables are distinguished by the distinct *e*, which is now more frequent.

All the pains taken to represent a babbling monologue perfectly by letters were fruitless, because these distinct and oft-repeated syllables alternated with indistinct loud and soft ones. Still, on the whole, of the consonants the most frequent at this period are *b*, *p*, *t*, *d*, *m*, *n*, and the new *r*; *l*, *g*, *k*, not rare. Of vowels the *a* has a decided preponderance. Both *u* and *o* are rare; *i* very rare. Yet a vowel is not repeated, either by itself or in a syllable, more than five times in succession without an interval. Commonly it is twice or three times. I have also noticed that the mechanical repetition of the same syllable, e. g., *papapa*, occurs far more often than the alternation of a distinctly spoken syllable with another distinctly spoken one, like *pata*. In the mean time it is certain that the child during his various movements of lips and tongue, along with contraction and expansion of the opening of the mouth, readily starts with surprise when he notices such a change of acoustic effect. It seems as if he were himself taking pleasure in practicing regularly all sorts of symmetrical and asymmetrical positions of the mouth, sometimes in silence, sometimes with loud voice, then again with soft voice. In the combinations of syllables, moreover, palpable accentuation somewhat like this, *appápapa atátata*, is by no means frequent. The surprisingly often repeated *dadada* has generally no accent.

With regard to the question whether in this period, especially important for the development of the apparatus of speech, any articulate utterance of sound stands in firm association with an idea, I have observed the child under the most varied circumstances possible without disturbing him; but I have ascertained only one such case with certainty. The *atta, hödda, hatta, hataï,* showed itself to be associated with the perception that something disappeared, for it was uttered when some one left the room, when the light was extinguished, and the like; also, to be sure, sometimes when such remarkable changes were not discoverable. Thus, the eleventh month ends without any other indubitable firm *association of articulation and idea.*

In the next four weeks, up to the *end of the first year* of life, there was no progress in this respect to record; but, from this time on, an eager desire—e. g., for a biscuit seen, but out of reach—was regularly announced by *ä-na*, *ä-nananana*, uttered loudly and with an expression of indescribable longing.

The attempts at imitation, too, are somewhat more successful, especially the attention is more strained. When, e. g., in the fifty-first week, I sang something for the child, he gazed fixedly more than a minute, with immovable countenance, without winking, at my mouth, and then moved his own tongue. Correct repetition of a syllable pronounced to him is, however, very rare. When I laugh, and the child observes it, he laughs likewise, and then crows, with strong abdominal pressure. This same loud expression of joy is exhibited when the child unexpectedly sees his parents at a distance. This peculiar pressure, with strong expiration, is in general associated with feelings of pleasure. The child almost seems to delight in the discovery of his own abdominal pressure, when he produces by means of it the very high crowing sounds with the vowel *i* or a genuine grunt.

Of articulate sounds, syllables, and combinations, made without suggestion from others in the twelfth month, I have caught the following particularly with accuracy: *haja, jajajajaja, aja, njaja, naïn-hopp, ha-a, pa-a, dēwär, han-na, mömma, allda, alldaï, apa-u-a, gägä, ka, ladn*. Besides, the earlier *atta* variously modified; no longer *dada*.

More important than such almost meaningless sound-formations, among which, by the way, appears for the first time *w*, is the now awakened *ability to discriminate between words heard*. The child turns around when his name is spoken in a loud voice; he does this, it is true, at other loud sounds also, but then with a dif-

ferent expression. When he hears a new tone, a new
noise, he is surprised, opens his eyes wide, and holds
his mouth open, without moving.

By frequent repetition of the words, "Give the
hand," with the holding out of the hand, I have brought
the child, in the fifty-second week, to the point of obey-
ing this command of himself—a sure proof that he distinguishes words heard. Another child did the same
thing in the seventh month. In this we can not fail to
see the beginning of communication by means of ordinary language, but this remained a one-sided affair till
past the third half-year, the child being simply recep-
tive. During this whole period, moreover, from birth
on, special sounds, particularly "sch (Eng., *sh*), ss, st,
pst," just the ones not produced by the child, had a remarkable effect of a quieting character. If the child
heard them when he was screaming, he became quiet,
as when he heard singing or instrumental music.

In the *first weeks of the second year of life*, the
child behaves just as awkwardly as ever in regard to
saying anything that is said to him but his attention
has become more lively. When anything is said to him
for him to say—e. g., *papa, mama, atta, tatta*—he
looks at the speaker with eyes wide open and mouth
half open, moves the tongue and the lips, often very
slightly, often vigorously, but can not at the same time
make his voice heard, or else he says, frequently with
an effort of abdominal pressure, *attaï*. Earlier, even
in the forty-fifth week, he had behaved in much the
same way, but to the word "papa," pronounced to him,
he had responded *rrra*. Once only, I remember, *papa*
was repeated correctly, in a faint tone, on the three

hundred and sixty-ninth day, almost as by one in a dream. With this exception, no word could be repeated on command, notwithstanding the fact that the faculty of imitation was already active in another department. The syllables most frequently uttered at this stage were *nja, njan, dada, atta, mama, papaï, attaï, na-na-na, hatta, meenĕ-meenĕ-meenĕ, mömm, mömma, ao-u.*

Of these syllables, *na-na* regularly denotes a desire, and the arms are stretched out in connection with it; *mama* is referred to the mother perhaps in the fifty-fourth week, on account of the pleasure she shows at the utterance of these syllables, but they are also repeated mechanically without any reference to her; *atta* is uttered now and then at going away, but at other times also. His joy—e. g., at recognizing his mother at a distance—the child expresses by crowing sounds, which have become stronger and higher than they were, but which can not be clearly designated; the nearest approach to a representation of them is *ăhijă.* Affirmation and negation may already be recognized by the tone of voice alone. The signification of the cooing and the grunting sounds remains the same. The former indicates desire of food; the latter the need of relieving the bowels. As if to exercise the vocal cords, extraordinarily high tones are now produced, which may be regarded as signs of pleasure in his own power. An imperfect language has thus already been formed imperceptibly, although no single object is as yet designated by a sound assigned to it *alone.* The articulation has made progress, for on the three hundred and sixty-eighth day appeared the first distinct *s,* in the syllable *ssi;* quite incidentally, to be sure.

The most important advance consists in the now awakened *understanding of spoken words*. The ability to learn, or the capability of being trained, has emerged almost as if it had come in a night.

For it did not require frequent repetition of the question, " How tall is the child ? " along with holding up his arms, in order to make him execute this movement every time that he heard the words, " Wie gross ? " (" How tall ? ") or " ooss," nay, even merely " oo." It was easy, too, to induce him to take an ivory ring, lying before him attached to a thread, into his hand, and reach it to me prettily when I held out my hand and said, " Where is the ring ? " and, after it had been grasped, said, " Give." In the same way, the child holds the biscuit, which he is carrying to his mouth, to the lips of the person who says pleasantly to him, " Give " ; and he has learned to move his head sidewise hither and thither when he hears " No, no." If we say to him, when he wants food or an object he has seen, " Bitte, bitte " (say " Please "), he puts his hands together in a begging attitude, a thing which seemed at first somewhat hard for him to learn. Finally, he had at this time been taught to respond to the question, " Where is the little rogue ? " by touching the side of his head with his hand (a movement he had often made of himself before).

From this it appears beyond a doubt that now (rather late in comparison with other children) the association of words heard with certain movements is established, inasmuch as upon acoustic impressions—at least upon combined impressions of hearing and of sight, which are repeated in like fashion — like movements follow, and indeed follow invariably with the expression of great satisfaction on the countenance. Yet this connection between the sensorium and the motorium is not yet stable, for there follows not seldom upon a command distinctly uttered, and without doubt correctly understood, the wrong movement—paramimy. Upon the question, " How tall?" the hands are put together for " Please," and the like. Once when I said, " How tall?" the child raised his arms a moment, then struck himself on the temples, and thereupon put his hands together, as if " rogue," and then " please," had been said to him. All three movements followed with the utmost swiftness, while the expression of face was that of a person confused, with wavering look. Evidently the child had *forgotten* which movement belonged with the " tall," and performed all the three tricks he had learned, *confounding* them one with another. This confounding of arm-raising, head-shaking, giving of the ring, putting the hands together, touching the head, is frequent. It is also to be noticed that some one of these five tricks is almost invariably performed by the child when some new command is given to him that he does not understand, as he perceives that something is required of him—the first conscious act of *obedience*, as yet imperfect.

In the fourteenth month there was no great increase in the number of independent utterances of sound that can be represented by syllables of the German language. Surprising visual impressions, like the brilliant Christmas-tree, and the observation of new objects, drew from the pleasurably excited child, without his having touched anything, almost the same sounds that he at other times made when in discontented mood, *ŭä, mŭä*, only softer; *mömö* and *mama*, and also *papa* are frequent expressions of pleasure. When the child is taken away, he often says *ta-ta* loudly, also, *atta* in a whisper. There can no longer be a doubt that in these syllables is now expressed simply the idea of "going." The labial *brrr*, the so-called "coachman's *R*," was practiced by the child, of his own accord, with special eagerness, and indeed was soon pronounced so cleverly that educated adults can not produce it in such purity and especially with so prolonged an utterance. The only new word is *dakku* and *daggn*, which is often uttered pleasantly with astonishing rapidity, in moments of enjoyment, e. g., when the child is eating food that tastes good. But it is also uttered so often without any assignable occasion, that a definite meaning can hardly be attributed to it, unless it be that of satisfaction. For it is never heard when the least thing of a disagreeable sort has happened to the child. The probability is obvious that we have here a case of imitation of the "Thanks" (Danke) which he has not seldom heard. But the modifications *taggn, attagn, attatn*, pass over into the word, undoubtedly the original favorite, *taï, ataï*.

Among all the indistinct and distinct sounds of the babbling monologues, no inspiratory ones appeared at this time either; but such did make their appearance now and then, in a passive manner, in swallowing and in the coughing that followed.

I spent much time in trying to get the child to repeat vowels and syllables pronounced to him, but always without special success. When I said plainly

11

to him " pá-pá-pá," he answered loudly *ta-taï*, or with manifest effort and a vigorous straining, *t-taï*, *k-taï*, *at-taï*, *hattaï*, and the same when " má-má " was said for him by any one, no matter whom. He also moved lips and tongue often, as if trying to get the sound in various ways; as if the *will* of the child, as he attentively observed the mouth of the speaker, were present, but not the ability to reproduce the sound-impression. Evidently he is taking pains to repeat what he has heard; and he laughs at the unsuccessful effort, if others laugh over it. The earliest success is with the repetition of the vowels " a-u-o," but this is irregular and inaccurate.

In contrast with these halting performances stands the precise, *parrot-like repetition* of such syllables as the child had uttered of his own accord, and which I had immediately after pronounced to him. Thus *attaï, taï, atta*, were often easily and correctly repeated, but, strangely enough, frequently in a whisper. The *ä-ĕ, ä-ö, ä-ĕ*, accompanied by oscillatory movements of the hand, when imitated directly by me was also produced again; in like manner, regularly, the *dakkn*, but this course did not succeed in the case of other primitive syllables or words, even under the most favorable circumstances: here it is to be borne in mind that the last-named utterances were precisely the most frequent at this period. When he was requested with emphasis to say *papa, mama, tata*, he would bring out one of the tricks he had been taught in the previous month; among others, that of moving the head to one side and the other as if in negation; but this it could not be, for this significance of the gesture was wholly unknown to

him at that time. Rather had the child received the
impression from my voice that he was to do something
that he was bidden, and he did what was easy to him
just at the moment, " mechanically," without knowing
which of the movements that he had learned was required (cf. p. 116).

In regard to the *understanding of words heard*,
several points of progress are to be noted; above all
a change of place in consequence of the question,
" Where is your clothes-press ? "   The child, standing
erect, being held by the hand, at these words turns his
head and his gaze toward the clothes-press, draws the
person holding him through the large room by the
hand, although he can not walk a step alone, and then
opens the press without assistance.   Here, at the beginning of the fourteenth month, is the *idea of a definite
stationary object associated with a sound heard*, and so
strongly that it is able to produce an independent act
of locomotion, the first one ; for, although before this
the clothes-press had often been named and shown, the
going to it is still the child's own performance.

It is now a matter of common occurrence that
other words heard have also a definite relation to objects seen. The questions, " Where is papa ? mamma ?
the light ? " are invariably answered correctly, after brief
deliberation, by turning the head (at the word " light,"
occasionally since the ninth month) and the gaze in the
proper direction, and by lifting the right arm, often also
the left, to point, the fingers of the outstretched hand
being at the same time generally spread out.   In the
previous month, only the association of the word *mama*
with the appearance of the mother was established.

The following are now added to the movements executed upon hearing certain words. The child likes to beat with his hands upon the table at which he is sitting. I said to him, "Play the piano," and made the movement after him. Afterward, when I merely said the word "piano" to the child (who was at the time quiet), without moving my hands, he *considered* for a few seconds, and then beat again with his hands on the table. Thus the recollection of the sound was sufficient to bring out the movement. Further, the child had accustomed himself, of his own accord, to give a regular *snort*, contracting the nostrils, pursing up the mouth, and breathing out through the nose. If now any one spoke to him of the "nose," this snorting was sure to be made. The word put the centro-motors into a state of excitement. The same is true of the command "Give!" since the child reaches out the object he is holding or is about to take hold of, in case any one puts out the hand or the lips to him. Some weeks ago this took place only with the ring and biscuit; now the word "give" has the same effect with any object capable of being grasped, but it operates almost like a reflex stimulus, "mechanically," without its being even once the case that the act of giving is a purely voluntary act or even occasioned by sympathy.

In these already learned co-ordinated movements made upon hearing the words "Please, How tall? rogue! no! piano! ring! give!" all of which are now executed with shorter intervals of deliberation as if by a well-trained animal, there is in general absolutely no deeper understanding present than that to this and the other sound-impression belong this and the other movement. By means of daily repetition of both, the time required for the production of the movement after the excitement of the auditory nerve becomes less and less, the doubt as to which movement follows this or that sound withdrawing more and more. At last the responsive movements followed without any remarkable strain of attention. They became habitual.

Now and then, however, the movements are still confounded. Upon "no! no!" follows the touching of the head ; upon "please," the shaking of the head ; upon "rogue," the putting of the hands together, etc. These errors become frequent when a new impression diverts the attention. They become more and more rare through repetition of the right movements made for the child to see and through guiding the limbs of the child. A further evidence of the increased ability to learn toward the end of the month is the fact that the hands are raised in the attitude of begging not only at the command "Please," but also at the question, " How does the good child behave ? " Thus, the experience is beginning to become a conscious one that, in order to obtain anything, the begging attitude is useful.

The fifteenth month brought no new definite independent utterances of sound with the exception of *wa*. Sensations and emotions, however, are indicated more and more definitely and variously by sounds that are inarticulate and sometimes unintelligible. Thus, astonishment is expressed by *hā-ā ĕā-ĕ ;* joy by vigorous crowing in very high tones and more prolonged than before ; further, very strong desire by repeated *häö, hä-ĕ ;* pain, impatience, by screaming in vowels which pass over into one another.

The only word that is unquestionably used of the child's own motion to indicate a class of perceptions is still *atta*, *ha-atta*, which during the following month also is uttered softly, for the most part, on going out, and which signifies "away" or "gone" (weg), and still continues to be used also as it was in the eleventh month, when a light is dimmed (by a lamp-shade). Beyond this no syllable can be named that marked the dawn of mental independence, none that testified to the voluntary use of articulate sounds for the purpose of announcing perceptions. For the *brrr*, the frequent *dakkn*, *mamam*, *mömö*, and *papap*, are without significance in the monologues. Even the saying of *atta*, with turning of the head toward the person going away, has acquired the meaning of "away" (fort) only through being repeatedly said to the child upon his being carried out; but no one said the word when the lamp was extinguished. Here has been in existence for some time not only the formation of the concept, but also the designation of the concept by syllables. The similarity in the very different phenomena of going away and of the dimming of the light, viz., the disappearance of a visual impression, was not only discovered, but was named by the child entirely independently in the eleventh month, and has kept its name up to the present time. He has many impressions; he perceives, he unites qualities to make concepts. This he has been doing for a long time without words; but only in this *one* instance does the child express one of his concepts in language after a particular instance had been thus named for him, and then the word he uses is one not belonging to his later language, but one that belongs to all children the world over.

In regard to the repeating of syllables pronounced
to him a marked advance is noticeable. The child can
not, indeed, by any means repeat *na* and *pa* and *o* or *e*
and *be*. He answers *a*, *taï*, *ta-a-o-ö-a*, and practices all
sorts of tongue- and lip-exercises. But the other syllables uttered by him, especially *anna*, *taï*, *dakkn*, *a*, he
says in response to any one who speaks them distinctly
to him, and he gives them easily and correctly in parrot
fashion. If a new word is said to him, e. g., "kalt"
(cold), which he can not repeat, he becomes vexed, turns
away his head, and screams, too, sometimes. I have
been able to introduce into his vocabulary only one new
word. In the sixty-third week he seized a biscuit that
had been dipped in hot water; let it fall, drew down the
corners of his mouth, and began to cry. Then I said
"heiss" (hot), whereupon the child, speedily quieted,
repeated *haï* and *haï-s* (with a just discernible *s*). Three
days later the same experiment was made. After this
the *haïs*, *haïsses*, with distinct *s*, was often heard without any occasion. Some days later I wanted him to
say "hand." The child observed my mouth closely,
took manifest pains, but produced only *ha-ïss*, then
very distinctly *hass* with sharp *ss*, and *ha-ith*, *hadith*,
with the English *th;* at another time distinctly *ha-its*.
Thus, at a time when *ts = z* can not be repeated, there
exists the possibility of pronouncing *z*. When I said
to him "warm," *ass* was pronounced with an effort and
distinctly, although the syllable *wa* belonged to the
child's stock of words. This was evidently a recollection of the previous attempts to repeat "heiss" and
"hand."

Corresponding to this inability to say words after

another's utterance of them is an articulation as yet very imperfect. Still, there is indication of progress in the distinctness of the *s*, the frequent English *th* with the thrusting out of the tip of the tongue between the incisors, the *w*, which now first appears often, as well as in the *smacking* first heard in the sixty-fifth week (in contented mood). The tongue is, when the child is awake, more than other muscles that in the adult are subject to cerebral volition, almost always in motion even when the child is silent. It is in various ways partly contracted, extended, bent. The lateral bending of the edges of the tongue downward and the turning back of the tip of the tongue (from left to right) so that the lower surface lies upward, are not easily imitated by adults. The mobility of my child's tongue is at any rate much greater than that of my tongue, notwithstanding the fact that, in consequence of varied practice from an early period in rapid speaking, the most difficult performances in rapid speaking are still easily executed by mine. The tongue is unquestionably the child's favorite plaything. One might almost speak of a lingual delirium in his case, as in that of the insane, when he pours forth all sorts of disconnected utterances, articulate and inarticulate, in confusion ; and yet I often saw his tongue affected with fibrillar contractions as if the mastery of the hypoglossus were not as yet complete. Quite similar fibrillar movements seem to be made by the tongue in bulbar paralysis, and in the case of dogs and guinea-pigs whose hypoglossus has been severed.

To the number of words heard that already produce a definite movement are added the following new ones.

The child is asked, "Where is the moon? the clock? the eye? the nose?" and he raises an arm, spreads the fingers, and looks in the proper direction. If I speak of "coughing," he coughs; of "blowing," he blows; of "kicking," he stretches out his legs; of "light," he blows into the air, or, if there is a lamp in sight, toward that, looking at it meantime—a reminiscence of the blowing out of matches and candles often seen by him. It requires great pains to get from him the affirmative nod of the head at the spoken "ja, ja." Not till the sixty-fourth week was this achieved by means of frequent repetition and forcible direction, and the movement was but awkwardly executed even later—months after. On hearing the "no, no," the negative shake of the head now appeared almost invariably, and this was executed as by adults without the least uncertainty.

The holding out of his hand at hearing "Give the hand," occurs almost invariably, but is not to be regarded as a special case of understanding of the syllable "give," for the word "hand" alone produces the same result.

All these accomplishments, attained by regular training, do not afford the least evidence of an understanding of what is commanded when the sound-impression is converted into motor impulse. It is rather a matter of the establishment of the recollection of the customary association of both during the interval of deliberation. The words and muscular contractions that belong together are less often confounded, and the physiological part of the process takes less time, but its duration is noticeably prolonged when the child is not quite well. He deliberates for as much as twelve seconds when the question is asked him, "Where is the rogue?" and then responds with the proper gesture (p. 115).

The sixteenth month brought few new articulate utterances of sound, none associated with a definite meaning; on the other hand, there was a marked progress in repeating what was said to the child, and especially in the understanding of words heard.

Among the sounds of his own making are heard—along with the *hä! hä-ö! ha-ĕ! hĕ-ĕ!* that even in the following months often expresses desire, but often also is quite without meaning—more seldom *hi, gö-gö, gö, f-pa* (the *f* for the first time), *aū*, and more frequently *ta, dokkn, tá-ha, a-bwa-bwa, bŭā-bŭ-ā*, and, as if by accident, once among all sorts of indefinable syllables, *dagon*. Further, the child—as was the case in the previous month—likes to take a newspaper or a book in his hands and hold the print before his face, babbling *ä-ĕ, ä-ĕ, ä-ĕ*, evidently in imitation of the reading aloud which he has often observed. By giving the command, "Read!" it was easy to get this performance repeated. Besides this, it is a delight to the child to utter a syllable—e. g., *bwa* or *ma*—over and over, some six times in succession, without stopping. As in the previous month, there are still the whispered *attö* and *hattö*, at the hiding of the face or of the light, at the shutting of a fan, or the emptying of a soup-plate, together with the *dakkn*, with the combinations of syllables made out of *ta, pa, ma, na, at, ap, am, an*, and with *mömö*. The *papa* and *mama* do not, however, express an exclusive relation to the parents. Only to the questions, "Where is papa?" "Where is mamma?" he points toward them, raising his hand with the fingers spread. Pain is an-

nounced by loud and prolonged screaming; joy by
short, high-pitched, piercing crowing, in which the
vowel *i* appears.

Of isolated vowels, *a* only was correctly repeated
on command. Of syllables, besides those of the previous month, *mö* and *ma;* and here the child's excessive gayety over the success of the experiment is worthy
of remark. He made the discovery that his parrot-like
repetition was a fresh source of pleasure, yet he could
not for several weeks repeat again the doubled syllables,
but kept to the simple ones, or responded with all sorts
of dissimilar ones, like *attob*, or said nothing. The syllable *ma* was very often given back as *hömá* and *hömö;*
pa was never given back, but, as had been the case previously, only *ta* and *taï* were the responses, made with
great effort and attention, and the visible purpose of
repeating correctly. To the word " danke," pronounced
for him with urgency innumerable times, the response
is *dakkn*, given regularly and promptly, and this in the
following months also. If all persuasion failed, and the
child were then left to himself without any direction of
his attention, then not infrequently new imitations of
sounds would be given correctly—e. g., when I said
" bo "—but these, again, would no longer succeed when
called for. Indeed, such attempts often broke down
utterly at once. Thus the child once heard a hen making a piteous outcry, without seeing the creature, and
he tried in vain to imitate the sound, but once only, and
not again. On the other hand, he often succeeds in repeating correctly movements of the tongue made for
him to see, as the thrusting out of the tongue between
the lips, by reason of the extraordinary mobility of his

tongue and lips; he even tries to smack in imitation. The more frequent partial contractions of the tongue, without attempts at speaking, are especially surprising. On one side, toward the middle of the tongue, rises a longitudinal swelling; then the edges are brought together, so that the tongue almost forms a closed tube; again, it is turned completely back in front. Such flexibility as this hardly belongs to the tongue of any adult. Besides, the lips are often protruded a good deal, even when this is not required in framing vocables.

The gain in the understanding of words heard is recognizable in this, that when the child hears the appropriate word, he takes hold, with thumb and forefinger, in a most graceful manner, of nose, mouth, beard, forehead, chin, eye, ear, or touches them with the thumb. But in doing this he often confounds ear and eye, chin and forehead, even nose and ear. "O" serves in place of "Ohr" (ear); "Au" in place of "Auge" (eye). In both cases the child soon discovered that these organs are in pairs, and he would seize with the right hand the lobe of my left and of my right ear alternately after I had asked "Ear?" How easily in such cases a new sound-impression causes confusion is shown by the following fact: After I had at one time pointed out one ear, and had said, "Other ear," I succeeded, by means of repetition, in getting him to point out this other one also correctly every time. Now, then, the thing was to apply what had been learned to the eye. When one eye had been pointed out, I asked, "Where is the other eye?" The child grasped at an ear, with the sight of which the sound "other" was now associated. Not till long after (in the twentieth month) did he learn to apply this sound of himself to different parts of the body. On the other hand, he understands perfectly the significance of the commands, "Bring, fetch, give ——"; he brings, fetches, gives desired objects, in which case, indeed, the gesture and look of the speaker are decisive; for, if these are only distinctly apprehended, it does not make much difference which word is said, or whether nothing is said.

In the seventeenth month, although no disturbance of the development took place, there was no perceptible advance in the utterance of thoughts by sounds, or in the imitation of syllables pronounced by others, or in articulation, but there was a considerable increase of the acoustic power of discrimination in words heard and of the memory of sounds.

Of syllables original with the child, these are new: *Bibi*, *nä-nä-nä*—the first has come from the frequent hearing of "bitte"; the last is an utterance of joy at meeting and an expression of the desire to be lifted up. Otherwise, longing, abhorrence, pleasure and pain, hunger and satiety, are indicated by pitch, accent, *timbre*, intensity of the vocal sounds, more decidedly than by syllables. A peculiar complaining sound signifies that he does not understand; another one, that he does not wish. In place of *atta*, at the change of location of an object perceived, comes often a *t-tó* and *höt-tó*, with the lips much protruded. But, when the child himself wishes to leave the room, then he takes a hat, and says *atta*, casting a longing look at his nurse, or repeatedly taking hold of the door.

Of voluntary attempts to imitate sounds, the most noteworthy were the efforts to give the noise heard on the winding of a time-piece, and to repeat tones sung.

The associations of words heard with seen, tangible objects on the one hand, and, on the other hand, with definite co-ordinated muscular movements, have become considerably more numerous. Thus the following are already correctly distinguished, being very rarely confounded : Uhr (clock), Ohr (ear) ; Schuh (shoe), Stuhl (chair), Schulter (shoulder), Fuss (foot) ; Stirn (forehead), Kinn (chin) ; Nase (nose), blasen (blow) ; Bart (beard), Haar (hair) ; heiss (hot), Fleisch (meat).

In addition to the above, eye, arm, hand, head, cheek, mouth, table, light, cupboard, flowers, are rightly pointed out.

The child so often obeys the orders he hears—" run," " kick," " lie down," " cough," " blow," " bring," " give," " come," " kiss "—that when he occasionally does not obey, the disobedience must be ascribed no longer, as before, to deficient understanding, but to caprice, or, as may be discerned beyond a doubt from the expression of his countenance, to a genuine roguishness. Thus the spoken consonants are at last surely recognized in their differences of sound.

In the eighteenth month this ability of the ear to discriminate, and with it the understanding of spoken words, increases. " Finger, glass, door, sofa, thermometer, stove, carpet, watering-pot, biscuit," are rightly pointed out, even when the objects, which were at first touched, or merely pointed at, along with loud and repeated utterance of those words, are no longer present, but objects like them are present. Say " Finger," and the child takes hold of his own fingers only ; " Ofen " (stove), then he invariably at first looks upward ("oben"). Besides the earlier commands, the following are correctly obeyed: "Find, pick up, take it, lay it down." Hand him a flower, saying, "Smell," and he often carries it to his nose without opening his mouth.

The repeating of syllables spoken for him is still rare; "mamma" is responded to by *ta*. The voluntary repeating of syllables heard by chance is likewise rare; in particular, "jaja" is now repeated with precision.

The *atta*, which used to be whispered when anything disappeared from the child's field of vision, has changed to *tto* and *t-tu* and *ftu*, with pouting of the lips.

In the monologues appear *näi*, *mimi*, *päpä*, *mimiä*, *pata*, *rrrrr*, the last uvular and labial for minutes at a time. But these meaningless utterances are simply signs of well-being in general, and are gladly repeated from pleasure in the exercise of the tongue and lips. The tongue still vibrates vigorously with fibrillar contractions when it is at rest, the mouth being open.

Characteristic for this period is the precision with which the various moods of feeling are expressed, without articulate sounds, by means of the voice, now become very high and strong, in screaming and crowing, then again in wailing, whimpering, weeping, grunting, squealing; so that the mood is recognized by the voice better than ever before, especially desire, grief, joy, hunger, willfulness, and fear. But this language can not be represented by written characters.

The same holds good of the nineteenth month, in which bawling and babbling are more rare, the spontaneous sound-imitations are more frequent, the vocal cords are strained harder, the mechanism of articulation

works with considerably more ease ; the understanding
and the retention of spoken words have perceptibly increased, but no word of the child's own, used always in
the same sense, is added.

When the child has thrown an object from the table
to the floor, he often follows it with his gaze and whispers, even when he does not know he is observed, *atta*
or *t-ta*, which is here used in the same sense with *tuff* or
ft or *ftu*, for " fort " (gone).

When he had taken a newspaper out of the paper-
basket and had spread it on the floor, he laid himself
flat upon it, holding his face close to the print, and said
—evidently of his own accord, imitating, as he had done
before, the reading aloud of the newspaper, which had
often been witnessed by him—repeating it for a long
time in a monotonous voice, *e-já-e-e-já nanana ána-ná-
na atta-ána āje-já sā*; then he tore the paper into many
small pieces, and next turned the leaves of books, uttering *pa-pa-ab ta hö-ö-ĕ mömömöm hö-önĕ*.

Such monologues are, however, exceptional at this
period, the rule being uniform repetitions of the same
syllable, e. g., *habb habb habb habb habbwa habbua*.

Screaming when water of 26° C. was poured over
him in the bath appeared, a few days after the first
experiment of this sort, even before the bathing, at
sight of the tub, sponge, and water. Previously, fear
had only in very rare cases occasioned screaming, now
the *idea* of the cold and wet that were to be expected
was enough to occasion violent screaming. After about
three weeks of daily bathing with water from 18 to 24°
C., however, the screaming decreased again. The experience that a pleasant feeling of warmth succeeded,

may have forced the recollection of the unpleasant feeling into the background. But the screaming can not at
all be represented by letters; *ä* and *ö* do not suffice.
The same is true of the screaming, often prolonged,
before falling asleep in the evening, which occurs not
seldom also without any assignable occasion, the child
making known by it his desire to leave the bed. As
this desire is not complied with, the child perceives the
uselessness of the screaming, and at length obeys the
command, "Lie down," without our employing force
or expedients for soothing him.

How far the power of imitation and of articulation
is developed, is shown especially by the fact that now,
at last, *pa* is correctly pronounced in response ; in the
beginning *ta* was still frequently the utterance, then *ba*,
finally *pa* almost invariably given correctly.

Further, these results were obtained :

Words said to him.	Response.
bitte . . .	*bis, bits, bit, bets, beest, be, bi, bit-th* (Eng., *th*).
hart . `. .	*hatt, att, haat.*
Fleisch . .	*da-ich, daï-s-ch, daï-s-j.*
ma	*mö, ma.*

In *bits* appears with perfect distinctness (as already in
the fifteenth month) the very rare *ts=z*. The "hart"
was once only confounded with "haar," and responded
to by grasping at the hair. The *bits* soon served to add
force to the putting together of the hands in the attitude of begging; it is thus the first attempt at the employment of a German word to denote a state of his
own, and that the state of desire. The other words
12

said to him, and illustrated by touching and putting the
hands upon objects, could not be given by him in response. When he was to say "weich" (soft), "kalt"
(cold), "nass" (wet), he turned his head away in repugnance, as formerly. To "nass" he uttered in reply,
once only, *na*. Smacking, when made for him, was
imitated perfectly. The early morning hours, in which
the sensibility of the brain is at its highest, are the best
adapted to such experiments; but these experiments
were not multiplied, in order that the independent development might not be disturbed.

The progress in the discrimination of words heard,
and in the firm retention of what has been repeatedly
heard, is shown particularly in more prompt obedience,
whether in abstaining or in acting.

To the list of objects correctly pointed out upon request are added "leg, nail, spoon, kettle," and others.
It is noteworthy, too, that now, if the syllables *pa* and
ma, or *papa* and *mamma*, are prefixed to the names of
the known parts of the face and head, the child points
these out correctly; e. g., to the question "Where is
Mamma-ear," the child responds by taking hold of the
ear of his mother, and to "papa-ear," of that of his
father; so with "nose, eye," etc. But if asked for
"mamma-beard," the child is visibly embarrassed, and
finally, when there is a laugh at his hesitation, he
laughs too.

The old tricks, "How tall is the child?" and
"Where is the little rogue?" which have not been
practiced for months past, have been retained in
memory, for when in the eighty-second week I
brought out both questions with urgency, the child be-

thought himself for several seconds, motionless, then suddenly, after the first question, raised both arms. After the other question he likewise considered for several seconds, and then pointed to his head as he used to do. His *memory* for sound-impressions often repeated and associated with specific movements is consequently good.

In the twentieth month there was an important advance to be recorded in his manner of repeating what was said to him. Suddenly, on the five hundred and eighty-fourth day, the child is repeating correctly and without difficulty words of two syllables that consist either of two like syllables—for the sake of brevity I will call these *like-syllabled*—or of syllables the second of which is the reverse of the first—such I call *reverse-syllabled*. Thus of the first class are *papa, mama, bebe, baba, neinei, jaja, bobo, bubu;* of the second class, *otto, enne, anna;* these are very frequently given back quickly and faultlessly at this period, after the repetition of the single syllables *pa, ma,* and others had gone on considerably more surely than before, and the child had more often tried of himself to imitate what he heard. These imitations already make sometimes the impression of not being voluntary. Thus the child once—in the eighty-third week—observed attentively a redstart in the garden for two full minutes, and then imitated five or six times, not badly, the piping of the bird, turning round toward me afterward. It was when he saw me that the child first seemed to be aware that he had made attempts at imitation at all. For his countenance was like that of one awaking from sleep, and he could not now be induced to imitate sounds. After five days the spectacle was repeated. Again the piping of the bird was reproduced, and in the afternoon the child took a cow, roughly carved out of wood, of the size of the redstart, made it move back and forth on the table, upon its feet, and chirped now as he had done at sight of the bird; *imagination* was here manifestly much excited. The wooden animal was to represent the bird, often observed in the garden, and nesting in the veranda; and the chirping and piping were to represent its voice.

On the other hand, words of unlike syllables, like "Zwieback" (biscuit), "Butterbrod," are either not given back at all or only in unrecognizable fashion, in spite of their being pronounced impressively for him. "Trock-en" (dry) yields sometimes *tokkĕ, tokko, otto.* Words of one syllable also offer generally great difficulties of articulation: thus "warm" and "weich" become *wāi,* "kalt" and "hart" become *hatt.* Although "bi" and "te" are often rightly given each by itself, the child can not combine the two, and turns away with repugnance when he is to reproduce "bi-te." The same thing frequently happens, still, even with "mamma" and "papa." But the child, when in lively spirits, very often pronounces of his own accord the syllables "bi" and "te" together, preferring, indeed, *bidih* (with English *th*) and *beet* to "bitte." In place of "adjö" (adieu) he gives back *adē* and *adjē.* Nor does he succeed in giving back three syllables; e. g., the child says *papa,* but not "papagei," and refuses altogether to repeat "gei" and "pagei." The same is true of "Gut," "Nacht," although he of himself holds out his hand for "Gute Nacht."

When others laugh at anything whatsoever, the child laughs regularly with them, a purely imitative movement.

It is surprising that the reproducing of what is said to him succeeds best directly after the cold bath in the morning, when the child has been screaming violently and has even been shivering, or when he is still screaming and is being rubbed dry, and, as if resigned to his fate, lies almost without comprehension. The will, it would seem, does not intrude here as a disturbing force, and echolalia manifests itself in its purity, as in the case of hypnotics. The little creature is subdued and powerless. But he speedily recovers himself, and then it is often quite hard to tell whether he *will* not or *can* not say the word that is pronounced to him.

The *understanding of single words*, especially of single questions and commands, is considerably more prompt than in the previous month. Without there being any sort of explanation for it, this extraordinary understanding is here, manifesting itself particularly when the child is requested to fetch and carry all sorts of things. He has observed and touched a great deal, has listened less, except when spoken to. All training in tricks and performances, an evil in the modern education of children hard to avoid, was, however, suppressed as far as possible, so that the only new things were " making a bow " and " kissing the hand." The child practices both of these toward the end of the month, without direction, at coming and going. Many new objects, such as window, bed, knife, plate, cigar, his own teeth and thumbs, are correctly pointed out, if only the corresponding word is distinctly pronounced. Yet " Ofen " and " oben " are still confounded.

To put into written form the syllables invented by

the child independently, and to get at a sure denotation of objects by them, is exceedingly difficult, particularly when the syllables are merely whispered as the objects are touched, which frequently occurs. At the sight of things rolled noisily, especially of things whirling in a circle, the child would utter *rodi*, *otto*, *rojo*, and like sounds, in general, very indistinctly. Only *one* new concept could with certainty be proved to be associated with a particular sound. With *dā* and *ndā*, frequently uttered on the sudden appearance of a new object in the field of vision, in a lively manner, loudly and with a peculiarly demonstrative accent—also with *tā* and *ntā* —the child associates, beyond a doubt, existence, coming, appearing, shooting forth, emerging, in contrast with the very often softly spoken, whispered *atta, f-tu, tuff,* which signifies "away" or "gone." If I cover my head and let the child uncover it, he laughs after taking off the handkerchief, and says loudly *da ;* if I leave the room, he says *atta* or *hätta,* or *ft* or *t-ta,* generally softly ; the last of these, or else *hata,* he says if he would like to be taken out himself. In the eighty-seventh week we went away on a journey, and on the railway-train the child, with an expression of terror or of anxious astonishment, again and again said *attah,* but without manifesting the desire for a change of place for himself, even by stretching out his arms.

Two words only—*papa* for father, and *bät* or *bit* for "bitte," are, besides, rightly applied of the child's own accord. The prolonged screaming, from wantonness, of *nānānānā, nom-nom, hāhā, lālā,* chiefly when running about, has no definite meaning. The child exercises himself a good deal in loud outcry, as if he wanted to test the power of his voice. These exercises evidently give him great pleasure. Still the highest crowing tones are no longer quite so high and piercing as they were formerly. The vocal cords have become larger, and can no longer produce such high tones. The screaming sounds of discontent, which continue to be repeated sometimes till hoarseness appears, but rarely in the night, have, on the contrary, as is the case with the shrill sounds of pain, scarcely changed their character, *hä-e*, *hä-ä-ä-ĕ*, *ĕ*. They are strongest in the bath, during the pouring on of cold water.

The child, when left to himself, keeps up all the time his loud readings ("Lesestudien"). He "reads" in a monotonous way maps, letters, newspapers, drawings, spreading them out in the direction he likes, and lies down on them with his face close to them, or holding the sheet with his hands close to his face, and, as before, utters especially vowel-sounds.

In the twenty-first month imitative attempts of this kind became more frequent; but singularly enough the babbling—from the eighty-ninth week on—became different. Before this time vowels were predominant, now more *consonants* are produced. When something is said for the child to reproduce that presents insuperable difficulties of articulation, then he moves tongue and lips in a marvelous fashion, and often says *ptö-ptö*, *pt-pt*, and *verlapp*, also *dla-dla*, without meaning, no matter what was the form of the word pronounced to him. In such practice there often appears likewise a wilfulness, showing itself in inarticulate sounds and the shaking of the head, even when it is merely the repetition of easy like-syllabled words that is

desired. Hence, in the case of new words, it is more
difficult than before, or is even impossible to determine
whether the child *will* not or whether he *can* not reproduce them. Words of unlike syllables are not repeated at all, not even " bitte." In place of " danke "
are heard *dang-gee* and *dank-kee;* the former favorite
dakkn is almost never heard. In most of the attempts
at sound imitation, the tendency to the doubling of syllables is worthy of notice. I say " bi," and the answer
is *bibi;* then I say " te," and the answer is *te-te.* If
I say " bi-te," the answer is likewise *bibi;* a single time
only, in spite of daily trial, the answer was *bi-te,* as if
by oversight.

This doubling of syllables, involuntary and surely contrary to the will of the child, stands in remarkable contrast with the indolence he commonly
shows in reproducing anything said, even when the
fault is not to be charged to teasing, stubbornness, or
inability. The child then finds more gratification in
other movements than those of the muscles of speech.
The babbling only, abounding in consonants, yields him
great pleasure, particularly when it is laughed at, although it remains wholly void of meaning as language.
Yet *bibi*, like *bäbä*, for " bitte," is correctly used by the
child of his own accord.

A new word, and one that gives notice of a considerable advance, is the term used by the child when
hungry and thirsty, for " milk " or " food." He says,
viz., with indescribable longing in his voice, *mimi*,
more rarely than before *mämä* and *mömöm* (page 85).
The first appellation was certainly taken from the
often-heard " milk " by imitation, and applied to biscuit

and other kinds of food. If the child, when he has
eaten enough, is asked, " Do you want milk ? " he says
without direction, *neinein ;* he has thus grasped
and turned to use already the signification of the
sound. The same is, perhaps, true also of " ja." For
previously, when I asked the child as he was eating, " Does it taste good ? " he was silent, and I would
say, " Say jaja," and this would be correctly repeated.
But in the ninety-first week he, of his own accord, answers the question with *jaja*—" yes, yes." This, too,
may rest simply on imitation, without a knowledge of
the meaning of the *ja*, and without an understanding
of the question ; yet there is progress in the recollection
of the connection of the sound " schmeckt's " with *jaja*,
the intermediate links being passed over.

In other cases, too, the strength of the memory for
sounds is plainly manifested. To all questions of an
earlier period, " Where is the forehead, nose, mouth,
chin, beard, hair, cheek, eye, ear, shoulder ? " the child
now at once pointed correctly in every instance, although he might not have answered them for anybody
even once for two weeks. Only the question, " Where
is the thumb ? " made him hesitate. But when the
thumb had been again shown to him (firmly pressed), he
knew it, and from that time pointed it out invariably
without delay. To the question, " Where is the eye ? "
he is accustomed to shut both eyes quickly at the same
time and to open them again, and then to point to my
eye ; to the question, " Axel's eye ? " he responds by
pointing to his own ; to the question, " The other eye ? "
by pointing to the one not touched.

In the understanding of what is spoken astonishing

progress has been made—e. g., if I say, "Go, take the hat and lay it on the chair!" the child executes the order without considering more than one or two seconds. He knows the meaning of a great number of words that no one has taught him—e. g., "whip, stick, match, pen." Objects of this sort are surely distinguished by the child, for, upon receiving orders, he gets, picks up, brings, lays down, gives these things each by itself.

This understanding of spoken words is the more surprising, as his repetition of them continues still to be of a very rudimentary character. With the exception of some interjections, especially *jäĕ* as a joyous sound and of crowing sounds, also screaming sounds, which, however, have become more rare, the child has but few expressions of his own with a recognizable meaning; *ndä, ndä, da* is demonstrative "da" ("there") at new impressions.

Att, att, att, is unintelligible, perhaps indicative of movement.

Attah means "we are off" (upon setting out) and "I want to go" (" ich will fort "); *tatass, tatass* is unintelligible, possibly a sound-imitation.

When traveling by rail the child tried several times to imitate the hissing of the steam of the locomotive.

In the twenty-second month again there are several observations to record, which show the progress in understanding, the strengthening of the memory, and the greater facility in articulation. The child executes the orders given him with surprising accuracy, although the words spoken have not previously been impressed on him separately. Here, indeed, it is essential to consider the looks and gestures of those who give the orders; but the child also does what I request of him without looking at me. Instances of confusion among the words known to him are also perceptibly more rare. Once I asked him very distinctly, " Where's the moon ? " (Mond) and for answer the child pointed to his mouth (Mund). But the error was not repeated.

The strength of the word-memory appears particularly in this, that all the objects learned are more quickly pointed out on request than they were previously, and the facility of articulation is perceived in the multiplying of consonants in the monologues and in the frequent spontaneous utterance of *pss*, *ps*, *ptsch* (once), and *pth* (Engl.). The child says, without any occasion, *pa-ptl-dä*, *pt*, and gives a loud greeting from a distance with *hāā-ö*, with *ada*, and *ana*.

It seemed to me remarkable that the boy began several times without the least incitement to *sing* tolerably well. When I expressed my approval of it, he sprang about, overjoyed. At one time he sang, holding his finger on his tongue, first *rollo*, *rollo*, innumerable times, then *mama*, *mama*, *mämä*, *mama*.

The progress in the sound-mechanism is most plainly discerned in the greater certainty in reproducing what is spoken. Thus, " pst " is correctly given, and of reverse-syllabled words, very accurately, "anna, otto, alla, appa, enne "; of unlike-syllabled words, " lina," but still, notwithstanding many trials, not yet " bitte." *For the first time three-syllabled words also, plainly pronounced to him, were correctly given back*, viz., *a-ma-ma* and *a-pa-pa*, as the child names his grandparents. Hitherto the vowels *e*, *i*, *o*, *u*, could not be correctly given every time, but " a " could be so given as before.

When the reproduction of any new word that is too hard is requested—e. g., "gute Nacht"—the child at this period regularly answers *tapĕta*, *pĕta*, *pta*, and *ptö-ptö*, also *rateratetat*, expressing thereby not merely his inability, but also, sometimes roguishly, his disinclination to repeat.

Ja ja and *nein nein*, along with *da* and *bibi* (with or without folding of the hands, for "bitte"), and *mimi*, continue still to be the only words taken from the language of adults that are used by the child in the proper sense when he desires or refuses anything. Apart from these appear inarticulate sounds, uttered even with the mouth shut. The intense cry of pain, or that produced by cold or wet or by grief at the departure of the parents (this with the accompaniment of abundant tears and the drawing of the corners of the mouth far down), makes the strongest contrast with the crowing for joy, particularly that at meeting again.

The twenty-third month brought at length *the first spoken judgment*. The child was drinking milk, carrying the cup to his mouth with both hands. The milk was too warm for him, and he set the cup down quickly and said, loudly and decidedly, looking at me with eyes wide open and with earnestness, *heiss* (hot). This single word was to signify "The drink is too hot!" In the same week, at the end of the ninety-ninth, the child of his own accord went to the heated stove, took a position before it, looked attentively at it, and suddenly said with decision, *hot* (*heiss*)! Again, a whole proposition in a syllable. In the sixty-third week for the first time the child had reproduced the word "hot" pronounced to him. Eight and a half months were required for the step from

the imitative *hot* to the independent *hot* as expressive of
his judgment. He progressed more rapidly with the
word " Wasser," which was reproduced as *watja*, and was
called out longingly by the thirsty child a few weeks
afterward. He already distinguishes water and milk in
his own fashion as *watja* and *mimi*. Yet *mimmi*,
mömö, and *māmā* still signify food in general, and are
called out often before meal-times by the impatient and
hungry child. The primitive word *atta* is likewise frequently uttered incidentally when anything disappears
from the child's field of vision or when he is himself
carried away. The other sound-utterances of this period
proceeding from the child's own impulse are interesting
only as exercises of the apparatus of articulation. Thus,
the child not seldom cries aloud *oi* or *eu* (*äu*); further,
unusually loud, *ana*, and for himself in play, *ida*, *didl*,
dadl, *dldo-dlda*, and in singing tone *cpojö*, *apojopojum
aui*, *heissa*. With special pleasure the child, when
talking to himself, said *papa*, *mama*, *māmä*, *mimi*,
momo, of his own accord, but not " mumu "; on the
other hand, *e-mama-ma-memama*, *mi*, *ma*, *mö*, *ma*.
His grandparents he now regularly designates by *e-papa*
and *e-mama*. He knows very well who is meant when
he is asked, " Where is grandmamma? Grandpapa?"
And several days after leaving them, when asked the
question, e. g., on the railway-train, he points out of the
window with a troubled look. The understanding of
words heard is, again, in general more easy. The child
for the most part obeys at once when I say, " drink, eat,
shut, open, pick it up, turn around, sit, run !" Only
the order "come!" is not so promptly executed, not,
however, on account of lack of understanding, but from

willfulness. That the word-memory is becoming firm
is indicated particularly by the circumstance that now
the separate parts of the face and body are pointed out,
even after pretty long intervals, quickly and upon request, on his own person and that of others. When I
asked about his beard, the child (after having already
pointed to my beard), in visible embarrassment, pointed
with his forefinger to the place on his face corresponding to that where he saw the beard on mine, and moved
his thumb and forefinger several times as if he were
holding a hair of the beard between them and pulling
at it, as he had had opportunity to do with mine. Here,
accordingly, memory and imagination came in as supplementary to satisfy the demand made by the acoustic
image.

The greatest progress is to be recorded in this month
in regard to the reproduction of syllables and words. A
perfecting of the process is apparent in the fact that
when anything is said for him to repeat, his head is not
turned away in unwillingness so often as before, in case
the new word said to him is too difficult, nor are all
sorts of incoherent, complicated sounds (*paterateratte*)
given forth directly upon the first failure of the attempt
at imitation. Thus, the following words were at this
period, without systematic exercises, incidentally picked
up (give, as before, the German pronunciation to the letters):

Spoken to him.	Reproduced.	Spoken to him.	Reproduced.
Ohr,	*Oa(r)*.	Wasser,	*Wass, Watja.*
Tisch,	*Tiss.*	Hand,	*Hann.*
Haus,	*Hausesess.*	Heiss,	*Haïss.*
Hemd,	*Hem.*	Auge,	*Autschge.*
Peitsche,	*Paitsch, Paitse.*	Butter,	*Buotö.*

Spoken to him.	Reproduced.	Spoken to him.	Reproduced.
Eimer,	*Aïma.*	Alle,	*Alla.*
Bitte,	*Bete, Bite.*	Leier,	*Laijai.*
Blatt,	*Batn.*	Mund,	*Munn.*
Tuch,	*Tuhs.*	Finger,	*Finge.*
Papier,	*Patn, Paï.*	Pferd,	*Pfowed, Fowid.*
Fort,	*Wott.*	Gute Nacht,	*Nag-ch Na.*
Vater,	*Fa-ata.*	Guten Tag,	*Tatách.*
Grete,	*Deete.*	Morgen,	*Moigjen.*
Karl,	*Kara.*	Axel,	*Akkes, Aje, Eja.*

The four words, *Paitsch* or *Paitse, Bite, Waïja,* and *Haïss,* are uttered now and then by the child without being said to him, and their use has regard to the meaning contained in them. His whip and his pail he learned to name quickly and correctly. His own name, Axel, on the contrary, he designates by the favorite interjections *Aje, Eja.* On the whole, variety of articulation is on the increase as compared with the previous month, but the ability to put syllables together into words is still but little developed. Thus, e. g., the child reproduces quite correctly " je," and " ja," and " na." But if any one says to him " Jena " or " Jana," the answer runs regularly *nena* or *nana,* and only exceptionally, as if by chance, *jena.* Further, he repeats correctly the syllables " bi" and " te " when they are given to him, and then also *bi-te ;* afterward, giving up the correct imitation, he says *beti,* but can not reproduce *ti-be* or *tebi.* " Bett, Karre, Kuk," are correctly repeated.

Finally, echolalia, not observed of late, appears again. If the child hears some one speak, he often repeats the last syllable of the sentence just finished, if the accent were on it—e. g., " What said the man ?"

man; or " Who is there?" *there?* "Nun?" (now) *nou*
(*noo*). Once the name "Willy" was called. Immediately the child likewise called *ŭilē*, with the accent on the
last syllable, and repeated the call during an hour several dozens of times; nay, even several days later he entertained himself with the stereotyped repetition. Had
not his first echo-play produced great merriment, doubtless this monotonous repetition would not have been
kept up. In regard to the preference of one or another
word the behavior of those about the child is not merely
influential, but is alone decisive. I observed here, as I
had done earlier, that urgent exhortations to repeat a
new word have generally a much worse result than is
obtained by leaving the child to himself. The correct,
or at any rate the best, repetitions were those made
when the child was not spoken to. Even adults can
imitate others in their manner of speaking, their dialect, even their voice, much better when not called upon
to do it, but left entirely to their own inclination. The
wish or command of others generates an embarrassment
which disturbs the course of the motor processes. I re-
solved, consequently, to abandon in the following month
all attempts to induce the child to reproduce sounds,
but to observe so much the more closely what he might
say of his own accord.

In the last month of the second year of his life this
leaving of him to himself proved fruitful in results to
this extent—that voluntary sound-imitations gained considerably in frequency and accuracy. Particularly,
genuine echolalia manifested itself more at this period
in the repeating of the last syllables of sentences heard,
the meaning of which remained unintelligible to the

child; and of single words, the sense of which became
gradually clear to him by means of accompanying gestures. Thus, the word "Herein!" (Come in!) was repeated as an empty sound, and then *arein, harrein, ha-
arein,* were shouted strenuously toward the door, when
the child wanted to be let in; *ab* (off) was uttered when
a neck-ribbon was to be loosened. *Moigen* signified
"Guten Morgen!" *na,* "Gute Nacht!" To the question, "Was thun wir morgen?" (What shall we do to-
morrow?) comes the echo-answer *moigen.* In general,
by far the greater part of the word-imitations are much
distorted, to strangers often quite unintelligible. *Ima* and
Imam mean "Emma," *dakkngaggngaggn* again means
"danke," and *betti* still continues to signify "bitte."
Only with the utmost pains, after the separate syllables
have been frequently pronounced, appear *dangēē* and
bittēē. An apple (Apfel) is regularly named *apfelēēlēē*
(from Apfelgelée); a biscuit (Zwieback), *wita,* then
wijak; butter, on the contrary, is often correctly named.
Instead of "Jawohl," the child almost invariably says
wolja; for "Licht" *list* and *lists;* for "Wasser," *watja*
still as before; for "pfui" he repeats, when he has been
awkward, *ūi,* and often adds a *pott* or *putt* in place of
"caput." "Gut" is still pronounced *ūt* or *tut,* and
"fort," *okk* or *ott.* All the defects illustrated by these
examples are owing rather to the lack of flexibility in
the apparatus of articulation—even stammering, *tit-t-t-t,*
in attempting to repeat "Tisch," appears—than to imperfect ability to apprehend sounds. For the deficiency
of articulation shows itself plainly when a new word
is properly used, but pronounced sometimes correctly
and sometimes incorrectly. Thus, the "tsch" hitherto

13

not often achieved (twentieth month), and the simple "sch" in *witschi* and *wesch*, both signifying "Zwetschen," are imperfect, although both sounds were long ago well understood as commands to be silent, and Zwetschen (plums) have been long known to the child. Further, the inability to reproduce anything is still expressed now and then by *rateratcratera;* the failure to understand, rather by a peculiar dazed expression of countenance, with an inquiring look.

With regard to the independent application of all the words repeated, in part correctly, in part with distortions, a multiplicity of meanings is especially noteworthy in the separate expressions used by the child. The primitive word *atta*, used with uncommon frequency, has now among others the following significations: "I want to go; he is gone; she is not here; not yet here; no longer here; there is nothing in it; there is no one there; it is empty; it is nowhere; out there; go out." To the question "Where have you been?" the child answers, on coming home, *atta*, and when he has drunk all there was in the glass, he likewise says *atta*. The concept common to all the interpretations adduced, "gone," seems to be the most comprehensive of all that are at the child's disposal. If we choose to regard a word like this *atta* as having the force of a whole sentence, we may note many such primitive sentences in this month. Thus, *mann* means, on one occasion, "A man has come," then almost every masculine figure is named *mann; auff*, accompanied with the offering of a key, signifies the wish for the opening of a box, and is cried with animation after vain attempts to open a watch. The concepts "male being" and "open" are thus not only clear, but are already named with the right words. The distinguishing of men from women appears for months past very strikingly in this, that the former only are greeted by reaching out the hand. The manifold meaning of a single word used as a sentence is shown particularly in the cry of *papa*, with gestures and looks corresponding to the different meanings of it. This one word, when called out to his father, means (1) "Come play with me"; (2) "Please lift me up"; (3) "Please give me that"; (4) "Help me get up on the chair"; (5) "I can't," etc.

The greatest progress, however, is indicated by the *combination of two words* into a sentence. The first sentence of this sort, spoken on the seven hundred and seventh day of his life at the sight of the house that was his home, was *haim, mimi,* i. e., "I would like to go home and drink milk." The second was *papa, mimi,* and others were similar. Contrasted with these first efforts at the framing of sentences, the earlier meaningless monologues play only a subordinate part; they become, as if they were the remains of the period of infancy, gradually rudimentary: thus, *pipapapaï, breit, laraï.* A more important fact for the recognition of progress in speaking is that the words are often *confounded*, e. g., *watja* and *buotö* (for *butter*). In gestures also and in all sorts of performances there are bad cases of confusion almost every day; e. g., the child tries to put on his shoes, holding them with the heel-end to his toes, and takes hold of the can out of which he pours the milk into his cup by the lip instead of the handle. He often affirms in place of denying. His joy is, however, regularly expressed by loud laughing and very high tones; his grief by an extraordinarily deep depression of the angles of the mouth and by weeping. Quickly as this expression of countenance may pass over into a cheerful one—often on a sudden, in consequence of some new impression—no confusion of *these* two *mimetic* movements takes place.

In the first month of the third year of life the progress is extraordinary, and it is only in regard to the articulatory mechanism that no important new actions are to be recorded. The child does not pronounce a perfect "u," or only by chance. Generally the lips are not enough protruded, so that "u" becomes "ou"; "Uhr" and "Ohr" often sound almost the same. The "i" also is frequently mixed with other vowel-sounds, particularly with "e." Probably the corners of the mouth are not drawn back sufficiently. With these exceptions the vowels of the German language now offer hardly any difficulties. Of the consonants, the "sch" and "cht" are often imperfect or wanting. "Waschtisch" is regularly pronounced *waztiz*, and "Gute Nacht" *gna*.

The sound-imitations of every kind are more manifold, eager, and skillful than ever before. Once the child even made a serious attempt to reproduce ten words spoken in close succession, but did not succeed. The attempt proves all the same that the word-imitation is now far beyond the lower echo-speech; yet he likes to repeat the last words and syllables of sentences heard by him even in the following months. Here belongs his saying *so* when any object is brought to the place appointed for it. When the reproduction is defective, the child shows himself to be now much more amenable to correction. He has become more teachable. At the beginning of the month he used to say, when he wanted to sit, *ette*, then *etse*, afterward *itse;* but he does not yet in the present month say " setzen " or " sitzen." Hitherto he could repeat correctly at the utmost two words said for him. Now he repeats three, and once even four, imperfectly : *papa, beene, delle,* means " Papa, Birne, Teller," and is uttered glibly ; but " Papa, Birne, Teller, bitte," or " Papa, Butter, bitte," is not yet re-peated correctly, but *pata, butte, betti,* and the like ; only very seldom, in spite of almost daily trial, *papa, beene, delle, bittee.*

Evidence of the progress of the memory, the under-standing, and the articulation, is furnished in the an-swers the child gave when I asked him, as I touched va-rious objects, " What is that ? "   He replied :

Autse,	for	Auge (eye).	*Hai,*	for	Haar (hair).
Nana,	"	Nase (nose).	*Uller,*	"	Schulter (shoulder).
Ba,	"	Backe (back).	*Aam,*	"	Arm (arm).
Baat,	"	Bart (beard).	*Ann,*	"	Hand (hand).
Oë, Oa,	"	Ohr (ear).	*Wiër,*	"	Finger (finger).
Opf,	"	Kopf (head).	*Daima,*	"	Daumen (thumb).
Tenn,	"	Kinn (chin).	*Anu,*	"	Handschuh (glove).
Täne,	"	Zähne (teeth).	*Bain,*	"	Bein (leg).

But not one word has the child himself invented. When a new expression appears it may be surely traced to what has been heard, as *uppe, oppee, appee, appei,* to " Suppe."   The name alone by which he calls on his nurse, *wolá*, seemed hard to explain.   If any one says, " Call Mary," the child invariably calls *wolá*.   It is probable, as he used to call it *wolja*, that the appellation has its origin in the often-heard " ja wohl."

The correct use of single words, picked up, one

might say, at random, increases in a surprising manner.
Here belong *baden*, *reiputtse*, for " Reissuppe," *la-ock*
for " Schlafrock," *boter* for " Butter," *Butterbrod*, *Uhr*,
Buch, *Billerbooch* for " Bilderbuch." In what fashion
such words now incorporated into the child's vocabulary
are employed is shown by the following examples: *Tul*
(for " Stuhl") means—(1) " I should like to be lifted up
on the chair ; (2) My chair is gone ; (3) I want this chair
brought to the table ; (4) This chair doesn't stand right."
If the chair or other familiar object is broken, then it
is still styled *putt* (for " caput," gone to smash) ; and
if the child has himself broken anything he scolds
his own hand, and says *oi* or *oui*, in place of " pfui "
(fie) ! He wants to write to his grandmother, and asks
for *Papier*, a *daitipf* (for " Bleistift," pencil), and says
raiwe (for " schreiben," write).

That misunderstandings occur in such beginnings of
speech seems a matter of course. All that I observed,
however, were from the child's standpoint rational.
Some one says, " Schlag das Buch auf " (Open the book,
but meaning literally " Strike upon the book "), and the
child strikes upon the book with his hands without
opening it. He does the same when one says, " Schlag
auf das Buch" (Strike upon the book). Or we say,
" Will you come? one, two!" and the child, without
being able to count, answers, " Three, four." He has
merely had the sequence 1, 2, 3, 4, said over to him frequently. But, on the whole, his *understanding* of words
heard, particularly of commands, has considerably advanced ; and how far the reasoning faculty has developed
is now easily seen in his independent designations for
concepts. For example, since his delight at gifts of all

sorts on his birthday, he says *burtsa* (for Geburtstag, birthday) when he is delighted by anything whatever. Another instance of childish induction was the following : The child's hand being slightly hurt, he was told to blow on his hand and it would be better. He did blow on his hand. In the afternoon he hit his head against something, and he began at once to blow of his own accord, supposing that the blowing would have a soothing effect, even when it did not reach the injured part.

In the forming of sentences considerable progress is to be recorded. Yet only once has the child joined more than four words in a sentence, and rarely three. His sentences consisting of two words, which express a fact of the present or of the immediate past, are often, perhaps generally, quite unintelligible to strangers. Thus, *danna kuha* signifies " Aunt has given me cake " ; *Kaffee naïn*, " There is no coffee here " ; and *mama etsee* or *etse* is intelligible only by means of the accompanying gesture as the expression of the wish, " Mamma, sit by me." *Helle pumme* signifies the wish to help (*helfen*) in pumping, and is uttered at the sight of persons pumping water.

The following sentence consisting of five words is particularly characteristic of this period, because it exhibits the first attempt to relate a personal experience. The child dropped his milk-cup and related *mimi atta teppa papa oï*, which meant " Milch fort [auf den] Teppich, Papa [sagte] pfui." (Milk gone [on] carpet, Papa [said] " Fie !") The words adopted by the child have often a very different meaning from that which they have in the language of adults, being not entirely misunderstood but peculiarly interpreted by the imitator. Thus, pronouns, which are not for a long time yet understood in their true sense, signify objects themselves or their qualities. *Dein bett* means " the large bed."

In the twenty-sixth month a large picture-book, with good colored pictures, was shown to the child by me every day. Then he himself would point out the separate objects represented, and those unknown to him were named to him, and then the words were repeated by him. Thus were obtained the following results:

Said to him.	His imitation.
Blasebalg (bellows),	*ba-a-bats, blasabalitz.*
Saugflasche (nursing-bottle),	*augflaze.*
Kanone (cannon),	*nanone.*
Koffer (trunk),	*towwer, toffer, pfoffa, poffa, toff-wa.*
Fuchs (fox),	*fuhts.*
Kaffeekanne (coffee-urn),	*taffeetanne, pfafee-tanne.*
Frosch (frog),	*frotz.*
Klingel (bell),	*linli* (learned as *ingeling* and *linlin*).
Besen (broom),	*bēsann, beedsen, beedsenn.*
Stiefel (boot),	*tiefel, stibbell, tihbell, tibl.*
Nest (nest),	*netz.*
Storch (stork),	*toich.*
Giesskanne (watering-pot),	*tietstanne, ihtstanne, ziesstanne.*
Fisch (fish),	*fiz.*
Zuckerhut (sugar-loaf),	*ukkahut.*
Vogel (bird),	*wodal.*
Kuchen (cake),	*tuche, tuchēn* (hitherto *kuha*).
Licht (light),	*lihts, lits.*
Schlitten (sled),	*lila, litta.*
Tisch (table),	*tiss.*
Nuss (nut),	*nuhuss, nuss.*
Kaffeetopf (coffee-pot),	*poffee-topf.*
Hund (dog),	*und.*
Brief (letter),	*dief.*
Elephant,	*elafant.*
Fledermaus (bat),	*lebamaunz, fleedermauz.*
Kamm (comb),	*damm, lamm, namm.*
Schwalbe (swallow),	*baubee.*
Staar (starling),	*tahr.*

Of his own accord the child pointed out with certainty in the picture-book—

häm, hä-em, hemm for	Helm (helmet).
hörz	" Hirsch (stag).
tawell	" Tafel (table).
lompee, lampé	" Lampe (lamp).
lotz	" Schloss (castle).
benne	" Birne (pear).
torb	" Korb (basket).
onne-erm	" Sonnenschirm (parasol).
flatse	" Flasche (bottle).
wetsa	" Zwetschen (plums).
clawelier	" Clavier (piano).
littl, litzl, lützl	" Schlüssel (key).
löwee	" Löwe (lion).
ofa	" Ofen (stove).
ūă	" Uhr (watch).
tint, kint	" Kind (child).
naninchä	" Kaninchen (rabbit).
manne	" Pfanne (pan).
tomml, tromml	" Trommel (drum).
tuhl	" Stuhl (chair).

With these words, the meaning of which the child knows well, though he does not yet pronounce them perfectly, are to be ranked many more which have not been taught him, but which he has himself appropriated Thus, *tola* for Kohlen (coals), *dals* for Salz (salt). Other words spontaneously appropriated are, however, already pronounced correctly and correctly used, as *Papier* (paper), *Holz* (wood), *Hut* (hat), *Wagen* (carriage), *Teppich* (carpet), *Deckel* (cover), *Milch, Teller* (often *tellĕ*), *Frau, Mann, Mäuse.* These cases form the minority, and are striking in the midst of the manifold mutilations which now constitute the child's speech. Of these mutilations some are, even to his nearest relatives who

are in company with the child every day, unintelligible
or only with great pains to be unriddled. Thus, the
child calls himself *Attall* instead of Axel; says also
rräus Atsl for "heraus Axel," i. e., "Axel wants to
go out." He still says *bita* for " bitte," and often *mima*
or *mami* for Marie; *apf* for "Apfel." The numerous
mutilations of the words the child undertakes to speak
are not all to be traced to defect of articulation. The
" sch " is already perfectly developed in *Handschuh;*
and yet in other words, as appears from the above examples, it is either simply left out or has its place supplied by *z* and *ss*. Further, it sounds almost like wantonness when frequently the surd consonant is put in
place of the sonant one or *vice versa;* when, e. g.,
puch (for Buch) *pücherr* is said on the one hand, and
wort instead of " fort " on the other. Here belongs
likewise the peculiar staccato manner of uttering the
syllables, e. g., *pil-ter-puch* (Bilder-buch—picture-book).
At other times is heard a hasty *billerbuch* or *piller-
puch.*

The babbling monologues have become infrequent
and more of a play with words and the syllables of
them, e. g., in the frequently repeated *papa-ŭ-á-ŭa.*

On the other hand, independent thoughts expressed
by words are more and more multiplied. Here is an
example : The child had been extraordinarily pleased
by the Christmas-tree. The candles on it had been
lighted for three evenings. On the third evening,
when only one of its many lights was burning, the child
could not leave it, but kept taking a position before it
and saying with earnest tone, *gunná-itz-boum,* i. e.,
" Gute nacht, Christbaum ! " The most of his sentences

still consist of two words, one of which is often a verb
in the infinitive.   Thus, *helle mama, helle mami,* i. e.,
" helfen (help) Mama, Marie! " and *bibak tommen,* i. e.,
" der Zwieback soll kommen " (let the biscuit come);
or *tsee machen* (make *c*)—on the piano the keys *c, d, e,*
had often been touched separately by the little fingers
accidentally, and the applause when in response to the
question, " Where is *c ?* " the right key was touched,
excited the wish for repetition; *roth, drün machen*
(make red or green)—the child was instructed by me in
the naming of colors; and *dekkn pilen,* i. e., " Ver-
stecken spielen " (play hide and seek).   In quite short
narratives, too, the verbs appear in the infinitive only.
Such accounts of every-day occurrences—important to
the child, however, through their novelty—are in general falling into the background as compared with the
expression of his wishes in words as in the last-mentioned cases.   Both kinds of initiatory attempts at speaking testify more and more plainly to awakening intellect, for, in order to use a noun together with a verb
in such a way as to correspond to a wish or to a fact
experienced, there must be added to the imitation of
words heard and to the memory of them something
which adapts the sense of them to the outward experiences at the time and the peculiar circumstances, and associates them with one another.   This something is the
intellect.   In proportion as it grows, the capacity for
being taught tricks decreases and the child is already
ashamed to answer by means of his former gestures the
old questions, " Where is the little rogue ? " " How
tall ? " etc.

But how far from the intellect of the older child is

that of the child now two years and two months old appears from this fact, that the latter has not the remotest notion of number. He repeats mechanically, many times over, the words said for him, *one, two, three, four, five ;* but when objects of the same sort are put before him in groups, he confounds all the numbers with one another in spite of countless attempts to bring the number 2 into firm connection' with the sound two, etc. Nor does he as yet understand the meaning of the frequently repeated " danke " (thanks), for, when the child has poured out milk for himself, he puts down the pitcher and says *dankee.*

One more remark is to be made about the names of animals. These names are multiplying in this period, which is an important one in regard to the genesis of mind. Ask, " What is the animal called ? " and the answer runs, *mumu, kikeriki, bauwau, piep-piep,* and others. No trace of onomatopoetic attempts can be discovered here. The child has received the names pronounced to him by his nurse and has retained them ; just so *hotto* for " Pferd " (horse), like *lingeling* for " Klingel " (bell). None the less every healthy child has a strong inclination to onomatopeia. The cases already reported prove the fact satisfactorily. The echolalia that still appears now and then really belongs to this. Inasmuch as in general in every onomatopoetic attempt we have to do with a sound-imitation or the reproducing of the oscillations of the tympanum as nearly as possible by means of the vocal cords, all attempts of the speechless child to speak are ultimately of onomatopoetic character in the earliest period ; but from the present time on sound-imitation retires before

the reasoning activity, which is now shooting forth vigorously in the childish brain.

In the twenty-seventh month the activity of thought
manifests itself already in various ways. The independent ideas, indeed, move in a narrowly limited
sphere, but their increasing number testifies to the
development of the intellect. Some examples may be
given :

The child sees a tall tree felled, and he says as it
lies upon the ground, *pick up!* Seeing a hole in a
dressing-gown, he says, *näĕn* (sew)! In his play he
sometimes says to himself, *dib acht* (take care)! To the
question, " Did it taste good ? " the child answers while
still eating, *mekk noch* (schmeckt noch), " It *does* taste
good," thus distinguishing the past in the question from
the present. The development of observation and *comparison* is indicated by the circumstance that salt is
also called *sand*. On the other hand, the feeling of
gratitude is as yet quite undeveloped. The child, as in
the previous month, says *dankee* to himself when, e. g.,
he has opened his wardrobe-door alone. The word is
thus as yet unintelligible to him, or it is used in the
sense of " so " or " succeeded." His frequent expressions of pity are striking. When dolls are cut out of
paper, the child weeps violently in the most pitiful manner, for fear that in the cutting a head (*Topf*) may be
taken off. This behavior calls to mind the cries of
arme wiebak (armer Zwieback—poor biscuit)! when a
biscuit is divided, and *arme holz* (poor wood)! when a
stick of wood is thrown into the stove. Nobody has
taught the child anything of that sort.

The independent observations which he expresses

correctly but very briefly in a form akin to the style of the telegraphic dispatch are now numerous, e. g.:

Tain milch : There is no milk here.

Lammee aus, lampee aus: The flame, the lamp, is gone out.

Dass la-okk: That is the dressing-gown (Schlafrock).

Diss nicht la-okk: This is not the dressing-gown.

His wishes the child expresses by means of *verbs* in the infinitive or of substantives alone. Thus, *papa auftehen* (papa, get up), *frü-tükken* (breakfast), *aus-taigen* (get out), *nicht blasen* (not blow—in building cardhouses), *pieldose aufziehn* (wind up the music-box), and *biback* (I should like a biscuit). Into these sentences of one, two, and three words there come, however, single adverbs not before used and indefinite pronouns, like *ēēn* and *ĕ* in *tann ēēn nicht* or *tannĕ nicht,* for " kann *er* nicht " or "kann *es* nicht." *Butter drauf* (butter on it), *Mama auch tommen* (mamma come, too), *noch mehr* (more), *blos Wasser* (only water), *hier* (here), are the child's own imperatives. *Schon wieder* (again) he does indeed say of his own accord on fitting occasions; but here he is probably repeating mechanically what he has heard. In all, the forming of a word that had not been heard as such, or that had not come from what had been heard through mutilation, has been surely proved in only a single instance. The child, viz., expressed the wish (on his seven hundred and ninety-sixth day) to have an apple pared or cut up, by means of the word *messen.* He knows a knife (Messer) and names it rightly, and while he works at the apple with a fork or a spoon or anything he can get hold of, or

merely points at it with his hand, he says repeatedly
messen ! Only after instruction did he say *Messer
neiden* (mit dem Messer schneiden—cut with the knife).
Here for the first time a wholly new word is formed.
The concept and the word "knife" ("Messer") and the
concept, "work with the knife," were present, but the
word "schneiden" (cut) for the last was wanting, as
also was "schälen" (pare). Hence, both in one were
named *messen* (for "messern," it may be). The two
expressions that used to be heard many times daily, the
name *wolà* for the nurse Mima (Mary) and *atta*, have
now almost disappeared. *Atta wesen* for "draussen
gewesen" (been out) is still used, it is true, but only
seldom. In place of it come now *weg, fort, aus*, and
allall, in the sense of "empty," "finished." The too
comprehensive, too indefinite concept *atta* has broken
up into more limited and more definite ones. It has
become, as it were, differentiated, as in the embryo the
separate tissues are differentiated out of the previously
apparently homogeneous tissue.

In the period of rapid development now attained,
the child daily surprises us afresh by his independent
applications of words just heard, although many are
not correctly applied, as *tochen haiss* (boiling hot), said
not only of the milk, but also of the fire.

When words clearly comprehended are used in a
different sense from that in which adults use them—
incorrectly used, the latter would say—there is, however, no *illogical* employment of them on the part of
the child. For it is always the fact, as in the last example, that the concept associated with the word is
taken in a more extended sense. The very young child

infers a law from a few, even from two observations, which present some agreement only in one respect, and that perhaps a quite subordinate respect. He makes inductions without deliberation. He has heard milk called " boiling hot," he feels its warmth, and then feels the warmth of the stove, consequently the stove also is " boiling hot"; and so in other cases. This logical activity, the *inductive* process, now prevails. The once favorite monologues, pure, meaningless exercises of articulation, of voice and of hearing, are, on the contrary, falling off. The frequent repetition of the same syllable, also of the same sentence (*lampee aus*), still survives particularly in animated expressions of wish, *erst essen* (first eat), *viel milch* (much milk), *mag-e-nicht* (don't like it). Desire for food and for playthings makes the child loquacious, much more than dislike does, the latter being more easily manifested by means of going away, turning around, turning away. The child can even beg on behalf of his carved figures of animals and men. Pointing out a puppet, he says *tint äin tikche apfl!* Für das kind *ein* Stückchen Apfel! (A bit of apple for the child.)

Notwithstanding these manifold signs of a use of words that is beginning to be independent, the sound and word imitation continues to exist in enlarged measure. Echolalia has never, perhaps, been more marked, the final words of sentences heard being repeated with the regularity of a machine. If I say, " Leg die Feder hin " (Lay the pen down)! there sounds in response a *feder hin*. All sorts of tones and noises are imitated with varying success; even the whistle of the locomotive, an object in which a passionate interest is displayed; the voices of animals; so also German, French, Italian, and English words. The French nasal " n " (in *bon, orange*), however—even in the following months—as well as the English " th," in *there* (in spite of the existence of the right formation in the fifteenth month), is not attained. The child still laughs regularly when others laugh, and on his part excites merriment through exact reproduction of separate fragments of a dialogue that he does not understand, and that does not concern him; e. g., *da hastn* (da hast Du ihn) (there you have him), or *aha siste* (siehst Du) (do you see)? or *um Gottes willen* (for God's sake), the accent in these cases being also imitated with precision. But in his independent use of words the accentuation varies in irregular fashion. Such an arbitrary variation is *bitté* and *bi-té*. *Beti* no longer appears.

As a noteworthy deficiency at this period is to be mentioned the feeble memory for often-prescribed answers to certain questions. To the question of a stranger, " What is your name?" the child for the first time gave of his own accord the answer *Attsell* (Axel), on the eight hundred and tenth day of his life. On the other hand, improper answers that have been seriously censured remain fixed in his recollection. The impression is stronger here. The weakness of memory is still shown most plainly when we try to make intelligible to the child the numerals one to five. It is a failure. The sensuous impression that *one* ball makes is so different from that which two balls make, the given words *one* and *two* sound so differently, that we can not help wondering how one and two, and likewise three, four, five, are confounded with one another.

14

A *question* has not yet been uttered by the child. The frequent *ist das* signifies merely " das ist," or it is the echo of the oft-heard question, " Was ist das ? " and is uttered without the tone of interrogation. The articles are not used at all yet; at any rate, if used, they are merely imitated without understanding.

The defects of articulation are now less striking, but only very slowly does the correct and distinct pronunciation take the place of the erroneous and indistinct. We still have regularly :

bücher-rank	for Bücherschrank (book-case).
fraï takkee	" Fräulein Starke (Miss Starke).
ērĕ, tseer	" Schere (shears).
raïbĕ, raiben	" Schreiben (u. Zeichnen) (write or draw).
nur	" Schnur (string).
neiderin	" Schneiderin (tailoress).
dsön (also *schön*)	" schön (pretty).
lafen	" schlafen (sleep).
pucken	" spucken (spit).
dsehen (also *sehen*)	" sehen (see).

The sounds " sch " and " sch " in the " st " as well as in the " sp " (" schneiden, Spiel ") are often omitted without any substitute (*naïdă, taign, piel*); more seldom their place is supplied by " s," as in *swer*=" schwer " for " müde." Yet *ks, ts* are often given with purity in *bex, bux, Axl*. The last word is often pronounced *Atsĕl* and *Atsli* (heard by him as " Axeli "), very rarely *Akkl* ; in " Aufziehen " the " z " is almost always correctly reproduced. Further, we still have

locotiwe for Locomotive.		*ann-nepf* for anknöpfen.	
nepf	" Knöpfe (buttons).	*nits*	" nichts (nothing).

" Milch " is now permanently named correctly ; no longer *mimi, mich ;* Wasser, *wassa*, no longer *watja*.

But "gefährlich" is called *fährlich;* "getrunken," *trunken.*

The twenty-eighth month is characterized by a rapid increase of activity in the formation of ideas, on the one hand, and by considerably greater certainty in the use of words, on the other. Ambition is developed and makes itself known by a frequent *laïnee (allein,* alone). The child wants to undertake all sorts of things without help. He asks for various objects interesting to him, with the words *Ding haben* (have the thing). That the faculty of observation and of combination is becoming perfected, is indicated by the following: The child sees an ox at the slaughter-house and says *mumu* (moo-moo); I add "todt" (dead); thereupon comes the response *mumu todt,* and after a pause the child says, of his own accord, *lachtett (geschlachtet,* slaughtered); then *Blut heraus* (blood out). The beginning of self-control is perceived in this, that the child often recollects, of himself, the strict commands he has received to refrain from this and that. Thus, he had been accustomed to strike members of the family in fun, and this had been forbidden him. Now, when the inclination seizes him still to strike, he says emphatically *nicht lagen (schlagen,* —not strike), *Axel brav* (good). In general the child names himself only by his name, which he also tells to strangers without being asked. His parents, and these alone, are mostly named *Papa* and *Mama,* but often also by their names.

The following is a proof of independent thinking while the understanding of language is still imperfect : At breakfast I say, "Axel is breakfasting with papa, is he not *(nicht wahr)* ? " He replies earnestly, with genuine child-logic, *doch wahr* (but he *is*)!

The earlier appellation *swer* and *wer* (schwer—heavy) for müde (tired) is preserved. This transference, like the other one, *locotiwe wassa trinkt*, when the engine is supplied with water, is the intellectual peculium of the child. The number of such childish conceptions has now become very large. On the other hand, the words independently formed out of what has been heard are not numerous:

beisst	for gebissen (bitten),	*wesen*	for gewesen (been),
reit	" geritten (ridden),	*austrinkt*	" ausgetrunken (drunk up),
esst	" gegessen (eaten),	*tschulter*	" Schulter (shoulder),

must be considered as mutilations, not as new formations. The great number of words correctly pronounced and used continues, on the other hand, to increase. There are even decided attempts to use single *prepositions: Nepfe* (Knöpfe) *für Mama* (buttons for mamma) may be simple repetition, like *Axel mit Papa;* but as utterances of this kind were not formerly repeated by him, though just as often made in his hearing, the understanding of the " für " and " mit " must now be awakened. From this time forth the understanding of several prepositions and the correct use of them abide. In addition there come into this period the first applications of the *article.* However often this part of speech may have been reproduced from the speech of others, it has never been said with understanding; but now in the expressions *um'n Hals* and *für'm Axel* (around the neck and for (the) Axel) there lies the beginning of right use of the article, and, indeed, also in the months immediately succeeding, almost solely of the definite article.

But more significant psychogenetically than all progress of this kind in the manipulation of language is the questioning that becomes active in this month. Although I paid special attention to this point from the beginning, I first heard the child ask a question of his own accord on the eight hundred and forty-fifth day of his life. He asked, "Where is Mima?" From that time on questions were more frequent; but in the time immediately following this his question was always one relating to something in space. The word "Where?" continued for a long time to be his only interrogative. He has also for a long time understood the "Where?" when he heard it. If, e. g., I asked, "Where is the nose?" without giving any hint by look or otherwise, this question has for months past been correctly answered by a movement of the child's arm to his nose. It is true that my question, "What is that?" a much more frequent one, is likewise answered correctly, although the word "What?" has never been used by the child.

His cleverness in reproducing even foreign expressions is surprising. The words pronounced for him by Italians (during a pretty long sojourn on Lake Garda), e. g., *uno, due, tre,* are given back without the least German accent. "Quattro," to be sure, became *wattro,* but *ancora piccolo* was absolutely pure. The imitation of the marching of soldiers, with the frequent cry *batelón eins sŭai* (battalion, one, two), already gives him the greatest pleasure. The imagination that is active in it is to be discerned, however, rather in gestures than in words. How lively the child's power of imagination is appears also in the fact that flat figures rudely cut out of newspaper, to represent glasses and cups, are carried to the mouth like real ones.

The *articulation* has again become a little more perfected, but in many respects it is still a good deal deficient; thus, in regard to the " sch," he says:

abneiden	for	abschneiden (cut off).
hirn	"	Stirn (forehead).
verbrochen	"	versprochen (promised).
lagn	"	schlagen (strike).
runtergeluckt	"	heruntergeschluckt (swallowed).
einteign	"	einsteigen (get in).

On the other hand, *aus-teign* (Aussteigen) (alight).

Other defects of articulation are shown by the following examples:

topf	for	klopfen (knock).
üffte	"	lüften (take the air).
leben	"	kleben (adhere).
viloa, viloja,	"	Viola.
dummi	"	Gummi (gum).

The *l mouillé* can not be at all successfully given at the beginning of this month (*batĕlōn* for " bataillon "), and the nasal sounds in " orange " and " salon " offer insuperable difficulties (up to the second half of the fourth year). At the end of this month, however, I heard a *ganzee bataljohn* (*j* like English *y*). " Orange " continued to be, after *oraanjee* had been given up, *or-ohsĕ*. The softening (mouilliren—*nj* = *ñ*) was inconvenient in this case.

Quite correctly named at this period were eye, nose, cheek, tongue, mouth, ear, beard, hair, arm, thumb, finger.

Meaningless chatter has become much more rare. On the other hand, the child is in the habit of making all sorts of remarks, especially in the morning early after waking, for a quarter of an hour at a time and longer without interruption, these remarks for the most part consisting of a noun and verb and relating to objects immediately about him. Monologues also are given in a singing voice, syllables without meaning, often a regular singing, the child meantime running many times around the table; besides, his strong voice is not seldom practiced in producing high tones without any outward occasion; and, finally, it is worthy of note that sometimes in sleep, evidently when the child has a vivid dream, a scream is uttered. Talking in his sleep first appeared in his fourth year.

The greatest advance in the twenty-ninth month consists in the employment of the personal pronoun in place of his own name: *bitte gib mir Brod* (please give me bread) was the first sentence in which it appeared. "Ich" (I) is not yet said, but if I ask "Who is 'me'?" then the child names himself with his own name, as he does in general. Through this employment, more and more frequent from this time forth, of the pronoun instead of the proper name, is gradually introduced the inflection of the verbs he has heard; but at this time the imperative has its place generally supplied by the infinitive: *Păpă sāgn* and *Ssooss sitzen.* Sentences composed by himself, or heard and then used by him, like *das meckt* (schmeckt) *sehr gut* (that tastes very good), are rare; yet the discrimination between regular and irregular verbs has already begun to be made. To be sure, the question "Where have you been?" is answered with *paziren gegeht* (goed to walk), and *ausge-zieht* is said for *ausgezogen* (drawed out), also *geseht* (seed) instead of *gesehen* (seen); but at the same time frequently *eingetigen* and *ausgetigen*, instead of *ein-* and *aus-geteigt*. An interesting, rare misformation was *grefessen* for " gefressen." The verbs most frequently used seem to be " haben" (have) and " kommen " (come), and the forms "hat " and " kommt " are indeed correctly used sometimes, e. g., *viel Rauch kommt heraus* (much smoke comes out), and *gleich kommt Kaffee* (the coffee is coming). While the infinitives "haben " and " kommen " are uttered several times a day, the infinitive " sein " (to be) is never heard; but of this auxiliary verb "ist" and "wesen " are used, the lat-ter for "gewesen." In every instance where the child expresses a desire by means of a verb, he simply takes the infinitive; e. g., he hears, as he sits in the room, the noise of the railway-train at a distance, and he says, *Locotiwe sehen.*

Further, *numbering* begins to be active to a note-worthy degree. Although the numerals are already well known to the child, he still confounds them on all occa-sions, and in view of the absolute failure of the many attempts to teach the child the significance of the num-bers 1, 2, 3, 4, 5, one might infer that he has not yet perceived the difference between, e. g., 3 matches and 4 matches; yet counting is already taking place, though in very unexpected fashion. The child began, viz., on the eight hundred and seventy-eighth day, suddenly, of his own accord entirely, to count with his nine-pins, put-ting them in a row, saying with each one, *eins* (one)! *eins! eins! eins!* afterward saying *eins! noch eins* (one more)! *noch eins! noch eins!* The process of adding is thus performed without the naming of the sums.

The questioning that appeared in the previous month, the surest sign of independent thought in the child, is somewhat more plainly manifest; but "Where" alone serves as the interrogative word, and that in its proper sense: Where is hat? "Which, who, why, when" are not spoken by the child and doubtless not understood, for, although succession in time is in many cases clear to him ("first cat," "then," "now"), yet in many other cases he does not know how to express distinctions of time; just as in comparing many and few, large and small objects, the quantity is wrongly given. Thus he says correctly, when many counters are to be brought together, *Zuviel* (too many), but says *Zuviel* wrongly for *Zuwenig* (too little) when there is too little butter on his bread. In this case the *Zuviel* (too much) sounds almost like irony, which, of course, is out of the question at his age. "Too much" and "too little" are confounded in the same way as 5 and 2. Yet, in another respect the memory has made a considerable gain. Expressions long since forgotten by those about the child are suddenly without assignable occasion sometimes uttered again with perfect distinctness, and the child even applies fitly what he has observed. Thus, he brings matches when he sees that some one wants to light a candle. I say to him, "Pick up the bread-crumbs." Upon this the child comes forward, though very slowly, cries out suddenly, *Get broom*, recollecting that he has seen the carpet swept, goes and gets the broom, and sweeps the crumbs away.

His memory for the utterances of animals as they have been made for him is very good. If I ask, e. g., " What does the duck say ? " the answer is *Kuak kuak*. He has gained also in certainty in naming the separate parts of a drawing, especially of a locomotive, so that one chief condition of speech, in the full sense of the word —memory—may be said to be well developed.

Articulation, on the contrary, makes slow progress. " Hirsch " is called *Hirss*, " Schwalbe" *Walbe*, "Flasche" *Flassee*. The following are generally correctly pronounced : *Treppe, Fenster, Krug, Kraut, Kuchen, Helm, Besen, Cigarre, Hut, Giesskanne, Dinte, Buch, Birne.* For " barometer, thermometer," he says *mometer,* for " Schrauben " *raubn,* for " frühstücken " (to breakfast) still often *fri-ticken.*

In the *thirtieth month* the independent activity of thought develops more and more. When the child is playing by himself, e. g., he often says to himself: *Eimerchen ausleeren* (make pail empty); *Hackemesser* (chopping-knife). Thus his small vocabulary serves him at any rate for making clear his own ideas. Already his thinking is often a low speaking, yet only in part. When language fails him, he first considers well. An example : The child finds it very difficult to turn crosswise or lengthwise one of the nine-pins which he wants to put into its box, and when I say, " Round the other way ! " he turns it around in such a way that it comes to lie as it did at the beginning, wrongly. He also pushes the broad side of the cover against the small end of the box. The child evidently understands the expression " Round the other way " ; but as the expression is ambiguous (the head of the nine-pin may go to the left, to the right, up, down, back, forward), we can understand that the pin should be turned now one way and again another way, and even brought back to its original position. Then appears the child's own deliberation without words—without any speaking at all, low or loud—until after frequently repeated packing and unpacking hardly any hesitation is shown. Many utterances show how easily at this period objects that have only a slight resemblance to one another or only a few qualities in common are included in one concept. When a roasted apple is peeled, the child sees the peel and says (thinking of his boiled milk, which he saw several hours previous, but which is not now present), *Milch auch Haut* (milk skin too). Similar is the expression *Kirche läutet* (church rings) when the tower-clock strikes.

The child forms concepts which comprehend a few qualities in unity, and indeed without designating the concept always by a particular word, whereas the developed understanding more and more forms concepts with many qualities and designates them by words. Hence the concepts of the child have less content and more extent than those of adults. For this reason they are less distinct also, and are often ephemeral, since they break up into narrower, more distinct concepts; but they always testify to activity of thought.

A greater intellectual advance, however, is manifested at this time in the first intentional use of language in order to bring on a game of hide-and-seek. A key falls to the floor. The child picks it up quickly, holds it behind him, and to my question, "Where is the key?" answers *nicht mehr da* (no longer there). As

I found in the following months no falsehood, in the
proper sense of the word, to record, but rather that the
least error, the most trivial exaggeration, was corrected
at once by the child himself, with peculiarly *naïve* seriousness, in a little story, with pauses between the separate words, so, too, in the present case the answer *nicht
mehr da* is no falsehood, but is to be understood as
meaning that the key is no longer to be seen. The expression of the face was roguish at the time.

The sole interrogative word continues still to be
" Where ? " e. g., *Where is ball ?* The demonstratives
da (there) and *dort* (yonder) (*dort ist nass*—wet) were
more frequently spoken correctly in answer.

The " I " in place of his own name does not yet appear, because this word does not occur frequently
enough in conversation with the child. The bad cus-
tom adults have of designating themselves in their talk
with little children, not as in ordinary conversation by
the word " I," but by the proper name, or as " aunt,"
" grandma," etc., postpones the time of saying " I " on
the part of children. *Me* is pretty often used at this
period, for the reason that it is frequently heard at meal-
times in " Give me ! "

Bitte, liebe Mama, gib mir mehr Suppe (Please, dear
mamma, give me more soup) is, to be sure, learned by
heart; but such sentences are at the proper time and
in the proper place modified and even independently
applied. *Noch mehr, immer noch mehr, vielleicht, fast*
(more, more yet, perhaps, almost), are also expressions
often properly employed, the last two, however, with
uncertainty still. *Fast gefallen* (almost fell) the child
says when he has actually fallen down.

Although declension and conjugation are as yet absolutely lacking, a transition has become established from the worst form of dysgrammatism to the beginning of correct diction by means of the more frequent use of the plural in nouns (*Rad, Räder*), the more frequent employment of the article (*för dĕ Papa*), the not very rare strong inflection (*gegangen* instead of the earlier *gegeht; genommen* instead of the earlier *genehmt*). To be sure, the infinitive still stands in the place of the participle and the imperative in by far the great majority of cases. The auxiliaries are often omitted or employed in strange misformations, e. g., "Where have you been?" Answer, *paziren gewarent* [something like *they wented 'all*] (wir waren spazieren, spazieren gewesen).

In *articulation* no perceptible progress is to be recorded. The objects known from the picture-book are indeed for the most part rightly named, but new ones often have their names very much distorted— e. g., "Violine" is persistently called *wilöine*. The "sch" is occasionally given correctly, but *s-trümpfe, auf-s-tehen* is the rule. The answer that has been learned to the question, "How old are you?" "Seit November zwei Jahre," is given *wember wai jahr*. The way in which the child learns the correct pronunciation is in general twofold : 1. Through frequent hearing of the correct words, since no one speaks as he himself does; thus, e. g., *genommen* took the place of *genehmt* without instruction. 2. Through having the words frequently pronounced on purpose for him to imitate with the utmost attention. Thus, e. g., the child up to this time always said *Locotiwe* and *Locopotiwe*. I exhorted him a few times earnestly to say "Locomotive." The result was *Loco-loco-loco-mo-tiwe*, and then *Locomotiwe*, with exact copying of the accent with which I spoke. Singing also is imitated.

His memory for words that denote objects is very good; but when expressions designating something not very apparent to the senses are to be learned, he easily fails. Thus, the left and the right foot or arm, the left and the right cheek or hand, are very often correctly named, but often falsely. The difference between left and right can not be exactly described, explained, or made imaginable to the child.

In the *thirty-first month* two new questions make their appearance: The child asks, *Welches Papier nehmen?* (What paper take?) after he has obtained permission to make marks with the pencil, i. e., to *raiben* (write and draw), and *Was kost die Trommel?* (What does the drum cost?)

Now the indefinite article appears oftener; it is distinctly audible in *Halt n biss-chen Wasser!* More surprising are individual new formations, which disappear, however, soon after their rise; thus, the comparative of " hoch." The child says with perfect distinctness *hocher bauen* (build higher) in playing with wooden blocks; he thus forms of himself the most natural comparative, like the participle *gegebt* for "gegeben." In place of "Uhrschlüssel" (watch-key) he says *Slüssl-Uhr* (key-watch), thus placing the principal thing first.

He makes use of the strange expression *heitgestern* in place of "heute" (to-day), and in place of "gestern" (yesterday). The two latter taken singly are confounded with each other for a long time yet.

Sentence-forming is still very imperfect: *is smoke* means "that is smoke" and "there is smoke"; and *kommt Locomotive* stands for "da kommt eine oder die Locomotive" (There comes a, or the, engine). At sight of the bath-tub, however, the child says six times in quick succession *Da kommt kalt Wasser rein, Marie* (Cold water is to go in here, Mary). He frequently makes remarks on matters of fact, e. g., *warm out there*. If he has broken a flower-pot, a bandbox, a glass, he says regularly, of his own accord, *Frederick glue again*, and he reports faithfully every little fault to his parents. But when a plaything or an object interesting to him vexes him, he says, peevishly, *stupid thing*, e. g., to the carpet, which he can not lift; and he does not linger long over one play. His occupation must be changed very often.

The imitations are now again becoming less frequent than in the past months, and expressions not understood are repeated rather for the amusement of the family than unconsciously; thus, *Ach Gott* (Oh God!) and *wirklich grossartig* (truly grand). Yet the child sometimes sings in his sleep, several seconds at a time, evidently dreaming.

The pronunciation of the "sch," even in the favorite succession of words, *Ganzes Batalljohn marss* (for "marsch") *eins, zwei*, is imperfect, and although no person of those about him pronounces the "st" in "Stall, stehen" otherwise than as "scht," the child keeps persistently to *S-tall, s-tehen*. The pronunciation "scht" began in the last six months of the fourth year of his life, and in the forty-sixth month it completely crowded out the "st," which seems the more remarkable as the child was taken care of by a Mecklenburg woman from the beginning of the fourth year.

In the *thirty-second month* the " I " began to displace his own name. *Mir* (*gib mir*) and *mich* (*bitte heb mich herauf*, please lift me up) had already appeared in the twenty-ninth to the thirty-first month; *ich komme gleich*, *Geld möcht ich haben* (I am coming directly, I should like money), are new acquirements. If he is asked " Who is *I?* " the answer is, *der Axel*. But he still speaks in the third person frequently; e. g., the child says, speaking of himself, *da ist er wieder* (here he is again), *Axel auch haben* (Axel have, too), and *mag-ĕ nicht*, thus designating himself at this period in fourfold fashion, by *I, he, Axel*, and by the omission of all pronouns and names. Although *bitte setz mich auf den Stuhl* (Please put me on the chair) is learned from hearing it said for him, yet the correct application of the sentence, which he makes of himself daily from this time on, must be regarded as an important advance. The same is true of the forming of clauses, which is now beginning to take place, as in *Weiss nicht, wo es ist* (Don't know where it is). New also is the separation of the particle in compound verbs, as in *fällt immer um* (keeps tumbling over).

Longer and longer names and sentences are spoken with perfect distinctness, but the influence of the dialect of the neighborhood is occasionally perceptible. His nurse is the one who talks most with him. She is from the Schwarzwald, and from her comes the omission of the " n " at the end of words, as in *Kännche, trocke*. Besides, the confounding of the surd, " p," with the sonant, " b " (*putter*), is so frequent that it may well be

taken from the Thuringian dialect, like the confounding of " eu " and " ei " (*heit*).   The only German
sounds that still present great difficulties are " sch " and
" chts " (in " nichts ").

The memory of the child has indeed improved, but
it has become somewhat fastidious.   Only that which
seems interesting and intelligible to the child impresses
itself permanently ; on the other hand, useless and unintelligible verses learned by rote, that persons have
taught him, though seldom, for fun, are forgotten after
a few days.

In the *thirty-third month* the strength of memory
already mentioned for certain experiences shows itself in many characteristic remarks.   Thus the child,
again absent from home with his parents for some
weeks, says almost every evening, *gleich blasen die
Soldaten* (the soldiers, i. e., the band, will play directly),
although no soldier is to be seen in the country far and
wide.   But at home the music was actually to be heard
every evening.

At sight of a cock in his picture-book the child says,
slowly, *Das ist der Hahn—kommt immer—das ganze
Stück fortnehmt — von der Hand — und laüft fort*
(" That is the cock—keeps coming—takes away the
whole piece—out of the hand—and runs off ").   This
narrative—the longest yet given, by the way—has reference to the feeding of the fowls, on which occasion
the cock had really carried off a piece of bread.   The
doings of animals in general excited the attention of
the child greatly.   He is capable even of forgetting
to eat, in order to observe assiduously the movements
of a fly.   *Jetzt geht in die Zeitung—geht in die Milch!*
15

Fort Thier! Geh fort! Unter den Kaffee! (Now
he is going into the newspaper—going into the milk!
Away, creature! go away! into the coffee!) His
interest is very keen for other moving objects also,
particularly locomotives.

How little clearness there is in his conceptions of
animal and machine, however, appears from the fact
that both are addressed in the same way. When his
father's brother comes, the child says, turning to his
father, *neuer* (new) *Papa;* he has not, therefore, the
slightest idea of that which the word " father " signifies.
Naturally he can have none. Yet selfhood (Ichheit) has
come forth at this period in considerably sharper manifestation. He cries, *Das Ding haben! das will ich,
das will ich, das will ich, das Spiel möcht ich haben!*
(Have the thing! I want it, I should like the game.)
To be sure, when one says " komm, ich knöpfs dir zu "
(come, I will button it for you), the child comes, and
says, as an echo, *ich knöpfs dir zu* (I will button it for
you), evidently meaning, " Button it for me "! He
also confounds *zu viel* (too much) with *zu wenig* (too
little), *nie* (never) with *immer* (always), *heute* (to-day)
with *gestern* (yesterday); on the contrary, the words
und, sondern, noch, mehr, nur, bis, wo (and, but, still,
more, only, till, where) are always used correctly. The
most striking mistakes are those of conjugation, which
is still quite erroneous (e. g., *getrinkt* and *getrunkt* along
with *getrunken*), and of articulation, the " sch " (*dsen*
for " schön ") being only seldom pure, mostly given as
" s " or " ts." " Toast " is called *Toos* and *Dose.*

After the first thousand days of his life had passed,
the observation of him was continued daily, but not the

record in writing. Some particulars belonging to the following months may be noted :

Many expressions accidentally heard by the child that excited the merriment of the family when once repeated by him, were rehearsed times without number in a laughing, roguish, obtrusive manner, thus, *du liebe Zeit.* The child also calls out the name of his nurse, *Marie,* often without meaning, over and over again, even in the night. He calls others also by this name in manifest distraction of mind, often making the correction himself when he perceives the mistake.

More and more seldom does the child speak of himself in the third person, and then he calls himself by his name, never saying "he" any more. Usually he speaks of himself as "I," especially "I will, I will have that, I can not." Gradually, too, he uses *Du* in address, e. g., *Was für hübsen Rock hast Du* (What a handsome coat you have)! Here the manner of using the "Was" is also new.

On the ten hundred and twenty-eighth day *warum* (why?) was first used in a question. I was watching with the closest attention for the first appearance of this word. The sentence ran, *Warum nach Hause gehen ? ich will nicht nach Hause* (Why go home? I don't want to go home). When a wheel creaked on the carriage, the child asked, *Was macht nur so* (What makes that) ? Both questions show that at last the instinct of causality, which manifested itself more than a year before in a kind of activity of inquiry, in experimenting, and even earlier (in the twelfth week) in giving attention to things, is expressed *in language ;* but the questioning is often repeated in a senseless way till

it reaches the point of weariness. *Warum wird das Holz
gesnitten ?* (for "gesägt"—Why is the wood sawed?)
Warum macht der Frödrich die [Blumen] Töpfe rein ?
(Why does Frederick clean the flower-pots?) are examples of childish questions, which when they receive an
answer, and indeed whatever answer, are followed by
fresh questions just as idle (from the standpoint of
adults); but they testify plainly to a far-reaching independent activity of thought. So with the frequent
question, *Wie macht man das nur ?* (How is that done?)

It is to be said, further, that I found the endeavor
impracticable to ascertain the order of succession in
which the child uses the different interrogative words.
It depends wholly on the company about him at what
time first this or that turn of expression or question is
repeated and then used independently. "Why" is
heard by him, as a rule, less often than "What?" and
"How?" and "Which?" Still, it seems remarkable
that I did not once hear the child say "When?" until
the close of the third year. The sense of space is, to
be sure, but little developed at that time, but the sense
of time still less. The use of the word "forgotten"
(*ich habe vergessen*) and of "I shall" (do this or that)
is exceedingly rare.

The articulation was speedily perfected; yet there
was no success at all in the repetition of French nasal
sounds. In spite of much pains "salon" remained
salo, "orange" *orose;* and the French "je" also presented insuperable difficulties. Of German sounds,
"sch" alone was seldom correct. It was still represented by *s ;* for example, in *sloss* for "Schloss," *ssooss*
for "Schooss."

His fondness for singing increases, and indeed all sorts of meaningless syllables are repeated with pleasure again and again, much as in the period of infancy, only more distinctly; but, just as at that time, they can not all be represented on paper or even be correctly reproduced by adults. For a considerable time he was fond of *ē-la, ē-la, la, la, la, la,* in higher and higher pitch, and with unequal intervals, *lálla-lálla, lilalula.* In this it was certainly more the joy over the increasing compass and power of his voice that stimulated him to repetition than it was the sound of the syllables; yet in the thirty-sixth month he showed great pleasure in his singing, of which peculiar, though not very pleasing, melodies were characteristic. The singing over of songs sung to him was but very imperfectly successful. On the other hand, the copying of the manner of speaking, of accent, cadence, and ring of the voices of adults was surprising, although echolalia proper almost ceased or appeared again only from time to time.

Grammatical errors are already becoming more rare. A stubborn fault in declension is the putting of *am* in place of *dem* and *der*, e. g., *das am Mama geben.* Long sentences are formed correctly, but slowly and with pauses, without errors, e. g., *die Blume—ist ganz durstig—möcht auch n bischen Wasser haben* (The flower is quite thirsty—would like a little water). If I ask now, " From whom have you learned that ? " the answer comes regularly, *das hab ich alleine gelernt* (I learned it alone). In general the child wants to manage for himself without assistance, to pull, push, mount, climb, water flowers, crying out repeatedly and passionately, *ich möcht ganz alleine* (I want to [do it] all alone). In

spite of this independence and these ambitious inclina-
tions, there seldom appears an invention of his own in
language.   Here belongs, e. g., the remark of the child,
das Bett ist zu holzhart (the bed is too wooden-hard),
after having hit himself against the bed-post.   Further,
to the question, "Do you like to sleep in the large
room?" he answered, *O ja ganz lieberich gern ;* and
when I asked, "Who, pray, speaks so?" the answer
came very slowly, with deliberation and with pauses,
nicht-nicht-nicht-nicht-nicht-niemand (not—nobody).

How far advanced is the use of the participles,
which are hard to master, is shown by the sentence, *die
Milch ist schon heiss gemacht worden* (the milk has already been made hot).

The child's manner of speaking when he was three
years old approximated more and more rapidly to that
of the family through continued listening to them and
imitation of them, so that I gave up recording it; besides, the abundant—some may think too abundant—
material already presented supplies facts enough to support the foundations of the history of the development
of speech in the child as I have attempted to set it
forth.   A systematic, thorough-going investigation requires the combined labor of many, who must all strive
to answer the same questions—questions which in this
chronological survey are, in regard to one single individual, in part answered, but in part could merely be
proposed.

To observe the child every day during the first thousand days of his life, in order to trace the historical development of speech, was possible only through self-
control, much patience, and great expenditure of time ;

but such observations are necessary, from the physiological, the psychological, the linguistic, and the pedagogic point of view, and nothing can supply their place.

In order to secure for them the highest degree of trustworthiness, I have adhered strictly, without exception, to the following rules:

1. I have not adopted a single observation of the accuracy of which I was not *myself* most positively convinced. Least of all can one rely on the reports of nurses, attendants, and other persons not practiced in scientific observing. I have often, merely by a brief, quiet cross-examination, brought such persons to see for themselves the erroneous character of their statements, particularly in case these were made in order to prove how " knowing " the infants were. On the other hand, I owe to the mother of my child, who has by nature a talent for observation such as is given to few, a great many communications concerning his mental development which have been easily verified by myself.

2. Every observation must *immediately* be entered in writing in a diary that is always lying ready. If this is not done, details of the observations are often forgotten; a thing easily conceivable, because these details in themselves are in many ways uninteresting—especially the meaningless articulations—and they acquire value only in connection with others.

3. In conducting the observations every artificial strain upon the child is to be avoided, and the effort is to be made as often as possible to observe without the child's noticing the observer at all.

4. All training of the one-year-old and of the two-

year-old child must be, so far as possible, prevented. I
have in this respect been so far successful that my child
was not until late acquainted with such tricks as children
are taught, and was not vexed with the learning by
heart of songs, etc., which he was not capable of understanding. Still, as the record shows, not all unnecessary
training could be avoided. The earlier a little child is
constrained to perform ceremonious and other conventional actions, the meaning of which is unknown to him,
so much the earlier does he lose the poetic naturalness
which, at any rate, is but brief and never comes again;
and so much the more difficult becomes the observation
of his unadulterated mental development.

5. Every interruption of one's observation for more
than a day demands the substitution of another observer,
and, after taking up the work again, a verification of
what has been perceived and noted down in the interval.

6. Three times, at least, every day the same child is
to be observed, and everything incidentally noticed is
to be put upon paper, no less than that which is me-
thodically ascertained with reference to definite questions.

In accordance with these directions, tested by myself, all my own observations in this book, and particularly those of this chapter, were conducted. Comparison
with the statements of others can alone give them a
general importance.

What has been furnished by earlier observers in regard to children's learning to speak is, however, not
extensive. I have collected some data in an appendix.

CHAPTER XIX.

DEVELOPMENT OF THE FEELING OF SELF, THE " I "-FEELING.

BEFORE the child is in a condition to recognize as belonging to him the parts of his body that he can feel and see, he must have had a great number of experiences, which are for the most part associated with *painful feelings.* How little is gained for the development of the notion of the " I " by means of the first movements of the hands, which the infant early carries to the mouth, and which must give him, when he sucks them, a different feeling from that given by sucking the finger of another person, or other suitable objects, appears from the fact that, e. g., my child for months tugged at his fingers as if he wanted to pull them off, and struck his own head with his hand by way of experiment. At the close of the first year he had a fancy for striking hard substances against his teeth, and made a regular play of gnashing the teeth. When on the four hundred and ninth day he stood up straight in bed, holding on to the railing of it with his hands, *he bit himself on his bare arm,* and that the upper arm, so that he immediately cried out with pain. The marks of the incisors were to be seen long afterward. The child did not a second time bite himself in the arm, but only bit his fingers, and inadvertently his tongue.

The same child, who likes to hold a biscuit to the mouth of any member of the family to whom he is favorably disposed, offered the biscuit in the same way, entirely of his own accord, to his own foot—sitting on the floor, holding the biscuit in a waiting attitude to his toes—and this strange freak was repeated many times in the twenty-third month. The child amused himself with it.

Thus, at a time when the attention to what is around is already very far developed, one's own person may not be distinguished from the environment. Vierordt thinks that a discrimination between the general feelings [i. e., those caused by bodily states] and the sensations that pertain to the external world exists in the third month. From my observations I can not agree with him; for, although the division may begin thus early, yet it does not become complete until much later. In the ninth month the feet are still eagerly felt of by the little hands, though not so eagerly as before, and the toes are carried to the mouth like a new plaything. Nay, even in the nineteenth month it is not yet clear how much belongs to one's own body. The child had lost a shoe. I said, " Give the shoe." He stooped, seized it, and gave it to me. Then, when I said to the child, as he was standing upright on the floor, " Give the foot," in the expectation that he would hold it out, stretch it toward me, he grasped at it with both hands, and labored hard to get it and hand it to me.

How little he understands, even after the first year of his life has passed, the difference between the parts of his own body and foreign objects is shown also in some strange experiments that the child conducted quite independently. He sits by me at the table and strikes very often and rapidly with his hands successive blows upon the table, at first gently, then hard; then, with the right hand alone, hard; next, suddenly strikes him-

self with the same hand on the mouth; then he holds
his hand to his mouth for a while, strikes the table again
with the right hand, and then on a sudden strikes his
own head (above the ear). The whole performance gave
exactly the impression of his having for the first time
noticed that it is one thing to strike oneself, one's
own hard head, and another thing to strike a foreign
hard object (forty-first week). Even in the thirteenth
month the child often raps his head with his hand to
try the effect, and seems surprised at the hardness of
the head. In the sixteenth month he used not unfrequently to set the left thumb against the left side of the
head, and at the same time the right thumb against the
right side of the head, above the ears, with the fingers
spread, and to push at the same time, putting on a strange,
wondering expression of face, with wide-open eyes.
This movement is not imitated and not inherited, but
invented. The child is doubtless making experiments
by means of it upon the holding of the head, head-
shaking, resistance of his own body, perhaps also upon
the management of the head, as at every thump of the
thumbs against the temporal bones a dull sound was
heard. The objectivity of the fingers was found out
not much before this time by involuntary, painful biting
of them, for as late as the fifteenth month the child bit
his finger so that he cried out with pain. Pain is the
most efficient teacher in the learning of the difference
between subjective and objective.

Another important factor is the *perception of a
change produced by one's own activity* in all sorts of
familiar objects that can be taken hold of in the neighborhood; and the most remarkable day, from a psycho-

genetic point of view, in any case an extremely significant day in the life of the infant, is the one in which he
first experiences the *connection of a movement executed
by himself with a sense-impression following upon it.*
The noise that comes from the tearing and crumpling
of paper is as yet unknown to the child. He discovers
(in the fifth month) the fact that he himself in tearing
paper into smaller and smaller pieces has again and
again the new sound-sensation, and he repeats the experiment day by day and with a strain of exertion until
this connection has lost the charm of novelty. At present there is not, indeed, as yet any clear insight into the
nexus of cause; but the child has now had the experience that he can himself be the cause of a combined
perception of sight and sound regularly, to the extent that
when he tears paper there appears, on the one hand, the
lessening in size ; on the other hand, the noise. The patience with which this occupation—from the forty-fifth
to the fifty-fifth week especially—is continued with pleasure is explained by the gratification at being a cause, at
the perception that so striking a transformation as that
of the newspaper into fragments has been effected by
means of his own activity. Other occupations of this
sort, which are taken up again and again with a persist-
ency incomprehensible to an adult, are the shaking of a
bunch of keys, the opening and closing of a box or
purse (thirteenth month); the pulling out and emptying, and then the filling and pushing in, of a table-
drawer ; the heaping up and the strewing about of gar-
den-mold or gravel ; the turning of the leaves of a book
(thirteenth to nineteenth month); digging and scraping
in the sand ; the carrying of footstools hither and thither ;

the placing of shells, stones, or buttons in rows (twenty-first month); pouring water into and out of bottles, cups, watering-pots (thirty-first to thirty-third months); and, in the case of my boy, the throwing of stones into the water. A little girl in the eleventh month found her chief pleasure in "rummaging" with trifles in drawers and little boxes. Her sister "played" with all sorts of things, taking an interest in dolls and pictures in the tenth month (Frau von Strümpell). Here, too, the eagerness and seriousness with which such apparently aimless movements are performed is remarkable. The satisfaction they afford must be very great, and it probably has its basis in the feeling of his own power generated by the movements originated by the child himself (changes of place, of position, of form) and in the proud feeling of being a cause.

This is not mere playing, although it is so called; it is *experimenting*. The child that at first merely played like a cat, being amused with color, form, and movement, has become a *causative being*. Herewith the development of the "*I*"-*feeling* enters upon a new phase; but it is not yet perfected. Vanity and ambition come in for the further development of it. Above all, it is *attention* to the *parts of his own body* and the *articles of his dress*, the nearest of all objects to the child's eye, that helps along the separation in thought of the child's body from all other objects.

I therefore made special observation of the directing of his look toward his own body and toward the mirror. In regard to the first I took note, among other facts, of the following:

17th week.—In the seizing movements, as yet imperfect, the gaze is fixed partly on the object, partly on *his own hand*, especially if the hand has once seized successfully.

18th week.—The very attentive regarding of the fingers in seizing is surprising, and is to be observed daily.

23d week.—When the infant, who often throws his hands about at random in the air, accidentally gets hold of one hand with the other, he regards attentively both his hands, which are often by chance folded.

24th week.—In the same way the child fixes his gaze for several minutes alternately upon a glove held by himself in his hands and upon his own fingers that hold it.

32d week.—The child, lying on his back, *looks* very frequently *at* his *legs* stretched up vertically, especially at his *feet*, as if they were something foreign to him.

35th week.—In every situation in which he can do so, the child tries to grasp a foot with both hands and carry it to his mouth, often with success. This monkey-like movement seems to afford him special pleasure.

36th week.—His own hands and feet are no more so frequently observed by him without special occasion. Other new objects attract his gaze and are seized.

39th week.—The same as before. In the bath, however, the child sometimes looks at and feels of *his own skin* in various places, evidently taking pleasure in doing so. Sometimes he directs his gaze to his legs, which are bent and extended in a very lively manner in the most manifold variety of positions.

55th week.—The child looks for a long time attentively at a person eating, and follows with his gaze every movement; grasps at the person's face, and then, after *striking himself on the head*, fixes his gaze on his own hands. He is fond of playing with the fingers of the persons in the family, and delights in the bendings and extensions, evidently comparing them with those of his own fingers.

62d week.—Playing with his own fingers (at which he looks with a protracted gaze) as if he would pull them off. Again, one hand is pressed down by the other flat upon the table until it hurts, as if the hand were a wholly foreign plaything, and it is still looked at wonderingly sometimes.

From this time forth the gazing at the parts of his own body was perceptibly lessened. The child *knew* them as to their form, and gradually learned to distinguish them from foreign objects as parts belonging to him; but in this he by no means arrives at the point of considering, "The hand is mine, the thing seized is not," or "The leg belongs to me," and the like; but because all the visible parts of the child's body, on account of very frequently repeated observation, no longer excite the optic center so strongly and therefore appear no longer interesting—because the experiences of touch combined with visual perceptions always recur in the same manner—the child has gradually become accustomed to them and *overlooks* them when making use of his hands and feet. He no longer represents them to himself separately, as he did before, whereas every new object felt, seen, or heard, is very interesting to him and is separately represented in idea. Thus arises the definite separation of object and subject in the child's intellect. In the beginning the child is new to him-

self, namely, to the representational apparatus that gets
its development only after birth ; later, after he has become acquainted with himself, after he, namely, his
body, has lost the charm of novelty for him, i. e., for
the representational apparatus in his brain, a dim feeling of the " I " exists, and by means of further abstraction the concept of the " I " is formed.

The progress of the intellect in the act of *looking
into the mirror* confirms this conclusion drawn from
the above observations.

For the behavior of the child toward his image in
the glass shows unmistakably the gradual growth of the
consciousness of self out of a condition in which objective and subjective changes are not yet distinguished
from each other.

Among the subjective changes is, without doubt, the
smiling at the image in the tenth week, which was probably occasioned merely by the brightness (Sigismund).
Another boy in the twenty-seventh week looked at himself in the glass with a smile (Sigismund).

Darwin recorded of one of his sons, that in the fifth
month he repeatedly smiled at his father's image and
his own in a mirror and took them for real objects; but
he was surprised that his father's voice sounded from
behind him (the child). " Like all infants, he much enjoyed thus looking at himself, and in less than two
months perfectly understood that it was an image, for
if I made quite silently any odd grimace, he would suddenly turn round to look at me. He was, however,
puzzled at the age of seven months, when, being out of
doors, he saw me on the inside of a large plate-glass
window, and seemed in doubt whether or not it was an

image. Another of my infants, a little girl, was not nearly so acute, and seemed quite perplexed at the image of a person in a mirror approaching her from behind. The higher apes which I tried with a small looking-glass behaved differently. They placed their hands behind the glass, and in doing so showed their sense; but, far from taking pleasure in looking at themselves, they got angry and would look no more." The first-mentioned child, at the age of not quite nine months, associated his own name with his image in the looking-glass, and when called by name would turn toward the glass even when at some distance from it. He gave to "Ah!" which he used at first when recognizing any person or his own image in a mirror, an exclamatory sound such as adults employ when surprised. Thus Darwin reports.

My boy gave me occasion for the following observations:

In the eleventh week he does not see himself in the glass. If I knock on the glass, he turns his head in the direction of the sound. His image does not, however, make the slightest impression upon him.

In the fourteenth and fifteenth weeks he looks at his image with utter indifference. His gaze is directed to the eyes in the image without any expression of pleasure or displeasure.

In the sixteenth week the reflected image is still either ignored or looked at without interest.

Near the beginning of the seventeenth week (on the one hundred and thirteenth day) the child for the first time regards his image in the glass with unmistakable attention, and indeed with the same expression with

16

which he is accustomed to fix his gaze on a strange face seen for the first time. The impression appears to awaken neither displeasure nor pleasure; the perception seems now for the first time to be distinct. Three days later the child for the first time undoubtedly laughed at his image.

When, in the twenty-fourth week, I held the child again before the glass, he saw my image, became very attentive, and suddenly turned round toward me, manifestly convincing himself that I stood near him.

In the twenty-fifth week he for the first time stretched out his hand toward his own image. He therefore regarded it as capable of being seized.

In the twenty-sixth week the child is delighted at seeing me in the glass. He turns round toward me, and evidently *compares* the original with the image.

In the thirty-fifth week the child gayly and with interest grasps at his image in the glass, and is surprised when his hand comes against the smooth surface.

In the forty-first to the forty-fourth week, the same. The reflected image is regularly greeted with a laugh, and is then grasped at.

All these observations were made before a very large stationary mirror.

In the fifty-seventh week, however, I held a small hand-mirror close to the face of the child. He looked at his image and then passed his hand behind the glass and moved the hand hither and thither as if searching. Then he took the mirror himself and looked at it and felt of it on both sides. When after several minutes I held the mirror before him again, precisely the same performance was repeated. It accords with what was observed by Darwin in the case of anthropoid apes mentioned above (p. 197).

In the fifty-eighth week I showed to the child his photograph, cabinet-size, in a frame under glass. He first turned the picture round as he had turned the hand-mirror. Although the photographic image was much smaller than the reflected one, it seemed to be equally esteemed. On the same day (four hundred and second) I held the hand-mirror before the boy again, pointing out to him his image in it; but he at once turned away obstinately (again like the intelligent animal).

Here the incomprehensible—in the literal sense— was disturbing. But very soon came the insight which is wanting to the quadrumana, for in the sixtieth week the child saw his mother in the mirror, and to the question, "Where is mamma?" he pointed to the image in the mirror and then turned round, laughing, to his mother. Now, as he had before this time behaved roguishly, there is no doubt that at this time, after fourteen months, original and image were distinguished with certainty as such, especially as his own photograph no longer excited wonder.

Nevertheless, the child, in the sixty-first week, is still trying to feel of his own image in the glass, and he licks the glass in which he sees it, and, in the sixty-sixth week, also strikes against it with his hand.

In the following week for the first time I saw the child make grimaces before the glass. He laughed as he did it. I stood behind him and called him by name. He turned around directly, although he saw me plainly

in the glass.   He evidently knew that the voice did not
come from the image.

In the sixty-ninth week signs of vanity are perceived.   The child looks at himself in the glass with
pleasure and often.   If we put anything on his head
and say, " Pretty," his expression changes.   He is gratified in a strange and peculiar fashion ; his eyebrows are
raised, and the eyes are opened wide.

In the twenty-first month the child puts some lace
or embroidered stuff about him, lets it hang down from
his shoulders, looks round behind at the train, advancing, stopping, eagerly throwing it into fresh folds.
Here there is a mixture of apish imitation with vanity.

As the child had, moreover, even in the seventeenth
month, been fond of placing himself before the glass
and making all sorts of faces, the experiments with the
mirror were no longer continued.

They show the transition from the infant's condition
previous to the development of the *ego*, when he can
not yet see distinctly, to the condition of the developed
ego, who consciously distinguishes himself from his
image in the glass and from other persons and their
images.   Yet for a long time after this step there exists a certain lack of clearness in regard to names.   In
the twenty-first month the child laughs at his image
in the glass and points to it when I ask, " Where is
Axel ? " and at my image when asked, " Where is papa ? "   But, being asked with emphasis, the child turns
round to me with a look of doubt.   I once brought a
large mirror near the child's bed in the evening after
he had gone to sleep, so that he might perceive himself
directly upon waking.   He saw his image immediately

after waking, seemed very much surprised at it, gazed fixedly at it, and when at last I asked, "Where is Axel?" he pointed not to himself but to the image (six hundred and twentieth day). In the thirty-first month it still afforded him great pleasure to gaze at his image in the glass. The child would laugh at it persistently and heartily.

Animals show great variety of behavior in this respect, as is well known. A pair of Turkish ducks, that I used to see every day for weeks, always kept themselves apart from other ducks. When the female died, the drake, to my surprise, betook himself by preference to a cellar-window that was covered on the inside and gave strong reflections, and he would stand with his head before this for hours every day. He saw his image there, and thought perhaps that it was his lost companion.

A kitten before which I held a small mirror must surely have taken the image for a second living cat, for she went behind the glass and around it when it was conveniently placed.

Many animals, on the contrary, are afraid of their reflected image, and run away from it.

In like manner little children are sometimes frightened by the discovery of their own shadows. My child exhibited signs of fear at his shadow the first time he saw it; but in his fourth year he was pleased with it, and to the question, "Where does the shadow come from?" he answered, to our surprise, "From the sun" (fortieth month).

More important for the development of the child's *ego* than are the observation of the shadow and of the image in the glass is the learning of speech, for it is not until words are used that the higher concepts are first marked off from one another, and this is the case with the concept of the *ego*. Yet the wide-spread view, that the " I "-*feeling* first appears with the beginning of the use of the word " I," is wholly incorrect. Many headstrong children have a strongly marked " I "-feeling without calling themselves by anything but their names, because their relatives in speaking with them do not call themselves " I," but " papa, mamma, uncle, O mamma," etc., so that the opportunity early to hear and to appropriate the words " I " and " mine " is rare. Others hear these words often, to be sure, especially from children somewhat older, and use them, yet do not understand them, but add to them their own names. Thus, a girl of two and a half years, named Ilse, used to say, *Ilse mein Tuhl* (Ilse, my chair), instead of " mein Stuhl " (Bardeleben). My boy of two and three fourths years repeated the " I " he heard, meaning by it " you." In the twenty-ninth month *mir* (me) was indeed said by him, but not " ich " (I), (p. 171). Soon, however, he named himself no more, as he had done in the twenty-third and even in the twenty-eighth month (pp. 147–167), by his first name. In the thirty-third month especially came *das will ich! das möcht ich!* (I wish that, I should like that) (p. 183). The fourfold designation of his own person in the thirty-second month (p. 180)—by his name, by " I," by " he," and by the omission of all pronouns—was only a brief transition-stage, as was also the misunderstanding of the " dein " (your) which for a time (p. 156) meant " gross " (large).

These observations plainly show that the " I "-feeling is not first awakened by the learning of words, for this feeling, according to the facts given above, is present much earlier; but by means of speech the *conceptual* distinction of the "I," the self, the mine, is first made exact; the development, not the origin, of the " I "-feeling is simply favored.

How obscure the " I " concept is even after learning the use of the personal pronouns is shown by the utterance of the four-year-old daughter of Lindner, named Olga, *die hat mich nass gemacht* (she has made me wet), when she meant that she herself had done it; and *du sollst mir doch folgen, Olga* (but you must follow me, Olga), the latter expression, indeed, being merely said after some one else. In her is noteworthy, too, the confounding of the possessives " his " and " her," e. g., *dem Papa ihr Buch auf der Mama seinen Platz gelegt* (her book, papa's, laid in his place, mamma's) (Lindner); and yet in these forms of speech there is an advance in the differentiation of the concepts.

All children are known to be late in beginning to speak about themselves, of what they wish to become, or of that which they can do better than others can, and the like. The *ego* has become an experience of consciousness long before this.

All these progressive steps, which in the individual can be traced only with great pains, form, as it were, converging lines that culminate in the fully developed feeling of the personality as exclusive, as distinct from the outer world.

Thus much the purely physiological view can admit without hesitation; but a further unification or indivisibility or unbroken permanence of the child's *ego*, it can not reconcile with the facts, perfectly well established by me, that are presented in this chapter.

For what is the significance of the fact, that "to the child his feet, hands, teeth, seem a plaything foreign to himself"? and that "the child bit his own arm as he was accustomed to bite objects with which he was not acquainted"? "Seem" to what part of the child? What is that which bites in the child as in the very young chick that seizes its own toe with its bill and bites it as if it were the toe of its neighbor or a grain of millet? Evidently the "subject" in the head is a different one from that in the trunk. The *ego* of the brain is other than the *ego* of the spinal marrow (the "spinal-marrowsoul" of Pflüger). The one speaks, sees, hears, tastes, smells, and feels; the other merely feels, and at the beginning, so long as brain and spinal marrow have only a loose organic connection and no functional connection at all with each other, the two *egos* are absolutely isolated from each other. Newly-born children with no brain, who lived for hours and days, as I myself saw in a case of rare interest, could suck, cry, move the limbs, and feel (for they stopped crying and took to sucking when something they could suck was put into their mouths when they were hungry). On the other hand, if a human being could be born with a brain but without a spinal marrow and could live, it would not be able to move its limbs. When a normal babe, therefore, plays with its feet or bites itself in the arm as it would bite a biscuit, we have in this a proof that the brain with its perceptive apparatus is independent of the spinal marrow. And the fact that acephalic new-born human beings and animal embryos deprived of brain, as Soltmann and I found, move their limbs just as sound ones do, cry just as they do, suck and respond to reflexes, proves that the functions of the spinal marrow (inclusive of the optic thalami, the corpora quadrigemina and the cervical marrow) are independent of the cerebral hemispheres (together with the corpus striatum, according to Soltmann).

Now, however, the brainless living child that sucks, cries, moves arms and legs, and distinguishes pleasure from displeasure, has indisputably an individuality, an *ego*. We must, then, of necessity admit two *egos* in the child that has both cerebrum and spinal marrow, and that represents to himself his arm as good to taste of, as something to like. But, if two, why not several? At the beginning, when the centers of sight, hearing, smell, and taste, in the brain are still imperfectly developed, each of these perceives for itself, the perceptions in the different departments of sense having as yet no connection at all with one another. The case is like that of the spinal marrow, which at first does not communicate, or only very imperfectly communicates, to the brain that which it feels, e. g., the effect of the prick of a needle, for the newly born do not generally react upon that. Only by means of very frequent coincidences of unlike sense-impressions, in tasting-and-touching, seeing-and-feeling, seeing-and-hearing, seeing-and-smelling, tasting-and-smelling, hearing-and-touching, are the intercentral connecting fibers developed, and then first can the various representational centers, these " I "-makers, as it were, contribute, as in the case of the ordinary formation of concepts, to the formation of the corporate " I," which is quite abstract.

This abstract "I"-concept, that belongs only to the adult, thinking human being, comes into existence in exactly the same way that other concepts do, viz., by means of the individual ideas from which it results, as e. g., the forest exists only when the trees exist. The subordinate "I's," that preside over the separate sense-departments, are in the little child not yet blended together, because in him the organic connections are still lacking; which, being translated into the language of psychology, means that he lacks the necessary power of abstraction. The co-excitations of the sensory centers, that are as yet impressed with too few memory-images, can not yet take place on occasion of a single excitation, the cerebral connecting fibers being as yet too scanty.

These co-excitations of parts of the brain functionally different, on occasion of excitation of a part of the brain that has previously often been excited together with those, form the physiological foundation of the psychical phenomenon of the formation of concepts in general, and so of the formation of the "I" concept. For the special ideas of all departments of sense have in all beings possessed of all the senses—or of four senses, or of three—the common quality of coming into existence only under conditions of time, space, and causality. This common property presupposes similar processes in every separate sense-center of the highest rank. Excitations of one of these centers easily effect similar co-excitations of centers that have often been excited together with them through objective impressions, and it is this similar co-excitement extending itself over the cerebral centers of all the nerves of sense that evokes the composite idea of the "I."

According to this view, therefore, the " I " can not exist as a unit, as undivided, as uninterrupted; it exists only when the separate departments of sense are active with their *egos*, out of which the " I " is abstracted; e. g., it disappears in dreamless sleep. In the waking condition it has continued existence only where the centro-sensory excitations are most strongly in force; i. e., where the attention is on the strain.

Still less, however, is the " I " an aggregate. For this presupposes the exchangeability of the component parts. The seeing *ego*, however, can just as little have its place made good by a substitute as can the hearing one, the tasting one, etc. The sum-total of the separate leaves, blossoms, stalks, roots, of the plant does not, by a great deal, constitute the plant. The parts must be joined together in a special manner. So, likewise, it is not enough to add together the characteristics common to the separate sense-representations in order to obtain from these the regulating and controlling " I." Rather there results from the increasing number and manifoldness of the sense-impressions a continually increasing growth of the gray substance of the child's cerebrum, a rapid increase of the inter-central connecting fibers, and through this a readier co-excitement — association, so called—which unites feeling with willing and thinking in the child.

This union is the " I," the sentient and emotive, the desiring and willing, the perceiving and thinking " I."

CHAPTER XX.

SUMMARY OF RESULTS.

OF all the facts that have been established by me through the observation of the child in the first years of his life, the *formation of concepts without language* is most opposed to the traditional doctrines, and it is just this on which I lay the greatest stress.

It has been demonstrated that the human being, at the very beginning of his life, not only distinguishes pleasure and discomfort, but may also have single, distinct sensations. He behaves on the first day differently, when the appropriate sense-impressions exist, from what he does when they are lacking. The first effect of these feelings, these few sensations, is the association of their traces, left behind in the central nervous system, with inborn movements. Those traces or central impressions develop gradually the personal *memory*. These movements are the point of departure for the primitive activity of the intellect, which separates the sensations both in time and in space. When the number of the memory-images, of distinct sensations, on the one hand, on the other, of the movements that have been associated with them—e. g., "sweet" and "sucking"—has become larger, then a firmer association of sensation-and-movement-memories, i. e., of excitations of sensory and motor ganglionic cells takes place, so that excitement of the one brings with it co-excitement of the other. Sucking awakens the recollection of the sweet taste; the sweet taste of itself causes sucking. This

succession is already a separation *in time* of two sensations (the sweet and the motor sensation in sucking).
The separation in space requires the recollection of two
sensations, each with one movement; the distinction
between sucking at the left breast and sucking at the
right is made after one trial. With this, the first act of
the intellect is performed, the first perception made,
i. e., a sensation first localized in time and space. The
motor sensation of sucking has come, like the sweet
taste, *after* a similar one, and it has come between two
unlike relations in space that were distinguished. By
means of multiplied perceptions (e. g., luminous fields
not well defined, but yet defined) and multiplied movements with sensations of touch, the perception, after
considerable time, acquires an object; i. e., the intellect,
which already allowed nothing bright to appear without
boundary-lines, and thus allowed nothing bright to appear except in space (whereas at the beginning brightness, as was the case even later with sound, had no
limitation, no demarcation), begins to assign a cause for
that which is perceived. Hereby perception is raised
to *representation*. The often-felt, localized, sweet,
warm, white wetness, which is associated with sucking,
now forms an idea, and one of the earliest ideas. When,
now, this idea has often arisen, the separate perceptions
that have been necessary to its formation are united
more and more firmly. Then, when one of these latter
appears for itself, the memory-images of the others will
also appear, through co-excitement of the ganglionic
cells concerned; but this means simply that the *concept*
is now in existence. For the concept has its origin in
the union of attributes. Attributes are perceived, and

the memory-images of them, that is, accordingly, memory-images of separate perceptions, are so firmly associated that, where only one appears in the midst of entirely new impressions, the concept yet emerges, because all the other images appear along with it. Language is not required for this. Up to this point, those born deaf behave exactly like infants that have all the senses, and like some animals that form concepts.

These few first ideas, namely, the individual ideas, or sense-intuitions that are generated by the first perceptions, and the simple general ideas (of a lower order), or concepts, arising out of these—the concepts of the child as yet without language, of microcephali also, of deaf-mutes, and of the higher animals—have now this peculiarity, that they have all been formed exactly in this way by the parents and the grandparents and the representatives of the successive generations (such notions as those of " food," " breast "). These concepts are not innate; because no idea can be innate, for the reason that several peripheral impressions are necessary for the formation of even a single perception. They are, however, inherited. Just as the teeth and the beard are not usually innate in man, but come and grow like those of the parents and are already implanted, piece for piece, in the new-born child, and are thus hereditary, so the first ideas of the infant, his first concepts, which arise unconsciously, without volition and without the possibility of inhibition, in every individual in the same way, must be called hereditary. Different as are the teeth from the germs of teeth in the newly-born, so different are the man's concepts, clear, sharply defined by words, from the child's ill-defined, obscure concepts, which arise quite independently of all language (of word, look, or gesture).

In this wise the old doctrine of "innate ideas" becomes clear. Ideas or thoughts are themselves either representations or combinations of representations. They thus presuppose perceptions, and can not accordingly be innate, but may some of them be inherited, those, viz., which at first, by virtue of the likeness between the brain of the child and that of the parent, and of the similarity between the external circumstances of the beginnings of life in child and parent, always arise in the same manner.

The principal thing is the innate aptitude to perceive things and to form ideas, i. e., the innate intellect. By aptitude (Anlage), however, can be understood nothing else at present than a manner of reacting, a sort of capability or excitability, impressed upon the central organs of the nervous system after repeated association of nervous excitations (through a great many generations in the same way).

The brain comes into the world provided with a great number of impressions upon it. Some of these are quite obscure, some few are distinct. Each ancestor has added his own to those previously existing. Among these impressions, finally, the useless ones must soon be obliterated by those that are useful. On the other hand, deep impressions will, like wounds, leave behind scars, which abide longer; and very frequently used paths of connection between different portions of the brain and spinal marrow and the organs of sense are easier to travel even at birth (instinctive and reflexive processes).

Now, of all the higher functions of the brain, the ordering one, which compares the simple, pure sensations, the original experiences, and first sets them in an order of succession, viz., arranges them in time, then puts them side by side and one above another, and, not till later, one behind another, viz., arranges them in space—this function is one of the oldest. This ordering of the sense-impressions is *an activity of the intellect that has nothing to do with speech*, and the *capacity* for it is, as Immanuel Kant discovered, present in man "as he now is" (Kant) *before* the activity of the senses begins ; but without this activity it can not assert itself.

Now, I maintain, and in doing so I take my stand upon the facts published in this book, that just as little as the intellect of the child not yet able to speak has need of words or looks or gestures, or any symbol whatever, in order to arrange in time and space the sense-impressions, so little does that intellect require those means in order to form concepts and to perform logical operations ; and in this fundamental fact I see the material for bridging over the only great gulf that separates the child from the brute animal.

That even physiologists deny that there is any passage from one to the other is shown by Vierordt in his " Physiology of Infancy " (1877).

The fundamental fact that a genuinely logical activity of the brain goes on without language of any sort, in the adult man who has the faculty of speech, was discovered by Helmholtz. The logical functions called by him " unconscious inferences " begin, as I think I have shown by many observations in the newly-born, immediately with the activity of the senses. Perception in the third dimension of space is a particularly clear example of this sort of logical activity without words, because it is developed slowly.

In place of the expression " unconscious," which, because it has caused much mischief, still prevents the term " unconscious inferences" from being naturalized in the physiology of the senses and the theory of perception, it would be advisable, since "instinctive" and "intuitive" are still more easily misunderstood, to say " wordless." Wordless ideas, wordless concepts, wordless judgments, wordless inferences, may be inherited. To these belong such as our progenitors often experienced at the beginning of life, such as not only come into existence without the participation of any medium of language whatever, but also are never even willed (intended, deliberate, voluntary), and can not under any circumstances be set aside or altered, whether to be corrected or falsified. An inherited defect can not be put aside, and neither can the inherited intellect. When the outer angle at the right of the eye is pressed upon, a light appears in the closed eye at the left, not at the right; not at the place touched. This optical illusion, which was known even in Newton's day, this wordless inductive inference, is hereditary and incorrigible; and, on the other hand, the hereditary wordless *concept* of food can neither be prevented from arising nor be set aside nor be formed otherwise than it was formed by our ancestors.

Innate, to make it once more prominent, is the faculty (the capacity, the aptitude, the potential function) of forming concepts, and some of the first concepts are

17

hereditary. New (not hereditary) concepts arise only after new perceptions, i. e., after experiences that associate themselves with the primitive ones by means of new connecting paths in the brain, and they begin in fact before the learning of speech.

A chick just out of the shell possesses the capacity to lay eggs—the organs necessary—in fact the future eggs are inborn in the creature; but only after some time does it lay eggs, and these are in every respect similar to the first eggs of its mother. Indeed, the chicks that come from these eggs resemble those of the mother herself; thus the eggs have hereditary properties. New eggs originate only by crossing, by external influences of all sorts, influences, therefore, of experience.

So, too, the new-born child possesses the capacity of forming concepts. The organs necessary for that are inborn in him, but not till after some time does he form concepts, and these are in all nations and at all times quite similar to the first concepts formed by the child's mother. Indeed, the inferences that attach themselves to the first concepts will resemble those which were developed in the mother or will be identical with them; these concepts have, then, hereditary properties. New concepts originate only through experience. They originate in great numbers in every child that learns to speak.

If the fact that children utterly ignorant of speech, even those born deaf, already perform logical operations with perfect correctness, proves the intellect to be independent of language, yet searching observation of the child that is learning to speak shows that only by means of verbal language can the intellect give precision to its primitive indistinct concepts and thereby develop itself further, connecting ideas appropriately with the circumstances in which the child lives.

It is a settled fact, however, that many ideas must already be formed in order to make possible the acquirement of speech. The existence of ideas is a necessary condition of learning to speak.

The greatest intellectual advance in this field consists in this, that the specific method of the human race is discovered by the speechless child—the method of expressing ideas aloud and articulately, i. e., by means of expirations of breath along with various positions of the larynx and the mouth and various movements of the tongue. No child *invents* this method, it is *transmitted;* but each individual child *discovers* that by means of sounds thus originating one can make known his ideas and thereby induce feelings of pleasure and do away with discomfort. Therefore he applies himself to this process of himself, without instruction, provided only that he grows up among speaking people; and even where hearing, which serves as a means of intercourse with them, is wanting from birth, a life rich in ideas and an intelligence of a high order may be developed, provided that written signs of sound supply the place of sounds heard. These signs, however, can be learned only by means of instruction. The way in which writing is learned is the same as the way in which the alalic child learns to speak. Both rest upon imitation.

I have shown that the first firm association of an idea with a syllable or with a word-like combination of syllables, takes place exclusively through imitation; but a union of this sort being once established, the child then freely invents new combinations, although to a much more limited extent than is commonly assumed. No one brings with him into the world a genius of such quality that it would be capable of inventing articulate speech. It is difficult enough to comprehend that imitation suffices for the child to learn a language.

What organic conditions are required for the imitation of sounds and for learning to speak I have endeavored to ascertain by means of a systematic collection, resting on the best pathological investigations, of all the disturbances of speech thus far observed in adults; and the daily observation of a sound child, who was kept away from all training as far as possible, as well as the frequent observation of other children, has brought me to the following important result:

That every known form of disturbance of speech in adults finds its perfect counterpart in the child that is learning to speak.

The child can not *yet* speak correctly, because his impressive, central, and expressive organs of speech are not yet completely developed. The adult patient can *no longer* speak correctly, because those parts are no longer complete or capable of performing their functions. The parallelism is perfect even to individual cases, if children of various ages are carefully observed in regard to their acquirement of speech. As to facts of a more general nature, we arrive, then, at the three following:

1. The normal infant understands spoken language much earlier than he can himself produce through imitation the sounds, syllables, and words he hears.

2. The normal child, however, before he begins to speak or to imitate correctly the sounds of language, forms of his own accord all or nearly all the sounds that occur in his future speech and very many others besides, and delights in doing it.

3. The order of succession in which the sounds of speech are produced by the infant is different with different individuals, and consequently is not determined by the principle of the least effort. It is dependent upon several factors—brain, teeth, size of the tongue, acuteness of hearing, motility, and others. Only in the later, intentional, sound-formations and attempts at speaking does that principle come under consideration.

In the acquirement of every complicated muscular movement, dancing, e. g., the difficult combinations which make a greater strain on the activity of the will are in like manner acquired last.

Heredity plays no part in this, for every child can learn to master perfectly any language, provided he hears from birth only the one to be learned. The plasticity of the inborn organs of speech is thus in the earliest childhood very great.

To follow farther the influence that the use of speech as a means of understanding has upon the intellectual development of the child lies outside the problem dealt with in this book. Let me, in conclusion, simply give a brief estimate of the questioning-activity that makes its appearance very early after the first attempts at speech, and also add a few remarks on the development of the " *I* "-*feeling*.

The child's questioning as a means of his culture is

almost universally underrated. The interest in causality that unfolds itself more and more vigorously with the learning of speech, the asking why, which is often almost unendurable to parents and educators, is fully justified, and ought not, as unfortunately is too often the case, to be unheeded, purposely left unanswered, purposely answered falsely. I have from the beginning given to my boy, to the best of my knowledge invariably, an answer to his questions intelligible to him and not contrary to truth, and have noticed that in consequence at a later period, in the fifth and the sixth and especially in the seventh year, the questions prove to be more and more intelligent, because the previous answers are retained. If, on the contrary, we do not answer at all, or if we answer with jests and false tales, it is not to be wondered at that a child even of superior endowments puts foolish and absurd questions and thinks illogically—a thing that rarely occurs where questions are rightly answered and fitting instruction is given, to say nothing of rearing the child to superstition. The only legend in which I allow my boy to have firm faith is that of the stork that brings new babes, and what goes along with that.

With regard to the development of the " I "-feeling the following holds good :

This feeling does not awake on the day when the child uses for the first time the word " I " instead of his own name—the date of such use varies according as those about it name themselves and the child by the proper name and not by the pronoun for a longer or a shorter period; but the " I " is separated from the " not-I " after a long series of experiences, chiefly of a painful bitter substances, on the first day (pp. 98, 121); nay, even by moistening the upper lip with bad-smelling substances (p. 131), and later by the sight of loathed food (p. 126).

Vomiting occurs both after overfilling the stomach with unsuitable liquid (even nurse's milk) and on putting the finger into the throat. In the fifth week I saw both cases, and observed how, without any external stimulus, the milk that had been swallowed shortly before sprang forth like a fountain, three or four inches high, from the mouth of the boy as he lay on his back. Eructation is not infrequent even in the first week.

Hiccough is observed to be very frequent in children in the first three months; much more frequent than in adults. I have observed it within the first twenty hours after the birth of the child. It can be stopped by putting upon the tongue half a spoonful of lukewarm sweetened water. After the swallowing of this small quantity, a very obstinate case of hiccough that I saw (in the tenth week) yielded; but I find no explanation for the effect of this simple remedy. For the diversion of attention is hardly sufficient here, since other sense-impressions do not produce the same result. The complicated mechanism for the movements of swallowing is inborn, and already performs its functions in man and in animals long before birth.

More important than all these typical reflexes, in their bearing on the genesis of mind, are the already-mentioned reflexive eye-movements and the movements of the limbs and of the head, following irritation of the skin, particularly by blowing and by tickling, and sound-impressions. Of the first sort frequent mention

door shows how high the developed human being tow-
ers above all his fellow-beings.

The key to the understanding of the great enigma,
how these extremes are connected, is furnished in the
history of the development of the mind of the child.

APPENDIXES.

A.

AMONG the earlier as among the later statements concerning the acquirement of speech, there are several that
have been put forth by writers on the subject without a
sufficient basis of observed facts. Not only Buffon, but
also Taine and his successors, have, from a few individual
cases, deduced general propositions which are not of general application.

Good observations were first supplied in Germany by
Berthold Sigismund in his pamphlet, "Kind und Welt"
("The Child and the World") (1856); but his observa-
tions were scanty.

He noted, as the first articulate sounds made by a child
from Thüringen (Rudolstadt), *ma, ba, bu, appa, ange, anne,
brrr, arrr:* these were made about the middle of the first
three months.

Sigismund is of the opinion that this first lisping, or
babbling, consists in the production of syllables with only
two sounds, of which the consonant is most often the
first; that the first consonants distinctly pronounced are
labials; that the lips, brought into activity by sucking, are
the first organs of articulation; but this conjecture lacks
general confirmation.

In the second three months (in the case of one child in the twenty-third week, with other healthy children considerably earlier) were heard, for the first time, the loud and high *crowing*-sounds, uttered by the child spontaneously, jubilantly, with lively movements of the limbs that showed the waxing power of the muscles: the child seemed to take pleasure in making the sounds. The utterance of syllables, on the other hand, is at this period often discontinued for weeks at a time.

In the third quarter of the first year, the lisping or stammering was more frequent. New sounds were added: *bä, fbu, fu;* and the following were among those that were repeated without cessation, *bäbäbä, dädädä;* also *adad, eded.*

In the next three months the child manifested his satisfaction in any object by the independent sound *ei, ei.* The first imitations of sounds, proved to be such, were made after the age of eleven months. But it is more significant, for our comprehension of the process of learning to speak, that long before the boy tried to imitate words or gestures, viz., at the age of nine months, he distinguished accurately the words "father, mother, light, window, moon, lane"; for he looked, or pointed, at the object designated, as soon as one of these words was spoken.

And when, finally, imitation began, musical tones, e. g., F, C, were imitated sooner than the spoken sounds, although the former were an octave higher. And the *ei, ei,* was repeated in pretty nearly the same tone or accent in which it had been pronounced for the child. Sneezing was not imitated till after fourteen months. The first word imitated by the child of his own accord (after fourteen months) was the cry "Neuback" (fresh-bake), as it resounded from the street; it was given back by the child, unsolicited, as *ei-a*. As late as the sixteenth month he replied to the word *papa*, just as he did to the word *Ida*, only with *atta ;* yet he had in the mean time learned to understand " lantern, piano, stove, bird, nine-pin, pot "—in all, more than twenty words—and to indicate by a look the objects named ; he had also learned to make the new imperfect sounds *pujéh, pujéh, tupe tupe téh, ämmäm, atta, ho.*

In the seventeenth month came in place of these sounds the babbled syllables *mäm, mam, mad-am, a-dam, das ;* in the case of other children, syllables different from these. Children often say several syllables in quick succession, " then suddenly stop as if they were thinking of something new—actually strain, as if they must exert themselves to bring their organs to utterance, until at last a new sound issues, and then this is repeated like the clack of a mill." Along with this appears the frequent doubling of syllables, as in *papa, mama.*

The boy, at twenty months, told his father the following, with pretty long pauses and animated gestures : *atten— beene—titten—bach—eine—puff—anna,* i. e., " Wir waren im Garten, haben Beeren und Kirschen gegessen, und in den Bach Steine geworfen ; dann kam Anna " (we were in the garden, ate berries and cherries, and threw stones into the brook ; then Anna came).

The observations of Sigismund are remarkable for their objectivity, their clearness of exposition, and their accuracy, and they agree with mine, as may easily be seen, in many respects perfectly. Unfortunately, this excellent observer (long since deceased) did not finish his work. The first part only has appeared. Moreover, the statements as to the date of the first imitations (see pp. 83, 108, 109, 118, 121) are not wholly in accord with one another.

I. E. Löbisch, likewise a physician, in his "Entwickel-ungsgeschichte der Seele des Kindes" ("History of the Development of the Mind of the Child," Vienna, 1851, p. 68), says: "Naturally the first sound formed in the mouth, which is more or less open, while the other organs of speech are inactive, is the sound resembling *a*, which approximates sometimes more, sometimes less, nearly to the *e* and the *o*.*

"Of the consonants the first are those formed by closing and opening the lips: *m*, *b*, *p* ; these are at first indistinct and not decidedly differentiated till later; then the *m* naturally goes not only before the *a* but also after it; *b* and *p* for a long time merely commence a syllable, and rarely close one until other consonants also have been formed. A child soon says *pa*, but certainly does not say *ab* until he can already pronounce other consonants also (p. 79).

"The order in which the sounds are produced by the child is the following: Of the vowels, first *a*, *e*, *o*, *u*, of course not well distinguished from *a* at the beginning; the last vowel is *i*. Of the consonants, *m* is the first, and it passes by way of the *w* into *b* and *p*. But here we may express our astonishment that so many writers on the subject of the order of succession of the consonants in the development of speech have assigned so late a date to the formation of the *w*; Schwarz puts it even after *t*, and before *r* and *s*. Then come *d*, *t* ; then *l* and *n* ; *n* is easily combined with *d* when it precedes *d* ; next *f* and the gutturals *h*, *ch*, *g*, *k*, the *g* and *k* often confounded with *d* and *t*. *S* and *r* are regarded as nearly simultaneous in their appearance; the gutturals as coming later, the latest of them being *ch*. Still, there is a difference in this

---

* The vowels have the Continental, not the English, sounds.

respect in different children. For many produce a sound resembling *r* among the first consonant sounds; so too *ä*, *ö*, *ü ;* the diphthongs proper do not come till the last."

These statements of Löbisch, going, as they do, far beyond pure observation, can not all be regarded as having general validity. For most German children, at least, even those first adduced can scarcely claim to be well founded.

H. Taine (in the supplement to his book on " Intelligence," which appeared in a German translation in 1880) noted, as expressions used by a French child in the fifteenth month, *papa, maman, tété* (nurse, evidently a word taken from the word *téter*, " to nurse or suck at the breast "), *oua-oua* (dog, in all probability a word said for the child to repeat), *koko* (cock, no doubt from *coq-coq*, which had been said for the child), *dada* (horse, carriage, indicating other objects also, no doubt; a demonstrative word, as it is with many German children). *Tem* was uttered without meaning for two weeks; then it signified " give, take, look, pay attention." I suspect that we have here a mutilation of the strongly accentuated *tiens*, which had probably been often heard. As early as the fourteenth month, *ham* signified " I want to eat " (*hamm*, then *am*, might have had its origin in the echo of *faim, as-tu faim?* (are you hungry?)). At the age of three and a half months this child formed only vowels, according to the account; at twelve months she twittered and uttered first *m-m*, then *kraaau, papa,* with varying intonation, but spoke no word with a recognizable meaning. In the tenth month there was an understanding of some questions. For the child, when asked " Where is grandpapa?" smiled at the portrait of the grandfather, but not at the one of the grandmother, which was not so good a likeness. In the eleventh

month, at the question "Where is mamma?" the child
would turn toward her mother, and in like manner toward
the father at the question, "papa"?

A second child observed by Taine made utterances
that had intellectual significance in the seventh week, for
the first time.   Up to the age of five months *ah, gue,
gre* (French) were heard ; in the seventh month, also
ata, ada.

In his reflections, attached to these and a few other
observations of his own, Taine rightly emphasizes the
great power of generalization and the peculiarity the very
young child had of associating with words it had heard
other notions than those common with us; but he as-
cribes too much to the child's inventive genius.   The child
guesses more than it discovers, and the very cases adduced
(*hamm, tem*), on which he lays great weight, may be traced,
as I remarked above parenthetically, to something heard
by the child; this fact he seems to have himself quite
overlooked.   It is true, that in the acquirement of speech
one word may have several different meanings in succession, as is especially the case with the word *bébé* (corresponding to the English word *baby*), almost universal with
French children; it is not true that a child without imitation of sounds invents a word with a fixed meaning, and
that, with no help or suggestion from members of the
family, it employs its imperfectly uttered syllables (Lall-
sylben) consistently for designating its ideas.

Among the notes of Wyma concerning an English
child ("The Mental Development of the Infant of To-
day," in the "Journal of Psychological Medicine and
Mental Pathology," vii, Part I, pp. 62–69, London, April,
1881), the following, relating to the acquisition of speech,
are to be mentioned :

At five months the child began to use a kind of language, consisting of six words, to indicate a desire or intention. *Ning* signified desire for milk, and was employed for that up to the age of two years. (The word may possibly have been derived from the word *milk*,* frequently heard.) At nine months the child made use of the words *pretty things* for animals; at ten months it formed many small sentences.

The child practiced itself in speaking, even without direct imitation of words just spoken, for at the age of two years it began to say over a number of nursery rhymes that nobody in the house knew, and that could not have been learned from other children, because the child had no intercourse with such. At a later period the child declared that the rhymes had been learned from a former nurse, whom it had not seen for nearly three months. Thus the articulation was perfecting itself for weeks before it was understood. The exercises of the child sounded like careless reading aloud.

The book of Prof. Ludwig Strümpell, of Leipsic, " Psychologische Pädagogik " (Leipsic, 1880, 368 pages), contains an appendix, " Notizen über die geistige Entwickelung eines weiblichen Kindes während der ersten zwei Lebensjahre " (" Notes on the Mental Development of a Female Child during the First Two Years of Life "); in this are many observations that relate to the learning of speech. These are from the years 1846 and 1847.

In the tenth week, *ah! ah!* was an utterance of joy; in the thirteenth, the child sings, all alone; in the nineteenth comes the guttural utterance, *grrr*, but no consonant is assigned to this period. In the first half-year are

---

* Or possibly for the word *drink*, which a child of my acquaintance called *ghing*.—EDITOR.

heard distinctly, in the order given, *ei, aga, eigei, ja, ede, dede, eds, edss, emme, meme, nene, nein.* In the eighth month, there is unmistakable understanding of what is said; e. g., " Where is the tick-tack? " In the ninth, *am, amme, ap, pap,* are said; she sings vowels that are sung for her. In the eleventh month, imitation of sounds is frequent, *kiss, kiss;* at sight of the tea-kettle, *ssi, ssi;* she knows all the people in the house; calls the birds by the strange name *tibu.* Echolalia. In the fourteenth month, needles are called *tick* (*stich* = prick or stitch). To the question, " Where is Emmy? " the child points, correctly, to herself; says distinctly, *Kopf* (head), *Buch* (book), *roth* (red), *Tante* (aunt), *gut* (good), *Mann* (man), *Baum* (tree); calls the eye (Auge) *ok*, Pruscinsky *prrti,* the dog *uf, uf.* In the seventeenth month, simple sentences are spoken; she speaks to herself. In the nineteenth month, she calls herself by her name, and counts *twei, drei, ümpf, exe, ibene, atte, neune* (zwei, drei, fünf, sechs, sieben, acht, neun—2, 3, 5, 6, 7, 8, 9); in the twenty-second month, she talks a good deal to herself, and makes very rapid progress in the correct use of words and the formation of sentences.

From the diary kept by Frau von Strümpell concerning this daughter and a sister of this one, and kindly placed at my disposal in the original, I take the following notes: In the eighth month, *mamma,* in the tenth, *papa,* without meaning. In the eleventh month, the child's understanding of what is said to her is surprising, and so is her imitation. To " Guten Tag " (good-day) she responds, *tata;* to " Adieu," *adaa.* A book, which the child likes to turn the leaves of, she calls *ade* (for a b c). The first certain association of a sound learned with a concept seems to be that of the *ee*, which has often been said to her, with wet, or with what is forbidden. *Amme am om*, "Amme komm" (nurse come) (both imitative), is most frequently repeated, *papa* seldom. The *r* guttural, or rattled, is imperfectly imitated. In the thirteenth month, the little girl says, *tippa tappa*, when she wants to be carried, and responds *te te* to "steh! steh" (stop)! She now calls the book *a-be-te* (for a b c). Pigeons she calls *kurru ;* men, in the picture-book, *mann mann.* When some one asked, "Where is the brush?" the child made the motion of brushing. To the questions, "Where is your ear, your tooth, nose, hand, your fingers, mamma's ear, papa's nose?" etc., she points correctly to the object. On her mother's coming into the room, *mamam ;* her father's, *papap.* When the nurse is gone, *amme om, amme am.* The mother asked some one, "Do you hear?" and the child looked at her and took hold of her own ears. To the question, "How do we eat?" she makes the motion of eating. She says *nein* when she means to refuse. "Dank" (thank) is pronounced *dakkn.* "Bitte" (I beg, or please) is correctly pronounced. She understands the meaning of spoon, dress, mirror, mouth, plate, drink, and many other words, and likes to hear stories, especially when they contain the words already known to her. In the fifteenth month "Mathilde" is given by her as *tilda* and *tida.* At sight of a faded bouquet she said *blom* (for Blume, flower). She says everything that is said to her, though imperfectly; produces the most varied articulate sounds; says *ta, papa, ta* when she hands anything to a person; calls the foot (Fuss) *pss*, lisping and thrusting out the tongue. She often says *omama* and *opapa.* In the seventeenth month, Ring is called *ning*, Wagen (carriage), *uagen*, Sophie, *dsofi*, Olga, *olla*, krank (ill), *kank*, Pflaume (plum), *pluma*, satt (satisfied, as to hunger), *datt*, Hände-waschen (washing the hands), *ander-uaschen*, Schuh and Tuch (shoe

18

and cloth), *tu*, Strumpf (stocking), *tumpf*, Hut (hat), *ut*,
Suppe (soup), *duppe*. *Mama kum bild dat bank*, is for
" Mama komm, ich habe das Bilderbuch, erzähle mir dazu
etwas, dort setz' Dich zu mir" (M., come, I have the
picture-book; tell me something in it; sit there by me).
In the eighteenth month, " Where is Omama?" is answered with *im garten ;* " How are Omama and Opapa?"
with *sund* (for gesund, well); " What is Omama doing?"
with *näht* (she is sewing). The black Apollo is called
pollo warz (schwarz, black).

The sister of this child, in the tenth month, applied
the word *mama* to her mother, *pap pap* and *papap* to her
father, but was less sure in this; *tjē-tē* were favorite syllables. When asked, " Where is Tick-tack ? " she looks at
the clock on the wall. A piercing scream is an utterance
of joy. In the fifteenth month, *Apapa* is her word for
grandfather, and is roguishly used for grandmother. She
says *aben* for " haben" (have), *tatta* for " Tante " (aunt),
apa (for *uppa*) means " I want to go up." Her imitation
of what is said is very imperfect, but her understanding
of it is surprising. In the nineteenth month she makes
much use of her hands in gesture instead of speaking.
Kuker is her word for " Zucker " (sugar), *bildebu* for " Bilderbuch " (picture-book). But she habitually calls a book
omama or *opapa* (from the letters of her grandparents).
Clara is pronounced *clala*, Christine, *titine*. In the twentieth month, her mother, after telling her a story, asked,
" Who, pray, is this, I ? " and the child replied, "*Mamma*."
" And who is that, you? " " *Bertha, Bertha* " (the child's
name) was the answer. At this period she said, *Bertha
will ;* also *paren* (for fahren, drive), *pallen* (fallen, fall),
bot, (Brot, bread), *atig* (artig, good, well-behaved), *mal*
(noch einmal, once more), *muna* (Mund, mouth), *aujen*
(Augen, eyes), *ol* (Ohr, ear), *tirn* (Stirn, forehead), *wanne*

(Wange, cheek, and Wanne, bath-tub), *aua* (August), *dute* (gute) *mama, päsche* (Equipage), *wasar tinken* (Wasser trinken, drink water) *dabel* (Gabel, fork), *lüssel* (Schlüssel, key), *is nits* (ist nichts, is nothing), *mula* (Milch, milk), *ass* (heiss, hot).

Another remarkable observation is the following from the fifteenth month. It reminds one of the behavior of hypnotized adults. On her grandmother's birthday the child said some rhymes that she did not easily remember (there were six short verses, thirty-four words). One night soon after the birthday festival the little girl said off the verses, "almost for the first time without any stumbling, in her sleep."

From this we see how much more quickly in regard to articulation and independent use of words both these girls (the first of whom weighed only six pounds at birth) learned to speak than did Sigismund's boy, my own boy, and others.

Darwin observed (*A Biographical Sketch of an Infant* in "Mind, a Quarterly Review of Psychology and Philosophy," July, 1877, pp. 285–294) in a son of his, on the forty-seventh day of his life, a formation of sounds without meaning. The child took pleasure in it. The sounds soon became manifold. In the sixth month he uttered the sound *da* without any meaning; but in the fifth he probably began to try to imitate sounds. In the tenth month the imitation of sounds was unmistakable. In the twelfth he could readily imitate all sorts of actions, such as shaking his head and saying "Ah." He also understood intonations, gestures, several words, and short sentences. When exactly seven months old, the child associated his nurse with her name, so that when it was called out he would look round for her. In the thirteenth month the boy used gestures to explain his wishes; for instance, he picked up a bit of paper and gave it to his father, pointing to the fire, as he had often seen and liked to see paper burned. At exactly the age of a year he called food *mum*, which also signified " Give me food," and he used this word instead of beginning to cry as formerly. This word with affixes signified particular things to eat; thus *shu-mum* signified sugar, and a little later licorice was called *black-shu-mum*. When asking for food by the word *mum* he gave to it a very strongly marked tone of longing (Darwin says an " interrogatory sound," which should mean the same thing). It is remarkable that my child also, and in the tenth week for the first time, said *mömm* when he was hungry, and that a child observed by Fritz Schultze (Dresden) said *mäm-mäm*. Probably the syllable has its origin from the primitive syllable *ma* and from hearing the word " mamma " when placed at the breast of the mother.

Of the facts communicated by the physiologist Vierordt concerning the language of the child (" Deutsche Revue " of January, 1879, Berlin, pp. 29–46) should be mentioned this, that a babe in its second month expressed pleasure by the vowel *a*, the opposite feeling by *ä*. This is true of many other children also. In the third and fourth months the following syllables were recognizable: *mam, ämma, fu, pfu, ess, äng, angka, acha, erra, hab*. A lisping babe said, countless times, *hab, hob, ha*. These syllables coincide in part with those given by other observers. The *pf* and *ss* only have not been heard by me at this age, and I doubt whether *f*, for which teeth are needed, was produced with purity so early. In the second and third years a child pronounced the following words: *beb* (for bös, naughty); *bebe* (Besen, *beesann*, broom); *webbe* (Wasser, *watja*, water); *wewe* (Löwe, *löwee*, lion); *ewebau* (Elephant, *elafant*); *webenau* (Fledermaus, *leba-*

maunz, bat); *babaube* (Blasebalg, *ba-abats,* bellows); *ade* (Hase, hare); *emele* (Schemel, footstool); *gɪgod* (Schildkröte, tortoise).

These examples illustrate very well the mogilalia and paralalia that exist in every child, but with differences in each individual. Sigmatism and parasigmatism and paralambdacism are strongly marked. At the same time the influence of dialect is perceptible (Tübingen). The pronunciations given in parentheses in the above instances were regularly used by my boy in his twenty-sixth month when he saw the pictures of the objects named in his picture-book. (In Jena.) One would not suppose beforehand that *watja* and *webbe* have the same meaning. From the ten examples may be seen, further, that *f, l, r, s, t* present more difficulties of articulation than *b, w, m, g,* and *d ;* but neither must this be made a general conclusion. The *w* (on account of the teeth) regularly comes later than the *b, m,* and *r.*

In the third year Vierordt noted down the following narration. I put in brackets the words omitted by the child:

id. mama . . papa gäge	[Es] ist [eine] mama [und ein] papa gewesen
unn die habe wai didi gabt	und diese haben zwei Kinder gehabt,
unn. didi . . . waud.	und [die] Kinder [sind in den] Wald [gegangen]
unn habe ohd duh	und haben Holz geholt;
na . . an e gugeeide guju	dann [sind sie] an ein Zuckerhäuschen gegangen
unn habe gäg	und haben gegessen ;
no ad die egg gag	dann hat die Hexe gesagt :
näg näg neidi	"Nucker, Nucker Neisle
wie. immi. eidi	wer [krabbelt] mir am Haüsle ?"
no habe die didi gag	dann haben die Kinder gesagt :
die wid, de immi immi wid	["Der Wind, der Wind, das himmlische Kind"] Der Wind, der himmlische, himmlische Wind.

(There were once a mama and a papa, and they had two children. And the children went into the woods and fetched wood. Then they came to a little sugar house and ate. Then the witch said: "Nucker, Nucker Neisle, who is crawling in my little house?" Then the children said: "The wind, the wind, the heavenly child" —The wind, the heavenly, heavenly wind.)

I told the same story to my boy for the first time when he was two years and eighteen days old. He repeated, with an effort:

Ess ets aine mama unn aįn papa edam (wesen).

unn (unt) diesa abn wais (twai) kinna (tinder) ghatf (dehappt).

unn die kinna sint (dsint) in den walt tegang (gangen).

unn-daben (habn) holz (olz) gehōl (ohlt).

dann sint (dsint) sie an ain utsom-händom (zukehäussn) zezan (gangn).

unn (unt) habn (abn) ge . . . (dessen).

dann hatt die hetse (hekksee) dsa (tsakt).

nanuck (nuke nuke) nana nainle (naisle).

wer . . (drabbelt) mir am häultje (äusle).

dann baben (habn) die . . . (tinder) ze-a (dsagt).

der wiĕds (wind) . . . (der fint).

dsēr wenn daz (das) himmelä (immlis) khint (tint).

Where the periods are, his attempts were all vain. At any rate, he would say *pta-pta* as he usually did in fruitless efforts at imitating sounds. Just two months after these first attempts, the same child recited for me the narrative, using the expressions in the parentheses; this indicated a distinct progress in articulation. A year after the first attempt, he easily repeated the whole, with only a single error. He still said *himmelä*, and then *himmliss*, for " himmlische."

A third boy (Düsseldorf) repeated the narrative much better, as early as his twenty-fifth month. He made only the following errors, which were noted by his mother, and kindly communicated by her to me :

gewesa	for gewesen	*fai*	for zwei
gehat	" gehabt	*kinner*	" kinder
gehat }	" gesagt	*wlad*	" Wald
gehakt }		*hol-l-l-t*	" Holz
gegannen	" gegangen	*uckerhäussen*	" Zuckerhäuschen
hamen	" haben	*hekes*	" Hexe
hind hie	" sind sie	*neissel*	" neisle
kabbell	" krabbelt	*häussel*	" Häusle
himmli-he	" himmlische		

The *ss* between two vowels was imperfect, reminding one of the English " th " and the German " sch " and " s." The child could not at this time be brought to learn by heart.

We see, from these three versions, how unequal the capacity for articulation is in its development, and how varied it is in regard to the omission of difficult consonants and the substitution of others in place of them, as well as in regard to transposition, e. g., in *wand, walt, wlad* (Wald), *wenn, wid, wiĕds, fint* (Wind)—and this even in the same individual.

As no one thus far has instituted comparisons of this sort, one more example may be given. The verses taught by Sigismund to his child (for whom I use the sign S) of twenty-one months, were often repeated by my boy (A), of twenty-five months, to me, and by the boy from Düsseldorf (D), in his twenty-fifth month, to his mother :

	S.	A.		D.
	21st month.	25th month.	27th month.	25th month.
Guter	tute	tuten	tuter	guter
Mond	bohnd	monn	mond	Mund
Du gehst	du tehz	du gehts	du dehst	du gehs
so stille	so tinne	so tilte	so tille	ho tille
durch die	duch die	durch die	durch die	durch die
Abendwolken	aten-bonten	aben-woltn	abendwolkn	abehtwolken
hin	in	in	in	hin
gehst so	tchz so	gehts so	dehst so	gehs so
traurig	tautech (atich)	treuja	trauig	terauhig
und ich	und ich	unn ich	und ich	und ich
fühle	büne	felam	fühle	fühle
dass ich	dass ich	dess ich	dass ich	dass ich
ohne Ruhe	one ule	ohno ruhge	ohne ruhe	ohni ruhe
bin	bin	bin	bin	bin
Guter	tute	hotten	tuter	guter
Mond	bohnd	mohn	mond	mond
du darfst	du atz	du dafp	du darfst	du darf
es wissen	es bitten	es witsen	es wissen	es wissen
weil du so	bein du so	leil du so	weil du so	weil du ho
verschwiegen	bieten	wereidsam	verwiegen	werwiegen
bist	bitz	bits	bist	bits
warum	amum	wa-um	warum	wahum
meine	meine	meine	meinhe	meine
Thränen	tänen	tänen	thränen	tänen
fliessen	bieten	flietjam	fliessen	fliessen
und mein	und mein	und mein	und mein	und mein
Herz so	ätz so	hetz so	erst so	hetz ho
traurig ist	atich iz	treutjam its	trauig ist	taudig ist
Errors	24	26	13	18

The errors are very unlike, and are characteristic for each child. The fact that in the case of A the errors diminished by half within two months is to be explained by frequency of recitation. I may add that the inclination to recite was so often lacking that a good deal of pains was required to bring the child to it.

From the vocabulary of the second year of the child's

life, according to the observations of Sigismund and my-self, the following words of frequent use are also worthy of notice:

	Vater (father)	Mutter (mother)	Anna	Milch (milk)	Kuh (cow)	Pferd (horse)
S.	atte ätte tate fatte	amme ämme ämmäm mämme matte	anne	minne	muh	hotto dodo päd
P.	va-ata papa	mama	anna	mimi	mumuh mukuh	otto pfowed fowid

	Vogel (bird)	Mund (mouth)	Nase (nose)	Ohr (ear)	Haare (hair)	Finger	Da (there)
S.	piep-piep	mund	ase	ohn	ale	finne	da
P.	piep, pipiep	mum	nane	o-a	ha-i	finge wi-er	da

	Adieu	Guten Tag (good-day)	Fort (away)	Ja (yes)	Nein (no)
S.	adé	tag	fot	ja	nein
P.	adjee	tatach	wott	ja; jaja	neinein

	Grossmutter (grandmother)	Kuk	Zucker (sugar)	Karl	Grete
S.	tosutte abutte osmutte	o-tute	zucke	all	ete
P.	a-mama e-mama	kuk	ucka	kara	dete

Sigismund noticed the following names of animals (in imitation of words given to the children): *bä, put, gik-gak, wäkwäk, huhu, ihz* (Hinz). I did not find these with my child. Sigismund likewise observed *baie-baie* for Wiege (cradle), which my child was not acquainted with; *päpä* for verborgen (hidden); *eichönten* for Eichhörnchen (squirrel); *äpften* for Äpfelchen (little apple); *mädsen* and *mädis* for Mädchen (girl); *atatt* for Bernhard; *hundis* for Hundchen, the Thüringian form of Hündchen (little dog); *pot* for Topf (pot); *dot* for dort (yonder). On the other hand, both children used *wehweh* for Schmerz (pain); *caput* for zerbrochen (broken to pieces); *schoos*, *sooss* for " auf den Schooss möcht ich " (I want to get up in the lap); *auf* for " hinauf möchte ich gehoben werden " (I want to be taken up); *toich* for Storch (stork); *tul* for Stuhl (chair). A third child in my presence called his grandmother *mama-mama*, i. e., twice-mamma, in distinction from the mother. This, however, does not necessarily imply a gift for invention, as the expression " Mamma's Mamma " may have been used of the grandmother in speaking to the child.

Other children of the same age do very much the same. The boy D, though he repeated cleverly what was said, was not good at naming objects when he was expected to do this of himself. He would say, e. g., *pilla* for Spiegel (mirror). At this same period (twenty-five months) he could not yet give the softened or liquid sound of consonants (mouilliren). He said *n* and *i* and *a* very plainly, and also *i-a*, but not *nja*, and not once " ja "; but, on the contrary, always turned away angrily when his father or I, or others, required it of him. But as late as the twenty-eighth month echolalia was present in the highest degree in this very vigorous and intelligent child, for he would at times repeat mechanically the last word of every sentence spoken in his hearing, and even a single word, e. g., when some one asked " Warum? " (why) he likewise said *warum* without answering the question, and he continued to do it for days again and again in a vacant way, with and without the tone of interrogation (which he did not understand). From this we see again plainly that the imitation of sounds is independent of the understanding of them, but is dependent on the functions of articulation.

These functions are discussed by themselves in the work of Prof. Fritz Schultze, of Dresden, "Die Sprache des Kindes" ("The Language of the Child," Leipsic, 1880, 44 pp.). The author defends in this the "principle of the least effort." He thinks the child begins with the sounds that are made with the least physiological effort, and proceeds gradually to the more difficult sounds, i. e., those which require more "labor of nerve and muscle." This "law" is nothing else than the "loi du moindre effort" which is to be traced back to Maupertuis, and which was long ago applied to the beginnings of articulation in children: e. g., by Buffon in 1749 ("Œuvres complètes," Paris, 1844, iv, pp. 68, 69), and, in spite of Littré, again quite recently by B. Perez* ("Les trois premières Années de l'Enfant," Paris, 1878, pp. 228–230, *seq.*) But this supposed "law" is opposed by many facts which have been presented in this chapter and the preceding one. The impossibility of determining the degree of "physiological effort" required for each separate sound in the child, moreover, is well known. Besides, every sound may be produced with very unequal expenditure of force; but the facts referred to are enough for refutation of the theory. According to Schultze, e. g., the vowels ought, in the process of development of the child's speech, to appear in the following order, separated in time by long intervals: 1. Ä; 2. A; 3. U; 4. O; 5. E; 6. I; 7. Ö; 8. Ü. It is correct that *ä* is one of the vowels that may be first plainly distinguished; but neither is it the first vowel audible

---

* "The First Three Years of Childhood," edited and translated by Alice M. Christie; published in Chicago, 1885.

—on the contrary, the first audible vowel is indistinct, and imperfectly articulated vowels are the first—nor can we admit that *ä* is produced with less of effort than is *a*. The reverse is the case. Further, *ö* is said to present "enormous difficulties," and hence has the place next to the last; but I have often heard the *ö*, short and long, perfectly pure in the second month, long before the *i*, and that not in my child alone. From the observations upon the latter, the order of succession appears to be the following: Indeterminate vowels, *u, ̮ä, a, ö, o, ai, ao, i, e, ü, oeu* (French sound in cœur), *au, oi*. Thus, for the above eight vowels, instead of 1, 2, 3, 4, 5, 6, 7, 8, the order 3, 1, 2, 7, 4, 6, 5, 8, so that only *i* and *ü* keep their place. But other children give a varying order, and these differences in the order of succession of vowels as well as of consonants will certainly not be referred to the "influence of heredity." Two factors of quite another sort are, on the contrary, to be taken into account here in the case of every normal child without exception, apart from the unavoidable errors in every assigned order growing out of incomplete observation. In the earliest period and when the babbling monologues begin, the cavity of the mouth takes on an infinitely manifold variety of forms—the lips, tongue, lower jaw, larynx, are moved, and in a greater variety of ways than ever afterward. At the same time there is expiration, often loud expiration, and thus originates entirely at random sometimes one sound, sometimes another. The child *hears* sounds and tones new to him, hears his own voice, takes pleasure in it, and delights in making sounds, as he does in moving his limbs in the bath. It is natural that he should find more pleasure in some sounds, in others less. The first are more frequently made by him on account of the motor memories that are associated with the acoustic memories, and an observer does not hear the others at all if he observes the child only from time to time. In fact, however, almost all simple sounds, even the most difficult, are formed in purity before they are used in speaking in the first eight months—most frequently those that give the child pleasure, that satisfy his desires, or lessen his discomfort. It is not to be forgotten that even the *ä*, which requires effort on account of the drawing back and spreading out of the tongue, diminishes discomfort. The fretful babe feels better when he cries *u-ä* than when he keeps silent. The second factor is determined by the surroundings of the child. Those sounds which the child distinctly hears he will be able to imitate correctly sooner than he will other sounds: but he will be in condition to hear most correctly, first of all, the sounds that are most frequent, just because these most frequently excite the auditory nerve and its tract in the brain; secondly, among these sounds that are acoustically most sharply defined, viz., first the vowels, then the resonants (m, n, ng); last, the compound "friction-sounds" (fl, schl). But it is only in part that the surroundings determine this order of succession for the sounds. Another thing that partly determines and modifies this order is the child's own unwearied practice in forming consonant-sounds. He hears his own voice now better than he did at an earlier period when he was forming vowels only. He most easily retains and repeats, among the infinitely manifold consonants that are produced by loud expiration, those which have been distinctly heard by him. This is owing to the association of the motor and the acoustic memory-image in the brain. These are the most frequent in his speech. Not until later does the mechanical difficulty of articulation exert an influence, and this comes in at the learning of the compound sounds. Hence there can not be any chronological order of succession of sounds that holds good universally in the language of the child, because each language has a different order in regard to the frequency of appearance of the sounds; but heredity can have no influence here, because every child of average gifts, though it may hear from its birth a language unknown to its ancestors, if it hears no other, yet learns to speak this language perfectly. What is hereditary is the great plasticity of the entire apparatus of speech, the voice, and with it a number of sounds that are not acquired, as *m*. An essential reason for the defective formation of sounds in children born deaf is the fact that they do not hear their own voice. This defect may also be hereditary.

The treatise of F. Schultze contains, besides, many good remarks upon the *technique* of the language of the child, but, as they are of inferior psychogenetic interest, they need not be particularly mentioned here. Others of them are only partially confirmed by the observations, as is shown by a comparison with what follows.

Gustav Lindner ("Twelfth Annual Report of the Lehrer-seminars at Zschopau," 1882, p. 13) heard from his daughter, in her ninth week, *arra* or *ärrä*, which was uttered for months. Also *äckn* appeared early. The principle of the least effort Lindner finds to be almost absolutely refuted by his observations. He rightly remarks that the frequent repetitions of the same groups of sounds, in the babbling monologues, are due in part to a kind of pleasure in success, such as urges adults also to repeat their successful efforts. Thus his child used to imitate the reading of the newspaper (in the second half-year) by *degattegattegatte*. In the eleventh and twelfth months the following were utterances of hers in repeating words heard : *ómama*, *oia* (Rosa), *batta* (Bertha), *ächard* (Richard), *wiwi* (Friedchen), *agga* (Martha), *olla olla* (Olga, her own name). Milch (milk) she called *mimi*, Stuhl (chair) *tuhl*, Laterne (lantern), *katonne*, the whistle of an engine in a neighboring factory, *wuh* (prolonged, onomatopoetic), Paul, *gouch*, danke (thank you), *dagn* or *dagni*, Baum (tree), *maum*. Another child substituted *u* for *i* and *e*, saying *hund* for " Kind," and *uluwant* for " Elephant ": thus, *ein fomme hund lass wäde much* for " ein frommes Kind lass werden mich " (let me become a pious child). Lindner's child, however, called " werden " not *wäde* but *wegen ;* and " turnen " she called *tung*, " blau " *balau*. At the end of the second year no sound in the German language presented difficulties to the child. Her pronunciation was, however, still incorrect, for the correct pronunciation of the separate sounds does not by any means carry with it the pronunciation of them in their combinations. This remark of Lindner's is directly to the point, and is also confirmed, as I find, by the first attempts of the child of four years to read a word after having learned the separate letters. The learning of the correct pronunciation is also delayed by the child's preference of his original incorrect pronunciation, to which he is accustomed, and which is encouraged by imitations of it on the part of his relatives. Lindner illustrates this by good examples. His child continued to say *mimela* after " Kamilla " was easy for him. Not till the family stopped saying it did " Kamilla " take its place. At the age of three and a half years the child still said *gebhalten* for " behalten " and *vervloren* for " verloren," as well as *gebhüte* for " behüte." " Grosspapa " was called successively *opapa, gropapa, grosspapa*. Grossmama had a corresponding development. " Fleisch " (meat) was first called *jeich*, then *leisch ;* " Kartoffeln " (potatoes) *kaffom*, then *kaftoffeln ;* " Zschopau " *sopau, schodau, tschopau ;* " Sparbüchse " (savings-box) *babichse, spabichse, spassbüchse, sparzbüchse ;* " Häring " (herring, also gold-fish) *hänging*. A sound out of the second sylla-

ble goes into the first. The first question, *isn das?* from
" Was ist denn das ? " (what is that, pray?) was noticed in
the twentieth month ; the interrogative word *was?* (what)
in the twenty-second month. Wo? (where) and Wohin?
(whither) had the same meaning (that of the French *où ?*),
and this as late as in the fourth year. The word " Ich "
(I) made its appearance in the thirtieth month. As to
verbs, it is to be mentioned that, with the child at two
years of age, before the use of the tenses there came the
special word denoting activity in general : thus he said,
when looking at a head of Christ by Guido Reni, *thut
beten*, instead of " betet " (" does pray," instead of " prays ").
The verb " sein " (be) was very much distorted : *Warum
warst du nicht fleissig gebist?* (gebist for gewesen) (why
have you not been industrious?). (Cf., pp. 172, 177.) He
inflected *bin, binst* (for bist), *bint* (ist), *binn* (sind), *bint*
(sind and seid), *binn* (sind). Further, *wir isn* (wir sind,
we are), and *nun sei ich ruhig* (sei for bin) (now I am
quiet), and *ich habe nicht ruhig geseit* (*habe* for " bin "
and *geseit* for " gewesen ") (I have not been quiet), are
worthy of note, because they show how strong an influence
in the formation of words during the transition period is
exerted by the forms most frequently heard—here the imperative. The child used first of all the imperative; last
the subjunctive. The superlative and comparative were
not used by this child until the fourth year.

The observations of Lindner (edited anew in the periodical " Kosmos " for 1882) are among the best we have.

In the case of four brothers and sisters, whose mother,
Frau Dr. Friedemann, of Berlin, has most kindly placed
at my disposal trustworthy observations concerning them,
the first articulate sounds heard were *ärä, hägä, äche*, and
a deep guttural, rattling or snarling sound (Schnarren);
but the last was heard from only one of the children.

The above syllables contain three consonants (*r, h, ch*) that are declared by many, wrongly, to be very late in their appearance. These children in their first attempts at speaking often left out the first consonant of a word pronounced for them, or else substituted for it the one last heard, as if their memory were not equal to the retaining of the sounds heard first: e. g., in the fifteenth month they would say *tĕ, t* for *Hut* (hat), *Lale* for *Rosalie ;* in the twenty-fourth, *kanke* for *danke* (thank you), *kecke* for *Decke* (covering), *kucker* for *Zucker* (sugar), *huch, huche* for *Schuh, Schuhe* (shoe, shoes), fifteenth month. In the last two cases comes in, to explain the omission, also the mechanical difficulty of the *Z* and *Sch.* The oldest of these children, a girl, when a year old, used to say, when she refused anything, *ateta*, with a shake of the head. She knew her own image in the glass, and pointed at it, saying *täte* (for *Käte*). In the following table the Roman figures stand for the month ; F₁, F₂, F₃, F₄, for the four children in the order of their ages. No further explanation will be needed :

VIII. *papa* distinctly (F₁); *dada, da, deda,* first syllables (F₄); *derta* for *Bertha* (F₁).

X. *dada,* name for all possible objects (F₂); *papa* (F₃); *ada, mama, detta* (F₄).

XII. *puppe* (doll) correctly; *täte* for *Käte* (F₁); *ida, papa, tata* for *Tante* (aunt); *täte* (F₄).

XIII. *mama, detta* for *Bertha ; wauwau* (F₂); *lala* (F₄).

XIV. *ba* for *baden* (bathe) (F₂).

XV. *hia* for *Ida ; ate* for *artig* (well-behaved); *da* for *danke ; bappen* for *essen* (eat); *piep ; ja, nein* (yes, no) correctly (F₁).

XVI. *ei* (egg) correctly; *feisch* for *Fleisch* (meat); *waffer* for *Wasser* (water); *wuffe* for *Suppe* (F₁); *tatte* for *Tante ; tittak ; Hut* (F₃).

19

XIX. *at* for *Katze* (cat); *duh* for *Kuh* (cow); *wän* for *Schwan* (swan); *nine* for *Kaninchen* (rabbit); *betta* for *Blätter* (leaves); *butta* for *Butterblume* (buttercup); *fiedemann* for *Friedemann; täti* for *Käti* (F_1); *gad* for *gerade* (straight); *kumm* for *krumm* (crooked) (F_3).

XX. *fidat* for *Zwieback* (biscuit); *tierdatten* for *Thiergarten* (zoölogical garden); *waden* for *wagen* (carriage); *nähnaden* for *Nähnadel* (needle); *wewette* for *serviette* (napkin); *teid* for *Kleid* (dress); *weife* for *Seife* (soap); *famm* for *Schwamm* (sponge); *tonnat* for *Konrad; potne* for *Portemonnaie; hauf* for *herauf* (up here); *hunta* for *herunter* (down here); *hiba papa* for *lieber* (dear) *papa* (F_1); *tü* for *Thür* (door); *bau* for *bauen* (build); *teta* for *Käte; manna* for *Amanda; ta* for *guten Tag* (good-day); *ku* for *Kugel* (ball) (F_2); *appudich* for *Apfelmuss* (applesauce); *mich* for *Milch* (milk); *ule pomm* for *Ulrich komm* (Ulrich come); *ku* for *Kuchen* (cake); *lilte* for *Mathilde* (F_3).

XXI. *teine* for *Steine* (stones); *bimelein* for *Blümelein* (little flowers); *mamase* for *Mamachen* (little mama); *tettern* for *klettern* (climb); *Papa weint nis* (Papa doesn't cry), first sentence (F_1); *Mamase, Täte artig—Tuss* (means *Mamachen, Käte ist wieder artig, gib ihr einen Kuss*) (Mamma, darling, Katy is good again, give her a kiss) (F_1); *Amanda's Hut, Mamases Hirm* (for *Schirm*) (Amanda's hat, mamma's umbrella), first use of the genitive case (F_1); *Mein Buch* (my book); *dein Ball* (thy ball) (F_1); *das?* for *was ist das?* (what is that?) in the tone of interrogation (F_1) *dida* for *Ida; lala* for *Rosalie; fadi* for *Fahne* (flag); *büda* for *Brüderchen* (little brother); *hu-e* for *Schuhe* (shoes); *mai maich*, for *meine Milch* (my milk) (F_2).

XXII. *kusch* for *Kuss* (kiss); *sch* generally used instead of *s* for months (F_3).

XXIII. *koka* for *Cacao;* *batt* for *Bett* (bed); *emmu* for *Hellmuth* (light-heartedness); *nanna mommom* (Bonbon); *papa, appel* for *Papa, bitte einen Apfel* (Papa, please, an apple) (F_2); *petscher* for *Schwester* (sister); *till* for *still;* *bils* for *Milch;* *hiba vata* for *lieber Vater* (dear father) (F_3).

XXIV. *pija eine* for *eine Fliege* (a fly); *pipik* for *Musik.* Sentences begin to be formed (F_3).

XXV. *pater* for *Vater* (father); *appelsine* for *Apfelsine* (orange) (F_2).

All these observations confirm my results in regard to articulation, viz., that in very many cases the more difficult sounds, i. e., those that require a more complicated muscular action, are either omitted or have their places supplied by others; but this rule does not by any means hold good universally: e. g., the sound preferred by F_3, *sch*, is more difficult than *s*, and my child very often failed to produce it as late as the first half of the fourth year.

In the twenty-second month, in the case of the intelligent little girl F_1, numbering began suddenly. She took small stones from a table in the garden, one after another, and counted them distinctly up to the ninth. The persons present could not explain this surprising performance (for the child had not learned to count) until it was discovered that on the previous day some one had counted the stairs for the child in going up. My child did not begin to count till the twenty-ninth month, and, indeed, although he knew the numbers (their names, not their meaning), he counted only by adding one to one (cf. above, p. 172). Sigismund's boy, long before he formed sentences, on seeing two horsemen, one following the other at a short interval, said, *eite* (for Reiter)! *noch eins!* This proves the activity of the faculty of numbering.

The boy F$_3$, at the age of two and two thirds years, still said *schank* for *Schrank* and *nopf* for *Knopf*, and, on being told to say *Sch-r-ank* plainly, he said *rrr-schank*. This child from the thirty-first month on made much use of the interrogative words. *Warum? weshalb?* he asked at every opportunity; very often, too, *was? wer? wo?* (Why? wherefore? what? who? where?); sometimes *was?* four or five times when he had been spoken to. When the meaning of what had been said was made plain, then the child stopped asking questions.

The little girl F$_4$, in her thirteenth month, always says, when she sees a clock, *didda* (for "tick-tack," which has been said to her), and imitates with her finger the movement of the pendulum. It was noticed of this child that, when not yet five months old, she would accompany a song, sung for her by her mother, with a continuous, drawling *äh-äh-äh;* but, as soon as the mother stopped, the child became silent also. The experiment was one day (the one hundred and forty-fifth of the child's life) repeated nine times, with the same result.

I have myself repeatedly observed that babes in the fourth month respond to words spoken in a forcible, pleasant manner with sounds indeterminate often, with *ö-ĕ* and other vowels. There is no imitation in this, but a reaction that is possible only through participation of the cerebrum, as in the case of the joyous sounds at music at an earlier period.

The date at which the words heard from members of the family are for the first time clearly imitated, and the time when the words of the mother-tongue are first used independently, depends, undoubtedly, with children in sound condition, chiefly upon the extent to which people occupy themselves with the children. According to Heinr. Feldmann (*De statu normali functionum corporis hu-*

mani. Inaugural dissertation, Bonn, 1833, p. 3), thirty-three children spoke for the first time (*prima verba fecerunt*) as follows :

14	15	16	17	18	19	Month.
1	8	19	3	1	1	Children.

Of these there could walk alone

8 9	10	11 12	Month.
3	24	6	Children.

According to this, it is generally the case (the author presumably observed Rhenish children) that the first independent step is taken in walking several months earlier than the first word is spoken. But the statement of Heyfelder is not correct, that the average time at which sound children learn to walk ("laufen lernen") comes almost exactly at the completion of the twelfth month. The greater part of them are said by him to begin to walk a few days before or after the 365th day. R. Demme observed that the greater part began to walk between the twelfth and eighteenth months, and my inquiries yield a similar result. Sigismund's boy could run before he imitated words and gestures, and he did not yet form a sentence when he had more than sixty words at his command. Of two sisters, the elder could not creep in her thirteenth month, could walk alone for the first time in the fifteenth month, step over a threshold alone in the eighteenth, jump down alone from a threshold in the nineteenth, run nimbly in the twentieth; the younger, on the other hand, could creep alone cleverly at the beginning of the tenth month, even over thresholds, could take the first unsteady steps alone in the thirteenth, and stride securely over the threshold alone in the fifteenth. In spite of this considerable start the younger child was not, by a great deal, so far advanced in articulation, in repeating words after others, and in the use of words, in her fifteenth month, as the elder was in her fifteenth. The latter spoke before she walked, the former ran before she spoke (Frau von Strümpell). My child could imitate gestures (beckoning, clinching the fist, nodding the head) and single syllables (*heiss*), before he could walk, and did not learn to speak till after that; whereas the child observed by Wyma could stand firmly at nine months, and walk soon after, and he spoke at the same age. Inasmuch as in such statistical materials the important thing is to know what is meant by " speaking for the first time," whether it be saying *mama*, or imitating, or using correctly a word of the language that is to be spoken later, or forming a sentence of more than one word—and yet on these points data are lacking—we can not regard the laborious inquiries and collections as of much value. Children in sound condition walk for the most part before they speak, and understand what is said long before they walk. A healthy boy, born on the 13th of July, 1873, ran alone for the first time on the 1st of November, 1874, and formed his first sentence, *hia muta ji* (" Marie! die Mutter ist ausgegangen," *ji* = adieu) (Mary, mother has gone out), on the 21st of November, 1875, thus a full year later (Schulte).

More important, psychogenetically, are observations concerning the forming of new words with a definite meaning before learning to speak—words not to be considered as mutilations, imperfectly imitated or onomatopoetic forms (these, too, would be imitations), or as original primitive interjections. In spite of observations and inquiries directed especially to this point, I have not been able to make sure that any inventions of that sort are made before there has taken place, through the medium of the child's relatives, the first association of ideas with articulate sounds and syllables. There is no reason for supposing them to be made by children. According to the foregoing data, they are not thus made. All the instances of word-inventions of a little boy, communicated by Prof. S. S. Haldemann, of the University at Philadelphia, in his " Note on the Invention of Words " (" Proceedings of the American Philological Association," July 14, 1880) are, like those noted by Taine, by Holden (see below), by myself, and others, onomatopoetic (imitative, pp. 160, 91). He called a cow *m*, a bell *tin-tin* (Holden's boy called a church-bell *ling-dong-mang* [communicated in correspondence]), a locomotive *tshu, tshu*, the noise made by throwing objects into the water *boom*, and he extended this word to mean throw, strike, fall, spill, without reference to the sound). But the point of departure here, also, was the sound. In consideration of the fact that a sound formed in imitation of it, that is, a repetition of the tympanic vibrations by means of the vibrations of the vocal cords, is employed as a *word* for a phenomenon associated with the sound—that this is done by means of the faculty of generalization belonging to children that are intelligent but as yet without speech—it is perfectly allowable, notwithstanding the scruples and objections of even a Max Müller, to look for the origin of language in the imitation of sounds and the repetition of our own inborn vocal sounds, and so in an imitation. For the power of forming concepts must have manifested itself in the primitive man, as is actually the case in the infant, by movements of many sorts before articulate language existed. The question is, not whether the roots of language originated onomatopoetically or interjectionally, but simply whether they originated through imitation or not. For interjections, all of them, could in no way come to be joined together so as to be means of mutual understanding, i. e., words, unless one person imitated those of another. Now if the alalic child be tested as to whether he forms new words in any other way than by imitation and transformation of what he imitates, i. e., whether he forms them solely of his own ability, be it by the combination of impulsive sounds of his own or of sounds accidentally arising in loud expiration, we find no sure case of it. Sound combinations, syllables—and those not in the least imitated—there are in abundance, but that even a single one is, without the intervention of the persons about the child, constantly associated with one and the same idea (before other ideas have received their verbal designation—likewise by means of the members of the family—and have been made intelligible to the child), can not be shown to be probable. My observations concerning the word *atta* (p. 122 *et al.*) would tend in that direction, were it not that the *atta*, uttered in the beginning without meaning, had first got the meaning of " away," through the fact that *atta* was once said by somebody at going away.

So long as proof is wanting, we can not believe that each individual child discovers anew the fundamental fact of the expression of ideas by movements of the tongue; but we have to admit that he has inherited the faculty for such expression, and simply manifests it when he finds occasion for imitations.

The first person that has attempted to fix the *number* of all the words used by the child, independently, before the beginning of the third year of life (and these only), is an astronomer, E. S. Holden, director of the Observatory of the University at Madison, Wisconsin. His results in the case of three children have been recently published (in the " Transactions of the American Philological Association," 1887, pp. 58–68).

Holden found, by help of Webster's "Unabridged Dictionary," his own vocabulary to consist of 33,456 words, with a probable error of one per cent. Allowing a probable error of two per cent, his vocabulary would be comprised between the limits of 34,125 words and 32,787 words. A vocabulary of 25,000 words and over is, according to the researches of himself and his friends, by no means an unusual one for grown persons of average intelligence and education.

Holden now determined in the most careful manner the words actually used by two children during the twenty-fourth month of their lives. A friend in England ascertained the same for a third child. All doubtful words were rigidly excluded. For example, words from nursery rhymes were excluded, unless they were independently and separately used in the same way with words of daily and common use. In the first two cases the words so excluded are above 500 in number. Again, the names of objects represented in pictures were not included unless they were often spontaneously used by the children. The lists of words are presented in the order of their initial letters, because the ease or difficulty of pronouncing a word, the author is convinced, largely determines its early or late adoption. In this I can not fully agree with him, on the ground of my own experience (particularly since I have myself been teaching my child English, in his fourth year; he learns the language easily). It is not correct that the pronunciation rather than the meaning makes the learning of a word difficult. Thus, in all three of Holden's cases, the words that have the least easy initial (s) predominate; the child, however, avoided them and substituted easy ones. Holden makes no mention of this; and in his list of all the words used he puts together, strangely, under one and the same letter, without regard to their sound- (phonic) value, vocables that begin with entirely different sounds. Thus, e. g., under *c* are found *corner* (*k*), *chair* (tsch), *cellar* (*s*); under *k*, actually *knee* (*n*) and *keep* (*k*), and, under *s*, words that begin with the same *s*-sound as in *cellar*, e. g., *soap*, and also words beginning with the *sch*-sound, *sugar*, and with *st*, *sw*, *sm*, and many others. As the words of the three children are grouped, not according to the *sounds* with which they begin, but according to their initial *letters*, into twenty-six classes, the author's conclusions can not be admitted. The words must first all be arranged according to their initial *sounds*. When this task is accomplished, which brings *no* and *know*, e. g., into one class, *wrap* and *rag* into a second— whereas they were put in four different classes—then we find by no means the same order of succession that Holden gives. The author wrote to me, however, in 1882, that his oldest child *understood* at least 1,000 words more than those enumerated here, i. e., than those published by him, and that with both children facility of pronunciation had more influence in regard to the use of words than did the ease with which the words could be understood; this, however, does not plainly follow from the printed statements before me, as he admits. When the first-born child was captivated by a new word, she was accustomed to practice it by herself, alone, and then to come and employ it with a certain pride. The second child did so, too, only in a less striking manner. The boy, on the contrary, who was four years old in December, 1881, and who had no ear for music and less pride than his sisters, did not do as they did.

Further, the statements of the number of all the nouns, adjectives, verbs, and adverbs used by a child of two years are of interest, although they present several errors: e. g., *supper* makes its appearance twice in the case of the same child under *s*, and *enough* figures as an adjective. For the three girls, in their twenty-fourth month, the results were:

Parts of Speech.	First child.	Second child.	Third child.
Nouns.....................	285	230	113
Verbs.....................	107	90	30
Adjectives..................	34	37	13
Adverbs...................	29	17	6
Other parts of speech........	28	25	11
Total...................	483	399	173

A fourth child, brother of the first and second, made use (according to the lists kindly communicated to me by the author), in his twenty-fourth month, of 227 nouns—some proper names among them—105 verbs, 22 adjectives, 10 adverbs, and 33 words of the remaining classes (all these figures being taken from the notes of the child's mother).

From these four vocabularies of the twenty-fourth month it plainly results that the stock of words and the kinds of words depend primarily on the words most used in the neighborhood of the child, and the objects most frequently perceived; they can not, therefore, be alike in different children. The daughters of the astronomer, before their third year, name correctly a portrait of Galileo, and one of Struve. A local " tone," or peculiarity of this sort, attaches to every individual child, a general one to the children of a race. I may add that the third child (in England) seems to have been less accurately observed than the others (in Madison, Wisconsin). Great patience and attention are required to observe and note down every word used by a child in a month.

Without mentioning the name of Holden, but refer-

ring to his investigations, which, in spite of the defects
mentioned, are of the very highest merit, M. W. Humphreys, Professor of Greek in Vanderbilt University, Nash-
ville, has published a similar treatise, based on observations of his own ("A Contribution to Infantile Linguistic,"
in the "Transactions of the American Philological Association," 1880, xi, pp. 6–17). He collected, with the help
of a dictionary, all the words that a little girl of just two
years "had full command of," whether correctly pronounced or not, and whether they appeared exactly in the
twenty-fourth month or earlier. He simply required to
be convinced that every one of the words was understood
and had been spontaneously used, and could still be used.
He did not include proper names, or words (amounting
to hundreds) from nursery-rhymes, or numerals, or names
of the days of the week, because he was not sure that
the child had a definite idea associated with them. The
vocabulary thus numbered 1,121 words: 592 nouns, 283
verbs, 114 adjectives, 56 adverbs, 35 pronouns, 28 prepositions, 5 conjunctions, and 8 interjections. In this table
irregular verb- and noun-forms are not counted as separate words, except in the case of defective verbs, as *am*,
was, *been*. The author presents the 1,121 words according
to their classification as parts of speech, and according to
initial *letters*, not according to initial *sounds*, although he
himself declares this an erroneous proceeding, as I did in
discussing Holden's paper. The only reason for it was
convenience.

In the adoption of a word by the child, difficulty of
utterance had some influence in the *first* year; when the
little girl was two years old, this had ceased to have any
effect whatever. She had by that time adopted certain
substitutes for letters that she could not pronounce, and
words containing these letters were employed by her as

freely as if the substitutes had been the correct sounds. In regard to the meaning, and the frequency of use dependent upon it, it is to be observed that the simplest ideas are most frequently expressed. When two words are synonymous, one of them will be used exclusively by a child, because of the rarer employment of the other by persons speaking in the child's presence. Here, too, the local "tone" that has been mentioned made itself felt; thus, the little girl used the word "crinoid" every day, to designate sections of fossil crinoid stems which abounded in neighboring gravel walks.

As to parts of speech, nouns were most readily seized; then, in order, verbs, adjectives, adverbs, pronouns. Prepositions and conjunctions the child began to employ early, but acquired them slowly. Natural interjections—*wah*, for instance—she used to some extent from the beginning; conventional ones came rather late.

The following observations by Humphreys are very remarkable, and are, in part, up to this time unique :

When about four months old the child began a curious and amusing mimicry of conversation, in which she so closely imitated the ordinary cadences that persons in an adjacent room would mistake it for actual conversation. The articulation, however, was indistinct, and the vowel-sounds obscure, and no attempt at separate words, whether real or imaginary, was made until she was six months old, *when she articulated most syllables distinctly*, without any apparent effort.

When she was eight months old it was discovered that she knew by name every person in the house, as well as most of the objects in her room, and the parts of the body, especially of the face. She also understood simple sentences, such as, " Where is the fire? " " Where is the baby in the glass? " to which she would reply by pointing. In

the following months she named many things correctly,
thus using words as words in the proper sense. The
pronunciation of some final consonants was indistinct, but
all initial consonants were distinctly pronounced, except
th, *t*, *d*, *n*, *l*. These the child learned in the eleventh
month. At this period she could imitate with accuracy
any sound given her, and had a special preference for *ng*
(*ngang*, *ngeng*), beginning a mimicry of language again,
this time using real or imaginary words, without reference
to signification. But an obscurity of vowel-sounds had
begun again. After the first year her facility of utterance
seemed to have been lost, so that she watched the mouths
of others closely when they were talking, and labored pain-
fully after the sounds. Finally, she dropped her mimicry
of language, and, at first very slowly, acquired words with
the ordinary infant pronunciation, showing a preference
for labials (*p*, *b*, *m*) and linguals (*t*, *d*, *n*, not *l*). Presently she substituted easy sounds for difficult ones. In the
period from eighteen months to two years of age, the following defects of articulation appeared regularly: *v* was
pronounced like *b*, *th* (*this*) like *d*, *th* (*thin*) like *t*, *z* like
d, *s* like *t*, *r* like *w*, *j* like *d*, *ch* like *t*, *sh* like *t ;* further:

Initial.	Final.
f like *w*,	*f* like *p*,
l not at all,	*l* correctly,
g like *d*,	*g* correctly,
k like *t*,	*k* correctly,

and in general correctly, *m*, *b*, *p*, *n*, *d*, *t*, *h*, *ng*, *w*. On the
other hand, the initial sounds *bl*, *br*, *pl*, *pr*, *fl*, *fr*, *dr*, *tr*,
thr, *sp*, *st*, became *b*, *b*, *p*, *p*, *w*, *w*, *d*, *t*, *t*, *p*, *t ;* and the initial sounds *sk*, *sw*, *sm*, *sn*, *sl*, *gl*, *gr*, *kw*, *kl*, *kr*, *hw*, became
t, *w*, *m*, *n*, *t* (for *s*), *d*, *w*, *w*, *t*, *w*, *hw* (*h* weak). The letter *y* was not pronounced at all, at first.

From this table, as Humphreys rightly observes, may

be drawn the following conclusions in regard to the initial sounds of words:

When a letter which could be pronounced correctly preceded another, the first was retained, but, if both were represented by substitutes, the second was retained. If, however, the second was one which the child made silent, then she pronounced the first. Thus, $tr = t$, $kr = w$ (for r), $kl = t$ (for k, l being one of her silent letters). With these results should be compared those presented in regard to German children, in the paper of Fritz Schultze (p. 239 above) (which likewise are not of universal application).

The accent was for the most part placed on the last syllable. Only one case of the invention of a new word could be established. When the child was about eighteen months old, a fly flew all about her plate when she was eating, and she exclaimed, " The old fly went wiggely-waggely." But at this time the child had already learned to speak; she knew, therefore, that perceptions are expressed by words. Notwithstanding, the original invention remains remarkable, unless there may be found in it a reminiscence of some expression out of nursery-talk (cf., p. 238). Until the eighteenth month, " no " signified both " yes " and " no."

At the end of two years subordinate propositions were correctly employed. This was the case also with a German girl in Jena, who, for instance, said, " The ball which Puck has " (P. Fürbringer). In the case of my boy such sentences did not make their appearance till much later.

I had hoped to find trustworthy observations in several other works besides those mentioned. Their titles led one to expect statements concerning the acquirement of speech by little children; thus, " Das Kind, Tagebuch eines Vaters " (" The Child, A Father's Diary "), by H. Semmig (second edition, Leipsic, 1876), and the book of B. Perez, already named (p. 239). But inasmuch as for the former of these writers the first cry of the newly-born is a "triumphal song of everlasting life," and for the second author "the glance" is associated with "the magnetic effluvia of the will," I must leave both of these works out of consideration. The second contains many statements concerning the doings and sayings of little children in France; but these can not easily be turned to account.

The same author has issued a new edition, in abridged form, of the "Memoirs," written, according to him, by Dietrich Tiedemann, of a son of Tiedemann two years of age (the biologist, Friedrich Tiedemann, born in 1781). (*Thierri Tiedemann et la science de l'enfant. Mes deux chats. Fragment de psychologie comparée par Bernard Perez.* Paris, 1881, pp. 7–38; Tiedemann, 39–78. "The First Six Weeks of Two Cats.") But it is merely on account of its historical interest that the book is mentioned here, as the scanty (and by no means objective) notes of the diary were made a hundred years ago. The treatises of Pollock and Egger, mentioned in the periodical "Mind" (London, July, 1881, No. 23), I am not acquainted with, and the same is true of the work of Schwarz (mentioned above, p. 224).

Very good general statements concerning the child's acquisition of speech are to be found in Degerando ("L'éducation des sourds-muets de naissance," 1 vol., Paris, 1827, pp. 32–57). He rightly maintains that the child learns to speak through his own observation, without attention from other persons, far more than through systematic instruction; the looks and gestures of the members of the family when talking with one another are especially observed by the child, who avails himself of them in divining the meaning of the words he hears. This divining, or guessing, plays in fact a chief part in the learning of speech, as I have several times remarked.

New comprehensive diaries concerning the actions of children in the first years of life are urgently to be desired. They should contain nothing but well-established *facts*, no hypotheses, and no repetitions of the statements of others.

Among the very friendly notes that have been sent to me, the following particularly conform to the above requirements. They were most kindly placed at my disposal by the Baroness von Taube, of Esthonia, daughter of the very widely and honorably known Count Keyserling. They relate to her first-born child, and come all of them from the mother herself :

In the first five months I heard from my son, when he cried, all the vowels. The sound *ä* was the first and most frequent. Of the consonants, on the other hand, I heard only *g*, which appeared after seven weeks. When the child was fretful he often cried *gege ;* when in good humor he often repeated the syllables *agu, agŏ, äou, ogŏ, eia ;* then *l* came in, *ül*.

The same sounds in the case of my daughter; but from her I heard, up to her tenth month, in spite of all my observation, no other consonants than *g, b, w,* rarely *l,* and finally *m*-sounds. With my son at the beginning of the seventh month an R-sound appeared —*grr, grrr,* plainly associated with *d* in *dirr dirr.* These sounds were decidedly sounds of discomfort, which expressed dissatisfaction, violent excitement, sleepiness ; and they are made even now by the boy at four years of age when, e. g., he is in pain. In the ninth month *dada* and *b, bab-a, bäb-ä* are added. *Agŏ* also is often said, and *ŏ* still more often. This *ŏ* is already a kind of conscious attempt at speaking, for he uses it when he sees anything new, e. g., the dog Caro, which he observes with eager attention, as he does the cat, uttering aloud meanwhile *ŏ, ŏ.*

If any one is called, the child calls in a very loud voice, *Ŏ, oe !* First imitation. (Gestures have been imitated since the eighth month, and the making of grimaces in the child's presence had to be strictly forbidden.) Understanding for what is said is also present,

20

for when one calls " Caro, Caro," in his hearing, he looks about him as if he were looking for the dog. In the tenth month he often repeats *Pap-ba*, but it has no significance.

If " Backe backe kuchen " (" bake cakes," corresponding to our "pat-a-cake ") is said to him, he immediately pats his hands as if preparing bread for baking. In the eleventh month *Pap-ba* is dropped. He now says often *dädädädä*, and, when he is dull or excited (*erregt*) or sleepy, *drin, drin*. These *r*-sounds do not occur with my daughter; but since her tenth month she uses *m*-sounds, *mämmä* when she is sleepy or dull. The boy now stretches out his hand and beckons when he sees any one at a distance. At sight of anything new, he no longer says *ö*, but *äda* (twelfth month). He likes to imitate gestures with his arms and mouth; he observes attentively the *movements of the lips of one who is speaking*, sometimes *touching* at the same time the *mouth of the speaker with his finger*.

At ten months the first teeth came. In the eleventh month the child was for the first time taken out into the open air. Now the *g*-sounds again become prominent—*aga. ga, gugag*. The child begins to creep, but often falls, and while making his toilsome efforts keeps crying out in a very comical manner, *äch, äch, äch!*

At eleven and a half months a great advance. The child is now much out of doors, and enjoys seeing horses, cows, hens, and ducks. When he sees the hens he says *gog, gog*, and even utters some croaking sounds. He can also imitate at once the sound *prrr* when it is pronounced to him. If *papa* is pronounced for him (he has lost this word), he responds regularly *wawa* or *wawawa*. I have only once heard *wauwau* from him. If he hears anybody cough, he immediately gives a little imitative cough in fun (vol. i, p. 288), and this sounds very comical.

He makes much use of *od, ädo*, and *äd*, and this also when he sees pictures. When the boy had reached the age of a year, he was weaned; from that time his mental development was very rapid. If any one sings to him gi ga gack, he responds invariably *gack*.

He begins to adapt sounds to objects: imitation of sound is the chief basis of this adaptation. He calls the ducks with *gäk, gäk*, and imitates the cock, after a fashion, names the dog *aua* (this he got from his nurse), not only when he sees the animal, but also when he hears him bark. E. g., the child is playing busily with pasteboard boxes; the dog begins to bark outside of the house; the child listens and says *aua*. I roll his little carriage back and forth; he immediately says *brrr*, pointing to it with his hand; he wants to ride, and I have to put him in (he had heard *burra*, as a name for riding, from his nurse). When he sees a horse, he says *prr* (this has likewise been said for him).

I remark here that the notion that the child thinks out its own language—a notion I have often met with, held by people not well informed in regard to this matter—rests on defective observation. The child has part of his language given to him by others; part is the result of his own sound-imitations—of animals, e. g.—and part rests on mutilations of our language. At the beginning of the thirteenth month he suddenly names all objects and pictures, for some days, *dodo, toto,* which takes the place of his former *ŏ;* then he calls them *niana,* which he heard frequently, as it means "nurse" in Russian. Everything now is called *niana : dirr* continues to be the sign of extreme discomfort.

Papba is no more said, ever; on the other hand, *mamma* appears for the first time, but without any significance, still less with any application to the mother.

The word *niana* becomes now the expression of desire, whether of his food or of going to somebody or somewhere. Sometimes, also, under the same circumstances, he cries *mămmă* and *mamma;* the dog is now decidedly called *aua,* the horse *prr.*

14th Month.—He now names also single objects in his picture-book: the dog, *aua,* the cats, *tith* (pronounced as in English), *kiss kiss* having been said for him; horses, *prr,* all birds, *gock* or *gack.* In the house of a neighbor he observes at once the picture, although it hangs high up on the wall, of the emperor driving in a sleigh, and cries *prrr.* Animals that he does not know he calls, whether in the book or the real animals, *aua* or *ua,* e. g. cows.

His nurse, to whom he is much attached, he now calls decidedly *niania,* although he continues to use this word in another sense also. If she is absent for some time, he calls, longingly, *niania, niania.* He sometimes calls me *mamma;* but not quite surely yet. He babbles a good deal to himself; says over all his words, and makes variations in his repertory, e. g., *niana, kanna, danna;* repeats syllables and words, producing also quite strange and unusual sounds, and accumulations of consonants, like *mba, mpta.* As soon as he wakes in the morning he takes up these meaningless language-exercises, and I hear him then going on in an endless babble.

When he does not want a thing, he shakes his head as a sign of refusal; this no one has taught him. Nodding the head as a sign of assent or affirmation he is not yet acquainted with, and learns it much later.

The nurse speaks with me of Caro; the child attends and says *aua ;* he knows what we were talking about. If his grandmother says, "Give the little hand," he at once stretches it out toward her. He understands what is said, and begins consciously to repeat it. His efforts to pronounce the word Grossmama (grandmamma) are comical; in spite of all his pains, he can not get beyond the *gr ;* says *Gr-mama,* and finally *Goo-mama,* and makes this utterance every time he sees his grandmother. At this time he learns also from his nurse the word *koppa* as a name for horse, instead of *prr, burra,* which, from this time forth, denotes only going in a carriage. *Koppa* is probably a formation from " hoppa koppati," an imitation of the sound of the hoofs.

At the end of the fourteenth month, his stock of words is much enlarged. The child plays much in the open air, sees much, and advances in his development; words and sounds are more and more suited to conceptions. He wakes in the night and says *appa,* which means " Give me some drink." The ball he calls *Ball ;* flower, *Bume* (for Blume); cat, *katz* and *kotz* (Katze)—what *kalla, kanna, kotta* signify we do not know. He imitates the barking of the dog with *auauauau.* He says *teine* for Steine (stones); calls Braten (roast meat) *pâati* and *pâa,* and Brod (bread) the same. If he hits against anything in creeping, he immediately says *ba* (it hurts). If he comes near a dangerous object, and some one says to him, *ba,* he is on his guard at once.

A decided step in advance, at the end of the fourteenth month, is his calling me *Mama.* At sight of me he often cries out, in a loud voice and in a coaxing tone, *ei-mamma !* just as he calls the nurse *ei-niana.* His father he now calls *Papa,* too, but not until now, although this sound, *papba,* made its appearance in the tenth month, after which time it was completely forgotten. His grandmother, as he can not get beyond the *gr,* is now called simply *grrru ;* not until later, *Go-mamma.*

15th Month.—He now says *Guten Tag* (good-day), but not always at the right time; also *Guttag.* He likes to see pictures, and calls picture-books *ga* or *gock,* probably because a good many birds are represented in them. He likes to have stories told to him, and to have pictures explained or rather named.

"Hinauf" (up) he calls *üppa*, e. g., when he is to be lifted into his chair. For "unten, hinab" (below, down), he says *patz*. Not long ago he repeated unweariedly *pka, pta* (pp. 139, 144), *mba, mbwa*.

At this period he begins to raise himself erect, holding on by chairs and such things.

Of horses he is passionately fond; but he begins to use the word *koppa*, as the Chinese do their words, in various meanings. He calls my large gold hair-pins *koppa*. Perhaps in his imagination they represent horses, as do many other objects also with which he plays. Berries he now calls *mamma*. He has a sharp eye for insects, and calls them all *putika*, from the Esthonian *puttukas* (beetle), which he has got from the maid.

All large birds in the picture-book he now calls *papa*, the word being probably derived from *Papagei* (parrot), which he also pronounces *papagoi*. The smaller birds are called *gog* and *gack*.

His image in the glass he calls *titta* (Esthonian designation for child, doll). Does he recognize himself in it (p. 196, *et seq.*)?

Once he heard me in the garden calling some one in a loud voice. He immediately imitated me, and afterward when he was asked "What does mamma do?" he understood the question at once, put out his lips, and made the same sound. He is very uneasy in strange surroundings, in strange places, or among strangers.

My bracelet, too, he now calls *kopita*. *Mann* is a new word. *O-patz* means "playing on the piano," as well as "below, down there." When the piano is played he sings in a hoarse voice, with lips protruded, as well as he can, but does not get the tune. He likes to dance, and always dances in time.

Nocho (noch, yet) is a new word, which he uses much in place of *mehr* (more), e. g., when he wants more food.

He often plays with apples, which for this reason, and very likely because they are round, he calls *Ball*, as he does his rubber ball. Yesterday he had baked apples, mashed, with milk. He recognized the apple at once in this altered form, and said as he ate, *Ball!* At this time he was not yet sixteen months old.

16th Month.—He is often heard to beg, or rather order, *Mamma opatz* (play the piano). If I do not at once obey, he moves his little hands like a piano-player and begs *tatata, tatata*, imitating the music. He likes also to hear songs sung, and can already tell some of them, as *Gigagack, kucka tralla*. He joins in singing the last of these.

17th Month.—He speaks his own name correctly, and when asked "Where is Adolph?" he points to his breast. As he is always addressed in the third person, i. e., by his name, he does not know any personal pronouns.

The syllable *ei* he often changes to *al;* e. g., he says *Papagal* instead of "Papagei."

He had some grapes given to him for the first time, and he at once called them *mammut* (berries). Being asked, "How do you like them?" he pressed his hand on his heart in an ecstasy of delight that was comical, crying *ach ! ach !*

18th Month.—He comprehends and answers questions; e. g., "Where are you going?" *Zu Tuhl* (to the chair). "What is that? *Bett tuddu,* i. e., a bed for sleeping. "Who gave you this?" *Mamma, Pappa.*

He can now say almost any word that is said to him, often mutilating it; but, if pains be taken to repeat it for him, he pronounces it correctly. He often tacks on the syllable *ga*, as if in endearment, *mammaga, pappaga, nianiaga.* The *forming of sentences is also beginning*, for he joins two words together, e. g., *Mamma kommt* (comes), *Papa gut* (good), *Ferd* (for *Pferd*) *halt* (horse stop). He says *wiebacka* for Zwieback (biscuit), *Brati* for Braten (roast meat), Goossmama for Grossmama (grandmamma). He pronounces correctly "Onkel Kuno, Suppe, Fuchs, Rabe, Kameel."

When others are conversing in his presence, he often says to himself the words he hears, especially the last words in the sentence. The word "Nein" (no) he uses as a sign of refusal; e. g., "Will you have some roast meat?" *Nein.* Ja (yes), on the other hand, he does not use, but he answers in the affirmative by repeating frequently with vehemence what he wants, e. g., "Do you want some roast?" *Brati, Brati* (i. e., I do want roast).

He gives names to his puppets. He calls them Grandmamma, Grandpapa, Uncle Kuno, Uncle Grünberg, gardener, cook, etc. The puppets are from his Noah's ark.

Now appear his first attempts at drawing. He draws, as he imagines, all kinds of animals: ducks, camels, tigers. He lately made marks, calling out *Torch und noch ein Torch* (a stork and another stork). (Cf. pp. 172, 247.)

The book of birds is his greatest delight. I have to imitate the notes of birds, and he does it after me, showing memory in it. He knows at once stork, woodpecker, pigeon, duck, pelican, siskin, and swallow. The little verses I sing at the same time amuse him, e. g., "Zeislein, Zeislein, wo ist dein Häuslein?" (Little siskin, where is your little house?); and he retains them when he hears them often. Russian words also are repeated by him.

For the first time I observe the attempt to communicate to others some experience of his own. He had been looking at the picture-book with me, and when he went to the nurse he told her, *Mamma, Bilder, Papagei* (Mamma, pictures, parrot).

19th Month.—From the time he was a year and a half old he has walked alone.

He speaks whole sentences, but without connectives, e. g., *Niana Braten holen* (nurse bring roast); *Caro draussen wauwau* (Caro outside, bow-wow); *Mamma tuddut* (sleeps, inflected correctly); *Decke um* (cover over); *Papa koppa Stadt* (Papa driven to city); *Mamma sitzt tuhl* (Mamma sits chair); *Adolph bei Mama bleiben* (Adolph stay with mamma); *Noch tanzen* (more dance); *Pappa Fuchs machen* (Papa make fox).

Certain words make him nervous. He does not like the refrain of the children's song of the goat. If I say "Darum, darum, meck, meck, meck," he looks at me indignantly and runs off. Sometimes he lays his hand on my mouth or screams loudly for the nurse. He gives up any play he is engaged in as soon as I say "darum, darum." *Pax vobiscum* has the same effect.

The songs amuse him chiefly on account of the words, particularly through the imitations of the sounds of animals.

He knows the songs and asks of his own accord for *Kucku Esaal, Kater putz, Kucku tralla,* but commonly hears only the first stanza, and then wants a different song. Lately, however, he listened very earnestly to the three stanzas of "Möpschen," and when I asked "What now?" he answered *Noch Mops* (more Mops). Playing with his puppets, he hummed to himself, *tu, tu, errsen, tu tu errsen.* I guessed that it was "Du, du liegst mir im Herzen," which he had on the previous day wanted to hear often and had tried to repeat.

20th Month.—Now for the first time *ja* is used for affirmation, chiefly in the form *ja wohl* (yes, indeed, certainly), which he retains. "Do you want this?" *Ja wohl.*

Being asked "Whose feet are these?" he answers correctly, *Mine;* but no personal pronouns appear yet. He often retains a new and difficult word that he has heard only once, e. g., "Chocolade."

To my question, after his grandfather had gone away, "Where is Grandpapa now?" he answers sorrowfully, *verloren* (lost). (Cf. p. 145.)

In his plays he imitates the doings and sayings of adults, puts a kerchief about his head and says, *Adolph go stable, give oats.*

Not long ago, as he said good-night to us, he went also to his image in the glass and kissed it repeatedly, saying, *Adolph, good-night!*

24th Month.—He knows a good many flowers, their names and colors; calls pansies "the dark flowers."

He also caught the air and rhythm of certain songs, e. g., *Kommt a Vogel angeflogen, Du, du, liegst mir im Herzen, machst mir viel Serzen*, and used to sing to himself continually when he was on a walk. Now that he is four years old, on the contrary, he hardly ever sings.

25th Month.—Beetles have a great interest for him. He brings a dead beetle into the parlor, and cries, "Run now!" His astonishment is great that the creature does not run.

If he sees something disagreeable (e. g., he saw the other day an organ-grinder with a monkey), he covers his face with his hands, weeping aloud and crying, *Monkey go away.* So, too, when he sees strangers.

The Latin names of flowers and insects are easily retained by him. They are not taught him, he simply hears them daily.

26th and 27th Months.—Of his childish language he has retained only the term *mammut*, for berries. Milk, which he used to call *mima*, is now called *milch* (cf., pp. 140, 157).

The child's use of the personal pronoun is strange. During my absence an aunt of his took my place, and she addressed him for the *first time* with the word "Du" (thou), and spoke of herself as "I," whereas I always called myself "Mama." The consequence was that the boy for a long time used "thou" as the first person, "I" as the second person, with logical consistency. He hands me bread, saying, *I am hungry*, or, when I am to go with him, *I come too.* Referring to himself, he says, *You want flowers; you will play with Niania.* All other persons are addressed with "I" instead of "you."

He tells his uncle, *There's an awfully pretty gentian in the yard.* He gets the nurse occasionally to repeat the Latin names, because they are difficult for her, and his correction of her is very comical.

28th Month.—He speaks long sentences. *Papa, come drink coffee, please do. Papa, I drive* (for " you drive ") *to town, to Reval, and bring some parrots (Bellensittiche).*

He often changes the form of words for fun, e. g., *guten Porgen* (for guten Morgen). On going out, he says, with a knowing air, "Splendid weather, the sun shines so warm." He alters songs also, putting in different expressions: e. g., instead of *Lieber Vogel fliege weiter, nimm a Kuss und a Gruss,* Adolph sings, *Lieber Vogel fliege weiter in die Wolken hinein* (dear bird, fly farther, *into the clouds,* instead of *take a kiss and a greeting*). It is a proof of logical thinking that he asks, at sight of the moon, *The moon is in the sky, has it wings ?*

I had.been sick; when I was better and was caressing him again, he said, *Mama is well, the dear Jesus has made mama well with sealing-wax.* " With sealing-wax ?" I asked, in astonishment. *Yes, from the writing-desk.* He had often seen his toys, when they had been broken, " made well," as he called it, by being stuck together with sealing-wax.

He now asks, *Where is the dear Jesus ?* " In heaven." *Can he fly then; has he wings ?*

Religious conceptions are difficult to impart to him, even at a much later period: e. g., heaven is too cold for him, his nose would freeze up there, etc.

He now asks questions a good deal in general, especially *What is that called ?* e. g., *What are chestnuts called ?* " Horse-chestnuts." *What are these pears called ?* " Bergamots." He jests: *Nein, Bergapots,* or, *What kind of mots are those ?* He will not eat an apple until he has learned what the name of it is.

He would often keep asking, in wanton sport, *What are books called ?* or *ducks ?* or *soup ?*

He uses the words "to-day, to-morrow," and the names of the days of the week, but without understanding their meaning.

Instead of saying " *zu Mittag gehen* " (go to noon-meal), he says, logically, " zu Nachmittag gehen " (go to afternoon-meal).

The child does not know what is true, what is actual. I never can depend on his statements, except, as it appears, when he tells what he has had to eat. If riding is spoken of, e. g., he has a vivid picture of riding in his mind. To-day, when I asked him " Did you see papa ride?" he answered, *Yes, indeed, papa rode away off into the woods.* Yet his father had not gone to ride at all.

In the same way he often denies what he has seen and done. He comes out of his father's room and I ask, " Well, have you said good-night to papa?" *No.* His father told me afterward that the child had done it.

In the park we see some crested titmice, and I tell the nurse that, in the previous autumn, I saw for the first time Finnish parrots or cross-bills here, but that I have not seen any since. When the child's father asked later, " Well, Adolph, what did you see in the park?" *Crested titmice, with golden crests* (he adds out of his own invention) *and Finnish parrots.* He mixes up what he has heard and seen with what he imagines.

Truth has to be taught to a child. The less this is done, the easier it is to inoculate him with religious notions, i. e., of miraculous revelation; otherwise one must be prepared for many questions that are hard to answer.

29th month.—Sad stories affect him to tears, and he runs away.

Names of animals and plants he remembers often more easily than I do, and informs me. He reasons logically. Lately, when he asked for some foolish thing, I said to him, "Sha'n't I bring the moon for you, too?" *No*, said he, *you can't do that, it is too high up in the clouds.*

30th to 33d months.—He now often calls himself "Adolph," and then speaks of himself in the third person. He frequently confounds "I" and "you," and does not so consistently use the first person for the second, and the reverse. The transition is very gradually taking place to the correct use of the personal pronoun. Instead of *my mamma*, he repeats often, when he is in an affectionate mood, *your mamma, your mamma.*

Some new books are given to him. In the book of beetles there are shown to him the party-colored and the gray, so-called "sad," grave-digger (*necrophorus*). The latter now becomes prominent in his plays. " Why is he called the sad?" I asked the child yesterday. *Ah! because he has no children*, he answered, sorrowfully. Probably he has at some time overheard this sentence, which has no meaning for him, from a grown person. Adult persons' ways of speaking are thus employed without an understanding of them; pure verbal memory.

In the same way, he retains the names, in his new book, of butterflies (few of them German) better than I do, however crabbed and difficult they may be.

This (pure) memory for mere sounds or tones has become less

strong in the now four-year-old boy, who has more to do with ideas and concepts, although his memory in other respects is good.

In the thirty-seventh month he sang, quite correctly, airs he had heard, and he could sing some songs to the piano, if they were frequently repeated with him. His fancy for this soon passed away, and these exercises ceased. On the other hand, he tells stories a great deal and with pleasure. His pronunciation is distinct, the construction of the sentences is mostly correct, apart from errors acquired from his nurse. The confounding of the first and second persons, the " I " and " you," or rather his use of the one for the other, has ceased, and the child designates himself by *I*, others by *thou* and *you*. Men are ordinarily addressed by him with *thou*, as his father and uncle are; women with *you*, as are even his mother and nurse. This continues for a long time. The boy of four years counts objects, with effort, up to six; numbers remain for a long time merely empty words (pp. 165, 172). In the same way, he has, as yet, but small notion of the order of the days of the week, and mixes up the names of them. To-day, to-morrow, yesterday, have gradually become more intelligible to him.

Notwithstanding the aphoristic character of these extracts from a full and detailed diary of observations, I have thought they ought to be given, because they form a valuable supplement to my observations in the nineteenth chapter, and show particularly how far independent thought may be developed, even in the second and third years, while there is, as yet, small knowledge of language. The differences in mental development between this child and mine are no less worthy of notice than are the agreements. Among the latter is the fact, extremely important in a pedagogical point of view, that, the less we teach the child the simple truth from the beginning, so much the easier it is to inoculate him permanently with religious notions, i. e., of " miraculous revelation." Fairy tales, ghost-stories, and the like easily make the childish imagination, of itself very active, hypertrophic, and cloud the judgment concerning actual events. Morals and nature offer such an abundance of facts with which we may connect the teaching of language, that it is better to dispense with legends. Æsop's fables combine the moral and the natural in a manner unsurpassable. My child tells me one of these fables every morning.

B.

NOTES CONCERNING LACKING, DEFECTIVE, AND ARRESTED MENTAL DEVELOPMENT IN THE FIRST YEARS OF LIFE.

THE data we have concerning the behavior of children born, living, without head or without brain, and of microcephalous children, as well as of idiots and cretins more advanced in age, are of great interest, as helping us to a knowledge of the dependence of the first psychical processes upon the development of the brain, especially of the cerebral cortex. Unfortunately, these data are scanty and scattered.

Very important, too, for psychogenesis, are reports concerning the physiological condition and activity of children whose mental development has seemed to be stopped for months, or to be made considerably slower, or to be unusually hastened.

Scanty as are the notes I have met with on this matter, after much search, yet I collect and present some of them, in the hope that they will incite to more abundant and more careful observation in the future than has been made up to this time.

A good many data concerning the behavior of cretin children are to be found in the very painstaking book, "Neue Untersuchungen über den Kretinismus oder die Entartung des Menschen in ihren verschiedenen Graden

und Formen " (" New Investigations concerning Cretin-
ism, or Human Deterioration, in its Various Forms and
Degrees "), by Maffei and Rösch (two vols, Erlangen, 1844).
But, in order that these data should be of value, the observed anomalies and defects of the cerebral functions
ought to be capable of being referred to careful morphological investigations of the cretin brain. As the authors
give no results of *post-mortem* examinations, I simply refer
to their work here.

I once had the opportunity myself of seeing a hemi-
cephalus, living, who was brought to the clinic of my
respected colleague, Prof. B. Schultze, in Jena. The child
was of the male sex, and was born on the 1st of July,
1883, at noon, along with a perfectly normal twin sister.
The parents are of sound condition. I saw the child for
the first time on the 3d of July, at two o'clock. I found
all the parts of the body, except the head, like those of
ordinary children born at the right time. The head had
on it a great red lump like a tumor, and came to an end
directly over the eyes, going down abruptly behind; but,
even if the tumor were supposed to be covered with skin,
there would by no means be the natural arched formation
of the cranium of a newly-born child. The face, too, absolutely without forehead, was smaller in comparison than
the rest of the body. I found now, in the case of this
child, already two days old, a remarkably regular breathing, a very cool skin—in the forenoon a specific warmth
of 32° C. had been found—and slight mobility. The eyes
remained closed. When I opened them, without violence,
the pupil was seen to be immobile. It did not react in the
least upon the direct light of the sun on either side. The
left eye did not move at all, the right made rare, convulsive, lateral movements. The conjunctiva was very much
reddened. The child did not react in the least to pricks

of a dull needle tried on all parts of the body, and reacted only very feebly to pinches; not at all to sound-stimuli, but regularly to stronger, prolonged cutaneous stimuli; in particular, the child moved its arms after a slap on the back, just like normal new-born children, and uttered very harsh, feeble tones when its back was rubbed. When I put my finger in its mouth vigorous sucking movements began, which induced me to offer the bottle—this had not yet been done. Some cubic centimetres of milk were vigorously swallowed, and soon afterward the breast of a nurse was taken. While this was going on I could feel quite distinctly with my finger, under the chin, the movements of swallowing. It was easy to establish the further fact that my finger, which I laid in the hollow of the child's hand, was frequently clasped firmly by the little fingers, which had well-developed nails. Not unfrequently, sometimes without previous contact, sometimes after it, the tip of the tongue, and even a larger part of the tongue, was thrust out between the lips, and once, when I held the child erect, he plainly gave a prolonged yawn. Finally, the fact seemed to me very noteworthy that, after being taken and held erect, sometimes also without any assignable outward occasion, the child inclined its head forward and turned it vigorously both to the right and to the left. When the child had sucked lustily a few times, it opened both eyes about two millimetres wide, and went on with its nursing. An assistant physician saw the child sneeze.

These observations upon a human child, two days old, unquestionably acephalous, i. e., absolutely without cerebrum, but as to the rest of its body not in the least abnormal, prove what I have already advanced (vol. i, p. 203), that the cerebrum takes no part at all in the first movements of the newly-born. In this respect the extremely rare case of an acephalous child, living for some days, supplies the place of an experiment of vivisection. Unfortunately, the child died so early that I could not carry on further observations and experiments. The report of the *post-mortem* examination will be published by itself.

Every observer of young children knows the great variety in the rapidity of their development, and will agree with me in general that a slow and steady development of the cerebral functions in the first four years, but especially in the first two years, justifies a more favorable prognosis than does a very hasty and unsteady development; but when during that period of time there occurs a complete and prolonged interruption of the mental development, then the danger is always great that the normal course will not be resumed. So much the more instructive, therefore, are the cases in which the children after such a standstill have come back to the normal condition. Four observations of this kind have been published by R. Demme ("19. Bericht über das Jenner'sche Kinderspital in Bern, 1882," S. 31 bis 52). These are of so great interest in their bearing on psychogenesis, and they confirm in so striking a manner some of the propositions laid down by me in this book, that I should like to print them here word for word, especially as the original does not appear to have found a wide circulation; but that would make my book altogether too large. I confine myself, therefore, to this reference, with the request that further cases of partial or total interruption of mental development during the first year of life, with a later progress in it, may be collected and made public.

It is only in rare cases that microcephalous children can be observed, while living, for any considerable length of time continuously. In this respect a case described by Aeby is particularly instructive.

A microcephalous boy was born of healthy parents—
he was their first child—about four weeks too soon. His
whole body had something of stiffness and awkwardness.
The legs were worse off in this respect than the arms;
they showed, as they continued to show up to the time of
his death, a tendency to become crossed. The boy was never
able to stand or walk. He made attempts to seize striking
objects, white or party-colored, but never learned actually
to hold anything. The play of feature was animated.
The dark eyes, shining and rapidly moving, never lingered
long upon one and the same object. The child was much
inclined to bite, and always bit very sharply. Mentally
there was pronounced imbecility. In spite of his four
years the boy never got so far as to produce any articulate
sounds whatever. Even simple words like "papa" and
"mamma" were beyond his ability. His desire for anything was expressed in inarticulate and not specially expressive tones. His sleep was short and light; he often
lay whole nights through with open eyes. He seldom
shed tears; his discomfort was manifested chiefly by shrill
screaming. He died of pulmonary paralysis at the end of
the fourth year.

The autopsy showed that the frontal lobes were surprisingly small, and that there was a partial deficiency of
the median longitudinal fissure. The fissure did not begin till beyond the crown of the head, in the region of the
occiput. The anterior half of the cerebrum consequently
lacked the division into lateral hemispheres. It had few
convolutions also, and the smoothness of its surface was
at once obvious. The *corpus callosum* and the *fornix*
were undeveloped. "The gray cortical layer attained in
general only about a third of the normal thickness, and
was especially weakly represented in the frontal region."
The cerebellum not being stunted, seemed, by the side of
the greatly shrunken cerebrum, surprisingly large.

In this case the microcephalus of four years behaves,
as far as the development of will is concerned, like the
normal boy of four months. The latter is, in fact,
superior to him in *seizing*, while the former in no
way manifests any advantage in a psychical point of
view.

Two cases of microcephaly have been described by Fletcher Beach (in the " Transactions of the International Medical Congress," London, 1881, iii, 615–626).

E. R. was, in May, 1875, received into his institution at the age of eleven years. She had at the time of her birth a small head, and had at no time manifested much intelligence. She could not stand or walk, but was able to move her arms and legs. Her sight and hearing were normal. She was quiet and obedient, and sat most of the time in her chair. She paid no attention to her bodily needs. She could not speak and had to be fed with a spoon. After six months she became a little more intelligent, made an attempt to speak, and muttered something indistinctly. She would stretch out her hand when told to give it, and she recognized with a smile her nurse and the physician. Some four months later she would grind her teeth when in a pleasant mood, and would act as if she were shy when spoken to, holding her hand before her eyes. She was fond of her nurse. Thus there was capacity of observation, there were attention, memory, affection, and some power of voluntary movement. She died in January, 1876. Her brain weighed, two days after her death, seven ounces. It is minutely described by the author—but after it had been preserved in alcohol for six years, and it then weighed only two ounces. The author found a number of convolutions not so far developed as in the fœtus of six months, according to Gratiolet, and he is of opinion that the cerebellum was further developed after the cerebrum had ceased to grow, so that there was not an arrest of the development but an irregularity. The cerebral hemispheres were asymmetrical, the frontal lobes, corresponding to the psychical performances in the case, being relatively pretty large, while the posterior portion of the third convolution on the left side, the island of Reil, and the operculum were very small, corresponding to the inability to learn to speak. The author connects the slight mobility with the smallness of the parietal and frontal ascending convolutions.

The other case is that of a girl of six years (E. H.), who came to the institution in January, 1879, and died in

21

July of the same year. She could walk about, and she had complete control of her limbs. She was cheerful, easy to be amused, and greatly attached to her nurse. She associated with other children, but could not speak a word. Her hearing was good, her habits bad. Although she could pick up objects and play with them, it did not occur to her to feed herself. She could take notice and observe, and could remember certain persons. Her brain weighed, two days after death, 20½ ounces, and was, in many respects, as simple as that of an infant; but, in regard to the convolutions, it was far superior to the brain of a monkey—was superior also to that of E. R. The ascending frontal and parietal convolutions were larger, corresponding to the greater mobility. The third frontal convolution and the island of Reil were small on both sides, corresponding to the alalia. The author is of opinion that the ganglionic cells in this brain lacked processes, so that the inter-central connections did not attain development.

A more accurate description of two brains of microcephali is given by Julius Sander in the "Archiv für Psychiatrie und Nerven-Krankheiten" (i, 299–307; Berlin, 1868), accompanied by good plates. One of these cases is that of which an account is given by Johannes Müller (in the "Medicinische Zeitung des Vereins für Heilkunde in Preussen," 1836, Nr. 2 und 3).

In the full and detailed treatises concerning microcephali by Karl Vogt ("Archiv für Anthropologie," ii, 2, 228) and Von Flesch ("Würzburger Festschrift," ii, 95, 1882) may be found further data in regard to more recent cases.

Many questions of physiological and psychological importance in respect to the capacity of development in cases of imperfectly developed brain are discussed in the "Zeitschrift für das Idioten-Wesen" by W. Schröter (Dresden) and E. Reichelt (Hubertusburg).

But thus far the methods of microscopical investigation of the brain are still so little developed that we can not yet with certainty establish a causal connection, in individual cases, between the deviations of microcephalic brains from the normal brain and the defects of the psychical functions. The number of brains of microcephali that have been examined with reference to this point is very small, although their scientific value, after thorough-going observation of the possessors of them during life, is immense. For microcephalous children of some years of age are a substitute for imaginary, because never practicable, vivisectory experiments, concerning the connection of body and mind.

To conclude these fragments, let me add here some observations concerning a case of rare interest, that of the microcephalous child, Margarethe Becker (born 1869), very well known in Germany. These observations I recorded on the 9th of July, 1877, in Jena, while the child was left free to do what she pleased.

The girl, eight years of age, born, according to the testimony of her father, with the frontal fontanelle (fonticulus anterior) closed and solid, had a smaller head than a child of one year. The notes follow the same order as that of the observations.

Time, 8.15 A. M.—The child yawns. She grasps with animation at some human skulls that she sees on a table near her, and directs her look to charts on the walls. She puts her fingers into her nostrils, brushes her apron with both hands, polishes my watch, which I have offered her and she has seized, holds it to one ear, then to one of her father's ears, draws her mouth into a smile, seems to be pleased by the ticking, holds the watch to her father's other ear, then to her own other ear, laughs, and repeats the experiment several times. Her head is very mobile.

The child now folds a bit of paper that I have given her, rolls it up awkwardly, wrinkling her forehead the while, chews up the paper and laughs aloud. Saliva flows from her mouth almost incessantly. Then the child begins to eat a biscuit, giving some of it, however, to her father and the attendant, putting her biscuit to their lips, and this with accuracy at once, whereas in the former case the watch was held at first near the ear, to the temple, and not till afterward to the ear itself.

The girl is very lively; she strikes about her in a lively manner with her hands, sees charts hanging high on the walls, points to them with her finger, throws her head back upon her neck to see them better, and *moves her fingers in the direction of the lines* of the diagrams. At last weariness seems to come on. The child puts an arm around the neck of her father, sits on his lap, but is more and more restless.

8.50.—Quiet. To appearance, the child has fallen asleep.

8.55.—Awake again. The child *sees* well, *hears* well, *smells* well; obeys some few commands, e. g., she gives her hand. But with this her intellectual accomplishments are exhausted. She does not utter a word.

Kollmann, who saw this microcephalous subject in September, 1877, writes, among other things, of her ("Correspondenzblatt der Deutschengesellschaft für Anthropologie," Nr. 11, S. 132):

"Her gait is tottering, the movements of the head and extremities jerky, not always co-ordinated, hence unsteady, inappropriate and spasmodic; her look is restless, objects are not definitely fixated. The normal functions of her mind are far inferior to those of a child of four years. The eight-year-old Margaret speaks only the word *Mama;* no other articulate sound has been learned by her. She makes known her need of food by plaints, by sounds of weeping, and by distortion of countenance; she laughs when presented with something to eat or with toys. It is only within the last two years that she has become cleanly; since then her appetite has improved. Her nutrition has gained, in comparison with the first years of life, and with it her comprehension also; she helps her mother set the table, and brings plates and knives, when requested to do so, from the place where they are kept. Further, she shows a tender sympathy with her microcephalous brother; she takes bread from the table, goes to her brother's bedside and feeds him, as he is not of himself capable of putting food into his mouth. She shows a very manifest liking for her relatives and a fear of strangers. When taken into the parlor she gave the most decided evidences of fear; being placed upon the table she hid her head in her father's coat, and did not become quiet until her mother took her in her arms. This awakening of mental activity shows that, notwithstanding the extremely small quantity of brain-substance, there exists a certain degree of intellectual development with advancing years. With the fourth year, in the case of M., independent movements began; up to that time she lay, as her five-year-old brother still lies, immovable in body and limbs, with the exception of slight bendings and stretchings."

Richard Pott, who (1879) likewise observed this microcephalous subject, found that she wandered about aimlessly, restlessly, and nimbly, from corner to corner [as if], groping and seeking; yet objects held before her were only momentarily fixated, scarcely holding her attention; often she did not once grasp at them. "The girl goes alone, without tottering or staggering, but her locomotive movements are absolutely without motive, having no end or aim, frequently changing their direction. Notwithstanding her size, the child gives the impression of the most extreme helplessness." She was fed, but was not indifferent as to food, seeming to prefer sour to sweet. She would come, indeed, when she was called, but seemed not to understand the words spoken to her; she spoke no word herself, but uttered shrill, inarticulate sounds; she felt shame when she was undressed, hiding her face in her sister's lap. The expression of her countenance was harmless, changeable, manifesting no definite psychical processes.

The statements contradictory to those of Kollmann are probably to be explained by the brevity of the observations.

Virchow ("Correspondenzblatt," S. 135), in his remarks upon this case, says: "I am convinced that every one who observes the microcephalic child will find that psychologically it has nothing whatever of the ape. All the positive faculties and qualities of the ape are wanting here; there is nothing of the psychology of the ape, but only the psychology of an imperfectly developed and deficient little child. Every characteristic is human; every single trait. I had the girl in my room a few months since, for hours together, and occupied myself with her; I never observed anything in her that reminds me even remotely of the psychological conditions of apes. She is a human being, in a low stage of development, but in no way deviating from the nature of humanity."

From these reports it is plain to be seen that for all mental development an hereditary physical growth of the cerebrum is indispensable. If the sensuous impressions experienced anew in each case by each human being, and the original movements, were sufficient without the development of the cerebral convolutions and of the gray cortex, then these microcephalous beings, upon whom the same impressions operated as upon other new-born children, must have had better brains and must have learned more. But the brain, notwithstanding the peripheral impressions received in seeing, hearing, and feeling, could not grow, and so the rudimentary human child could not learn anything, and could not even form the ideas requisite for articulate voluntary movement, or combine these ideas. Only the motor centers of lower rank could be developed.

In peculiar contrast with these cases of genuine microcephaly stands the exceedingly remarkable case, observed by Dr. Rudolf Krause (Hamburg), of a boy whose brain is not at all morbidly affected or abnormally small, but exhibits decidedly the type of the brain of the ape. The discoverer reported upon it to the Anthropological Society (" Correspondenzblatt a.a. O., S. 132–135) the following facts among others:

" The skull and brain belonged to a boy who was born on the 4th of October, 1869, the last of four children. Paul was scrofulous from his youth. He did not get his teeth until the end of his second year, and they were quite brown in color and were soon lost. According to the statement of Paul's mother, he had several successive sets of teeth. It was not until the fifth year that he learned to walk. He was cleanly from the third year, but not when he felt ill. His appetite was always good up to his last sickness of four weeks. His sleep was habitually undisturbed. He was of a cheerful temperament, and inclined to play; as soon as he heard music he would dance, and sing to the music in rather unmelodious tones. When teased he could be very violent; he would throw anything he could lay his hands on at the head of the offender. He liked the company of others, especially of men. By the time he was four years old he had learned to eat without help. Paul was very supple, was fond of climbing, and had great strength in his arms and hands especially; these had actually a horny appearance, and thus reminded one of the hands of the chimpanzee. He could sit on the ground with his legs wide apart. His gait was uncertain, and he was apt to tumble; he ran with knees bent forward and legs crooked; he was fond of hopping, and seemed particularly ape-like when doing so. The great-toe of each foot stood off at an angle from the foot, and thus gave the impression of a prehensile toe. I thought at first that this deviation had its origin in the fact that the child, on account of his uncertainty in walking, wanted to get a broader basis of support; but I afterward gave up that opinion, because I have never found an instance of a similar habit in other children with diseased heads, e. g., hydrocephalous children. Paul could speak but little, could say hardly any words except *Papa* and *Mama*, and even these he did not until late learn to pronounce in two syllables; he uttered for the most part only sounds that resembled a grunt. He imitated the barking of a dog by the sound *rrrrrr*. He frequently stamped with feet and hands, clapped his hands together, and ejaculated a sort of grunting sound, just as I have observed in the case of gorillas and chimpanzees.

"Paul was smaller than children of his age; on his right eye he had from his youth a large leucoma; the eyelids had generally a catarrhal affection, and were in a state of suppuration. The head looked sore; the forehead was small. Paul had a strongly marked tendency to imitation. His whole being, his movements, were strikingly ape-like. He was decidedly neglected by his parents, was generally dirty in appearance, and I really think the early death of the child was induced by the slight care taken of him. Paul was taken sick at the beginning of December, 1876, with an acute bronchial catarrh, and died on the 5th of January, 1877, at the age of seven and a quarter years.

"If you look at the cranium and the brain here, which belonged to the child just described, there are lacking in the first place all the characteristics of microcephaly. The cranium possesses a capacity of 1,022 cubic centimetres, and the brain weighs 950 grammes; they do not deviate, therefore, from the normal condition. But let the cranium, where it is laid open by the saw, be observed from within, and we notice an *asymmetry of the two hemispheres of the brain;* the cranium is pushed somewhat forward and to the right. The *partes orbitales* of the frontal bone are higher and more arched than is usual, in consequence of which the *lamina cribrosa* of the ethmoid bone lies deeper, and room is given for the well-known conformation of the ethmoidal process in the brain. The cerebral convolutions are plainly marked upon the inner surface of the cranium. The facial cranium shows no deviations. There is no prognathism. The formation of the teeth alone is irregular; one pre-molar tooth is lacking above and below in the jaw, and, in fact, there is no place for it. The incisors and the pre-molar teeth are undergoing change.

"The two cerebral hemispheres are asymmetrical; in the region where the parieto-occipital fissure is situated on the left hemisphere, the two hemispheres diverge from each other and form an edge which curves outward and backward, so that the cerebellum remains uncovered. On the lower surface of the frontal lobes there exists a strongly marked ethmoidal prominence. Neither of the fissures of Sylvius is quite closed, the left less so than the right; the operculum is but slightly developed, and the island of Reil lies with its fissures almost entirely uncovered. This conformation reminds us throughout of the brain of the anthropoid apes. The two *sulci centrales sive fissuræ Rolandi* run straight to the border of the hemisphere, less deeply impressed than is normally the case, without forming an angle with each other. Very strongly and deeply impressed *sulci præcentrales* seem to serve as substitutes for them. The *sulcus interparietalis*, which begins farther outward than in the ordinary human being, receives the *sulcus parieto-occipitalis*—a structure in conformity with the typical brain of the ape. The *sulcus occipitalis transversus*, which is generally lightly stamped in man, extends here as a deep fissure across over the occipital lobe, thus producing a so-called simian fissure, and the posterior part of the occipital lobe has the appearance of an operculum. The *fissura calcarina* has its origin directly on the surface of the occipital lobe, does not receive until late the *fissura parieto-occipitalis*, and goes directly, on the right side, into the *fissura hippocampi*. This abnormal structure also is typical for the brain of the ape.

"The *gyrus occipitalis primus* is separated from the upper parietal lobe by the *sulcus parieto-occipitalis*, a formation that, according to Gratiolet, exists in many apes. The *gyrus temporalis superior* is greatly reduced on both sides, and has an average breadth of only five millimetres; it is the one peculiarity that recalls emphatically the brain of the chimpanzee, which always has this reduced upper temporal convolution.

" We have here, then, a brain that scarcely deviates from the normal brain in volume, that possesses all the convolutions and fissures, seeming, perhaps, richer than the average brain in convolutions, and that is in every respect differentiated; and notwithstanding all this it approximates, in its whole structure, to the simian rather than to the human type. Had the brain been placed before me without my knowing its origin, I should have been perfectly justified in assigning this brain to an anthropoid ape standing somewhat nearer to man than does the chimpanzee."

No second case of this sort has thus far been observed.

C.

REPORTS CONCERNING THE PROCESS OF LEARNING TO SEE, ON THE PART OF PERSONS BORN BLIND, BUT ACQUIRING SIGHT THROUGH SURGICAL TREATMENT. ALSO SOME CRITICAL REMARKS.

I. The Chesselden Case.

THE following extracts are taken from the report published by Will. Chesselden in the " Philosophical Transactions for the Months of April, May, and June, 1728 " (No. 402, London, pp. 447–450), or the " Philosophical Transactions from 1719 to 1733, abridged by J. Eames and J. Martyn " (vii, 3, pp. 491–493, London, 1734):

" Though we say of the gentleman that he was blind, as we do of all people who have ripe cataracts, yet they are never so blind from that cause but that they can discern day from night, and, for the most part, in a strong light distinguish black, white, and scarlet; but they can

not perceive the shape of anything. . . . And thus it was
with this young gentleman, who, though he knew these
colors asunder in a good light, yet when he saw them after
he was couched, the faint ideas he had of them before
were not sufficient for him to know them by afterward,
and therefore he did not think them the same which he
had known before by those names. . . .

"When he first saw, he was so far from making any
judgment about distances, that he thought all objects
whatever touched his eyes (as he expressed it) as what he
felt did his skin, and thought no objects so agreeable as
those which were smooth and regular. He knew not the
shape of anything nor any one thing from another, however different in shape or magnitude; but upon being told
what things were, whose form he before knew from feeling, he would carefully observe, that he might know them
again. But, having too many objects to learn at once, he
forgot many of them, and (as he said) at first he learned
to know and again forgot a thousand things in a day.
Having often forgot which was the cat and which the dog,
he was ashamed to ask; but catching the cat (which he
knew by feeling), he was observed to look at her stead-
fastly, and then, setting her down, said, 'So, puss, I shall
know you another time.' He was very much surprised that
those things which he had liked best did not appear most
agreeable to his eyes, expecting those persons would appear
most beautiful that he loved most, and such things to be
most agreeable to his sight that were so to his taste. We
thought he soon knew what pictures represented which
were showed to him, but we found afterward we were mistaken, for about two months after he was couched he discovered at once they represented solid bodies, when to that
time he considered them only as party-colored planes or
surfaces diversified with variety of paint; but even then
he was no less surprised, expecting the pictures would feel
like the things they represented, and was amazed when he
found those parts, which by their light and shadow appeared now round and uneven, felt only flat like the rest,
and asked which was the lying sense, feeling or seeing?

"Being shown his father's picture in a locket at his
mother's watch and told what it was, he acknowledged a

likeness, but was vastly surprised, asking how it could be that a large face could be expressed in so little room.

"At first he could bear but very little sight, and the things he saw he thought extremely large; but, upon seeing things larger, those first seen he conceived less, never being able to imagine any lines beyond the bounds he saw. The room he was in he said he knew to be but part of the house, yet he could not conceive that the whole house could look bigger. Before he was couched he expected little advantage from seeing, except reading and writing. Blindness, he observed, had this advantage, that he could go anywhere in the dark much better than those who could see, and after he had seen he did not soon lose this quality nor desire a light to go about the house in the night.

"A year after first seeing, being carried upon Epsom Downs and observing a large prospect, he was exceedingly delighted with it and called it a new kind of seeing; and now being lately couched of his other eye, he says that objects at first appeared large to this eye but not so large as they did at first to the other, and, looking upon the same object with both eyes, he thought it looked about twice as large as with the first couched eye only, but not double, that we can anywise discover."

Remark on the First Case.

Although this Chesselden case is the most famous of all, and the most frequently cited, it belongs, nevertheless, to those most inaccurately described. It is, however, not only the first in the order of time, but especially important for the reason that it demonstrates in a striking manner the slow acquirement of space-perception by the eye, and also the acquirement of the first and second dimensions of space (cf. vol. i, p. 57).

II., III. The Ware Cases.

One of these cases is that of a boy, who at the age of seven years recovered his sight which he had lost in the first half-year of his life. The surgeon who performed the operation, James Ware, writes (" Philosophical Transactions of the Royal Society for 1801," ii, London, 1801, pp. 382–396):

" The young W. appeared to be a healthy, perfect child; his eyes in particular were large and rather prominent. About the end of his first year, a number of persons passing in procession near his father's house, accompanied with music and flags, the child was taken to see them; but, instead of looking at the procession, it was observed that, though he was evidently much pleased with the music, his eyes were never directed to the place from whence the sound came. His mother, alarmed by this discovery, held silver spoons and other glaring objects before him at different distances, and she was soon convinced that he was unable to perceive any of them. A surgeon was consulted, who, on examining the eyes, pronounced that there was a complete cataract in each. All thoughts of assisting his sight were (for the present) relinquished. As soon as he could speak it was observed that when an object was held close to his eyes he was able to distinguish its color if strongly marked, but on no occasion did he ever notice its outline or figure. I performed the operation on the left eye on the 29th of December, 1800. The eye was immediately bound up, and no inquiries made on that day with regard to his sight. On the 30th I found that he had experienced a slight sickness on the preceding evening. On the 31st, as soon as I entered his chamber, the mother with much joy informed me that her child could see. About an hour before my visit he was standing near the fire, with a handkerchief tied loosely over his eyes, when he told her that under the handkerchief, which had slipped upward, he could distinguish the table by the side of which she was sitting. It was about a yard and a half from him, and he observed that it was covered with a green cloth (which was really the case), and that it was a little farther off than he was able to reach. . . . Desirous to ascertain whether he was able to distinguish objects, I held a letter before him at the distance of about twelve inches, when he told me, after a short hesitation, that it was a piece of paper; that it was square, which he knew by its corners; and that it was longer in one direction than it was in the other. On being desired to point to the corners, he did it with great precision and readily carried his finger in the line of its longest diameter. I then showed him a small oblong bandbox covered with red leather, which he said was red and square, and pointed at once to its four corners. After this I placed before him an oval silver box, which he said had a shining appearance, and presently afterward that it was round, because it had not corners. A white stone mug he first called a white basin, but soon after, recollecting himself, said it was a mug because it had a handle. I held the objects at different distances from his eye and inquired very particularly if he was sensible of any difference in their situation, which he always said he was, informing me on every change whether they were brought nearer to or carried farther from him. I again inquired, both of his mother and himself, whether he had ever before this time distinguished by sight any sort of object, and I was assured by both that he never had on any occasion, and that when he wished to discover colors, which he could only do when they were very strong, he had always been obliged to hold the colored object close to his eye and a little on one side to avoid the projection of the nose. No further experiments were made on that day. On the 1st of January I found that he felt no uneasiness on the approach of light. I showed him a table-knife, which at first he called a spoon, but soon rectified the mistake, giving it the right name and distinguishing the blade from the handle by pointing to each as he was desired. He called a yellow pocket-book by its name, taking notice of the silver lock in the cover. I held my hand before him, which he knew, but could not at first tell the number of my fingers nor distinguish one of them from another. I then held up his own hand and desired him to remark the difference between his thumb and his fingers, after which he readily pointed out the distinctions in mine also. Dark-colored and smooth objects were more agreeable to him than those which were bright and rough. On the 3d of January he saw from the drawing-room window a dancing bear in the street and distinguished a number of boys that were standing round him, noticing particularly a bundle of clothes which one of them had on his head. On the same evening I placed him before a looking-glass and held up his hand. After a little time he smiled and said he saw the shadow of his hand as well as that of his head. He could not then distinguish his features; but on the following day, his mother having again placed him before the glass, he pointed to his eyes, nose, and mouth. The young W., a remarkably intelligent boy (of seven years), gave the most direct and satisfactory answers to every question that was put to him, and, though not born blind, certainly had not any recollection of having ever seen. The right eye was operated upon a month after the left, but without the least success."

In regard to the other case, Ware writes: "In the instance of a young gentleman from Ireland, fourteen years old, from each of whose eyes I extracted a cataract in the year 1794, and who, before the operation, assured me, as did his friends, that he had never seen the figure of any object, I was astonished by the facility with which, on the first experiment, he took hold of my hand at different distances, mentioning whether it was brought nearer to or carried farther from him, and conveying his hand to mine in a circular direction, that we [Ware and another physician] might be the better satisfied of the accuracy with which he did it." In this case, as in others of like nature, Ware could not, "although the patients had certainly been blind from early infancy," satisfy himself "that they had not, before this period, enjoyed a sufficient degree of sight to impress the image of visible objects on their minds, and to give them ideas which could not afterward be entirely obliterated."

Ware found, moreover, that, in the case of two children between seven and eight years of age, both blind from birth, and on whom no operation had been performed, the knowledge of colors, limited as it was, was sufficient to enable them to tell whether colored objects were brought nearer to or carried farther from them; for instance, whether they were at the distance of two inches or four inches from their eyes; and he himself observes that they were not, in strictness of speech, blind, though they were deprived of all useful sight.

Remarks on the Second and Third Cases.

It is a surprising thing, in the account of the former case, that nothing whatever is said of the behavior of the patient on the first and on the fourth day after the operation. We must assume that he passed the first day wholly with his eyes bandaged. Further, the boy pointed out four corners of a box, while the box had eight; yet no inference can be drawn from this, for possibly only one side of the box was shown to him. The most remarkable thing is the statement of the patient that he saw the *shadow* of his hand in the glass. This circumstance, and the astonishing certainty, at the very first attempts to estimate space-relations, in the discrimination of round and angular, and in the observation that the table was somewhat farther from him than he could reach, show what influence the mere ability to perceive colors has upon vision in space. Before the operation, W. distinguished only striking colors from one another; but he could perceive nearness and distance of colored objects, within narrow limits, by the great differences in the luminous intensity of the colors. He distinguished with certainty dimness from brightness. Accordingly, when he noticed a decrease in the brightness of a color, he inferred the distance of the colored object from the eye, regulating his judgment also by touch. Thus the boy had, before the operation, some perception of space with the eye, and it is not much to be wondered at, considering his uncommon intelligence, that he, soon after the operation (probably attempts at seeing were secretly made by the patient on the first day) learned to judge pretty surely of space-relations—much more surely than a person born blind learns to judge in so short a time. Besides, it is not to be forgotten that, while it is true that the cataract had become completely developed at the end of the first year of life, there is no proof that the child was unable to see during the first months. At that time images, as in the second case, may have unconsciously impressed themselves, with which, at a later period, more accurate space-ideas may have been associated, through the sense of touch, than is the case with persons born completely blind. Ware concludes, from his observations—

1. " When children are born blind, in consequence of having cataracts in their eyes, they are never so totally deprived of sight as not to be able to distinguish colors; and, though they can not see the figure of an object, nor even its color, unless it be placed within a very short distance, they nevertheless can tell whether, when within this distance, it be brought nearer to or carried farther from them.

2. " In consequence of this power, whilst in a state of comparative blindness, children who have their cataracts removed are enabled immediately on the acquisition of sight to form some judgment of the distance, and even of the outline, of those strongly defined objects with the color of which they were previously acquainted."

Both these conclusions are simply matter of fact. It only needs explanation how the distance and outlines of objects can be known after the operation *in consequence of* the ability described in the first proposition. That distance is actually estimated at once in consequence of this power, is clear; not so with the outlines. How can round and angular be distinguished, when only colors and gross differences of intensity and saturation are perceived? Ware gives no solution of the difficulty, but thinks that, because the colors appeared more intense, the previously

22

imperfect ideas concerning distances might be improved
and extended, so that they would even give a knowledge of
the boundary-lines and of the form of those things with
the color of which the patients were previously acquainted.
But this improvement of the ideas concerning distance
can not lead directly to discrimination of the limits of objects, and is itself hypothetical, inasmuch as we might
expect, *immediately* after the operation, on account of the
enormous difference in the luminous intensity, an uncertainty in the judgment.   But such uncertainty appeared
only in a slight degree in both the cases, a thing possible
only because there had already been sufficient experiences
with the eye.   But these experiences, as is frequently
stated, were absolutely lacking in regard to the limits and
the form of objects.   Here another thing comes in to help.
Evidently, an eye that distinguishes only colors sees these
colors always only as limited ; even if it saw only a single
color that occupied the whole field of vision, the field
would still be a limited one.   But the colored field may
be small or large, and this difference may be noticed before
the operation.   If the object—one of vivid coloring—is
long and narrow, the patient, even before the operation,
will see it otherwise than if it is, with the same coloring,
short and broad.   And suppose he merely observes that
not the whole field of vision is colored.   If the whole field
is colored, there is, of course, an entire lack of angles ; on
the other hand, if the whole field of vision is not filled by
the colored object, then it is—however faintly—divided,
and the lines of division, i. e., the indistinct boundary-lines
of the objects whose color is perceived, may be either like
the natural limits of the entire field of vision, i. e., "round,"
or unlike them, i. e., "angular."   If, now, the obstacle is
suddenly removed, the patient (even if he did not before
the operation distinguish angular and round by the eye)

must yet perceive which of the objects before him resemble in contour the previous field of vision, i. e., are round, and which do not; for the round contour of his field of vision is familiar to him. But W. had learned, through the sense of touch, that what is not round is angular. He would, therefore, even if he could perceive colors when the whole field of vision was filled—a matter on which we have no information—be able to guess the outlines of some objects soon after the operation, merely on the ground of his experiences before it. It was guess-work every time, as appears from the confounding of knife and spoon, mug and basin. The boy must have thought, " How would it be if I felt of it?" and, as he had before the operation frequently observed that whatever had the same contour as his field of vision, or a contour similar to that, was round, he could, after the operation, distinguish round and not round—a thing which a person born blind, on the other hand, and knowing nothing of his field of vision, because he has never had any, can never do.

On the whole, the two Ware cases are by no means so important as the Franz (see below) and Chesselden cases, because the boy, W., had ample opportunity up to his seventh year for learning to distinguish different colors according to their quality and luminous intensity; because he must have known the limits of his field of vision, and could in any case, by means of touch, correct and relatively confirm his very frequent attempts to guess at forms and distances by the eye. Finally, it is not known whether he became blind before or immediately after his birth, or, as is most probable, not till some months after birth. The same is true of the second case.

IV, V. The Home Cases.

Everard Home makes the following statement in the "Philosophical Transactions of the Royal Society," London, 1807, i, pp. 83–87, 91:

"1. William Stiff, twelve years of age, had cataracts in his eyes, which, according to the account of his mother, existed at the time of birth. From earliest infancy he never stretched out his hand to catch at anything, nor were his eyes directed to objects placed before him, but rolled about in a very unusual manner. The eyes were not examined till he was six months old, and at that time the cataracts were as distinct as when he was received into the hospital. He could at that time (July 17, 1806) distinguish light from darkness, and the light of the sun from that of a fire or candle; he said it was redder and more pleasant to look at, but lightning made a still stronger impression on his eyes. All these different lights he called red. The sun appeared to him the size of his hat. The candle-flame was larger than his finger and smaller than his arm. When he looked at the sun, he said it appeared to touch his eye. When a lighted candle was placed before him, both his eyes were directed toward it, and moved together. When it was at any nearer distance than twelve inches, he said it touched his eyes. When moved farther off he said it did not touch them, and at twenty-two inches it became invisible.

"On the 21st of July the operation of extracting the crystalline lens was performed on the left eye. Light became very distressing to his eye. After allowing the eyelids to remain closed for a few minutes, and then opening them, the pupil appeared clear, but he could not bear exposure to light. On my asking him what he had seen, he said, 'Your head, which seemed to touch my eye,' but he could not tell its shape. On the 22d the light was less offensive. He said he saw my head, which touched his eye. On the 23d the eye was less inflamed, and he could bear a weak light. He said he could see several gentlemen round him, but could not describe their figure. My face, while I was looking at his eye, he said was round and red.

From the 25th of July to the 1st of August there was inflammation. On the 4th of August an attempt was made to ascertain the powers of vision; it became necessary to shade the glare of light by hanging a white cloth before the window. The least exertion fatigued the eye, and the cicatrix on the cornea, to which the iris had become attached, drew it down so as considerably to diminish the pupil. The attempt had therefore to be postponed.

" On the 16th of September the right eye was couched. The light was so distressing to his eye that the lids were closed as soon as it was over. The eyes were not examined with respect to their vision till the 13th of October; the boy remained quiet in the hospital. On this day he could discern a white, red, or yellow color, particularly when bright and shining. The sun and other objects did not now seem to touch his eyes as before, they appeared to be at a short distance from him. The right eye had the most distinct vision, but in both it was imperfect. The distance at which he saw best was five inches. When the object was of a bright color, and illuminated by a strong light, he could make out that it was flat and broad; and when one corner of a square substance was pointed out to him, he saw it, and could find out the other, which was at the end of the same side, but could not do this under less favorable circumstances. When the four corners of a white card were pointed out, and he had examined them, he seemed to know them; but when the opposite surface of the same card, which was yellow, was placed before him, he could not tell whether it had corners or not, so that he had not acquired any correct knowledge of them, since he could not apply it to the next colored surface, whose form was exactly the same with that, the outline of which the eye had just been taught to trace. . . .

" 2. John Salter, seven years of age, was admitted into St. George's Hospital on the 1st of October, 1806, with cataracts in both eyes, which, according to the accounts of his relations, had existed from his birth. The pupils contracted considerably when a lighted candle was placed before him, and dilated as soon as it was withdrawn. He was capable of distinguishing colors with tolerable accuracy, particularly the more bright and vivid ones. On the

6th of October the left eye was couched. The eye was allowed ten minutes to recover itself; a round piece of card, of a yellow color, one inch in diameter, was then placed about six inches from it. He said immediately that it was yellow, and, on being asked its shape, said, ' Let me touch it, and I will tell you.' Being told that he must not touch it, after looking for some time, he said it was round. A square, blue card, nearly the same size, being put before him, he said it was blue and round. A triangular piece he also called round. The different colors of the objects placed before him he instantly decided on with great correctness, but had no idea of their form. He saw best at a distance of six or seven inches. He was asked whether the object seemed to touch his eye; he said, ' No,' but when desired to say at what distance it was, he could not tell. The eye was covered, and he was put to bed and told to keep himself quiet; but upon the house-surgeon going to him half an hour afterward, his eye was found uncovered, and he was looking at his bed-curtains, which were close drawn. The bandage was replaced, but so delighted was the boy with seeing, that he again immediately removed it. The house-surgeon could not enforce his instructions, and repeated the experiment about two hours after the operation. Upon being shown a square, and asked if he could find any corners to it, the boy was very desirous of touching it. This being refused, he examined it for some time, and said at last that he had found a corner, and then readily counted the four corners of the square; and afterward, when a triangle was shown him, he counted the corners in the same way; but in doing so his eye went along the edge from corner to corner, naming them as he went along. Next day he told me he had seen ' the soldiers with their fifes and pretty things.' The guards in the morning had marched past the hospital with their band; on hearing the music, he had got out of bed and gone to the window to look at them. Seeing the bright barrels of muskets, he must in his mind have connected them with the sounds which he heard, and mistaken them for musical instruments. Twenty-four hours after the operation the pupil of the eye was clear. A pair of scissors was shown him, and he said it was a knife. On being told he was wrong, he could not make them out; but the moment he touched them he said they were scissors, and seemed delighted with the discovery.

" From this time he was constantly improving himself by looking at, and examining with his hands, everything within his reach, but he frequently forgot what he had learned. On the 10th I saw him again. He went to the window and called out, ' What is that moving?' I asked him what he thought it was. He said: ' A dog drawing a wheelbarrow. There is one, two, three dogs drawing another. How very pretty!' These proved to be carts and horses on the road, which he saw from a two-pair-of-stairs window.

" On the 19th the different colored pieces of card were separately placed before his eye, and so little had he gained in thirteen days that he could not, without counting their corners one by one, tell their shape. This he did with great facility, running his eye quickly along the outline, so that it was evident he was still learning, just as a child learns to read. He had got so far as to know the angles, when they were placed before him, and to count the number belonging to any one object. The reason of his making so slow a progress was, that these figures had never been subjected to examination by touch, and were unlike anything he had been accustomed to see. He had got so much the habit of assisting his eyes with his hands, that nothing but holding them could keep them from the object.

" On the 26th the experiments were again repeated on the couched eye. It was now found that the boy, on looking at any one of the cards in a good light, could tell the form nearly as readily as the color."

From these two instructive cases Home concludes:

" That, where the eye, before the cataract is removed, has only been capable of discerning light, without being able to distinguish colors, objects after its removal will seem to touch the eye, and there will be no knowledge of their outline, which confirms the observations made by Chesselden.

" That where the eye has previously distinguished colors, there must also be an imperfect knowledge of dis-

tances, but not of outline, which, however, will be very
soon acquired, as happened in Ware's cases. This is proved
by the history of the first boy, who, before the operation
had no knowledge of colors or distances, but after it, when
his eye had only arrived at the same state that the second
boy's was in before the operation, he had learned that the
objects were at a distance and of different colors.

" That when a child has acquired a new sense, nothing
but great pain or absolute coercion will prevent him from
making use of it."

VI. The Wardrop Case.

James Wardrop reports (" Philosophical Transactions
of the Royal Society for 1826," iii, 529–540, London,
1826):

" A girl who was observed, during the first months of
her infancy, to have something peculiar in the appearance
of her eyes and an unusual groping manner which made
her parents suspect that she had defective vision, had an
operation performed on both eyes at the age of about six
months The right eye was entirely destroyed in consequence. The left eye was preserved, but the child could
only distinguish a very light from a very dark room without having the power to perceive even the situation of the
window through which the light entered, though in sunshine or in bright moonlight she knew the direction from
which the light emanated. In this case no light could
reach the retina except such rays as could pass through
the substance of the iris. Until her forty-sixth year the
patient could not perceive objects and had no notion of
colors. On the 26th of January I introduced a very
small needle through the cornea and the center of the
iris; but I could not destroy any of the adhesions which
had shut up the pupillar opening. After this operation
she said she could distinguish more light, but she could
perceive neither forms nor colors. On the 8th of February the iris (a portion of it) was divided. The light became offensive to her. She complained of its brightness,
and was frequently observed trying to see her hands ; but

it was evident that her vision was very imperfect, for, although there was an incision made in the iris, some opaque matter lay behind the opening, which must have greatly obstructed the entrance of light.

"On the 17th of February a third operation. The opening was enlarged and the opaque matter removed. The operation being performed at my house, she returned home in a carriage, with her eye covered only with a loose piece of silk, and the first thing she noticed was a hackney-coach passing, when she exclaimed, 'What is that large thing that has passed by us?' In the course of the evening she requested her brother to show her his watch, concerning which she expressed much curiosity, and she looked at it a considerable time, holding it close to her eye. She was asked what she saw, and she said there was a dark and a bright side; she pointed to the hour of twelve, and smiled. Her brother asked her if she saw anything more. She replied, 'Yes,' and pointed to the hour of six and to the hands of the watch. She then looked at the chain and seals, and observed that one of the seals was bright, which was the case. The following day I asked her to look again at the watch, which she refused to do, saying that the light was offensive to her eye and that she felt very stupid, meaning that she was much confused by the visible world thus for the first time opened to her.

"On the third day she observed the doors on the opposite side of the street and asked if they were red, but they were, in fact, of an oak-color. In the evening she looked at her brother's face and said that she saw his nose. He asked her to touch it, which she did. He then slipped a handkerchief over his face and asked her to look again, when she playfully pulled it off and asked, 'What is that?'

"On the sixth day she told us that she saw better than she had done on any preceding day; 'but I can not tell what I do see. I am quite stupid.' She felt disappointed in not having the power of distinguishing at once by her eye objects which she could so readily distinguish from one another by feeling them.

"On the seventh day she observed that the mistress of the house was tall. She asked what the color of her gown was, to which she was answered that it was blue. 'So is that thing on your head,' she then observed, which was the case; 'and your handkerchief, that is a different color,' which was also correct. She added, ' I see you pretty well, I think.' The teacups and saucers underwent an examination. ' What are they like? ' her brother asked her. ' I don't know,' she replied, ' they look very queer to me, but I can tell what they are in a minute when I touch them.' She distinguished an orange, but could form no notion of what it was till she touched it. She seemed now to have become more cheerful, and she was very sanguine that she would find her newly acquired faculty of more use to her when she returned home, where everything was familiar to her.

" On the eighth day she asked her brother ' what he was helping himself to? ' and when she was told it was a glass of port wine, she replied, ' Port wine is dark, and looks to me very ugly.' She observed, when candles were brought into the room, her brother's face in the mirror as well as that of a lady who was present; she also walked for the first time without assistance from her chair to a sofa which was on the opposite side of the room and back again to the chair. When at tea she took notice of the tray, observed the shining of the japan-work, and asked ' what the color was round the edge? ' she was told that it was yellow, upon which she remarked, ' I will know that again.'

" On the ninth day she came down-stairs to breakfast in great spirits. She said to her brother, ' I see you very well to-day,' and came up to him and shook hands. She also observed a ticket on a window of a house on the opposite side of the street ('a lodging to let'), and her brother, to convince himself of her seeing it, took her to the window three several times, and to his surprise and gratification she pointed it out to him distinctly on each trial.

" She spent a great part of the eleventh day looking out of the window, and spoke very little.

" On the twelfth day she went to walk with her brother. The clear blue sky first attracted her notice, and she said, ' It is the prettiest thing I have ever seen yet, and equally pretty every time I turn round and look at it.' She distinguished the street from the foot-pavement distinctly, and stepped from one to the other like a person accustomed to the use of her eyes. Her great curiosity, and the manner in which she stared at the variety of objects and pointed to them, exciting the observation of many by-standers, her brother soon conducted her home, much against her will.

" On the evening of the thirteenth day she observed that there was a different tea-tray, and that it was not a pretty one, but had a dark border, which was a correct description. Her brother asked her to look in the mirror and tell him if she saw his face in it, to which she answered, evidently disconcerted : ' I see my own ; let me go away.'

" On the fourteenth day she drove in a carriage four miles, and noticed the trees, and likewise the river Thames as she crossed Vauxhall Bridge. At this time it was bright sunshine, and she said something dazzled her when she looked on the water.

" On the fifteenth day she walked to a chapel. The people passing on the pavement startled her, and once when a gentleman was going past her who had a white waistcoat and a blue coat with yellow buttons, which the sunshine brought full in her view, she started so as to draw her brother, who was walking with her, off the pavement. She distinguished the clergyman moving his hands in the pulpit, and observed that he held something in them. This was a white handkerchief.

" On the sixteenth day she went in a coach through the town, and appeared much entertained with the bustle in the streets. On asking her how she saw on that day, she answered : ' I see a great deal, if I could only tell what I do see ; but surely I am very stupid.'

" On the seventeenth day, when her brother asked her how she was, she replied : ' I am well, and see better ; but don't tease me with too many questions till I have learned a little better how to make use of my eye. All that I can say is, that I am sure, from what I do see, a great change has taken place, but I can not describe what I feel.'

" On the eighteenth day, when pieces of paper one inch

and a half square, differently colored, were presented to her, she not only distinguished them at once from one another, but gave a decided preference to some colors, liking yellow most, and then pale pink. When desirous of examining an object, she had considerable difficulty in directing her eye to it and finding out its position, moving her hand as well as her eye in various directions, as a person when blindfolded or in the dark gropes with his hands for what he wishes to touch. She also distinguished a large from a small object when they were both held up before her for comparison. She said she saw different forms in various objects which were shown to her. On asking what she meant by different forms, such as long, round, and square, and desiring her to draw with her finger these forms on her other hand, and then presenting to her eye the respective forms, she pointed to them exactly; she not only distinguished small from large objects, but knew what was meant by above and below. A figure, drawn with ink, was placed before her eye, having one end broad and the other narrow, and she saw the positions as they really were, and not inverted.

" She could also perceive motions, for, when a glass of water was placed on the table before her, on approaching her hand near it, it was moved quickly to a greater distance, upon which she immediately said : ' You move it ; you take it away.'

" She seemed to have the greatest difficulty in finding out the distance of any object; for, when an object was held close to her eye, she would search for it by stretching her hand far beyond its position, while on other occasions she groped close to her own face for a thing far removed from her.

" She learned with facility the names of the different colors, and two days after the colored papers had been shown to her, on coming into a room the color of which was crimson, she observed that it was red. She also observed some pictures hanging on the red wall of the room in which she was sitting, distinguishing several small figures in them, but not knowing what they represented, and admiring the gilt frames. On the same day she walked round a pond, and was pleased with the glistening of the sun's rays on the water, as well as with the blue sky and green shrubs, the colors of which she named correctly.

"She had as yet acquired, by the use of her sight, but very little knowledge of any forms, and was unable to apply the information gained by this new sense, and to compare it with what she had been accustomed to acquire by her sense of touch. When, therefore, a silver pencil-case and a large key were given her to examine with her hands, she discriminated and knew each distinctly; but when they were placed on the table, side by side, though she distinguished each with her eye, yet she could not tell which was the pencil-case and which was the key.

"On the twenty-fifth day after the operation she drove in a carriage for an hour in the Regent's Park, and asked more questions, on her way there, than usual, about the objects surrounding her, such as, 'What is that?' 'It is a soldier,' she was answered. 'And that? See, see!' These were candles of various colors in a tallow-chandler's window. 'Who is that that has passed us just now?' It was a person on horseback. 'But what is that on the pavement, red?' It was some ladies who wore red shawls. On going into the park she was asked if she could guess what any of the objects were. 'Oh, yes,' she replied, 'there is the sky; that is the grass; yonder is water, and two white things,' which were two swans.

"When she left London, forty-two days after the operation, she had acquired a pretty accurate notion of colors and their different shades and names. She had not yet acquired anything like an accurate knowledge of distance or of forms, and, up to this period, she continued to be very much confused with every new object at which she looked. Neither was she yet able, without considerable difficulty and numerous fruitless trials, to direct her eye to an object; so that, when she attempted to look at anything, she turned her head in various directions, until her eye caught the object of which it was in search."

Remarks on the Sixth Case.

This case has been adduced as a proof that the sense of sight is sufficient, without aid from the sense of touch, to perceive whether an object is brought nearer the eye or carried farther from it. But John Stuart Mill rightly observes, in opposition to this ("Dissertations and Discussions," ii, 113; London, 1859), that the observation we are concerned with was not made "till the eighteenth day after the operation, by which time a middle-aged woman might well have acquired the experience necessary for distinguishing so simple a phenomenon." Besides, she was very uncertain in her judgment of distances, and, in her attempts to seize with the hand new and distant objects, she frequently acted exactly like an infant.

VII. The Franz Case.

J. C. A. Franz, of Leipsic, communicates the following to the "Philosophical Transactions of the Royal Society" (by Sir Benjamin C. Brodie), (London, 1841; i, pp. 59-69):

"F. J. is the son of a physician. He is endowed with an excellent understanding, quick power of conception, and retentive memory. At his birth, both eyes were found to be turned inward to such an extent that a portion of the cornea was hidden by the inner canthus, and in both pupils there was a yellowish-white discoloration. That the strabismus and cataract of both eyes in this case were congenital is evident from the testimony both of the parents and of the nurse. The latter held a light before the eyes of the child when he was a few months old, of which he took no notice. I ascertained also from her that the eyeballs did not move hither and thither, but were always turned inward, and that but rarely either the one or the other was moved from the internal canthus.

"Toward the end of the second year, as was stated to me, the operation of keratonyxis was performed on the right eye, upon which a severe iritis ensued, terminating in atrophy of the eyeball. Within the next four years two similar operations were performed on the left eye without success. The color of the opacity became, however, of a clearer white, and the patient acquired a certain sensation of light, which he did not seem to have had before the operation.

"At the end of June, 1840, the patient, being then seventeen years of age, was brought to me. I found the condition of things as follows: Both eyes were so much inverted that nearly one half the cornea was hidden. The left eye he could move voluntarily outward, but not without exertion; it returned immediately inward when the influence of the will had ceased. The left eyeball was of the natural size and elasticity. The patient had not the slightest perception of light with the right eye; the stimulus of light had no effect on the pupil. The pupil of the left eye, which was not round, but drawn angularly downward and inward, did not alter in dimension with the movements of the eye nor from the stimulus of light. On examining the eye by looking straight into it through the pupil, the anterior wall of the capsule appeared opaque in its whole extent, and of a color and luster like mother-of-pearl. On looking from the temporal side in an oblique direction into the pupil, there was visible in the anterior wall of the capsule a very small perpendicular cleft of about one line and a quarter in length.

"This cleft was situated so far from the center of the pupil that it was entirely covered by the iris. With this eye the patient had a perception of light, and was even capable of perceiving colors of an intense and decided tone. He believed himself, moreover, able to perceive about one third of a square inch of any bright object, if held at the distance of half an inch or an inch from the eye, and obliquely in such a direction as to reflect the light strongly toward the pupil. But this, I am convinced, was a mere delusion, for all rays of light falling in the direction of the optic axis must have been intercepted and reflected by the opaque capsule. By these rays, therefore, a perception of light, indeed, might be conveyed, but certainly no perception of objects. On the other hand, it seems probable that the lateral cleft in the capsule permitted rays of light to pass into the interior of the eye. But as this small aperture was situated entirely behind the iris, those rays only would have permeated which came in a very oblique direction from the temporal side. Admitting, then, these rays of light to pass through the cleft, still on account of their obliquity they could produce but a very imperfect image, because they impinged upon an unfavorable portion of the retina. Moreover, I satisfied myself by experiments, that the patient could not in the least discern objects by sight. My experiments led me to the conclusion that his belief that he really saw objects resulted solely from his imagination combined with his power of reasoning. In feeling an object and bringing it in contact with the eyelids and the cheek, an idea of the object was produced, which was judged of and corrected according to the experience he had gained by constant practice.

" The patient's sense of touch had attained an extraordinary degree of perfection. In order to examine an object minutely he conveyed it to his lips.

" On the 10th of July, 1840, I performed an operation on the left eye. The light was so painful to him that I could not try any experiments immediately after the operation. Both eyes were closed with narrow strips of courtplaster, and treated with iced water for forty-eight hours. The patient suffered from *muscæ volitantes*, and could not bear even a mild degree of light falling on the closed lids. After the lapse of a few weeks, the *muscæ volitantes* were greatly mitigated, and the intolerance of light ceased.

" On opening the eye for the first time on the third day after the operation, I asked the patient what he could see; he answered that he saw an extensive field of light, in which everything appeared dull, confused, and in motion. He could not distinguish objects. The pain produced by the light forced him to close the eye immediately.

" Two days afterward the eye, which had been kept closed by means of court-plaster, was again opened. He now described what he saw as a number of opaque watery spheres, which moved with the movements of the eye, but when the eye was at rest remained stationary, and then partly covered each other. Two days after this the eye was again opened. The same phenomena were again observed, but the spheres were less opaque and somewhat transparent; their movements more steady; they appeared to cover each other more than before. He was now for the first time able, as he said, to look through the spheres, and to perceive a difference, but merely a difference, in the surrounding objects. When he directed his eye steadily toward an object, the visual impression produced by the object was painful and very imperfect, because the eye, on account of its intolerance of light, could not be kept open long enough for the formation of the idea as derived from visual sensation. The appearance of spheres diminished daily; they became smaller, clearer, and more pellucid, allowed objects to be seen more distinctly, and disappeared entirely after two weeks. The *muscæ volitantes*, which had the form of black, immovable, and horizontal stripes, appeared, every time the eye was opened, in a direction upward and inward. When the eye was closed he observed, especially in the evening, in an outward and upward direction, an appearance of dark blue, violet, and red colors; these colors became gradually less intense, were shaded into bright orange, yellow, and green, which latter colors alone eventually remained, and in the course of five weeks disappeared entirely. As soon as the intolerance of light had so far abated that the patient could observe an object without pain, and for a sufficient time to gain an idea of it, the following experiments were made on different days.

"*First Experiment.*—Silk ribbons of different colors, fastened on a black ground, were employed to show the complementary colors. The patient recognized the different colors, with the exception of yellow and green, which he frequently confounded, but could distinguish when both were exhibited at the same time. He could point out each color correctly when a variety was shown him at the same time. Gray pleased him best; the effect of red, orange, and yellow was painful; that of violet and brown not painful, but disagreeable. Black produced subjective colors, and white occasioned the recurrence of *muscæ volitantes* in a most vehement degree.

"*Second Experiment.*—The patient sat with his back to the light, and kept his eye closed. A sheet of paper on which two strong black lines had been drawn, the one

23

horizontal, the other vertical, was placed before him, at the distance of about three feet. He was now allowed to open the eye, and after attentive examination he called the lines by their right denominations. When I asked him to point out with his finger the horizontal line, he moved his hand slowly, as if feeling, and pointed to the vertical; but after a short time, observing his error, he corrected himself. The outline in black of a square [six inches in diameter], within which a circle had been drawn, and within the latter a triangle, was, after careful examination, recognized and correctly described by him. When he was asked to point out either of the figures, he never moved his hand directly and decidedly, but always as if feeling, and with the greatest caution; he pointed them out, however, correctly. A zigzag and a spiral line, both drawn on a sheet of paper, he observed to be different, but could not describe them otherwise than by imitating their forms with his finger in the air. He said he had no idea of those figures.

"*Third Experiment.*—The windows of the room were darkened, with the exception of one, toward which the patient, closing his eye, turned his back. At the distance of three feet, and on a level with the eye, a solid *cube* and a *sphere*, each of four inches diameter, were placed before him. I now let him open his eye. After attentively examining these bodies, he said he saw a *quadrangular* and a *circular* figure, and after some consideration he pronounced the one a *square* and the other a *disk*. His eye being then closed, the cube was taken away, and a disk of equal size substituted and placed next to the sphere. On again opening his eye he observed no difference in these objects, but regarded them both as disks. The solid cube was now placed in a somewhat oblique position before the eye, and close beside it a figure cut out of pasteboard, representing a plane outline prospect of the cube when in this position. Both objects he took to be something like flat quadrates. A pyramid, placed before him with one of its sides toward his eye, he saw as a plane triangle. This object was now turned a little, so as to present two of its sides to view, but rather more of one side than of the other; after considering and examining it for a long time, he said that this was a very extraordinary figure; it was neither a triangle, nor a quadrangle, nor a circle; he had no idea of it, and could not describe it. 'In fact,' said he, 'I must give it up.' On the conclusion of these experiments I asked him to describe the sensations the objects had produced, whereupon he said that immediately on opening his eye he had discovered a difference in the two objects, the cube and the sphere, placed before him, and perceived that they were not drawings; but that he had not been able to form from them the idea of a square and a disk, *until he perceived a sensation of what he saw in the points of his fingers*, as if he really touched the objects. When I gave the three bodies, the sphere, cube, and pyramid, into his hand, he was much surprised that he had not recognized them as such by sight, as he was well acquainted with them by touch. These experiments prove the correctness of the hypothesis I have advanced elsewhere on the well-known question put by Mr. Molyneux to Locke, which was answered by both these gentlemen in the negative.

"*Fourth Experiment.*—In a vessel containing water to about the depth of one foot was placed a musket-ball, and on the surface of the water a piece of pasteboard of the same form, size, and color as the ball. The patient could perceive no difference in the position of these bodies; he believed both to be upon the surface of the water. Pointing to the ball, I desired him to take up this object. He made an attempt to take it from the plane of the water; but, when he found he could not grasp it there, he said he had deceived himself, the objects were lying in the water, upon which I informed him of their real position. I now desired him to touch the ball which lay in the water with a small rod. He attempted this several times, but always missed his aim. He could never touch the object at the first movement of his hand toward it, but only by feeling about with the rod. On being questioned with respect to reflected light, he said that he was always obliged to bear in mind that the looking-glass was fastened to the wall in order to correct his idea of the apparent situation of objects behind the glass.

" When the patient first acquired the faculty of sight, all objects appeared to him so near that he was sometimes afraid of coming in contact with them, though they were in reality at a great distance from him. He saw everything much larger than he had supposed from the idea obtained by his sense of touch. Moving and especially living objects, such as men, horses, etc., appeared to him very large. If he wished to form an estimate of the distance of objects from his own person or of two objects from each other without moving from his place, he examined the objects from different points of view by turning his head to the right and to the left. Of perspective in pictures he had, of course, no idea; it appeared to him unnatural that the figure of a man represented in the front of a picture should be larger than a house or mountain in the background. All objects appeared to him perfectly flat. Thus, although he very well knew by his touch that the nose was prominent and the eyes sunk deeper in the head, he saw the human face only as a plane. Though he possessed an excellent memory, this faculty was at first quite deficient as regarded visible objects: he was not able, for example, to recognize visitors, unless he heard them speak, till he had seen them very frequently. Even when he had seen an object repeatedly he could form no idea of its visible qualities without having the real object before him. Heretofore when he dreamed of any persons, of his parents, for instance, he felt them and heard their voices, but never saw them; but now, after having seen them frequently, he saw them also in his dreams. The human face pleased him more than any other object. Although the newly-acquired sense afforded him many pleasures, the great number of strange and extraordinary sights was often disagreeable and wearisome to him. He said that he saw too much novelty which he could not comprehend; and, even though he could see both near and remote objects very well, he would nevertheless continually have recourse to the use of the sense of touch."

Final Remarks.

To the seven reports upon cases of persons born blind and afterward surgically treated, which are here presented in abridged form from the English originals, may be added some more recent and more accessible ones, one by Hirschberg (" Archiv für Opthalmologie," xxi, 1. Abth., S. 29 bis 42, 1875), one by A. von Hippel (ibid., xxi, 2. Abth., S. 101), and one by Dufour (" Archives des Sciences physiques et naturelles," lviii, No. 242, April, 1877, p. 420). The cases reported here are those most discussed. I have given them considerably in detail in order that the reader may form an independent judgment concerning the behavior of persons born blind and then operated upon, as that behavior is described *before* the modern physiological controversy over empiricism and nativism. Helmholtz (" Physiologische Optik," § 28) mentions, besides those of Chesselden and Wardrop and Ware, which he gives in abridged form, some other cases also. Others still may be found in Froriep's " Notizen " (xi, p. 177, 1825, and iv, p. 243, 1837, also xxi, p. 41, 1842), partly reported, partly cited (the latter according to Franz).

In addition to the cases here given of persons born blind and then surgically treated—persons not able to see things in space-relations before becoming blind—one more case is to be mentioned; it is that of a girl who in her seventh year (probably in consequence of the effect of dazzling sunlight) lost her sight completely, but recovered it again at the age of seventeen years after being treated with electricity. She had to begin absolutely anew to learn to name colors like a child; all measure of distance, perspective, size, had been lost for her *by lack of practice* (as O. Heyfelder relates in his work " Die Kindheit des Menschen," second edition, Erlangen, 1858, pp. 12–15). He says, p. 12, that the patient had been eight years blind ; p. 13, that she had been ten years so. Such cases prove the great influence of experience upon vision in space, and show how little of this vision is inborn in mankind.

When we compare the acquirement of sight by the

normal newly-born child and the infant with that of those
born blind, we should, above all, bear in mind that the latter in general could make use of only *one* eye, and also
that on account of the long inactivity of the retina and the
absence of the crystalline lens, as well as in consequence
of the numerous experiences of touch, essential differences
exist. Notwithstanding this, there appears an agreement
in the manner in which in both cases vision is learned, the
eye is practiced, and the association of sight and touch is
acquired. The seventh case in particular shows plainly
how strong the analogies are.

These cases are sufficient to refute some singular assertions, e. g., that all the newly-born must see objects reversed, as even a Buffon ("Œuvres complètes," iv, 136;
Paris, 1844) thought to be the fact. My boy, when I had
him write, in his fifth year, the ordinary figures after a
copy that I set for him, imitated the most of them, to my
surprise, always in a reversed hand (Spiegelschrift, "mir-
ror-hand"); the 1 and the 4 he continued longest to
write thus, though he often made the 4 the other way,
too, whereas he always wrote the 5 correctly. This, however, was, of course, not owing to imperfect sight, but to
incomplete transformation of the visual idea into the
motor idea required for writing. Other boys, as I am
given to understand, do the same thing. For myself, I
found the distinction between "right" and "left" so difficult in my childhood, that I remember vividly the trouble
I had with it.

Singularly enough, Buffon assumed, in 1749, that the
neglect of the double images does not yet take place at the
beginning of life. Johannes Müller, in 1826, expresses
the same view. But, inasmuch as in the first two or three
weeks after the birth of a human being, in contrast with
many animals, nothing at all can as yet be distinctly seen,

it is not allowable to maintain that everything must be seen double. Rather is it true that everything is seen neither single nor double, since the very young child perceives, as yet, no forms (boundary-lines) and no distances, but merely receives impressions of light, precisely as is the case with the person born blind, in the period directly after an operation has been performed upon his eyes.

Schopenhauer (in his treatise on "Sight and Colors," first edition, Leipsic, 1816, p. 14) divined this truth. He says, "If a person who was looking out upon a wide and beautiful prospect could be in an instant wholly deprived of his intellect, then nothing of all the view would remain for him except the sensation of a very manifold reaction of his retina, which is, as it were, the raw material out of which his intellect created that view."

The new-born child has, as yet, no intellect, and therefore can not, as yet, at the beginning, see; he can merely have the sensation of light.

This opinion of mine, derived from observation of the behavior of newly-born and of very young infants (cf. the first chapter of this book), seems to me to be practically confirmed in an account given by Anselm von Feuerbach in his work on Kaspar Hauser (Anspach, 1832, p. 77).

"In the year 1828, soon after his arrival in Nuremberg, Kaspar Hauser was to look out at the window in the Vestner Tower, from which there was a view of a broad and many-colored summer landscape. Kaspar Hauser turned away; the sight was repugnant to him. At a later period, long after he had learned to speak, he gave, when questioned, the following explanation :

"'When I looked toward the window it always seemed to me as if a shutter had been put up close before my eyes, and that upon this shutter a colorer had wiped off his brushes of different colors, white, blue, green, yellow, and

red, all in motley confusion. Individual things, as I now
see them, I could not, at that time, perceive and distinguish upon it; it was absolutely hideous to look upon.'"

By this, as well as by the experiences with persons born
blind and afterward surgically treated, it is clearly demonstrated that colors and degrees of brightness are severally
apprehended before forms and distances can be perceived.
The case must be the same with the normal human child
in the first weeks after birth.

After discrimination of the luminous sensations, the
boundary-lines of bright plane surfaces are next clearly
discerned; then come forms, and, last of all, the distances
of these.

With reference to this progress of the normal infant
in learning to see, the accounts of persons born blind and
afterward surgically treated are again of great value.
After the famous question put by Molyneux to Locke,
whether an intelligent person, blind from birth, would be
able immediately after an operation to distinguish a sphere
from a cube by means of the eye alone, had been answered
in the negative, the opinion was accepted as satisfactory
that such a person learns the distinction only by means of
the sense of touch. Thus, the perception of difference
would come later, after the sight of different forms, only
by means of the tactual memory.

In truth, however, very many forms are discerned as
different purely by means of the eye, without the possibility of aid from any other sense. Phenomena exclusively
optical, which, like the rainbow, can not be apprehended
by touch or by hearing, are distinctly perceived by the child
at a very early period. Without touching, the different
forms of objects would be perceived by means of sight
alone, and that even by a child unable to touch, through
movements of the eyes and head, changes of bodily posi-

tion, of attitude and posture, and through practice in accommodation and in the observation of differences of brightness.

The fact correctly predicted by Molyneux, that those born blind but afterward surgically treated can not, by means of the eye alone, distinguish the form of a sphere from that of a cube, must accordingly be supplemented to this extent, viz., that such persons are capable, just as are normal children who can see, of learning this difference of form by means of the eye alone without the direct intervention of the sense of touch; for the co-ordination of the retinal excitations in space and time by means of the intellect, quite independently of all impressions from other departments of sense, is possible, and is in countless cases actual, just as is the learning of differences of form solely by means of the sense of touch in children who are born blind and never learn to see.

THE END.

CLASSICS IN PSYCHOLOGY

AN ARNO PRESS COLLECTION

Angell, James Rowland. **Psychology: On Introductory Study of the Structure and Function of Human Consciousness.** 4th edition. 1908

Bain, Alexander. **Mental Science.** 1868

Baldwin, James Mark. **Social and Ethical Interpretations in Mental Development.** 2nd edition. 1899

Bechterev, Vladimir Michailovitch. **General Principles of Human Reflexology.** [1932]

Binet, Alfred and Th[éodore] Simon. **The Development of Intelligence in Children.** 1916

Bogardus, Emory S. **Fundamentals of Social Psychology.** 1924

Buytendijk, F. J. J. **The Mind of the Dog.** 1936

Ebbinghaus, Hermann. **Psychology: An Elementary Text-Book.** 1908

Goddard, Henry Herbert. **The Kallikak Family.** 1931

Hobhouse, L[eonard] T. **Mind in Evolution.** 1915

Holt, Edwin B. **The Concept of Consciousness.** 1914

Külpe, Oswald. **Outlines of Psychology.** 1895

Ladd-Franklin, Christine. **Colour and Colour Theories.** 1929

Lectures Delivered at the 20th Anniversary Celebration of Clark University. (Reprinted from *The American Journal of Psychology*, Vol. 21, Nos. 2 and 3). 1910

Lipps, Theodor. **Psychological Studies.** 2nd edition. 1926

Loeb, Jacques. **Comparative Physiology of the Brain and Comparative Psychology.** 1900

Lotze, Hermann. **Outlines of Psychology.** [1885]

McDougall, William. **The Group Mind.** 2nd edition. 1920

Meier, Norman C., editor. **Studies in the Psychology of Art: Volume III.** 1939

Morgan, C. Lloyd. **Habit and Instinct.** 1896

Münsterberg, Hugo. **Psychology and Industrial Efficiency.** 1913

Murchison, Carl, editor. **Psychologies of 1930.** 1930

Piéron, Henri. **Thought and the Brain.** 1927

Pillsbury, W[alter] B[owers]. **Attention.** 1908

[Poffenberger, A. T., editor]. **James McKeen Cattell: Man of Science.** 1947

Preyer, W[illiam] **The Mind of the Child: Parts I and II.** 1890/1889

The Psychology of Skill: Three Studies. 1973

Reymert, Martin L., editor. **Feelings and Emotions: The Wittenberg Symposium.** 1928

Ribot, Th[éodule Armand]. **Essay on the Creative Imagination.** 1906

Roback, A[braham] A[aron]. **The Psychology of Character.** 1927

I. M. Sechenov: Biographical Sketch and Essays. (Reprinted from *Selected Works* by I. Sechenov). 1935

Sherrington, Charles. **The Integrative Action of the Nervous System.** 2nd edition. 1947

Spearman, C[harles]. **The Nature of 'Intelligence' and the Principles of Cognition.** 1923

Thorndike, Edward L. **Education: A First Book.** 1912

Thorndike, Edward L., E. O. Bregman, M. V. Cobb, et al. **The Measurement of Intelligence.** [1927]

Titchener, Edward Bradford. **Lectures on the Elementary Psychology of Feeling and Attention.** 1908

Titchener, Edward Bradford. **Lectures on the Experimental Psychology of the Thought-Processes.** 1909

Washburn, Margaret Floy. **Movement and Mental Imagery.** 1916

Whipple, Guy Montrose. **Manual of Mental and Physical Tests: Parts I and II.** 2nd edition. 1914/1915

Woodworth, Robert Sessions. **Dynamic Psychology.** 1918

Wundt, Wilhelm. **An Introduction to Psychology.** 1912

Yerkes, Robert M. **The Dancing Mouse** and **The Mind of a Gorilla.** 1907/1926